P9-DBT-264

*f*P

Measures for Clinical Practice

A SOURCEBOOK

Third Edition

Volume 1. Couples, Families, and Children

KEVIN CORCORAN
JOEL FISCHER

THE FREE PRESS

New York   London   Toronto   Sydney   Singapore

THE FREE PRESS
A Division of Simon & Schuster Inc.
1230 Avenue of the Americas
New York, NY 10020

Copyright © 1994, 2000 by Joel Fischer and Kevin Corcoran
Copyright © 1987 by The Free Press

All rights reserved,
including the right of reproduction
in whole or in part in any form.

THE FREE PRESS and colophon are trademarks
of Simon & Schuster Inc.

Manufactured in the United States of America

10 9 8 7 6 5 4 3 2 1

Library of Congress Cataloging-in-Publication Data

Corcoran, Kevin (Kevin J.)
    Measures for clinical practice : a sourcebook / Kevin Corcoran,
    Joel Fischer.—3rd ed.
        p.   cm.
    Includes bibliographical references.
    ISBN 0-684-84830-9 (v. 1)—ISBN 0-684-84831-7 (v. 2)
        I. Psychological tests.   I. Fischer, Joel.   II. Title.

BF176.C66 2000
150'.28'7—dc21
                                            00-037132

ISBN 0-684-84830-9

The instruments in this book are reprinted with the permission of the authors
and publishers. In no uncertain terms, these acts of kindness do not relinquish or
weaken the author's and/or publisher's copyright. Reproduction in any form
without permission is restricted by law.

To Sug Olivetti and J. Spencer Siegerson, whose romance redefined love

To Art Vandalay, architect of dreams, and to Renee and Schmoopie
for virtually everything else

CONTENTS

VOLUME 1

List of Instruments for Couples ix
List of Instruments for Families xi
List of Instruments for Children xiv
List of Instruments for Adults (Vol. 2) xvii
List of Instruments Cross-Indexed by Problem Area (Vols. 1 and 2) xxx
Foreword by David H. Barlow xlix
Preface to the Third Edition liii

PART
I MEASUREMENT AND PRACTICE

1. *Introduction* 3
2. *Basic Principles of Measurement* 11
3. *Types of Measurement Tools* 27
4. *Advantages and Disadvantages of Rapid Assessment Instruments* 43
5. *Selecting Measures for Practice* 49
6. *Administering the Instruments* 63

PART
II INSTRUMENTS FOR PRACTICE

Introduction 77
Instruments for Couples 81
Instruments for Families 197
Instruments for Children 449

References 633

VOLUME 2

List of Instruments for Adults ix
List of Instruments for Couples (Vol. 1) xxii
List of Instruments for Families (Vol. 1) xxiv
List of Instruments for Children (Vol. 1) xxvii
List of Instruments Cross-Indexed by Problem Area
  (Vols. 1 and 2) xxx
Foreword by David H. Barlow xlix
Preface to the Third Edition liii

INSTRUMENTS FOR PRACTICE

Introduction to Volume 2 1
Instruments for Adults 5

INSTRUMENTS FOR COUPLES
(Volume 1)

BEIER-STERNBERG DISCORD
QUESTIONNAIRE   81
E. G. Beier and D. P.
Sternberg

COMPETITIVENESS SCALE   84
M. R. Laner

CONSTRUCTION OF PROBLEMS
SCALE   87
L. Heatherington

DOMINANCE-ACCOMMODATION
SCALE   92
C. N. Hoskins

DUAL EMPLOYED COPING SCALES   96
D. A. Skinner and H. I.
McCubbin

DUAL-CAREER FAMILY SCALE   104
B. F. Pendleton, M. M.
Poloma, and T. N. Garland

DYADIC ADJUSTMENT SCALE   108
G. B. Spanier

EQUITY/INEQUITY SCALE   112
J. Traupmann, R. Petersen,
M. Utne, and E. Hatfield

HYPOTHETICAL, JEALOUSY-
PRODUCING EVENTS SCALE   116
G. L. Hansen

INDEX OF MARITAL SATISFACTION
119
W. W. Hudson

KANSAS MARITAL CONFLICT SCALE
122
K. Eggeman, V. Moxley, and
W. R. Schumm

KANSAS MARITAL GOALS
ORIENTATION SCALE   125
K. Eggeman, V. Moxley, and
W. R. Schumm

KANSAS MARITAL SATISFACTION
SCALE   127
W. R. Schumm, L. A. Paff-
Bergen, R. C. Hatch, F. C.
Obiorah, J. M. Copeland,
L. D. Meens, and M. A.
Bugaighis

LIFE DISTRESS INVENTORY   129
E. J. Thomas, M. Yoshioka,
and R. D. Ager

LOCKE-WALLACE MARITAL
ADJUSTMENT TEST   133
H. J. Locke and K. M.
Wallace

MARITAL ALTERNATIVES SCALE   136
J. R. Udry

MARITAL COMPARISON LEVEL INDEX
138
R. M. Sabatelli

MARITAL CONVENTIONALIZATION
SCALE   142
V. H. Edmonds

MARITAL HAPPINESS SCALE   144
N. H. Azrin, B. T. Naster,
and R. Jones

MARITAL INSTABILITY INDEX   146
J. N. Edwards, D. R.
Johnson, and A. Booth

x Contents

MILLER MARITAL LOCUS OF CONTROL SCALE 150 — P. C. Miller, H. M. Lefcourt, and E. E. Ware

NON-PHYSICAL ABUSE OF PARTNER SCALE 154 — J. W. Garner and W. W. Hudson

PARTNER ABUSE SCALE: NON-PHYSICAL 156 — W. W. Hudson

PARTNER ABUSE SCALE: PHYSICAL 158 — W. W. Hudson

PASSIONATE LOVE SCALE 160 — E. Hatfield and S. Sprecher

PHYSICAL ABUSE OF PARTNER SCALE 163 — J. W. Garner and W. W. Hudson

POSITIVE FEELINGS QUESTIONNAIRE 165 — K. D. O'Leary, F. Fincham, and H. Turkewitz

PRIMARY COMMUNICATION INVENTORY 168 — H. J. Locke, F. Sabaght, and M. M. Thomes

RELATIONSHIP ASSESSMENT SCALE 171 — S. S. Hendrick

RELATIONSHIP EVENTS SCALE 173 — C. E. King and A. Christensen

SEMANTIC DIFFERENTIAL OF SEX ROLES 175 — R. J. Hafner

SPOUSE ENABLING INVENTORY 178 — E. J. Thomas, M. Yoshioka, and R. D. Ager

SPOUSE SOBRIETY INFLUENCE INVENTORY 184 — E. J. Thomas, M. Yoshioka, and R. D. Ager

SPOUSE TREATMENT MEDIATION INVENTORIES 191 — R. D. Ager and E. J. Thomas

INSTRUMENTS FOR FAMILIES
(Volume 1)

ADOLESCENT-FAMILY INVENTORY OF LIFE EVENTS AND CHANGES   197 — H. I. McCubbin, J. M. Patterson, E. Bauman, and L. H. Harris

ADULT-ADOLESCENT PARENTING INVENTORY   204 — S. J. Bavolek

ATTITUDE TOWARD THE PROVISION OF LONG-TERM CARE   207 — W. Klein

BECK CODEPENDENCE ASSESSMENT SCALE   210 — W. H. Beck

BOUNDARY AMBIGUITY SCALES—1–6   214 — P. Boss, J. Greenberg, and D. Pearce-McCall

CO-DEPENDENCY INVENTORY   222 — S. Stonebrink

CODEPENDENT QUESTIONNAIRE   225 — P. V. Roehling and E. Gaumond

CONFLICT TACTICS SCALES   229 — M. A. Straus

COPING HEALTH INVENTORY FOR PARENTS   237 — H. I. McCubbin, M. A. McCubbin, R. S. Nevin, and E. Cauble

ENVIRONMENTAL ASSESSMENT INDEX   243 — R. H. Poresky

FAMILY ADAPTABILITY AND COHESION EVALUATION SCALE   246 — D. H. Olson, J. Portner, and Y. Lavee

FAMILY ASSESSMENT DEVICE   250 — N. B. Epstein, L. M. Baldwin, and D. S. Bishop

FAMILY ATTACHMENT AND CHANGEABILITY INDEX 8   254 — H. McCubbin, A. Thompson, and K. Elver

FAMILY AWARENESS SCALE   259 — M. S. Kolevzon and R. G. Green

FAMILY BELIEFS INVENTORY   263 — P. V. Roehling and A. L. Robin

FAMILY CELEBRATIONS INDEX   280 — H. I. McCubbin and A. I. Thompson

FAMILY COPING COHERENCE INDEX   282 — H. McCubbin, A. Larsen, and D. Olson

FAMILY COPING INDEX   284 — H. McCubbin, A. Thompson, and K. Elver

FAMILY COPING INVENTORY   288 — H. I. McCubbin, P. G. Boss, G. R. Wilson, and B. B. Dahl

FAMILY CRISIS ORIENTED PERSONAL
  EVALUATION SCALES   294
H. I. McCubbin, D. H.
  Olson, and A. S. Larsen

FAMILY DISTRESS INDEX   298
H. I. McCubbin, A. I.
  Thompson, and K. Elver

FAMILY EMOTIONAL INVOLVEMENT
  AND CRITICISM SCALE   300
C. G. Shields, P. Franks,
  J. J. Harp, S. H. McDaniel,
  and T. L. Campbell

FAMILY EMPOWERMENT SCALE   302
P. E. Koren, N. DeChillo,
  and B. J. Friesen

FAMILY FUNCTIONING SCALE   307
M. L. Tavitian, J. Lubiner, L.
  Green, L. C. Grebstein,
  and W. F. Velicer

FAMILY HARDINESS INDEX   312
M. A. McCubbin, H. I.
  McCubbin, and A. I.
  Thompson

FAMILY INVENTORY OF LIFE EVENTS
  AND CHANGES   315
H. I. McCubbin, J. M.
  Patterson, and L. R.
  Wilson

FAMILY INVENTORY OF RESOURCES
  FOR MANAGEMENT   322
H. I. McCubbin, J. K.
  Comeau, and J. A. Harkins

FAMILY MEMBER WELL-BEING   329
H. McCubbin and J.
  Patterson

FAMILY-OF-ORIGIN SCALE   331
A. J. Hovestadt, W. T.
  Anderson, F. P. Piercy, S.
  W. Cochran, and M. Fine

FAMILY ORGANIZED COHESIVENESS
  SCALE   336
L. Fischer

FAMILY PRESSURES SCALE—ETHNIC
  338
H. McCubbin, A.
  Thompson, and K. Elver

FAMILY PROBLEM SOLVING
  COMMUNICATION   342
M. McCubbin, H.
  McCubbin, and A.
  Thompson

FAMILY RESPONSIBILITY INDEX   345
P. M. Bjorkquist

FAMILY SCHEMA—ETHNIC   351
H. McCubbin, A.
  Thompson, K. Elver, and
  K. Carpenter

FAMILY SENSE OF COHERENCE AND
  FAMILY ADAPTATION SCALES   354
A. Antonovsky and T.
  Sourani

FAMILY TIMES AND ROUTINES INDEX
  363
H. I. McCubbin, M. A.
  McCubbin, and A. I.
  Thompson

FAMILY TRADITIONS SCALE   370
H. I. McCubbin and A. I.
  Thompson

FETAL HEALTH LOCUS OF CONTROL
SCALE   372 — S. M. Labs and S. K. Wurtele

INDEX OF BROTHER AND SISTER
RELATIONS   376 — W. W. Hudson, G. MacNeil, and J. Dierks

INDEX OF FAMILY RELATIONS   379 — W. W. Hudson

INDEX OF PARENTAL ATTITUDES   382 — W. W. Hudson

KANSAS FAMILY LIFE SATISFACTION
SCALE   384 — W. R. Schumm, A. P. Jurich, and S. R. Bollman

KANSAS PARENTAL SATISFACTION
SCALE   386 — W. R. Schumm and J. Hall

LEVEL OF EXPRESSED EMOTION   388 — J. D. Cole and S. S. Kazarian

MEMORY AND BEHAVIOR PROBLEMS
CHECKLIST   392 — S. H. Zarit and J. M. Zarit

PARENT AFFECT TEST   397 — M. N. Linehan

PARENT'S REPORT   408 — E. Dibble and D. J. Cohen

PARENT-CHILD RELATIONSHIP
SURVEY   416 — M. A. Fine, J. R. Moreland, and A. Schwebel

PARENTAL AUTHORITY
QUESTIONNAIRE   420 — J. R. Buri

PARENTAL BONDING INSTRUMENT   424 — G. Parker, H. Tupling, and L. B. Brown

PARENTAL NURTURANCE SCALE   427 — J. R. Buri, T. M. Misukanis, and R. A. Mueller

PARENTAL TOLERANCE SCALE   429 — R. J. Butler

PARENTING SCALE   431 — D. S. Arnold, S. G. O'Leary, L. S. Wolff, and M. M. Acker

PERINATAL GRIEF SCALE   436 — L. Potvin, J. Lasker, and T. Toediter

REALIZATIONS OF FILIAL
RESPONSIBILITY   438 — W. C. Seelbach

SELF-REPORT FAMILY INSTRUMENT
441 — W. R. Beavers, R. B. Hampson, and Y. F. Hulgus

SOCIAL SUPPORT INDEX   446 — H. McCubbin, J. Patterson, and T. Glynn

INSTRUMENTS FOR CHILDREN
(Volume 1)

ADOLESCENT CONCERNS EVALUATION 449 — D. W. Springer

ADOLESCENT COPING ORIENTATION FOR PROBLEM EXPERIENCES 454 — J. M. Patterson and H. I. McCubbin

ASSERTIVENESS SCALE FOR ADOLESCENTS 459 — D. Y. Lee, E. T. Hallberg, A. G. Slemon, and R. F. Haase

BEHAVIORAL SELF-CONCEPT SCALE 469 — R. L. Williams and E. A. Workman

BEHAVIOR RATING INDEX FOR CHILDREN 473 — A. R. Stiffman, J. G. Orme, D. A. Evans, R. A. Feldman, and P. A. Keeney

BODY INVESTMENT SCALE 476 — I. Orbach and M. Mikulincer

CHILD DENTAL CONTROL ASSESSMENT 480 — P. Weinstein, P. Milgrom, O. Hoskoldsson, D. Golletz, E. Jeffcott, and M. Koday

CHILD REPORT OF POSTTRAUMATIC SYMPTOMS AND PARENT REPORT OF POSTTRAUMATIC SYMPTOMS 484 — R. Greenwald and A. Rubin

CHILDHOOD PERSONALITY SCALE 488 — E. Dibble and D. J. Cohen

CHILD'S ATTITUDE TOWARD FATHER AND MOTHER SCALES 495 — W. W. Hudson

CHILDREN'S ACTION TENDENCY SCALE 499 — R. H. Deluty

CHILDREN'S ATTRIBUTIONAL STYLE QUESTIONNAIRE—REVISED 505 — M. Thompson, N. J. Kaslow, B. Weiss, and S. Nolen-Hoeksema

CHILDREN'S BELIEFS ABOUT PARENTAL DIVORCE SCALE 509 — L. A. Kurdek and B. Berg

CHILDREN'S COGNITIVE ASSESSMENT QUESTIONNAIRE 513 — S. Zatz and L. Chassin

CHILDREN'S LONELINESS QUESTIONNAIRE 517 — S. R. Asher

CHILDREN'S PERCEIVED SELF-CONTROL SCALE 519 — L. L. Humphrey

CHINESE WAYS OF COPING QUESTIONNAIRE 521 — D. W. Chan

COMMON BELIEF INVENTORY FOR STUDENTS 524 — S. R. Hooper and C. C. Layne

COMPANION ANIMAL BONDING SCALE   528 — R. H. Poresky, C. Hendrix, J. E. Mosier, and M. L. Samuelson

COMPULSIVE EATING SCALE   530 — D. M. Kagan and R. L. Squires

CONCERN OVER WEIGHT AND DIETING SCALE   532 — D. M. Kagan and R. L. Squires

DEPRESSION SELF-RATING SCALE   535 — P. Birleson

DRINKING MOTIVES QUESTIONNAIRE   537 — M. L. Cooper

EYBERG CHILD BEHAVIOR INVENTORY   540 — S. Eyberg

FAMILY, FRIENDS, AND SELF FORM   545 — D. Simpson and A. A. McBride

HARE SELF-ESTEEM SCALE   550 — B. R. Hare

HOMEWORK PROBLEM CHECKLIST   553 — K. M. Anesko, B. Scholock, R. Ramirez, and F. M. Levine

HOPELESSNESS SCALE FOR CHILDREN   556 — A. E. Kazdin

HOSPITAL FEARS RATING SCALE   558 — B. G. Melamed and M. A. Lumley

IMPULSIVITY SCALE   560 — P. P. Hirschfield, B. Sutton-Smith, and B. G. Rosenberg

INDEX OF PEER RELATIONS   562 — W. W. Hudson

INVENTORY OF PARENT AND PEER ATTACHMENT   564 — G. C. Armsden and M. T. Greenberg

MOOD THERMOMETERS   574 — B. W. Tuckman

MULTI-ATTITUDE SUICIDE TENDENCY SCALE   576 — I. Orbach, I. Milstein, D. Har-Even, A. Apter, S. Tiano, and A. Elizur

MULTIGROUP ETHNIC IDENTITY MEASURE   581 — J. S. Phinney

NOWICKI-STRICKLAND LOCUS OF CONTROL SCALE   584 — S. Nowicki, Jr. and B. R. Strickland

OREGON MENTAL HEALTH REFERRAL CHECKLIST   587 — K. Corcoran

PAIN RESPONSE INVENTORY   591 — L. S. Walker, C. A. Smith, J. Garber, and D. A. Van Slyke

PEER AND SELF-RATING SCALE   595 — R. A. Glow and P. H. Glow

PERSISTENCE SCALE FOR CHILDREN   600 — D. Lufi and A. Cohen

PERSONAL ATTRIBUTE INVENTORY
FOR CHILDREN AND NONSEXIST
PERSONAL ATTRIBUTE INVENTORY
603   T. S. Parish

REASON FOR LIVING INVENTORY
FOR ADOLESCENTS   606   A. Osman, W. R. Downs,
T. M. Besett, B. A.
Kopper, F. X. Barrios, and
M. M. Linehan

ROSENBERG SELF-ESTEEM SCALE   610   M. Rosenberg

SCALE OF RACIAL SOCIALIZATION
FOR ADOLESCENTS   612   H. C. Stevenson

SELF-CONCEPT SCALE FOR
CHILDREN   617   L. P. Lipsitt

SELF-CONTROL RATING SCALE   619   P. C. Kendall and L. E.
Wilcox

SPIDER PHOBIA QUESTIONNAIRE
FOR CHILDREN   623   M. Kindt, J. F. Brosschot,
and P. Muris

YOUNG CHILDREN'S SOCIAL
DESIRABILITY SCALE   625   L. H. Ford and B. M. Rubin

YOUTH COPING INDEX   628   H. McCubbin, A.
Thompson, and K. Elver

INSTRUMENTS FOR ADULTS
(Volume 2)

ACCEPTING THE PAST/REMINISCING
ABOUT THE PAST   5
    D. A. Santor and D. C. Zuroff

ACCULTURATION RATING SCALE FOR
MEXICAN-AMERICANS—II   9
    I. Cuellar, B. Arnold, and R. Maldonado

ACHIEVEMENT ANXIETY TEST   20
    R. Alpert and R. N. Haber

ACTIVITY-FEELING SCALE II   24
    J. Reeve

ADHERENCE DETERMINANTS
QUESTIONNAIRE   27
    M. R. DiMatteo et al.

ADULT HEALTH CONCERNS
QUESTIONNAIRE   31
    R. L. Spoth and D. M. Dush

ADULT SELF-EXPRESSION SCALE   34
    M. L. Gay, J. G. Hollandsworth, Jr., and J. P. Galassi

AFFECT BALANCE SCALE   38
    N. Bradburn and E. Noll

AGGRESSION INVENTORY   40
    B. A. Gladue

AGGRESSION QUESTIONNAIRE   43
    A. H. Buss and M. Perry

AGORAPHOBIC COGNITIONS
QUESTIONNAIRE   46
    D. L. Chambless, G. C. Caputo, P. Bright, and R. Gallagher

ALCOHOL BELIEFS SCALE   48
    G. J. Connors and S. A. Maisto

ALCOHOL OUTCOME EXPECTANCIES
SCALE   53
    B. C. Leigh and A. W. Stacy

ANGER IDIOMS SCALE   55
    R. G. Malgady, L. H. Rogler, and D. E. Cortes

ARGUMENTATIVENESS SCALE   57
    D. A. Infante and A. S. Rancer

AROUSABILITY PREDISPOSITION
SCALE   59
    S. Coren

ASCRIPTION OF RESPONSIBILITY
QUESTIONNAIRE   61
    A. R. Hakstian and P. Suedfeld

ASSERTION INVENTORY   64
    E. Gambrill and C. Richey

ASSERTION QUESTIONNAIRE IN DRUG
USE   68
    D. A. Callner and S. M. Ross

ASSERTION SELF-STATEMENT TEST—
REVISED   71
    R. G. Heimberg, E. J. Chiauzzi, R. E. Becker, and R. Madrazo-Peterson

ASSERTIVE JOB-HUNTING SURVEY
75
    H. A. Becker

ASSERTIVENESS SELF-REPORT
INVENTORY   77
    S. D. Herzberger, E. Chan, and J. Katz

ASSERTIVENESS SELF-STATEMENT TEST 80 — R. M. Schwartz and J. M. Gottman

AUDITORY HALLUCINATIONS QUESTIONNAIRE 85 — H. H. Hustig and R. J. Hafner

AUTHORITARIANISM SCALE (REVISED F-SCALE) 89 — P. C. L. Heaven

AUTHORITY BEHAVIOR INVENTORY 91 — K. Rigby

AUTOMATIC THOUGHTS QUESTIONNAIRE 94 — P. C. Kendall and S. D. Hollon

BAKKER ASSERTIVENESS-AGGRESSIVENESS INVENTORY 96 — C. B. Bakker, M. K. Bakker-Rabdau, and S. Breit

BARNETT LIKING OF CHILDREN SCALE 101 — M. A. Barnett and C. S. Sinisi

BARRATT IMPULSIVENESS SCALE 11 104 — E. S. Barratt

BELIEF IN PERSONAL CONTROL SCALE 107 — J. L. Berrenberg

BELIEFS ASSOCIATED WITH CHILDHOOD SEXUAL ABUSE 111 — D. Jehu, C. Klassen, and M. Gazan

BIDIMENSIONAL ACCULTURATION SCALE FOR HISPANICS 114 — G. Marin and R. J. Gamba

BODY IMAGE AVOIDANCE QUESTIONNAIRE 120 — J. C. Rosen, D. Srebnik, E. Saltzberg, and S. Wendt

BODY SENSATIONS QUESTIONNAIRE 123 — D. L. Chambless, G. C. Caputo, P. Bright, and R. Gallagher

BODY SHAPE QUESTIONNAIRE 125 — P. J. Cooper, M. J. Taylor, Z. Cooper, and C. G. Fairburn

BOREDOM PRONENESS 129 — R. Famer and N. D. Sundberg

BREAST SELF-EXAMINATION SCALE 131 — K. E. H. Race and J. A. Silverberg

BRIEF DEPRESSION RATING SCALE 134 — R. Kellner

BRIEF SCREEN FOR DEPRESSION 138 — A. R. Hakstian and P. D. McLean

BULIMIA TEST—REVISED 140 — M. H. Thelen and M. Smith

BULIMIC AUTOMATIC THOUGHTS TEST 148 — D. L. Franco and D. C. Zuroff

CAREGIVER STRAIN INDEX 150 — B. C. Robinson

CAREGIVER'S BURDEN SCALE 152 — S. H. Zarit, K. E. Reever, and J. Bach-Peterson

CENTER FOR EPIDEMIOLOGIC STUDIES-DEPRESSED MOOD SCALE 155 — L. S. Radloff

CHINESE DEPRESSIVE SYMPTOM SCALE   157 — N. Lin

CHRONIC PAIN INTRUSION AND ACCOMMODATION SCALE   160 — M. C. Jacob, R. D. Kerns, R. Rosenberg, and J. Haythornthwaite

CLIENT EXPERIENCES QUESTIONNAIRE 163 — J. R. Greeley and J. S. Greenberg

CLIENT MOTIVATION FOR THERAPY SCALE   168 — L. G. Pelletier, K. M. Tuson, and N. K. Haddad

CLIENT SATISFACTION INVENTORY   172 — S. L. McMurty and W. W. Hudson

CLIENT SATISFACTION QUESTIONNAIRE   174 — C. C. Attkisson

CLINICAL ANXIETY SCALE   177 — B. A. Thyer

COGNITIVE COPING STRATEGY INVENTORY   179 — R. W. Butler, F. L. Damarin, C. Beaulieu, A. Schwebel, and B. E. Thorn

COGNITIVE PROCESSES SURVEY   189 — R. F. Martinetti

COGNITIVE SLIPPAGE SCALE   193 — T. C. Miers and M. L. Raulin

COGNITIVE-SOMATIC ANXIETY QUESTIONNAIRE   196 — G. E. Schwartz, R. L. Davidson, and D. J. Goleman

COGNITIVE TRIAD INVENTORY   198 — E. E. Beckham, W. R. Leber, J. T. Watkins, J. L. Boyer, and J. B. Cook

COLLECTIVE SELF-ESTEEM SCALE   203 — R. Luhtanen and J. Crocker

COMBAT EXPOSURE SCALE   206 — T. M. Keane, J. A. Fairbank, J. M. Caddell, R. T. Zimmering, K. L. Taylor, and C. A. Mora

COMPULSIVENESS INVENTORY   208 — D. M. Kagan and R. L. Squires

CONCERN ABOUT DEATH-DYING AND COPING CHECKLISTS   210 — P. S. Fry

COSTELLO-COMREY DEPRESSION AND ANXIETY SCALES   213 — C. G. Costello and A. L. Comrey

CULTURAL CONGRUITY SCALE   219 — A. M. Gloria and S. E. Robinson-Kurpius

DATING AND ASSERTION QUESTIONNAIRE   221 — R. W. Levenson and J. M. Gottman

DEATH DEPRESSION SCALE   225 — D. I. Templer, M. LaVoie, H. Chalgujian, and S. Thomas-Dobson

xx   *Contents*

DEFENSE STYLE QUESTIONNAIRE-40   G. Andrews, M. Singh,
227   and M. Bond
DENTAL ANXIETY SCALE   231   N. Corah, E. N. Gale, and S.
                                   J. Illig
DENTAL FEAR SURVEY   233   R. A. Kleinknecht, R. K.
                                   Klepac, L. D. Alexander,
                                   and D. A. Bernstein

DEPRESSION ANXIETY AND STRESS   S. H. Lovibond and P. F.
   SCALES   237   Lovibond
DEPRESSION-HAPPINESS SCALE   240   S. Joseph and C. A. Lewis
DEPRESSIVE PERSONALITY DISORDER   S. K. Huprich, J. Margrett,
   INVENTORY   242   K. J. Barthelemy, and M.
                                   A. Fine
DETOX FEAR SURVEY SCHEDULE-27   M. A. Gentile and J. B.
245   Milby
DIETARY INVENTORY OF EATING   D. G. Schlundt and R. T.
   TEMPTATIONS   248   Zimering
DISSOCIATIVE EXPERIENCES SCALE   E. M. Bernstein and F. W.
254   Putnam
DRUG ABUSE SCREENING TEST   260   H. A. Skinner
DYSFUNCTIONAL ATTITUDE SCALE   A. Weissman
263
EATING ATTITUDES TEST   267   D. M. Garner and P. E.
                                   Garfinkel
EATING QUESTIONNAIRE—REVISED   D. A. Williamson, C. J.
270   Davis, A. J. Goreczny, S.
                                   J. McKenzie, and P.
                                   Watkins
EATING SELF-EFFICACY SCALE   273   S. M. Glynn and A. J.
                                   Ruderman
EGO IDENTITY SCALE   275   A. L. Tan, R. J. Kendis, J.
                                   Fine, and J. Porac
EMOTIONAL ASSESSMENT SCALE   278   C. R. Carlson, F. L. Collins,
                                   J. F. Stewart, J. Porzelius,
                                   J. A. Nitz, and C. O. Lind
EMOTIONAL/SOCIAL LONELINESS   H. Vincenzi and F. Grabosky
   INVENTORY   281
FEAR-OF-INTIMACY SCALE   284   C. J. Descutner and M.
                                   Thelen
FEAR OF NEGATIVE EVALUATION   287 D. Watson and R. Friend
FEAR QUESTIONNAIRE   291   I. M. Mark and A. M.
                                   Mathews
FEAR SURVEY SCHEDULE-II   294   J. H. Geer

FREQUENCY OF SELF REINFORCEMENT
QUESTIONNAIRE 296

E. M. Heiby

FRIENDLINESS–UNFRIENDLINESS
SCALE (SACRAL) 299

J. M. Reisman

FROST MULTIDIMENSIONAL
PERFECTIONISM SCALE 302

R. O. Frost, P. Martin, C.
Lahart, and R. Rosenblate

GAMBLING ATTITUDES SCALE 306

J. I. Kassinove

GENERALIZED CONTENTMENT SCALE
310

W. W. Hudson

GENERALIZED EXPECTANCY FOR
SUCCESS SCALE—REVISED 313

W. D. Hale and C. D. Cochran

GERIATRIC DEPRESSION SCALE 315

T. L. Brink, J. A. Yesavage,
O. Lum, P. Heersema, V.
Huang, T. L. Rose, M.
Adey, and V. O. Leirer

GOLDFARB FEAR OF FAT SCALE 318

L. A. Goldfarb

HARDER PERSONAL FEELINGS
QUESTIONNAIRE 320

D. W. Harder

HARDINESS SCALE 322

P. T. Bartone, R. J. Ursano,
K. M. Wright, and L. H.
Ingraham

HEALTH SURVEY SHORT FORMS 327

J. E. Ware, Jr.

HELPLESS BEHAVIOR
QUESTIONNAIRE 334

C. Peterson

HENDRICK SEXUAL ATTITUDE SCALE
336

S. Hendrick and C. Hendrick

HOMESICKNESS AND CONTENTMENT
SCALE 339

H. Shin and N. Abell

HUNGER-SATIETY SCALES 343

P. E. Garfinkel

HYPERCOMPETITIVE ATTITUDE
SCALE 347

R. M. Ryckman, M.
Hammer, L. M. Kaczor,
and J. A. Gold

HYPOCHONDRIASIS SCALE FOR
INSTITUTIONAL GERIATRIC
PATIENTS 350

T. L. Brink, J. Bryant, J.
Belanger, D. Capri, S.
Jasculca, C. Janakes, and
C. Oliveira

ILLNESS ATTITUDE SCALE 352

R. Kellner

ILLNESS BEHAVIOR INVENTORY 356

I. D. Turkat and L. S.
Pettegrew

ILLNESS BEHAVIOR QUESTIONNAIRE
358

I. Pilowsky and N. D. Spence

IMPACT OF EVENT SCALE 363

M. J. Horowitz

IMPOSTER PHENOMENON SCALE 365

P. R. Clance

INDECISIVENESS SCALE   369   R. O. Frost and D. L. Shows
INDEX OF ALCOHOL INVOLVEMENT   G. MacNeil
    372
INDEX OF ATTITUDES TOWARD   W. W. Hudson and W.
    HOMOSEXUALS   374   Ricketts
INDEX OF CLINICAL STRESS   376   N. Abell
INDEX OF DRUG INVOLVEMENT   378   A. C. Faul and W. H.
                                               Hudson
INDEX OF JOB SATISFACTION   381   C. K. Pike and W. H.
                                               Hudson
INDEX OF SELF-ESTEEM   383   W. W. Hudson
INDEX OF SEXUAL HARASSMENT   386   W. H. Hudson and A. L.
                                               Decker
INDEX OF SEXUAL SATISFACTION   388   W. W. Hudson
INTERACTION AND AUDIENCE   M. R. Leary
    ANXIOUSNESS SCALES   391
INTERNAL CONTROL INDEX   394   P. Duttweiler
INTERNAL VERSUS EXTERNAL   L. L. Tobias and M. L.
    CONTROL OF WEIGHT SCALE   397   MacDonald
INTERNALIZED HOMOPHOBIA SCALE   M. W. Ross and B. R. S.
    399   Rosser
INTERPERSONAL DEPENDENCY   R. M. A. Hirschfield, G. L.
    INVENTORY   401   Klerman, H. G. Gough, J.
                                               Barrett, S. J. Korchin, and
                                               P. Chodoff
INTIMACY SCALE   405   A. J. Walker and L.
                                               Thompson
INVENTORY TO DIAGNOSE   M. Zimmerman, W. Coryell,
    DEPRESSION   407   C. Corenthal, and S.
                                               Wilson
INVENTORY OF DYADIC HETEROSEXUAL   D. M. Purnine, M. P. Carey,
    PREFERENCES   413   and R. S. Jorgensen
IRRATIONAL VALUES SCALE   418   A. P. MacDonald
IRRITABILITY/APATHY SCALE   421   A. Burns, S. Folstein, J.
                                               Brandt, and M. Folstein
JOB INTERVIEW SELF-STATEMENT   R. G. Heimberg, K. E.
    SCHEDULE   424   Keller, and T. Peca-Baker
LIFE EVENTS QUESTIONNAIRE   430   T. S. Brugha
LIFE SATISFACTION INDEX-Z   432   B. Neugarten, R. J.
                                               Havighurst, and S. S.
                                               Tobin
LIKING PEOPLE SCALE   434   E. E. Filsinger

LONELINESS RATING SCALE 436 — J. J. Scalise, E. J. Ginter, and L. H. Gerstein

LOVE ATTITUDES SCALE 440 — C. Hendrick and S. S. Hendrick

MAGICAL IDEATION SCALE 443 — M. Eckblad and L. J. Chapman

MATHEMATICS ANXIETY RATING SCALE—REVISED 446 — B. S. Plake and C. S. Parker

MAUDSLEY OBSESSIONAL-COMPULSIVE INVENTORY 448 — R. J. Hodgson and S. Rachman

MCGILL PAIN QUESTIONNAIRE 450 — R. Melzack

MCMULLIN ADDICTION THOUGHT SCALE 452 — R. F. McMullin

MEDICAL AVOIDANCE SURVEY 455 — R. A. Kleinknecht

MEDICAL FEAR SURVEY 459 — R. A. Kleinknecht

MENSTRUAL SYMPTOM QUESTIONNAIRE 463 — M. Chesney

MICHIGAN ALCOHOLISM SCREENING TEST 466 — M. K. Selzer

MILLER SOCIAL INTIMACY SCALE 469 — R. S. Miller and H. M. Lefcourt

MISSISSIPPI SCALE 472 — T. Keane, J. M. Caddell, and K. L. Taylor

MOBILITY INVENTORY FOR AGORAPHOBIA 478 — D. L. Chambless, G. C. Caputo, S. E. Jasin, E. Gracely, and C. Williams

MOOD-RELATED PLEASANT EVENTS SCHEDULE 482 — D. J. MacPhillamy and P. M. Lewinsohn

MOOD SURVEY 486 — B. Underwood and W. J. Froming

MULTIDIMENSIONAL BODY-SELF RELATIONS QUESTIONNAIRE 488 — T. F. Cash

MULTIDIMENSIONAL DESIRE FOR CONTROL SCALES 492 — L. A. Anderson

MULTIDIMENSIONAL HEALTH LOCUS OF CONTROL SCALES 495 — K. A. Wallston, B. S. Wallston, and R. DeVellis

MULTIDIMENSIONAL LOCUS OF CONTROL SCALES FOR PSYCHIATRIC PATIENTS 500 — H. Levenson

MULTIDIMENSIONAL SCALE OF PERCEIVED SOCIAL SUPPORT 502 — G. D. Zimet, N. W. Dahlem, S. G. Zimet, and G. K. Farley

MULTIDIMENSIONAL SENSE OF HUMOR
  SCALE   504   J. A. Thorson and F. C.
                                         Powell
MULTIDIMENSIONAL SUPPORT SCALE   H. R. Winefield, A. H.
  507   Winefield, and M.
                                         Tiggemann

NEGATIVE ATTITUDES TOWARD   P. R. Abramson and D. L.
  MASTURBATION INVENTORY   512   Mosher
NETWORK ORIENTATION SCALE   515   A. Vaux, P. Burda, and D.
                                       Stewart

NEUROTIC PERFECTIONISM   S. F. Mitzman, P. Slade,
  QUESTIONNAIRE   518   and M. E. Dewey
NONCONTINGENT OUTCOME   J. P. Shapiro
  INSTRUMENT   522
OBSESSIVE-COMPULSIVE INVENTORY   E. B. Foa, M. J. Kazak,
  524   and P. M. Salkovskis
OBSESSIVE-COMPULSIVE SCALE   529   G. D. Gibb, J. R. Bailey, R.
                                       H. Best, and T. T.
                                       Lambirth

ORGANIZATIONAL CLIMATE SCALE   531   A. Thompson and H.
                                       McCubbin

ORTHOGONAL CULTURE   F. Beauvais and E. R.
  IDENTIFICATION SCALE   535   Oetting
PADUA INVENTORY   539   E. Sanavio
PAIN CATASTROPHIZING SCALE   544   M. L. Sullivan, S. R. Bishop,
                                       and J. Pivik
PAIN-RELATED SELF STATEMENTS   H. Flor, D. J. Behle, and
  SCALE AND PAIN-RELATED CONTROL   N. Birbaumer
  SCALE   547
PANIC ATTACK COGNITIONS   G. A. Clum, S. Broyles, J.
  QUESTIONNAIRE   551   Borden, and P. L. Watkins
PANIC ATTACK SYMPTOMS   G. A. Clum, S. Broyles, J.
  QUESTIONNAIRE   553   Borden, and P. L. Watkins
PATIENT REACTIONS ASSESSMENT   556   J. P. Galassi, R. Schanberg,
                                       and W. B. Ware
PENN STATE WORRY QUESTIONNAIRE   T. J. Meyer, M. L. Miller,
  559   R. L. Metzger, and T. D.
                                       Borkovec

PERCEIVED GUILT INDEX—STATE AND   J. R. Otterbacher and D. C.
  PERCEIVED GUILT INDEX—TRAIT   562   Munz

PERCEIVED SOCIAL SUPPORT—FRIEND   M. E. Procidano and K.
  SCALE AND PERCEIVED SOCIAL   Heller
  SUPPORT—FAMILY SCALE   565

PERCEIVED STRESS SCALE 570 — S. Cohen, T. Kamarck, and R. Mermelstein

PERSONAL ASSERTION ANALYSIS 573 — B. L. Hedlund and C. U. Lindquist

PERSONAL STYLE INVENTORY 576 — C. J. Robins and A. G. Luten

PHYSICAL SELF-EFFICACY SCALE 586 — R. M. Ryckman, M. A. Robbins, B. Thornton, and P. Cantrell

POSITIVE AND NEGATIVE SUICIDE IDEATION INVENTORY 589 — A. Osman, B. A. Kopper, F. X. Barrios, and P. M. Gutierrez

PROBLEM-SOLVING INVENTORY 591 — P. P. Heppner

PROCRASTINATION ASSESSMENT SCALE—STUDENTS 595 — L. J. Solomon and E. D. Rothblum

PROCRASTINATION SCALE 602 — B. W. Tuckman

PROVISION OF SOCIAL RELATIONS 604 — R. J. Turner, B. G. Frankel, and D. M. Levin

PURSUING-DISTANCING SCALE 606 — D. M. Bernstein, J. Santelli, K. Alter-Reid, and V. Androsiglio

QUESTIONNAIRE OF EXPERIENCES OF DISSOCIATION 611 — K. C. Riley

RAPE AFTERMATH SYMPTOM TEST 613 — D. G. Kilpatrick

RATHUS ASSERTIVENESS SCHEDULE 618 — S. A. Rathus

RATIONAL BEHAVIOR INVENTORY 621 — C. T. Shorkey and V. C. Whiteman

RAULIN INTENSE AMBIVALENCE SCALE 625 — M. L. Raulin

REACTION INVENTORY INTERFERENCE 628 — D. R. Evans and S. S. Kazarian

REASONS FOR LIVING INVENTORY 631 — M. M. Linehan

REID-GUNDLACH SOCIAL SERVICE SATISFACTION SCALE 635 — P. N. Reid and J. P. Gundlach

RESTRAINT SCALE 638 — C. P. Herman

REVISED KINSHIP SCALE 640 — K. G. Bailey and G. R. Nava

REVISED MARTIN-LARSEN APPROVAL MOTIVATION 642 — H. J. Martin

REVISED UCLA LONELINESS SCALE 644 — D. Russell, L. Peplau, and C. Cutrona

ROLE PERCEPTION SCALE 646 — M. S. Richardson and J. L. Alpert

SATISFACTION WITH APPEARANCE   J. W. Lawrence et al.
   SCALE   650
SATISFACTION WITH LIFE SCALE   652   E. Diener, R. A. Emmons,
                                      R.J. Larsen, and
                                      S. Griffin

SCALE FOR THE ASSESSMENT OF   N. C. Andreasen
   NEGATIVE SYMPTOMS AND SCALE
   FOR THE ASSESSMENT OF POSITIVE
   SYMPTOMS   654
SELF-ADMINISTERED ALCOHOLISM   W. M. Swenson and
   SCREENING TEST   662   R. M. Morse
SELF-ATTITUDE INVENTORY   667   M. Lorr and R. A.
                                      Wunderlich
SELF-CONSCIOUSNESS SCALE   671   M. F. Scheier
SELF-CONTROL QUESTIONNAIRE   673   L. P. Rehm
SELF-CONTROL SCHEDULE   677   M. Rosenbaum
SELF-EFFICACY SCALE   681   M. Sherer, J. E. Maddux, B.
                                      Mercandante, S. Prentice-
                                      Dunn, B. Jacobs, and R.
                                      W. Rogers

SELF-EFFICACY SCALE FOR   B. McDermott
   SCHIZOPHRENICS   683
SELF-ESTEEM RATING SCALE   690   W. R. Nugent and J. W.
                                      Thomas
SELF-RATING ANXIETY SCALE   693   W. W. K. Zung
SELF-RATING DEPRESSION SCALE   695   W. W. K. Zung
SELF-RIGHTEOUSNESS SCALE   697   T. Falbo
SELFISM   699   E. J. Phares and N. Erskine
SEMANTIC DIFFERENTIAL FEELING   M. Lorr and R. A.
   AND MOOD SCALES   702   Wunderlich
SENSATION SCALE   705   S. A. Maisto, V. J. Adesso,
                                      and R. Lauerman
SENSE OF SYMBOLIC IMMORTALITY   J.-L. Drolet
   SCALE   708
SEPARATION-INDIVIDUATION PROCESS   R. M. Christenson and W. P.
   INVENTORY   712   Wilson
SESSION EVALUATION   W. B. Stiles
   QUESTIONNAIRE   715
SEVERITY OF SYMPTOMS SCALE   717   B. Vitiello, S. Spreat, and D.
                                      Behar
SEXUAL AROUSABILITY INVENTORY   E. F. Hoon and D. L.
   AND SEXUAL AROUSABILITY   Chambless
   INVENTORY—EXPANDED   720

SEXUAL ASSAULT SYMPTOM SCALE 724 — L. O. Ruch, J. W. Gartell, S. R. Amedeo, and B. J. Coyne

SEXUAL ATTITUDE SCALE 728 — W. W. Hudson, G. J. Murphy, and P. S. Nurius

SEXUAL BEHAVIOR INVENTORY— FEMALE 730 — P. M. Bentler

SEXUAL BEHAVIOR INVENTORY— MALE 733 — P. M. Bentler

SHORT ACCULTURATION SCALE FOR HISPANICS 736 — G. Marin

SIMPATIA SCALE 743 — J. D. Griffith, G. W. Joe, L. R. Chatham, and D. D. Simpson

SIMPLE RATHUS ASSERTIVENESS SCHEDULE 746 — I. A. McCormick

SMOKING SELF-EFFICACY QUESTIONNAIRE 749 — G. Colletti and J. A. Supnick

SOCIAL ADJUSTMENT SCALE—SELF REPORT 752 — M. M. Weissman and E. S. Paykel

SOCIAL ANXIETY THOUGHTS QUESTIONNAIRE 763 — L. M. Hartman

SOCIAL AVOIDANCE AND DISTRESS SCALE 765 — D. Watson and R. Friend

SOCIAL FEAR SCALE 767 — M. L. Raulin and J. L. Wee

SOCIAL INTERACTION SELF- STATEMENT TEST 769 — C. R. Glass, T. V. Merluzzi, J. L. Biever, and K. H. Larsen

SOCIAL PROBLEM-SOLVING INVENTORY 772 — T. J. D'Zurilla and A. M. Nezu

SOCIAL RHYTHM METRIC 780 — T. Monk, J. F. Flaherty, E. Frank, and D. J. Kupfer

SOCIAL SUPPORT APPRAISALS SCALE 783 — A. Vaux, J. Phillips, L. Holley, B. Thompson, D. Williams, and D. Stewart

SOCIAL SUPPORT BEHAVIORS SCALE 786 — A. Vaux, S. Riedel, and D. Stewart

SOCIOPOLITICAL CONTROL SCALE 791 — M. A. Zimmerman and J. H. Zahniser

SOMATIC, COGNITIVE, BEHAVIORAL ANXIETY INVENTORY 793 — P. M. Lehrer and R. L. Woolfolk

SOMATOFORM DISSOCIATION QUESTIONNAIRE 799 — E. R. S. Nijenhuis, O. van der Hart, and J. Vanderlinden

SOUTH OAKS GAMBLING SCREEN   803   H. R. Lesieur and S. B. Blume

SPLITTING SCALE   807   M.-J. Gerson
STATE HOPE SCALE   809   C. R. Snyder et al.
STATE-TRAIT ANGER SCALE   811   C. Spielberger and P. London

STRESS-AROUSAL CHECKLIST   814   C. Mackay and T. Cox
STRESSFUL SITUATIONS QUESTIONNAIRE   816   W. F. Hodges and J. P. Felling
STUDENT JENKINS ACTIVITY SURVEY 819   P. R. Yarnold and F. B. Bryant
SURVEY OF HETEROSEXUAL INTERACTIONS   824   C. T. Twentyman and R. M. McFall
SYMPTOM QUESTIONNAIRE   830   R. Kellner
SYMPTOMS CHECKLIST   834   P. T. Bartone, R. J. Ursano, K. M. Wright, and L. H. Ingraham

TCU DEPRESSION AND TCU DECISION-MAKING SCALES   836   G. W. Joe, L. Knezek, D. Watson, and D. D. Simpson

TEMPLER DEATH ANXIETY SCALE   838   D. I. Templer
TEMPORAL SATISFACTION WITH LIFE SCALE   840   W. Pavot, E. Diener, and E. Suh
TEST OF NEGATIVE SOCIAL EXCHANGE   843   L. S. Ruehlman and P. Karoly
THOUGHT CONTROL QUESTIONNAIRE 845   A. Wells and M. I. Davies
THREAT APPRAISAL SCALE   849   K. E. Hart
TIME URGENCY AND PERPETUAL ACTIVATION SCALE   851   L. Wright, S. McCurdy, and G. Rogoll
TRUST IN PHYSICIAN SCALE   858   L. A. Anderson and R. F. Dedrick

UNIVERSITY ENVIRONMENT SCALE 860   A. M. Gloria and S. E. R. Kurpius
VALUES CONFLICT RESOLUTION ASSESSMENT   862   R. T. Kinnier

VERBAL AGGRESSIVENESS SCALE   868   D. A. Infante and C. J. Wigley, III

WAY OF LIFE SCALE   870   L. Wright, K. von Bussmann, A. Friedman, M. Khoury, F. Owens, and W. Paris

WEST HAVEN–YALE MULTI-DIMENSIONAL PAIN INVENTORY   873   R. D. Kerns, D. C. Turk, and T. E. Rudy

WHITE BEAR SUPPRESSION INVENTORY 882 — D. M. Wegner and S. Zanakos

WILLINGNESS TO CARE SCALE 884 — N. Abell

WORKING ALLIANCE INVENTORY 888 — A. O. Horvath

YOUNG ADULT FAMILY INVENTORY OF LIFE EVENTS AND CHANGES 892 — H. I. McCubbin, J. M. Patterson, and J. R. Grochowski

YOUNG ADULT SOCIAL SUPPORT INVENTORY 897 — H. I. McCubbin, J. M. Patterson, and J. R. Grochowski

INSTRUMENTS CROSS-INDEXED BY PROBLEM AREA

(Instruments in **boldface** are in Volume 1 and those in standard type are in Volume 2.)

PROBLEM AREA	INSTRUMENT
Abuse (also see Rape)	Index of Sexual Harassment 386 **Non-Physical Abuse of Partner Scale 154** **Partner Abuse Scale: Non-Physical 156** **Partner Abuse Scale: Physical 158** **Physical Abuse of Partner Scale 163**
Acculturation	Acculturation Rating Scale for Mexican-Americans-II 9 Bidimensional Acculturation Scale 339 Cultural Congruity Scale 219 Homesickness and Contentment Scale 339 **Multigroup Ethnic Identity Scale 581** Orthogonal Cultural Identification Scale 535 **Scale for Racial Socialization for Adolescents 612** Short Acculturation Scale for Hispanics 936 University Environment Scale 860
Addiction (also see Substance Abuse)	Gambling Attitudes Scale 306 South Oaks Gambling Screen 803
Anger and Hostility	Aggression Inventory 40 Aggression Questionnaire 43 Anger Idioms Scale 55 Argumentativeness Scale 57 Bakker Assertiveness-Aggressiveness Inventory 96 **Conflict Tactics Scales 229**

[Anger and Hostility]

Anxiety and Fear
   (also see Mood, Phobias)

State-Trait Anger Scale   811
Symptom Questionnaire   830

Achievement Anxiety Test   20
**Children's Cognitive Assessment
   Questionnaire   513**
Clinical Anxiety Scale   177
Cognitive-Somatic Anxiety
   Questionnaire   196
Combat Exposure Scale   206
Concern About Death-Dying and
   Coping Checklists   210
Costello-Comrey Anxiety Scale
   213
Dental Anxiety Scale   231
Dental Fear Survey   233
Depression Anxiety and Stress
   Scales   237
Fear-of-Intimacy Scale   284
Fear of Negative Evaluation   287
**Hospital Fears Rating Scale
   558**
Interaction and Audience
   Anxiousness Scales   391
Mathematics Anxiety Rating Scale—
   Revised   446
Penn State Worry Questionnaire   559
Self-Consciousness Scale   671
Self-Rating Anxiety Scale   693
Social Anxiety Thoughts
   Questionnaire   763
Social Avoidance and Distress Scale
   765
Social Fear Scale   767
Social Interaction Self-Statement
   Test   769
Somatic, Cognitive, Behavioral
   Anxiety Inventory   793
Stressful Situations Questionnaire
   816
Symptom Questionnaire
   830
Threat Appraisal Scale   849

PROBLEM AREA   INSTRUMENT

Assertiveness   Assertion Inventory   64
  (also see Anxiety, Inter-   Assertion Self-Statement Test—
  personal Behavior)   Revised   71
                                 Assertive Job-Hunting Survey
                                   75
                                 **Assertiveness Scale for
                                   Adolescents   459**
                                 Assertiveness Self-Report Inventory
                                   77
                                 Assertiveness Self-Statement Test
                                   80
                                 Bakker Assertiveness-Aggressiveness
                                   Inventory   96
                                 **Children's Action Tendency Scale
                                   499**
                                 Conflict Tactics Scales   229
                                 Personal Assertion Analysis   573
                                 Rathus Assertiveness Schedule
                                   618
                                 Simple Rathus Assertiveness
                                   Schedule   746

Beliefs (Rational and Irrational)   Ascription of Responsibility
                                   Questionnaire   61
                                 Authoritarianism Scale   89
                                 Beliefs Associated with Childhood
                                   Sexual Abuse   111
                                 Cognitive Triad Inventory   198
                                 **Common Belief Inventory for
                                   Students   524**
                                 Family Beliefs Inventory   263
                                 Hardiness Scale   322
                                 Imposter Phenomenon Scale   365
                                 Irrational Values Scale   418
                                 Neurotic Perfectionism Questionnaire
                                   518
                                 Rational Behavior Inventory   621
                                 Self-Righteousness Scale   697
                                 Separation-Individuation Process
                                   Inventory   712

PROBLEM AREA	INSTRUMENT
Children's Behaviors/Problems	**Adolescent Concerns Evaluation 449**
	Behavior Rating Index for Children 473
	Child Dental Control Assessment 480
	Childhood Personality Scale 488
	Children's Attributional Style Questionnaire 505
	Children's Beliefs about Parental Divorce Scale 509
	Child Report of Posttraumatic Symptoms 484
	Parent Report of Posttraumatic Symptoms 484
	Companion Animal Bonding Scale 528
	Eyberg Child Behavior Inventory 540
	Homework Problem Checklist 553
	Oregon Mental Health Referral Checklist 587
	Peer and Self-Rating Scale 595
	Persistence Scale for Children 600
	Self-Control Rating Scale 619
	Spider Phobia Questionnaire for Children 623
	Youth Coping Index 628
Client Motivation	Client Motivation for Therapy Scale 168
	Drinking Motives Questionnaire 537
Coping	**Adolescent Coping Orientation for Problem Experiences 454**
	Chinese Ways of Coping Questionnaire 521
	Concern About Death-Dying and Coping Checklists 210

PROBLEM AREA	INSTRUMENT

PROBLEM AREA

[Coping]

Couple Relationship
  (see Marital/Couple Relationship)

Death Concerns

Depression and Grief
  (also see Mood, Suicide)

INSTRUMENT

[Coping]
**Coping Health Inventory for
  Parents　237**
**Family Coping Coherence Index
  282**
Family Coping Index　284
Hardiness Scale　322
State Hope Scale　809
Youth Coping Index　628

Death Concerns
Concern About Death-Dying and
  Coping Checklists　210
Death Depression Scale　225
Sense of Symbolic Immortality
  Scale　708
Templer Death Anxiety Scale　838

Depression and Grief
Accepting the Past/Reminiscing
  About the Past　5
Automatic Thoughts Questionnaire
  94
Brief Depression Rating Scale　134
Brief Screen for Depression　138
Center for Epidemiologic Studies-
  Depressed Mood Scale　155
**Children's Attributional Style
  Questionnaire　505**
Chinese Depressive Symptom Scale
  157
Costello-Comrey Depression Scale
  213
Depression Anxiety and Stress
  Scales　237
Depression-Happiness Scale　240
Depression Self-Rating Scale　535
Depressive Personality Disorder
  Inventory　242
Dysfunctional Attitude Scale
  263

PROBLEM AREA   INSTRUMENT

[Depression and Grief]   Frequency of Self Reinforcement
                                              Questionnaire   296
                                          Generalized Contentment Scale   310
                                          Helpless Behavior Questionnaire
                                              334
                                          Homesickness and Contentment
                                              Scale   339
                                          **Hopelessness Scale for Children
                                              556**
                                          Inventory to Diagnose Depression
                                              407
                                          Mood-Related Pleasant Events
                                              Schedule   482
                                          Perinatal Grief Scale   436
                                          Personal Style Inventory   576
                                          Self-Control Questionnaire   673
                                          Self-Rating Depression Scale   695
                                          Social Rhythm Metric   780
                                          Symptom Questionnaire
                                              830

Eating Problems   Bulimic Automatic Thoughts Test
                                              148
                                          Bulimia Test—Revised   140
                                          Body Shape Questionnaire   125
                                          Compulsive Eating Scale   530
                                          **Concern over Weight and Dieting
                                              Scale   532**
                                          Dietary Inventory of Eating
                                              Temptations   248
                                          Eating Attitudes Test   267
                                          Eating Questionnaire—Revised   270
                                          Eating Self-Efficacy Scale   273
                                          Goldfarb Fear of Fat Scale   318
                                          Hunger-Satiety Scales   343
                                          Internal Versus External Control of
                                              Weight Scale   397
                                          Restraint Scale   638

Ethnic Identity   Acculturation Rating Scale for
                                              Mexican-Americans-II   9

PROBLEM AREA   INSTRUMENT

[Ethnic Identity]   Bidimensional Acculturation Scale
                                   114
                                Cultural Congruity Scale   219
                                Homesickness and Contentment
                                   Scale   339
                                **Multigroup Ethnic Identity Scale
                                   581**
                                Orthogonal Cultural Identification
                                   Scale   535
                                **Scale for Racial Socialization for
                                   Adolescents   612**
                                Short Acculturation Scale for
                                   Hispanics   736
                                University Environment Scale   860

Family Functioning   **Boundary Ambiguity Scales   214**
   (also see Parent-Child   **Construction of Problems Scale
   Relationships)   87**
                                **Environmental Assessment Index
                                   243**
                                **Family Adaptability and Cohesion
                                   Evaluation Scale   246**
                                Family Assessment Device   250
                                **Family Attachment and
                                   Changeability Index   254**
                                Family Awareness Scale   259
                                Family Celebrations Index   280
                                **Family Coping Coherence Index
                                   282**
                                Family Coping Index   284
                                **Family Crisis Oriented Personal
                                   Evaluation Scales   294**
                                **Family Emotional Involvement and
                                   Criticism Scale   300**
                                Family Distress Index   298
                                **Family, Friends, and Self Form
                                   545**
                                Family Functioning Scale   307
                                **Family Inventory of Resources for
                                   Management   322**

PROBLEM AREA INSTRUMENT

[Family Functioning] **Family Member Well-Being 329**
Family-of-Origin Scale 331
Family Organized Cohesiveness Scale 336
Family Pressures Scale—Ethnic 338
Family Problem Solving Communication 342
Family Responsibility Index 345
Family Schema—Ethnic 351
Family Sense of Coherence and Family Adaptation Scales 354
Family Times and Routines Index 363
Family Traditions Scale 370
Index of Brother and Sister Relations 376
Index of Family Relations 379
Kansas Family Life Satisfaction Scale 384
Level of Expressed Emotion 388
Self-Report Family Instrument 441
Separation-Individuation Process Inventory 712

Geriatric Accepting the Past/Reminiscing
(also see listings under About the Past 5
problem areas) **Attitude Toward the Provision of Long-Term Care 207**
Caregiver Strain Index 150
Caregiver's Burden Scale 152
Concern About Death-Dying and Coping Checklists 210
Geriatric Depression Scale 315
Irritability/Apathy Scale 421
Memory and Behavior Problems Checklist 392
Realizations of Filial Responsibility 438
Willingness to Care Scale 884

PROBLEM AREA	INSTRUMENT

Guilt
  (also see Anxiety, Beliefs)
	Harder Personal Feelings
	  Questionnaire 320
	Perceived Guilt Index—State and
	  Perceived Guilt Index—Trait
	  562

Health Issues	Adherence Determinants
	  Questionnaire 27
	Adult Health Concerns
	  Questionnaire 31
	Breast Self-Examination Scale 131
	Child Dental Control Assessment
	480
	Cognitive Coping Strategy
	  Inventory 179
	Coping Health Inventory for
	Parents 237
	Health Survey Short Forms 327
	Hospital Fears Rating Scale 558
	Hypochondriasis Scale for
	  Institutional Geriatric Patients
	  350
	Illness Attitude Scale 356
	Illness Behavior Inventory 356
	Illness Behavior Questionnaire
	  358
	McGill Pain Questionnaire 450
	Medical Avoidance Survey 455
	Medical Fear Survey 459
	Menstrual Symptom Questionnaire
	  463
	Multidimensional Body-Self
	  Relations Questionnaire 488
	Multidimensional Health Locus of
	  Control Scales 495
	Patient Reactions Assessment 556
	Parental Tolerance Scale 429
	Symptom Questionnaire 830
	Time Urgency and Perpetual
	  Activation Scale 851
	Trust in Physician Scale 858

PROBLEM AREA INSTRUMENT

[Health Issues]   West Haven–Yale Multidimensional
                           Pain Inventory   873

Identity   Ego Identity Scale   275
                           Imposter Phenomenon Scale   365
                           Separation-Individuation Process
                               Inventory   712

Impulsivity   Barratt Impulsiveness Scale 11
                               104
                           Impulsivity Scale   560

Interpersonal Behavior   Argumentativeness Scale   57
   (also see related issues)   Authority Behavior Inventory   91
                           Barnett Liking of Children Scale
                               101
                           Boredom Proneness   129
                           Conflict Tactics Scales   229
                           Dating and Assertion Questionnaire
                               221
                           Friendliness–Unfriendliness Scale
                               (SACRAL)   299
                           Hypercompetitive Attitude Scale
                               347
                           Index of Attitudes Toward
                               Homosexuals   374
                           Index of Peer Relations   562
                           Interpersonal Dependency Inventory
                               401
                           Job Interview Self-Statement
                               Schedule   424
                           Liking People Scale   434
                           Miller Social Intimacy Scale   469
                           Pursuing-Distancing Scale   606
                           Revised Martin-Larsen Approval
                               Motivation   642
                           Separation-Individuation Process
                               Inventory   712
                           Test of Negative Social Exchange
                               843
                           Verbal Aggressiveness Scale   868

PROBLEM AREA   INSTRUMENT

[Interpersonal Behavior]   **Young Children's Social
                                           Desirability Scale   625**

Locus of Control   Ascription of Responsibility
                                           Questionnaire   61
                                       Belief in Personal Control Scale
                                           107
                                       Family Empowerment Scale   302
                                       **Fetal Health Locus of Control
                                           Scale   372**
                                       Generalized Expectancy for Success
                                           Scale—Revised   313
                                       Hardiness Scale   322
                                       Internal Control Index   394
                                       Internal Versus External Control of
                                           Weight Scale   397
                                       **Miller Marital Locus of Control
                                           Scale   150**
                                       Multidimensional Desire for Control
                                           Scales   492
                                       Multidimensional Health Locus of
                                           Control Scales   495
                                       Multidimensional Locus of Control
                                           Scales for Psychiatric Patients
                                           500
                                       Noncontingent Outcome Instrument
                                           522
                                       **Nowicki-Strickland Locus of
                                           Control Scale   584**
                                       Sociopolitical Control Scale   791
                                       Way of Life Scale   870

Loneliness   **Adolescent-Family Inventory of
   (also see Interpersonal Behavior)   Life Events and Changes   197**
                                       **Children's Loneliness
                                           Questionnaire   517**
                                       Emotional/Social Loneliness
                                           Inventory   281
                                       Loneliness Rating Scale   436
                                       Revised UCLA Loneliness Scale
                                           644

PROBLEM AREA

INSTRUMENT

Love

Intimacy Scale   405
Love Attitudes Scale   440
Parental Nurturance Scale   429
Passionate Love Scale   160
Revised Kinship Scale   640

Marital/Couple Relationship
   (also see Sexuality)

**Beier-Sternberg Discord
   Questionnaire   81**
Competitiveness Scale   84
Construction of Problems Scale   87
**Dominance-Accommodation Scale
   92**
Dual Employed Coping Scales   96
Dual-Career Family Scale   104
Dyadic Adjustment Scale   108
Equity/Inequity Scale   112
**Hypothetical, Jealousy-Producing
   Events Scale   116**
Index of Marital Satisfaction   119
Kansas Marital Conflict Scale   122
**Kansas Marital Goals Orientation
   Scale   125**
**Kansas Marital Satisfaction Scale
   127**
Life Distress Inventory   129
**Locke-Wallace Marital Adjustment
   Test   133**
Marital Alternatives Scale   136
**Marital Comparison Level Index
   138**
**Marital Conventionalization Scale
   142**
Marital Happiness Scale   144
Marital Instability Index   146
**Positive Feelings Questionnaire
   165**
**Primary Communication
   Inventory   168**
**Relationship Assessment Scale
   171**
Relationship Events Scale   173

PROBLEM AREA	INSTRUMENT

[Marital/Couple Relationship]

Semantic Differential of Sex Roles 175

Spouse Treatment Mediation Inventories   191

Mood
(also see Depression)

Mood Survey   486

Mood Thermometers   574

Semantic Differential Mood Scale 702

Narcissism

Selfism   699

Obsessive-Compulsive

Compulsiveness Inventory   208

Indecisiveness Scale   369

Maudsley Obsessional-Compulsive Inventory   448

Obsessive-Compulsive Scale   529

Padua Inventory   539

Reaction Inventory Interference   628

Severity of Symptoms Scale   717

Pain

Chronic Pain Intrusion and Accommodation Scale   160

McGill Pain Questionnaire   450

Pain Catastrophizing Scale   544

Pain Response Inventory   591

Pain-Related Control Scale and Pain-Related Self-Statements   547

West Haven–Yale Multidimensional Pain Inventory   873

Parent-Child Relationship
(also see Family Functioning)

Adult-Adolescent Parenting Inventory   204

Child's Attitude Toward Father and Mother Scales   495

Conflict Tactics Scales   229

Family Empowerment Scale   302

Inventory of Parent and Peer Attachment   564

Kansas Parental Satisfaction Scale 386

PROBLEM AREA	INSTRUMENT

[Parent-Child Relationship]

Parent Affect Test   397
Parent's Report   408
**Parent-Child Relationship Survey
   416**
Parenting Scale   431
**Parental Authority Questionnaire
   420**
**Parental Bonding Instrument
   424**
Parental Nurturance Scale   427
Parental Tolerance Scale   429

Perfectionism

Frost Multidimensional Perfectionism
   Scale   302

Phobias
   (see also Anxiety)

Agoraphobic Cognitions
   Questionnaire   46
Body Sensations Questionnaire
   123
Fear Questionnaire   291
Fear Survey Schedule-II   294
Hospital Fears Rating Scale   558
Internalized Homophobia Scale
   399
Mobility Inventory for Agoraphobia
   478
Panic Attack Cognitions
   Questionnaire   551
Panic Attack Symptoms
   Questionnaire   553
**Spider Phobia Questionnaire for
   Children   623**

Posttraumatic Stress

**Child Report of Posttraumatic
   Symptoms/Parent Report of Post-
   traumatic Symptoms   484**
Combat Exposure Scale   206
Impact of Event Scale   363
Mississippi Scale   477

Problem-Solving

Problem-Solving Inventory   591

PROBLEM AREA   INSTRUMENT

[Problem-Solving]   Social Problem-Solving Inventory
                                             772
                                          Values Conflict Resolution
                                             Assessment   862

Procrastination   Indecisiveness Scale   369
                                          Procrastination Assessment Scale—
                                             Students   591
                                          Procrastination Scale   595

Psychopathology (General) and   Activity-Feeling Scale II   24
   Psychiatric Symptoms   Auditory Hallucinations
                                             Questionnaire   85
                                          Body Image Avoidance
                                             Questionnaire   120
                                          Body Investment Scale   476
                                          Defense Style Questionnaire-40
                                             227
                                          Dissociative Experiences Scale   254
                                          Emotional Assessment Scale   278
                                          Family, Friends, and Self Form   545
                                          Hardiness Scale   372
                                          **Oregon Mental Health Referral
                                             Checklist   587**
                                          Questionnaire of Experiences of
                                             Dissociation   611
                                          Raulin Intense Ambivalence Scale
                                             625
                                          Scale for the Assessment of Negative
                                             Symptoms   654
                                          Scale for the Assessment of Positive
                                             Symptoms   654
                                          Separation-Individuation Process
                                             Inventory   712
                                          Student Jenkins Activity Survey
                                             819
                                          Symptom Questionnaire   830
                                          Symptoms Checklist   834
                                          White Bear Suppression Inventory
                                             882

PROBLEM AREA	INSTRUMENT
Rape	Rape Aftermath Symptom Test 613 Sexual Assault Symptom Scale 724
Satisfaction with Life (also see Depression)	Client Experiences Questionnaire 163 Life Satisfaction Index-Z 432 Satisfaction with Life Scale 652
Schizotypal Symptoms	Cognitive Slippage Scale 193 Magical Ideation Scale 443 Raulin Intense Ambivalence Scale 625 Somatoform Dissociation Questionnaire 799 Splitting Scale 807 Thought Control Questionnaire 845
Self-Concept and Esteem	Affect Balance Scale 38 **Behavioral Self-Concept Scale 469** Collective Self-Esteem Scale 203 Ego Identity Scale 275 **Hare Self-Esteem Scale 550** Index of Self-Esteem 383 **Personal Attribute Inventory for Children and Nonsexist Personal Attribute Inventory 603** Satisfaction with Appearance Scale 650 **Self-Concept Scale for Children 617** Self-Esteem Rating Scale 691 **Semantic Differential of Sex Roles 175**
Self-Control (also see Locus of Control)	**Children's Perceived Self-Control Scale 519** **Impulsivity Scale 560** **Peer and Self-Rating Scale 595**
Self-Efficacy	Physical Self-Efficacy Scale 586

PROBLEM AREA   INSTRUMENT

[Self-Efficacy]   Self-Efficacy Scale   681
                                Self-Efficacy Scale for Schizophrenics
                                   683
                                Smoking Self-Efficacy
                                   Questionnaire   749

Sexuality   Hendrick Sexual Attitude Scale   336
                                Index of Sexual Satisfaction   388
                                Inventory of Dyadic Heterosexual
                                   Preferences   413
                                Negative Attitudes Toward
                                   Masturbation Inventory   512
                                Sexual Arousability Inventory   720
                                Sexual Arousability Inventory—
                                   Expanded   720
                                Sexual Attitude Scale   728
                                Sexual Behavior Inventory—Female
                                   730
                                Sexual Behavior Inventory—Male
                                   733
                                Survey of Heterosexual Interactions
                                   824

Smoking   Smoking Self-Efficacy
                                   Questionnaire   749

Social Functioning   Mood-Related Pleasant Events
   (also see Interpersonal Behavior)   Schedule   482
                                Social Adjustment Scale—Self-
                                   Report   752

Social Support   Multidimensional Scale of Perceived
                                   Social Support   502
                                Multidimensional Support Scale
                                   507
                                Network Orientation Scale   515
                                Perceived Social Support—Family
                                   Scale   565
                                Perceived Social Support—Friend
                                   Scale   565
                                Provision of Social Relations   604

PROBLEM AREA	INSTRUMENT

[Social Support]

Social Support Appraisals Scale 583
Social Support Behaviors Scale   786
Social Support Index   446
Young Adult Social Support Inventory   897

Stress

Adolescent Coping Orientation for Problem Experiences   454
Adolescent-Family Inventory of Life Events and Changes   197
Depression Anxiety and Stress Scales 237
Family Hardiness Index   312
Family Inventory of Life Events and Changes   315
Hardiness Scale   322
Impact of Event Scale   363
Index of Clinical Stress   376
Life Events Questionnaire   430
Perceived Stress Scale   570
Self-Control Schedule   677
Stress-Arousal Checklist   814
Young Adult Family Inventory of Life Events and Changes   892

Suicide
(also see Depression, Satisfaction with Life)

Hopelessness Scale for Children 556
Multi-Attitude Suicide Tendency Scale   576
Positive and Negative Suicide Ideation Inventory   589
Reasons for Living Inventory 631
Reasons for Living Inventory— Adolescents   606

Treatment Satisfaction

Client Experiences Questionnaire 163
Client Satisfaction Inventory 172

Contents

PROBLEM AREA	INSTRUMENT
[Treatment Satisfaction]	Client Satisfaction Questionnaire 174
	Reid-Gundlach Social Service Satisfaction Scale 635
	Session Evaluation Questionnaire 715
	Working Alliance Inventory 888
Substance Abuse	Alcohol Beliefs Scale 48
	Alcohol Outcome Expectancies Scale 53
	Assertion Questionnaire in Drug Use 68
	Beck Codependence Assessment Scale 210
	Co-dependency Inventory 222
	Codependent Questionnaire 225
	Detox Fear Survey Schedule—27 245
	Drinking Motives Questionnaire 537
	Drug Abuse Screening Test 260
	Index of Alcohol Involvement 372
	Index of Drug Involvement 378
	McMullin Addiction Thought Scale 452
	Michigan Alcoholism Screening Test 466
	Self-Administered Alcoholism Screening Test 662
	Sensation Scale 705
	Simpatia Scale 743
	Spouse Enabling Inventory 178
	Spouse Sobriety Influence Inventory 184
	TCU Depression and TCU Decision-Making Scales 836

FOREWORD

Historians of behavioral science reviewing progress in the provision of human services at some point in the future will have to confront a curious issue. They will note that the twentieth century witnessed the development of a science of human behavior. They will also note that from mid-century on, clinicians treating behavioral and emotional disorders began relying more heavily on the systematic application of theories and facts emanating from this science to emotional and behavioral problems. They will make observations on various false starts in the development of our therapeutic techniques, and offer reasons for the initial acceptance of these "false starts" in which clinicians or practitioners would apply exactly the same intervention or style of intervention to every problem that came before them. But in the last analysis historians will applaud the slow but systematic development of ever more powerful specific procedures and techniques devised to deal successfully with the variety of specific emotional and behavioral problems. This will be one of the success stories of the twentieth century.

Historians will also note a curious paradox which they will be hard pressed to explain. They will write that well into the 1990s few practitioners or clinicians evaluated the effects of their new treatments in any systematic way. Rather, whatever the behavioral or emotional problem, they would simply ask clients from time to time how they were feeling or how they were doing. Sometimes this would be followed by reports in an official chart or record duly noting clients' replies. If families or married couples were involved, a report from only one member of the interpersonal system would often suffice. Occasionally, these attempts at "evaluation" would reach peaks of quantifiable objectivity by presenting the questions in somewhat different ways such as "how are you feeling or doing compared to a year ago when you first came to see me?"

Historians will point out wryly that this practice would be analogous to physicians periodically asking patients with blood infections or fractures "how are you feeling" without bothering to analyze blood samples or take X rays. "How could this have been?" they will ask. In searching for answers they will examine records of clinical practice in the late twentieth century and find that the most usual response from clinicians was that they were simply too busy to evaluate what they were doing. But the real reason, astute historians will note, is that they never learned how.

Our government regulatory agencies, and other institutions, have anticipated these turn-of-the-century historians with the implementation of procedures requiring practitioners to evaluate what they do. This practice, most often subsumed under the rubric of "accountability," will very soon have a broad and deep hold on the practice of countless human service providers. But more important than the rise of new regulations will be the full realization on the part of all practitioners of the ultimate logic and wisdom of evaluating what they do. In response to this need, a number of books have appeared of late dealing with methods to help practitioners evaluate what they do. Some books even suggest that this will enable clinicians to make direct contributions to our science. Using strategies of repeated measurement of emotional and behavioral problems combined with sophisticated case study procedures and single case experimental designs, the teaching of these methods is increasing rapidly in our graduate and professional schools. But at the heart of this process is measurement, and the *sine qua non* of successful measurement is the availability of realistic and practical measures of change. Only through wide dissemination of realistic, practical, and accurate measures of change will practitioners be able to fulfill the requirements of accountability as well as their own growing sense of personal obligation to their clients to evaluate their intervention. Up until now this has been our weakness, not because satisfactory measures did not exist, but because so many widely scattered measurement tools existed that it was impossible for any one practitioner to keep track of these developments, let alone make a wise choice of which measures might be useful.

Corcoran and Fischer have accomplished this task and the result is this excellent book, now in its 3rd edition, that not only describes the essentials of measurement but also presents the most up-to-date and satisfactory measures of change for almost any problem a practitioner might encounter. Concentrating on what they call rapid assessment instruments (RAIs), they present a series of brief questionnaires most of which fulfill the criterion of being under 50 items, thereby requiring no more than several minutes to fill out. By cross-referencing these RAIs by problem areas, no practitioner need take more than a few minutes to choose the proper questionnaire for any problem or combination of problems with which he or she might be confronted. With its well-written and easy-to-read chapters on what makes a brief questionnaire measure satisfactory or unsatisfactory, this book should be on the shelf of every practitioner working in a human service setting. Through the use of this book practitioners will not only be able to meet growing demands for accountability, but also satisfy their own desires for objective, quantifiable indications of progress in a manner that can be accomplished in no more than several minutes. As this activity becomes an integral part of the delivery of human services, the value of this book will increase.

David H. Barlow, Ph.D.
Center for Anxiety and Related Disorders
at Boston University

PREFACE TO THE THIRD EDITION

The purpose of this book, like the first and second editions, is to provide practitioners and students with a number of instruments that they can use to help them monitor and evaluate their practice. These instruments were specifically selected because they measure most of the common problems seen in clinical practice, they are relatively short, easy to score and administer, and because we believe they really will help you, the reader, in your practice. This edition, like the second edition, comes in two volumes. Volume 1 contains measures for couples, families, and children. Volume 2 contains measures for adults with problems outside the context of the family.

We know through our own practice, and the practice of our students and colleagues, how difficult it sometimes is to be clear about where you are going with a client and whether or not you actually get there. We also realize the frustrations of trying to help a client be specific about a particular problem rather than leaving the problem defined in some global, vague—and therefore, unworkable—way.

These essentially are problems in *measurement:* being able to be as clear as possible about what you and the client are working on. Without a clear handle on the problem, the typical frustrations of practice are multiplied many times. We believe the instruments we present in this book will help relieve some of the frustrations you may have experienced in attempting to be precise about clients' problems. We also hope that we will be able to overcome the old myth of clinical practice that "most of our clients' problems really aren't measurable." We plan to show you that they are, and just how to go about doing it.

Practitioners in all the human services—psychology, social work, counseling, psychiatry, and nursing—increasingly are being held accountable for monitoring and evaluating their practice. One of the simplest yet most productive ways of doing this is to have available a package of instruments that measure the wide range of problems that practitioners typically face. Then you simply would select the instruments most appropriate for the problem of the client (individual, couple, group, or family) and use those to monitor practice with that client or system.

There are a number of such instruments available. Unfortunately, they are widely scattered throughout the literature. With this book, we hope to save you the time and energy required to go into the literature to find and select the appropriate instrument. We not only provide information about those instruments, we include copies of them so that you can immediately assess their utility for your practice. We also provide information as to where you can obtain copies of the instruments if you want to use them.

This book is addressed to members of all the helping professions who are engaged in clinical or therapeutic work with individuals, couples, groups, or families. Further, we believe the instruments contained in this book will be useful to practitioners from all theoretical orientations who are interested in monitoring or evaluating their practice. Indeed, one of the great appeals of these instruments is that they are not limited to use by adherents of only one or even a few clinical schools of thought or theoretical orientations. If you believe that it is useful to be able to keep track of changes in your client's problem as your intervention proceeds, then we think this book is for you.

Although we don't mean to oversimplify the task, we believe this book can be useful to students and practitioners with very little experience in using measures such as we have included here. Of course, we will provide information on how to use these instruments, including relevant data on their reliability and validity and other characteristics. Indeed, we believe this book also will be useful to researchers who will be able to use these instruments to help them conduct their studies in a wide range of problem areas.

We hope this book will prove useful to you. Most of all, we hope it will help you enhance the efficiency and effectiveness of your practice.

ORGANIZATION OF THE BOOK

Volume 1 includes an introduction to the basic principles of measurement, an overview of different types of measures, and an introduction to the rapid assessment inventories included in this book: how we selected them, how to administer and score them, and how to avoid errors in their use. Volume 1 also contains copies of actual instruments for use with couples, families, and children. Volume 2 contains instruments to be used with adults when the problem of concern is not focused on the family or couple relationship.

In both volumes, the measures are listed alphabetically. However, for more help in finding an instrument that is specially designed for a particular problem area, consult the third part of the Table of Contents. We have presented a list of instruments cross-indexed by problem area. Thus, if you need an instrument for evaluating your client's anxiety, you could look under Anxiety in the Table of Contents and see which instruments are designed for measurement of anxiety. We hope this will facilitate the selection process.

ACKNOWLEDGMENTS

We are very grateful to several people who have helped us complete this book. Hisae Tachi, Renee Furuyama, Carolyn Brooks, and Al Mann have provided a tremendous amount of help and support. And we'd also like to note that the order of our names in this book has nothing to do with how much either of us contributed to its completion, despite the fact that each of us is convinced that he did most of the work.

PART

I

Measurement and Practice

1

INTRODUCTION

Your client has come to you with a number of
complaints. "I just feel lousy. I don't have any energy, I
just never want to go out anymore. Sometimes, especially
at night, I find myself crying over nothing. I don't even
feel like eating. My boss pushes me around at work: he
makes me do all kinds of things that the other employees
don't have to do. But I can't tell him I won't do the work.
Then I feel even worse." After a good deal of exploration,
you help the client focus the complaints until you see
certain patterns. Among them, the client seems to be
depressed, have low self-esteem, and to be very
unassertive. You devise an intervention program to work
with all of these areas, but one thing is missing. Although
you're pretty sure your interventions will be the right
ones, other than asking the client how she feels and
maybe making a few observations on your own, you
don't have a clear way of assessing accurately whether or
not there will be real improvement in each of these areas.
After all, they are pretty hard to measure with any degree
of objectivity. Or are they?

This book will help you answer that question. Although
we don't pretend to have all the answers to all the questions you might have on
how to measure your client's problems, we hope to be able to help you grapple
with a most important issue for clinical practice: how we can more or less
accurately and objectively, and without a lot of aggravation and extra work,
measure some of the most commonly encountered clinical problems.

In the short case example at the beginning of this chapter, there actually
are several ways a practitioner could have measured the client's problems. We
will briefly examine several methods of measurement in this book, but the main

focus is on one: the use of instruments that the client can fill out himself or herself, and that give a fairly clear picture of the intensity or magnitude of a given problem. In the case example presented earlier, the practitioner might have selected one of several readily accessible, easy-to-use instruments to measure the client's degree of depression, level of self-esteem, or assertiveness. Indeed, instruments to measure each of these problems are included in Part II of this volume and all of Volume 2.

ACCOUNTABILITY IN PRACTICE

The last decade or so has seen increasing pressure brought to bear on practitioners to be "accountable" for what they do in practice. Although the term accountability has several meanings, we believe the most basic meaning of accountability is this: we have to be responsible for what we do with our clients. The most crucial aspect of that responsibility is a commitment to delivering effective services.

There are very few in the human services who would deny the importance of providing effective services to clients as a major priority. Where the differences come about is in deciding how to go about implementing or operationalizing this commitment to providing effective services. Conscientious monitoring and measurement of one's practice and the client's functioning is a primary way to fulfill this commitment.

Use of Research in Practice

Let's face it. Many human services practitioners are not very enamored with research, often because they do not see its value—how it can really make a difference in practice.

Part of the problem may be that researchers have not done their best to demystify the research process. Most research texts reflect a way of thinking about many phenomena that is very different from the way many practitioners view the world. After all, most of us in the helping professions are there because we want to work with people, not numbers.

But research does offer some very concrete ways of enhancing our practice. First of all, recent years have seen a tremendous increase in the number of studies with positive outcomes. Many hundreds of studies point to a wide range of clinical techniques and programs that have been successful in helping clients with a multitude of problems (Acierno et al., 1994; Barlow, 1993; Chambless et al., 1996; Cormier and Cormier, 1998; Fischer, 1981, 1993; Nathan and Gorman, 1998; Pikoff, 1996; Reid, 1997; Roth and Foragy, 1996; Sanderson and Woody, 1995;

Thyer and Wodarski, 1998; Wodarski and Thyer, 1998). Thus, practitioners can now select a number of intervention techniques or programs on the basis of their demonstrated success with one or more problem configurations as documented in numerous studies (e.g., see Barlow, 1985; Corcoran, 1992). A second practical value of research is the availability of a range of methods to help us monitor how well we are doing with our clients, that is, to keep track of our clients' problems over time and, if necessary, make changes in our intervention program if it is not proceeding as well as desired. This is true whether our clients are individuals, couples, families, or other groups.

And third, we also have the research tools to *evaluate* our practice, to make decisions about whether or not our clients' problems are actually changing, and also whether it was our interventions that helped them to change. Both of these areas—the monitoring and the evaluating of practice—are obviously of great importance to practitioners, and the practical relevance of the research tools is what makes recent developments in research so exciting for all of us.

By and large, the recent developments that have made research more accessible to practitioners have come about in two areas: evaluation designs for practice, and new measurement tools. While the focus of this book is on measurement, we will provide a brief review of designs for practice, and the relationship of these designs to measurement.

EVALUATION DESIGNS FOR PRACTICE

There is a wide variety of evaluation designs that can provide useful information for practice. The most common—the ones most practitioners learned about in their educational programs—are the experimental designs, field studies, and surveys in which the researcher collects data on large groups of people or events and then analyzes those data using a variety of mathematical and statistical techniques. Some of these designs (e.g., those using random assignment, control and contrast groups) are best suited for informing our practice about what interventions work best with what clients with what problems in what situations. But despite their value these designs are rarely used in actual practice by practitioners, because they often require more sophisticated knowledge, time, or resources than are available to most practitioners.

A second set of designs that can be of value to practitioners are the *single-system designs*. These designs, which allow practitioners to monitor and evaluate each case, have been called by a number of terms: single case experimental designs, single subject or single *N* designs, time series designs, and single organism designs. While all these terms basically refer to the same set of operations, we prefer the term single-system design because it suggests that the designs do not have to be limited to a single client but can be used with couples, families, groups, organizations, or larger collectivities.

These designs, elaborated in several recent books (Bloom, Fischer, and Orme, 1994, 1999; Bloom and Fischer, 1982; Jayaratne and Levy, 1979; Kazdin, 1982; Barlow et al., 1984; Barlow and Hersen, 1984; Kratochwill, 1978), are a relatively new development for the helping professions. And while this new technology is increasingly being made available to practitioners, a brief review of the basic components of single-system designs is in order.

The first component of single-system designs is the specification of a problem which the practitioner and client agree needs to be worked on. This problem can be in any of the many areas of human functioning—behavioral, cognitive, affective, or the activities of individuals or groups.

The second component is selecting a way to measure the problem. In the past, finding ways to measure problems has been a major stumbling block for many practitioners. But there are now a wide variety of ways to measure problems—some of which were once thought to be "unmeasurable"—available to practitioners of diverse theoretical orientations. These will be discussed throughout the rest of this book.

The third component is the implementation of the design itself—the systematic collection of information about the problem on a regular basis. This generally starts before the intervention proper is begun—the baseline—and continues over time until the intervention is completed. This use of "repeated measures"—collecting information on a problem over time—is a hallmark of single-system designs, and provides the basis for the monitoring and evaluation functions described earlier.

The essence of single-system designs is the comparison of the intensity, level, magnitude, frequency, or duration of the problem across different phases of the process. These comparisons are typically plotted on a graph, as shall be illustrated below, to facilitate visual examination. For example, one might concoct an elementary study of a client's progress by comparing information collected during the baseline on the client's level of depression with information collected during the intervention period to see if there is any change in the problem. A graphed example of such a design, called an A-B design (A = baseline; B = intervention), is presented in Figure 1.1. As with all single-system designs, the level of the problem is plotted along the vertical axis and the time period is plotted along the horizontal axis. In this case, the client was assessed using a self-administered depression scale once a week. During a three-week assessment period (the baseline) the client filled out the questionnaire three times. The intervention was begun the fourth week and the steady decline in scores shows that the level of the client's depression was decreasing.

A more sophisticated design, combining or alternating different intervention or nonintervention (baseline) phases, can indicate not only whether the

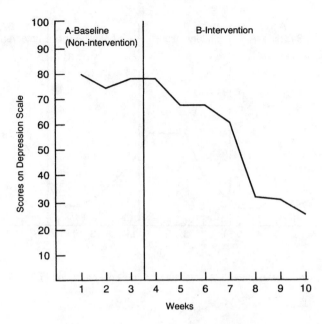

Figure 1.1. Changes in Client's Depression Scores over a Period of 10 Weeks

client's problem changed, but whether the practitioner's intervention program is responsible for the change. An example of one of several designs that can provide evidence of the relationship between the intervention and the change in the client's problems is presented in Figure 1.2. This example, in which the goal is to increase the client's assertiveness, is called an A-B-A-B (reversal or withdrawal) design. Evidence of the link between intervention and a change in the problem is established by the fact that the problem diminishes only when the intervention is applied and returns to its previous level when the intervention is withdrawn or applied to another problem.

As the practitioner collects information on the problem, he or she also is getting feedback on whether the intervention is producing the desired effects and therefore should be continued, or is not producing the desired effects and therefore should be changed; this is the monitoring function. An example of the effects of such monitoring is presented in Figure 1.3. In this example, the practitioner was not satisfied with the slow progress shown in the first intervention period (Phase B) and changed his intervention to produce a more positive result (Phase C).

Finally, a review of all the information collected will provide data on success in attaining the desired goal—the evaluation of the outcome.

Single-system designs seem to offer excellent opportunities for actual utilization. They can be built into practice with each and every case; they

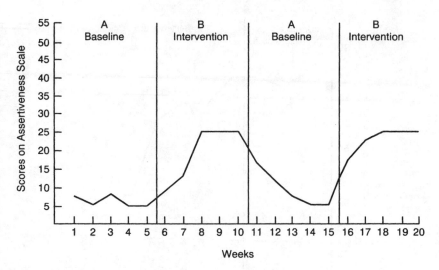

Figure 1.2.   Changes in Client's Assertiveness Scores over a Period of 20 Weeks

provide direct feedback enabling the practitioner to readily assess, monitor, and evaluate the case, and they allow the practitioner to make changes in the intervention program if it appears not to be working. Thus, the instruments described in this book will probably find their most frequent use in the context of single-system designs.

However, the same instruments can be—and have been—used in classical research. The selection of a design depends on the question one is asking: for some questions, a classical design is more appropriate; for others, one of the single-system designs would be the design of choice. (A comparison of the characteristics, advantages, and disadvantage of classical and single-system designs is available in Bloom, Fischer, and Orme, 1999). The use and administration of the measure would vary with the design, from once in a cross-sectional survey to pre- and post-test administration in a classical experiment, to repeated administration perhaps once or twice weekly—in a single-system design that lasts for several weeks or longer.

The Role of Measurement

One of the key challenges of all types of research, and practice as well, is finding a way to measure the problem. Measurement helps us be precise in defining problems and goals. It is measurement of the client's problems that allows feedback on the success or failure of treatment efforts, indicating when changes in the intervention program are necessary. Measurement procedures help standardize and objectify both research and practice. Using procedures that can

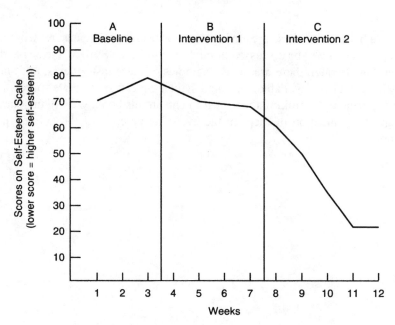

Figure 1.3. Changes in Intervention (Phases B and C) and Concurrent Change in Client's Self-Esteem Scores

also be used by others provides a basis for comparing results of different intervention programs.

Measurement has been particularly well received and promoted in managed care settings (Corcoran and Vandiver, 1996) where observable goals and structured interventions are commonplace. Practitioners in these settings frequently use instruments such as those presented here to monitor outcome. With a little effort, short but accurate assessment tools may be used to establish treatment necessity when a score is noticeably different from a norm (Corcoran, 1997) and then throughout the managed care process. In a word, measurement of our clients' problems helps us know where we are going and when we get there.

Because formal measurement procedures provide some of the best bases for evaluating what we do, they are essential components of responsible, accountable practice. In Chapter 3 we will review a range of measurement procedures available to practitioners. However, the focus of this book is on one type of measure: standardized paper-and-pencil questionnaires that can be filled out by the client in a relatively short period of time, that can be easily administered and scored by the practitioner, and that give fairly accurate pictures of the client's condition at any point in time and/or over a period of many administrations. These types of measures have been called rapid assessment instruments (RAIs) by Levitt and Reid (1981).

We believe that these are among the most useful of all measurement tools for reasons that will be discussed throughout this book. Suffice it to say at this point that although there are many examples of these instruments, until now they have not been available, reprinted in their entirety, in a single source. It is our hope that by compiling these instruments in this book, we will encourage far greater utilization of them in the everyday practice of the helping professions.

2

BASIC PRINCIPLES
OF MEASUREMENT

In this chapter we will review some basic principles of measurement. The major purpose of this review is to acquaint you with some of the terms we use in Part II and in Volume 2 in describing the instruments there, and to help you in selecting measures. Since the topic can be difficult, we will try to present it in an understandable way by dividing the material into four areas: a definition of measurement, the research principles defining a "good" measure, the statistical principles involved in interpreting scores, and the practice principles involved in using measures.

MEASUREMENT DEFINED

Measurement can actually be defined simply, although some writers have developed complex, technical and intimidating definitions. Researchers in measurement are like other scientists as they, too, create a new vocabulary for concepts most of us already know. For example, a mathematician works with "integers," while the rest of us use numbers.

Most simply, measurement is the systematic process of assigning a number to "something" (Nunnally, 1978, p. 3). The "thing" is known as a variable. The variables of concern to clinical practice tend to be a client's behavior, thoughts, feelings, or situation (the dependent or outcome variable); treatment goals; and theoretical concepts such as self-esteem. The number assigned represents a quantified attribute of the variable.

This simple definition of measurement reflects the process of quantifying the "thing." Quantification is beneficial in work with clients because it allows you to monitor change mathematically. The mathematical procedures of interest to us are addition, subtraction, multiplication, and division. For example, suppose you have successfully treated "an explosive personality" such that at the end of therapy you conclude the "explosive personality is in remission." By assigning a number to, say, the symptom of anger by using Spielberger's (1982) State-Trait Anger Scale, you can mathematically monitor how this symptom has changed during treatment. It would be impossible, on the other hand, to subtract an explosive personality in remission from an explosive personality.

In determining which math procedures to use, the first consideration is known as the "level of measurement," of which there are four: nominal, ordinal, interval, and ratio. These four levels differ from each other by the presence or absence of four characteristics: exclusiveness, order, equivalency, and absoluteness.

The *nominal* level of measurement possesses only exclusiveness, which means the number assigned to an attribute is distinct from others as it represents one and only one attribute. With a nominal level the number is essentially the same as a name given to the attribute. An example of a nominal variable is "sex" with the attributes of "male" and "female." It is impossible to use mathematics with nominal measures, just as it is with terms like "explosive personality."

The *ordinal* level of measurement possesses exclusiveness, but is also ordered. To say the numbers are ordered means the numbers have a ranking. An example of an ordinal level of measurement is the severity of a client's problems or the ranking of a client's social functioning, as described in the *DSM IV* (American Psychiatric Association, 1994). With ordinal measures you can compare the relative positions between the numbers assigned to some variable. For example, you can compare "poor functioning"—which is assigned the number 5—in relation to "superior functioning"—which is assigned the number 1. While you can compare the relative rankings of an ordinal level of measurement, you cannot determine how much the two attributes differ by using the mathematic procedures of addition, subtraction, multiplication, and division. In other words, you cannot subtract "superior" from "poor."

The use of math procedures is appropriate with measures at the *interval* level. An interval measure possesses exclusiveness and is ordered, but differs from ordinal measures in having equivalency. Equivalency means the distances between the numbers assigned to an attribute are equal. For example, the difference, or distance, between 2 and 4 on a seven-point scale is equal to the difference between 5 and 7.

With interval level measures, however, we do not have an absolute zero. This means either that complete absence of the variable never occurs or that our tool cannot assess it. For example, self-esteem is never completely absent as illustrated with the Index of Self-Esteem (Hudson, 1992). Consequently, we really should not multiply or divide scores from interval level measures since a score of 30 on an assertiveness questionnaire, for example, may not reflect twice as much assertion as a score of 60. Another example of this issue is temperature; 90 degrees is not twice as hot as 45 degrees.

The problem caused by not having an absolute zero is resolved by assuming the measurement tool has an arbitrary zero. By assuming there is an arbitrary score which reflects an absence of the variable, we can use all four mathematical procedures: addition, subtraction, multiplication, and division.

The fourth level of measurement is *ratio*. Measures that are at a ratio level possess exclusiveness, order, equivalency, and have an absolute zero. The only difference between a ratio and an interval level of measurement is this characteristic. With an interval level measure, we had to assume an arbitrary zero instead of actually having and being able to measure an absolute zero. This means there is an absolute absence of the variable which our measurement tool can ascertain. Ratio measures are fairly rare in the behavioral and social sciences, although numerous everyday variables can be measured on a ratio scale, such as age, years of marriage, and so on. However, the assumption of an arbitrary zero allows us to use all the mathematical procedures to monitor our practice.

The benefits of measurement, namely our ability to better understand what is happening in our practice, is a result of our using math to help us monitor practice. The levels of measurement that result from how a number is assigned to something determines what math procedures you will be able to use. As the remainder of this book will show you, measures at the interval and ration levels allow you to determine the effects of your intervention most clearly and, therefore, to be a more accountable professional.

RESEARCH PRINCIPLES UNDERLYING MEASUREMENT

A good measure essentially is one that is reliable and valid. Reliability refers to the consistency of an instrument in terms of the items measuring the same entity and the total instrument measuring the same way every time. Validity pertains to whether the measure accurately assesses what it was designed to assess. Unfortunately, no instrument available for clinical practice is completely reliable or valid. Lack of reliability and lack of validity are referred to as random and systematic error, respectively.

Reliability

There are three basic approaches to determining an instrument's reliability: whether the individual items of a measure are consistent with each other;

whether scores are stable over time; and whether different forms of the same instrument are equal to each other. These approaches to estimating reliability are known as internal consistency, test-retest reliability, and parallel forms reliability.

Internal consistency.   Items of an instrument that are not consistent with one another are most likely measuring different things, and thus do not contribute to—and may detract from—the instrument's assessment of the particular variable in question. When using measures in practice you will want to use those tools where the items are all tapping a similar aspect of a particular construct domain.

The research procedure most frequently used to determine if the items are internally consistent is Cronbach's coefficient alpha. This statistic is based on the average correlations among the items. A correlation is a statistic reflecting the amount of association between variables. In terms of reliability, the alpha coefficient has a maximum value of 1.0. When an instrument has a high alpha it means the items are tapping a similiar domain, and, hence, that the instrument is internally consistent. While there are no hard and fast rules, an alpha coefficient exceeding .80 suggests the instrument is more or less internally consistent.

In addition to Cronbach's alpha, there are other similar methods for estimating internal consistency. The essential logic of the procedures is to determine the correlation among the items. There are three frequently encountered methods. The "Kuder-Richardson formula 20" is an appropriate method for instruments with dichotomous items, such as true-false and forced-choice questions. "Split-half reliability" is a method that estimates the consistency by correlating the first half of the items with the second half; this method can also divide the items into two groups by randomly assigning them. A special form of split-half reliability is known as "odd-even." With odd-even reliability the odd items are correlated with the even items. Any method of split-half reliability underestimates consistency because reliability is influenced by the total number of items in an instrument. Because of this, you will often find references to the "Spearman-Brown formula," which corrects for this underestimation.

Test-retest reliability.   Reliability also can be assessed in terms of the consistency of scores from different administrations of the instrument. If in actuality the variable has not changed between the times you measure it, then the scores should be relatively similar. This is known as test-retest reliability and refers to the stability of an instrument. Test-retest reliability is also estimated from a correlation. A strong correlation, say above .80, suggests that the instrument is more or less stable over time.

When you use an instrument over a period of time—for example, before, during, and after therapy—test-retest reliability becomes very important. How, after all, can you tell if the apparent change in your client's problem is real change if the instrument you use is not stable? Without some evidence of stability you are less able to discern if the observed change was real or simply reflected error in your instrument. Again, there are no concrete rules for determining how strong the test-retest coefficient of stability needs to be. Correlations of .69 or better for a one-month period between administrations is considered a "reasonable degree of stability" (Cronbach, 1970, p. 144). For shorter intervals, like a week or two, we suggest a stronger correlation, above .80, as an acceptable level of stability.

Parallel forms. A third way to assess reliability is to determine if two forms of the same instrument are correlated. When two forms of the same measure exist, such as the long and short forms of the Rathus Assertiveness Schedule (Rathus, 1973; McCormick, 1985), then the scores for each should be highly correlated. Here, correlations of above .80 are needed to consider two parallel forms consistent.

Error. All three approaches to reliability are designed to detect the absence of error in the measure. Another way to look at reliability is to estimate directly the amount of error in the instrument. This is known as the standard error of measurement (SEM), and is basically an estimate of the standard deviation of error. The SEM is calculated by multiplying the standard deviation by the square root of 1 minus the reliability coefficient ($SD \times \sqrt{1 - \text{rel}}$). As an index of error, the SEM can be used to determine what change in scores may be due to error. For example, if the instrument's SEM is 5 and scores changed from 30 to 25 from one administration to the next, this change is likely due to error in the measurement. Thus, only change greater than the SEM may be considered real change.

The SEM is also an important way to consider reliability because it is less easily influenced by differences in the samples from which reliability is estimated. The SEM has limitations because the number reflects the scale range of the measurement tool. You cannot directly compare the SEM from different instruments unless they have the same range of scores. For example, Zung's (1965) Self-Rating Depression scale has a range of 20 to 80. Hudson's (1992) Generalized Contentment scale, however, has a range of zero to 100. The size of the SEM of both scales is affected by their respective ranges. However, in general, the smaller the SEM, the more reliable the instrument (the less measurement error).

One way to solve this problem is to convert the SEM into a percentage, by dividing the SEM by the score range and multiplying by 100. This gives you the percentage of scores which might be due to error. By making this conversion you will be able to compare two instruments and, all other things being equal, use the one with the least amount of error.

Validity

The validity of an instrument refers to how well it measures what it was designed to measure. There are three general approaches to validity: content validity, criterion validity, and construct validity. The literature, however, is full of inconsistent—and occasionally incorrect—use of these terms.

Content validity.   Content validity assesses whether the substance of the items taps the entity you are trying to measure. More specifically, since it is not possible to ask every question about your client's problem, content validity indicates whether these particular scale items are a representative sample of the content area.

There are two basic approaches to content validity, face and logical content validity. Face validity asks if the items appear on the surface to tap the content. Face validity is determined by examining the items and judging if they appear to actually be measuring the content they claim to be measuring. To illustrate this, select any instrument from Part II and look at the items. In your judgment do they look like they measure the content they are supposed to? If so, you would say the instrument has face validity.

This exercise demonstrates the major problem with face validity: it is basically someone's subjective judgment. Logical content validity, however, is more systematic. It refers to the procedure the instrument developer used to evaluate the content of the items and whether they cover the entire content domain. That is, do the items on the measure appear to be representative of all content areas that should be included? When this information is available, it will be presented by the researcher in a manual or in the research article on the instrument. While you will want to use an instrument that has logical content validity, the necessary information frequently is not available. Consequently, you will often have to settle for your own judgment of face validity.

Criterion validity.   This approach to validity has several different names, and therefore generates a great deal of confusion. It is also known as empirical validity or predictive validity, among other terms. In general, criterion validity asks whether the measure correlates significantly with other relevant variables. Usually, these other variables are already established as valid measures. There are two basic types of criterion validity: *predictive validity* asks whether the instrument is correlated with some event that will occur in the future; *concur-*

rent validity refers to an instrument's correlation with an event that is assessed at the same time the measure is administered.

These approaches to validity are empirically based and are more sophisticated than content validity. Quite simply, both approaches to criterion validity are estimates of an instrument's association with some other already valid measure where you would most likely expect to find a correlation. When such information is available, you can be more confident that your instrument is accurately measuring what it was designed to measure.

Another approach to criterion validity is *known-groups validity*. This procedure (sometimes called discriminant validity) compares scores on the measure for a group that is known to have the problem with a group that is known not to have the problem. If the measure is valid, then these groups should have significantly different scores. Different scores support the validity by suggesting that the measure actually taps the presence of the variable.

Construct validity. The third type of validity asks whether the instrument taps a particular theoretical construct. For example, does the Splitting Scale (Gerson, 1984) really measure this defense mechanism? The answer can be partially determined from criterion validity, of course, but a more convincing procedure is construct validation. In order to consider an instrument as having construct validity, it should be shown to have convergent validity *and* discriminant validity, although some authors use the terms as if they were separate types of validity.

Convergent validity asks if a construct, such as loneliness, correlates with some theoretically relevant variable, such as the amount of time a person spends by him or herself. Other examples could be whether the measurement of loneliness correlates with the number of friends or feelings of alienation. In other words, do scores on a measure converge with theoretically relevant variables? With convergent validity you want to find statistically significant correlations between the instrument and other measures of relevant variables. *Discriminant validity* (sometimes called divergent validity), on the other hand, refers to the way theoretically nonrelevant and dissimilar variables should not be associated with scores on the instrument. Here you would want to find instruments that are not significantly correlated with measures with which they should not be correlated, in order to believe the score is not measuring something theoretically irrelevant.

Another approach to construct validity is *factorial validity*, by which researchers determine if an instrument has convergent and discriminant validity (Sundberg, 1977, p. 45). Factorial validity can be determined with a statistical procedure known as factor analysis designed to derive groups of variables that measure separate aspects of the problem, which are called "factors." If the variables were similar, they would correlate with the same factor and would suggest convergent validity. Since this statistical procedure is designed to detect relatively uncorrelated factors, variables not associated with a particular factor suggest discriminant validity.

This approach to factorial validity is often a statistical nightmare. First of all, one needs a large number of subjects to use the statistic appropriately. Moreover, the statistical procedure has numerous variations which are frequently misapplied, and the specific values used for decision making—known as eigenvalues—may not be sufficiently stringent to actually indicate the variables form a meaningful factor. Consequently, the construct validity findings can be misleading (Cattell, 1966; Comrey, 1978).

A second way to estimate factorial validity is to determine if individual items correlate with the instrument's total score and do not correlate with unrelated variables. This procedure, nicely demonstrated by Hudson (1982), again tells you if the instrument converges with relevant variables and differs from less relevant ones. Factorial validity, then, helps you decide if the theoretical construct is indeed being measured by the instrument.

Summary

Let us now summarize this material from a practical point of view. First of all, to monitor and evaluate practice you will want to use instruments that are reliable and valid. You can consider the instrument to be reliable if the items are consistent with each other and the scores are stable from one administration to the next; when available, different forms of the same instrument need to be highly correlated in order to consider the scores consistent.

Additionally, you will want to use measures that provide relatively valid assessments of the problem. The simplest way to address this issue is to examine the content of the items and make a judgment about the face validity of the instrument. More sophisticated methods are found when the researcher correlates the scores with some criterion of future status (predictive validity) or present status (concurrent validity). At times you will find measures that are reported to have known-groups validity, which means the scores are different for groups known to have and known not to have the problem. Finally, you may come across instruments that are reported to have construct validity, which means that within the same study, the measure correlates with theoretically relevant variables and does not correlate with nonrelevant ones.

For an instrument to be valid, it must to some extent be reliable. Conversely, a reliable instrument may not be valid. Thus, if an instrument reports only information on validity, we can assume some degree of reliability but if it reports only information on reliability, we must use more caution in its application.

It is important to look beyond these validity terms in assessing research or deciding whether to use a scale, because many researchers use the terms inconsistently. Moreover, we must warn you that you will probably never find all of this information regarding the reliability and validity of a particular instrument. Since no measure in the behavioral and social sciences is completely reliable and valid, you will simply have to settle for some error in measurement. Consequently, you must also be judicious in how you interpret and use scores from instruments. However, we firmly believe that a measure without some substantiation is usually better than a measure with no substantiation or no measure at all.

STATISTICAL PRINCIPLES OF INTERPRETATION

We are now at a point to discuss the next of our four basic sets of principles, namely how to make meaningful the number assigned to the variable being measured.

In order for a number to be meaningful it must be interpreted by comparing it with other numbers. This section will discuss different scores researchers may use when describing their instruments and methods of comparing scores in order to interpret them. If you want to understand a score, it is essential that you be familiar with some elementary statistics related to central tendency and variability.

Measures of Central Tendency and Variability

In order to interpret a score it is necessary to have more than one score. A group of scores is called a sample, which has a distribution. We can describe a sample by its central tendency and variability.

Central tendency is commonly described by the mean, mode, and median of all the scores. The mean is what we frequently call the average (the sum of all scores divided by the number of scores). The mode is the most frequently occurring score. The median is that score which is the middle value of all the scores when arranged from lowest to highest. When the mean, mode, and median all have the same value, the distribution is called "normal." A normal distribution is displayed in Figure 2.1.

By itself, a measure of central tendency is not very informative. We also need to know how scores deviate from the central tendency, which is variability. The basic measures of variability are range, variance, and standard deviation. The range is the difference between the lowest and highest scores. The number tells us very little, besides the difference between the two extreme scores. The

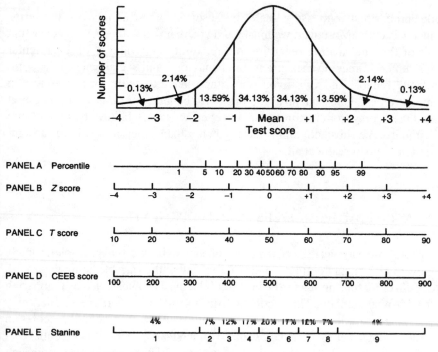

Figure 2.1. Normal Distribution and Transformed Scores

variance, on the other hand, is a number representing the entire area of the distribution, that is, all the scores taken together, and refers to the extent to which scores tend to cluster around or scatter away from the mean of the entire distribution. Variance is determined by the following formula:

$$\Sigma (X - M)^2 \div n - 1$$

In this formula X represents each score, from which the mean (M) is subtracted. The result is then squared and added together (Σ); this number is then divided by the sample size (n) minus one.

The square root of the variance is the standard deviation, which reflects the deviation from the mean, or how far the scores on a measure deviate from the mean. The standard deviation can also indicate what percentage of scores is higher or lower than a particular score. With a normal distribution, half of the area is below the mean and half is above. One standard deviation above the mean represents approximately 34.13% of the area away from the mean. As Figure 2.1 illustrates, an additional standard deviation incorporates another

13.6% of the distribution, while a third standard deviation includes approximately 2.1% more, and a fourth represents about .13%.

These concepts are important because you can use them with different types of scores, as well as with some methods of comparing scores; when they are available, we will present them for each scale in the book.

Raw scores and transformed scores. We now consider some of the different types of scores you might obtain yourself or come across in the literature. The basic types are raw scores and transformed scores, of which we will consider percentile ranks, standard scores, and three different standardized scores. Raw scores are the straightforward responses to the items on a measure. In your use of an instrument to monitor your practice you will most likely only need to use raw scores.

Raw scores from instruments with different possible ranges of scores, however, cannot be compared with each other. Consider the same issue we discussed earlier in terms of comparing different SEMs. A score of 30 on a 20 to 80 scale cannot be compared directly with a score of 35 on a zero to 100 scale. In order to compare scores from such measures you will need to transform the scores so that the ranges are the same.

Probably the most widely used transformed score—although not the best for our purposes—is a percentile rank. A percentile rank represents the proportion of scores which are lower than a particular raw score. With percentile ranks the median score is the 50th percentile, which is displayed in Panel A of Figure 2.1. Because percentile ranks concern one person's score in comparison to others' scores in the same sample, its use in practice evaluation is infrequent. Rather, you will be concerned with your client's score in relation to his or her previous scores.

You could use percentile rank, however, by comparing the percentile rank at the end of treatment with that at the beginning of treatment. To do so, you would simply count all scores with values less than the one you are interested in, divide by the total number of scores, and then multiply by 100. If you did this with two instruments with different ranges, you could compare the performances as reflected in percentile ranks.

A more useful transformed score is the standard score. Standard scores are also known as "Z scores." Standard scores convert a raw score to a number that reflects its distance from the mean. This transformed score derives its name from the standard deviation as it is essentially a measure of the score in terms of the extent of its deviation from the mean. The standard score, therefore, usually has a range from −4 to +4. A standard score of +1 would indicate that the score was 34.1% above the mean. With standard scores the mean is always zero. The standard score is displayed in Panel B of Figure 2.1.

Standard scores are derived from the following formula:

$$Z = (X - M) \div SD$$

where Z is the transformed score, X is the raw score, M is the sample mean, and SD is the standard deviation. By using this formula you can transform raw scores from different instruments to have the same range, a mean of zero and a standard deviation of one. These transformed scores then can be used to compare performances on different instruments. They also appear frequently in the literature.

Raw scores can also be transformed into standardized scores. Standardized scores are those where the mean and standard deviation are converted to some agreed-upon convention or standard. Some of the more common standardized scores you'll come across in the literature are T scores, CEEBs, and stanines.

A T score has a mean of 50 and a standard deviation of 10. T scores are used with a number of standardized measures, such as the Minnesota Multiphasic Inventory (MMPI). This is seen in Panel C of Figure 2.1. A CEEB, which stands for College Entrance Examination Board, has a mean of 500 and a standard deviation of 100. The CEEB score is found in Panel D of Figure 2.1. The stanine, which is abbreviated from standard nine, has a mean of 4.5, and a range of one to nine. This standardized score is displayed in Panel E of Figure 2.1.

To summarize, transformed scores allow you to compare instruments that have different ranges of scores; many authors will report data on the instruments in the form of transformed scores.

Methods of comparing raw and transformed scores. As we stated earlier, in order for a score to be interpreted it must be compared with other scores. We will consider two basic procedures for comparing scores: norm-referenced comparisons and self-referenced comparisons.

Norm-referenced comparisons allow you to interpret a score by comparing it with an established "norm." Ideally, these normative data should be representative of a population. When you compare your client's score with a norm, you can interpret it in terms of how the performance relates to the sample mean and standard deviation, in other words, how much above or below the mean your client is in relation to the norm.

Unfortunately, we do not have many instruments for rapid assessment that have well-established norms. Norm-referenced comparisons also have many limitations. One limitation is that the samples used to develop instruments are frequently not representative of a larger population. Secondly, even if the sample is representative, it is quite possible that your client is dissimilar enough to make the norm-referenced data noncomparable. Consider two examples. The

Selfism scale (Phares and Erskine, 1984) was designed to measure narcissism and was developed with undergraduates; these data might not be an appropriate norm with which to compare a narcissistic client's scores. It would make sense, though, to make norm-referenced comparisons between an adult client whose problem is due to irrational beliefs on Shorkey's Rational Behavior Scale (Shorkey and Whiteman, 1977), since these normative data are more representative of adult clients. Additionally, norms represent performance on an instrument at a specific point in time. Old normative data, say ten years or older, may not be relevant to clients you measure today.

To avoid these and other problems with normative comparisons, an alternative method of interpreting scores is to compare your client's scores with his or her previous performance. This is the basis of the single-system evaluation designs we discussed in Chapter 1 as an excellent way to monitor practice.

When used in single-system evaluation, self-referenced comparison means you interpret scores by comparing performance throughout the course of treatment. Clearly, this kind of comparison indicates whether your client's scores reveal change over time.

There are several advantages to self-referenced comparisons. First of all, you can usually use raw scores. Additionally, you can be more certain the comparisons are relevant and appropriate since the scores are from your own client and not some normative data which may or may not be relevant or representative. Finally, self-referenced comparisons have the advantage of being timely—or not outdated—since the assessment is occurring over the actual course of intervention.

PRACTICE PRINCIPLES INVOLVED IN MEASUREMENT

Having discussed what a "good" instrument is and how to statistically interpret scores, we turn now to the actual use of measures to monitor your client's progress and evaluate your effectiveness. In choosing to use a particular instrument you need to consider several factors that determine its practical value. These include utility, suitability and acceptability, sensitivity, directness, nonreactivity, and appropriateness. All of these issues concern the practical value of using instruments in your practice.

Utility

Utility refers to how much practical advantage you get from using an instrument (Gottman and Leiblum, 1974). In clinical practice, an instrument which helps you plan—or improve upon—your services, or provides accurate feedback regarding your effectiveness would be considered to have some utility (Nelson, 1981).

Certain features of an instrument influence its utility. Chief among these are the measure's purpose, length, your ability to score it, and the ease of interpreting the score. Instruments that tap a clinically relevant problem, are short, easy to score, and easy to interpret are the most useful for practice.

Suitability and Acceptability

A second element of an instrument's practical value is how suitable its content is to your client's intellectual ability and emotional state. Many require fairly sophisticated vocabulary or reading levels and may not be suitable for clients with poor literacy skills or whose first language is not English. Similarly, instruments may require the ability to discriminate between different emotional states, a set of skills which may not be developed in young children or severely disturbed clients. Psychotic clients, for example, are usually unable to accurately fill out most instruments.

If the scores are not accurate reflections of your client's problem, then the use of the instrument has little practical advantage. Furthermore, in order for an instrument to have practical value, your client will need to perceive the content as acceptable (Haynes, 1983), and the process of measuring the problem throughout treatment as important. If your client does not realize that measuring his or her problem is important, then the instrument may not be given serious attention—or even completed at all. Similarly, if your client sees the content as offensive, which might occur with some of the sexuality instruments, the responses may be affected. As we will discuss later, in these circumstances you will need to familiarize your client with the value of measurement in practice, and select an instrument with an understanding of your client's point of view.

Sensitivity

Since measurement in practice is intended to observe change over time, you will need to use instruments that are sensitive to tapping those changes. Without a sensitive instrument your client's progress may go undetected. You might ask, though, "Aren't scores supposed to be stable as an indicator of reliability?" Yes, and in fact, you will want an instrument that is both stable and sensitive. In other words, you will want to use instruments that are stable unless actual change has occurred. When real change does occur you will want an instrument that is sensitive enough to reveal that change. Sensitivity usually is revealed when the instrument is used as a measure of change in a study with actual clients.

Directness

Directness refers to how the score reflects the actual behavior, thoughts, or feelings of your client. Instruments that tap an underlying disposition from which you make inferences about your client are considered indirect. Direct measures, then, are *signs* of the problem, while indirect ones are *symbols* of the problem. Behavioral observations are considered relatively direct measures, while the Rorschach Inkblot is a classic example of an indirect measure. Most instruments, of course, are somewhere between these extremes. When deciding which instrument to use you should try to find ones that measure the actual problem as much as possible in terms of its manifested behavior or the client's experience. By avoiding the most indirect measures, not only are you preventing potential problems in reliability, but you can more validly ascertain the magnitude or intensity of the client's problem.

Nonreactivity

You will also want to try to use instruments that are relatively nonreactive. Reactivity refers to how the very act of measuring something changes it. Some methods of measurement are very reactive, such as the self-monitoring of cigarette smoking (e.g., Conway, 1977), while others are relatively nonreactive. Nonreactive measures are also known as unobtrusive. Since you are interested in how your treatment helps a client change, you certainly want an instrument that in and of itself, by the act of measurement, does not change your client.

At first glance, reactivity may seem beneficial in your effort to change a client's problem. After all, if measuring something can change it, why not just give all clients instruments instead of delivering treatment? However, the change from a reactive measure rarely produces long-lasting change, which therapeutic interventions are designed to produce. Consequently, you should attempt to use instruments that do not artificially affect the results, that is, try to use relatively nonreactive instruments. If you do use instruments that could produce reactive changes, you have to be aware of this in both your administration of the measure—and try to minimize it (see Bloom, Fischer, and Orme, 1999, for some suggestions)—and in a more cautious interpretation of results.

Appropriateness

This final criterion of an instrument's practical value is actually a composite of all the previous principles. Appropriateness refers to how compatible an instrument is for single-system evaluation. In order for it to be appropriate for routine use it must require little time for your client to complete and little time for you to score. Instruments that are lengthy or complicated to score may provide valuable information, but cannot be used on a regular and frequent basis throughout the course of treatment because they take up too much valuable time.

Appropriateness is also considered in the context of the information gained from using an instrument. In order for the information to be appropriate it must be reliable and valid, have utility, be suitable and acceptable to your client, sensitive to measuring real change, and measure the problem in a relatively direct and nonreactive manner. Instruments that meet these practice principles can provide important information which allows you to more fully understand your client as you monitor his or her progress.

3

TYPES OF
MEASUREMENT
TOOLS

For many years, a large number of practitioners in the human services thought that many of the problems they worked with were "unmeasurable." How, went the question, can you really measure what a person thinks or feels about himself or herself? How can you measure affect, attitudes, quality of life, and so on?

But in recent years, there has been a gradual shift in thinking among human service professionals. More and more of us are convinced that most if not all of the problems with which we work are indeed measurable—in terms that lead to increased precision and objectivity in our practice. In fact, one practitioner/ researcher put the issue bluntly: "If you cannot measure the client's problem, it does not exist" (Hudson, 1978).

The point, perhaps, is that while it may be difficult to measure our client's problems, it is not impossible. Many of our clients do indeed bring us problems that are globally or vaguely defined at first. The task for the practitioner is to help the client define (or redefine) the problem in terms that are amenable to measurement. This is not because measurement is an end in itself. Rather, it is because once a problem is measurable, it will also be clear enough to work with in an intervention program. Thus, your job as a practitioner is to find some *indicator* of the problem that can be measured so that you will know just how well you are doing with your intervention program. Examples of such indicators abound: a score on a self-esteem questionnaire can be an indicator of how a person feels about himself or herself, a score on a depression scale is an indicator of the intensity of one's depression, and so on.

Again, the goal here is not measurement for the sake of measurement. The goal is responsible, accountable practice. From the point of view of measurement, this means finding some indicator of the problem that is representative, that will be accessible to measurement, and that will provide leads for both conducting your intervention and evaluating its effects. Without these dimensions, we never could lay claim to being accountable practitioners.

The remainder of this chapter provides an overview of a number of ways to measure clients' problems. Although the central concern of this book is standardized rapid assessment instruments, we do not believe these instruments are the only way clients' problems can be measured. There are other complementary methods of measurement, to be selected depending on the needs of the individual case. The methods we will be discussing here include behavioral observations, individualized rating scales, client logs, unobtrusive measures, electro-mechanical measures, and of course, standardized questionnaire measures. Since each of these sections will simply be an overview of the area, we hope you will be encouraged to pursue the literature for further information on each method. (Some comprehensive references on measurement of practice problems include Bellack and Hersen, 1988; Goldstein and Hersen, 1990; Hersen and Bellack, 1988; Hudson, 1982, 1992; Barlow, 1981; Mash and Terdal, 1988; Haynes and Wilson, 1979; Cone and Hawkins, 1977; Ciminero et al., 1977; Kendall and Hollon, 1981; Haynes, 1978; Nay, 1979; Bloom, Fischer, and Orme 1994, 1999; see also Table 5.2 in Chapter 5.) We also hope that by the end of this chapter, you will agree that just about any problem—behavior, feeling, attitude, thought, activity—can be measured.

BEHAVIORAL OBSERVATIONS

When you think of observing behaviors, you probably think of behaviors that you actually can see. But we have a broader definition. By behavior, we mean just about anything people do, whether it is overt (kissing, walking) or covert (thinking or feeling). The key here is that the behavior must be measurable and countable by someone, whether it is the client counting his or her negative thoughts or number of cigarettes smoked (called *self-monitoring*), or someone else observing the number of times a child swears.

Behavioral measures, based on observation of the client's actual functioning, are particularly useful because they typically are the most direct expression of the problem and therefore tend to have a great deal of validity. Also, because behavior can be counted and defined fairly specifically, this form of measurement can add a good deal to the precision and reliability of one's assessment. Moreover, the behaviors can be a ready target for intervention efforts.

There are three basic ways of measuring or counting behavior: frequency, duration, and interval counts. Frequency measures involve simply counting how often a problem behavior occurs. The key consideration in deciding to use a frequency count is that the problem occurs too often and needs to be decreased (say, negative self-thoughts, anxiety, number of cigarettes smoked), or the problem does not occur often enough and needs to be increased (number of chores completed, number of meetings attended).

The second type of behavioral measure is a duration count. Duration counts are used when the problem involves time, that is, a problem occurs for too long a period (tantrums, crying, tension, headaches), or does not occur for a long enough period (studying, exercise, maintenance of penile erections). Duration counts require a timepiece such as a stop watch to keep track of how long a behavior lasts. It is, of course, crucial to be absolutely clear about when a behavior begins and ends to be certain about how long it lasts.

The third type of behavior observation is an interval count. This might be used when a behavior occurs so often or for so long a period, or is so difficult to break into discrete units, that it becomes problematic to use frequency or duration recording. In interval recording, a period of observation is selected and then divided into equal blocks of time. Then all the observer has to do is record whether or not the behavior is displayed at all during each of the recording intervals. The behavior is recorded as occurring only once per interval no matter how long or how many times it has occurred.

With all three forms of behavior observation, it is very important for the practitioner and whoever is doing the counting to have the problem specifically defined and to be clear about the time period involved in the recording. To this end, it is particularly important to have two observers, say the practitioner and the person who will be doing the observing, engage in "reliability checks." In these, the two recorders observe the problem behavior and then compare their observations. To obtain a reliability coefficient (a measure of how much or little the score depends on the particular scorer) one observer's figures are divided into the other's (always the largest into the smallest). For frequency measures, you would divide the largest number of observed behaviors (say 12) into the smallest (say 10) and come up with a figure of .83 or 83 percent reliability. For duration measures, the same method is used, dividing the smaller duration by the larger (10 minutes of observed problems divided by 12 minutes equals .83). For interval measures, you would divide the number of intervals in which two observers agreed the problem did or did not occur by the total number of intervals to get your reliability figure.

Behavioral observation is often accompanied by the use of coding forms or other tools, such as prepared checklists, 3×5 cards to keep track of behavior, stop watches, golf counters to tally up everything from calories to negative thoughts, cassette tape recorders, coins to move from one pocket to another, and so on. The methods of counting are limited only by your own imagination, as long as they are portable and relatively unobtrusive. Behavioral observation is one of the most flexible, useful, and important types of measurement you can implement in order to monitor and evaluate your client's progress.

INDIVIDUALIZED RATING SCALES

Individualized rating scales (IRS) are scales that you and the client can devise to measure a particular problem. The three main types of IRSs are self-anchored scales, rating scales, and target complaint scales (see Bloom, Fischer, and Orme, 1999).

The *self-anchored scale* is so flexible and can be used with so many problems and in so many situations that it has been dubbed "the all purpose measurement procedure" (Bloom, 1975). The practitioner and client together can construct a self-anchored scale to measure any given problem. All you do is establish a range that focuses on the intensity of the problem as perceived by the client, that is, the degree or extent to which the client experiences some feeling, thought, or condition. Any number of problems can be measured by this procedure: thoughts and feelings, the intensity of pain, fear, sexual excitement, and so on. These scales are very easy to construct and can be used as many times per day as the occasion calls for. Indeed, for many problems on which only the client himself or herself can report, this may be the only kind of measurement available.

The process of developing a scale is relatively straightforward. Once the problem area is defined, you present to the client a picture of a social or psychological thermometer, with one end being the most intense end of the problem and the other the least intense. Then you select the number of points for the scale. We usually recommend 0–10 or 1–9, although if the client has difficulty in discriminating among that many points, you can collapse the scale to 1–7 or 1–5 points. Make sure you are clear with the client that they are equal intervals, so that the difference between 1 and 2 on the scale is no greater than the difference between 5 and 6. Finally, you and the client attempt to anchor the scale points using as much concrete detail to define each point as possible. Thus, if level 9 is the most intense level of the problem, you would try to help the client describe what he or she is experiencing at that level. A self-anchored scale measuring intensity of cognitions of sadness might look like this:

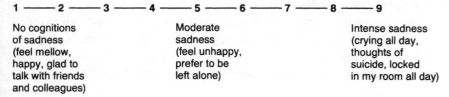

1 ——— 2 ——— 3 ——— 4 ——— 5 ——— 6 ——— 7 ——— 8 ——— 9

| No cognitions of sadness (feel mellow, happy, glad to talk with friends and colleagues) | Moderate sadness (feel unhappy, prefer to be left alone) | Intense sadness (crying all day, thoughts of suicide, locked in my room all day) |

Rating scales are constructed pretty much the same way as self-anchored scales, with one difference: the client does not rate himself or herself. Instead, someone else uses the scale to rate the client. These scales have a number of uses. They can be used when the client is unable to rate himself or herself or when an additional perspective on the problem is needed. They can even be used as "analogue measures," for example, to rate an artificially created situation such as a structured role play which the practitioner sets up to evaluate the progress of clients on selected behaviors (say, in the learning of job interview skills).

Target complaint scales (TCS) are based on the client's initial statement of the problem. Once you and the client agree on a particular problem as the focus of intervention, you simply ask the client periodically to rate either severity or improvement; these ratings would be made using a scale such as "much worse–worse–little change–better–much better."

Self-anchored, rating, and target complaint scales are very easy to use and their flexibility and face validity recommend them highly.

CLIENT LOGS

One of the most important tasks of the practitioner is to collect from the client as much systematic and accurate information as possible in order to develop and evaluate the optimal intervention plan. One way of facilitating this process is through use of client logs. These essentially are journals kept by clients of events they consider relevant to their problem. The logs are more or less formal records of these events that can be used to minimize distortion when the client presents information to the practitioner.

Client logs have two purposes. The first one is to aid in the overall assessment by helping pinpoint problems. Part of this process is to use the material collected in the log as a source for hypotheses about events that seem related to the client's problems as well as the client's reaction to these events.

The second purpose is for evaluation. Client logs provide an on-going record of the client's activities involving the problem being worked on. The value of the client logs can be greatly expanded by, first, using each incident recorded as a behavioral count of the occurrence of the problem, and second, adding a self-anchored scale on which the client records the intensity of his or her feelings about the recorded event.

You can use the same format for all client logs. This consists of a prepared form which lists across the top of the page the types of information that should be collected. This information, of course, varies with the nature of the problem, but usually includes a brief description of the event, what preceded or followed it, who was present, and what the client did, thought, or felt about it. Along the

| CLIENT NAME _____ | DATE _____ |

TIME:	EVENT:	WHO WAS PRESENT	CLIENT'S REACTION
_____	_____	_____	_____
	_____	_____	_____
	_____	_____	_____
_____	_____	_____	_____
	_____	_____	_____
	_____	_____	_____
_____	_____	_____	_____
	_____	_____	_____
	_____	_____	_____
_____	_____	_____	_____
	_____	_____	_____
	_____	_____	_____
_____	_____	_____	_____
	_____	_____	_____
	_____	_____	_____
	_____	_____	_____
_____	_____	_____	_____
	_____	_____	_____
	_____	_____	_____
_____	_____	_____	_____
	_____	_____	_____

Figure 3.1. General Model for Client Logs *(adapted from Bloom, Fischer, and Orme, 1999)*

left-hand side of the page, the time of each event is recorded. A general model for client logs is presented in Figure 3.1.

Client logs essentially vary according to the time and the category of the problem. Regarding time, the client can be asked to record whenever an event occurs or at specifically preset intervals. Categories of problems can also vary from relatively open (record any event you think is critical) to very specific including a number of different categories (e.g., who was present, what did he or she say, what did you say, what was their reaction, and so on). A number of examples of these different types of logs are available in Bloom, Fischer, and Orme (1999) and Schwartz and Goldiamond (1975).

UNOBTRUSIVE MEASURES

An obvious concern you might have in using measurement procedures with your client is that the actual act of measurement might affect or change the client's problem before you even begin your intervention, thereby distorting your results. We described this in Chapter 2 as reactivity, and indeed, the potential for change due to measurement itself is an ever-present danger. There are procedures for overcoming reactivity in some measures and even using it to clinical advantage (see, e.g., Nay, 1979), which we will discuss further in Chapter 6. But there are also some measures that were designed specifically to avoid the problem of reactivity; these are called unobtrusive measures (Webb et al., 1966). Essentially, these are measures where the client is not aware of being measured so that there is little chance that the act of measurement itself can produce change.

There are several types of unobtrusive measures that might be useful. Behavioral products enable one to measure the effects of behavior (e.g., items left on the floor or the number of cigarette butts in an ashtray). Physical traces are evidence left by an individual or group without the knowledge it will be used for other purposes. Simple observation involves the act of observing the client without being seen or noticed (e.g., through a one-way mirror).

One other unobtrusive measure that is particularly useful is the archival record, involving data that are kept for one purpose, but can be used to help evaluate an intervention program. Indeed, in some instances, these records might directly reflect the problem on which the practitioner is working (school attendance, school grades, recidivism rates, agency record data, etc.).

It is important to be aware of the fact that archival data can also present some frustrations because often they are incomplete, lost, or access to them is difficult. However, because they do overcome problems of reactivity they can be a particularly valuable measurement tool.

ELECTRO-MECHANICAL MEASURES

One area of measurement that usually receives fairly scant attention in the practice literature is the use of electro-mechanical devices for psychophysiological assessment. This oversight may be due to a natural aversion on the part of many human service practitioners to hook clients up to mechanical devices.

Further, these devices tend to be expensive and/or complicated to use, and are usually not available to practitioners.

On the other hand, in certain circumstances these devices may be the measurement procedure of choice. This obviously is in a situation when the physiological measures are clearly related to the social or psychological problem. The broad range of electro-mechanical devices available and their increasing utilization in areas such as behavioral medicine, sex therapy, and treatment of anxiety and stress suggest their potential importance for practitioners.

Among the most commonly used devices are the electromyogram (EMG) to measure muscle action; the electrocardiogram (EKG) for cardiac reactions; blood pressure readings; skin resistance level (SRL) and response (SRR) to measure sweat gland activity; the electroencephalogram (EEG) to monitor brain functions; and strain gauges and plethysmographs to monitor sexual arousal. These devices are most useful when one can be relatively certain the devices possess an adequate degree of reliability and validity, and when there appears to be a unique physiological response that can provide information on social or psychological variables that would permit an appropriate intervention plan (Kallman and Feuerstein, 1986). Some additional sources that can be reviewed for information on electro-mechanical measures include Rugh et al. (1986), Lang (1977), Epstein (1976), Haynes (1978), and Ray and Raczynski (1984).

STANDARDIZED MEASURES

Our main reason for the discussion of other measurement procedures is that they are available, they have important uses, and although we are focusing on standardized, self-report instruments, we don't mean to exclude other methods. In fact, our basic recommendations for measuring client problems are first, use the best (most direct, valid, reliable, sensitive) measure available every time you can; and second, whenever possible, try to use more than one measure because problems usually are not confined to only one area of human functioning. Two measures can provide a far broader and more accurate picture of changes in a client's problem than one. And standardized, self-report instruments are only one of several types of measures available.

In fact, though, just about all of the rest of the book will be concerned with the use of standardized measures. A standardized measure is one that has uniform procedures for administration and scoring, and contains a series of structured questions or statements designed to elicit information from the client. These statements do not vary each time the questionnaire is administered. In addition, standardized measures usually provide a numerical score for estimating the magnitude, intensity, or degree of the client's problem (Levitt and Reid, 1981). There is usually information available about the psychometric properties of the measure, including all or most of the following: the purpose and interpretation of the measure, its reliability and validity, scoring and administration, and sometimes norms for comparison of individual scores with the scores of groups who have been evaluated on the measure previously.

There are literally thousands of standardized measures available for just about any type of problem a practitioner might have to deal with in practice. Similarly, there are many different types of standardized measures including scales, checklists, inventories, indexes, and so on. Further, these measures have been developed to be filled out not only by the client (self-report), but by professionals and significant others. However, many of these measures are excessively long, complicated, difficult to score and/or interpret, and have weak or questionable psychometric information available about them. Indeed, precisely because there are so many of these measures available, we consider the primary purpose of this book the selection of those instruments that would be most useful to you in your practice.

Our effort to select from the many thousands of available instruments and develop a useful set of measures focused on rapid assessment instruments (RAIs). Several characteristics distinguish RAIs from other forms of standardized measures (Levitt and Reid, 1981):

1. They are self-report measures, filled out by the client.
2. They tend to be short (one to two pages), easy to administer, and easy to complete (usually in less than 15 minutes).
3. They are generally written in a clear, simple language that the client can understand.
4. They can be scored rapidly, often in the presence of the client.
5. The interpretation of the measure is straightforward and clear.
6. Use of the measure by the practitioner does not require extensive knowledge of testing procedures.
7. They do not require subscription to a particular theoretical perspective.
8. They provide a systematic overview of the client's problem as well as information on individual aspects that may be discussed in the interview.
9. The overall score provides an index of the degree, intensity, or magnitude of the client's problem.
10. They can provide a structured means for collecting data that is standardized and comparable across applications of the measure, both for individual clients, and across all clients.
11. They can be used on a one-time basis, or as repeated measures, thereby producing information on changes in the client's problem over time by comparing scores from one administration to another.

The scores obtained can be plotted on a single-system design chart such as those illustrated in Chapter 1, allowing easy, visual inspection of changes.

As you can see, these instruments have a great deal of potential for adding immensely useful information to practice. They can be used as a guide to treatment planning, can provide feedback regarding progress, can provide evidence as to overall effectiveness, and can even provide information that will be useful to the practitioner in the give and take of the clinical interview. All of this can be accomplished within the context of the interview; very little additional time is required for the client to complete and practitioner to score the measure.

Now while it might seem as though these instruments are the answer to the practitioner's dream, even a panacea for all measurement problems, in fact, some problems do exist in using these measures. In the remainder of Part I, we will discuss standardized measures in more detail, including their strengths and limitations, and particularly, how you can administer them in a way that will provide you with optimal results.

The Issue of Standardization

Because there are so many measures available, it is important to have clear criteria for selecting a measure. In this section we explain the criteria we used in selecting the instruments included in this book. Essentially, all of the measures we selected can be considered standardized. There are two main aspects of standardization. The first is that a standardized measure has uniform items, scoring procedures, and method of administration that do not change no matter how many times you administer the instrument or to whom you administer it. (The one exception to this might be the extra care you would want to take to explain the instrument to people who have trouble in understanding its application.)

Secondly, standardized measures generally have certain types of information available about them. That is, it is the responsibility of the developer of an instrument to provide sufficient information about it to allow a potential user to make a sound judgment about the measure's value. The areas of information include purpose and interpretation, reliability, validity, scoring, administration, and norms. (Norms refer to interpreting the meaning of a score on an instrument in relation to scores of other groups of people who have taken it, or in relation to achievement of some preset criterion, e.g., qualifying for some type of license. All of these areas are discussed in more detail in Chapter 2, and in publications by Ciarlo et al., 1986; the American Psychological Association, 1985; Anastasi, 1988; Cronbach, 1970).

Just because a measure does not have all of this information does not mean it is not standardized. Instruments vary on the extent to which complete information is available, especially concerning validity, because of the difficulty of developing such information. This is particularly true if the measure is relatively new. On the other hand, to the extent that information from all or most of these categories is available for any given measure, you can make a more rational decision and select a better instrument than if only some of this information is available.

Standardization is not the same thing as "objectivity" (Cronbach, 1970). If a measure is "objective," then every observer who sees a performance arrives at exactly the same report. The more two observers disagree, the more subjective is the observation and evaluation.

Problems Addressed

As we indicated earlier, there are standardized measures available for just about any area of human functioning. Measures are available that examine general or broadly defined dimensions such as environments, including ward, treatment, and correctional environments (Moos, 1974, 1975a and b, 1979); personality; adjustment; competence; and mental health (see, e.g., the collections of measures listed in Chapter 5, Table 5.2.) But standardized measures also address just about any specific problem area you might conceivably face in practice. One sourcebook alone (Comrey et al., 1973) lists 45 categories of measures in specific problem areas ranging from alcoholism to juvenile delinquency to sex to vocational tests. The measures available span the full range of human functioning including behaviors, cognitions, attitudes, and feelings.

Of course, most of these measures are not included in this book for reasons indicated earlier: some are too sophisticated or require too much training to be easily used in practice, many are simply too long or difficult for the client to fill out readily, many do not have sufficient psychometric data to allow a reasoned judgment about their practical advantages, and many are not feasible for use in single-system designs as repeated measures.

Focus of Measures

There are a number of different dimensions that characterize an instrument. One is the degree to which the measure assesses a range, from the client's global perceptions to more specific reactions. The client may be asked to describe his or her feelings in general about some state of affairs ("Do you feel depressed?"), or at the other end of the continuum, might be asked to indicate how many hours he or she cries per day.

Another related dimension distinguishes broad personality measures from measures of specific problem areas. Some of the broader personality measures, such as the Rorschach Test or the Thematic Apperception Test (TAT), focus on the client's reaction to ambiguous visual stimuli and produce broadly based diagnostic categories regarding the client's psychological functioning. At the other end of the continuum, some instruments are focused around specific problem areas, for example, a scale on sexual satisfaction which provides a specific index of the level of the client's sexual satisfaction with his or her partner.

Instruments may also be categorized as state versus trait measures. In essence, a "trait," is viewed as a relatively enduring or stable characteristic of an individual, and is broadly defined. A "state," on the other hand, is seen as a more transitory emotional condition typically elicited by a particular stimulus or environmental condition. Though controversy continues over whether human personality and functioning are best conceptualized in terms of traits or states, both kinds of measures have value to the extent that they facilitate the prediction and modification of behavior (Mischel, 1968). And while we cannot hope to resolve this controversy here, we do want you to be aware that a few of the instruments in this book do make this distinction.

Yet another dimension of standardized measures is their directness. As we discussed in Chapter 2, directness refers to the extent to which you have to make an inference regarding the behavior, cognition, or feelings being assessed. All things being equal (which they rarely are), we believe that the more direct the measure, the more potential value it has for your practice. Thus, in choosing between two instruments, if one produces a score from which you need to make an inference about the client's condition, and the other produces a score that directly reflects the client's problem, we would suggest the latter measure is a more useful one.

More or less direct measures can include observations of specific behaviors, self-reports of clients of their thoughts and feelings, and any other method of measurement that requires minimal inference about the client's condition. Although we have attempted to locate as many direct measures as possible, we actually have provided a broad range—from more or less direct to more or less indirect—because many standardized measures do require some degree of inference about the client's condition yet contain reliability and validity information that is as good as the more direct measures.

Standardized measures also differ in who is to fill them out. Some are designed to be filled out by practitioners or significant others about someone else (e.g., a parent or counselor checking items on an inventory about a child's behavior). Others, including most of the instruments in this book, are designed as self-report measures, in that the person filling out the questionnaire responds with his or her thoughts or feelings to items on the instrument that typically refer to the respondent's own condition, problem, or circumstances.

Some standardized measures have cutting scores. These are scores, based on the norms for that measure, that distinguish different groups of respondents. Thus, if research on a particular measure has shown that people who score above a certain point can be distinguished from people below that point with regard to possession of certain characteristics, that would be a cutting point. For example, based on extensive research on the WALMYR Assessment Scales (Hudson, 1992), scores of approximately 30 on each instrument tend to distinguish people who have a clinically significant problem on that particular measure from those who do not. Other instruments may have cutting scores that distinguish different categories of respondents, for example, not depressed, moderately depressed, and severely depressed. While cutting scores can be a great advantage to the practitioner in interpreting a given measure, they generally should be used with caution and not too rigidly; a few-point difference in one person's score as compared to someone else's may not, in reality, reflect a true difference between those two people, even though one may be on one side of the cutting score and the other person on the other side.

Finally, standardized measures also vary according to the age of the target group of users. Some measures are designed for children and adolescents, some for both children and adults, and a few target the elderly. We have tried to include a cross-section of available measures for all groups. However, because there are natural limitations on children's abilities to fill out questionnaires, there are fewer instruments available for them. Most measures for children are actually rating scales that are filled out by adults about children, and only a few of this type of instrument are included in this book.

Procedures for Developing Standardized Measures

In this section we will try to clarify some of the terms used to describe a variety of different types of measure. Although we will be using standard references as guides (e.g., Anastasi, 1988; Cronbach, 1970; Miller, 1977), we must admit that there is not universal acceptance of all these terms.

Standardized measures are developed in any number of ways: The author may intuitively think up items that could be included on an instrument, he or she may select items based on a review of the literature (both of these using a face validity criterion), or by using more empirically oriented methods. Instruments developed empirically have been described by Golden et al. (1984) as having three basic methodologies: (1) developing items on the basis of their ability to discriminate between two other groups (say, between depressed and nondepressed clients); (2) using items that show a high correlation with an external variable of interest (e.g., correlation of items on a depression scale with psychiatric ratings); (3) using items that group together empirically on the basis of factor analysis (i.e., intercorrelations of certain items from a pool of items).

Standardized measures also vary according to the number of dimensions included within one measure. The scores on some measures reflect only one dimension, such as overall magnitude of depression. These measures are called unidimensional. Some measures are multidimensional; they include subdimensions or subscales (often based on factor analysis). For example, an overall score dealing with self-esteem may encompass subscales reflecting feelings of self-worth under different circumstances. Some researchers believe unidimensional measures are more desirable because they are more efficient—easier to use—and because multidimensional measures, to some extent, consist of several unidimensional measures collected on one instrument. On the other hand, if all subdimensions of a multidimensional measure have good reliability and validity, the multidimensional instrument can be at least as useful as several unidimensional measures, and perhaps more efficient.

Finally, there are different categories of measures including inventories, indexes, and scales, although the terms are often used interchangeably. The most generic term for these measures is "questionnaire" because they all require someone to write responses on a piece of paper. Inventories and checklists typically include a range of behaviors, thoughts, or feelings and the respondent indicates whether or not these appear to be present.

Indexes and scales, the most commonly used (and confused) terms, are really variations of the same phenomenon. Both are composite measures constructed from two or more indicators or items. Some researchers believe the distinction between the two is that indexes produce ordinal levels of measurement while scales produce interval levels (Hudson, 1981). Others claim that both indexes and scales are ordinal measures, but distinguish between the two according to the manner in which their scores are assigned. Indexes are said to be constructed through the simple accumulation of scores assigned to individual attributes, while scales are constructed by assigning scores to patterns of attributes (Babbie, 1983). Thus, scales are seen as taking advantage of the intensity structure that may exist among attributes.

Basically, though, both indexes and scales are developed using logical inference and a numerical scale that assumes some underlying continuity and which the respondent can realistically act upon in self-rating (Miller, 1977). However, there are so many different types of measures that are differentiated on a technical basis that a brief review of these measures, based on the work of Miller (1977), follows. The most commonly used standardized measures fall into the following categories:

Thurstone equal appearing scale. This is a scale comprising a number of items whose position on the scale is determined by ranking operations, i.e., in its development experts make judgments as to the order of the items. The respondent then selects the responses that best describe how he or she feels.

Likert-type scale. This commonly used scale is comprised of a series of items to which the client responds. The scores on each item are summed to produce an overall score. The client indicates agreement or disagreement with each item on an intensity scale. It is particularly useful in ordering people regarding attitudes.

Guttman scale-analysis. This technique is an attempt to describe the unidimensionality of a scale. Only items meeting a criterion of reproducibility are acceptable (i.e., if we know a respondent's extreme position, we should be able to reproduce all of his or her responses). If this scale is unidimensional, a person who has a more favorable attitude about some variable than another person should respond to each item with equal or greater favorableness than the other. Each score on the scale corresponds to a response pattern or scale type; thus, the score can be used to predict the response of all items.

Scale discrimination techniques. These techniques also seek to develop a set of items that are unidimensional, have equal-appearing intervals, and measure intensity. Aspects of the first three types of scales described above and, hence, their advantages, are combined here.

Rating scales. This type of procedure is an attempt to obtain an evaluation or quantitative judgment about personality, group, or institutional characteristics based upon personal judgments. The respondent or rater places the person or object being rated at a point along the continuum or in one of an ordered series of categories, and then a numerical value is assigned to the point or category. Rating scales can be used to assess a wide variety of attitudes, values, and social activities.

Paired comparison. This procedure attempts to assess psychological values of qualitative stimuli without knowledge of any corresponding respondent values. Respondents are asked to select the more favorable of a pair of statements or objects over a set of several pairs, and an attempt is made to order the statements or objects along a continuum. This procedure is often called "forced choice."

Semantic differential. This type of measure attempts to assess the meaning of an object to the respondent. The respondent is asked to rate a given concept on a series of seven-point, bipolar rating scales. The rating is made according to the respondent's perception of the relatedness or association of the adjective (e.g., good-bad, fair-unfair) to the concept being rated.

Other available techniques include multidimensional scaling (Miller, 1977) and item-response theory (Reckase, 1984). These are more complicated and beyond the scope of this book. However, some of the procedures described above are represented in Part II and Volume 2; hence, their brief description here.

THE RAI: FULL CIRCLE

Rapid Assessment Instruments—as standardized measures—are not limited to one type of scale or index. Any measure we could locate that was standardized, short, easy to administer and score, based on self-reports, focused on a problem that you might see in clinical practice, and that contained relatively useful psychometric properties was reviewed for inclusion in this book.

4

ADVANTAGES AND DISADVANTAGES OF RAPID ASSESSMENT INSTRUMENTS

In Chapter 3 we discussed a variety of tools for measuring your practice. Though rapid assessment instruments (RAIs) are most amenable to routine use with most clients, their use is not without limitations. In this chapter we will discuss some of the advantages and disadvantages of using RAIs to monitor your client's progress and evaluate practice.

ADVANTAGES

We believe, as do others (e.g., Bloom, Fischer, and Orme, 1999); Wittenborn, 1984), that using RAIs in practice has enormous value in terms of enhancing effectiveness and accountability. Among the advantages of particular importance to your practice are efficiency, accessibility, disclosure, comparability, and the potential for theoretical neutrality.

Efficiency

Perhaps the major strength of RAIs is their efficiency. Rapid assessment instruments are efficient because they are easy to administer, do not require extensive training, and tend to be short in length; thus, they do not require much time for scoring. RAIs are efficient also because they are readily available in the professional literature and are usually inexpensive to use. Any clinician can easily have available right at his or her desk a number of RAIs to apply with clients depending on the problem and situation.

Accessibility

RAIs can provide access to information about the client that may be hard to observe overtly. As this book illustrates, RAIs have been developed to measure a large variety of attitudes, feelings, and behaviors. RAIs also have the potential of providing information about certain behaviors that are only observable through self-reports, such as magical thinking or a client's feelings. In addition, self-report instruments indicate how important a problem is to the client in terms of its level or magnitude.

Disclosure

RAIs enable the client to disclose sensitive information that he or she might find difficult to verbalize (Fischer and Gochros, 1975; Hudson, 1982). This is particularly advantageous during the initial phases of treatment before you and your client have developed a trusting relationship. For example, during an initial interview a client may be reluctant to discuss particular sexual behaviors or dissatisfaction (Wincze and Lange, 1982). This type of information, however, may be disclosed by completing the Sexuality Arousability Inventory (Hoon and Chambless, 1987) or the Index of Sexual Satisfaction (Hudson, 1992).

Comparability

Another advantage of RAIs is comparability. You can make comparisons two ways: by comparing scores with some established norm or by comparing a client's performance with previous scores. The advantage of self-referenced comparison, you will remember, is that you can monitor your client's progress throughout treatment.

Neutrality

A final advantage to consider is that many RAIs have the potential of being theoretically neutral. We say potential because many instruments are germane to a theory and most of our knowledge in clinical practice is derived from theoretical constructs. Nonetheless, many instruments do not require that you adhere to a particular theory in order to use them to help you monitor treatment.

Clearly, neutrality is not an absolute characteristic of instruments. In fact, many are designed to assess a problem from a specific theoretical perspective, such as the Rational Behavior Inventory (Shorkey and Whiteman, 1977). On the other hand, instruments like the WALMYR Assessment Scales (Hudson, 1982, 1992) or Stiles' (1980) Session Evaluation Questionnaire are not theoretically based. More importantly, even those instruments that have been developed within a particular theoretical framework may be used to monitor practice even if you do not adhere to the theory, or are using a treatment approach derived from a different theoretical orientation.

DISADVANTAGES

In spite of their many advantages, RAIs are not a panacea. In fact, clinical measures have several limitations. These disadvantages tend to relate to psychometrics, practical utility, and the agency context in which you might work. As we shall point out, however, many of these limitations may be minimized by the way you use the RAIs.

Psychometric Disadvantages

Four of the basic disadvantages of using RAIs pertain to psychometrics. First of all, while many instruments have reliability and validity data, these research findings are only estimates based on particular groups. The psychometric data come from a group and it is difficult to determine if, indeed, the instrument would be reliable and valid for your particular client. In clinical practice your client's problem would probably not be reflective of the norm for, say, a group of college sophomores. The focus of your practice is most likely a single system, such as an individual or a family.

One way to minimize the adverse effect of this issue is to be judicious about accepting scores as "truth." Any score is simply an estimate of some attribute, and should not be accepted uncritically. Moreover, scores contain error, which means that decisions about practice can be incorrect if based strictly on any instrument. You should never, for example, terminate treatment based solely on the score from a rapid assessment instrument. In other words, we suggest you use scores as indicators in monitoring practice but never rely on a score too much. In this respect, rapid assessment instruments should be used in conjunction with other methods of evaluating progress, such as supervision and case consultations.

RAIs also tend to be obtrusive and may cause some reactive effect in your client. As explained above, reactivity occurs when the assessment process alters the actual problem. While reactivity is more often found in self-monitoring behavioral observations (e.g., Johnson and Bolstad, 1973; Kazdin, 1982), RAIs can induce reactivity by sensitizing your client toward the content.

Similarly, RAIs are susceptible to distorted responses by your client. A client may distort the truth to provide socially desirable responses, or to suggest that it is too early to terminate treatment or that clinical services are not needed.

As we will discuss more fully in Chapter 6, you can minimize these potential disadvantages by informing your client of the importance of measurement in practice. Moreover, you must reassure your client that his or her honest responses will be helpful to treatment. After all, as Mischel (1981) has noted, "We cannot expect honest self-reports unless people are convinced that their honesty will not be used against them" (p. 482). This reassurance will need to be presented explicitly, and evidenced throughout the course of intervention.

A fourth disadvantage related to reliability and validity is that while many instruments focus on a particular problem, most are not specific enough to measure its nuances. Depression, for example, has many dimensions relating to social behavior, cognitions, biochemistry, and affect. Many instruments, although certainly not all, are simply too general to tap these subtleties. Consequently, you may not find an instrument that addresses the specific aspects of your client's problem.

The most feasible way to minimize this limitation is to use RAIs that are as specific and direct as possible. This will allow more confidence in the validity of the scores, although you should always remain somewhat critical. Additionally, we suggest you use more than one instrument whenever possible. The use of multiple measures can further increase your confidence in the scores.

Practical Disadvantages

Another set of disadvantages pertains to how RAIs are used in your practice. One limitation is that since RAIs are so easy to administer, score, and interpret they can be overused. This can occur by administering a scale too frequently or by relying too much on what you think the score means.

The most direct way to minimize this is to allow sufficient time to elapse between administrations. We suggest about one week between administrations for most rapid assessment instruments, though some can be administered twice a week. Finally, you can minimize overuse of an instrument by using parallel forms when they exist. For example, you could use the Rathus Assertion Schedule and the Simplified Rathus Assertion Schedule on alternating weeks. However, using parallel forms may mean you have to transform the scores in order to compare them, and parallel forms frequently are not available.

Another practical disadvantage is that rapid assessment instruments are relatively new to the literature. Consequently, instruments may not exist to measure a client's problem, or even more likely, its nuances. In such circumstances you may very well have to use a measure you consider second choice, one that may not be as direct or specific as you would like.

You may also find practical limitations due to your client's abilities and/or awareness of the problem. For example, a young child's reading level may not be sufficient for RAIs, or the child's awareness and memory may not be adequate to provide valid information.

The most obvious way to minimize these potential problems is to find instruments that are appropriate for your client's ability. You should also try to be creative in solving each unique problem as it arises, such as reading the instrument to the child or administering it frequently enough to allow the child to be able to respond accurately. When you do apply creative ways of resolving these types of problems, you also should remember that these instruments are standardized, and in order to keep scores as valid as possible you should follow the same procedures each time you use the instrument with the client.

Agency Disadvantages

You may encounter other obstacles to the use of RAIs in an agency setting (Corcoran, 1993; Thomas, 1978; Toseland and Reid, 1985). There may be open opposition from colleagues and supervisors who are unfamiliar with the value of monitoring practice. Or there may be demanding caseloads, back-to-back treatment sessions, and paperwork that take up too much of your time.

The latter restraints are minimized, as you know, by the fact that RAIs are short and do not take much time to complete and score. Moreover, the administration of RAIs is flexible enough so that your client can complete them outside the office or just prior to the interview with you.

Open opposition to monitoring and evaluating your practice may be more difficult to overcome. In part it may necessitate taking a leadership role and educating your colleagues about the benefits of measurement in practice. (You might even consider giving them copies of this book; your colleagues—and the authors—will thank you for it.)

On the other hand, agencies can provide a context in which the use of measurements is enhanced (Austin, 1981). For example, you can encourage your agency to use RAIs by obtaining a variety of different measures that assess the clinical problems most frequently seen in your agency. Agencies can also arrange for release time for you to search for additional instruments to add to your repertoire, as well as providing group supervision to improve staff ability to use instruments to monitor and evaluate practice.

RAIs are like all other assessment procedures, including clinical judgments: they are not perfect. But, like clinical judgment, when used wisely in the context of the entire therapeutic relationship and all the information available about the client, they can be invaluable to effective practice.

5

SELECTING
MEASURES FOR
PRACTICE

While this book provides many of the instruments you will need in your evaluation of practice, there will be many times when you will want additional ones or even other types of measures. This is especially true since the field of measurement is growing very rapidly and more and more instruments are becoming available. In this chapter we will discuss how you can go about selecting RAIs. We will consider what you will be measuring within certain important contexts and will show you how to locate measures. We will also suggest questions you can ask to help you evaluate which measure to use. Our emphasis is on short, standardized RAIs, but we will mention additional types of measurement tools when appropriate.

DEFINING WHAT YOU NEED TO MEASURE

By the end of your assessment interviews you will probably have a pretty good idea about your client's problem and some of the objectives of intervention. It is helpful to have the problem or treatment goals narrowed down in fairly concrete terms. You will then not only be more likely to effect change, but you will have a better chance of finding an appropriate tool to measure this change. Thus, one guideline to consider as you define your measurement need is to be concrete and specific about what your client is to change and the goals of treatment.

Once you have decided what you intend to measure, whether it is a specific client behavior—like the length of a temper tantrum—or a less direct construct, such as self-esteem or marital discord, you will need to decide what type of measurement tool to use.

First consider the source of the observations. Who could complete a behavioral rating scale, or is it better to have the client use a self-report instrument? You have three choices here: the client, a significant other, or you as the clinician.

With children you might very well need a significant other, such as a parent or teacher. The reason for this is that children are not the most reliable and valid sources of observations; plus, they may be limited by reading ability, recall, and awareness. Consequently, you might very well need to use behavioral rating scales. For example, you might consider having a teacher complete the Teacher's Self-Control Rating Scale to use in conjunction with the Children's Perceived Self-Control Scale (Humphrey, 1982). Using more than one measure will enhance the validity of your observations, and allow you to be more certain about the change you are monitoring in your client.

You can also measure the problem or treatment goals yourself. We usually do this anyway, and call it clinical judgment. By using a standardized measurement tool your accuracy may substantiate the clinical judgment as well as improve it. Another tool to help evaluate your own practice is the Session Evaluation Questionnaire (Stiles, 1980). This instrument assesses the depth and smoothness of a therapy session and can serve as an indicator of the quality of each treatment session. Such instruments give you more feedback on how well your clinical work is progressing.

We believe a very good observer of the client's problem and treatment goals is, of course, the client. In fact, as we mentioned before, some clinical problems can be measured only by the client. But clearly clients are not the only source of information. In deciding which source to use you should first consider which person will be the most reliable and valid observer. Then, if it is at all possible to use more than one source, do so. This will increase the amount and quality of information you receive and enable you to be more confident about what you are measuring.

Another factor in defining what is to be measured is your practice approach. While we argued earlier that one advantage of RAIs is the potential of being theoretically neutral, you may very well want a measure consistent with a particular theory, or you may want to avoid certain theoretically based instruments. For example, the clinician working with a borderline personality may want a theoretically based instrument like the Selfism Scale (Phares and Erskine, 1984) or the Ego Identity Scale (Tan et al., 1977). The cognitive-behaviorist, on the other hand, might prefer the Ellis Irrational Values Scale (McDonald and Games, 1972). In deciding what to measure, then, you should ask if the specific problem or treatment goal implies a certain theoretical perspective. Also, consider whether what you are measuring can be tapped by measurement tools from different theories. This may broaden not only your clinical orientation, but the range of possible instruments from which to select.

In deciding what to measure you should also consider where the measurement will occur. This is important because many client problems differ across various settings (Kazdin, 1979; Wicker, 1981). Similarly, observations in one environment may not generalize to other environments (Bellack and Hersen, 1977; Mischel, 1968). One guideline in deciding where to make the observations is whether the clinical problem is seen as a state or trait. As we mentioned in Chapter 3, state problems are considered more transitory and tend to be more apparent in specific settings. Trait behaviors, on the other hand, are believed to be more stable characteristics of an individual's general behavior (Levy, 1983), and therefore should be evident in a variety of settings.

If you consider your client's problem as a state, we suggest you use measurement tools that are completed in the appropriate environment, such as in a classroom or at the family dinner table if these are the specific places the problem occurs. If you believe the problem is more of a trait of your client, then you can be more flexible in where the measure is used. But you will need to be consistent, and make certain that the measurement is always recorded in the same setting, a topic we'll discuss more fully in the following chapter.

Whenever possible, the selection of instruments for monitoring practice should not be limited to one type of measurement tool, or even one source of observations. An optimal assessment package includes a self-report rapid assessment instrument, observations by significant others, a behavioral observation if possible, and perhaps a client log. Admittedly, it may be difficult to include all of these in daily practice with each and every client. You should, however, try to use as many as possible, provided they give you information you think relates to the client problem or treatment goals. This not only allows for more reliable and valid observations, but enables you to assess different aspects of the same problem.

How, though, do you decide on particular instruments for a particular client with a particular problem? The first step, of course, is to have a concrete and observable definition of the problem. Secondly, make sure the measures you are considering are relatively reliable and valid, and suitable to the respondent's reading level and ability to understand and complete the instruments. Next, familiarize yourself with the different self-reports and other types of measurement devices by completing them yourself. You should consider each item in terms of whether it is a sample of the client's problem. This will not only give you an understanding of the instruments, but will allow you to select the one that is most reflective of the subtleties of your client's problem. Once you have familiarized yourself with the different measurements, consider using as many as possible. However, the entire time for any individual respondent to complete the instruments should not exceed ten to fifteen minutes. Before asking a significant other (spouse, parent, roommate) to make some observations, make certain the person is invested in the client's progress and willing to comply with the task. Finally, consider if the measures are appropriate for your treatment approach; many are theoretically neutral, so this may not be much of a problem.

These considerations are illustrated by the following case example. Therapy was initiated for a family who sought treatment from one of the authors because of disciplinary problems with the teenage daughter who reportedly was "not herself." The child was "doing as she pleased," was truant from school for weeks at a time, and was arguing with her parents. At times she would lose control and hit or shove the mother. The assessment suggested that the mother, father, and daughter did not have age appropriate interpersonal boundaries (Minuchin, 1974), and that the child—not the parents—was in control of the family. Since most of the discord was between the mother and daughter, the former completed the Index of Parental Attitudes and the latter completed the Child's Attitude Toward Mother Scale (Hudson, 1982, 1992). To further evaluate the treatment the father was instructed to complete the Index of Family Relations (Hudson, 1982, 1992), and the school registrar reported the frequency of attendance. These theoretically neutral measures were assessed weekly over the course of treatment using structural family therapy techniques. This assessment package provided a sound picture of the family members' interpersonal relationships and one manifestation of the child's disciplinary problem.

LOCATING MEASUREMENT TOOLS

Once you have a good idea about what specifically you want to measure and with what type of tool, you have to find the measurement device. This book, of course, is designed to be one source of locating appropriate instruments. There may be occasions when you will need different types of measurement tools or additional instruments. Consequently, we offer some suggestions about where to start looking.

There are two general outlets for measurement tools: publishing houses and the professional literature. Publishing houses market measurement tools for profit. The cost may vary considerably, although most instruments are relatively inexpensive. In fact, an agency may be able to purchase a large number of instruments at a substantial savings. A list of some of the major publishers is presented in Table 5.1.

You can also find instruments in the journal literature, but this may require an expensive computer literature search. Consequently, you may decide to manually search reference indexes like *The Twelfth Mental Measurements Yearbook* (Conoley and Kramer, 1995), or review some of the seminal volumes on measurement. A list of works available since 1970 is presented in Table 5.2.

TABLE 5.1

List of Publishers Marketing Measurement Devices

Academic Therapy Publications, 20 Commercial Boulevard, Novato, California 94947; (415) 883-3314; (800) 422-7249

Thomas Achenbach, Department of Psychiatry, 1 S. Prospect Street, University of Vermont, Burlington, Vermont 05401

Associates for Research in Behavior, Inc. (ARBOR), The Science Center, 34th & Market Streets, Philadelphia, Pennsylvania 19104; (215) 387-5300

Behavior Science Press, 3710 Resource Drive, Tuscaloosa, Alabama 35401; (205) 759-2089

Biometrics Research, Research Assessment and Training Unit, New York State Psychiatric Institute, 722 West 168th Street, Room 341, New York, New York 10032; (212) 960-5534

Bureau of Educational Measurements, Emporia State University, Emporia, Kansas 66801; (316) 343-1200

Center for Epidemiologic Studies, Department of Health and Human Services, 5600 Fishers Lane, Rockville, Maryland 20857; (301) 443-4513

Clinical Psychometric Research, P.O. Box 619, Riderwood, Maryland 21139; (800) 245-0277

Consulting Psychologists Press, Inc., P.O. Box 10096, Palo Alto, California 94306; (415) 857-1444

CTB/McGraw-Hill, 20 Ryan Ranch Road, Monterey, California 93940; (408) 393-0700; (800) 538-9547, in California (800) 682-9222

Devereux Foundation, 19 South Waterloo Road, Devon, Pennsylvania 19333; (610) 964-3000

Educational and Industrial Testing Service (EDITS), P.O. Box 7234, San Diego, California 92107; (619) 222-1666

Family Life Publications, Inc., Box 427, Saluda, North Carolina 28773; (704) 749-4971

Hamanics Psychological Test Corporation, 1482 Mecaslin Street, NW, Atlanta, Georgia 30357-0400; (800) 874-8844

Institute for Personality and Ability Testing, Inc. (IPAT), P.O. Box 188, 1801 Woodfield Drive, Champaign, Illinois 61824; (217) 352-4739

Medical Outcomes Trust, 20 Park Plaza, Suite 1014, Boston, Massachusetts 02116; (617) 426-4046; www.outcomes-trust.org

Merrill (Charles E.) Publishing Company, 1300 Alum Creek Drive, Box 508, Columbus, Ohio 43216; (614) 258-8441

NCS Assessments, 5605 Green Circle Drive, P.O. Box 1416, Minnetonka, Minnesota 55440; (800) 348-4966

Nursing Research Associates, 3752 Cummings Street, Eau Claire, Wisconsin 54701; (715) 836-4731

TABLE 5.1 (cont.)

Personnel Research Institute (PRI), Psychological Research Services, Case Western Reserve University, 11220 Bellflower Road, Cleveland, Ohio 44106; (216) 368-3546

Person-O-Metrics, Inc., Evaluation and Development Services, 20504 Williamsburg Road, Dearborn Heights, Michigan 48127; no business phone

Preventive Measures, Inc., 1115 W. Campus Road, Lawrence, Kansas 66044; (913) 842-5078

PRO-ED, Inc., 8700 Shoal Creek Boulevard, Austin, Texas, 78757-6897; (512) 451-3246

PRO-Health Publications, P.O. Box 682, College Station, Texas 77841

Psychological Assessment and Services, Inc., P.O. Box 1031, Iowa City, Iowa 52240; no business phone

Psychological Assessment Resources, Inc., P.O. Box 998, Odessa, Florida 33556; (813) 920-6357

The Psychological Corporation, 555 Academic Court, San Antonio, Texas 78204; (800) 228-0752

Psychological Services, Inc., 100 W. Broadway, Suite 1100, Glendale, California 91210; (818) 244-0033

Psychological Test Specialists, P.O. Box 9229, Missoula, Montana 59807; (406) 728-1702

Research Concepts, A Division of Test Maker, Inc., 1368 East Airport Road, Muskegon, Michigan 49444; (616) 739-7401

Research Press, Box 317760, Champaign, Illinois 61820; (217) 352-3272

Research Psychologists Press, Inc., P.O. Box 984, Port Huron, Michigan 48060; (313) 982-4556

Science Research Associates, Inc. (SRA), 155 North Wacker Drive, Chicago, Illinois 60606; (800) 621-0664, in Illinois (312) 984-2000

Scott, Foresman and Company, Test Division, 1900 East Lake Avenue, Glenview, Illinois 60025; (312) 729-3000

United States Department of Defense, Testing Directorate, Headquarters, Military Enlistment Processing Command, Attn: MEPCT, Fort Sheridan, Illinois 60037; (312) 926-4111

United States Department of Labor, Division of Testing, Employment and Training Administration, Washington, D.C. 20213; (202) 376-6270

University Associates, Inc., Learning Resources Corporation, 8517 Production Avenue, P.O. Box 26240, San Diego, California 92126; (714) 578-5900

WALMYR Publishing Co., P.O. Box 12217, Tallahassee, Florida, 32317-2217; (850) 383-0045

Western Psychological Services, 12031 Wilshire Boulevard, Los Angeles, California 90025; (213) 478-2061

XICOM, Inc., RR#2, Woods Road, Tuxedo, New York 10987; (800) 759-4266

TABLE 5.2

Selected Volumes Since 1970 on Measurement Devices

Volumes Reprinting Measures
       Cautela (1977, 1981)
       Hudson (1982, 1992)
       McCubbin and Thompson (1991)
       McCubbin et al. (1996)
       McDowell and Newell (1996)
       Moos (1974, 1975, 1979)
       Robinson and Shaver (1973)
       Schutte and Malouff (1995)

Volumes Describing and Referencing Measures
       Anastasi (1988)
       Andrulis (1977)
       Beere (1979)
       Bellack and Hersen (1988)
       Brodsky and Smitherman (1983)
       Chun, Cobb, and French (1975)
       Ciarlo et al. (1986)
       Comrey, Barkey, and Galser (1975)
       Conoley and Kramer (1989, 1995)
       Dana (1993)
       Fredman and Sherman (1987)
       Goldman and Busch (1978, 1982)
       Goldman and Sanders (1974)
       Grotevant and Carlson (1989)
       Hammill et al. (1989)
       Hersen and Bellack (1988)
       Holman (1983)
       Johnson (1976)
       Johnson and Bommarito (1971)
       Kamphaus (1996)
       Kestenbaum and Williams (1988)
       Lake, Miles, and Earle (1973)
       McDowell and Newell (1987, 1996)
       McReynolds (1981)
       Miller (1977)
       Mitchell (1985)
       Olin and Keatinge (1998)
       Sawin and Harrigan (1994)
       Scholl and Schnur (1976)
       Southworth, Burr, and Cox (1981)

TABLE 5.2 (cont.)

Sweetland and Keyser (1991)
Thompson (1989)
Touliatos, Permutter, and Straus (1990)
van Riezen and Segal (1988)
Wetzler (1989)

Other Volumes Discussing Measurement Methods
Barlow (1981)
Ciminero, Calhoun, and Adams (1977)
Cone and Hawkins (1977)
Goldman, Stein, and Guerry (1983)
Goldstein and Hersen (1990)
Haynes (1978)
Haynes and Wilson (1979)
Hersen and Bellack (1988)
Jacob and Tennenbaum (1988)
Lambert, Christensen, and DeJulio (1983)
Lauffer (1982)
Mash and Terdal (1988)
Merluzzi, Glass, and Genest (1981)
Ogles and Masters (1996)
Olldenick and Hersen (1992)
Pecora et al. (1995)
Reynolds and Kamphaus (1990)
Rutter, Tuma, and Lann (1988)
Sederer and Dickey (1996)
Suzuki, Meller, and Ponterotto (1996)
Waskow and Parloff (1975)
Woody (1980)

All of these books either discuss different methods of measurement or present measurement devices, many of which are relevant to clinical practice. Another alternative is to examine the abstracts in certain journals that tend to emphasize measurement. Table 5.3 lists several journals that frequently publish instruments.

QUESTIONS TO ASK IN EVALUATING INSTRUMENTS

Between the publishing houses, books, and journals you will probably find at least one or two instruments for your measurement need. The question becomes, then, which measurement tool to use and how to select it. This issue actually addresses much of what we have considered throughout this book. On a general level, you will want to select the most reliable, valid, and practical instrument

TABLE 5.3

Journals Frequently Publishing New Measurement Tools

American Journal of Psychiatry
Applied Behavioral Measurement
Behavior Assessment
Behavior Therapy
Behaviour Research and Therapy
Educational and Psychological Measurement
Evaluation Family Practice
Family Process
Hispanic Journal of Behavioral Sciences
Journal of Behavioral Assessment and Psychopathology
Journal of Black Psychology
Journal of Clinical Psychology
Journal of Consulting and Clinical Psychology
Journal of Mental and Nervous Disease
Journal of Personality Assessment
Measurement and Evaluation in Counseling and Development
Psychological Assessment

---

for your purpose. If no instrument meets these criteria, remember you can always construct an individualized rating scale or use another type of measure.

While there are no definitive rules for evaluating measures, we suggest you consider instruments in the context of the research principles and practice principles we discussed in Chapter 2. To facilitate your evaluation of instruments from this perspective, we have categorized the research and practice criteria into 20 questions relating to the sample, reliability, validity, and practicality of an instrument. These questions are presented in Table 5.4, which can be used to facilitate your evaluation of measures.

Questions Regarding the Sample

When evaluating a measure consider the sample or samples from which the instrument was developed. If you intend to compare your client's scores with the normative data available, you should ask if the population is appropriate for your client. By appropriate we mean that your client could be considered a member of the population. It will be of little value for you to compare your

TABLE 5.4.

Questions to Consider in Evaluating Measurement Tools

Questioning the Sample

1. Are the samples sizes sufficiently large?
2. Are the samples representative of a relevant population?
3. Are the data from the samples current or up-to-date?

Questioning the Reliability

4. Is there sufficient evidence of internal consistency, say above .80?
5. Is there stability over a relevant period of time?
6. If more than one form is available, are they parallel?

Questioning the Validity

7. Do the items appear to have content validity?
8. Is there evidence of predictive or current validity?
9. Are the criterion variables themselves reliable and valid?
10. If there is known-groups validity, do the samples have different scores?
11. Are scores correlated with relevant variables and uncorrelated with irrelevant ones?
12. Are there cross-validation studies that also support the measure?

Questioning the Practicality

13. Is the instrument short enough for rapid completion?
14. Is the content socially acceptable to your client?
15. Is the instrument feasible for your client to complete?
16. Does the instrument seem to have utility?
17. Is the instrument sensitive to measuring change?
18. Does the instrument tap the problem in a relatively direct manner?
19. Is the instrument relatively nonreactive?
20. Is the instrument easy to score?

client to a norm from a dissimilar population or with old data. Many times instruments are developed on undergraduate students, a group that really may not be clinically relevant for your purposes. This does not mean you should necessarily reject the instrument. However, you can be more comfortable with the reliability and validity of an instrument if the sample is sufficiently large and representative of a pertinent population, and the data are fairly current.

Questions Regarding Reliability

In order for an instrument to be helpful to your practice, you must be convinced it is a fairly reliable measure of the problem. Of course there will be times when you do not have information on a measure's reliability and you will need to be more critical when interpreting the scores. When possible, though, we suggest you use an instrument that has internal consistency coefficients of at least .80.

Another reliability question is whether an instrument is appropriate for repeated measurement throughout the course of intervention. As we have discussed before, you will want to try to find instruments that are stable over time. Unstable measures introduce mistakes or error in the information you use to monitor your clients. It is not possible to evaluate practice if the information contains too much error. We suggest you look first for those instruments that have test-retest reliability correlations of around .80. This is high enough to suggest the instrument is sufficiently free of error and stable over time.

Infrequently, you may be fortunate enough to have two forms of the same instrument, enabling you to alternate the administration of the instruments as you monitor your client. By doing so you minimize error due to such factors as memory, practice, and instrument decay (Kazdin, 1980). You will remember from our previous discussion in Chapter 2 that the two instruments are called parallel forms or alternate forms. These two forms should correlate at a high magnitude, say above .80.

There will be times when no instrument tested for reliability is available and you will need to use an instrument that has no reliability data. In such cases you should be even more judicious in your reliance on the scores.

Questions Regarding Validity

Once you are satisfied with the instrument's reliability you should consider its validity. You will undoubtedly not find a measure that provides all the validity data you might desire, but at a minimal level the content of the instrument should have face validity. In other words, the instrument should appear to measure what it was designed to measure.

A more important validity consideration concerns criterion validity, either concurrent or predictive. When considering the criterion validity of an instrument we recommend that you also question whether the criterion itself is reliable and valid. Evidence of criterion validity is of little value if those variables are unreliable or invalid. In general, when predictive or concurrent validity data are available you would expect to find moderate to high correlations between the instrument and the criterion variable.

Alternatively, you might find instruments that are reported to have known-groups validity. Here you should consider if the subjects with the particular problem have scores that are different from a group of subjects without the problem. For example, scores on the Bulimia Test (Smith and Thelen, 1984) are different for people with an eating disorder compared to those without such a problem.

Finally, you might come across a measure that is reported to have construct validity. Often, this information is misleading because construct validity requires both convergent and discriminant estimates. When evaluating your instruments for construct validity, you will be looking for evidence that scores converge with theoretically relevant variables, such that statistically significant correlations are reported. Additionally, you may find evidence that the instrument is not associated with nonrelevant variables. Here you would hope to find instruments that are uncorrelated with the nonrelevant variables, that is, are not statistically significant.

Your review of an instrument's validity, whether one of the criterion validity procedures or construct validity, will probably be based on only one study. There is nothing wrong with selecting a measure based on just one study. However, some instruments have received a good deal of attention and may have cross-validation studies. If the findings from these studies attest to the instrument's validity, they enable you to select the instrument for your use with greater confidence.

Questions Regarding Practicality

Another set of questions to ask in evaluating instruments concerns practice principles. Here you will find it helpful to consider the practical advantages of using a particular measure with a particular client who has a particular problem.

The first three practicality questions will help you determine the likelihood that your client will complete the instruments you have selected to measure the problem. Even the most reliable and valid instrument is of no practical value if your client leaves it unanswered.

There are three major aspects of an instrument that can influence whether you should select it for measuring your practice: its length, the social acceptability of its content, and the ability of your client to complete it. Lengthy instruments that are not acceptable or comprehensible to your client might cause him or her to become frustrated, offended, and less committed to observing the problem with rapid assessment instruments. This complicates the treatment process instead of complementing it, preventing you from determining whether change is actually occurring. Consequently, we recommend you select instruments that are short, that ask questions your client will consider socially and culturally acceptable, and that your client can readily comprehend.

You will also want to consider the practical advantage of the information gained from using an instrument, and whether the information would be available otherwise. Here we are speaking of an instrument's utility, and the point of concern is that the measure provide you with information useful to monitoring practice. For example, in treating a client complaining of feeling depressed because of too few dates you might consider measuring his or her social isolation, feelings of loneliness, depression, or dating and assertion skills. Feelings of isolation, loneliness, and depression may very well be the consequence of too few dates, while the lack of dating and assertiveness may be the actual reason he or she is not getting dates. If this were the case, then you would want to select a measure of these social skills, such as the Dating and Assertion Questionnaire (Levenson and Gottman, 1978) which appears in this book. By using these instruments you will gain valuable information about how well you and your client are treating the actual problem.

Since the purpose of measuring your practice is to determine when change is occurring, you will need to ask if the instrument also is sensitive. When data on sensitivity are available, they are often in the form of change scores before and after a clinical intervention. This information is frequently not available on measurement tools; thus, you might have to use the instrument to see if it indeed registers change in your client's behavior.

When selecting a measure, we recommend you use those that seem relatively direct. Instruments differ in their degree of directness, and while you will rarely find an instrument that is as direct as you might like, we recommend that you try not to use measures that clearly consider the score to be a symbol of some problem as opposed to a sign of the problem. Most of the instruments in this volume are not totally direct, but only a few assume indirect dispositions of the problem. Measures that ask for responses about the frequency, intensity, or experience of a clinical problem are considered direct because the items are a sample of the problem. Instruments that assume some underlying cause or disposition to the problem, are indirect. The essential feature of our recommendation for using as direct a measure as possible is to select instruments which are not one step removed from what you are measuring. We recommend that you try to use instruments containing items that are considered examples or samples of the problem, and thus require less inference in interpreting the scores.

Additionally, in your evaluation of instruments, you should ask if a measure is nonreactive. Unfortunately, few measurement tools are totally nonreactive, so you will have to settle for the possibility of some change in your client due to the act of measurement. This is less of a problem with RAIs than with other tools, such as self-monitoring of specific behaviors like smoking. When selecting an instrument, consider whether it will appear to induce change in your client when none is occurring and use the tool that appears the most nonreactive. For example, does the client appear to be changing before the treatment has actually begun, such as during the baseline phase? If so, we would suggest you consider using another type of measurement tool or at least interpret the results with caution.

An additional practicality question to ask when deciding whether to use a measure is how easy it is to score. Those tools that are difficult and time consuming to score may be less feasible for your purpose of measuring practice. Consider for example, how frequently you would actually use an instrument that required anything more than ten or fifteen minutes to score. Thus, the size and structure of rapid assessment instruments, which make them fairly easy to score, are significant advantages.

6

ADMINISTERING
THE INSTRUMENTS

Selecting the right measure for your client is only a first step. Like everything else in practice, if the measure isn't *used*, whatever effort you've put in to this point will amount to nothing. Perhaps even more important than selecting the right instrument is gaining the client's cooperation in completing it. This chapter presents some guidelines for administering measures that we hope will help you utilize them in an optimum way. The chapter is divided into two sections—the mechanics of administration and the skills of administration.

MECHANICS OF ADMINISTRATION

Several aspects of administering measures involve such "mechanics" as when, where, and how often they should be used. While we consider these to be the mechanics of administration, it is especially important to note here, as we will later in the chapter, the way you *present* the mechanics may be more important than the mechanics themselves.

Knowledge of Your Measure

There can be no substitute for the practitioner being well informed about the instrument. One suggestion we have is for you to administer to yourself any instrument you plan to use with clients. Get a feel for what it is like. In addition, you want to be knowledgeable about the meaning and interpretation of the instrument, its scoring, and its varied uses. Try to be prepared for any question the client could ask you about the measure. The best way to do this is to try to locate the original reference sources on the instrument so that you can be familiar with its functions. Once you read this material, take the instrument yourself, and interpret your own score, you will be better prepared to deal with the client's questions.

Where to Administer Your Measure

The instrument can be completed by the client in your office (or wherever your interview is conducted) or elsewhere. If you administer the instrument in your office, you again have two choices: it can be administered prior to your interview, say by a receptionist or intake worker, or by you during the interview. Part of the consideration here is time and the availability of other personnel. If someone else presents the instrument to the client, he or she should be able to answer questions about it. If you do the administering of the instrument, you should be sure you have the time available during the interview so that you and the client won't feel rushed. In both circumstances, you should attempt to provide the client with a quiet place to fill out the instrument so the client won't feel that others are observing his or her completion of the instrument. This can be embarrassing and may lead to distorted results.

On the other hand, having the client fill out the instrument at home can serve as a successful "homework" assignment, a task the client takes responsibility for completing on a regular basis. This can provide structure for your intervention program. Also, the client will be able to complete the instrument without the feeling of being watched. Filling out the instrument at home also may give the client more time to think about his or her responses, providing more thoughtful answers and possibly even additional material for your interview session.

Time of Administration

It should be clear to both you and the client that the instrument should be filled out at roughly the same time and place each time it is completed. If the client is to complete the instrument at home, and you have seen a pattern in the most likely times for the client to experience the problem, you might instruct the client to fill out the instrument in those circumstances at that time each week. This should minimize the possibility that the client's responses will change only because the conditions in which he or she completes the instrument change.

Number of Administrations

You, of course, have to decide how often the instrument should be administered, although some instruments come with instructions on this point. In general, the longer or more difficult the instrument is, the less frequently you would ask the client to complete it. An obvious consideration is how willing the client is to complete it. If he or she appears bored, annoyed, or reluctant to complete the instrument, or appears to be answering in patterned or repetitious ways, this is pretty clear feedback that you might be asking the client to fill it out too many times. It is important to get feedback on this each time the client turns in the questionnaire. You simply might ask, "How's the questionnaire going? Are you having a hard time filling it out?"

Another consideration is the extent to which you rely on the instrument as your sole source of feedback on the client. The more you rely on it as a major source of information, the more often you would want to administer the instrument. As we mentioned earlier, whenever possible multiple measures should be the rule rather than the exception.

A general guideline for most of the instruments included in this book is that they be used no more than twice per week, with once a week being the most typically recommended frequency of administration. In any case, the goal is to make completion of the measure as nonaversive as possible.

Scoring

Unfortunately, though there are some similarities among many of the instruments included in this book as to how they are scored (just about all of them total the individual items to come up with an overall score), there also are many differences among them. Thus, we cannot provide you with one or two clear guidelines on how these instruments are scored except to say most can be done in just a few minutes with little or no training and no need for specialized mathematical skills. However, specific instructions for scoring the instruments in this book are provided in the comments accompanying each instrument.

On the other hand, you do have some options regarding when and where you score an instrument. The first option is to score the instrument when the client is not there. This is most obvious when the client mails the instrument in to you or the instrument cannot be readily scored in just a few minutes.

The second option is to score the instrument while the client is watching. This, of course, provides the most rapid feedback to the client. (We suggest providing feedback on the score and the meaning of the score as soon as possible no matter when the scoring is done.) But scoring while the client is watching does have its drawbacks. You might become flustered and make an error in your scoring, or the silence while you are scoring or the experience of watching you score could make the client uncomfortable and anxious. In these circumstances, you might make a few remarks to the client while you are scoring, suggest that he or she does not have to remain seated, or provide some reading material (a good time for bibliotherapy) for the client.

Once you have scored the instrument, we suggest plotting the scores on a chart such as those illustrated in Chapter 1. Not only does this allow easy visual analysis of changes, but if the client is comfortable posting it in a conspicuous place in his or her residence, it can serve as a motivating factor as well.

USE OF COMPUTERS IN ADMINISTERING MEASURES

All of the measures described in this book are paper-and-pencil instruments that are filled out by the client, and in a few instances, by the practitioner. However, there are an increasing number of opportunities to administer questionnaires with microcomputers. Given the general availability of computers in just about all agencies and practice contexts, this possibility should not be overlooked.

Of course, computers have a wide variety of potential uses in clinical practice. These range from the obvious—as a way of managing data and word processing—to the less obvious and more innovative—as a method for providing ongoing support in practice, to aid in various activities of the practice process such as assessment, record keeping, monitoring of treatment, evaluation, or even in providing advice as expert systems (see Videka-Sherman and Reid, 1990, for several examples of computer-assisted practice, and Bloom, Fischer, and Orme, 1999, for an overview of the use of computers in measurement along with references to the most recent literature on the topic such as Karger and Levine, 1999).

But computers can also be used to administer, score, chart, and even interpret the types of measures described in this book. There are several advantages to use of computers in this way. Computers are fast, of course, and also extremely efficient. Their very speed and efficiency can provide the client and practitioner with more time to work on other areas. Computers also don't make mistakes; they are completely reliable. Computers can be easier for clients to respond to than live interviews, perhaps relieving some of the discomfort or embarrassment of providing deeply personal responses to humans when greater privacy may be more desired. And computers are increasingly flexible, able to deal with a growing number of vagaries and issues of the clinical situation.

Of course, computers have their drawbacks. Practitioners must be able and willing to use them. This means they need an even broader knowledge base than was required in the past. For clients, computer programs must be easy to use and nonthreatening. Computers may be perceived not as objective but as impersonal and even dehumanizing, so that both practitioners and clients may be unwilling to use them.

One computer program that seems to feature the advantages described above and to overcome most of the drawbacks is the Computer-Assisted Social Services (CASS) system, developed by Walter Hudson and available through WALMYR Publishing, P.O. Box 12217, Tallahassee, FL, 32317-2217 (see also Nurius and Hudson, 1993). This innovative program stores and produces instruments such as those described in this book, administers these instruments directly to clients, scores the measures, interprets them, prepares graphs, develops single-system designs, and conducts a variety of other procedures including development of agency forms, social histories, and so on. It allows for the inclusion of any number of tests and examinations of any length and even has a student version for teaching practitioners how to use microcomputers and the CASS system. In essence, CASS provides a huge part of the basis for conducting a computer-based practice. In fact, the CASS system includes some 20 of the measures included in this book, the WALMYR Assessment Scales (Hudson, 1992).

Overall, computer-assisted practice in general, or even in its specific applications to the use of the types of measures included in this book, is a growing and increasingly important component of clinical practice, one that may be one of the hallmarks of practice in the twenty-first century.

THE SKILLS OF ADMINISTERING MEASURES

A number of key principles underlie the smooth and effective administration of instruments. Essentially, these are all interpersonal skills; good rapport and a good relationship with the client will provide tremendous advantages for your work by facilitating cooperative give-and-take between you and the client.

Be Confident

We can't think of a more important piece of advice. Few, if any, clients will be willing to participate in any program (let alone fill out some strange question-naire) with a practitioner who stumbles or makes apologies to the client for administering one of these measures. It is essential to appear confident to a client who may be very unsure of himself or herself or anxious and insecure in a new situation. Part of your confidence will come from familiarity with the instrument and experience in administering it. But we also urge you to engage in some structured role playing with colleagues prior to your first administration of one of these instruments; this practice experience may be just what it takes to provide you with the confidence to inspire the client to really want to cooperate with you.

Structure the Situation

In all therapeutic endeavors, it is very important that you explain to the client what you are doing, why you are doing it, how important it is, and, in the case of one of these instruments, how the scores will be used. Many people have built-in mistrust of questionnaires (they see them as "tests"), and it is important for you to overcome that lack of trust. A good way of doing it is to provide the client with a clear rationale for the use of the measure. Assure the client of confidentiality of his or her scores (within organizational constraints). Perhaps use a medical analogy: "Just as your physician has to take your blood pressure to monitor how well you are doing, we have to have this information to ensure we are on the right track." This kind of structure has been shown to be very effective in a whole range of situations when introducing new material to the client. Further, it is very important to explain to the client that this is not a "test" and that there are no right or wrong answers.

Sensitivity

Just as with any interview situation, you have to be very sensitive to the nuances in the client's response to your request to fill out the questionnaire. Perhaps this is just part of good interviewing behavior—the interpersonal skills that form the heart of therapeutic work anyway. This includes being sensitive to your client's reaction to determine whether he or she finds the content socially acceptable. But you have to be aware that some people may be concerned about what the questionnaire means, but will not voice their questions or objections uninvited. Therefore, unless you give them an opportunity to express themselves, your entire effort may be undermined. The guideline here: encourage the client to express doubts, fears, and concerns about use of the measure.

Ethnic and Cultural Differences

Most of the measures in this book have been used largely with a white, middle-class American population. Thus, we urge that you use extreme care in utilization and interpretation of these instruments with clients from other ethnic or socioeconomic groups. This does not mean that these measures are inappropriate for people of color or extremely poor clients; only that data are not always available to attest to the utility of the measure for those groups.

If you do decide to use one of these instruments with a minority or poor client, we urge again that you be especially sensitive. First of all, the whole context of use of questionnaires may have a different meaning to someone from a minority ethnic group. It is crucial to explore this with the client. Second, it is important to ascertain with each client whether he or she understands how to use the questionnaire and the meaning of every item. You would be shocked to find how many presumably "simple" words are not understood even by middle-class, white Americans. Imagine then the complications of using these measures with someone whose English vocabulary may be even more limited.

In some cases, RAIs have been translated into other languages. To ensure a good translation, a different person should translate the foreign language version of the instrument back into English. If the two English language versions coincide, you have a good translation. Then, all you have to be concerned about is the cultural appropriateness of the translated measure, taking special care to use caution and sensitivity in the cross-cultural application and interpretation of the measure.

You might go over some or all of the items orally with your client to make sure he or she understands it. In fact, some practitioners, with some of the briefer instruments, routinely read each item aloud to the client, after which the client provides the responses orally. This can also be done in work with children. The problem with this method is that it may have a serious effect on the reliability and validity of the questionnaire because the practitioner could subtly influence responses by the way he or she presents the items.

Response Problems

All questionnaires are subject to certain types of bias. The first is called *response bias* in which the client responds to each item in a questionnaire in the same or patterned way (for example, all fours on a six-point scale). Another problem is called *social desirability response set* in which the client responds on the basis of what he or she thinks the response *should* be rather than on what he or she actually thinks or feels.

Some questionnaires are structured with an eye toward addressing these problems. For example, response bias can be handled by varying the directionality of items so that a four on one item might mean something negative and a four on another item might mean something positive. Some questionnaires attempt to control for social desirability response set by wording items in such a way that they do not obviously reflect social values.

But let's face it. Our clients are only human. There are many characteristics of a therapeutic setting that could encourage them to provide distorted answers on their questionnaires. These so-called demand characteristics include subtle cues from the practitioner which lead the client to think he or she "has" to improve. Or the client's payment of fees may lead him or her to focus on what he or she is getting for the money. Another related bias is the client's deliberate falsification of information on the questionnaire in order to achieve some goal—such as release from a court order or from prison, change in job or school status, or even a child or spouse falsifying information for fear that a parent or spouse might be hurt.

Unfortunately, there are no easy solutions to these problems. Perhaps the most important way to deal with them is for the practitioner to be "up front" about them. All of these questionnaires are indeed easy to falsify. It is very important for the practitioner to let the client know that he or she is well aware of how the measure can be distorted. In the context of a sensitive and trusting relationship and confidentiality regarding the client's responses, the practitioner might say:

> Look, I realize just how easy it is to put just about anything you want on these questionnaires to make yourself look better (or worse as the case might be). But it is very important that you and I have as honest and accurate answers as possible in this questionnaire. Otherwise, I just won't be able to know how well we're doing, and this means I won't be able to develop the best possible program to help you with your problems.

Clinical Uses

One advantage of these instruments is that they can provide "grist for the therapeutic mill"—more information for you and the client to discuss. There are numerous examples of interactions that can be centered on the instruments your client may be filling out.

Inconsistent responses.   Inconsistencies in the client's responses may appear in the form of differences between a client's verbal responses and scores on the instrument or differences between scores on similar items on the instrument. In both instances, it is the practitioner's responsibility to inquire about and discuss those inconsistencies with the client. A good deal of clinical skill is called for here, because the purpose is not to "catch" the client in an error or lie. The purpose is to help the client clarify which response is most accurate and perhaps to review items on the instruments that may not be clear.

Careful, sensitive exploration with the client of these inconsistencies could enhance both the relationship and use of the instrument.

Changes in scores. It is important for the practitioner to be alert to any changes—positive or negative—in the client's scores on the instrument and to discuss these with the client. This is, in essence, the monitoring function of these measures: keeping track of changes as the relationship progresses. It is important that the practitioner not be too overenthusiastic about positive changes or too disturbed about negative changes. First, one must be alert to the fact that the changes may not be due to the practitioner's interventions, but may be due to other events, client distortion, or the client's desire to please the practitioner. Second, the practitioner by his or her response could subtly encourage the client to keep reporting progress when no progress is being made, or conversely, discourage honesty if the client is doing poorly.

On the other hand, it is crucial for the practitioner to be able to encourage the client to report changes as honestly as the client can—whether they are negative or positive changes. This can be done by being straightforward about the importance of honest recording as an aid to treatment planning. Further, when the practitioner is relatively certain that positive changes are accurate, those changes can be used to support the intervention program and motivate the client to continue participating.

Individual items. Most RAIs included in this book have fairly good reliability as a complete instrument. Often, individual items have much lower reliability. Thus, discussion of individual items with clients is somewhat risky and one should not depend heavily on their interpretation. On the other hand, examining individual items—especially if the client initiates such examination—can prove useful. It can serve as a communication tool as you and the client open up discussion about a particular topic based on scores on that item. Individual items can provide clues to problems that need further exploration; for example, when one item changes very rapidly or doesn't change at all. Looking at individual items can clarify for the client how the instrument as a whole can be used to monitor progress. And a review of individual items can also enhance the relationship between the practitioner and client because it will highlight the practitioner's sensitivity to specific components of the client's problem.

In general, when using RAIs for clinical purposes, one must be prepared for a variety of reactions from the client, including anger, defensiveness, enthusiasm, happiness over changes, reluctance to speak about the scores, and so on. Each reaction, of course, must be dealt with not only as it affects the measurement procedure, but as it affects the overall treatment process. Sensitivity and empathy about presumably small issues such as those discussed above can pay large dividends in enhancing the clinical process.

Further, it is important to remember that use of RAIs constitutes only one part of the intervention process. Many conditions can affect changes in scores on a given measure, and, therefore, one must avoid overreliance on one score on one measure as the only indicator of change. In addition to sensitive clinical observation of changes in the client, this is one of the reasons we have encouraged use of more than one measure to monitor and evaluate changes.

A Program for Cooperation

The success or failure of any measurement program—indeed any activities requiring some outside effort on the part of the client—depends on how well the practitioner is able to elicit the client's cooperation. The suggestions in this chapter are an attempt to provide some ideas specific to the administration of standardized measures that we hope will enhance that cooperation.

But there is another way to approach the problem. The clinical literature increasingly is concerned with enhancing the client's cooperation in a whole range of other tasks and activities such as homework and task assignments. This literature typically uses the term "compliance"—a term borrowed from the medical literature essentially referring to the carrying out of an assignment in the manner described by the person who assigned the task. There is increasing empirical evidence about a number of effective ways to gain such compliance or cooperation from the client. Following the work of Shelton and Levy (1981), these procedures will be briefly described here.

1. Assignments should be clear. Give specific details regarding when, where, how long, and under what circumstances the questionnaire should be completed. Provide written instructions when possible.
2. Give direct skill training and practice when needed. If the client has trouble filling out a questionnaire, practice filling it out in the office.
3. Reinforce cooperation. Provide praise and support for efforts at completing the instrument. Encourage others in the client's environment to do so too.
4. Begin small. Do not ask the client to do too much too often. You can gradually increase what you do both quantitatively and in complexity as the client masters the earlier tasks.
5. Use prompts, cues, or reminders. You might have a copy of the instrument assignment posted where the client is likely to see it. You might even give the client a call once in a while in between

contacts just to keep in touch and to indicate your support, inquiring at the same time how he or she is doing in filling out the questionnaire.

6. Have the client make a commitment to cooperate. This might be done in a form of an oral commitment, or better yet, a written contract.

7. Help the client make a private commitment to cooperate. Elicit the client's thoughts and feelings about filling out the questionnaire. Find out if he or she has had experience with that type of assignment before. Give a clear rationale to the client so he or she will accept the importance of the measure. Prepare the client for potential problems. If it is possible, have the client help select which instrument he or she will use.

8. Use a cognitive rehearsal strategy. Have the client relax, visualize the task, visualize successful completion, and engage in self-reinforcing statements or images.

9. Try to anticipate any negative effects of cooperation and prepare the client to deal with them.

10. The more sources that keep track of how well the client is doing, the more likely it is that the client will cooperate. This is another reason why it might be useful to post the client's chart in a conspicuous place.

11. Make sure you have a good relationship with the client and that he or she trusts you before you assign a task. Show empathy, caring, and warmth. Present the assignment with confidence and sincerity.

PART II

Instruments for Practice

INTRODUCTION

So far in this book we have reviewed the role of measurement to help in monitoring your client's progress and in evaluating your effectiveness using single-system research designs. Our discussion included an overview of the basic principles of reliable and valid measures, the principles related to using measures in practice, and issues regarding interpreting scores. We also discussed some of the different types of measures, including the advantages and disadvantages of rapid assessment instruments. While we clearly believe this type of measure is particularly valuable, we know that there may be times when you will want other measurement tools as well as additional rapid assessment instruments. To this end we presented information on determining what to measure within the context of practice, how to locate measures, and pertinent questions you might ask when evaluating which measure to use. Finally, we presented some guidelines for you to consider when administering instruments.

We now turn to the rationale and procedures we used to locate and select the instruments presented in both volumes. We have not included all rapid assess- ment instruments in existence, but we believe that the measures that are includ- ed cover most of the client problem areas commonly encountered in practice.

The primary rationale for including an instrument in these volumes was that it measures some specific client problem or treatment goal relevant to clinical practice. Thus, we excluded certain instruments that we believed just were not relevant to treatment. For example, a measure of one's personal epistemology was not included because this is not a frequently seen clinical problem.

We also excluded instruments that measure *practitioner* behaviors that might occur during your interventions. While there is indeed a growing concern for measuring what you do as a clinician, we believe you would more likely want to measure particular *client* problems or treatment goals. This, after all, is one of the best ways to monitor practice.

We also decided to include mainly self-report instruments that could be used for rapid assessment. While numerous other types of measurement tools are available, as we discussed in Chapter 3, we believe you are more likely to monitor your practice with those on which your client directly reports his or her perceptions, feelings, or experiences. Not only are clients often the best source of this information, but RAIs can be used in conjunction with your own clinical assessment.

In the same vein, we included only those instruments that are relatively short. While there is no concrete agreement on how short an instrument should be in order to be used for rapid completion and scoring, we have included mainly those that are 50 items or less. There are a few, however, that are somewhat longer; we included these because shorter measures were not available for a particular problem, because the instrument has subscales that can be used for rapid assessment, or because the instrument can be completed quickly despite its length.

Finally, just about all of the instruments we include have demonstrated some evidence of reliability and/or validity. All have some practice utility, providing information that will help you monitor your client's progress and evaluate your effectiveness. In order to facilitate your use of these instruments, we have used a standardized format to critique each one, to help you make judgments about which instruments would be best for your particular purposes. Like many measures in the behavioral and social sciences, some of those included here lack convincing reliability, validity, or other important data. This is not to imply that no data were available, just that more is needed to be thoroughly convincing. When you use one of these instruments, even those with sufficient reliability and validity data for that matter, we hope you will approach it with a judicious degree of caution and your own critique.

LOCATING THE INSTRUMENTS

In order to locate measurement tools, we began with a computer literature search. Additionally, we identified key volumes and journals that pertained to measurement in practice and reviewed them for appropriate instruments. (See Chapter 5, Tables 5.2 and 5.3.) For the journals we identified, all volumes were reviewed from 1974, except the *Journal of Clinical Psychology* and the *Journal of Personality Assessment*, which were reviewed from 1964 through 1998. For journals that first appeared later than 1974, all volumes were reviewed.

THE FINAL SELECTION

Whenever possible, we have tried to include more than one instrument to measure a problem, not only to provide a choice, but because different instruments tap different aspects of a problem. For example, you will notice there are several measures of anxiety. One of these may be more appropriate for your measurement need with a given client than others. Finally, there are obviously more instruments available to measure certain types of problems than other types. For example, relatively few measures are available to assess children because children tend to have more difficulty in filling out self-report instruments than adults. Thus, while we included as many self-report RAIs for children as we could, we also included some observer rating scales for children. In this and a few other areas as well, where the nature of the people or problem suggests that self-report measures may be difficult to administer, observer rating scales would be an appropriate substitute.

In this volume, we have focused solely on measures for couples, families, and children. We recognize that categorizing measures in this way—with measures for adults where the problem does not seem primarily concerned with other family members being included in Volume 2—leaves something to be desired. There is obvious overlap among many of the categories for several problems. Nevertheless, we hope this organization of the two volumes will make selection of measures for your practice as smooth as possible.

In sum, we have not included all available self-report rapid assessment instruments. For example, a few that we would have chosen to include, such as the Beck Depression Inventory (Beck et al., 1961), were not available for reproduction. Some we have included are sold commercially, such as the WALMYR Assessment Scales (Hudson, 1992). However, we believe the instruments we have chosen cover most of the client problem areas commonly encountered in practice. Nevertheless, we must stress that other measures are available, and you should consider using them in conjunction with the RAIs included here. We have been fortunate to be permitted to reprint the instruments in this volume and Volume II. We are able to do so with the kind permission of the authors and—when the author did not retain the copyright—the publishers of the instruments. We need to point out that while the measures are reprinted here, the authors and/or publishers retain ownership. Reproduction in any form, electronic or even simply turning this book over on the photocopy machine and punching the "copy" button, is restricted by law. We reproduce the measures in these works so you can examine them to determine which are useful for you. It is important for you to get permission before you actually use them. We hope the instruments presented in these two volumes will get you started and help you develop an increasing number of measurement tools for use in monitoring clients and evaluating your practice effectiveness.

INSTRUMENTS FOR
COUPLES

BEIER-STERNBERG DISCORD QUESTIONNAIRE (DQ)

AUTHORS: Ernest G. Beier and Daniel P. Sternberg
PURPOSE: To measure marital conflict and unhappiness.
DESCRIPTION: The DQ is a 10-item instrument designed to measure two dimensions of a marital relationship: discord or conflict and the degree of unhappiness attached to such discord. The items on the DQ were selected based on a review of literature that revealed these topics to be major sources of marital disagreement. Each respondent first scores each topic with regard to the amount of conflict it generates in the marriage and then evaluates the extent to which such discord produces unhappiness. The items are scored individually. Although there is not a great deal of psychometric information available about the DQ, its utility stems from the ability to analyze separately each relevant dimension of a couple's relationship.
NORMS: The data for the DQ were generated from a series of studies involving newly married couples who responded to letters soliciting their cooperation. The couples were heterogenous in background, and were contacted shortly after marriage and one year later. Means are available for each item in the DQ for these couples at both time periods. There was a slight increase in conflict for the couples over the period of a year with an overall conflict mean of 33.92 shortly after marriage and 36.55 a year later.
SCORING: Each item is scored separately on a 7-point scale with higher scores indicating more conflict and more unhappiness. The individual items can be summed for a total score, but the meaning of that score is not clear.

81

RELIABILITY: No information is available.

VALIDITY: The DQ has some degree of concurrent validity in that conflict ratings are significantly correlated with unhappiness ratings, and there is some correlation between scores on the DQ and a range of intimate behavior ratings. Also, there is a significant change over the first year of marriage for wives (total mean moved from 19 to 25.33), suggesting some degree of predictive validity for the DQ.

PRIMARY REFERENCE: Beier, E. G. and Sternberg, D. P. (1977). Marital communication, *Journal of Communication*, 27, 92–100. Instrument reproduced with permission of Ernest G. Beier and Daniel P. Sternberg.

AVAILABILITY: Dr. Daniel P. Sternberg, Psychiatric Associates, 3540 South 4000 West, Suite 310, West Valley City, UT 84120.

DQ

With these scales, we want to find out what you believe are the areas of agreement or disagreement in your marriage. We also want to find out if these areas of agreement and disagreement make you feel happy, sad, or indifferent. For example, if money is a topic of much disagreement in your marriage, you could make a mark in *Scale 1: Degree of Agreement* under the numbers 5, 6, or 7 depending on the extent of your disagreement. If you were to make a mark under the number 7, this would mean that you feel there is much disagreement about money in your marriage. If you were to mark under the number 5, this means you feel there is some disagreement about money.

With *Scale 1* we want to find out how you differ from your spouse in looking at things. In *Scale 2* we want to find out how you feel about these differences. If, for example a disagreement were to make you very unhappy, as in the "Money" example given above, you would mark 6 or 7 on *Scale 2: Results of Agreement or Disagreement*. Please check each item in both scales. Remember, the *higher* the number the *more* disagreement or conflict over a partlcular topic, the *lower* the number, the *more* agreement.

		Scale 1: Degree of Agreement							Scale 2: Results of Agreement or Disagreement						
		Agree					Disagree		Happy					Unhappy	
		1	2	3	4	5	6	7	1	2	3	4	5	6	7
1.	Money														
2.	Children														
3.	Sex														
4.	Concern and love														
5.	Doing things together (in spare time)														
6.	Friends and social life														
7.	Getting ahead, ambition														
8.	Politics														
9.	Children's education														
10.	Religion														
	Other(s): please specify														

COMPETITIVENESS SCALE (CS)

AUTHOR: Mary R. Laner

PURPOSE: To measure a partner's competitiveness in a relationship.

DESCRIPTION: The CS is a 50-item instrument designed to measure a partner's competitiveness in relationships. The CS is divided into three subscales, as indicated on the measure itself, based on whether the behaviors were likely to be experienced as pleasant (P), unpleasant (U) or aggressive/abusive (A). These subscales were developed by independent raters with an agreement rate of 88%. The CS can be very useful in identifying and exploring issues of competitiveness with couples experiencing problems in their relationships.

NORMS: The CS was studied initially with 99 male and 81 female, mainly white, students in a large southwestern university. The large majority were never married and middle class; 80% of the women were aged 20 or younger and 74% of the men were 21 or older. Actual norms are not available, though men and women score the same on all but 8 of the pleasant items, all but 2 of the unpleasant items, and on all of the aggressive/abusive items.

SCORING.   The CS is easily scored by giving each "typical" and "occasional" response one point, then summing these for each subscale. Pleasant has a maximum of 20 points, unpleasant a maximum of 22 points, and aggressive/ abusive has a maximum of 8 points.

RELIABILITY: Data are not available.

VALIDITY: Although data are limited, the unpleasant subscale is associated with combativeness scores as measured by the Index of Spouse Abuse.

PRIMARY REFERENCE: Laner, M. R. (1986). Competition in courtship, *Family Relations*, 35, 275–279.

AVAILABILITY: Dr. Mary Laner, Professor, Department of Sociology, Arizona State University, Tempe, AZ 85287.

CS

Please think carefully about the behaviors, traits, or qualities that your partner displays in your relationship to get his or her own way. For each of the items shown below, place an X in the column that comes closest to describing your partner's traits, qualities, or behaviors toward you.

		To get his/her own way, my partner:	*This trait/quality/behavior is*		
			Quite typical	Used only occasionally	Never used
U	1.	Displays brute strength	( )	( )	( )
U	2.	Cheats	( )	( )	( )
P	3.	Shows flexibility	( )	( )	( )
P	4.	Shows tenacity (sticks to things)	( )	( )	( )
U	5.	Uses silence (is uncommunicative)	( )	( )	( )
A	6.	Uses physical violence	( )	( )	( )
U	7.	Lies	( )	( )	( )
P	8.	Perseveres (is persistent)	( )	( )	( )
P	9.	Is industrious (works hard)	( )	( )	( )
P	10.	Behaves stoically (is uncomplaining)	( )	( )	( )
A	11.	Is ruthless	( )	( )	( )
U	12.	Is cunning, shrewd	( )	( )	( )
P	13.	Displays intelligence, wit, knowledgeability	( )	( )	( )
A	14.	Bullies, threatens, intimidates	( )	( )	( )
P	15.	Displays courage	( )	( )	( )
P	16.	Uses charm	( )	( )	( )
U	17.	Behaves recklessly	( )	( )	( )
U	18.	Uses "smooth talk"	( )	( )	( )
P	19.	Displays endurance (tolerance)	( )	( )	( )
U	20.	Uses cajolery (flattery, coaxing)	( )	( )	( )
A	21.	Inspires fear and/or anxiety	( )	( )	( )
U	22.	Acts flamboyantly ("flashy")	( )	( )	( )
U	23.	Stresses past achievements	( )	( )	( )
P	24.	Uses humor, irony	( )	( )	( )
P	25.	Displays expertise, competence	( )	( )	( )
A	26.	Is insulting, abusive, rude	( )	( )	( )
U	27.	Acts snobbishly	( )	( )	( )
P	28.	Displays stamina, energy	( )	( )	( )
P	29.	Acts like a "good sport"	( )	( )	( )
P	30.	Displays patience	( )	( )	( )
U	31.	Acts haughty, superior	( )	( )	( )
U	32.	Uses satire, ridicule	( )	( )	( )
P	33.	Acts exuberant, enthusiastic	( )	( )	( )
U	34.	Displays power, authority, influence, string-pulling	( )	( )	( )
U	35.	Acts sophisticated, "worldly wise"	( )	( )	( )
A	36.	Displays anger	( )	( )	( )

		To get his/her own way, my partner:	*This trait/quality/behavior is*		
			Quite typical	Used only occasionally	Never used
U	37.	Is sarcastic	( )	( )	( )
P	38.	Is careful, a planner	( )	( )	( )
U	39.	Inspires guilt	( )	( )	( )
U	40.	Is boastful	( )	( )	( )
U	41.	Uses guile (subterfuge)	( )	( )	( )
P	42.	Shows self-awareness	( )	( )	( )
A	43.	Challenges, confronts	( )	( )	( )
U	44.	Is deceitful	( )	( )	( )
P	45.	Is self-reliant	( )	( )	( )
U	46.	Pretends weakness (acts like a martyr)	( )	( )	( )
P	47.	Acts calmly (shows equanimity)	( )	( )	( )
U	48.	Pretends love	( )	( )	( )
U	49.	Pretends stupidity	( )	( )	( )
P	50.	Is diplomatic, tactful	( )	( )	( )

CONSTRUCTION OF PROBLEMS SCALE (CPS)

AUTHOR: Laurie Heatherington

PURPOSE: To assess the private cognitive construction of problems.

DESCRIPTION: This 27-item instrument is designed to assess an individual's private cognitive construction of a presenting problem. The CPS was developed for use in families, but is also useful for couples in conflicts. The premise of the CPS is to ascertain how different family members construe problems such that the beliefs restrict one's identity and bind one to distressful emotions and dysfunctional relationships. This premise is found in a number of contemporary therapeutic interventions, including narrative therapy, solution-focused treatment and some systemic approaches such as structural family therapy. The CPS includes an open-ended question where the respondent describes the problem and then assesses the causal attributions of the problem. It takes about 15 minutes to complete the CPS, and it is appropriate for adults and adolescents. The CPS has two subscales, problems which are other or interpersonal focus (OIF items, 3, 5, 9, 11, 12, 16, 17, 24, and 27), and problems which are self-focused (SF items 4, 20, 21, 23, 25, and 26). Subscale scores may be used, but the CPS was designed to compare each item response of one person in a family or couple dyad with the item scores of another member of the unit.

NORMS: Each item on the CPS is scored separately. Using a combined sample of 221 adults and adolescents, item means (standard deviations) were:

1.	3.16	(.94)	15.	1.6	(1.11)
2.	2.48	(1.38)	16.	3.05	(1.34)
3.	3.38	(1.5)	17.	3.54	(1.33)
4.	1.82	(1.1)	18.	1.24	(.75)
5.	2.67	(1.21)	19.	2.24	(1.33)
6.	2.71	(1.48)	20.	2.01	(1.23)
7.	1.16	(.6)	21.	2.25	(1.16)
8.	1.86	(1.47)	22.	1.31	(.75)
9.	2.74	(1.35)	23.	2.01	(1.21)
10.	2.02	(1.32)	24.	3.18	(1.23)
11.	2.7	(1.34)	25.	1.74	(1.09)
12.	3.07	(1.41)	26.	1.87	(1.15)
13.	2.03	(1.29)	27.	3.11	(1.28)
14.	3.36	(1.14)			

Normative data are not reported on the subscales.

SCORING: The subscale scores are the sum of the item scores. The CPS is designed to use each item separately and to compare members on each item.

The scoring, then, is simply the individual item scores. In order to compare all the item scores, it is best to construct a profile of all item scores. A summary profile form is reprinted here as part of the CPS to facilitate this type of scoring.

RELIABILITY: The items of the CPS were assessed for test-retest reliability over a 3 to 4 week period. The average item correlation between the two testing periods was .72. Correlations ranged from .44 for item 6 to .87 for item 20.

VALIDITY: The CPS has good evidence of criterion related validity. In a sample of 39 volunteers with marital conflicts, particular items on the CPS correlated with scores on the Locke-Wallace Marital Adjustment Test. A second study had 50 mothers and 50 adolescent daughters complete the CPS separately. Certain item scores correlated with cohesion, expressiveness, and conflict. The validity of the CPS is also supported with factor analysis where the two separate subscale items were identified.

PRIMARY REFERENCE: Heatherington, L., Freidlander, M. L., Johnson, B., Buchanan, R. M., Burke, L. E., and Shaw, D. M. (1998). Assessing individual family members' constructions of family problems, *Family Process*, 37, 167–187.

AVAILABILITY: Laurie Heatherington, Ph.D., Department of Psychology, Williams College, Williamstown, MA 01267.

CPS

We would like to know your own opinions about what the problem or situation is that has brought you or your family here. Would you kindly use the space below to describe the problem or situation and also what you think the causes of it are.

Next, the following questions each state a possible cause of the problem situation. For each question, consider how much that is or is not a cause of the problem you just wrote about. Simply read the question and check the circle that best describes *your opinion* regarding that particular cause.

	Not at all	A little	Somewhat	A lot	Completely
1. To what extent is this a family problem (vs. an individual problem)?	4	3	2	1	0
2. Is this problem caused by circumstances in the environment which are beyond the control of the people involved (e.g., accident, laid off from job, etc.)?	4	3	2	1	0
3. Does this problem result from the way two or more people in the family relate or communicate with each other?	4	3	2	1	0
4. Are you to blame or at fault for this problem?	4	3	2	1	0
5. Is some other family member to blame or at fault for this problem?	4	3	2	1	0
6. Is this problem related to certain family events or situations that occurred in the family in which you were raised?	4	3	2	1	0
7. Is this problem caused by your own physical illness or condition?	4	3	2	1	0
8. Is this problem caused by the physical illness or condition of a family member other than yourself?	4	3	2	1	0
9. Is this problem caused by the way two (or more) people behave together in a "vicious circle" (e.g., the more a wife nags the more her husband withdraws and the more he withdraws the more she nags, or the more a brother teases his sister the more she tattles and the more she tattles the more he teases her)?	4	3	2	1	0
10. Is this problem a matter of bad luck?	4	3	2	1	0
11. Is someone in the family other than yourself responsible for the cause of this problem?	4	3	2	1	0

12.	Is this problem due to family members not seeing things from one another's point of view?	4	3	2	1	0
13.	Is this problem due to the genetic makeup of someone in the family other than yourself?	4	3	2	1	0
14.	Is this problem solvable?	4	3	2	1	0
15.	Is this problem caused by the mental disorder of someone in the family other than yourself?	4	3	2	1	0
16.	Is this problem caused by how family members other than yourself think about, or view, the situation?	4	3	2	1	0
17.	Is this problem due to the personality traits of a family member other than yourself?	4	3	2	1	0
18.	Is this problem caused by your own mental disorder?	4	3	2	1	0
19.	Is this problem related to family events or situations that occurred in previous generations, i.e., things that happened when your parents or grandparents were growing up?	4	3	2	1	0
20.	Is this problem due to your personality traits?	4	3	2	1	0
21.	Do you have any power or control over resolving this problem?	4	3	2	1	0
22.	Is this problem due to your genetic makeup?	4	3	2	1	0
23.	Is this problem caused by how you think about, or view, the problem?	4	3	2	1	0
24.	Do family members other than yourself have any power or control over resolving the problem?	4	3	2	1	0
25.	Are you responsible for the cause of this problem?	4	3	2	1	0
26.	Is this problem caused by your attitude?	4	3	2	1	0
27.	Is this problem caused by the attitude of someone in the family other than yourself?	4	3	2	1	0

CONSTRUCTIONS OF PROBLEMS SCALE: SUMMARY PROFILE

NAME _____

DATE _____

Completely	5	.	.	.	.	.	.	.	.	.	.	.	.	.
A lot	4	.	.	.	.	.	.	.	.	.	.	.	.	.
Somewhat	3	.	.	.	.	.	.	.	.	.	.	.	.	.
A little	2	.	.	.	.	.	.	.	.	.	.	.	.	.
Not at all	1	.	.	.	.	.	.	.	.	.	.	.	.	.
		1	**2**	**3**	**4**	**5**	**6**	**7**	**8**	**9**	**10**	**11**	**12**	**13**

1. Family problem
2. Environment
3. Communication
4. Blame—self
5. Blame—other
6. Family of origin
7. Physical illness—self
8. Physical illness—other
9. Vicious circle
10. Bad luck
11. Responsible—other
12. Different points of view
13. Genetics—other
14. Solvable

Completely	5	.	.	.	.	.	.	.	.	.	.	.	.	.
A lot	4	.	.	.	.	.	.	.	.	.	.	.	.	.
Somewhat	3	.	.	.	.	.	.	.	.	.	.	.	.	.
A little	2	.	.	.	.	.	.	.	.	.	.	.	.	.
Not at all	1	.	.	.	.	.	.	.	.	.	.	.	.	.
		15	**16**	**17**	**18**	**19**	**20**	**21**	**22**	**23**	**24**	**25**	**26**	**27**

15. Mental disorder—other
16. Thinking—others'
17. Personality—others
18. Mental disorder—self
19. Previous generations
20. Personality—self
21. Power/control—self
22. Genetics—self
23. Thinking—self
24. Power/control—other
25. Responsible—self
26. Attitude—self
27. Attitude—other

DOMINANCE-ACCOMMODATION SCALE (DA)

AUTHOR: Carol Noll Hoskins

PURPOSE: To measure dominance-accommodation in couples and families.

DESCRIPTION: The DA is a 37-item instrument designed to measure dominance and accommodation in interpersonal relationships, particularly in couples and families. Dominance was defined as attempts to control one's environment: expression of opinions, preferences, or attitudes in a verbal or nonverbal manner that tends to strongly influence or direct the behaviors of one's partner. Thus, an individual high on dominance would be seen as trying to control the partner. An individual high on accommodation was defined as accepting blame and criticism when not deserved; tending to be self-effacing; avoiding risk of physical or emotional harm; seeking to maximize personal psychological safety, well-being, or stability. The DA has two factors or subscales: self-referent accommodation (items 2, 3, 5–7, 9–11, 13, 14, 16–18, 20, 21, 23, 25, 26, 28–30, 35–37) and couple referent accommodation (items 1, 3, 4, 6, 8, 9, 12, 13, 15–26, 28, 31, 33). Separate factor scores are recommended for use, with higher scores on the first factor meaning there is a tendency to accommodate to the partner and a lower score indicating self-assertion. Higher scores on the second factor indicate respondents perceive little appreciation of their own needs.

NORMS: The DA has been studied with several samples, most recently with 78 couples (156 individuals) with a mean age of 39, mean of 11.6 years in the relationship; 87% were professionals, and 78% had a college or graduate school education. The mean score for the whole scale was 164.4 (SD = 19.2).

SCORING: The DA is scored by reverse-scoring all items on the second factor and then summing item values for the subscale and total scores.

RELIABILITY: The DA has fair to good reliability with an overall alpha of .84; factor one has an alpha of .79 and factor two an alpha of .65. Data on stability were not reported.

VALIDITY: The DA has fair concurrent validity, with significant correlations between both subscales and several subscales of the Personality Research Form—E, including abasement, aggression, dependence, dominance, harm avoidance, social recognition, and understanding.

PRIMARY REFERENCE: Hoskins, C. N. (1986). Measuring perceived dominance-accommodation: Development of a scale, *Psychological Reports*, 58, 627–642.

AVAILABILITY: Dr. Carol Hoskins, New York University, 429 Shimkin Hall, Washington Square, New York, NY 10003.

DA

On the following pages you will find a series of sentences that describe feelings about your relationship to your partner. Please read each sentence carefully and respond according to HOW YOU FEEL in general. Please mark all the items.

A rating scale is provided for your response. If you circle *SA* it means you *strongly agree*. If you circle *A* it means you *agree*. If you circle *U* it means you are *undecided*. If you circle *D* it means you *disagree*. If you circle *SD* it means you *strongly disagree*.

1.	I know my partner takes me seriously when I'm concerned about conditions in today's world.	SA A U D SD
2.	Even if I could sleep late, I usually get up because my partner wants me to.	SA A U D SD
3.	When I need help from my partner in the house, I insist on it.	SA A U D SD
4.	My partner is good about getting together with my friends even though he/she may not like them as well as I do.	SA A U D SD
5.	I usually give in for the sake of peace if my partner explains why he/she thinks my views are wrong.	SA A U D SD
6.	I insist on having my say about how much free time we spend with friends.	SA A U D SD
7.	If my partner wakes me up, I try to be pleasant even if I don't feel that way.	SA A U D SD
8.	Even though my partner has work to do, I know he/she will put it aside if I need to have time together.	SA A U D SD
9.	When it's my partner's turn to clean up after dinner, I don't do it.	SA A U D SD
10.	If my partner didn't understand my need to have some money of my own, I wouldn't make an issue over it.	SA A U D SD
11.	I try to go along with my partner's ideas for weekend activities even if I have other thoughts.	SA A U D SD

12. We spend money according to whether we both   SA A U D SD
     agree that we can afford it.

13. If I feel like eating before my partner gets home,   SA A U D SD
     I do.

14. My partner usually decides when it is time for us to SA A U D SD
     call it a day and retire.

15. My partner considers my interests as much as   SA A U D SD
     his/hers when planning for leisure time.

16. If I don't have to be up in the morning, I expect my SA A U D SD
     partner to get going by himself/herself.

17. When we disagree over some aspect of our sex life,   SA A U D SD
     I express my views.

18. When our ideas for the weekend are different, I say   SA A U D SD
     so.

19. When I make plans with friends, my partner will   SA A U D SD
     adjust his/her schedule.

20. If my partner is late getting home, he/she can get   SA A U D SD
     his/her own dinner.

21. If my partner awakens me when I want to sleep, I   SA A U D SD
     let him/her know about it.

22. Because our basic values are similar, I am satisfied SA A U D SD
     with our life style.

23. If my partner makes love in a way that I find   SA A U D SD
     disagreeable, I don't go along with it.

24. When I let my partner know I need to be close, I   SA A U D SD
     know he/she will take time for it.

25. Even though I can tell when my partner wants sex, I   SA A U D SD
     don't feel I have to accommodate him/her.

26. I don't quit what I'm doing and go to bed just   SA A U D SD
     because my partner is ready.

27. My partner doesn't seriously consider my worries   SA A U D SD
     about social conditions.

28. I try to maintain friendships even if my partner isn't   SA   A   U   D   SD
    interested.

29. If my partner objects to my telling a waitress that   SA   A   U   D   SD
    she charged too little, I don't do it.

30. My partner's interests come first when planning   SA   A   U   D   SD
    leisure time.

31. When we disagree on what to eat, my partner gives   SA   A   U   D   SD
    in as much as I do.

32. I prefer to back off if my partner doesn't respond to   SA   A   U   D   SD
    me sexually.

33. I am comfortable talking about life and its meaning   SA   A   U   D   SD
    with my partner because he/she shows respect for
    my beliefs.

34. If I need to be close, I can't count on my partner to   SA   A   U   D   SD
    put other demands aside.

35. I feel obligated to serve dinner even if my partner is   SA   A   U   D   SD
    late.

36. I am often reluctant to spend money without   SA   A   U   D   SD
    consulting my partner.

37. Even if I get hungry before my partner gets home, I   SA   A   U   D   SD
    feel better if I wait.

Copyright © 1986 Carol Noll Hoskins, Ph.D.

DUAL EMPLOYED COPING SCALES (DECS)

AUTHORS: Denise A. Skinner and Hamilton I. McCubbin

PURPOSE: To measure coping behaviors in families with two employed spouses.

DESCRIPTION: The DECS is a 58-item instrument designed to measure the coping behaviors spouses find helpful in managing work and family roles when both partners are employed outside the home. Given the increasing need of both spouses to be employed in American society, this measure can be very useful in helping practitioners assess and keep track of changes in coping behaviors that could negatively affect family interactions. The DECS has four factors or subscales described in detail in the primary reference: maintaining the family system, procurement of support, modifying roles and standards, and maintaining perspective/reducing tension. However, the DECS also can be used as an overall measure of coping by using the total score.

NORMS: The DECS has been studied with several samples of families including parents of children with serious illness. No other demographic data are available. Overall means are 173.9 for wives and 162.3 for husbands. In all studies, there were significant differences between wives' and husbands' scores with wives using coping behaviors to a greater extent than husbands.

SCORING: After reverse-scoring item 45, all items are simply summed for a total score.

RELIABILITY: The DECS has very good internal consistency with an overall alpha of .86. Data on stability were not available.

VALIDITY: The DECS has fair concurrent validity correlating with a measure of family adaptation. The DECS also has fair known-groups validity, distinguishing between parents from balanced and extreme families (in terms of adaptation).

PRIMARY REFERENCE: McCubbin, H. I. and Thompson, A. I. (eds.) (1991). *Family Assessment Inventories for Research and Practice*. Madison, WI: University of Wisconsin.

AVAILABILITY: Dr. Hamilton McCubbin, Dean, School of Family Resources and Consumer Services, Madison, WI 53706-1575.

DECS

Purpose:
The Dual-Employed Coping Scales is designed to record what spouses find helpful to them in managing family and work roles when both spouses are employed outside the home. Coping is defined as personal or collective (with other individuals, programs) efforts to manage the demands associated with the dual-employed family.

Directions:
First, read the list of "Coping behaviors" on the left, below, one at a time.
Second, decide how well each statement describes your coping. If the statement describes your coping *very well*, then circle the number 5 indicating that you STRONGLY AGREE. If the statement does not describe your coping at all, then circle the number 1 indicating that you STRONGLY DISAGREE; if the statement describes your coping to some degree, then select a number 2, 3, or 4 to indicate how much you agree or disagree with the statement about your coping behavior.

COPING BEHAVIORS: I "cope" with the demands of our dual-employed family by:	Strongly disagree	Moderately disagree	Neither agree nor disagree	Moderately agree	Strongly agree	No child
1. Becoming more efficient; making better use of my time "at home"	1	2	3	4	5	
2. Using modern equipment (e.g., microwave oven, etc.) to help out at home	1	2	3	4	5	
3. Believing that we have much to gain financially by our both working	1	2	3	4	5	
4. Working out a "fair" schedule of household tasks for all family members	1	2	3	4	5	
5. Getting by on less sleep than I'd ideally like to have	1	2	3	4	5	

COPING BEHAVIORS: I "cope" with the demands of our dual-employed family by:	Strongly disagree	Moderately disagree	Neither agree nor disagree	Moderately agree	Strongly agree	No child
6. Ignoring comments of how we "should" behave as men and women (e.g., women shouldn't work; men should clean house)	1	2	3	4	5	
7. Deciding I will do certain housekeeping tasks at a regular time each week	1	2	3	4	5	
8. Buying convenience foods which are easy to prepare at home	1	2	3	4	5	
9. Believing that my working has made me a better parent than I otherwise would be	1	2	3	4	5	NC
10. Leaving some things undone around the house (even though I would like to have them done)	1	2	3	4	5	NC
11. Getting our children to help out with household tasks	1	2	3	4	5	
12. Ignoring criticisms of others about parents who both work outside the home	1	2	3	4	5	NC
13. Making friends with other couples who are both employed outside the home	1	2	3	4	5	
14. Specifically planning "family time together" into our schedule; planning family activities for all of us to do together	1	2	3	4	5	

COPING BEHAVIORS: I "cope" with the demands of our dual-employed family by:	Strongly disagree	Moderately disagree	Neither agree nor disagree	Moderately agree	Strongly agree	No child
15. Hiring outside help to assist with our housekeeping and home maintenance	1	2	3	4	5	
16. Overlooking the difficulties and focusing on the good things about our lifestyle	1	2	3	4	5	
17. Planning for various family relations to occur at a certain regular time each day or week (e.g., "from the time we get home until their bedtime is the "children's time")	1	2	3	4	5	
18. Eating out frequently	1	2	3	4	5	
19. Believing that my working has made me a better spouse	1	2	3	4	5	
20. Hiring help to care for the children	1	2	3	4	5	NC
21. Relying on extended family members for encouragement	1	2	3	4	5	
22. Covering household family responsibilities for each other when one spouse has extra work	1	2	3	4	5	
23. Leaving work and work-related problems at work when I leave at the end of the day	1	2	3	4	5	
24. Having friends at work whom I can talk to about how I feel	1	2	3	4	5	
25. Planning for time alone with my spouse	1	2	3	4	5	

COPING BEHAVIORS: I "cope" with the demands of our dual-employed family by:	Strongly disagree	Moderately disagree	Neither agree nor disagree	Moderately agree	Strongly agree	No child
26. Modifying my work schedule (e.g., reducing amount of time at work or working different hours)	1	2	3	4	5	
27. Relying on extended family members for financial help when needed	1	2	3	4	5	
28. Negotiating who stays home with an ill child on a "case-by-case" basis	1	2	3	4	5	NC
29. Planning work changes (e.g., transfer, promotion, shift change), around family needs	1	2	3	4	5	
30. Relying on extended family members for childcare help	1	2	3	4	5	NC
31. Identifying one partner as primarily responsible for child-rearing tasks	1	2	3	4	5	NC
32. Believing that we are good "role models" for our children by our both working	1	2	3	4	5	NC
33. Identifying one partner as primarily responsible for household tasks	1	2	3	4	5	
34. Planning time for myself to relieve tensions (jogging, exercising, meditating, etc.)	1	2	3	4	5	
35. Buying more goods and services (as opposed to "do-it-yourself" projects)	1	2	3	4	5	

COPING BEHAVIORS: I "cope" with the demands of our dual-employed family by:	Strongly disagree	Moderately disagree	Neither agree nor disagree	Moderately agree	Strongly agree	No child
36. Encouraging our children to help each other out when possible (e.g., homework, rides to activities, etc.)	1	2	3	4	5	NC
37. Trying to be flexible enough to fit in special needs and events (e.g., child's concert at school, etc.)	1	2	3	4	5	
38. Planning ahead so that major changes at home (e.g., having a baby) will not disturb our work requirements	1	2	3	4	5	
39. Making better use of time at work	1	2	3	4	5	
40. Having good friends whom I talk to about how I feel	1	2	3	4	5	
41. Limiting our home entertaining to only our close friends	1	2	3	4	5	
42. Believing that, with time, our lifestyle will be easier	1	2	3	4	5	
43. Planning schedules out ahead of time (e.g., who takes kid(s) to the doctor; who works late)	1	2	3	4	5	
44. Sticking to an established schedule of work and family-related activities	1	2	3	4	5	
45. Believing that I must excel at both my work and my family roles	1	2	3	4	5	

COPING BEHAVIORS: I "cope" with the demands of our dual-employed family by:	Strongly disagree	Moderately disagree	Neither agree nor disagree	Moderately agree	Strongly agree	No child
46. Cutting down on the amount of "outside activities" in which I can be involved	1	2	3	4	5	
47. Establishing whose role responsibility it is to stay home when child(ren) are ill	1	2	3	4	5	NC
48. Identifying one partner as primarily responsible for bread-winning	1	2	3	4	5	
10. Believing that working is good for my personal growth.	1	2	3	4	5	
50. Believing that, overall, there are more advantages than disadvantages to our lifestyle	1	2	3	4	5	
51. Limiting job involvement in order to have time for my family	1	2	3	4	5	
52. Lowering my standards for "how well" household tasks must be done	1	2	3	4	5	
53. Encouraging our child(ren) to be more self-sufficient, where appropriate	1	2	3	4	5	
54. Eliminating certain activities (home entertaining, volunteer work, etc.)	1	2	3	4	5	
55. Frequent communication among all family members about individual schedules, needs, and responsibilities	1	2	3	4	5	

	Strongly disagree	Moderately disagree	Neither agree nor disagree	Moderately agree	Strongly agree	No child
COPING BEHAVIORS: I "cope" with the demands of our dual-employed family by:						
56. Maintaining health (eating right, exercising, etc.)	1	2	3	4	5	
57. Believing that I need a lot of stimulation and activity to keep from getting bored	1	2	3	4	5	
58. Limiting my involvement on the job—saying "no" to some of the things I could be doing	1	2	3	4	5	

Please check all 58 items to be sure you have circled a number for each one. Thank you!

Copyright © 1991 H. McCubbin and A. I. Thompson

DUAL-CAREER FAMILY SCALE (DCFS)

AUTHORS: Brian F. Pendleton, Margaret M. Poloma, and T. Neal Garland.

PURPOSE: To measure characteristics of dual-career families.

DESCRIPTION: The DCFS is a 31-item instrument that is composed of six scales measuring the following characteristics of dual-career families as indicated on the scale: (1) marriage type (MT), (2) domestic responsibility (DR), (3) satisfaction (S), (4) self-image (S-I), (5) career salience (CS), and (6) career line (CL). The items for these scales were developed out of theoretical work on families and tested empirically with ambiguous items dropped. Since dual-career families are a relatively new area of practice and research, these scales can be viewed as an initial basis for continuing exploration in practice and research.

NORMS: The data on which these scales were based came from a study of 45 wives who were employed as attorneys, professors, or physicians. No other demographic information was provided nor were actual norms.

SCORING: The DCFS is scored on 5-point Likert-type scales ranging from "strongly agree" (1) to "strongly disagree" (5). The scale scores are simply a sum of individual items. A total combined score for all six scales is not recommended.

RELIABILITY: Internal consistency for the six scales is rather weak, with alpha coefficients ranging from .42 to .76 (mean alpha = .61) with the self-image and career line scales having the best internal consistency (.73 and .76 respectively). The scales were also subject to Guttman analyses involving coefficients of reproducibility (predictability of scores from one item to the next). Coefficients of reproducibility exceeded the requirement of .85 for three of the scales (domestic responsibility, satisfaction, and self-image) while the other three scales ranged from .76 to .81.

VALIDITY: No real validity data are presented. However, the authors maintain that some degree of construct validity can be garnered by a matrix of scale intercorrelations in which 5 of 15 intercorrelations were significant in predictable ways.

PRIMARY REFERENCE: Pendleton, B. F., Poloma, M. M., and Garland, T. N. (1980). Scales for investigation of the dual-career family, *Journal of Marriage and the Family, 42, 269–276. Instrument reprinted by permission of the National Council on Family Relations.*

AVAILABILITY: Dr. T. Neal Garland, Department of Sociology, University of Akron, Akron, OH 44325.

DCFS

Please circle the number that indicates the extent to which you agree or disagree with the item.

1 = Strongly agree
2 = Agree
3 = No opinion
4 = Disagree
5 = Strongly disagree

Marriage Type

1. If a child were ill and needed to remain home from school, I would be (have been) more likely to stay home with him/her than my husband.   1 2 3 4 5

2. Given the structure of our society, it is important that the woman assume primary responsibility for child care.   1 2 3 4 5

0. I consider my husband to be the main breadwinner in the family.   1 2 3 4 5

4. My income is as vital to the well-being of our family as is my husband's.   1 2 3 4 5

5. I would not work if my husband did not approve.   1 2 3 4 5

6. I would not attend a professional convention if it inconvenienced my husband.   1 2 3 4 5

Domestic Responsibility

7. Although my husband may assist me, the responsibility for homemaking tasks is primarily mine.   1 2 3 4 5

8. If a wife and mother feels she is not meeting her domestic responsibilities due to her career involvement, she should cut back her career demands.   1 2 3 4 5

9. I bend over backwards not to have to make demands on my husband that his colleagues (with nonemployed wives) do not have to meet.   1 2 3 4 5

Satisfaction

10. I would be a less fulfilled person without my experience of family life.   1 2 3 4 5

11. If I had it to do over again, I would not have had any children.   1 2 3 4 5

12. If I had it to do over again, I would not have trained for my particular profession.   1 2 3 4 5

Self-Image

13. My career has made me a better wife than I would have been otherwise.   1 2 3 4 5

14. Married professional women have the best of two worlds: professional employment combined with a full family life.   1 2 3 4 5

15. My career has made me a better mother than I otherwise would have been.   1 2 3 4 5

16. I spend (spent) as much or more actual time with my children as my non-working neighbors who are active in community affairs.   1 2 3 4 5

Career Salience

17. I view my work more as a job that I enjoy than as a career.   1 2 3 4 5

18. I have cut back on my career involvement in order not to threaten my marriage.   1 2 3 4 5

19. My career is as important to my husband as it is to me.   1 2 3 4 5

20. I am as career-oriented as my male colleagues.   1 2 3 4 5

21. I would recommend that any young woman contemplating a career complete her professional training before marriage.   1 2 3 4 5

22. In case of conflicting demands, a professional woman's primary responsibilities are to her husband and children.   1 2 3 4 5

23. It is possible for a husband and wife to work in separate
    cities to maximize career possibilities and have a
    successful marriage at the same time.   1 2 3 4 5

24. If I were to receive an exceptional job offer in another
    city (one that I wanted to accept), I would not expect my
    husband to accompany me unless he were sure of a
    suitable position for himself.   1 2 3 4 5

Career Line

25. A married woman's career history should be considered
    in light of the two sets of demands she faces as a wife
    and as a professional.   1 2 3 4 5

26. Most single career women have greater opportunities to
    succeed in a profession than do married career women.   1 2 3 4 5

27. A married woman's career goals tend to be more
    modest than those of her male colleagues.   1 2 3 4 5

28. I have cut back on my career involvement in order to
    meet the needs of my family.   1 2 3 4 5

29. My career has suffered due to the responsibilities I have
    (had) as a mother.   1 2 3 4 5

30. It is impossible in our present society to combine a
    career, in the fullest sense of the term (uninterrupted,
    full-time work with a high degree of commitment and
    desire for success) with the demands of a family.   1 2 3 4 5

31. I consider myself a working woman (have professional
    employment) rather than a career woman (to whom
    advancement and exceptional achievement in a
    profession is important).   1 2 3 4 5

Copyright © 1980 National Council on Family Relations.

DYADIC ADJUSTMENT SCALE (DAS)

AUTHOR: Graham B. Spanier

PURPOSE: To assess the quality of marriage or similar dyads.

DESCRIPTION: This 32-item instrument is designed to assess the quality of the relationship as perceived by married or cohabiting couples. The instrument was designed to serve a number of needs. It can be used as a general measure of satisfaction in an intimate relationship by using total scores. Factor analysis indicates that the instrument measures four aspects of the relationship: dyadic satisfaction (DS), dyadic cohesion (DCoh), dyadic consensus (DCon) and affectional expression (AE). The instrument may be adapted for use in interviews.

NORMS: The DAS was developed on a sample of married ($n = 218$) and divorced persons ($n = 94$). The average age of the married people was 35.1 years, while the divorced sample was slightly younger, 30.4 years. The married sample had been married an average of 13.2 years while the average length of the marriages for the divorced sample was 8.5 years. The mean score on the total DAS was 114.8 with a standard deviation of 17.8 for the married sample. The mean for the divorced sample was 70.7 with a standard deviation of 23.8.

SCORING: Three different types of rating scales are used with the DAS. Total scores are the sum of all items, ranging from 0 to 151. Higher scores reflect a better relationship. The factor items are as follows: DS: 16, 17, 18, 19, 20, 21, 22, 23, 31, 32; DCoh: 24, 25, 26, 27, 28; DCon: 1, 2, 3, 5, 7, 8, 9, 10, 11, 12, 13, 14, 15; AE: 4, 6, 29, 30.

RELIABILITY: As a total score, the DAS has impressive internal consistency, with an alpha of .96. The subscales have fair to excellent internal consistency: DS = .94, DCoh = .81, DCon = .90, and AE = .73.

VALIDITY: The instrument was first checked with logical content validity procedures. The DAS also has shown known-groups validity by discriminating between married and divorced couples on each item. The instrument also has evidence of concurrent validity, correlating with the Locke-Wallace Marital Adjustment Scale.

PRIMARY REFERENCE: Spanier, G. B. (1976). Measuring dyadic adjustment: New scales for assessing the quality of marriage and similar dyads, *Journal of Marriage and the Family*, 38, 15–28. Instrument reproduced with permission of Graham B. Spanier.

AVAILABILITY: Journal article.

DAS

Most persons have disagreements with their relationships. Please indicate below the appropriate extent of the agreement or disagreement between you and your partner for each item on the following list.

5 = Always agree
4 = Almost always agree
3 = Occasionally disagree
2 = Frequently disagree
1 = Almost always disagree
0 = Always disagree

_____ 1. Handling family finances
_____ 2. Matters of recreation
_____ 3. Religious matters
_____ 4. Demonstration of affection
_____ 5. Friends
_____ 6. Sex relations
_____ 7. Conventionality (correct or proper behavior)
_____ 8. Philosophy of life
_____ 9. Ways of dealing with in-laws
_____ 10. Aims, goals, and things believed important
_____ 11. Amount of time spent together
_____ 12. Making major decisions
_____ 13. Household tasks
_____ 14. Leisure time interests
_____ 15. Career decisions

Please indicate below approximately how often the following items occur between you and your partner.

1 = All the time
2 = Most of the time
3 = More often than not
4 = Occasionally
5 = Rarely
6 = Never

_____ 16. How often do you discuss or have you considered divorce, separation, or terminating the relationship?
_____ 17. How often do you or your mate leave the house after a fight?
_____ 18. In general, how often do you think things between you and your partner are going well?
_____ 19. Do you confide in your mate?
_____ 20. Do you ever regret that you married? (*or lived together*)
_____ 21. How often do you and your partner quarrel?
_____ 22. How often do you and your mate "get on each other's nerves?"

23.   Do you kiss your mate?

	Almost			
Every day	every day	Occasionally	Rarely	Never
4	3	2	1	0

24.   Do you and your mate engage in outside interests together?

All of	Most of	Some of	Very few	None of
them	them	them	of them	them
4	3	2	1	0

How often would you say the following events occur between you and your mate?

1 = Never
2 = Less than once a month
3 = Once or twice a month
4 = Once a day
5 = More often

_____   25.   Have a stimulating exchange of ideas
_____   26.   Laugh together
_____   27.   Calmly discuss something
_____   28.   Work together on a project

There are some things about which couples sometimes agree and sometimes disagree. Indicate if either item below caused differences of opinions or problems in your relationship during the past few weeks. (Circle yes or no)

Yes No   29.   Being too tired for sex
Yes No   30.   Not showing love

31.   The numbers on the following line represent different degrees of happiness in your relationship. The middle point, "happy," represents the degree of happiness of most relationships. Please circle the number that best describes the degree of happiness, all things considered, of your relationship.

0	1	2	3	4	5	6
Extremely	Fairly	A little	Happy	Very	Extremely	Perfect
unhappy	unhappy	unhappy		happy	happy	

32. Please circle the number of *one* of the following statements that best describes how you feel about the future of your relationship.

   5   I want desperately for my relationship to succeed, and *would go to almost any length* to see that it does

   4   I want very much for my relationship to succeed, and *will do all that I can* to see that it does

   3   I want very much for my relationship to succeed, and *will do my fair share* to see that it does

   2   It would be nice if my relationship succeded, but *I can't do much more than I am doing* now to make it succeed.

   1   It would be nice if it succeeded, but *I refuse to do any more than I am doing* now to keep the relationship going.

   0   My relationship can never succeed, and *there is no more that I can do* to keep the relationship going.

EQUITY/INEQUITY SCALE (E/I)

AUTHORS: Jane Traupmann, Robert Petersen, Mary Utne, and Elaine Hatfield
PURPOSE: To measure equity in intimate relationships.
DESCRIPTION: The E/I is a 26-item instrument designed to measure levels of
    equity intimate couples perceive in their relationship. Two separate scores
    are available from the E/I, a global score of equity based on one item; and a
    score for detailed areas of an intimate relationship, namely, personal con-
    cerns, emotional concerns, day-to-day concerns, and opportunities gained
    and lost (25 items). The E/I is a useful measure for research and practice
    with couples in intimate relationships. The global E/I scale takes approxi-
    mately 2 minutes to complete, while the detailed E/I takes about 15 minutes.
    Scores range from +3.00 to −3.0. Scores between +3 and +1.5 reflect a
    partner who is over-benefiting in the relationship; scores between +1.49 to
    −1.49 suggest a degree of equity in the relationship; and scores from −1.50
    to −3.0 indicate a partner who is underburdened in the relationship.
NORMS: The E/I was developed in three studies including pretest, a reliability
    assessment, and a validity assessment. These studies included 118 couples
    who had applied for marriage licenses in a four-month period in a Wisconsin
    community, 36 people (including 16 married couples) recruited by news-
    paper advertisement, and 123 subjects (60 daters including 29 males and 31
    females, and 63 married including 36 males and 27 females) recruited from
    a variety of sources in Wisconsin. Norms are not reported.
SCORING: The 26 items of the E/I are scored on a Likert-type scale that ranges
    from +3 to −3 for each item. The ratings are summed. The sum of the ratings
    for the detailed E/I is divided by 25. Four scores for each respondent can be
    derived (when partners also fill out the questionnaire): own inputs (sum of
    all scale items on the input scale), sum of own outcomes, sum of partner's
    inputs, and sum of partner's outcomes. The discrepancies between the scores
    can be seen as issues in the equity arrangements within couples.
RELIABILITY: The Detailed E/I has good to excellent internal consistency, with
    Cronbach's alphas for total inputs being .90 and for total outcomes .87. No
    data on stability were reported.
VALIDITY: The E/I was reported as having good construct validity in that it
    correlated with other constructs predicted by equity theory, affect (content-
    ment versus anger), and satisfaction (happiness with the relationship).
PRIMARY REFERENCE: Traupmann, J., Petersen, R., Utne, M., and Hatfield,
    E. (1981). Measuring equity in intimate relations, *Applied Psychological
    Measurement*, 5, 467–480.
AVAILABILITY: Dr. Jane Traupmann, Center for Research on Women, Welles-
    ley College, Wellesley, MA 02181.

E/I

GLOBAL MEASURE OF EQUITY/INEQUITY

Considering what you put into your (dating relationship) (marriage), compared with what you get out of it, and what your partner puts in, compared with what (s)he gets out of it, how does your (dating relationship) (marriage) "stack up"? Record the number that best describes how you rate your relationship. _____

+3 = I am getting a much better deal than my partner.
+2 = I am getting a somewhat better deal.
+1 = I am getting a slightly better deal.
 0 = We are both getting an equally good . . . or bad . . . deal.
−1 = My partner is getting a slightly better deal.
−2 = My partner is getting a somewhat better deal.
−3 = My partner is getting a much better deal than I am.

DETAILED MEASURE OF EQUITY/INEQUITY

Here is a list of some critical areas in any relationship. The headings give you a sense of the ground that will be covered: you and your partner's personal concerns, your emotional concerns, your day-to-day concerns, and a little about the things the two of you feel you gain or lose—simply by being married. Read each statement and rate it using the following scale. Record your ratings in the space to the left of each statement.

Considering what you put into your (dating relationship) (marriage) in this area, compared to what you get out of it, and what your partner puts in, compared to what (s)he gets out of it, how does your (dating relationship) (marriage) "stack up"?

+3 = I am getting a much better deal than my partner.
+2 = I am getting a somewhat better deal.
+1 = I am getting a slightly better deal.
 0 = We are both getting an equally good . . . or bad . . . deal.
−1 = My partner is getting a slightly better deal.
−2 = My partner is getting a somewhat better deal.
−3 = My partner is getting a much better deal than I am.

AREAS INVOLVED IN THE GIVE AND TAKE

PERSONAL CONCERNS

_____ 1. Social grace: Some people are sociable, friendly, relaxed in social settings. Others are not.
_____ 2. Intelligence: Some people are intelligent and informed.
_____ 3. Physical attractiveness: Some people are physically attractive.

_____ 4. Concern for physical appearance and health: Some people take care of their physical appearance and conditioning, through attention to such things as their clothing, cleanliness, exercise, and good eating habits.

EMOTIONAL CONCERNS

_____ 5. Liking: Some people like their partners and show it. Others do not express their feelings.

_____ 6. Love: Some people feel and express love for their partners.

_____ 7. Understanding and concern: Some people know their partner's personal concerns and emotional needs and respond to them.

_____ 8. Accepting and encouraging role flexibility: Some people let their partner try out different roles occasionally, for example, letting their partner be a "baby" sometimes, a "mother," a colleague, or a friend, an aggressive as well as a passive lover, and so on.

_____ 9. Expression of appreciation: Some people openly show appreciation for their partner's contributions to the relationship; they don't take their partner for granted.

_____ 10. Showing Affection: Some people are openly affectionate, touching, hugging, kissing.

_____ 11. Sexual pleasure: Some people participate in the sexual aspect of a relationship: working to make it mutually satisfying and fulfilling.

_____ 12. Sexual fidelity: Some people live up to (are "faithful" to) their agreements about extramarital relations.

_____ 13. Commitment: Some people commit themselves to their partner and to the future of their relationship together.

_____ 14. Respecting partner's need to be a free and independent person: Some people allow their partners to develop as an individual in the way that they choose: for example, they allow their partners freedom to go to school or not, to work at the kind of job or career they like, to pursue outside interests, to do things by themselves or with friends, to simply be alone sometimes.

_____ 15. Plans and goals for the future: Some people plan for and dream about their future together.

DAY-TO-DAY CONCERNS

_____ 16. Day-to-day maintenance: Some people contribute time and effort to household responsibilities such as grocery shopping, making dinner, cleaning, and car maintenance. Others do not.

_____ 17. Finances: Some people contribute income to the couple's joint account.

_____ 18. Easy-to-live-with: Some people are easy to live with on a day-to-day basis; that is, they have a sense of humor, aren't too moody, don't get drunk too often, and so on.

_____ 19. Companionship: Some people are good companions, who suggest interesting activities for both of them to do together, as well as going along with their partner's ideas about what they might do for fun.

_____ 20. Conversation: Some people tell their partner about the day's events and what's on their mind and are also interested in hearing about their partner's concerns and daily activities.

_____ 21. Fitting in: Some people are compatible with their partner's friends and relatives; they like the friends and relatives, and the friends and relatives like them.

_____ 22. Decision-making: Some people take their fair share of the responsibility for making and carrying out decisions that affect both partners.

_____ 23. Remembering special occasions: Some people are thoughtful about sentimental things, such as remembering birthdays, your anniversary, and other special occasions.

OPPORTUNITIES GAINED AND LOST

_____ 24. Chance to be married: Marriage gives many people the opportunity to partake of the many life experiences that depend upon being married; for example, the chance to become a parent and even a grandparent, the chance to be included in "married couple" social events, and finally, having someone to count on in old age.

_____ 25. Opportunities foregone: Marriage necessarily requires people to give up certain opportunities in order to be in this relationship. The opportunities could have been other possible mates, a career, travel, etc.

HYPOTHETICAL, JEALOUSY-PRODUCING
EVENTS SCALE (HJPE)

AUTHOR: Gary L. Hansen

PURPOSE: To measure marital jealousy.

DESCRIPTION: The HJPE is an 8-item instrument designed to measure marital
jealousy using hypothetical, jealousy-producing events as stimuli. The HJPE
is based on the notion that jealousy comprises two factors. The first is an
individual's definition of a partner's actual or imagined behavior as conflicting with his or her own definition of the relationship. The second involves
the individual viewing the relationship as valuable. Respondents are presented with series of situations and are asked to rate each on an 11-point
scale regarding how pleased (or bothered) they would be about that situation.
The HJPE can be a useful measure for tracking changes in jealousy in a
couple counseling program.

NORMS: The HJPE initially was studied with 108 males and 112 female
undergraduates in a large Southern university; 91% of the subjects were
white and their mean age was 20.3. Means for the eight events were as
follows: 1 = 8.19, 2 = 4.41, 3 = 3.32, 4 = 4.38, 5 = 6.14, 6 = 6.84, 7 = 9.95,
8 = 10.54. The overall mean score was 56.27. There were no significant
differences between males and females.

SCORING: The total score is calculated by simply summing scores on the eight
individual items.

RELIABILITY: The HJPE has fair internal consistency, with an alpha of .65.
Test-retest data are not available.

VALIDITY: The HJPE had fair concurrent validity, correlating positively with
gender-role traditionalism, negatively with marital alternatives, and negatively with self-esteem in females.

PRIMARY REFERENCE: Hansen, G. L. (1982). Reactions to hypothetical,
jealousy-producing events, *Family Relations*, 31, 513–518. Instrument reprinted by permission of the National Council on Family Relations.

AVAILABILITY: Journal article.

HJPE

By circling a number, please indicate how you would feel about your mate's behavior in each of the following hypothetical (imaginary) situations. In each case, "1" indicates that you would be extremely pleased with the situation while "11" indicates that you would be extremely disturbed or bothered by the situation.

1. Your mate has a job which requires him/her to work a normal 40 hours per week. In addition to working these 40 hours per week, your mate feels very committed to his/her job and devotes, on the average, an additional 10 hours per week to work-related activities which require him/her to go back to the office in the evenings and on weekends. Your mate does not receive extra pay for these activities.

    1   2   3   4   5   6   7   8   9   10   11

2. Your mate enjoys a personal hobby such as painting, photography, etc., and devotes a large proportion of his/her leisure time (approximately 15 hours per week) to its pursuit. This hobby is one you do not share with your mate so he/she engages in it alone. (The hobby does not impose a financial burden on your family.)

    1   2   3   4   5   6   7   8   9   10   11

3. You and your mate have just had a baby. Your mate is very devoted to the child and concerned about its welfare. As a result of this devotion and concern, your mate devotes nearly all of his/her free time to playing with and taking care of the child, which has drastically reduced the amount of time you and your mate have for doing things alone with each other.

    1   2   3   4   5   6   7   8   9   10   11

4. Your mate regularly enjoys playing cards or other types of games with his/her same-sex friends. Your mate's "night with the boys/girls" occurs about once a week.

    1   2   3   4   5   6   7   8   9   10   11

5. Your mate has become good friends with a co-worker of the opposite sex who you do not know very well. Your mate and his/her friend enjoy having lunch together, discussing their respective lives, and providing each other emotional support. (Their relationship does not have a sexual component.)

    1   2   3   4   5   6   7   8   9   10   11

6. You and your mate live in the same town as his/her parents and siblings. Your mate has set aside Sunday afternoons for doing things (e.g. going fishing, playing golf, visiting) with his/her family members. You do not participate with your mate in these activities with his/her family.

    1   2   3   4   5   6   7   8   9   10   11

7. Your mate returns from a business trip to a different city and informs you that he/she met a member of the opposite sex that he/she found very physically attractive. They ended up engaging in sexual relations. Your mate informs you that their relationship was purely physical (not emotional) and that they will never be seeing each other again.

    1   2   3   4   5   6   7   8   9   10   11

8. Your mate has developed an ongoing emotional and sexual relationship with a member of the opposite sex. Your mate receives a high degree of satisfaction from this relationship and plans to continue it. Both you and your mate have been happy and pleased with your own relationship. Your mate views his/her outside relationship as a supplement to, not a substitute for, the relationship between the two of you.

    1   2   3   4   5   6   7   8   9   10   11

Copyright © 1982 National Council on Family Relations.

INDEX OF MARITAL SATISFACTION (IMS)

AUTHOR: Walter W. Hudson

PURPOSE: To measure problems in the marital relationship.

DESCRIPTION: The IMS is a 25-item instrument designed to measure the degree, severity, or magnitude of a problem one spouse or partner has in the marital relationship. It does not characterize the relationship as a unitary entity but measures the extent to which one partner perceives problems in the relationship. The IMS does not measure marital adjustment since a couple may have arrived at a good adjustment despite having a high degree of discord or dissatisfaction. The IMS has two cutting scores. The first is a score of 30 (±5); scores below this point indicate absence of a clinically significant problem in this area. Scores above 30 suggest the presence of a clinically significant problem. The second cutting score is 70. Scores above this point nearly always indicate that clients are experiencing severe stress with a clear possibility that some type of violence could be considered or used to deal with problems. The practitioner should be aware of this possibility. Another advantage of the IMS is that it is one of several scales of the WALMYR Assessment Scales package reproduced here, all of which are administered and scored the same way.

NORMS: The IMS respondents who participated in the development of this scale included single and married individuals, clinical and nonclinical populations, high school and college students and nonstudents. Respondents were primarily Caucasian, but also included Japanese and Chinese Americans, and a smaller number of members of other ethnic groups. Actual norms are not available.

SCORING: Like most WALMYR Assessment Scales instruments, the IMS is scored by first reverse-scoring items listed at the bottom of the page (1, 3, 5, 8, 9, 11, 13, 16, 17, 19, 20, 21, and 23), summing these and the remaining scores, subtracting the number of completed items, multiplying this figure by 100, and dividing by the number of items completed times 6. This will produce a range from 0 to 100 with higher scores indicating greater magnitude or severity of problems.

RELIABILITY: The IMS has a mean alpha of .96, indicating excellent internal consistency, and an excellent (low) Standard Error of Measurement of 4.00. The IMS also has excellent short-term stability with a two-hour test-retest correlation of .96.

VALIDITY: The IMS has excellent concurrent validity, correlating significantly with the Locke-Wallace Marital Adjustment Test. The IMS also has very good known-groups validity discriminating significantly between couples known to have marital problems and those known not to. The IMS also has good construct validity, correlating poorly with measures with which it should not correlate, and correlating significantly with several measures with which it should correlate, such as sexual satisfaction and marital problems.

PRIMARY REFERENCE: Hudson, W. W. (1997). *The WALMYR Assessment Scales Scoring Manual.* Tallahassee, FL: WALMYR Publishing Company.

AVAILABILITY: This scale cannot be reproduced or copied in any manner and must be obtained by writing to the WALMYR Publishing Company, PO Box 12217, Tallahassee, FL 32317-2217 or by calling (850) 383-0045.

INDEX OF MARITAL SATISFACTION (IMS)

Name: _____ Today's Date: _____

This questionnaire is designed to measure the degree of satisfaction you have with your present marriage. It is not a test, there are no right or wrong answers. Answer each item as carefully and as accurately as you can by placing a number side each one as follows.

1 = None of the time
2 = Very rarely
3 = A little of the time
4 = Some of the time
5 = A good part of the time
6 = Most of the time
7 = All of the time

1. _____ My partner is affectionate enough.
2. _____ My partner treats me badly.
3. _____ My partner really cares for me.
4. _____ I feel that I would not choose the same partner if I had it to do over again.
5. _____ I feel that I can trust my partner.
6. _____ I feel that our relationship is breaking up.
7. _____ My partner really doesn't understand me.
8. _____ I feel that our relationship is a good one.
9. _____ Ours is a very happy relationship.
10. _____ Our life together is dull.
11. _____ We have a lot of fun together.
12. _____ My partner does not confide in me.
13. _____ Ours is a very close relationship.
14. _____ I feel that I cannot rely on my partner.
15. _____ I feel that we do not have enough interests in common.
16. _____ We manage arguments and disagreements very well.
17. _____ We do a good job of managing our finances.
18. _____ I feel that I should never have married my partner.
19. _____ My partner and I get along very well together.
20. _____ Our relationship is very stable.
21. _____ My partner is a real comfort to me.
22. _____ I feel that I no longer care for my partner.
23. _____ I feel that the future looks bright for our relationship.
24. _____ I feel that our relationship is empty.
25. _____ I feel there is no excitement in our relationship.

Copyright (c) 1992, Walter W. Hudson   **Illegal to Photocopy or Otherwise Reprod**

1, 3, 5, 8, 9, 11, 13, 16, 17, 19, 20, 21, 23.

KANSAS MARITAL CONFLICT SCALE (KMCS)

AUTHORS: Kenneth Eggeman, Virginia Moxley, and Walter R. Schumm
PURPOSE: To measure marital conflict.
DESCRIPTION: The KMCS is a series of three scales designed to measure the
stages of marital conflict; the first stage has 11 items, the second stage has
5 items, and the third stage has 11 items for a total of 27 items. The scale is
based on observational research that shows that distressed and nondistressed
couples differ in substantial ways over three phases of marital conflict, the
first being agenda building, the second being arguing, and the third being
negotiation. This scale is viewed as useful for evaluating marital therapy, particularly since it is the only scale to measure the patterns in marital conflict
over distinct stages.
NORMS: The KMCS was studied initially with 10 couples, predominantly
white, who volunteered for a marriage enrichment program in Kansas. The
mean age of wives was 22.4 and of husbands 24.4. Wives averaged 15.5
years of education and husbands 16.2 years. The average duration of marriage was 19.4 months. The mean scores, prior to treatment, for husbands
were: Stage 1—36.0 (SD = 9.8), Stage 2—57.56 (SD = 12.44), Stage 3—
42.1 (SD = 7.89). The scores for wives were: Stage 1—35.4 (SD = 10.57),
Stage 2—57.7 (SD = 12.47), Stage 3—38.5 (SD = 8.02).
SCORING: Scores are developed for each separate stage by simply summing
the individual item scores. In Stage 1, items 5, 7, 9, and 11 are reverse scored;
in Stage 2, all items except "respect toward you" are reverse-scored; and in
Stage 3, items 2, 4, 5, 6, and 7 are reverse-scored. Higher scores represent
lower conflict.
RELIABILITY: The KMCS has excellent internal consistency, with alphas for
all stages for men in the range of .91 to .95 and alphas for women ranging
from .88 to .95. Stability of the measure also is very good with six-month
test-retest correlations of the three stages that range from .64 to .96.
VALIDITY: The scales have good known-groups validity for wives, significantly distinguishing between distressed and nondistressed marriages in
terms of marital satisfaction. The correlations also were positive for husbands but not always significantly so. The KMCS scales also correlated with
a number of other scales, suggesting good to excellent construct validity.
Those scales include FACES II; measures of empathy, regard, and congru-
ence; several subscales of the Marital Communication Inventory; apprehen-
sion about communication, and marital goal-orientation.
PRIMARY REFERENCE: Eggeman, K., Moxley, V., and Schumm, W. R. (1985).
Assessing spouses' perceptions of Gottman's Temporal Form in marital
conflict, *Psychological Reports*, 57, 171–181.
AVAILABILITY: Journal article.

KMCS

Please use the following scale and indicate how often you and your spouse engage in the activities mentioned in each question. Please indicate how often by recording the number in the space to the left of each item.

1 = Never
2 = Once in a while
3 = Sometimes
4 = Frequently
5 = Almost always

When you and your husband are beginning to discuss a disagreement over an important issue, how often:

___ 1. Do you both begin to understand each other's feelings reasonably quickly?
___ 2. Do you both get your points across to each other without too much trouble?
___ 3. Do you both begin to appreciate each other's points of view on the matter fairly soon?
___ 4. Does your husband seem to be supportive of your feelings about your disagreement?
___ 5. Does your husband tell you that you shouldn't feel the way you do about the issue?
___ 6. Is your husband willing to really hear what you want to communicate?
___ 7. Does your husband insist on contradicting many of your ideas on the issue before he even understands what your ideas are?
___ 8. Does your husband make you feel that your views, even if different from his, are really important to him?
___ 9. Does your husband seem more interested in justifying his own point of view rather than in understanding yours?
___ 10. Does your husband let you feel upset or angry without putting you down for it?
___ 11. Does your husband blame you for any of your feelings of frustration or irritation as if they were mostly your own fault, none of his?

After you and your husband have been discussing a disagreement over an important issue for a while, how often:

___ 1. Are you able to clearly identify the specific things about which you disagree?
___ 2. Are you able to identify clearly the specific things about which you do agree?
___ 3. Are you both able to express how the other feels about the issue?
___ 4. Are you both able to express the other's viewpoint nearly as well as you could your own viewpoint?

     5. Does your husband's *facial* expression and tone of voice convey a sense of:

___ discouragement	
___ anger	___ frustration
___ disgust	___ bitterness
___ condescension	___ self-pity (for himself)
___ resentment	___ cynicism
___ hostility	___ respect toward you

About the time you and your husband feel you are close to a solution to your disagreement over an important issue, how often:

___   1. Are you able to completely resolve it with some sort of compromise that is OK with both of you?

___   2. Do you end up with very little resolved after all?

___   3. Do you quickly bring the matter to a conclusion that is satisfactory for both of you?

___   4. Do you realize the matter will have to be reargued in the near future because at least one of you is still basically unhappy with the apparent solution?

___   5. Do you find that just as soon as you think you have gotten things resolved, your husband comes up with a new idea for resolving the issue?

___   6. Does your husband keep on trying to propose things that are not mutually acceptable ways of resolving the issue at hand?

___   7. Does it seem that no matter what you suggest, your husband keeps on finding new, supposedly better solutions?

___   8. Are you both willing to give and take in order to settle the disagreement?

___   9. Are you and your husband able to give up some of what you wanted in order to bring the issue to a close?

___   10. Are you and your husband able to keep coming closer together on a mutually acceptable solution until you achieve it?

___   11. Are you and your husband able to reach a mutually acceptable contract for resolving the disagreement?

KANSAS MARITAL GOALS ORIENTATION SCALE (KMGOS)

AUTHORS: Kenneth Eggeman, Virginia Moxley, and Walter R. Schumm

PURPOSE: To measure intentionality in a marital relationship

DESCRIPTION: The KMGOS is a 7-item instrument designed to measure intentionality in a couple's marital relationship. Intentionality is defined as the extent to which a couple is working to improve its relationship, now and for the future. The KMGOS was designed to assess one focus of marital enrichment programs, which is to facilitate couples taking a more active role in improving their current and future relationship. The KMGOS is very easy to administer and score and takes only two to three minutes to complete. The reprinted version is for wives; by changing the word "husband" to "wife" on the scale, it will be adapted for husbands.

NORMS: The KMGOS was administered to 10 couples who volunteered to participate in a marriage-enrichment program in Kansas. The wives' mean age was 22.4 (SD = 2.63) and the husbands' mean age was 24.4 (SD = 2.53). Wives averaged 15.5 years of education and husbands 16.2 years. The mean duration of marriage was 19.4 months (SD = 13.8); all subjects were Caucasian except for one Hispanic male. The mean score for husbands was 21.20 (SD = 6.88) and for wives was 21.30 (SD = 5.76).

SCORING: The KMGOS is easily scored by summing the individual items for a potential range of 7 to 35.

RELIABILITY: The KMGOS has very good to excellent internal consistency, with alphas of .94 and .95 for husbands and .86 and .90 for wives. Stability of the KMGOS was excellent, with test-retest correlations of .91 for husbands and .89 for wives.

VALIDITY: The KMGOS has very good concurrent validity with significant correlations for both husbands and wives between the KMGOS and marital conflict scales.

PRIMARY REFERENCE: Eggeman, K., Moxley, V., and Schumm, W. R. (1985). Assessing spouses' perceptions of Gottman's Temporal Form in marital conflict, *Psychological Reports*, 57, 171–181.

AVAILABILITY: Journal article.

KMGOS

1 = Almost never
2 = Once in a while
3 = Sometimes
4 = Frequently
5 = Almost always

_____ 1. How often do you and your husband discuss the way you would like your marriage to be five years from now?

_____ 2. How often do you and your husband make deliberate, intentional changes in order to strengthen your relationship?

_____ 3. How often do you and your husband make specific changes in your priorities in order to enhance your marriage?

_____ 4. To what extent do you think you and your husband agree on long-term goals for your marriage?

_____ 5. How often does your husband make a deliberate effort to learn more about you so he can be more pleasing to you?

_____ 6. How often does your husband consider specific ways in which he can change in order to improve your relationship?

_____ 7. How often do you and your husband discuss the primary objectives you have for your relationship/marriage?

KANSAS MARITAL SATISFACTION SCALE (KMS)

AUTHORS: Walter R. Schumm, Lois A. Paff-Bergen, Ruth C. Hatch, Felix C. Obiorah, Janette M. Copeland, Lori D. Meens, and Margaret A. Bugaighis

PURPOSE: To measure marital satisfaction.

DESCRIPTION: The KMS is a 3-item instrument designed to provide a brief measure of marital satisfaction. The rationale for development of this measure was that other measures of marital satisfaction may be too long for use under certain circumstances. The items for the KMS were designed from the theory that there were conceptual differences between questions on spouses, marriage, and the marital relationship. The KMS is viewed as useful for assessing the satisfaction dimension of marital quality.

NORMS: The KMS was studied with 61 wives randomly selected from a nine-state research project on stress and coping. The respondents had a mean age of 44.5 years (SD = 7.95), mean duration of 22 years of marriage, and a mean education of 14.72 years (SD = 2.79). Item means were 6.21 (SD = .84), 6.11 (SD = .84), and 5.95 (SD = 1.04) for satisfaction with husband as a spouse, with marriage, and with relationship with husband, respectively.

SCORING: The KMS is easily scored by summing the individual item scores for a possible range of 3 to 21, with higher scores reflecting greater satisfaction.

RELIABILITY: The KMS has excellent internal consistency for such a short scale, with an alpha of .93. No test-retest data were reported.

VALIDITY: The KMS has excellent concurrent validity, significantly correlating with the Dyadic Adjustment Scale and the Quality of Marriage Index. The KMS also is correlated with a measure of marital social desirability, suggesting some degree of bias in responses.

PRIMARY REFERENCE: Schumm, W. R., Paff-Bergen, L. A., Hatch, R. C., Obiorah, F. C., Copeland, J. M., Meens, L. D., and Bugaighis, M. A. (1986). Concurrent and discriminant validity of the Kansas Marital Satisfaction Scale, *Journal of Marriage and the Family*, 48, 381–387. Instrument reprinted by permission of the National Council on Family Relations.

AVAILABILITY: Dr. Walter Schumm, Department of Human Development and Family Studies, Justin Hall, Kansas State University, Manhattan, KS 66506-1403.

KMS

	Extremely dissatisfied	Very dissatisfied	Somewhat dissatisfied	Mixed	Somewhat satisfied	Very satisfied	Extremely satisfied
1. How satisfied are you with your marriage?	1	2	3	4	5	6	7
2. How satisfied are you with your husband as a spouse?	1	2	3	4	5	6	7
3. How satisfied are you with your relationship with your husband?	1	2	3	4	5	6	7

Copyright © 1986 National Council on Family Relations.

LIFE DISTRESS INVENTORY (LDI)

AUTHORS: Edwin J. Thomas, Marianne Yoshioka, and Richard D. Ager

PURPOSE: To assess the level of distress associated with 18 areas of life.

DESCRIPTION: This 18-item inventory is a self-rating instrument intended to measure the current level of distress experienced across 18 areas of life. Developed as a clinical research instrument, the LDI has been successfully employed for rapid clinical assessment and monitoring of spouse distress, for evaluating treatment to reduce such distress, and for examining the correlates of life distress. Along with a total score for general distress, subscores may be obtained for five areas based on a factor analysis described below.

NORMS: The LDI was developed on a sample of spouses—primarily white, educated, middle-class females—of alcohol abusers who refused to stop drinking or to enter treatment ($N = 77$). The sample was recruited to receive unilateral family therapy to assist the spouse with the abuser's alcohol problem. Factor analysis indicated that the instrument measures distress related to marital concerns (MC), career concerns (CC), outside activities (OA), self and family (SF), and life satisfaction/optimism (SO). The mean LDI score for general distress was 3.27 (SD = .82). Means for the subscales are given below.

SCORING: Total distress scores are the sum for all items, which can range from 0 to 126. Higher scores reflect greater distress. The factor items are as follows: MC: 1, 2, 3, 16; CC: 8, 9, 13; OA: 10, 11; SF: 4, 5, 6, 7, 14; SO: 17, 18.

RELIABILITY: Test-retest reliability for the total score over a 6-month interval for the 42 spouses who did not receive immediate treatment in the experimental evaluation was $r = .66$, indicating relatively good temporal stability. Internal consistency for the total score was high, with an alpha of .85. Alphas for the subscales indicate fair to good internal consistency: MC = .84, CC = .55, OA = .76, SF = .71, and SO = .77.

VALIDITY: A factor analysis of the LDI produced a five-factor solution described above that explained 52% of the variance. Loadings ranged from .40 to .89 with an average of .63. (Items 8 and 15 were not included in this solution.) The factors provided evidence of content validity for the LDI. The means for the factors indicated more distress for MC (4.9) and SO (4.2), as one would expect for this sample of spouses living with alcohol abusers who resist treatment, than for the other areas (CC = 2.4, OA = 2.8, and SF = 2.7). The LDI was found to correlate positively with the Global Severity Index of the Brief Symptom Inventory, thus supporting its convergent validity, and was not associated with SES, education, or religion, indicating discriminant validity.

PRIMARY REFERENCE: Thomas, E. J., Yoshioka, M. R., and Ager, R. D. (1993). The Life Distress Inventory: Reliability and validity. Manuscript submitted for publication. Instrument reprinted with the permission of Edwin J. Thomas.

AVAILABILITY: Dr. Edwin J. Thomas, University of Michigan, School of Social Work, Ann Arbor, MI 48109-1285.

LDI

This scale is intended to estimate your *current* level of distress with each of the eighteen areas of your life listed below. Please circle one of the numbers (1–7) beside each area. Numbers toward the left end of the seven-unit scale indicate higher levels of distress, while numbers toward the right end of the scale indicate lower levels of distress. Try to concentrate on how distressed you *currently* feel about each area.

	The most distress I've ever felt	Extremely distressed	Very distressed	Moderately distressed	Somewhat distressed	Very little distressed	No distress
Marriage	7	6	5	4	3	2	1
Sex	7	6	5	4	3	2	1
Relationship to spouse	7	6	5	4	3	2	1
Relationship to children	7	6	5	4	3	2	1
Relationship to other relatives	7	6	5	4	3	2	1
Household management	7	6	5	4	3	2	1
Financial situation	7	6	5	4	3	2	1
Employment	7	6	5	4	3	2	1
Education	7	6	5	4	3	2	1
Recreation/leisure	7	6	5	4	3	2	1
Social life	7	6	5	4	3	2	1
Religion	7	6	5	4	3	2	1
Management of time	7	6	5	4	3	2	1
Physical health	7	6	5	4	3	2	1

	The most distress I've ever felt	Extremely distressed	Very distressed	Moderately distressed	Somewhat distressed	Very little distressed	No distress
Personal independence	7	6	5	4	3	2	1
Role of alcohol in home	7	6	5	4	3	2	1
Satisfaction with life	7	6	5	4	3	2	1
Expectations for future	7	6	5	4	3	2	1

Please circle one number for each item.

Copyright © 1992 Edwin J. Thomas and The University of Michigan.

LOCKE-WALLACE MARITAL ADJUSTMENT TEST (LWMAT)

AUTHORS: Harvey J. Locke and Karl M. Wallace

PURPOSE: To measure marital adjustment

DESCRIPTION: This 15-item instrument was one of the first short measures of marital adjustment. Marital adjustment is defined as the accommodation of partners to each other at any given time. The first item is a general index of marital happiness and is given extra weight in scoring. Scores of 100 or less are considered cutting scores, indicating maladjustment in the marital relationship. The instrument is rather global and may not be very helpful in treatment planning where behavioral specificity is important.

NORMS: Normative data are available on a sample of 236 married couples. The sample was predominantly white and was approximately 30 years old. A subsample of "adjusted" respondents had a mean score of 135.9 while a subsample of "maladjusted" respondents had a mean of 71.7.

SCORING: Items are scored with different weights, as indicated on the instrument. Item 12 is scored 10 points if respondents indicate both spouses prefer to "stay at home," 3 points if both spouses prefer to be "on the go" and 2 points if the spouses' preferences differ. Scores are the sum of each item and range from 2 to 158.

RELIABILITY: The internal consistency was estimated using the Spearman-Brown formula and was very good, with a correlation of .90. No information is available on test-retest reliability.

VALIDITY: The LWMAT has evidence of known-groups validity, with scores discriminating between adjusted and maladjusted couples. There is also some evidence of concurrent validity with scores on the instrument correlating with the Locke-Wallace Marital Predictions Test, a measure of predicted future adjustment.

PRIMARY REFERENCE: Locke, H. J. and Wallace, K. M. (1959). Short marital-adjustment and prediction tests: Their reliability and validity, *Marriage and Family Living*, 21, 251–255. Instrument reproduced with permission of Harvey J. Locke and Karl M. Wallace.

AVAILABILITY: Journal article.

LWMAT

1. Circle the dot on the scale line below which best describes the degree of happiness, everything considered, of your present marriage. The middle point, "happy," represents the degree of happiness which most people get from marriage, and the scale gradually ranges on one side to those few who are very unhappy in marriage, and on the other, to those few who experience extreme joy or felicity in marriage.

0	2	7	15	20	25	35
•	•	•	•	•	•	•

Very unhappy			Happy			Perfectly happy

State the approximate extent of agreement or disagreement between you and your mate on the following items by circling a number for each item.

	Always agree	Almost always agree	Occa- sionally disagree	Fre- quently disagree	Almost always disagree	Always disagree
2. Handling family finances	5	4	3	2	1	0
3. Matters of recreation	5	4	3	2	1	0
4. Demonstration of affection	8	6	4	2	1	0
5. Friends	5	4	3	2	1	0
6. Sex relations	15	12	9	4	1	0
7. Conventionality (right, good, or proper conduct)	5	4	3	2	1	0
8. Philosophy of life	5	4	3	2	1	0
9. Ways of dealing with in-laws	5	4	3	2	1	0

10. When disagreements arise, they usually result in:
    0   husband giving in
    2   wife giving in
    10   agreement by mutual give and take

11. Do you and your mate engage in outside interests together?
    10   All of them
    8   Some of them
    3   Very few of them
    0   None of them

12. In leisure time do you generally prefer: to be "on the go"   _____
                                           to stay at home?   _____

    Does your mate generally prefer: to be "on the go"   _____
                                           to stay at home?   _____

13. Do you ever wish you had not married?
    0   Frequently
    3   Occasionally
    8   Rarely
    15   Never

14. If you had your life to live over, do you think you would:
    15   marry the same person
    0   marry a different person
    1   not marry at all

15. Do you confide in your mate:
    0   almost never
    2   rarely
    10   in most things
    10   in everything

MARITAL ALTERNATIVES SCALE (MAS)

AUTHOR: J. Richard Udry

PURPOSE: To measure perceptions of alternatives to marriage.

DESCRIPTION: The MAS is an 11-item instrument designed to measure the perception of how much better or worse off a person would be without his or her present spouse, and how easily that spouse would be replaced with one of comparable quality. The measure is grounded in the theory of spouse "availability" that holds that one is constantly comparing one's "marital bargain" with other possible marital bargains, as well as with potential benefits from not being married at all. Two separate factors were identified: (1) spouse replacement (items 1, 2, and 9 for husbands and wives) and (2) economic level maintenance (items 5, 6, 7, and 10 for husbands and items 5, 7, and 10 for wives). The MAS is seen as a better predictor of marital disruption than marital satisfaction. The forms for men and women are the same except for changing the gender to fit the respondent.

NORMS: The MAS was developed from a series of interviews over three time periods in the 1970s that included 375 to 400 couples. The participants were said to be representative of young, urban, white, low- and middle-income couples in the United States. Specific demographic data were not reported nor were actual norms.

SCORING: Item responses range from 1 to 4 and the MAS is scored by simply summing the items. Higher scores equal greater dissatisfaction. It is also possible to divide scores into categories by dichotomizing the scores of each sex at their respective means (e.g., husband and wife both low or both high, etc.).

RELIABILITY: The MAS has fair internal consistency with split-half reliabilities of .70 for both men and women. No data on stability are provided.

VALIDITY: The MAS has good concurrent and predictive validity significantly predicting disruption (divorce or separation) and significantly correlating with several resources of the self, such as parity, socio-economic status, income and personal appearance, especially for wives.

PRIMARY REFERENCE: Udry, J. R. (1981). Marital Alternatives and Marital Disruption, *Journal of Marriage and the Family*, 43, 889–897. Instrument reprinted by permission of the National Council on Family Relations.

AVAILABILITY: Journal article.

MAS (Wives)

These days it seems like a lot of marriages are breaking up. Of course, this isn't likely, but just suppose your husband were to leave you this year. How likely do you imagine each of the following would be? Decide whether you think each item would be impossible, possible, probable, or certain. (Circle the appropriate number below.)

How likely is it that:	Impossible	Possible, but unlikely	Probable	Certain
1. You could get another man better than he is?	1	2	3	4
2. You could get another man as good as he is?	1	2	3	4
3. You would be quite satisfied without a man?	1	2	3	4
4. You would be sad, but get over it quickly?	1	2	3	4
5. You would be able to live as well as you do now?	1	2	3	4
6. You would be able to take care of yourself?	1	2	3	4
7. You would be better off economically?	1	2	3	4
8. Your prospects for a happy future would be bleak?	1	2	3	4
9. There are many other men you could be happy with?	1	2	3	4
10. You could support yourself at your present level?	1	2	3	4
11. Your life would be ruined?	1	2	3	4

Copyright © 1981 National Council on Family Relations.

MARITAL COMPARISON LEVEL INDEX (MCLI)

AUTHORS: Ronald M. Sabatelli

PURPOSE: To assess spouses' perceptions of their marital relationship.

DESCRIPTION: The MCLI is a 32-item instrument designed to measure an individual's perception of the degree to which his or her marital relationship is living up to his or her expectations. The MCLI can be viewed as a global assessment of the respondent's complaints about his or her marital relationship. It is based on the notion that one complains about some aspect of the marriage only when that aspect fails to meet one's expectations. The items were initially generated from theory based on comprehensive review of the marital satisfaction/adjustment literature. Through factor analysis, with the elimination of four items, the MCLI was found to be unidimensional. In order to assess marital outcomes relative to expectations, each item was scored on a 7-point scale with the midpoint on the scale reflecting the respondent's expectation level. This allows respondents to indicate the degree to which their relationship outcomes fall above or below expectations.

NORMS: A sample of 300 married couples was selected from a Wisconsin university. The sample had a mean age of 36.1 for women and 38 for men, and consisted primarily of upper middle-class, professional families. Means on the MCLI for men were 144.7 and for women 149.7.

SCORING: The MCLI is scored by assigning 1 point to an answer of −3, 2 points to −2, 3 points to −1, 4 points when a person circles "0" (the midpoint), 5 points to +1, 6 points to +2, and 7 when a person circles +3. The individual item scores are then summed, with higher scores indicating more favorable evaluation of outcomes relative to expectations.

RELIABILITY: The MCLI has excellent internal consistency with an alpha of .93. A very low Standard Error of Measurement of 1.38 also indicates excellent reliability. No test-retest data were reported.

VALIDITY: The MCLI has good concurrent validity, correlating significantly with scores on measures of relational equity and marital commitment.

PRIMARY REFERENCE: Sabatelli, R. M. (1984). The Marital Comparison Level Index: A measure for assessing outcomes relative to expectations, *Journal of Marriage and the Family*, 46, 651–662. Instrument reprinted with permission of the National Council on Family Relations.

AVAILABILITY: Dr. Ronald M. Sabatelli, Human Development Center, U 117, Storrs, CT 06268.

MCLI

Indicate by circling the appropriate number how your current experiences compare to your expectations.

−3	−2	−1	0	+1	+2	+3
Worse than I expect			About what I expect			Better than I expect

1. The amount of companionship you experience   −3 −2 −1 0 +1 +2 +3

2. The amount your partner is trusting of you   −3 −2 −1 0 +1 +2 +3

3. The amount of sexual activity that you experience   −3 −2 −1 0 +1 +2 +3

4. The amount of confiding that occurs between you and your spouse   −3 −2 −1 0 +1 +2 +3

5. The amount of conflict over daily decisions that exists   −3 −2 −1 0 +1 +2 +3

6. The amount of time you spend together   −3 −2 −1 0 +1 +2 +3

7. The amount of affection your partner displays   −3 −2 −1 0 +1 +2 +3

8. The amount the responsibility for household tasks is shared   −3 −2 −1 0 +1 +2 +3

9. The amount your partner is willing to listen to you   −3 −2 −1 0 +1 +2 +3

10. The amount of relationship equality you experience   −3 −2 −1 0 +1 +2 +3

11. The amount of conflict over money you experience   −3 −2 −1 0 +1 +2 +3

12. The amount of compatibility that you experience   −3 −2 −1 0 +1 +2 +3

13. The amount of conflict over the use of leisure time that you experience −3 −2 −1 0 +1 +2 +3

14.	The amount of disagreement over friends that you experience	−3	−2	−1	0	+1	+2	+3
15.	The amount of interest in sex your partner expresses	−3	−2	−1	0	+1	+2	+3
16.	The fairness with which money is spent	−3	−2	−1	0	+1	+2	+3
17.	The amount of criticism your partner expresses	−3	−2	−1	0	+1	+2	+3
18.	The amount of mutual respect you experience	−3	−2	−1	0	+1	+2	+3
19.	The degree to which your interpersonal communications are effective	−3	−2	−1	0	+1	+2	+3
20.	The amount of love you experience	−3	−2	−1	0	+1	+2	+3
21.	The degree to which your needs are met	−3	−2	−1	0	+1	+2	+3
22.	The amount of freedom you experience in pursuing other friendships	−3	−2	−1	0	+1	+2	+3
23.	The amount of responsibility your partner accepts for household chores	−3	−2	−1	0	+1	+2	+3
24.	The amount that you and your partner discuss sex	−3	−2	−1	0	+1	+2	+3
25.	The amount of privacy you experience	−3	−2	−1	0	+1	+2	+3
26.	The amount to which your spouse supports your choice of an occupation	−3	−2	−1	0	+1	+2	+3
27.	The amount to which you and your spouse agree on your life-style	−3	−2	−1	0	+1	+2	+3
28.	The amount to which you and your spouse agree on the number of children to have	−3	−2	−1	0	+1	+2	+3
29.	The degree of physical attractiveness of your partner	−3	−2	−1	0	+1	+2	+3
30.	The amount of arguing over petty issues that you experience	−3	−2	−1	0	+1	+2	+3

31. The amount of jealousy your partner   −3   −2   −1   0   +1   +2   +3
    expresses

32. The amount of commitment you   −3   −2   −1   0   +1   +2   +3
    experience from your spouse

Copyright © 1984 National Council on Family Relations.

MARITAL CONVENTIONALIZATION SCALE (MCS)

AUTHOR: Vernon H. Edmonds

PURPOSE: To measure distortion in appraising one's marriage.

DESCRIPTION: The MCS is a 15-item true/false instrument measuring the extent to which a person distorts the appraisal of his or her marriage in the direction of social desirability. The focus of this scale is on "conventionalization," the tendency to act as if something is the case with too little concern about whether it actually is the case. The idea underlying development of the MCS was that conventionalization is a special problem in self-report measures of marital relationships because social approval and consequent ego involvement—the main determinants of conventionalization—are greater here than in any other area of life. While the MCS was developed solely as a research instrument to control for conventionalization in studying marital relationships, the scale may have interesting clinical utility in helping practitioners discover clients' unrealistic or inflated views of their partners—the "pedestal effect."

NORMS: The MCS was studied initially with 100 randomly selected married students from Florida State University, with a mean length of marriage of above five years. No other demographic data were provided. The mean score on the long form of the MCS (50 items) was 12 (SD = 8) and on the 15-item short form, reproduced here, and which correlated about .99 with the long form, was 34 (SD = 30). The short-form scores are weighted (see Scoring, below).

SCORING: Each item that is answered in a conventionalized way is weighted by the figure in the parentheses following the item. Scored responses are True to items 3, 4, 6, 7, 8, 9, 11, 12, 13, and 14 and False to the remainder. Thus, if an individual circled "false" for item 1, the score would be 6 for that item. The weights are proportional to the correlations between each item and the total MCS score on the long form. Individual items are summed for the total score.

RELIABILITY: No data reported.

VALIDITY: The MCS has fair concurrent validity, correlating .63 with the Locke-Wallace Short Scale of Marital Adjustment. The long and short forms also were correlated .44 and .39 respectively with the Lie Scale of the MMPI, a correlation in line with the idea that conventionalization is a form of self-other deception.

PRIMARY REFERENCE: Edmonds, V. H. (1967). Marital conventionalization: Definition and measurement, *Journal of Marriage and the Family*, 29, November 1967, 681–688. Instrument reprinted by permission of the National Council on Family Relations.

AVAILABILITY: Journal article.

MCS

Read each statement and decide whether it is true as applied to you, your mate, or your marriage. If it is true as applied to you, your mate, or your marriage circle the letter T. If it is false as it applies to you, your mate, or your marriage circle the letter F.

T F 1. I have some needs that are not being met by my marriage. (W = 6)

T F 2. My marriage could be happier than it is. (W = 6)

T F 3. If every person in the world of the opposite sex had been available and willing to marry me, I could not have made a better choice (W= 4)

T F 4. I don't think any couple could live together with greater harmony than my mate and I. (W = 5)

T F 5. There are times when I do not feel a great deal of love and affection for my mate. (W = 6)

T F 6. I have never regretted my marriage, not even for a moment. (W = 5)

T F 7. We are as well adjusted as any two persons in this world can be. (W = 6)

T F 8. I don't think anyone could possibly be happier than my mate and I when we are with one another. (W = 6)

T F 9. My mate completely understands and sympathizes with my every mood. (W = 5)

T F 10. My marriage is not a perfect success. (W = 8)

T F 11. Every new thing I have learned about my mate has pleased me. (W = 6)

T F 12. My mate has all of the qualities I've always wanted in a mate. (W = 8)

T F 13. If my mate has any faults I am not aware of them. (W = 8)

T F 14. My mate and I understand each other completely. (W = 8)

T F 15. There are times when my mate does things that make me unhappy. (W = 10)

Copyright © 1967 National Council on Family Relations.

MARITAL HAPPINESS SCALE (MHS)

AUTHORS: Nathan H. Azrin, Barry T. Naster, and Robert Jones

PURPOSE: To measure current levels of marital happiness.

DESCRIPTION: This 10-item instrument was originally designed to test the effects of reciprocity counseling, a behavioral approach to marital counseling. The MHS assesses marital happiness in nine different areas of interaction, with a global single-item index measuring general happiness. Attention is given to the content of each item separately. The instrument seems particularly useful for couples dealing with the distribution of responsibility.

NORMS: Normative data are not available. The instrument was originally tested with 24 couples.

SCORING: Each item can be treated as a separate index of marital happiness for specific areas of marital interaction. Scores, thus, are the item responses having a range from 1 to 10. Scores on all items can be summed to produce a general index of marital happiness, with scores ranging from 10 to 100.

RELIABILITY: Data are not presented in primary reference.

VALIDITY: The couples used in the development of the MHS participated first in catharsis counseling and then in reciprocity counseling. Scores during the first treatment condition were lower than scores during the reciprocity counseling, suggesting the instrument is sensitive to measuring change. No other validity evidence is available.

PRIMARY REFERENCE: Azrin, N. H., Naster, B. J., and Jones, R. (1973). Reciprocity counseling: A rapid learning-based procedure for marital counseling, *Behavioral Research and Therapy*, 11, 365–382. Instrument reproduced with permission of Dr. N. Azrin.

AVAILABILITY: Dr. N. Azrin, 5151 Bayview Drive, Ft. Lauderdale, FL 33308.

MHS

This scale is intended to estimate your *current* happiness with your marriage on each of the ten dimensions listed. You are to circle one of the numbers (1–10) beside each marriage area. Numbers toward the left end of the ten-unit scale indicate some degree of unhappiness and numbers toward the right end of the scale indicate varying degrees of happiness. Ask yourself this question as you rate each marriage area: "If my partner continues to act in the future as he (she) is acting *today* with respect to this marriage area, how happy will I be *with this area of our marriage*?" In other words, state according to the numerical scale (1–10) exactly how you feel today. Try to exclude all feelings of yesterday and concentrate only on the feelings of today in each of the marital areas. Also try not to allow one category to influence the results of the other categories.

	Completely unhappy								Completely happy	
Household responsibilities	1	2	3	4	5	6	7	8	9	10
Rearing of children	1	2	3	4	5	6	7	8	9	10
Social activities	1	2	3	4	5	6	7	8	9	10
Money	1	2	3	4	5	6	7	8	9	10
Communication	1	2	3	4	5	6	7	8	9	10
Sex	1	2	3	4	5	6	7	8	9	10
Academic (or occupational) progress	1	2	3	4	5	6	7	8	9	10
Personal independence	1	2	3	4	5	6	7	8	9	10
Spouse independence	1	2	3	4	5	6	7	8	9	10
General happiness	1	2	3	4	5	6	7	8	9	10

MARITAL INSTABILITY INDEX (MII)

AUTHORS: John N. Edwards, David R. Johnson, and Alan Booth

PURPOSE: To measure marital instability

DESCRIPTION: The MII is a 14-item instrument designed to measure marital instability and, especially, proneness to divorce. The MII is based on the idea that both cognitions and behaviors have to be taken into account when evaluating the instability and potential for divorce of a couple. This scale can be easily administered by an interviewer and scored within a few minutes. The MII is seen as particularly useful the more recently it is administered to the specified cognitions and behaviors. It holds promise as a counseling tool in that it can help the counselor determine with greater accuracy the predicted outcome for a particular marital relationship. The MII is reproduced here (as Part I) along with a measure of several other risk factors (Part II) that the practitioner can administer that can increase its accuracy.

NORMS: The MII was studied initially with 2034 married men and women under 55 years of age in 1980 and with 1578 (78%) of that sample in 1983. No actual norms are reported nor are other demographic data.

SCORING: The MII is easily scored by following the instructions right on the instrument. The number of "divorce prone" answers are summed and recorded at the bottom of the measure where a corresponding "chance of divorce" figure is also presented. An example for using Part II is presented at the end of Part II.

RELIABILITY: The MII has excellent internal consistency with an alpha of .93. No data on stability are reported.

VALIDITY: The MII has very good predictive validity. Of the people reporting no signs of mental instability in 1980, only 3% had permanently dissolved their marriages in 1983, whereas people scoring at the other extreme had a dissolution rate of 27%, 9 times higher. The MII also has been shown to have good construct validity in subsequent research, correlating positively with measures of marital problems and marital "disagrees", and negatively with marital happiness and marital interaction.

PRIMARY REFERENCE: Edwards, J. N., Johnson, D. R., and Booth, A. (1987). Coming apart: A prognostic instrument of marital breakup, *Family Relations*, 36, 168–170. Instrument reprinted by permission of the National Council on Family Relations.

AVAILABILITY: Journal article.

.

MII

Part I. Assessing Divorce Proneness

ASK THE QUESTION FOR EACH INDICATOR AND CIRCLE ONE OF THE ANSWERS GIVEN:

	Not Divorce Prone	*Divorce Prone*
Smetimes married people think they would enjoy living apart from their spouse. How often do you feel this way? Would you say very often, often, occasionally, or never?	Occasionally or never	Very often or often
Even people who get along quite well with their spouse sometimes wonder whether their marriage is working out. Have you thought your marriage might be in trouble within the last 3 years?	No	Yes
As far as you know, has your spouse ever thought your marriage was in trouble?	No	Yes
Have you talked with family members, friends, clergy, counselors, or social workers about problems in your marriage within the last 3 years?	No	Yes
As far as you know, has your (husband/wife) talked with relatives, friends, or a counselor about problems either of you were having with your marriage?	No	Yes
Has the thought of getting a divorce or separation crossed your mind in the last 3 years?	No	Yes
As far as you know, has the thought of divorce or separation crossed your (husband's/wife's) mind in the last 3 years?	No	Yes
Have you or your spouse seriously suggested the idea of divorce in the last 3 years?	No	Yes
Have you talked about dividing up the property?	No	Yes
Have you talked about consulting an attorney?	No	Yes
Have you or your spouse consulted an attorney about a divorce or separation?	No	Yes
Because of problems people are having with their marriage, they sometimes leave home either for a short time or as a trial separation. Has this happened in your marriage within the last 3 years?	No	Yes

	Not Divorce Prone	Divorce Prone
	Occasionally or never	Very often or often
Have you talked with your spouse about filing for divorce or separation?	No	Yes
Have you or your (husband/wife) filed for a divorce or separation petition?	No	Yes

COUNT THE NUMBER OF DIVORCE PRONE ANSWERS
(include "don't know" as a "yes") AND RECORD HERE: _____

CIRCLE THE CHANCES OF DIVORCE IN THE NEXT 3 YEARS AS FOLLOWS:

Proneness to Divorce Score	Chance of Divorce
0–2	22
3–4	26
5–6	31
7–9	38
10+	43

Part II. Attractions and Barriers to Divorce

ASK THE QUESTIONS BELOW AND ADD OR SUBTRACT POINTS FROM THE
CHANCE OF DIVORCE SCORE ACCORDING TO THE ANSWERS.

Below are some of the things couples sometimes do together.
For each one, please tell how often you and your spouse do this
together.

Number
of
Answer

How often do you eat your main meal together—almost always,
usually, occasionally, or never?

    1 Never   2 Occasionally   3 Usually   4 Almost always   _____

How often do you visit friends together?

    1 Never   2 Occasionally   3 Usually   4 Almost always   _____

How often do you work together on projects around the house?

    1 Never   2 Occasionally   3 Usually   4 Almost always   _____

When you go out—say, to play cards, bowling, or a movie—how often do you do this together?

1 Never   2 Occasionally   3 Usually   4 Almost always   _____

ADD THE NUMBERS FOR FREQUENCY OF DOING THINGS TOGETHER. IF THE TOTAL IS BETWEEN 13 AND 16, SUBTRACT 12 FROM DIVORCE CHANCE SCORE AND IF TOTAL IS BETWEEN 9 AND 12, SUBTRACT 10.

NEW DIVORCE CHANCE SCORE   _____

If you had to do it all over again, would you (a) marry the same person, (b) marry someone else, or (c) not marry at all?

IF ANSWER IS NOT MARRY AT ALL (c), ADD 11 TO THE LAST DIVORCE CHANCE SCORE. IF (a) OR (b), PROCEED TO THE NEXT ITEM.

NEW DIVORCE CHANCE SCORE   _____

Do you own or rent your home?

IF HOME IS OWNED, SUBTRACT 6 FROM LAST DIVORCE CHANCE SCORE.

NEW DIVORCE CHANCE SCORE   _____

In general, how much would you say your religious beliefs influence your daily life—very much, quite a bit, some, a little, or none?

IF SOME, QUITE A BIT, OR VERY MUCH, SUBTRACT 4 FROM LAST DIVORCE CHANCE SCORE.

NEW DIVORCE CHANCE SCORE   _____

How many years have you been married to your spouse?

IF COUPLE HAS BEEN MARRIED LESS THAN FIVE YEARS, ADD 3 TO LAST DIVORCE CHANCE SCORE.

FINAL DIVORCE CHANCE SCORE   _____

Example:
A person who scores 1 on the divorce proneness scale would start with a 22% chance of getting a divorce within 3 years. But if a person does a lot of things with his/her spouse (e.g., scores 14 on frequency of doing things together), the probability is lowered by 12 points to 10%. If a couple is buying their home, subtract another 6 points, lowering their divorce proneness to 4%. Finally, if religion has at least some importance in their lives, the score would be reduced to 0.

Copyright © 1987 National Council on Family Relations.

MILLER MARITAL LOCUS OF CONTROL SCALE (MMLOC)

AUTHORS: Philip C. Miller, Herbert M. Lefcourt, and Edward E. Ware

PURPOSE: To measure locus of control in marital relationships.

DESCRIPTION: This 26-item instrument measures locus of control in marital relationships. Internal-external locus of control has been widely researched, and is an important moderator of stress. The MMLOC considers the characteristics of the partners in the relationship that enhance stability and satisfaction. It was developed with sound psychometric procedures. The 26 items were derived from a sample of 78 items that measure four dimensions related to marital outcome: ability, effort, context, and luck. Generally, in the marital relationship, one who scores higher on internality tends to have greater marital satisfaction and intimacy than one who scores higher on externality.

NORMS: Based on a sample of 230 married college students, scores were not significantly different for men and women. Means were 133.42 (SD = 19.83) for men, and 131.43 (SD = 19.59) for women.

SCORING: Total scores are determined by the following formula: 132 + External Score − Internal Score. External score = items 1 + 2 + 4 + 6 + 10 + 12 + 13 + 15 + 17 + 21 + 22 + 24 + 27 + 28 + 30 + 32 + 35 + 37 + 39 + 41 + 42 + 44. Internal score = items 3 + 5 + 7 + 8 + 9 + 11 + 14 + 16 + 18 + 19 + 20 + 23 + 25 + 26 + 29 + 31 + 33 + 34 + 36 + 38 + 40 + 43. Adding a constant and subtracting internal items effectively recodes internal items in the external direction. The four attributional subscale scores are: Effort = 3 + 5 + 7 + 9 + 14 + 18 + 23 + 29 + 31 + 40; Ability = 8 + 11 + 16 + 19 + 20 + 25 + 26 + 33 + 34 + 36 + 38 + 43; Context = 1 + 2 + 6 + 10 + 12 + 13 + 17 + 24 + 27 + 28 + 35 + 37 + 39 + 41 + 42; Luck = 4 + 15 + 21 + 22 + 30 + 32 + 44. Higher scores reflect *externality* for marital locus of control.

RELIABILITY: The MMLOC has very good internal consistency, with an alpha of .83. Data on stability are not reported.

VALIDITY: The MMLOC has evidence of concurrent validity as seen by a correlation with scores on a measure of social intimacy. The validity of the MMLOC is also seen from the correlation between an external locus of control and the discrepancy between husband's and wife's scores, i.e., those respondents who are more external than internal had more discrepancy between their scores. MMLOC scores also correlated with marital satisfaction and general life satisfaction.

PRIMARY REFERENCES: Miller, P. C., Lefcourt, H. M., and Ware, E. E. (1983). The construction and development of the Miller Marital Locus of Control Scale, *Canadian Journal of Behavioral Science*, 15, 266–279. Miller, P. C., Lefcourt, H. M., Holme, J. G., Ware, E. E., and Saleh, W. E. (1986). Marital locus of control and marital problem-solving, *Journal of Personality and Social Psychology*, 51, 161–169. Instrument reproduced with permission of Herbert M. Lefcourt and the Canadian Psychological Association.

AVAILABILITY: Journal article.

MMLOC

The statements in this questionnaire express opinions on a number of issues in the marital relationship. You may find yourself agreeing strongly with some of the statements, disagreeing just as strongly with others and perhaps feeling uncertain about others. Your reactions reflect your own opinions and there are no right or wrong answers. Whether you agree or disagree with any statement, you can be sure that there are many people who feel the same way you do.

Mark each statement in the left margin according to how much you agree or disagree with it. Please mark every one.

Write +1, +2, 0, −1, −2 depending on how you feel in each case.

> +1 = I agree a little
> +2 = I agree very much
> 0 = Neither agree nor disagree
> −1 = I disagree a little
> −2 = I disagree very much

Remember that the best answer is whatever your personal opinion is and this is usually reflected in your *first* reaction to an item, rather than after long debates with yourself over particular experiences.

_____ 1. When I want my spouse to do something she/he hadn't planned on, there's little that I can do to bring her/him around to my way of thinking.

_____ 2. I am often at a loss as to what to say or do when I'm in disagreement with my spouse.

_____ 3. More often than not some effort on my part can help to resolve marital problems.

_____ 4. I can often help to bring about a reconciliation when my spouse and I have an argument.

_____ 5. My spouse's moods are often mysterious to me, in that I have little idea as to what may have set them off.

_____ 6. I often find my spouse's behavior to be unpredictable.

_____ 7. During disagreements I can often do or say something that will improve the situation.

_____ 8. My spouse's behavior is understandable to me.

_____ 9. Happy times in our marriage just seem to happen with little or no effort on my part.

_____ 10. Often my spouse's mood state will be in response to something I've said or done.

_____ 11. There are things I can do that will help to end an argument with my spouse that leave us feeling better.

_____ 12. Circumstances of one sort or another play a major role in determining whether my marriage functions smoothly.

_____ 13. When we're in conflict my spouse will more often be the one to help us become reconciled.

_____ 14. Some effort is usually required on my part in order to bring about pleasant experiences in our marriage.

_____ 15. When we have unpleasant experiences in our marriage I can often see how I have helped to bring them about.

_____ 16. It's more often up to my spouse to make an argument end peaceably.

_____ 17. The unhappy times in our marriage just seem to happen regardless of what I am doing.

_____ 18. When we have difficulties in our marriage there seems to be little that my spouse and I are able to do to bring about a reconciliation.

_____ 19. I can often persuade my spouse to do something that he/she hadn't planned on doing.

_____ 20. Circumstances play a very limited role in causing marital satisfaction; it is largely effort and concern that matter.

_____ 21. I often find that men are more difficult to understand than are women.

_____ 22. When I have difficulties in my interactions with men, I find that time is a better healer than anything I could do.

_____ 23. Men seem less predictable than women.

_____ 24. Women are more perplexing to me than are men.

_____ 25. When I encounter problems in my interactions with women there seems to be little I can do to turn the situation around.

_____ 26. Women are more reliable in their interactions with me than are men.

Copyright © 1983 Canadian Psychological Association.

NON-PHYSICAL ABUSE OF PARTNER SCALE (NPAPS)

AUTHORS: James W. Garner and Walter W. Hudson

PURPOSE: To measure non-physical abuse that clients report they have inflicted on a spouse or partner.

DESCRIPTION: The NPAPS is a 25-item instrument that is designed to measure the degree or magnitude of perceived non-physical abuse that clients report they have inflicted on a spouse or partner. The NPAPS was developed for use with heterosexual or homosexual couples who are dating or living together as married or unmarried couples. This scale is one of the few to examine perceptions of the abuser as to the amount of abuse he or she perceives as inflicting. As such, it can be very useful as a device for tracking the abuser's perceptions over time during an intervention program. Another advantage of the NPAPS is that it is one of several instruments of the WALMYR Assessment Scales package reproduced here, all of which are administered and scored the same way.

NORMS: Not available.

SCORING: Like most WALMYR Assessment Scales instruments, the NPAPS is scored by summing the scores, subtracting the number of completed items, multiplying this figure by 100, and dividing by the number of items completed times 6. This will produce a range from 0 to 100 with higher scores indicating greater magnitude or severity of problems.

RELIABILITY: The NPAPS has excellent internal consistency, with an alpha in excess of .90. Data on stability are not available.

VALIDITY: The NPAPS is reported as having good content and factorial validity, plus beginning evidence of construct validity.

PRIMARY REFERENCE: Hudson, W. W. (1997). *The WALMYR Assessment Scales Scoring Manual.* Tallahassee, FL: WALMYR Publishing Company.

AVAILABILITY: This scale cannot be reproduced or copied in any manner and must be obtained by writing to the WALMYR Publishing Company, PO Box 12217, Tallahassee, FL 32317-2217 or by calling (850) 383-0045.

NON-PHYSICAL ABUSE
OF PARTNER SCALE (NPAPS)

Name: _____ Today's Date: _____

This questionnaire is designed to measure the degree of satisfaction you have with your present marriage. It is not a te
so there are no right or wrong answers. Answer each item as carefully and as accurately as you can by placing a numb
beside each one as follow.

> 1 = None of the time
> 2 = Very rarely
> 3 = A little of the time
> 4 = Some of the time
> 5 = A good part of the time
> 6 = Most of the time
> 7 = All of the time

1. _____ I make fun of my partner's ability to do things.
2. _____ I expect my partner to obey.
3. _____ I become very upset and angry if my partner says that I have been drinking too muc
4. _____ I demand my partner to perform sex acts that he or she does not enjoy or like.
5. _____ I become very upset if my partner's work is not done when I think it should be.
6. _____ I don't want my partner to have any male friends.
7. _____ I tell my partner he or she is ugly and unattractive.
8. _____ I tell my partner that he or she really couldn't manage without me.
9. _____ I expect my partner to hop to it when I give him or her an order.
10. _____ I insult or shame my partner in front of others.
11. _____ I become angry if my partner disagrees with my point of view.
12. _____ I carefully control the money I give my partner.
13. _____ I tell my partner that he or she is dumb or stupid.
14. _____ I demand that my partner stay home.
15. _____ I don't want my partner to work or go to school.
16. _____ I don't want my partner socializing with his or her female friends.
17. _____ I demand sex whether my partner wants it or not.
18. _____ I scream and yell at my partner.
19. _____ I shout and scream at my partner when I'm drinking.
20. _____ I order my partner around.
21. _____ I have no respect for my partner's feelings.
22. _____ I act like a bully towards my partner.
23. _____ I frighten my partner.
24. _____ I treat my partner like he or she is a dimwit.
25. _____ I'm rude to my partner.

Copyright (c) 1992, James W. Garner & Walter W. Hudson   **Illegal to Photocopy or Otherwise Reprodu**

PARTNER ABUSE SCALE: NON-PHYSICAL (PASNP)

AUTHOR: Walter W. Hudson

PURPOSE: To measure perceived non-physical abuse.

DESCRIPTION: The PASNP is a 25-item instrument designed to measure the degree or magnitude of perceived non-physical abuse that clients report they have received from a spouse or partner. The scale is designed to be used by heterosexual or homosexual couples who are dating or living together as married or unmarried couples. Given the importance of this area to clinical practitioners, and the fact that non-physical abuse often is overlooked, this is one of the few short-form scales available for measuring this serious and widespread problem. Another advantage of the PASNP is that it is one of several instruments of the WALMYR Assessment Scales package reproduced here, all of which are administered and scored the same way.

NORMS: Not available.

SCORING: Like most WALMYR Assessment Scales instruments, the PASNP is scored by summing the scores, subtracting the number of completed items, multiplying this figure by 100, and dividing by the number of items completed times 6. This will produce a range from 0 to 100 with higher scores indicating greater magnitude or severity of problems.

RELIABILITY: The PASNP has excellent internal consistency with an alpha in excess of .90. Data on stability are not available.

VALIDITY: The PASNP is reported as having good content and factorial validity along with beginning evidence of construct validity.

PRIMARY REFERENCE: Hudson, W. W. (1997). *The WALMYR Assessment Scales Scoring Manual.* Tallahassee, FL: WALMYR Publishing Company.

AVAILABILITY: This scale cannot be reproduced or copied in any manner and must be obtained by writing to the WALMYR Publishing Company, PO Box 12217, Tallahassee, FL 32317-2217 or by calling (850) 383-0045.

PARTNER ABUSE SCALE: Non-Physical (PASNP)

Name: _____ Today's Date: _____

This questionnaire is designed to measure the non-physical abuse you have experienced in your relationship with your parner. It is not a test, so there are no right or wrong answers. Answer each item as carefully and as accurately as you can placing a number beside each one as follows:

1 = None of the time
2 = Very rarely
3 = A little of the time
4 = Some of the time
5 = A good part of the time
6 = Most of the time
7 = All of the time

1. ____ My partner belittles me.
2. ____ My partner demands obedience to his or her whims.
3. ____ My partner becomes surly and angry if I say he or she is drinking too much.
4. ____ My partner demands that I perform sex acts that I do not enjoy or like.
5. ____ My partner becomes very upset if my work is not done when he or she thinks it sho be.
6. ____ My partner does not want me to have any male friends.
7. ____ My partner tells me I am ugly and unattractive.
8. ____ My partner tells me I couldn't manage or take care of myself without him or her.
9. ____ My partner acts like I am his or her personal servant.
10. ____ My partner insults or shames me in front of others.
11. ____ My partner becomes very angry if I disagree with his or her point of view.
12. ____ My partner is stingy in giving me money.
13. ____ My partner belittles me intellectually.
14. ____ My partner demands that I stay home.
15. ____ My partner feels that I should not work or go to school.
16. ____ My partner does not want me to socialize with my female friends.
17. ____ My partner demands sex whether I want it or not.
18. ____ My partner screams and yells at me.
19. ____ My partner shouts and screams at me when he or she drinks.
20. ____ My partner orders me around.
21. ____ My partner has no respect for my feelings.
22. ____ My partner acts like a bully towards me.
23. ____ My partner frightens me.
24. ____ My partner treats me like a dunce.
25. ____ My partner is surly and rude to me.

Copyright (c) 1992, Walter W. Hudson   **Illegal to Photocopy or Otherwise Reproc**

PARTNER ABUSE SCALE: PHYSICAL (PASPH)

AUTHOR: Walter W. Hudson

PURPOSE: To measure perceived physical abuse.

DESCRIPTION: The PASPH is a 25-item instrument designed to measure the degree or magnitude of perceived physical abuse which clients receive from a spouse or partner. The scale is designed to be used by heterosexual or homosexual couples who are dating or living together as married or unmarried couples. Given the importance of this area to clinical practitioners, this is one of the few short-form scales available to measure this serious and widespread problem. Another advantage of the PASPH is that it is one of several instruments of the WALMYR Assessment Scales package to be reproduced here, all of which are administered and scored the same way.

NORMS: Not available.

SCORING: Like most WALMYR Assessment Scales instruments, the PASPH is scored by summing the scores, subtracting the number of completed items, multiplying this figure by 100, and dividing by the number of items completed times 6. This will produce a range from 0 to 100 with higher scores indicating greater magnitude or severity of problems.

RELIABILITY: The PASPH has excellent internal consistency with an alpha in excess of .90. Data on stability are not available.

VALIDITY: The PASPH is reported as having good content and factorial validity along with beginning evidence in support of construct validity.

PRIMARY REFERENCE: Hudson, W. W. (1997). *The WALMYR Assessment Scales Scoring Manual.* Tallahassee, FL: WALMYR Publishing Company.

AVAILABILITY: This scale cannot be reproduced or copied in any manner and must be obtained by writing to the WALMYR Publishing Company, PO Box 12217, Tallahassee, FL 32317-2217 or by calling (850) 383-0045.

PARTNER ABUSE SCALE: Physical (PASPH)

Name: _____ Today's Date: _____

This questionnaire is designed to measure the physical abuse you have experienced in your relationship with your part
It is not a test, so there are no right or wrong answers. Answer each item as carefully and as accurately as you can by p
ing a number beside each one as follows:

1 = None of the time
2 = Very rarely
3 = A little of the time
4 = Some of the time
5 = A good part of the time
6 = Most of the time
7 = All of the time

1. ____ My partner physically forces me to have sex.
2. ____ My partner pushes and shoves me around violently.
3. ____ My partner hits and punches my arms and body.
4. ____ My partner threatens me with a weapon.
5. ____ My partner beats me so hard I must seek medical help.
6. ____ My partner slaps me around my face and head.
7. ____ My partner beats me when he or she drinks.
8. ____ My partner makes me afraid for my life.
9. ____ My partner physically throws me around the room.
10. ____ My partner hits and punches my face and head.
11. ____ My partner beats me in the face so badly that I am ashamed to be seen in public.
12. ____ My partner acts like he or she would like to kill me.
13. ____ My partner threatens to cut or stab me with a knife or other sharp object.
14. ____ My partner tries to choke or strangle me.
15. ____ My partner knocks me down and then kicks or stomps me.
16. ____ My partner twists my fingers, arms, or legs.
17. ____ My partner throws dangerous objects at me.
18. ____ My partner bites or scratches me so badly that I bleed or have bruises.
19. ____ My partner violently pinches or twists my skin.
20. ____ My partner badly hurts me while we are having sex.
21. ____ My partner injures my breasts or genitals.
22. ____ My partner tries to suffocate me with pillows, towels, or other objects.
23. ____ My partner pokes or jabs me with pointed objects.
24. ____ My partner has broken one or more my bones.
25. ____ My partner kicks my face and head.

Copyright (c) 1992, Walter W. Hudson   Illegal to Photocopy or Otherwise Reprod

PASSIONATE LOVE SCALE (PLS)

AUTHORS: Elaine Hatfield and Susan Sprecher

PURPOSE: To measure passionate love.

DESCRIPTION: The PLS is a 30-item instrument designed to measure passionate love, especially in adolescents. Passionate love is defined by the scale's authors as a state of intense longing for union with another, a state of intense psychological arousal. Passionate love is comprised of at least three components, all of which are represented on the PLS: cognitive, emotional, and behavioral. The PLS was developed by identifying the components of passionate love from the literature and interviews. Then a series of studies was conducted to select the most discriminating items. The PLS is a unidimensional scale that can be very useful in research or in clinical practice for helping focus discussions with clients around skill development for shaping passionate encounters into rewarding relationships. Asterisks indicate items for the short-form PLS.

NORMS: The PLS initially was studied with 60 male and 60 female sociology undergraduates at the University of Wisconsin. Almost all respondents (119) were Caucasian, most were from middle and upper-class families. The mean age was 20.1 years. The mean score for the men was 204.75 (SD = 37.22) and for women was 209.12 (SD = 38.12); this difference was not statistically significant.

SCORING: The PLS is scored by simply summing the individual items for a total score.

RELIABILITY: The PLS has excellent internal consistency, with an alpha of .94. No data on stability were provided.

VALIDITY: The PLS has excellent concurrent validity, correlating significantly with a variety of variables involving love, intimacy, and desire for interactions, including Rubin's Love and Liking scales. The PLS has some degree of construct validity as well, correlating to a significantly greater degree with variables that are most closely related conceptually to the construct of passionate love. The PLS also is free from social desirability response bias.

PRIMARY REFERENCE: Hatfield, E. and Sprecher, S. (1986). Measuring passionate love in intimate relationships, *Journal of Adolescence*, 9, 383–410. Instrument reprinted by permission of Academic Press, Inc., London, England.

AVAILABILITY: Journal article.

PLS

In this questionnaire you will be asked to describe how you feel when you are passionately in love. Some common terms for this feeling are passionate love, infatuation, love sickness, or obsessive love.

Please think of the person whom you love most passionately *right now*. If you are not in love right now, please think of the last person you loved passionately. If you have never been in love, think of the person whom you came closest to caring for in that way. Keep this person in mind as you complete the questionnaire. (The person you choose should be of the opposite sex if you are heterosexual or of the same sex if you are homosexual.) Try to tell us how you felt at the time when your feelings were the most intense. All of your answers will be strictly confidential. Use the following scale, and write the number closest to your response in the space to the left of each statement.

Possible responses to each item range from:

1	2	3	4	5	6	7	8	9
Not at all true				Moderately true				Definitely true

_____ 1. Since I've been involved with _____, my emotions have been on a roller coaster.

_____ *2. I would feel deep despair if _____ left me.

_____ 3. Sometimes my body trembles with excitement at the sight of _____.

_____ 4. I take delight in studying the movements and angles of _____'s body.

_____ *5. Sometimes I feel I can't control my thoughts; they are obsessively on _____.

_____ *6. I feel happy when I am doing something to make _____ happy.

_____ *7. I would rather be with _____ than anyone else.

_____ *8. I'd get jealous if I thought _____ were falling in love with someone else.

_____ 9. No one else could love _____ like I do.

_____ *10. I yearn to know all about _____.

_____ *11.   I want _____—physically, emotionally, mentally.

_____ 12.   I will love _____ forever.

_____ 13.   I melt when looking deeply into _____'s eyes.

_____ *14.   I have an endless appetite for affection from _____.

_____ *15.   For me, _____ is the perfect romantic partner.

_____ 16.   _____ is the person who can make me feel the happiest.

_____ *17.   I sense my body responding when _____ touches me.

_____ 18.   I feel tender toward _____.

_____ *19.   _____ always seems to be on my mind.

_____ 20.   If I were separated from _____ for a long time, I would feel intensely lonely.

_____ 21.   I sometimes find it difficult to concentrate on work because thoughts of _____ occupy my mind.

_____ *22.   I want _____ to know me—my thoughts, my fears, and my hopes.

_____ 23.   Knowing that _____ cares about me makes me feel complete.

_____ *24.   I eagerly look for signs indicating _____'s desire for me.

_____ 25.   If _____ were going through a difficult time, I would put away my own concerns to help him/her out.

_____ 26.   _____ can make me feel effervescent and bubbly.

_____ 27.   In the presence of _____, I yearn to touch and be touched.

_____ 28.   An existence without _____ would be dark and dismal.

_____ *29.   I possess a powerful attraction for _____.

_____ *30.   I get extremely depressed when things don't go right in my relationship with _____.

PHYSICAL ABUSE OF PARTNER SCALE (PAPS)

AUTHORS: James W. Garner and Walter W. Hudson

PURPOSE: To measure physical abuse that clients report they have inflicted on a spouse or partner.

DESCRIPTION: The PAPS is a 25-item instrument that is designed to measure the degree or magnitude of perceived physical abuse that clients report they have inflicted on a spouse or partner. The PAPS was developed for use with heterosexual or homosexual couples who are dating or living together as married or unmarried couples. This scale is one of the few to examine perceptions of the abuser as to the amount of abuse he or she perceives as inflicting. As such, it can be very useful as a device for tracking the abuser's perceptions over time during an intervention program. Another advantage of the PAPS is that it is one of several instruments of the WALMYR Assessment Scales package reproduced here, all of which are administered and scored the same way.

NORMS: Not available.

SCORING: Like most WALMYR Assessment Scales instruments, the PAPS is scored by summing the scores, subtracting the number of completed items, multiplying this figure by 100, and dividing by the number of items completed times 6. This will produce a range from 0 to 100 with higher scores indicating greater magnitude or severity of problems.

RELIABILITY: The PAPS has excellent internal consistency, with an alpha in excess of .90. Data on stability are not available.

VALIDITY: The PAPS is reported as having good content and factorial validity, plus beginning evidence of construct validity.

PRIMARY REFERENCE: Hudson, W. W. (1997). *The WALMYR Assessment Scales Scoring Manual.* Tallahassee, FL: WALMYR Publishing Company.

AVAILABILITY: This scale cannot be reproduced or copied in any manner and must be obtained by writing to the WALMYR Publishing Company, PO Box 12217, Tallahassee, FL 32317-2217 or by calling (850) 383-0045.

PHYSICAL ABUSE OF PARTNER SCALE (PAPS)

Name: _____ Today's Date: _____

This questionnaire is designed to measure the physical abuse you have delivered upon your partner. It is not a test, so there are not right or wrong answers. Answer each item as carefully and as accurately as you can by placing a number beside each one as follows.

1 = Never
2 = Very rarely
3 = A little of the time
4 = Some of the time
5 = A good part of the time
6 = Very frequently
7 = All of the time

1. _____ I physically force my partner to have sex.
2. _____ I push and shove my partner around violently.
3. _____ I hit and punch my partner's arms and body.
4. _____ I threaten my partner with a weapon.
5. _____ I beat my partner so hard he or she must seek medical help.
6. _____ I slap my partner around his or her face and head.
7. _____ I beat my partner when I'm drinking.
8. _____ I make my partner afraid for his or her life.
9. _____ I physically throw my partner around the room.
10. _____ I hit and punch my partner's face and head.
11. _____ I beat my partner in the face so that he or she is ashamed to be seen in public.
12. _____ I act like I would like to kill my partner.
13. _____ I threaten to cut or stab my partner with a knife or other sharp object.
14. _____ I try to choke or strangle my partner.
15. _____ I knock my partner down and then kick or stomp him or her.
16. _____ I twist my partner's fingers, arms or legs.
17. _____ I throw dangerous objects at my partner.
18. _____ I bite or scratch my partner so badly that he or she bleeds or has bruises.
19. _____ I violently pinch or twist my partner's skin.
20. _____ I hurt my partner while we are having sex.
21. _____ I injure my partner's breasts or genitals.
22. _____ I try to suffocate my partner with pillows, towels, or other objects.
23. _____ I poke or jab my partner with pointed objects.
24. _____ I have broken one or more of my partner's bones.
25. _____ I kick my partner's face and head.

Copyright (c) 1992, James W. Garner & Walter W. Hudson   Illegal to Photocopy or Otherwise Reproduce

POSITIVE FEELINGS QUESTIONNAIRE (PFQ)

AUTHORS: K. Daniel O'Leary, Francis Fincham, and Hillary Turkewitz

PURPOSE: To measure positive feelings toward one's spouse.

DESCRIPTION: The PFQ is a 17-item instrument designed to measure positive affect or love toward one's spouse. The PFQ assesses how touching, being alone with a spouse, kissing, and sitting close affect the spouse. The PFQ is written for a seventh grade reading level and is easily administered and scored, making it a very useful measure for couple counseling and therapy.

NORMS: The PFQ has been studied with several samples including 46 men and 46 women recruited from a newspaper ad and 58 men and 56 women described as distressed couples seen at a university marital therapy clinic. Means for community men were 100.52 (SD = 12.4) and for community women were 104.26 (SD = 9.7); means for clinic men were 83.98 (SD = 18.2) and for clinic women were 73.86 (SD = 22.4).

SCORING: The PFQ is easily scored by summing items for a total score.

RELIABILITY: The PFQ has excellent internal consistency with an alpha of .94. Data on stability were not reported.

VALIDITY: The PFQ has very good concurrent validity with significant correlations with the Marital Adjustment Test, Navran Communication Scale, Beck Depression Inventory, spouses' rating of commitment to marriage, and ratings of hypothetical positive actions by their spouses. Women had significantly lower PFQ scores than men in the distressed group but not in the community group. The PFQ also is sensitive to changes due to treatment.

PRIMARY REFERENCE: O'Leary, K. D., Fincham, F., and Turkewitz, H. (1983). Assessment of positive feelings toward spouse, *Journal of Consulting and Clinical Psychology*, 51, 949–951.

AVAILABILITY: K. Daniel O'Leary, Psychology Department, SUNY, Stony Brook, NY 11794.

PFQ

Below is a list of 17 questions about various feelings between engaged/married people. Answer each one of them in terms of how you *generally* feel about your mate/spouse, taking into account the last few months. The rating you choose should reflect how you *actually* feel, not how you think you should feel or would like to feel.

Please answer each question by choosing the best number to show how you have generally been feeling in the past few months. Choose *only one number* for each question.

```
1 = Extremely negative
2 = Quite negative
3 = Slightly negative
4 = Neutral
5 = Slightly positive
6 = Quite positive
7 = Extremely positive
```

1. How do you feel about your spouse as a friend to you? 1 2 3 4 5 6 7

2. How do you feel about the future of your marital relationship? 1 2 3 4 5 6 7

3. How do you feel about marrying/having married your spouse? 1 2 3 4 5 6 7

4. How do you feel about your spouse's ability to put you in a good mood so that you can laugh and smile? 1 2 3 4 5 6 7

5. How do you feel about your spouse's ability to handle stress? 1 2 3 4 5 6 7

6. How do you feel about the degree to which your spouse understands you? 1 2 3 4 5 6 7

7. How do you feel about the degree to which you can trust your spouse? 1 2 3 4 5 6 7

8. How do you feel about how your spouse relates to other people? 1 2 3 4 5 6 7

The following 9 items are in the form of statements rather than questions. However, please complete them in the same manner, remembering to base your responses on how *you generally* feel about your spouse, taking into account the last few months.

1 = Extremely negative
2 = Quite negative
3 = Slightly negative
4 = Neutral
5 = Slightly positive
6 = Quite positive
7 = Extremely positive

1. Touching my spouse makes me feel   1 2 3 4 5 6 7

2. Being alone with my spouse makes me feel   1 2 3 4 5 6 7

3. Having sexual relations with my spouse makes me feel   1 2 3 4 5 6 7

4. Talking and communicating with my spouse makes me feel   1 2 3 4 5 6 7

5. My spouse's encouragement of my individual growth makes me feel   1 2 3 4 5 6 7

6. My spouse's physical appearance makes me feel   1 2 3 4 5 6 7

7. Seeking comfort from my spouse makes me feel   1 2 3 4 5 6 7

8. Kissing my spouse makes me feel   1 2 3 4 5 6 7

9. Sitting or lying close to my spouse makes me feel   1 2 3 4 5 6 7

PRIMARY COMMUNICATION INVENTORY (PCI)

AUTHORS: H. J. Locke, F. Sabaght, and Mary M. Thomes

PURPOSE: To measure marital communication.

DESCRIPTION: The PCI is a 25-item instrument designed to assess marital communication. The overall score on the PCI is a good indicator of the soundness of communication between two members of a couple. Various subscales have been used by different investigators, including verbal and nonverbal communication subscales determined by face validity, and two subscales determined by factor analysis: (1) the individual's perception of his or her own communication ability, and (2) the partner's perception of the individual's communication abilities (Beach and Arias, 1983). In view of the discrepancies regarding the subscales and problems in interpreting them, it is recommended that the overall score be used. Both members of a couple must fill out the PCI for the instrument to be scored accurately.

NORMS: Several studies of the PCI have been conducted with distressed and nondistressed couples. In an early study 24 unhappy married couples were compared with 24 happily married couples. All the couples were from the same socioeconomic class (union workers and their spouses) and their mean age was in the mid-thirties. Mean scores for the happily married husbands and wives were virtually identical, 105.1 and 105.4 respectively. Means for the unhappily married husbands and wives were also similar, 81.6 and 81.1.

SCORING: The PCI is scored by reverse-scoring items 8, 15, and 17, transposing items 5, 6, 7, 9, 11, 13, 15, 21, and 24 from the partner's questionnaire (i.e., an individual's score for each of these items is the rating given by the partner), and then summing all these items for the individual score. Higher scores mean better or more positively viewed communication. (It is also possible to subtract a partner's ratings from the other person's self-ratings to determine dyadic disagreement in the perceptions of the other person's communication ability.)

RELIABILITY: Data are not available.

VALIDITY: The PCI has excellent concurrent validity, correlating strongly and significantly with the Locke-Wallace Marriage Relationship Inventory. The PCI also has excellent known-groups validity, distinguishing in several studies between distressed and nondistressed couples and couples seeking marital therapy and nonclinic couples. The PCI also has been found to be sensitive to changes due to therapeutic interventions.

PRIMARY REFERENCE: Navran, L. (1967). Communication and adjustment in marriage, *Family Process*, 6, 173–184. Instrument reproduced with permission of *Family Process*.

AVAILABILITY: Journal article.

PCI

Below is a list of items on communication between you and your spouse. Using the scale described here, fill in the blank space next to each item with the number which best represents the extent to which you and your spouse behave in the specified way.

$$1 = \text{Never}$$
$$2 = \text{Seldom}$$
$$3 = \text{Occasionally}$$
$$4 = \text{Frequently}$$
$$5 = \text{Very frequently}$$

_____ 1. How often do you and your spouse talk over pleasant things that happen during the day?

_____ 2. How often do you and your spouse talk over unpleasant things that happen during the day?

_____ 3. Do you and your spouse talk over things you disagree about or have difficulties over?

_____ 4. Do you and your spouse talk about things in which you are both interested?

_____ 5. Does your spouse adjust what he/she says and how he/she says it to the way you seem to feel at the moment?

_____ 6. When you start to ask a question, does your spouse know what it is before you ask it?

_____ 7. Do you know the feelings of your spouse from his/her facial and bodily gestures?

_____ 8. Do you and your spouse avoid certain subjects in conversation?

_____ 9. Does your spouse explain or express himself/herself to you through a glance or gesture?

_____ 10. Do you and your spouse discuss things together before making an important decision?

_____ 11. Can your spouse tell what kind of day you have had without asking?

_____ 12. Your spouse wants to visit some close friends or relatives. You don't particularly enjoy their company. Would you tell him/her this?.

_____ 13. Does your spouse discuss matters of sex with you?

_____ 14. Do you and your spouse use words which have a special meaning not understood by outsiders?

_____ 15. How often does your spouse sulk or pout?

_____ 16. Can you and your spouse discuss your most sacred beliefs without feelings of restraint or embarrassment?

_____ 17. Do you avoid telling your spouse things that put you in a bad light?

_____ 18. You and your spouse are visiting friends. Something is said by the friends which causes you to glance at each other. Would you understand each other?

_____ 19. How often can you tell as much from the tone of voice of your spouse as from what he/she actually says?

_____ 20. How often do you and your spouse talk with each other about personal problems?

____ 21. Do you feel that in most matters your spouse knows what you are trying to say?

____ 22. Would you rather talk about intimate matters with your spouse than with some other person?

____ 23. Do you understand the meaning of your spouse's facial expressions?

____ 24. If you and your spouse are visiting friends or relatives and one of you starts to say something, does the other take over the conversation without the feeling of interrupting?

____ 25. During marriage, have you and your spouse, in general, talked most things over together?

RELATIONSHIP ASSESSMENT SCALE (RAS)

AUTHOR: Susan S. Hendrick

PURPOSE: To measure relationship satisfaction.

DESCRIPTION: The RAS is a 7-item instrument designed to measure satisfaction in relationships. This measure was designed to be a brief, easily administered and scored measure of satisfaction in romantic relationships in general. It is not limited to marital relationships, and can be used to give a clinician a good estimate of relationship satisfaction that is more informative than just a single item.

NORMS: The RAS was studied initially with two samples of college students; the first was 235 undergraduates (118 males, 117 females) enrolled in psychology courses in a southwestern university, and the second was 57 dating couples at that university. For sample 1, the mean score was 29.14 (SD = 6.4). For sample 2, the mean for couples that subsequently stayed together was 4.34 and for those who broke up was 3.33.

SCORING: After reverse-scoring items 4 and 7, items are summed for a total score (A = 1, E = 5). Scores can range from 7 (low satisfaction) to 35 (high satisfaction).

RELIABILITY: The RAS has very good internal consistency, with an alpha of .86. No data on stability were reported.

VALIDITY: The RAS has good concurrent validity, with significant correlations with a number of the subscales of the love attitudes scale and Dyadic Adjustment Scale. The RAS also has good predictive validity, significantly distinguishing between couples who subsequently stayed together or broke up.

PRIMARY REFERENCE: Hendrick, S. S. (1988). A generic measure of relationship satisfaction, *Journal of Marriage and the Family*, 50, 93–98. Instrument reprinted by permission of the National Council on Family Relations.

AVAILABILITY: Dr. Susan Hendrick, Department of Psychology, Texas Tech University, Lubbock, TX 79409.

RAS

Please mark on the answer sheet the letter for each item which best answers that item for you:

1. How well does your partner meet your needs?

A	B	C	D	E
Poorly		Average		Extremely well

2. In general, how satisfied are you with your relationship?

A	B	C	D	E
Unsatisfied		Average		Extremely satisfied

3. How good is your relationship compared to most?

A	B	C	D	E
Poor		Average		Excellent

4. How often do you wish you hadn't gotten in this relationship?

A	B	C	D	E
Never		Average		Very often

5. To what extent has your relationship met your original expectations?

A	B	C	D	E
Hardly at all		Average		Completely

6. How much do you love your partner?

A	B	C	D	E
Not much		Average		Very much

7. How many problems are there in your relationship?

A	B	C	D	E
Very few		Average		Very many

Copyright © 1988 National Council on Family Relations.

RELATIONSHIP EVENTS SCALE (RES)

AUTHORS: Charles E. King and Andrew Christensen

PURPOSE: To measure courtship progress.

DESCRIPTION: The RES is a 19-item instrument designed to measure courtship progress, reflecting increasing intimacy, interdependence, and commitment in dating relationships. The RES is based on the ideas that progress in courtship is indicated by certain important events, that couples can reliably report on these events, and that courtship progress is unidimensional. A Guttman scale technique was used wherein items are ranked in a hierarchy so that endorsement of an item high on the scale is expected to produce endorsement of all items ranked lower. The RES is a useful measure for evaluating the progress of dating couples.

NORMS: Tho RES was initially studied with 222 female and 136 male volunteers who were currently involved in a romantic relationship. All were enrolled in introductory psychology courses at the University of California (Los Angeles). The mean age was 18.2; 80% were freshmen. Half of the respondents had been dating their partners less than 6 months. The mean for the entire sample was 3.48 (SD = 1.52) with a mode and median of 4.

SCORING: The RES is divided into six levels. To pass each level, one or two items must be indicated as "true." For each level passed, the respondent is given a score of 1. This results in a range of scores from 0 (did not pass any levels) to 6 (passed all levels). The levels, items, and "pass criteria" are: level 1—items 1, 7, 8, 14, 16, (pass 2); level 2—items 12, 15, 18 (pass 1); level 3—items 2, 3, 9, 11 (pass 2); level 4—items 4, 17 (pass 1); level 5—items 6, 10, 13 (pass 2); level 6—items 5, 19 (pass 1).

RELIABILITY: The RES has excellent reproducibility, with a coefficient of .942. There is a median of 93% agreement between couples in one sample, with a median Kappa of .55 (an index of agreement adjusted for chance agreement). The correlation between male and female scores of members of couples was .81.

VALIDITY: The RES has very good concurrent validity, with significant correlations with the Love Scale and with measures of durability, commitment, and emotional involvement. The RES also has very good predictive validity, with significant associations between RES scores and the outcome of relationships (those with lower RES scores were less likely to survive).

PRIMARY REFERENCE: King, C. A. and Christensen, A. (1983). The Relationship Events Scale: A Guttman scaling of progress in courtship, *Journal of Marriage and the Family*, 45, 671–678. Instrument reprinted by permission of the National Council on Family Relations.

AVAILABILITY: Dr. Andrew Christensen, Department of Psychology, University of California (Los Angeles), Los Angeles, CA 90024.

RES

Listed below are events that occur in many relationships. Mark the item T (true) if the event has ever happened in your relationship or F (false) if the event has not happened in your relationship.

_____ 1. My partner has called me an affectionate name (sweetheart, darling, etc.)
_____ 2. My partner has said "I love you" to me.
_____ 3. My partner does not date anyone other than myself.
_____ 4. We have discussed the possibility of getting married.
_____ 5. We have lived together or we live together now.
_____ 6. I have lent my partner more than $20 for more than a week.
_____ 7. I have called my partner an affectionate name (sweetheart, darling, etc.)
_____ 8. We have felt comfortable enough with each other so that we could be together without talking or doing an activity.
_____ 9. I do not date anyone other than my partner.
_____ 10. We have spent a vacation together that lasted longer than three days.
_____ 11. I have said "I love you" to my partner.
_____ 12. I have referred to my partner as my girlfriend/boyfriend.
_____ 13. My partner has lent me more than $20 for more than a week.
_____ 14. We have spent a whole day with just each other.
_____ 15. My partner has referred to me as his/her girlfriend/boyfriend.
_____ 16. We have arranged to spend time together without planning any activity.
_____ 17. We have discussed living together.
_____ 18. We have received an invitation for the two of us as a couple.
_____ 19. We are or have been engaged to be married.

Copyright © 1983 National Council on Family Relations.

SEMANTIC DIFFERENTIAL OF SEX ROLES (SDSR)

AUTHOR: R. Julian Hafner

PURPOSE: To measure three aspects of sex roles in marital relationships.

DESCRIPTION: This 15-item instrument measures sex roles in a marital relationship. The instrument is completed four times in response to four "concepts": "Myself as I AM" (actual self, AS), "Myself as I would like to BE" (ideal self, IS), "My partner as he/she IS" (actual partner, AP) and "My partner as I would like him/her to BE" (ideal partner, IP). Forms of the SDSR are changed by recording a different "concept" in the space provided at the top of the instrument. The SDSR has three subscales: power (items a, d, g, j, l, n); empathy (items b, e, h, k, m, o) and autonomy (items c, f, i). Subscale scores for the four different "concepts" are used four different ways: one, as a measure of overt marital dissatisfaction (IP scores minus AP scores); two, as a measure of dissatisfaction with oneself (IS minus AS scores); three, as a measure of sex role stereotyping and androgyny (as reflected in higher scores on all three of the subscale scores for each of the separate "concepts"); and four, as a measure of denied marital conflict (one partner's AS scores minus the other partner's AP scores, where greater discrepancy reflects marital problems).

NORMS: Means and standard deviations are available from a sample of 68 married couples for each of the 15 words in the SDSR. The subscales of power, empathy, and autonomy had means and standard deviations of 24.6 (8.9), 29.8 (7.9), 16.7 (5.7) for males' AS raw scores, and 21.8 (8.0), 26.4 (5.9), 14.7 (4.0) for females' AS raw scores. Means and standard deviations for the three subscales were 22.6 (8.3), 32.5 (8.1), 14.7 (4.2) for males' AP concept and 25.2 (8.8), 31.3 (7.7), 17.3 (3.6) for females' AP concept. No other normative data are available.

SCORING: Subscales scores are the sum of each subscale item score; these raw scores are then divided by the number of items in the subscale to produce a score ranging from 1 to 7. Higher scores reflect more power, empathy, and autonomy.

RELIABILITY: Reliability data are not reported in the primary reference.

VALIDITY: The SDSR has evidence of concurrent validity as it correlates with measures of marital adjustment, self-concept, and sex roles. A similar semantic differential measure predicted outcome of therapy for couples with an agoraphobic member.

PRIMARY REFERENCE: Hafner, R. J. (1984). The marital repercussions of behavior therapy for agoraphobia, *Psychotherapy*, 21, 530–542. Instrument reproduced with permission of R. Julian Hafner.

AVAILABILITY: R. Julian Hafner. M.D., Didner Research Unit, Glenside Hospital, 226 Fullarton Road, Eastwood S.A. 5063 Australia.

SDSR

The fifteen attributes listed here allow you to describe _____. Place an X in *ONE* of the seven boxes in line with each attribute.

	Never	Rarely	Sometimes	Half the time	Often	Nearly always	Always
	1	2	3	4	5	6	7
a. Assertive							
b. Sympathetic							
c. Self-reliant							
d. Strong personality							
e. Understanding							
f. Independent							
g. Forceful							
h. Compassionate							
i. Self-sufficient							
j. Dominant							

176

	Never	Rarely	Sometimes	Half the time	Often	Nearly always	Always
	1	2	3	4	5	6	7
k. Warm	|	|	|	|	|	|	|
l. Aggressive	|	|	|	|	|	|	|
m. Tender	|	|	|	|	|	|	|
n. Acts as leader	|	|	|	|	|	|	|
o. Gentle	|	|	|	|	|	|	|

SPOUSE ENABLING INVENTORY (SEI)

AUTHORS: Edwin J. Thomas, Marianne R. Yoshioka, and Richard D. Ager

PURPOSE: To assess spouse behaviors that enable alcohol use of a marital partner.

DESCRIPTION: This 47-item instrument asks respondents to rate the frequency with which they engage in 47 specific behaviors or activities that can enable alcohol use of a marital partner. Developed as a clinical and research instrument, the SEI has been successfully employed for rapid clinical assessment and monitoring of spouse enabling, for evaluating intervention to reduce such enabling, and for examining the correlates of spouse enabling. In addition to a total enabling score, the instrument provides scores for Type I enabling, consisting of those behaviors that serve to accelerate potential increasers of the marital partner's drinking (e.g., suggesting attending events where alcoholic beverages are served); and Type II enabling, comprised of behaviors that serve to decelerate potential decreasers of partner drinking (e.g., calling in sick for the drinker when he or she misses work because of the drinking).

NORMS: The SEI was developed on a sample of spouses—primarily white, educated, middle-class females—of alcohol abusers unmotivated to stop drinking or to enter treatment ($N = 74$). The sample was recruited to receive unilateral family therapy to assist the spouse with the abuser's alcohol problem. The mean total enabling score was 1.60 (SD = 37) for this sample, with subscore means of 1.71 (SD = .54) for Type I enabling and 1.56 (SD = .40) for Type II enabling.

SCORING: Score values range from 1 (always) to 5 (never), which are reversed in scoring (e.g., 1 = 5, 2 = 4, etc.). Scores are determined by summing item scores, which range from 0 to 235, and dividing by the number of items. Item numbers for the Type I subscale are 1, 2, 7, 8, 9, 10, 11, 14, 15, 28, 29, 30, 31, 32, 44, 46, and 47; the rest of the items comprise the Type II subscale.

RELIABILITY: The SEI has good to excellent internal consistency, with alphas of .89 for the total score, .90 for Type I enabling, and .86 for Type II enabling. Test-retest coefficients computed over a six-month interval were available for subjects who did not receive immediate treatment in the evaluation experiment ($N = 42$). The correlations were .70 for the total score, .79 for Type I enabling, and .72 for Type II enabling, suggesting very good stability.

VALIDITY: The items were based upon inductively derived instances of enabling behavior or activities of spouses of alcohol abusers. Content validity of the scale is further indicated by the logical relationship of each item to one or the other of the two theoretical types of enabling. Construct validity was indicated by (a) the results of an analysis of factorial validity, and (b) a factor analysis, accounting for 50% of the extracted variance, that disclosed that 5 of the 6 factors clearly fell into either Type I or Type II enabling. Drawing on a set of variables correlated differentially with the types of enabling, multiple regression analyses indicated that the predictors of Type I enabling (e.g., spouse alcohol consumption and marital happiness scores) were different from those of Type II enabling (e.g., hypomania, perception of being trapped, and depression).

PRIMARY REFERENCE: Thomas, E. J., Yoshioka, M. R., and Ager, R. D. (1993). The Spouse Enabling Inventory: Reliability and validity. Manuscript submitted for publication. Instrument reproduced with the permission of Edwin J. Thomas.

AVAILABILITY: Dr. Edwin J. Thomas, University of Michigan School of Social Work, Ann Arbor, MI 48109-1285.

SEI

This checklist is intended to provide us with information about aspects of your behavior as it relates to your marital partner's drinking. The behaviors in the list below are among those that many spouses engage in. Please indicate how often you have engaged in each of these behaviors in the past six months by circling your response for each question. This is not a test, so there are no right or wrong answers

AS IT INVOLVES THE DRINKER IN THE LAST SIX MONTHS, HOW OFTEN HAVE YOU:	Always	Frequently	Occasionally	Rarely	Never
1. Told amusing stories about others who drank a lot	1	2	3	4	5
2. Spoken admiringly of the ability of others to hold their drink	1	2	3	4	5
3. Had the drinker's car repaired after an alcohol-related accident	1	2	3	4	5
4. Paid fines for drunk driving offenses	1	2	3	4	5
5. Bailed the drinker out of jail because of a drink-related offense	1	2	3	4	5
6. Returned beer bottles and/or collected and washed glasses used for drinking by the drinker	1	2	3	4	5
7. Suggested that the drinker attend activities where alcohol was to be served	1	2	3	4	5
8. Invited friends over to drink	1	2	3	4	5
9. Gone to bars with the drinker	1	2	3	4	5
10. Bought alcohol and kept it in the home	1	2	3	4	5
11. Served alcohol with meals or snacks	1	2	3	4	5
12. Helped the drinker find his/her things lost while drunk	1	2	3	4	5

AS IT INVOLVES THE DRINKER IN THE LAST SIX MONTHS, HOW OFTEN HAVE YOU:	Always	Frequently	Occasionally	Rarely	Never
13. Provided the drinker with clean clothes after he/she soiled them due to use of alcohol	1	2	3	4	5
14. Gone to drinking parties with the drinker	1	2	3	4	5
15. Arranged parties where alcohol was served and which were attended by the drinker	1	2	3	4	5
16. Made hangover remedies	1	2	3	4	5
17. Cleaned up alcohol-related messes (e.g., spilled drinks, vomit, urine)	1	2	3	4	5
18. Tended to the drinker's alcohol-related injuries	1	2	3	4	5
19. Put the drinker to bed when he/she has been drinking	1	2	3	4	5
20. Avoided social contact with friends to cover up the drinking	1	2	3	4	5
21. Avoided relationships with neighbors and others who might drop in, to cover up the drinking	1	2	3	4	5
22. Avoided social contact with the extended family to cover up the drinking	1	2	3	4	5
23. Encouraged children to be silent about the drinking	1	2	3	4	5
24. Called the drinker's place of employment to say he/she was sick when he/she could not or would not go to work because of the drinking	1	2	3	4	5
25. Taken responsibility for awakening the drinker the morning after a night of drinking so that he/she would not be late for work	1	2	3	4	5

AS IT INVOLVES THE DRINKER IN THE LAST SIX MONTHS, HOW OFTEN HAVE YOU:	Always	Frequently	Occasionally	Rarely	Never
26. Canceled appointments and social engagements for the drinker because of his/her drinking	1	2	3	4	5
27. Made excuses for the drinker's behavior when he/she was drunk or had been drinking	1	2	3	4	5
28. Taken responsibility for keeping his/her drinks cold (e.g., beer, wine, mixers)	1	2	3	4	5
29. Spoken admiringly of the drinker's ability to hold his/her drink	1	2	3	4	5
30. Bought devices especially for the drinker such as shot glasses, bottle openers, drinking glasses	1	2	3	4	5
31. Said the drinker behaved better when drinking (e.g., is easier to get along with)	1	2	3	4	5
32. Offered drinks to the drinker	1	2	3	4	5
33. Given him/her something to eat when he/she got drunk to reduce the effects of the drinking	1	2	3	4	5
34. Explained, justified, or made excuses to the drinker for the drinker's drinking	1	2	3	4	5
35. Explained, justified, or made excuses to others for the drinker's drinking	1	2	3	4	5
36. Reassured the drinker that his/her inappropriate and/or embarrassing behavior when under the influence of alcohol was not all that bad	1	2	3	4	5
37. Comforted the drinker about his/her feelings of guilt about drinking	1	2	3	4	5

AS IT INVOLVES THE DRINKER IN THE LAST SIX MONTHS, HOW OFTEN HAVE YOU:	Always	Frequently	Occasionally	Rarely	Never
38. Said to the drinker or others that the amount of alcohol drunk was less than actually was drunk	1	2	3	4	5
39. Softened or covered up the obvious signs of alcohol abuse (e.g., blackouts, tremors, puffy face, bloodshot eyes, hangovers)	1	2	3	4	5
40. Minimized the seriousness of the drinking (e.g., ignored it, said it was not a problem, said the drinker could control it when he/she could not)	1	2	3	4	5
41. Minimized the consequences of drinking	1	2	3	4	5
42. Concealed his/her drinking from others	1	2	3	4	5
43. Cut down on household expenses (e.g., groceries) to provide drinking money for the drinker	1	2	3	4	5
44. Given the drinker money for drinking	1	2	3	4	5
45. Consumed alcoholic beverages with the drinker	1	2	3	4	5
46. Told the drinker it was OK with you that he/she drank	1	2	3	4	5
47. Suggested to the drinker that he/she have a drink	1	2	3	4	5

Copyright © 1988 by Edwin J. Thomas, Marianne Yoshioka, Richard Ager, and the University of Michigan.

SPOUSE SOBRIETY INFLUENCE INVENTORY (SSII)

AUTHORS: Edwin J. Thomas, Marianne Yoshioka, and Richard D. Ager

PURPOSE: To assess spouse efforts intended to change the partner's drinking behavior.

DESCRIPTION: This 52-item inventory is intended to assess two separate aspects of spouse efforts to change the partner's drinking behavior. The 45-item Drink Control Scale (DCS) measures spouse efforts intended to control the partner's drinking (e.g., nagging or punishing the partner for drinking); and the 7-item Sobriety Support Scale (SSS) measures spouse efforts intended to increase nondrinking behaviors (e.g., suggesting non-alcohol-related activities). Developed as a clinical and research instrument, the SSII has been successfully employed for rapid clinical assessment and monitoring of each aspect of spouse sobriety influence, for evaluating interventions relating to such behaviors, and for examining the correlates of each aspect of sobriety influence.

NORMS: The SSII was developed on a sample of spouses—primarily white, educated, middle-class females—of alcohol abusers who were unmotivated to stop drinking or to enter treatment ($N = 74$). The sample was recruited to receive unilateral family therapy for the marital partner's alcohol problem. The sample means were 2.32 (SD = .50) on the DCS and 2.85 (SD = .69) on the SSS.

SCORING: The scores range from 1 (always) to 5 (never), which are reversed in scoring (e.g., 1 = 5, 2 = 4, etc.). Item numbers in the SSS are 13, 15, 16, 20, 28, 29, and 31; the rest of the items compose the DCS. Only separate scores for the DCS or the SSS are used, not total scores for the SSII.

RELIABILITY: The internal consistency of the DCS was excellent (alpha = .92) and moderate for the SSS (alpha = .72; N =74). Test-retest coefficients computed over a six-month interval were available for subjects who did not receive immediate treatment in the evaluation experiment ($N = 42$). The scores were $r = .75$ for the DCS and $r = .51$ for the SSS, suggesting very good stability.

VALIDITY: In support of their content validity, the items were based on a sample of inductively derived instances of sobriety influence of spouses of uncooperative alcohol abusers. Items were then assigned by logical analysis to one or the other of the two SSII scales corresponding to the two types of sobriety influence. Empirical findings from an analysis of factorial validity supported the item assignment. In support of construct validity, the DCS was negatively related to measures of marital happiness and adjustment and positively related to measures of life distress and psychopathology, whereas SSS was unrelated to these measures.

PRIMARY REFERENCE: Thomas, E. J., Yoshioka, M. R., and Ager, R. D. (1993). The Spouse Sobriety Influence Inventory: Theory and measurement. Manuscript submitted for publication. Instrument reprinted with permission of Edwin J. Thomas. For additional discussion of the inventory, see the following reference: Yoshioka, M. R., Thomas, E. D., and Ager, R. D. (1992). Nagging and other drinking control efforts of spouses of uncooperative alcohol abusers: Assessment and modification, *Journal of Substance Abuse*, 4, 309–318.

AVAILABILITY: Dr. Edwin J. Thomas, University of Michigan School of Social Work Ann Arbor, MI 48109-1285.

SSII

This questionnaire is designed to measure aspects of your relationship with your spouse as they involve ways by which you have tried to get your spouse to stop or reduce his/her drinking. Listed below are different ways many spouses have tried to get their marital partner to stop or reduce his/her drinking. Please indicate how often in the past six months you have engaged in each of the following behaviors by circling the number of your response for each question. This is not a test, so there are no right or wrong answers.

IN THE PAST SIX MONTHS, HOW OFTEN HAVE YOU:	Always	Frequently	Occasionally	Rarely	Never
1. Given the drinker written information about the harmful effects of alcohol (e.g., pamphlets, books)?	1	2	3	4	5
2. Expressed disapproval of the drinking?	1	2	3	4	5
3. Asked the drinker to stop or reduce his/her drinking?	1	2	3	4	5
4. Reminded the drinker of the things he/she said or did when he/she was drunk or had been drinking?	1	2	3	4	5
5. Spoke to the drinker before he/she went out in order to get him/her to drink less or not at all in that situation?	1	2	3	4	5
6. Encouraged the drinker to enter an alcohol treatment program, seek medical assistance, or to attend an alcohol education program?	1	2	3	4	5
7. Sought professional help yourself about the drinking problem (e.g., went to a physician, psychologist, psychiatrist, counselor, social worker, or clergy member)?	1	2	3	4	5
8. Hidden or threw out alcohol?	1	2	3	4	5

IN THE PAST SIX MONTHS, HOW OFTEN HAVE YOU:	Always	Frequently	Occasionally	Rarely	Never
9. Hidden money or the checkbook or spent all the money so that there was little left for alcohol?	1	2	3	4	5
10. Hit or tried to hurt the drinker physically to make him/her stop drinking?	1	2	3	4	5
11. Made a rule that the drinker cannot drink in the house?	1	2	3	4	5
12. Tried to get the drinker to reduce his/her drinking while at a social function (e.g., a party, bar, or club) or to leave a social function before he/she became drunk?	1	2	3	4	5
13. Told the drinker that you enjoyed his/her company when he/she was not drinking?	1	2	3	4	5
14. Served meals at a different time to interrupt the drinker's drinking?	1	2	3	4	5
15. Suggested or served the drinker non-alcoholic beverages instead of alcoholic beverages?	1	2	3	4	5
16. Suggested activities that do not involve alcohol?	1	2	3	4	5
17. Hidden valuables or household things so that the drinker could not pawn or sell them to buy alcohol?	1	2	3	4	5
18. Cut back on your own drinking to set a good example for the drinker?	1	2	3	4	5
19. Questioned the drinker regarding his/her whereabouts or how money was spent when you suspected that he/she had been drinking?	1	2	3	4	5

IN THE PAST SIX MONTHS, HOW OFTEN HAVE YOU:	Always	Frequently	Occasionally	Rarely	Never
20. Praised the drinker for not drinking or for a reduction in drinking?	1	2	3	4	5
21. Tried to stop the drinker from drinking too much by creating a scene or by attempting to make him/her feel small or ridiculous in public?	1	2	3	4	5
22. Shown the drinker that his/her drinking is making you upset or ill?	1	2	3	4	5
23. Withheld Information as punishment for the drinking?	1	2	3	4	5
24. Had arguments about problems related to the drinking?	1	2	3	4	5
25. Requested that you or someone else accompany the drinker as a means of controlling his/her drinking?	1	2	3	4	5
26. Avoided entertaining to prevent the opportunities to drink?	1	2	3	4	5
27. Prevented drinking friends from coming to the house?	1	2	3	4	5
28. Suggested that you eat in restaurants which do not serve alcohol?	1	2	3	4	5
29. Suggested social activities at which alcohol is not available?	1	2	3	4	5
30. Tried to stop the drinker from drinking too much by inviting friends or relatives in?	1	2	3	4	5
31. Tried to stop the drinker from drinking too much by getting him/her to engage in social activities with nondrinking companions?	1	2	3	4	5

IN THE PAST SIX MONTHS, HOW OFTEN HAVE YOU:	Always	Frequently	Occasionally	Rarely	Never
32. Tried to stop the drinker from drinking too much by getting him/her to reduce the number of social activities with drinking companions?	1	2	3	4	5
33. Threatened to contact someone for help to try to stop him/her from drinking?	1	2	3	4	5
34. Asked his/her employer or supervisor to step in?	1	2	3	4	5
35. Checked his/her whereabouts to see if he/she was drinking?	1	2	3	4	5
36. Tried to reduce problems or stress for the drinker so that he/she would drink less?	1	2	3	4	5
37. Tried to stop him/her from drinking too much by actually getting drunk yourself?	1	2	3	4	5
38. Refused to talk to the drinker when he/she was drunk or had been drinking?	1	2	3	4	5
39. Said that if the drinker loved you or the children he/she would stop drinking?	1	2	3	4	5
40. Told the drinker that the children would lose their respect for him/her because of the drinking?	1	2	3	4	5
41. Told the drinker that you were hurt by the drinking or by what he/she did when drinking?	1	2	3	4	5
42. Made sarcastic remarks about the drinking?	1	2	3	4	5
43. Refused to share the bed with the drinker when he/she was drunk or had been drinking?	1	2	3	4	5

IN THE PAST SIX MONTHS, HOW OFTEN HAVE YOU:	Always	Frequently	Occasionally	Rarely	Never
44. Withheld sex or other forms of affection because of the drinker's drinking?	1	2	3	4	5
45. Left home, even for part of a day, because of the drinking?	1	2	3	4	5
46. Threatened divorce or separation if the drinker did not stop drinking?	1	2	3	4	5
47. Demonstrated your strong feelings about his/her drinking by threatening to kill yourself?	1	2	3	4	5
48. Cried to reduce the drinker's drinking?	1	2	3	4	5
49. Tried to get even because of the drinking?	1	2	3	4	5
50. Said that the drinker must leave or kept him/her out of the house because of his/her drinking?	1	2	3	4	5
51. Threatened the drinker about what you would do if he/she continued to drink?	1	2	3	4	5
52. Ignored the drinker to get back at him/her when he/she was drunk, had been drinking, or after a drinking episode?	1	2	3	4	5

Copyright © 1988 by Edwin J. Thomas, Marianne Yoshioka, Richard Ager, and the University of Michigan.

SPOUSE TREATMENT MEDIATION INVENTORIES (STMI)

AUTHORS: Richard D. Ager and Edwin J. Thomas

PURPOSE: To assess a spouse's potential to function as a mediator of planned therapeutic change.

DESCRIPTION: This 43-item instrument is intended to assess a spouse's capability to function as a mediator of planned change between a therapist and a target person who may or may not participate in the treatment. There are four subinventories in the STMI, each of which measures a different systemic component of the treatment mediation system. They are the therapist-mediator subinventory (T-M), the mediator subinventory (M), the mediator/target person subinventory (M-TP), and the target person subinventory (TP).

NORMS: The STMI was developed on a sample of spouses—primarily white, educated, middle-class females—of alcohol abusers unmotivated to stop drinking or to enter treatment ($N = 75$). The sample was recruited to receive unilateral family therapy for the marital partner's alcohol problem. The sample means were 3.42 (SD = .38) on the total STMI, 4.02 (SD = .54) on T-M, 3.62 (SD = .62) on M, 3.38 (SD = .45) on M-TP, and 2.13 (SD = .79) on the TP.

SCORING: Scores range from 1 to 5, with higher scores reflecting better treatment mediation potential. Scores are determined by summing scores for items, with values for the odd-numbered items reversed. Total scores are computed from all items. Item numbers for the subinventories are as follows: T-M: 2, 29, 39, 43; M: 8, 10, 16, 19, 20, 27, 31, 33, 42; M-TP: 1, 3, 4, 5, 6, 7, 9, 11, 12, 13, 14, 15, 17, 18, 21, 23, 24, 25, 26, 28, 30, 34, 35, 36, 37, 38, 40, 41; TP: 22, 32.

RELIABILITY: The subinventories showed varying degrees of internal consistency. Alphas were .80 for the total score, .79 for M-TP, .71 for M, .19 for the T-M, and –.01 for TP ($N = 75$). Test-retest coefficients for the six-month interval for the 42 subjects who did not receive immediate treatment in the evaluation experiment likewise indicated varying degrees of temporal stability. The correlations were .72 for the total score, .25 for T-M, .69 for M, .74 for T-M, and .49 for TP.

VALIDITY: The content validity of items was indicated by logical analysis and/or justification in the psychological and treatment literature. Support for the construct validity of M and M-TP was obtained in a factor analysis. Support for the construct validity of M, M-TP, and TP was obtained in an analysis of correlates in which it was found that there were significant negative correlations of M scores with diverse measures of spouse psychopathology and of the M-TP scores with several measures of marital discord. There were insufficient data to provide an adequate examination of the construct validity of T-M.

PRIMARY REFERENCE: Ager, R. D. and Thomas, E. J. (1993). The Spouse Treatment Mediation Inventory: Reliability and validity. Manuscript submitted for publication. Instrument reproduced by permission of Richard D. Ager and Edwin J. Thomas.

AVAILABILITY: Dr. Richard D. Ager, School of Social Work, Tulane University, New Orleans, LA 70118-5672.

STMI

This questionnaire is designed to measure aspects of your relationship with your spouse as it involves treatment, including how you influence your spouse. It is not a test, so there are no right or wrong answers. Answer each item as carefully and accurately as you can by encircling the number of your response for each question.

		Strongly agree	Somewhat agree	Neither agree nor disagree	Somewhat disagree	Strongly disagree
1.	When I have difficulties my spouse is very understanding.	1	2	3	4	5
2.	It is difficult for me to accept help from others.	1	2	3	4	5
3.	My spouse is willing to work hard to make our marriage work.	1	2	3	4	5
4.	I would have serious problems if my marriage ended.	1	2	3	4	5
5.	It is important to me that my spouse change.	1	2	3	4	5
6.	My spouse does not love me.	1	2	3	4	5
7.	I know how to please my spouse.	1	2	3	4	5
8.	I am often overwhelmed by my responsibilities.	1	2	3	4	5
9.	When we disagree, I try to understand my spouse's point of view.	1	2	3	4	5
10.	I rarely have the energy to complete the things I set out to do.	1	2	3	4	5
11.	I initiate most of the activities in my marriage.	1	2	3	4	5

		Strongly agree	Somewhat agree	Neither agree nor disagree	Somewhat disagree	Strongly disagree
12.	I can not openly express love and affection in my marriage.	1	2	3	4	5
13.	My spouse sees me as competent and knowledgeable.	1	2	3	4	5
14.	My spouse rarely talks to me about things that are important to him/her.	1	2	3	4	5
15.	When it really matters, I know I can depend on my spouse.	1	2	3	4	5
16.	It seems as if my life is one crisis after another.	1	2	3	4	5
17.	When we disagree, my spouse tries to understand my point of view.	1	2	3	4	5
18.	I do not provide much emotional support for my spouse.	1	2	3	4	5
19.	I can stand up for my point of view without being overly aggressive or apologetic.	1	2	3	4	5
20.	I often forget or put off things I promised to do.	1	2	3	4	5
21.	My spouse is sexually attracted to me.	1	2	3	4	5
22.	When it comes to change, my spouse is inflexible.	1	2	3	4	5
23.	I am willing to work hard to make my marriage work.	1	2	3	4	5
24.	My spouse has the final say in most of the family decisions.	1	2	3	4	5

		Strongly agree	Somewhat agree	Neither agree nor disagree	Somewhat disagree	Strongly disagree
25.	When my spouse has difficulties, I am very understanding.	1	2	3	4	5
26.	I am fed up with trying to help my spouse change.	1	2	3	4	5
27.	I am good at keeping track of things I might otherwise forget.	1	2	3	4	5
28.	When my spouse makes a promise to me, he/she rarely keeps it.	1	2	3	4	5
29.	I am highly motivated to make changes through participating in this treatment program.	1	2	3	4	5
30.	My spouse believes that I am not interested in his/her well being.	1	2	3	4	5
31.	I learn new things quickly.	1	2	3	4	5
32.	My spouse's problem which brings me here is extremely serious.	1	2	3	4	5
33.	I am a good observer of what other people do.	1	2	3	4	5
34.	There is a lot of conflict in my marriage.	1	2	3	4	5
35.	I make most of the decisions about how the family money is used.	1	2	3	4	5
36.	I am sometimes afraid of my spouse.	1	2	3	4	5
37.	My spouse wants to please me.	1	2	3	4	5

		Strongly agree	Somewhat agree	Neither agree nor disagree	Somewhat disagree	Strongly disagree
38.	I rarely spend time alone with my spouse.	1	2	3	4	5
39.	I need someone outside of my family to talk to about my problems.	1	2	3	4	5
40.	I am not able to confront my spouse when I have concerns about him/her.	1	2	3	4	5
41.	I am able to get my spouse to do things that he/she would not otherwise do.	1	2	3	4	5
42.	When I obtain medical assistance, I often do not follow the advice I receive.	1	2	3	4	5
43.	I believe that participating in this treatment program will help me with my personal concerns.	1	2	3	4	5

Copyright © 1987 by Richard D. Ager and Edwin J. Thomas, The University of Michigan.

INSTRUMENTS FOR FAMILIES

ADOLESCENT-FAMILY INVENTORY OF LIFE EVENTS AND CHANGES (A-FILE)

AUTHORS: Hamilton I. McCubbin, Joan M. Patterson, Edward Bauman, and Linda Hall Harris

PURPOSE: To measure an adolescent's perspective on family changes as a measure of family stress.

DESCRIPTION: The A-FILE is a 50-item instrument designed to measure an adolescent's perceptions of life events and changes experienced by his or her family. These changes are evaluated as occurring within the past year, and a subset of 27 items evaluates changes prior to that. The selection of items for the A-FILE was guided by research and clinical experience and by other available instruments regarding experiences to which an adolescent could be sensitive. The focus of the A-FILE is on changes of sufficient magnitude to require some adjustment in the regular behaviors or interactions of family members. While the A-FILE contains several subscales, only use of the total score is recommended. The A-FILE can be used as a measure of family stress from an adolescent's perspective.

NORMS: The A-FILE was studied with 500 junior and senior high school students. No other demographic information was provided. The mean for total recent life changes was 7 (SD = 4), and for total past life changes was 8 (SD = 6).

SCORING: The A-FILE is easily scored by assigning a 1 to each yes answer and summing all items for the total score. Higher scores indicate greater stress. The A-FILE also can be assigned weights (indicated on the instrument) reflecting the magnitude of change each life event requires for the family. These weights can then be summed for a total stress score.

RELIABILITY: The A-FILE has fair internal consistency, with an alpha for total recent life changes of .69. The A-FILE has very good stability with a two-week test-retest correlation of .82 for total recent life changes and .84 for total past life changes.

VALIDITY: The A-FILE has fair predictive validity, with low correlations between the A-FILE and adolescent substance use and abuse and with the Multidimensional Health Locus of Control Scale.

PRIMARY REFERENCE: McCubbin, H. I. and Thompson, A. I. (eds.) (1991). *Family Assessment Inventories for Research and Practice*. Madison, WI: University of Wisconsin.

AVAILABILITY: Dr. Hamilton McCubbin, Dean, School of Family Resources and Consumer Services, Madison, WI 53706-1575.

A-FILE

Purpose:
To record what family life changes adolescent members experience. The following list of family life changes can happen in a family at any time. Because family members are connected to each other in some way, a life change for any one member affects all the other persons in the family to some degree.

"FAMILY" means a group of persons who are related to each other by marriage, blood, or adoption, who may or may not live with you. Family includes stepparents, stepbrothers and stepsisters.

REMEMBER: Anytime the words "parent," "mother," "father," "brother," "sister" are used, they also mean "stepparent," "stepbrother," etc.

Directions:
Please read each family life change and decide whether it happened to any member of your family—*including you*. First, decide if it happened any time *during* the last 12 months and check YES or NO. Second, for *some family changes* decide if it happened any time *before* the last 12 months and check YES or NO. It is okay to check YES twice if it happened both times—before last year and during the past year.

| | DID THE CHANGE HAPPEN IN YOUR FAMILY? | | | |
| | *During* last 12 months | | *Before* last 12 months | |
FAMILY LIFE CHANGES	Yes	No	Yes	No
I. TRANSITIONS				
1. Family member started new business (farm, store, etc).	☐ 41	☐	☐	☐ 41
2. Parent quit or lost a job.	☐ 69	☐	☐	☐
3. Parents separated or divorced.	☐ 82	☐	☐	☐
4. Parent remarried.	☐ 64	☐	☐	☐
5. Family member was found to have a learning disorder.	☐ 57	☐	☐	☐ 49

	DID THE CHANGE HAPPEN IN YOUR FAMILY?			
	During last 12 months		*Before* last 12 months	
FAMILY LIFE CHANGES	Yes	No	Yes	No
6. Family member was married.	☐ 46	☐		
7. Parents adopted a child.	☐ 45	☐		
8. A member started junior high or high school.	☐ 23	☐		
9. Child or teenage member transferred to a new school.	☐ 37	☐		
10. Parent started school.	☐ 43	☐		
11. Brother or sister moved away from home.	☐ 78	☐		
12. Young adult member entered college, vocational training or armed forces.	☐ 41	☐		
13. Parent(s) started or changed to a new job.	☐ 47	☐		
14. Family moved to a new home.	☐ 61	☐		

II. SEXUALITY

	Yes	No	Yes	No
15. Unmarried family member became pregnant.	☐ 69	☐	☐	☐ 60
16. Family member had an abortion.	☐ 71	☐	☐	☐
17. Birth of a brother or sister.	☐ 38	☐		
18. Teenager began having sexual intercourse.	☐ 55	☐		

		DID THE CHANGE HAPPEN IN YOUR FAMILY?			
		During last 12 months		*Before* last 12 months	
	FAMILY LIFE CHANGES	Yes	No	Yes	No

III. LOSSES

19. Family went on welfare.
    ☐ 72 ☐ ☐ ☐

20. Damage to or loss of family property due to fire, burglary, or other disaster.
    ☐ 71 ☐ ☐ ☐

21. Brother or sister died.
    ☐ 90 ☐ ☐ ☐ 70

22. Parent died.
    ☐ 94 ☐ ☐ ☐

23. Close family relative died.
    ☐ 84 ☐ ☐ ☐

24. Death of a close friend of family member.
    ☐ 82 ☐ ☐ ☐

25. Family member or close family friend attempted or committed suicide.
    ☐ 87 ☐ ☐ ☐ 78

IV. RESPONSIBILITIES AND STRAINS

26. Family member became seriously ill or injured (NOT hospitalized).
    ☐ 61 ☐ ☐ ☐ 13

27. Family member was hospitalized.
    ☐ 50 ☐ ☐ ☐

28. Family member became physically disabled or was found to have a long-term health problem (allergies, asthma, diabetes, etc.).
    ☐ 61 ☐ ☐ ☐

29. Family member has emotional problems.
    ☐ 60 ☐ ☐ ☐

30. Grandparent(s) became seriously ill.
    ☐ 77 ☐ ☐ ☐

		DID THE CHANGE HAPPEN IN YOUR FAMILY?			
		During last 12 months		Before last 12 months	
	FAMILY LIFE CHANGES	Yes	No	Yes	No
31.	Parent(s) have more responsibility to take care of grandparent(s).	☐ 55	☐	☐	☐
32.	Family member ran away.	☐ 73	☐	☐	☐
33.	More financial debts due to use of credit cards or charges.	☐ 63	☐	☐	☐ 27
34.	Increased family living expenses for medical care, food, clothing, energy costs (gasoline, heating).	☐ 59	☐		
35.	Increase of parent's time away from family.	☐ 55	☐		
36.	Child or teenage member resists doing things with family.	☐ 43	☐		
37.	Increase in arguments between parents.	☐ 60	☐		
38.	Children or teenagers have more arguments with one another.	☐ 40	☐		
39.	Parent(s) and teenager(s) have increased arguments (hassles) over *use of car or hours to stay out*.	☐ 49	☐		
40.	Parent(s) and teenager(s) have increased arguments (hassles) over *choice of friends and/or social activities*.	☐ 49	☐		
41.	Parent(s) and teenager(s) have increased arguments (hassles) over *attendance at religious activities*.	☐ 43	☐		
42.	Parent(s) and teenager(s) have increased arguments (hassles) over *personal appearance (clothes, hair, etc.)*.	☐ 43	☐		

		DID THE CHANGE HAPPEN IN YOUR FAMILY?			
		During last 12 months		*Before* last 12 months	
FAMILY LIFE CHANGES		Yes	No	Yes	No

		Yes	No	Yes	No
43.	Increased arguments about getting the jobs done at home.	☐ 50	☐		
44.	Increased pressure for a member in school to get "good" grades or do well in sports or school activities.	☐ 38	☐		

V. SUBSTANCE USE

		Yes	No	Yes	No
45.	Family member uses drugs (not given by doctor).	☐ 76	☐	☐	☐ 40
46.	Family member drinks too much alcohol.	☐ 75	☐	☐	☐
47.	Child or teenage member was suspended from school or dropped out of school.	☐ 59	☐	☐	☐
48.	Parent(s) and teenager(s) have increased arguments (hassles) over *use of cigarettes, alcohol, or drugs*.	☐ 62	☐		

VI. LEGAL CONFLICT

		Yes	No	Yes	No
49.	Family member went to jail, juvenile detention, or was placed on court probation.	☐ 80	☐	☐	☐
50.	Family member was robbed or attacked (physically or sexually).	☐ 83	☐	☐	☐ 49

Copyright © 1991 H. McCubbin and A. I. Thompson.

ADULT-ADOLESCENT PARENTING INVENTORY (AAPI)

AUTHOR: Stephen J. Bavolek

PURPOSE: To assess parenting and child rearing attitudes.

DESCRIPTION: The AAPI is a 32-item instrument, written in simple language, designed to help professionals assess parenting and child rearing strengths and weaknesses in four areas: (1) inappropriate developmental expectations of children, (2) lack of empathy toward children's needs, (3) belief in the use of corporal punishment, and (4) reversing parent-child roles. The AAPI can be used to assess attitudes of prospective parents, to assess changes in parenting attitudes before and after treatment, to screen and train foster parent applicants, and to assess attitudes of professionals and parapro-fessionals. Two forms are used when pre- and posttesting is called for. An excellent handbook describing all details of the psychometric properties, administration, and scoring is available from the author.

NORMS: Extensive norms are available based on 782 abusive adults, 1239 nonabusive adults, 305 abused adolescents, and 6480 nonabused adolescents. These respondents come from all over the United States and include both males and females and blacks and whites. These norms allow easy comparison of individual scores with norms. The AAPI is designed specifically for adolescents ages 12 to 19 and adults 20 and over.

SCORING: The AAPI requires the use of scoring stencils for each test form. Raw scores are easily converted into standard scores by using the tables in the handbook. These tables give information on the four parenting subscales and provide standard scores for abusive and nonabusive adults and adolescents.

RELIABILITY: Internal consistency, using coefficient alpha, ranges from .70 for the construct of inappropriate expectations of children (for adolescents) to .86 for the construct of family role-reversal (for adults). Test-retest reliability (stability) is .39 for inappropriate expectation of children, .65 for empathic awareness of children's needs, .85 for family role-reversal, and .89 for empathic awareness. Total test-retest correlation is .76, indicating fairly good stability.

VALIDITY: Extensive validity information is available, including excellent content validity based on expert judgments, construct validity data, and excellent concurrent and known-groups validity indicating that the AAPI was clearly able to discriminate among different groups.

PRIMARY REFERENCE: Bavolek, S. J. (1984). *Handbook for the Adult-Adolescent Parenting Inventory*. Eau Claire, Wisconsin: Family Development Associates, Inc. Instrument reproduced with permission of S. J. Bavolek.

AVAILABILITY: Family Development Resources, Inc., 767 Second Ave., Eau Claire, WI 54703.

AAPI

There are 32 statements in this questionnaire. They are statements about parenting and raising children. You decide the degree to which you agree or disagree with each statement by indicating the appropriate number at the left. If you strongly support the statement, or feel this statement is true most or all the tlme, indicate *Strongly agree*. If you support the statement or feel this statement is true some of the time, indicate *agree*. If you feel strongly against the statement or feel this statement is not true most or all the time, indicate *strongly disagree*. If you feel you cannot support the statement or that the statement is not true some of the time, indicate *disagree*. Use *uncertain* only when it is absolutely impossible to decide on one of the other choices.

Please keep these four points in mind:

1. Answer the questions frankly and truthfully. There is no advantage in glving an untrue answer because you think it is the right thing to say.

2. Answer the questions as quickly as you can. Don't spend too much time thlnking about what to answer. Give the first natural answer that comes to mind.

3. Don't skip any questions or provide two answers to any question. Make sure you respond to every statement with only one answer.

4. Although some questions may seem much like others, there are no two statements exactly alike so make sure you respond to every statement.

If there is anything you don't understand, please ask your questions now. If you come across a word you don't know while answering a question, ask the examiner for help.

1 = Strongly agree
2 = Agree
3 = Uncertain
4 = Disagree
5 = Strongly disagree

_____ 1. Young children should be expected to comfort their mother when she's feellng blue.

_____ 2. Parents should teach their children right from wrong by sometimes using physical punishment.

_____ 3. Children should be the main source of comfort and care for their parents.

_____ 4. Young children should be expected to hug their mother when she is sad.

_____ 5. Parents will spoil their children by picking them up and comforting them when they cry.

_____ 6. Children should be expected to verbally express themselves before the age of one year.

_____ 7. A good child will comfort both of his/her parents after the parents have argued.

_____ 8. Children learn good behavior through the use of physical punishment.

_____ 9. Children develop good, strong characters through very strict discipline.

_____ 10. Parents should expect their children who are under three years to begin taking care of themselves.

_____ 11. Young children should be aware of ways to comfort their parents after a hard day's work.

_____ 12. Parents should slap their chld when she/he has done something wrong.

_____ 13. Children should always be spanked when they misbehave.

_____ 14. Young children should be responsible for much of the happiness of their parents.

_____ 15. Parents have a responsibility to spank their child when she/he misbehaves.

_____ 16. Parents should expect children to feed themselves by twelve months.

_____ 17. Parents should expect their children to grow physically at about the same rate.

_____ 18. Young children who feel secure often grow up expecting too much.

_____ 19. Children should always "pay the price" for misbehaving.

_____ 20. Children should be expected at an early age to feed, bathe, and clothe themselves.

_____ 21. Parents who are sensitive to their children's feelings and moods often spoil their children.

_____ 22. Children deserve more discipline than they get.

_____ 23. Children whose needs are left unattended will often grow up to be more independent.

_____ 24. Parents who encourage communication with their children only end up listening to complaints.

_____ 25. Children are more likely to learn appropriate behavior when they are spanked for misbehaving.

_____ 26. Children will quit crying faster if they are ignored.

_____ 27. Children five months of age ought to be capable of sensing what their parents expect.

_____ 28. Children who are given too much love by their parents will grow up to be stubborn and spoiled.

_____ 29. Children should be forced to respect parental authority.

_____ 30. Young children should try to make their parent's life more pleasurable.

_____ 31. Young children who are hugged and kissed often will grow up to be "sissies."

_____ 32. Young children should be expected to comfort their father when he is upset.

ATTITUDE TOWARD THE PROVISION OF LONG-TERM CARE (ATPLTC)

AUTHOR: Waldo Klein

PURPOSE: To measure attitude toward the provision of informal long-term care for family members.

DESCRIPTION: This 26-item instrument is designed to measure the attitude of persons providing informal support to frail, impaired, or disabled family members on an ongoing basis. The ATPLTC was developed to assist in identifying the role and level of participation of family members in caring for impaired relatives. By identifying the underlying attitude that caregivers may hold in relation to the caregiving role, care plans may be developed that address the needs of caregivers and the primary client.

NORMS: The author developed the ATPLTC with individuals providing informal supportive care to either frail elderly family members or developmentally disabled children. Among caregivers to frail elderly family members, the average ATPLTC score was 35 with a standard deviation of 15.4; caregivers to developmentally disabled children averaged 31 on the ATPLTC with a standard deviation of 13.1.

SCORING: Scoring of the ATPLTC begins by reverse-scoring items 1, 5, 9, 11, 12, 18, 20, 21, 22, 23, and 25 and totaling the item scores. Using this item total, the following formula produces a score ranging from zero to 100 with lower scores indicating a more positive attitude toward providing care: score = 100 (item total − N)/25N where, N = the number of completed items. This formula offers the convenient advantage of adjusting an individual's score in cases that include uncompleted items.

RELIABILITY: The scale has very good internal consistency, with a Cronbach's alpha of .88 among caregivers to elderly family members and .86 among caregivers to developmentally disabled children. Data on stability were not available.

VALIDITY: Initial assessment of the ATPLTC scale suggests fairly good concurrent validity, correlating with self-reports concerning family relationships and various aspects of long-term caregiving. Factor analysis also supports construct validity. The scale shows no statistically significant relationships with age, education, gender, religion, or ethnicity.

PRIMARY REFERENCE: Klein, W. C. (1992). Measuring caregiver attitude toward the provision of long-term care, *Journal of Social Service Research*, 16, 147–162. Instrument reproduced with permission of Waldo Klein.

AVAILABILITY: Dr. Waldo C. Klein, School of Social Work, University of Connecticut, 1798 Asylum Avenue, West Hartford, CT 06117-2698.

ATPLTC

The following statements refer to personally providing care on an ongoing basis to a family member who is unable to meet all of his or her own needs in performing various activities of daily living. These activities include such things as preparing meals, bathing, going to the bathroom, and dressing. This disability may result from a birth defect, an accident, a stroke, a chronic disease, or growing old. Please respond to each statement by placing the number of the statement that best expresses your attitude on the line provided.

1 = Strongly agree
2 = Moderately agree
3 = Neither agree nor disagree
4 = Moderately disagree
5 = Strongly disagree

_____ 1. It is *not* fair that adult children should have to give up so much to care for frail elderly parents.

_____ 2. Families should *not* place severely retarded children in institutions.

_____ 3. A parent should look after his/her child even if that child is severely disabled.

_____ 4. Families that really want to provide care for a disabled relative will find a way to do so.

_____ 5. Nursing homes or institutions can provide better care for disabled relatives than families.

_____ 6. The physical demands of providing care to a disabled family member are manageable.

_____ 7. It is the responsibility of families to care for their disabled members.

_____ 8. This society will collapse if family members do *not* provide care for their disabled members.

_____ 9. Family members who *cannot* bathe or dress themselves are better off in nursing homes or institutions.

_____ 10. Providing care for a disabled family member is one of the basic responsibilities of a family.

_____ 11. It is *not* fair that young parents should have to give up so much to care for retarded children.

_____ 12. Any right-thinking person would have second thoughts about providing care to a disabled family member.

_____ 13. People should be willing to quit their jobs in order to provide care to impaired family members.

_____ 14. Providing ongoing care for a disabled relative would be one of the most meaningful things a person could do.

_____ 15. Providing care to a disabled family member is a basic human responsibility.

_____ 16. Families should plan for the possibility of providing care for an elderly disabled family member.

_____ 17. Families should rearrange their schedules in order to provide care to disabled family members.

_____ 18. Providing care for disabled family members at home is useless since most of them will end up in institutions or nursing homes anyway.

_____ 19. Although medical advances have increased the need for extended care, family members should continue to provide this care to dependent family members.

_____ 20. Disabled children over the age of six years who *cannot* bathe or dress themselves are an unfair burden to their parents.

_____ 21. When people can no longer care for themselves, it would be better for them to die than to be dependent on family to provide care.

_____ 22. Providing care for a disabled family member is mentally exhausting.

_____ 23. It should be the responsibility of government programs rather than families to provide care for disabled people.

_____ 24. Families are just as good at providing care to dependent family members as organizations that specialize in providing those kind of services.

_____ 25. Older family members who *cannot* bathe or dress themselves are an unfair burden to their children.

_____ 26. Humankind is benefited by families that care for their disabled members.

Copyright © 1988 W. C. Klein

BECK CODEPENDENCE ASSESSMENT SCALE (BCAS)

AUTHOR: William H. Beck

PURPOSE: To measure codependence.

DESCRIPTION: The BCAS is a 35-item instrument designed to measure co-dependence, defined as chronic enabling or caretaking behaviors toward a dysfunctional significant other. The BCAS was developed by identifying a set of diagnostic behaviors and cognitions more likely to be typical of those who are codependent than those who are not. The BCAS has three subscales (factors): control (C; items 1, 4, 8, 12, 17, 22, 24, 31, 33, 35 [marked with an asterisk on the answer sheet]); social concern (S; items 2, 5, 11, 15, 16, 19, 21, 26, 28, 30 [marked with a solid bullet on the answer sheet]); and family conflict (F; items 3, 6, 7, 9, 10, 13, 14, 18, 20, 23, 25, 27, 29, 32, 34 [marked with a hyphen on the answer sheet]).

NORMS: The BCAS was studied with 100 university students, of whom 50 were diagnosed as codependent and 50 as non-codependent. The groups were equally divided between males and females, predominantly white, with between 18% and 28% Black, Hispanic, and Asian. Mean scores for the codependent group ranged from 7 to 10 with an overall mean of 8.54 (SD = 1.03) and were all either 1 or 2 for the non-codependent group with a mean of 1.16 (SD = .42).

SCORING: Items 2, 3, 5, 11, 13, 15, 17, 19, 21, 26, 28, and 32 are reverse-scored. Then, item responses are summed for the overall and subscale scores.

RELIABILITY: The BCAS has good internal consistency, with an alpha for the family conflict subscale of .89 (other alphas were not available). The BCAS has excellent stability with a test-retest reliability coefficient of .86.

VALIDITY: The BCAS has excellent predictive and known-groups validity, with three subscales predicting codependence with a .85 overall predictive accuracy (using discriminant function analysis). The BCAS is slightly affected by social desirability response bias as shown by a significant correlation with the Crowne-Marlowe Social Desirability Scale.

PRIMARY REFERENCE: Beck, W. H. (1991). *Codependence Assessment Manual*. Chicago: Administrative Services.

AVAILABILITY: W. H. Beck, P.O. Box 138392, Chicago, IL 60613.

BCAS

Please mark how often each statement describes you by checking the appropriate box. Some statements express a thought. In that case your choice would indicate how often you have that thought. Other statements describe feelings or situations, and in each case, you would mark the choice describing the frequency with which the statement describes you or the situation in which you have been involved.

PLEASE REMEMBER TO ANSWER EACH QUESTION.

		Almost never	Rarely	Sometimes	Frequently	Almost always
1.	I feel that my significant other does not understand me.	☐	☐	☐	☐	☐
2.	I let others make their own choices even when I think they are wrong.	☐	☐	☐	☐	☐
3.	As a child, I was encouraged to express myself.	☐	☐	☐	☐	☐
4.	I feel frustrated because I cannot keep my significant other from behaving self-destructively.	☐	☐	☐	☐	☐
5.	If my friend or significant other wants to get drunk or take drugs, it's not my problem.	☐	☐	☐	☐	☐
6.	If my parents fought, I felt it was my fault.	☐	☐	☐	☐	☐
7.	When growing up, I felt no one really understood me.					
8.	I have sex when I don't want to.	☐	☐	☐	☐	☐
9.	There was a lot of tension in my family when I was growing up.	☐	☐	☐	☐	☐
10.	One or both of my parents told me I was worthless.	☐	☐	☐	☐	☐
11.	It's not my responsibility to take care of other people.	☐	☐	☐	☐	☐

		Almost never	Rarely	Sometimes	Frequently	Almost always
12.	I say what I hope will make people do as I want.	☐	☐	☐	☐	☐
13.	I feel loved and accepted by my family.	☐	☐	☐	☐	☐
14.	As a child, I was anxious.	☐	☐	☐	☐	☐
15.	If other people get mad, it's not my problem.	☐	☐	☐	☐	☐
16.	My significant other is sick.	☐	☐	☐	☐	☐
17.	I let everyone make their own choices.	☐	☐	☐	☐	☐
18.	My parents let me down as a child.	☐	☐	☐	☐	☐
19.	I do not like to do for other people what they can do for themselves.	☐	☐	☐	☐	☐
20.	In my family, I had to learn not to show my emotions.	☐	☐	☐	☐	☐
21.	I can't control other people.	☐	☐	☐	☐	☐
22.	I have used guilt to make other people do what I wanted.	☐	☐	☐	☐	☐
23.	It was not OK to talk about problems in my family.	☐	☐	☐	☐	☐
24.	Because I feel responsible for other people, I try to control what they do.	☐	☐	☐	☐	☐
25.	My parents were angry.	☐	☐	☐	☐	☐
26.	If my friend drinks too much, I don't worry about it.	☐	☐	☐	☐	☐
27.	In my family, it was not acceptable to express my feelings.	☐	☐	☐	☐	☐

	Almost never	Rarely	Sometimes	Frequently	Almost always
28. If two friends don't like each other, it's not my problem.	☐	☐	☐	☐	☐
29. As a child, I expected something terrible to happen.	☐	☐	☐	☐	☐
30. I try to keep my friends and family out of trouble.	☐	☐	☐	☐	☐
31. I know what's best for other people.	☐	☐	☐	☐	☐
32. When I have been in trouble, I knew I could go to my parents for help.	☐	☐	☐	☐	☐
33. I think I know best how people should behave.	☐	☐	☐	☐	☐
34. I had to be careful to avoid making my parents angry.	☐	☐	☐	☐	☐
35. I don't know how I do it, but I find myself involved in other people's business.	☐	☐	☐	☐	☐

Copyright © 1991 William H. Beck.

BOUNDARY AMBIGUITY SCALES—1–6 (BAS—1–6)

AUTHORS: Pauline Boss, Jan Greenberg, and Debra Pearce-McCall

PURPOSE: To measure family boundary ambiguity.

DESCRIPTION: The BAS—1-6 is a set of six scales, each of which measures a different type of boundary ambiguity. Scale 1 is for wives of men declared missing-in-action and contains 18 items; Scale 2 is for widows and contains 12 items; Scale 3 is for parents of adolescents leaving home and contains 9 items; Scale 4 is for adolescent and adult children of divorce and contains 25 items; Scale 5 is for divorced adults and contains 22 items; and Scale 6 is for caregivers of patients with dementia and contains 14 items. Boundary ambiguity is defined as the family not knowing who is in and who is out of the system. Members of families may perceive a physically absent member as psychologically present or may perceive a physically present member as psychologically absent. In both cases the family boundary is considered to be ambiguous. The BAS—1-6 are individual measures of different types of boundary ambiguity for different types of situations. The scales measure boundary ambiguity through self reports of family members' perceptions of psychological presence with physical absence (Scales 1 and 5) or physical presence with psychological absence (Scale 6). The importance of these scales is that they allow better understanding of stressed families on the grounds that the greater the family boundary ambiguity, the higher the stress for the family, and the greater the individual and family dysfunction. Therefore, the Boundary Ambiguity Scales can focus practitioners on family process as a primary medium for intervention.

NORMS: Each of the six Boundary Ambiguity Scales was studied with respondents appropriate to the purpose of the individual scale. Norms on some of the scales are available in the original publication and norms for the remaining scales may be available from the author.

SCORING: An individual's boundary ambiguity score is simply the sum of responses across items after answers to particular items have been reverse scored. For Scale 1, items 1, 2, 6, 8, 11, 13, and 15 should be reverse scored. For Scale 2, items 1, 2, 3, 4, and 12. For Scale 3, reverse-score item 2. For Scale 4, reverse-score items 3, 11, 12, 13, 19, 21, and 25. For Scale 5, reverse-score items 2, 9, 11, 17, 19, 20, and 22. For Scale 6, no items are reverse scored. With all scales the higher the score the more that respondent perceives his or her family boundary as ambiguous.

RELIABILITY: In the original publication the availability of reliability figures for the individual scales varied. For Scale 1 reliability data were not reported. For Scale 2 reliability data were found to be very low in a sample of 80 urban and rural women, with internal consistency reliability of .58. For Scale 3 the alpha was .74 indicating fair reliability. For Scale 4 the alpha was .75. No data were available for Scale 5. For Scale 6 reliability data were not reported.

VALIDITY: A variety of different types of validity information was available on some of the scales in the original reports. For Scale 1 the scores on the scale were significant predictors of respondents' functioning. For Scale 2 the authors report a number of correlations between boundary ambiguity and the time of death of a spouse that were consistent with predictions. For Scale 3 the authors report fair construct validity with significant correlations between scores on the scale and respondents' ratings of stress. For Scale 4 a number of significant correlations supported both the general theory of boundary ambiguity and the validity of the scale. For Scale 5 data on validity were not available. The validity of Scale 6 is under study and the data are available from the author. Overall the validity of the Boundary Ambiguity Scale varies from scale to scale.

PRIMARY REFERENCES: Boss, P. G., Greenberg, J. R., and Pearce-McCall, D. (1990). *The Measurement of Boundary Ambiguity.* Minneapolis: University of Minnesota Agriculture Experiment Station Publication 593. Boss, P. et al. (1990). Predictors of depression in caregivers of dementia patients: Boundary ambiguity and mastery, *Family Process,* 29, 245–254.

AVAILABILITY: Pauline Boss, Ph.D., Boundary Ambiguity Project, Family Social Science Department, University of Minnesota, 290 McNeal Hall, St. Paul, MN 55108.

BAS

BAS-1
FOR WIVES OF MEN DECLARED MISSING-IN-ACTION (MIA)

The following statements are about the changes in your family since your husband was declared missing-in-action. Using the scale provided as your guideline, choose the number that best shows how you feel and place it in the blank to the left of each item. There are no right or wrong answers.

For questions 1–18, use the following scale as a guide in answering:

1 = Strongly disagree
2 = Disagree
3 = Neutral
4 = Agree
5 = Strongly agree

_____ 1. I no longer consider myself an "MIA" wife.

_____ 2. I feel I have prepared myself for a change in status (to widow).

_____ 3. I find myself still wondering if my husband is alive.

_____ 4. I continue to keep alive my deepest hope that my husband will return.

_____ 5. I feel guilty about dating (or wanting to date).

_____ 6. I feel I am able to plan my future without feeling guilty for not continuing to wait for my husband.

_____ 7. I will never be satisfied until I have positive proof of my husband's death.

_____ 8. I hope to remarry.

_____ 9. I think about my husband a lot.

_____ 10. I feel it will be difficult, if not impossible, to carve out a new life for myself without my husband.

_____ 11. The Armed Services have done everything reasonably possible to account for my husband.

_____ 12. I feel incapable of establishing a meaningful relationship with another man.

_____ 13. My children are able to talk about their father without becoming emotionally upset.

_____ 14. My children still believe that their father is alive.

_____ 15. My children are aware of all "the facts" and have reconciled their father's loss.

_____ 16. My children and I talk about their father seemingly quite often.

_____ 17. Conflicts with my own parents over my husband's change of status have presented a problem for me.

_____ 18. My in-laws do not or would not approve of my plans to develop a life for myself.

BAS-2
FOR WIDOWS

The following statements are about the changes in status from wife to widow. Using the scale provided as your guideline, choose the number that best shows how you feel and place it in the blank to the left of each item. There are no right or wrong answers.

For questions 1–12, use the following scale as a guide in answering:

1 = Strongly disagree
2 = Disagree
3 = Agree
4 = Strongly agree

____ 1. I no longer consider myself a wife.
____ 2. I feel I have prepared myself for a change in status (to widow).
____ 3. I feel I am able to plan my future without feeling guilty for not continuing to mourn for my husband.
____ 4. I hope to remarry.
____ 5. I find myself wondering if my husband is alive in a different dimension.
____ 6. I continue to keep alive my deepest hope that I will be with my husband again some day.
____ 7. I feel guilty about dating (or wanting to date).
____ 8. I still talk to or communicate with my husband.
____ 9. I think about my husband a lot.
____ 10. I feel it will be difficult, if not impossible, to carve out a new life for myself without my husband.
____ 11. I feel incapable of establishing meaningful relationships with other men.
____ 12. My children are able to talk about their father without becoming emotionally upset.

BAS-3
FOR PARENTS OF ADOLESCENTS LEAVING HOME

The following statements are about the changes in your family as your adolescent or young adult leaves home. (As you read, imagine his or her name in the space in the sentence.) Using the scale provided as your guideline, choose the number that best shows how you feel and place it in the blank to the left of each item. There are no right or wrong answers.

Birthdate for this child: _____

Year adolescent left home: _____

For questions 1–4, use the following scale as a guide in answering:

> 1 = Strongly disagree
> 2 = Moderately disagree
> 3 = Neutral
> 4 = Moderately agree
> 5 = Strongly agree

_____ 1. I feel that it will be difficult for me now that _____ has left home.
_____ 2. I feel that I prepared myself for _____ leaving home.
_____ 3. I have difficulty accepting that _____ has grown up.
_____ 4. I continue to keep alive my hope that _____ will return home to live.

For questions 5–9, use the following scale as a guide in answering:

> 1 = Never
> 2 = Rarely
> 3 = Sometimes
> 4 = Often
> 5 = Almost always

_____ 5. Our family talks about _____ quite often.
_____ 6. I think about _____ a lot.
_____ 7. I find myself thinking about where _____ is and what s/he is doing.
_____ 8. I am bothered because I miss my son/daughter.
_____ 9. Since _____ left, I am bothered by feelings of loneliness.

BAS-4
FOR ADOLESCENT AND ADULT CHILDREN OF DIVORCE

The following statements are about the changes in your family since the divorce of your parents. Using the scale provided as your guideline, choose the number that best shows how you feel and place it in the blank to the left of each item. There are no right or wrong answers.

For questions 1–25, use the following scale as a guide in answering:

> 1 = Never
> 2 = Rarely
> 3 = Sometimes
> 4 = Often
> 5 = Almost always

_____ 1. I hope that my parents' relationship with each other will improve.
_____ 2. I worry about whether I am spending enough time with each of my parents.
_____ 3. My parents and I can solve family problems together.
_____ 4. I find myself being a go-between for my parents (e.g., carrying messages, making arrangements).
_____ 5. I feel as though each of my parents wants me to be on his/her side.

_____ 6. Since the divorce, I find it more difficult to talk with my father about things I may need from him (money, time, advice).

_____ 7. Since the divorce, I find it more difficult to talk with my mother about things I may need from her (money, time, advice).

_____ 8. My feeling about whom I consider a member of my family and who is not a member of my family continues to change.

_____ 9. I still feel disturbed about my parents' divorce.

_____ 10. I think about my mother and my father as a unit, as "my parents."

_____ 11. I feel comfortable talking about my mother in front of my father.

_____ 12. I feel comfortable talking about my father in front of my mother.

_____ 13. My family has clear rules about how money and financial arrangements should be handled.

_____ 14. When I think about important future occasions (e.g., graduations, weddings, newborn children) where my parents will be together, I worry about how they will behave.

_____ 15. People on my father's side of my family secretly ask me about my mother or ask me to say hello for them.

_____ 16. People on my mother's side of my family secretly ask me about my father or ask me to say hello for them.

_____ 17. I worry about which family members I should or will be with on important holidays and special occasions.

_____ 18. My parents say things about each other to me that make me feel uncomfortable.

_____ 19. In both of my parents' homes, I feel comfortable, like I belong.

_____ 20. It is unclear how the relationships between my extended family (grandparents, uncles, aunts, cousins) will be affected by the divorce.

If one or both of your parents has remarried or has been cohabiting for over one year, answer the following items. If neither parent has remarried or been cohabiting for over one year, skip items 21–25.

_____ 21. It took time, but now I have a good feeling about how we all fit together as a family.

_____ 22. I will always think of my original nuclear family as my real family.

_____ 23. I am confused about whether or not I accept my mother's partner as part of my family.

_____ 24. I am confused about whether or not I accept my father's partner as part of my family.

_____ 25. I am clear about what type of relationship(s) I want to have with my stepsibling(s) or my parent's partners' children.

BAS-5
FOR DIVORCED ADULTS

The following statements are about the changes in your family since your divorce. Using the scale provided as your guideline, choose the number that best shows how you feel and place it in the blank to the left of each item. There are no right or wrong answers.

For questions 1–22, use the following scale as a guide in answering:

> 1 = Never
> 2 = Rarely
> 3 = Sometimes
> 4 = Often
> 5 = Almost always

_____ 1. I still consider myself a wife/husband to my former spouse.

_____ 2. Calling myself a divorced person feels comfortable to me now.

_____ 3. I feel upset when I imagine my former spouse with another man/woman.

_____ 4. I find myself wondering about where my former spouse is and what s/he is doing.

_____ 5. I feel that in some sense I will always be attached to my former spouse.

_____ 6. I still get my former spouse's advice about important personal decisions (e.g., health, career).

_____ 7. I continue to keep alive my hope that I will be reunited with my former spouse.

_____ 8. I continue to hope that my relationship with my former spouse will improve.

_____ 9. I feel competent performing the household or outside tasks that my former spouse used to do.

_____ 10. I feel guilty about dating (or wanting to date).

_____ 11. I feel that I have completely recovered from my divorce.

_____ 12. I still consider some members of my former spouse's family to be part of my family.

_____ 13. I feel incapable of establishing meaningful relationships with another man/woman.

_____ 14. I find myself asking my former spouse for advice about the areas s/he used to handle.

_____ 15. I often wonder what my former spouse's opinion or comment would be on events that happen or things I see during the day.

_____ 16. My former spouse and I discuss our new relationships with each other.

If you do not have children, stop here. If you do have children, answer items 17–22:

_____ 17. My children and I are able to talk about my former spouse without becoming emotionally upset.

____ 18. I worry that my children feel caught in the middle between me and my former spouse.

____ 19. My former spouse and I agree on how to share the responsibilities of parenting.

____ 20. My children are aware of the facts and are reconciled to the divorce.

____ 21. My former spouse and I have difficulty discussing financial matters involving the children.

____ 22. It feels like a complete family when the children and I are together without my former spouse.

BAS-6
FOR CAREGIVERS OF PATIENTS WITH DEMENTIA

The following statements are about your relationship with the Alzheimer's patient. (As you read, imagine his or her name in the blank space in each sentence.) Using the scale provided as a guideline, choose the number that best shows how you feel and place it in the blank to the left of each item. There are no right or wrong answers. It is important that you answer every item, even if you are unsure of your answer.

For questions 1–14, use the following scale as a guide in answering:

1 = Strongly disagree
2 = Disagree
3 = Agree
4 = Strongly agree
5 = Unsure how I feel

____ 1. I feel guilty when I get out of the house to do something enjoyable while ____ remains at home.

____ 2. I feel it will be difficult if not impossible to carve out my own life as long as ____ needs my help.

____ 3. I feel incapable of establishing new friendships right now.

____ 4. I feel I cannot go anywhere without first thinking about ____'s needs

____ 5. I feel like I have no time to myself.

____ 6. Sometimes I'm not sure where ____ fits in as part of the family.

____ 7. I'm not sure what I should expect ____ to do around the house.

____ 8. I often feel mixed up about how much I should be doing for ____.

____ 9. I put ____'s needs before my own.

____ 10. My family and I often have disagreements about my involvement with ____.

____ 11. When I'm not with ____, I find myself wondering how s/he is getting along.

____ 12. Family members tend to ignore ____.

____ 13. ____ no longer feels like my spouse/parent/sibling.

____ 14. I think about ____ a lot.

Copyright © 1990 Minnesota Agricultural Experiment Station, University of Minnesota.

CO-DEPENDENCY INVENTORY (CODI)

AUTHOR: Sandra Stonebrink

PURPOSE: To measure co-dependency in family and friends of substance abusers.

DESCRIPTION: The CODI is a 29-item instrument designed to study co-dependency in family and friends of substance abusers. Co-dependency was defined as enabling the abuser to continue to use chemicals and/or trying to control the abusers' use of alcohol and/or drugs. Items and subscales were developed from the literature that suggests co-dependency is characterized by: the need to control (C; items 1, 5, 9, 13, 17, 21, 25); interpersonal dependency (ID; items 2, 6–10, 14, 18, 22, 26, 29); self-alienation (SA; items 3, 7, 11, 15, 19, 23, and 27); and enmeshment (E; items 4, 8, 12, 16, 20, 24, 28). Given the abundance of literature on co-dependency but the lack of adequate measures of the concept, the CODI is an important instrument for use in measuring co-dependency.

NORMS: The CODI was studied with 48 friends or family members of individuals receiving treatment at a medical center's alcohol and addiction program in Kailua, Hawaii; 69% were female and 31% male, and the sample had a mean age of 43 years. Sixty percent were married, 65% were Caucasian. Parents comprised 37.5% of the sample, spouses 35.4%, lovers/partners 12.5%, children 6.3%, siblings 4.2% and friends 2.1%. Actual norms are not available.

SCORING: The CODI is scored by summing item scores for subscale and total scores after reverse-scoring items 9, 13, 17, and 25.

RELIABILITY: The CODI has fair internal consistency, with an overall alpha of .79 and subscale alphas that ranged from .45 for control to .75 for interpersonal dependency. Data on stability were not reported.

VALIDITY: The CODI has fair construct validity with significant relationships, with identification with stereotyped feminine sex-role characteristics, and, for females only, with dysfunctional family of origin environment. For both males and females, the self-alienation component of the CODI was related to dysfunctional family of origin environment.

PRIMARY REFERENCE: Stonebrink, S. (1988). *A measure of co-dependency and the impact of socio-cultural characteristics.* Unpublished Master's Thesis, University of Hawaii, School of Social Work.

AVAILABILITY: The Free Press.

CODI

In answering the following questions, please circle the response which best describes your relationship with the person you care about who is currently chemically dependent.

0 = Never
1 = Sometimes
2 = Often
3 = Always

1. I try to take charge of things when I am with people I care about.   0 1 2 3

2. Disapproval by someone I care about is very painful for me.   0 1 2 3

3. I often do things without knowing why.   0 1 2 3

4. I put the needs of people I care about before my own needs.   0 1 2 3

5. I try to have other people do things the way I want them done.   0 1 2 3

6. I would be completely lost if I didn't have someone special.   0 1 2 3

7. I often feel like a stranger to myself.   0 1 2 3

8. I am loyal to others I care about even though they don't deserve my loyalty.   0 1 2 3

9. I let other people I care about decide what to do.   0 1 2 3

10. I tend to expect too much from others who are important to me.   0 1 2 3

11. I often hide my true feelings from people I care about.   0 1 2 3

12. I blame myself for things that go wrong in my relationships.   0 1 2 3

13. I let other people who are important to me influence my actions.   0 1 2 3

14. I feel that I never get all that I need from people I care about.   0 1 2 3

15. Sometimes it's hard for me to make up my mind because I don't know how I really feel about anything.   0 1 2 3

16.	Sometimes I let down my standards and accept less from people who are important to me.		0 1 2 3
17.	I let other people take charge of things.		0 1 2 3
18.	I think most people don't realize how easily they can hurt me.		0 1 2 3
19.	I avoid talking about my problems.		0 1 2 3
20.	I don't spend as much time with my friends as I would like to.		0 1 2 3
21.	I try to influence the people who are important to me.		0 1 2 3
22.	I tend to imagine the worst if someone I love doesn't arrive when expected.		0 1 2 3
23.	Sometimes I don't know what I want so I do what other people want me to do.		0 1 2 3
24.	I am influenced by the feelings of people I care about.		0 1 2 3
25.	I am easily led by people who are important to me.		0 1 2 3
26.	I have always had a terrible fear that I will lose the love and support of people I care about.		0 1 2 3
27.	I often pretend things are fine when really they are not.		0 1 2 3
28.	I often take on the responsibilities of people who are important to me.		0 1 2 3
29.	I would feel helpless if I was deserted by someone I love.		0 1 2 3

CODEPENDENT QUESTIONNAIRE (CdQ)

AUTHORS: Patricia V. Roehling and Eva Gaumond

PURPOSE: To measure codependence

DESCRIPTION: The CdQ is a 36-item instrument designed to measure codependency among families where at least one member has some psychological disorder such as alcohol abuse. The CdQ was designed to measure four essential features of codependence: responsibility (assuming responsibility for meeting other's needs to the exclusion of acknowledging one's own needs), control (continued investment of self-esteem and the ability to influence and or control feelings and behaviors in one's self and others in the face of obvious adverse consequences), enmeshment (enmeshment in relationships with people with personality disorders, drug dependency, or impulse disorders), and intimacy (anxiety and boundary distortions in situations of intimacy and separation). The CdQ allows practitioners to assess codependency, to relate codependency to other possible disorders, and to track progress in attempting to treat codependency.

NORMS: The CdQ was developed in two studies; the first study was conducted with 48 undergraduate psychology students of whom 37 were female and all were Caucasian. The mean age of this group was 21. The second study was conducted with 42 clients receiving psychotherapy at a private outpatient clinic; 33 were female, 9 were male. The mean age of the clients was 38 with a range of 23 to 63 years. Actual norms were not provided.

SCORING: There are four subscales of the CdQ: intimacy (items 1, 10, 12, 17, 21, 22, 24, 30, 32, and 35), control (items 2, 4, 7, 16, 18, 25, 26, 27, 29, and 34), responsibility (items 3, 5, 6, 8, 11, 14, 15, 19, and 28), and enmeshment (items 9, 13, 20, 23, 31, 33, and 36). The scores for the CdQ and the subscales are obtained by simply summing the individual item scores for either the total scale or the subscales after reverse-scoring items 9, 18, 27, and 30. Total scores range from 36 to 180 with higher scores indicating greater codependency.

RELIABILITY: The CdQ has good internal consistency with an overall alpha of .85 for the total scale; alphas for the subscales were lower, ranging from a low of .50 for intimacy to a high of .77 for responsibility. The CdQ has very good test-retest reliability with a 3-week test-retest reliability of .80 for the total scale and 3-week test-retest reliabilities that range from .46 for control to .85 for responsibility.

VALIDITY: The CdQ has good criterion-related validity with client scores on the CdQ correlating significantly with therapists' ratings of codependency for the total scale as well as all subscales. The CdQ also demonstrates good concurrent validity based upon a number of significant correlations between the CdQ overall score and subscale scores and several items on the Miloon Clinical Multiaxial Inventory.

PRIMARY REFERENCE: Roehling, P. V. and Gaumond, E., (1996). Reliability and validity of the codependent questionnaire, *Alcoholism Treatment Quarterly,* 14, 85–95.

AVAILABILITY: P.V. Roehling, Ph.D., Cornell University, Cornell Careers Institute, G21, MVR Hall, Ithaca, NY, 14853-4401.

CdQ

Please rate on a scale of 1 to 5 how strongly the following statements represent your feelings:

1 = I never feel this way
2 = I rarely feel this way
3 = I sometimes feel this way
4 = I often feel this way
5 = I always feel this way

Record your feelings in the space to the left of the item.

____ 1. Feelings often build up inside me that I do not express.
____ 2. When I am unable to help someone, I feel inadequate.
____ 3. I tend to place the needs of others ahead of my own.
____ 4. I get angry when things do not go my way.
____ 5. I think that others take advantage of me.
____ 6. I am unaware of what I want from others.
____ 7. I feel that without my effort and attention, everything would fall apart.
____ 8. I feel that it is my fault when someone gets angry or upset.
____ 9. It is easy for me to say no to others.
____ 10. It makes me feel uncomfortable to share my feelings with others.
____ 11. I try to please other people.
____ 12. When I am not intimately involved with someone, I feel worthless.
____ 13. I get a great deal of satisfaction from helping others.
____ 14. People will not like me if I talk to them about my problems.
____ 15. Even with good friends, I am afraid that someday they will reject me.
____ 16. I often feel depressed even when things are going well.
____ 17. I tend to either really like a person or really dislike them.
____ 18. I usually do not care about what others think of me.
____ 19. I am comfortable letting others into my life and revealing the "real me" to them.
____ 20. I seem to get involved with people with personal problems.
____ 21. I worry a great deal about what others think of me.
____ 22. It bothers me when friends try to get too close.
____ 23. Most of my friends have many problems.
____ 24. I am overly sensitive to the feelings of those who are important to me.
____ 25. I am highly critical of the things that I do and say.
____ 26. If I work hard enough I should be able to solve almost any problem or make things better for people.
____ 27. My mood is fairly stable and unaffected by the problems and moods of those close to me.
____ 28. I tend to avoid close relationships.
____ 29. If things are going to be done correctly, I must do them myself.
____ 30. I am very open with others about my feelings, no matter what they are.
____ 31. When there is a great deal of activity going on around me, I tend to get a headache.

_____ 32. When I become closely involved with someone, I begin to adopt their values and tastes.
_____ 33. I often get caught in the middle of an argument between other people.
_____ 34. As a child, it seemed like nothing I did was good enough.
_____ 35. Sometimes I do not know how I really feel.
_____ 36. Most of my friends rely upon my guidance and advice.

Copyright © 1996 Roehling and Gaumond.

CONFLICT TACTICS SCALES (CT)

AUTHOR: Murray A. Straus

PURPOSE: To measure reasoning, verbal aggression, and violence in the family.

DESCRIPTION: The CT scale is a 15-item instrument designed to measure three tactics in resolving conflict between family members—reasoning, verbal aggression, and violence. The CT is perhaps the most widely used measure of family conflict. There are three forms of the CT: Conflict with Brother or Sister, Conflict with Parents, and Mother-Father Conflict Resolution. The CT items are actions one might take in a conflict with a family member, and scores are the number of times the action has occurred over the past year. A respondent assesses the frequency of each action for himself or herself and the other person in the conflict. Caution in relying on the CT scores is necessary in clinical samples because people may tend to underreport their own verbal and physical aggression while overreporting the rate of aggression by the relevant other.

NORMS: Normative data vary considerably based on the family members involved, for example, conflicts between brothers compared to mother-father conflicts. The primary reference provides norms on the incident rates of each conflict tactic for several types of family relationships.

SCORING: There are several ways to score the CT scales, including Guttman scale scores, summative scores, rates of conflict tactics, and typology of aggression; these are available in the primary reference. Scores on the chronicity of conflict tactics are useful in clinical practice and are the sum of each item score. For each CT scale the reasoning subscale scores are items A through E. Verbal aggression scores are the sum of items F through J, and physical aggression consists of items K through O. Scores for one's own conflict tactics and those of the other in the conflict are tallied separately. Scores range from 0 to 15 and higher scores reflect more use of the particular tactic.

RELIABILITY: As summarized in the primary reference, six studies have supported the internal consistency of the reasoning, verbal aggression, and physical aggression subscales. For the reasoning subscale, 12 alpha coefficients range from .42 to .76. For the verbal aggression subscale 16 alphas are available and range from .62 to .88. Seventeen alphas are available on the physical aggression subscale and range from .42 to .96. The internal consistency of the reasoning subscale seems lower because the form used in the study had fewer items, and thus the version presented here is probably more reliable. Data on stability were not available.

VALIDITY: The CT scales have received extensive support regarding their validity. First, several studies support the factor structure of reasoning, verbal aggression, and physical aggression. Concurrent validity is evidenced by the agreement between different family members about the conflict tactics. The CT scales do not seem to correlate with social desirability. Extensive construct validity data are also available, including correlations between CT scores and risk factors of family violence, antisocial behaviors by child victims, levels of affection between family members, and self-esteem.

PRIMARY REFERENCE: Straus, M. A. and Gelles, R. J. (1990). *Physical Violence in American Families: Risk Factors and Adaptations to Violence in 8,145 Families*. New Brunswick, NJ: Transaction. Instruments reproduced with permission of Murray A. Straus.

AVAILABILITY: Murray A. Straus, Family Research Laboratory, University of New Hampshire, Durham, NH 03824.

Conflict with Brother or Sister

Here is a list of things that you and your brother or sister might have done when you had a conflict. Now taking *all* disagreements into account, we would like you to say how often you had done the things listed at any time during the last year. Answer by circling one of these numbers for your brother or sister and one for yourself.

0 = Never
1 = Once that year
2 = Two or three times
3 = Often, but less than once a month
4 = About once a month
5 = More than once a month

	Brother or Sister	Me
A. *Tried* to discuss the issue relatively calmly	0 1 2 3 4 5	0 1 2 3 4 5
B. *Did* discuss the issue relatively calmly	0 1 2 3 4 5	0 1 2 3 4 5
C. Got information to back up his/her side of things	0 1 2 3 4 5	0 1 2 3 4 5
D. Brought in someone else to help settle things (or tried to)	0 1 2 3 4 5	0 1 2 3 4 5
E. Argued heatedly but short of yelling	0 1 2 3 4 5	0 1 2 3 4 5
F. Yelled and/or insulted	0 1 2 3 4 5	0 1 2 3 4 5

		Brother or Sister	Me
G.	Sulked and/or refused to talk about it	0 1 2 3 4 5	0 1 2 3 4 5
H.	Stomped out of the room	0 1 2 3 4 5	0 1 2 3 4 5
I.	Threw something (but not at the other) or smashed something	0 1 2 3 4 5	0 1 2 3 4 5
J.	Threatened to hit or throw something at the other	0 1 2 3 4 5	0 1 2 3 4 5
K.	Threw something *at the other*	0 1 2 3 4 5	0 1 2 3 4 5
L.	Pushed, grabbed, or shoved the other	0 1 2 3 4 5	0 1 2 3 4 5
M.	Hit (or tried to hit) the other person but *not* with anything	0 1 2 3 4 5	0 1 2 3 4 5
N.	Hit or tried to hit the other person with something hard	0 1 2 3 4 5	0 1 2 3 4 5
O.	Other. Please describe:	0 1 2 3 4 5	0 1 2 3 4 5

Conflict with Parents

Here is the same list of things that you and your father and mother might have done when you had a conflict. Now taking into account *all* disagreements (not just the most serious one), we would like you to say how often you had done the things listed at any time during the last year. Answer by circling one of these numbers for each person.

0 = Never
1 = Once that year
2 = Two or three times
3 = Often, but less than once a month
4 = About once a month
5 = More than once a month

	Father	Me	Mother	Me
A. *Tried* to discuss the issue relatively calmly	0 1 2 3 4 5	0 1 2 3 4 5	0 1 2 3 4 5	0 1 2 3 4 5
B. *Did* discuss the issue relatively calmly	0 1 2 3 4 5	0 1 2 3 4 5	0 1 2 3 4 5	0 1 2 3 4 5
C. Got information to back up his/her side of things	0 1 2 3 4 5	0 1 2 3 4 5	0 1 2 3 4 5	0 1 2 3 4 5
D. Brought in someone else to help settle things (or tried to)	0 1 2 3 4 5	0 1 2 3 4 5	0 1 2 3 4 5	0 1 2 3 4 5
E. Argued heatedly but short of yelling	0 1 2 3 4 5	0 1 2 3 4 5	0 1 2 3 4 5	0 1 2 3 4 5

Father	Me		Mother	Me
0 1 2 3 4 5	0 1 2 3 4 5	F. Yelled and/or insulted	0 1 2 3 4 5	0 1 2 3 4 5
0 1 2 3 4 5	0 1 2 3 4 5	G. Sulked and/or refused to talk about it	0 1 2 3 4 5	0 1 2 3 4 5
0 1 2 3 4 5	0 1 2 3 4 5	H. Stomped out of the room	0 1 2 3 4 5	0 1 2 3 4 5
0 1 2 3 4 5	0 1 2 3 4 5	I. Threw something (but not at the other) or smashed something	0 1 2 3 4 5	0 1 2 3 4 5
0 1 2 3 4 5	0 1 2 3 4 5	J. Threatened to hit or throw something at the other	0 1 2 3 4 5	0 1 2 3 4 5
0 1 2 3 4 5	0 1 2 3 4 5	K. Threw something *at the other*	0 1 2 3 4 5	0 1 2 3 4 5
0 1 2 3 4 5	0 1 2 3 4 5	L. Pushed, grabbed, or shoved the other	0 1 2 3 4 5	0 1 2 3 4 5
0 1 2 3 4 5	0 1 2 3 4 5	M. Hit (or tried to hit) the other person but *not* with anything	0 1 2 3 4 5	0 1 2 3 4 5
0 1 2 3 4 5	0 1 2 3 4 5	N. Hit or tried to hit the other person with something hard	0 1 2 3 4 5	0 1 2 3 4 5
0 1 2 3 4 5	0 1 2 3 4 5	O. Other. Please describe:	0 1 2 3 4 5	0 1 2 3 4 5

Father-Mother Conflict Resolution

We have the same list of things your father and mother might have done when they had a conflict. Now taking *all* disagreements into account (not just the most serious one), how often did they do the things listed at any time during the last year?

0 = Never
1 = Once that year
2 = Two or three times
3 = Often, but less than once a month
4 = About once a month
5 = More than once a month

		Father						Mother					
A.	*Tried* to discuss the issue relatively calmly	0	1	2	3	4	5	0	1	2	3	4	5
B.	*Did* discuss the issue relatively calmly	0	1	2	3	4	5	0	1	2	3	4	5
C.	Got information to back up his/her side of things	0	1	2	3	4	5	0	1	2	3	4	5
D.	Brought in someone else to help settle things (or tried to)	0	1	2	3	4	5	0	1	2	3	4	5
E.	Argued heatedly but short of yelling	0	1	2	3	4	5	0	1	2	3	4	5
F.	Yelled and/or insulted	0	1	2	3	4	5	0	1	2	3	4	5
G.	Sulked and/or refused to talk about it	0	1	2	3	4	5	0	1	2	3	4	5
H.	Stomped out of the room	0	1	2	3	4	5	0	1	2	3	4	5

I.	Threw something (but not at the other) or smashed something	0	1	2	3	4	5	0	1	2	3	4	5
J.	Threatened to hit or throw something at the other	0	1	2	3	4	5	0	1	2	3	4	5
K.	Threw something *at the other* person	0	1	2	3	4	5	0	1	2	3	4	5
L.	Pushed, grabbed, or shoved the other	0	1	2	3	4	5	0	1	2	3	4	5
M.	Hit (or tried to hit) the other person but *not* with anything	0	1	2	3	4	5	0	1	2	3	4	5
N.	Hit or tried to hit the other person with something hard	0	1	2	3	4	5	0	1	2	3	4	5
O.	Threatened to break up the marriage by separation or divorce	0	1	2	3	4	5	0	1	2	3	4	5
P.	Other. Please describe:	0	1	2	3	4	5	0	1	2	3	4	5

COPING HEALTH INVENTORY FOR PARENTS (CHIP)

AUTHORS: Hamilton I. McCubbin, Marilyn A. McCubbin, Robert S. Nevin, and Elizabeth Cauble

PURPOSE: To measure a family's coping with chronic illness of a child.

DESCRIPTION: The CHIP is a 45-item instrument designed to measure parents' response to management of family life when they have a child who is seriously and/or chronically ill. Items for the CHIP were developed by use of items from previous research in family stress and from theory from several areas pertinent to families and health. The CHIP has three subscales developed through factor analysis: maintaining family integration, cooperation, and an optimistic definition of the situation (I; items 1, 3, 6, 8, 11, 13, 23, 26, 28, 31, 36, 38, 41, 43, 44, 45); maintaining social support, self-esteem and psychological stability (II; items 2, 4, 7, 9, 12, 14, 17, 19, 22, 24, 27, 29, 32, 33, 34, 37, 39, 42); understanding the medical situation through communication with other parents and consultation with medical staff (III; items 5, 10, 15, 20, 25, 30, 35, 40).

NORMS: The CHIP was studied with 308 parents who have a chronically ill child (no other demographic data reported). Mean scores on Factor I were 40 (SD = 15) for mothers and 36 (SD = 20) for fathers: on Factor II—28 (SD = 12) for mothers and 25 (SD = 15) for fathers; and on Factor III—15 (SD = 7) for mothers and 12 (SD = 8) for fathers.

SCORING: Scores for each subscale are simply a sum of items on that subscale. The column "CB Not Used" is ignored. Developing profiles of coping patterns using the questionnaire are described in the primary reference.

RELIABILITY: The CHIP has good internal consistency with alphas of .79 for the first two factors and .71 for Factor III. No data on stability were available.

VALIDITY: The CHIP has fair concurrent validity with several correlations with the Family Environment Scales. The CHIP also has good known-groups validity, significantly discriminating between high and low conflict families. Results from some 22 other studies of the CHIP are summarized in the primary reference.

PRIMARY REFERENCE: McCubbin, H. I. and Thompson, A. I. (eds.) (1991). *Family Assessment Inventories for Research and Practice*. Madison, WI: University of Wisconsin.

AVAILABILITY: Dr. Hamilton McCubbin, Dean, School of Family Resources and Consumer Services, Madison, WI 53706-1575.

CHIP

Purpose:
CHIP—The Coping-Health Inventory for Parents was developed to record what parents find helpful or not helpful to them in the management of family life when one or more of its members is ill for a brief period or has a medical condition which calls for continued medical care. Coping is defined as personal or collective (with other individuals, programs) efforts to manage the hardships associated with health problems in the family.

Directions:
To complete this inventory you are asked to read the list of "Coping Behaviors" below, one at a time.

For each coping behavior you used, please record how helpful it was. Circle ONE number:

> 3 = Extremely helpful
> 2 = Moderately helpful
> 1 = Minimally helpful
> 0 = Not helpful

For each coping behavior (CB) you did *not* use please record your reason by checking *one* of the boxes: "Chose not to use it" or "Not possible."

Please begin: Please read and record your decision for EACH and EVERY coping behavior listed below.

COPING BEHAVIORS	Extremely helpful	Moderately helpful	Minimally helpful	Not helpful	CB Not Used Reasons Chose not to	Not possible
1. Trying to maintain family stability	3	2	1	0	☐	☐
2. Engaging in relationships and friendships which help me to feel important and appreciated	3	2	1	0	☐	☐
3. Trusting my spouse (or former spouse) to help support me and my child(ren)	3	2	1	0	☐	☐
4. Sleeping	3	2	1	0	☐	☐

COPING BEHAVIORS	Extremely helpful	Moderately helpful	Minimally helpful	Not helpful	CB Not Used Reasons	
					Chose not to	Not possible
5. Talking with the medical staff (nurses, social worker, etc.) when we visit the medical center	3	2	1	0	☐	☐
6. Believing that my child(ren) will get better	3	2	1	0	☐	☐
7. Working, outside employment	3	2	1	0	☐	☐
8. Showing that I am strong	3	2	1	0	☐	☐
9. Purchasing gifts for myself and/or other family members	3	2	1	0	☐	☐
10. Talking with other individuals/parents in my same situation	3	2	1	0	☐	☐
11. Taking good care of all the medical equipment at home	3	2	1	0	☐	☐
12. Eating	3	2	1	0	☐	☐
13. Getting other members of the family to help with chores and tasks at home	3	2	1	0	☐	☐
14. Getting away by myself	3	2	1	0	☐	☐
15. Talking with the doctor about my concerns about my child(ren) with the medical condition	3	2	1	0	☐	☐
16. Believing that the medical center/hospital has my family's best interest in mind	3	2	1	0	☐	☐
17. Building close relationships with people	3	2	1	0	☐	☐

	COPING BEHAVIORS	Extremely helpful	Moderately helpful	Minimally helpful	Not helpful	CB Not Used Reasons	
						Chose not to	Not possible
18.	Believing in God	3	2	1	0	☐	☐
19.	Developing myself as a person	3	2	1	0	☐	☐
20.	Talking with other parents in the same type of situation and learning about their experiences	3	2	1	0	☐	☐
21.	Doing things together as a family (involving all members of the family)	3	2	1	0	☐	☐
22.	Investing time and energy in my job	3	2	1	0	☐	☐
23.	Believing that my child is getting the best medical care possible	3	2	1	0	☐	☐
24.	Entertaining friends in our home	3	2	1	0	☐	☐
25.	Reading about how other persons in my situation handle things	3	2	1	0	☐	☐
26.	Doing things with family relatives	3	2	1	0	☐	☐
27.	Becoming more self-reliant and independent	3	2	1	0	☐	☐
28.	Telling myself that I have many things I should be thankful for	3	2	1	0	☐	☐
29.	Concentrating on hobbies (art, music, jogging, etc.)	3	2	1	0	☐	☐

	COPING BEHAVIORS	Extremely helpful	Moderately helpful	Minimally helpful	Not helpful	CB Not Used Reasons	
						Chose not to	Not possible
30.	Explaining our family situation to friends and neighbors so they will understand us	3	2	1	0	☐	☐
31.	Encouraging child(ren) with medical condition to be more independent	3	2	1	0	☐	☐
32.	Keeping myself in shape and well-groomed	3	2	1	0	☐	☐
33.	Involvement in social activities (parties, etc.) with friends	3	2	1	0	☐	☐
34.	Going out with my spouse on a regular basis	3	2	1	0	☐	☐
35.	Being sure prescribed medical treatments for child(ren) are carried out at home on a daily basis	3	2	1	0	☐	☐
36.	Building a closer relationship with my spouse	3	2	1	0	☐	☐
37.	Allowing myself to get angry	3	2	1	0	☐	☐
38.	Investing myself in my child(ren)	3	2	1	0	☐	☐
39.	Talking to someone (not professional counselor/doctor) about how I feel	3	2	1	0	☐	☐
40.	Reading more about the medical problem which concerns me	3	2	1	0	☐	☐
41.	Talking over personal feelings and concerns with spouse	3	2	1	0	☐	☐

COPING BEHAVIORS	Extremely helpful	Moderately helpful	Minimally helpful	Not helpful	CB Not Used Reasons	
					Chose not to	Not possible
42. Being able to get away from the home care tasks and responsibilities for some relief	3	2	1	0	☐	☐
43. Having my child with the medical condition seen at the clinic/hospital on a regular basis	3	2	1	0	☐	☐
44. Believing that things will always work out	3	2	1	0	☐	☐
45. Doing things with my children	3	2	1	0	☐	☐

Copyright © 1991 H. McCubbin and A. I. Thompson.

ENVIRONMENTAL ASSESSMENT INDEX (EAI)

AUTHOR: Robert H. Poresky

PURPOSE: To assess the quality of children's home environments.

DESCRIPTION: The EAI is a 44-item (short-form = 22 items) instrument designed to assess the educational/developmental quality of children's home environments. (The short-form items are indicated by asterisks on the questionnaire.) The EAI was developed for use as a home (maternal) interview and observation procedure for assessing the homes of children between ages 3 and 11. A home visitor scores each item "yes" or "no" based on either direct observation or information from the child's mother. The EAI is viewed as being useful in assisting with child placements, assessing the effectiveness of home interventions, and understanding the home environment's influence on children's development.

NORMS: The EAI was studied for norms with 62 children from 12 randomly selected midwestern, nonurban counties with two-parent families who had lived on a farm for at least five years. Data were collected in a three-year longitudinal study. Children had to be within the age range of 3 to 11 years. Scores on the EAI (long form) ranged from 70 to 88 with a mean of 82.18 (SD = 3.96).

SCORING: Each "yes" answer is scored 2 and each "no" is scored 1. The total score is the sum of all items (long-form range = 44 to 88; short-form range = 24 to 48).

RELIABILITY: The Cronbach alpha is .84 for the EAI long form and .82 for the short form, both coefficients suggesting good internal consistency. The correlation between the long and short forms was .93, suggesting excellent alternate form reliability. The EAI is an extremely stable measure with three-year test-retest reliability coefficients for the long form that ranged from .67 to .96.

VALIDITY: The EAI has very good concurrent and predictive validity with significant correlations between both forms and measures of intellectual functioning.

PRIMARY REFERENCE: Poresky, R. H. (1987). Environmental Assessment Index: Reliability, stability and validity of the long and short forms, *Educational and Psychological Measurements*, 47, 969–975.

AVAILABILITY: Journal article.

EAI

Interview/Observation Items

Yes	No	*1.	Things requiring visual discrimination (toy typewriter, pressouts, play school, peg boards, hidden face games, or toys making use of color discrimination).
Yes	No	2.	Toys or games facilitating learning letters, words, writing, or reading (books about letters, labeling books, toy typewriter, letter sticks, pencils, stencils, blocks with letters).
Yes	No	*3.	Three or more puzzles.
Yes	No	4.	Two toys or tools necessitating finger and whole hand movement (dolls and doll clothing, toy pistols, clay or play dough, pliers or drill).
Yes	No	*5.	Record player and at least five records appropriate to the child's age (or tape cassette player and tapes).
Yes	No	6.	Real or toy musical instrument (piano, drum, toy xylophone, or guitar).
Yes	No	7.	Toy or game encouraging free expression (finger paints, play dough, crayons, paints and paper, art supplies, drawing paper, colored pencils).
Yes	No	8.	Toys or games necessitating fine motor coordination (paint by numbers, dot book, paper dolls, pick-up-sticks, model airplanes).
Yes	No	9.	Opportunity to learn about animals (animals, books, 4-H).
Yes	No	*10.	Toys or games facilitating learning numbers and math concepts (blocks with numbers, books about numbers, number cards, flash cards).
Yes	No	11.	Building toys (building blocks, Lincoln logs, tinker toys, zig-zag puzzles, erector set).
Yes	No	12.	Family buys a newspaper daily and reads it.
Yes	No	13.	Family subscribes to at least one magazine.
Yes	No	14.	Child has been to a museum, historical or art, in the past year.
Yes	No	15.	Child goes to town at least once a week (do not credit school attendance).
Yes	No	*16.	Child goes to the library at least once a month (do not credit school library).
Yes	No	*17.	Family has a TV, and it is used judiciously, not left on continuously (No TV requires automatic "No", any scheduling scores "Yes").
Yes	No	18.	Parent turns on special TV programs regarded "good" by the mother for the children.
Yes	No	19.	Someone reads stories with the child or discusses pictures in magazine at least five times weekly.
Yes	No	*20.	Child has a special place in which to keep his/her things and "treasures" (other than clothing).
Yes	No	*21.	Child is encouraged to learn to use numbers or mathematics.
Yes	No	22.	Child is encouraged to learn to tell time.

Yes	No	23.	Child is encouraged to learn to make bed, pick up toys, and clean his/her room without help.
Yes	No	24.	Child is taught rules of social behavior, which involve recognition of rights of others.
Yes	No	25.	Parent teaches child some simple manners—to say "Please," "Thank you," "I'm sorry."
Yes	No	26.	Some delay of food gratification is demanded of the child.

By Observation ONLY:

Yes	No	*27.	Ten or more children's books are present and visible in the home.
Yes	No	*28.	At least ten other books are visible in the home.
Yes	No	*29.	Child's outside play environment appears safe and free of hazards.
Yes	No	*30.	The interior of the home is not dark or perceptibly monotonous (yes = 2 = light).
Yes	No	*31.	House is not overly noisy—TV, shouts of children, radio, etc.
Yes	No	*32.	The rooms are not overcrowded with furniture (yes = 2 = not overcrowded).
Yes	No	*33.	All visible rooms of the house are reasonably clean and minimally cluttered.
Yes	No	34.	Mother used complex sentence structure and some long words in conversing.
Yes	No	*35.	Mother used correct grammar and pronunciation.
Yes	No	*36.	Mother's speech is distinct, clear, and audible.
Yes	No	*37.	Child's art work or awards are displayed some place in the house (anything that the child makes).
Yes	No	38.	Mother introduces interviewer to child.
Yes	No	39.	Mother converses with child at least twice during the visit (scolding and skeptical comments not counted).
Yes	No	*40.	Mother answers child's questions or requests verbally.
Yes	No	*41.	Mother usually responds verbally to child's talking.
Yes	No	*42.	Mother spontaneously praises child's appearance or behavior at least once during the visit.
Yes	No	*43.	When speaking of or to child, mother's voice conveys positive feeling.
Yes	No	44.	Mother sets up situation that allows child to show off during visit.

FAMILY ADAPTABILITY AND COHESION EVALUATION SCALE (FACES-III)

AUTHORS: David H. Olson, Joyce Portner, and Yoav Lavee

PURPOSE: To measure family cohesion and family adaptability.

DESCRIPTION: FACES-III is a 20-item instrument designed to measure two main dimensions of family functioning: cohesion and adaptability. FACES-III is based on the Circumplex Model of family functioning which asserts that there are three central dimensions of family behavior: cohesion, adaptability (ability to change), and communication. FACES-III is the third in a series of instruments designed to measure two out of three of these dimensions. The instrument is designed to place families within the Circumplex Model and does so by assessing how family members see their family (perceived) and how they would like it to be (ideal). Thus, the same 20 items on the FACES-III are responded to in two different ways. FACES-III can also be used with couples simply by changing the wording on some of the items (e.g., the first item becomes, "We ask each other for help"). Clinical rating scales for therapists are also available for each of the three dimensions of family functioning.

NORMS: Extensive research on FACES-III has involved 2453 adults across the life cycle and 412 adolescents. Norms are available for families, families with adolescents, and young couples in different stages of the life cycle. Cutting scores also are available that distinguish among rigid, structured, flexible, and chaotic families on the adaptability dimension, and among disengaged, separated, connected, and enmeshed families on the cohesion dimension.

SCORING: FACES-III is scored by summing all items to obtain the total score, summing odd items to obtain the cohesion score, and summing even items to obtain the adaptability score. The higher the cohesion score, the more enmeshed the family is said to be. The higher the adaptability score, the more chaotic it is.

RELIABILITY: FACES-III has only fair internal consistency, with an overall alpha of .68 for the total instrument, .77 for cohesion, and .62 for adaptability. Test-retest data are not available but for FACES-II, there was a four to five-week test-retest correlation of .83 for cohesion and .80 for adaptability showing very good stability.

VALIDITY: FACES-III appears to have good face validity, but data were not available demonstrating any other type of validity. On the other hand, a number of studies have shown FACES-II to have fair known-groups validity in being able to discriminate among extreme, mid-range, and balanced families in several problem categories. A good deal of research currently is being conducted on FACES-III which might generate more information on validity.

PRIMARY REFERENCES: Olson, D. H. (1986) Circumplex Model VII: Validation studies and FACES-III. *Family Process*, 25, 337–351. Olson. D. H., Portner, J., and Lavee, Y. (1985). FACES-III, Family Social Science, University of Minnesota, 290 McNeal Hall, St. Paul, Minnesota, 55108. Instrument reproduced with permission of David H. Olson.

AVAILABILITY: Dr. David H. Olson, Family Social Science, University of Minnesota, 290 McNeal Hall, 1985 Buford Avenue, St. Paul, MN 55108.

FACES-III

Please use the following scale to answer both sets of questions:

1 = Almost never
2 = Once in a while
3 = Sometimes
4 = Frequently
5 = Almost always

DESCRIBE YOUR FAMILY NOW:

____ 1. Family members ask each other for help.
____ 2. In solving problems, the children's suggestions are followed.
____ 3. We approve of each other's friends.
____ 4. Children have a say in their discipline.
____ 5. We like to do things with just our immediate family.
____ 6. Different persons act as leaders in our family.
____ 7. Family members feel closer to other family members than to people outside the family.
____ 8. Our family changes its way of handling tasks.
____ 9. Family members like to spend free time with each other.
____ 10. Parent(s) and children discuss punishment together.
____ 11. Family members feel very close to each other.
____ 12. The children make the decisions in our family.
____ 13. When our family gets together for activities, everybody is present.
____ 14. Rules change in our family.
____ 15. We can easily think of things to do together as a family.
____ 16. We shift household responsibilities from person to person.
____ 17. Family members consult other family members on their decisions.
____ 18. It is hard to identify the leader(s) in our family.
____ 19. Family togetherness is very important.
____ 20. It is hard to tell who does which household chores.

IDEALLY, HOW WOULD YOU LIKE YOUR FAMILY TO BE:

____ 21. Family members would ask each other for help.
____ 22. In solving problems, the children's suggestions would be followed.
____ 23. We would approve of each other's friends.
____ 24. The children would have a say in their discipline.
____ 25. We would like to do things with just our immediate family.
____ 26. Different persons would act as leaders in our family.
____ 27. Family members would feel closer to each other than to people outside the family.
____ 28. Our family would change its way of handling tasks.
____ 29. Family members would like to spend free time with each other.
____ 30. Parent(s) and children would discuss punishment together.
____ 31. Family members would feel very close to each other.
____ 32. Children would make the decisions in our family.

_____ 33. When our family got together, everybody would be present.
_____ 34. Rules would change in our family.
_____ 35. We could easily think of things to do together as a family.
_____ 36. We would shift household responsibilities from person to person.
_____ 37. Family members would consult each other on their decisions.
_____ 38. We would know who the leader(s) was (were) in our family.
_____ 39. Family togetherness would be very important.
_____ 40. We could tell who does which household chores.

FAMILY ASSESSMENT DEVICE (FAD)

AUTHORS: Nathan B. Epstein, Lawrence M. Baldwin, and Duane S. Bishop

PURPOSE: To evaluate family functioning.

DESCRIPTION: The FAD is a 60-item questionnaire designed to evaluate family functioning according to the McMaster Model. This model describes structural, occupational, and transactional properties of families and identifies six dimensions of family functioning: problem solving, communication, roles, affective responsiveness, affective involvement, and behavior control. Accordingly, the FAD is made up of six subscales to measure each of these dimensions plus a seventh subscale dealing with general functioning. A clinical rating scale, used by clinicians in evaluating family functioning, is also available.

NORMS: The FAD was developed on the basis of responses of 503 individuals of whom 294 came from a group of 112 families. The bulk (93) of these families had one member who was an inpatient in an adult psychiatric hospital. The remaining 209 individuals in the sample were students in an introductory psychology course. No other demographic data were presented. Means and standard deviations for clinical and nonclinical samples are:

Scale	Clinical	Nonclinical
Problem Solving (PS)	2.20	2.38
Communication (C)	2.15	2.37
Roles (R)	2.22	2.47
Affective Responsiveness (AR)	2.23	2.42
Affective Involvement (AI)	2.05	2.23
Behavior Control (BC)	1.90	2.02
General Functioning (GF)	1.96	2.26

Although the current version of the scale has 60 items, the original studies were based on a 53-item measure. Seven items were added which are reported to increase reliability of the subscales to which they were added. The items on the subscales are indicated on the instrument.

SCORING: Each item is scored on a 1 to 4 basis using the following key: SA = 1, A = 2, D = 3, SD = 4. Items describing unhealthy functioning are reverse-scored. Lower scores indicate healthier functioning. Scored responses to the items are averaged to provide seven scale scores, each having a possible range from 1.0 (healthy) to 4.0 (unhealthy). Scoring sheets and keys are available to make the scoring process relatively simple and to indicate the items of each subscale.

RELIABILITY: The FAD demonstrates fairly good internal consistency, with alphas for the subscales ranging from .72 to .92. No reliability figures are reported for the overall measure; test-retest reliability data are not available.

VALIDITY: When the general functioning subscale is removed from the analysis, the six other subscales appear relatively independent. The FAD demonstrates some degree of concurrent and predictive validity. In a separate study of 178 couples in their sixties, the FAD was moderately correlated with the Locke-Wallace Marital Satisfaction Scale and showed a fair ability to predict scores on the Philadelphia Geriatric Morale Scale. Further, the FAD has good known-groups validity, with all seven subscales significantly distinguishing between individuals from clinical families and those from nonclinical families.

PRIMARY REFERENCE: Epstein, N. B., Baldwin, L. M., and Bishop, D. S. (1983). The McMaster Family Assessment Device, *Journal of Marital and Family Therapy*, 9, 171–180. Instrument reproduced with permission of Nathan Epstein and Duane Bishop.

AVAILABILITY: Family Research Program, Butler Hospital, 345 Blackstone Boulevard, Providence, RI 92906.

FAD

Following are a number of statements about families. Please read each statement carefully, and decide how well it describes your own family. You should answer according to how you see your family.

For each statement there are four (4) possible responses:

1 = Strongly agree   Select 1 if you feel that the statement describes
                          your family very accurately.

2 = Agree   Select 2 if you feel that the statement describes
                          your family for the most part.

3 = Disagree   Select 3 if you feel that the statement does not
                          describe your family for the most part.

4 = Strongly disagree   Select 4 if you feel that the statement does not
                          describe your family at all.

Try not to spend too much time thinking about each statement, but respond as quickly and as honestly as you can. If you have trouble with one answer with your first reaction. Please be sure to answer *every* statement and mark all your answers in the *space provided to the left* of each statement.

_____ 1.   Planning family activities is difficult because we misunderstand each other. (G)
_____ 2.   We resolve most everyday problems around the house. (PS)
_____ 3.   When someone is upset the others know why. (C)
_____ 4.   When you ask someone to do something, you have to check that they did it. (R)
_____ 5.   If someone is in trouble, the others become too involved (AI)
_____ 6.   In times of crisis we can turn to each other for support. (G)
_____ 7.   We don't know what to do when an emergency comes up. (BC)
_____ 8.   We sometimes run out of things that we need. (G)
_____ 9.   We are reluctant to show our affection for each other. (AR)
_____ 10. We make sure members meet their family responsibilities. (R)
_____ 11. We cannot talk to each other about the sadness we feel. (G)
_____ 12. We usually act on our decisions regarding problems. (PS)
_____ 13. You only get the interest of others when something is important to them. (AI)
_____ 14. You can't tell how a person is feeling from what they are saying. (C)
_____ 15. Family tasks don't get spread around enough. (R)
_____ 16. Individuals are accepted for what they are. (G)
_____ 17. You can easily get away with breaking the rules. (BC)
_____ 18. People come right out and say things instead of hinting at them. (C)
_____ 19. Some of us just don't respond emotionally. (AR)
_____ 20. We know what to do in an emergency. (BC)
_____ 21. We avoid discussing our fears and concerns. (G)

_____ 22. It is difficult to talk to each other about tender feelings. (AI)
_____ 23. We have trouble meeting our bills. (R)
_____ 24. After our family tries to solve a problem, we usually discuss whether it worked or not. (PS)
_____ 25. We are too self-centered (AI)
_____ 26. We can express feelings to each other. (G)
_____ 27. We have no clear expectations about toilet habits. (BC)
_____ 28. We do not show our love for each other. (AR)
_____ 29. We talk to people directly rather than through go-betweens. (C)
_____ 30. Each of us has particular duties and responsibilities. (R)
_____ 31. There are lots of bad feelings in the family. (G)
_____ 32. We have rules about hitting people. (BC)
_____ 33. We get involved with each other only when something interests. (AI)
_____ 34. There's little time to explore personal interests. (R)
_____ 35. We often don't say what we mean. (AR)
_____ 36. We feel accepted for what we are. (G)
_____ 37. We show interest in each other when we can get something out of it personally. (AI)
_____ 38. We resolve most emotional upsets that come up. (PS)
_____ 39. Tenderness takes second place to other things in our family. (AR)
_____ 40. We discuss who is to do household jobs. (R)
_____ 41. Making decisions is a problem for our family. (G)
_____ 42. Our family shows interest in each other only when they can get something out of it. (AI)
_____ 43. We are frank with each other. (C)
_____ 44. We don't hold to any rules or standards. (BC)
_____ 45. If people are asked to do something, they need reminding. (R)
_____ 46. We are able to make decisions about how to solve problems. (G)
_____ 47. If the rules are broken, we don't know what to expect. (BC)
_____ 48. Anything goes in our family. (BC)
_____ 49. We express tenderness. (AR)
_____ 50. We confront problems involving feelings. (PS)
_____ 51. We don't get along well together. (G)
_____ 52. We don't talk to each other when we are angry. (C)
_____ 53. We are generally dissatisfied with the family duties assigned to us. (R)
_____ 54. Even though we mean well, we intrude too much into each others' lives. (AI)
_____ 55. There are rules about dangerous situations. (BC)
_____ 56. We confide in each other. (G)
_____ 57. We cry openly. (AR)
_____ 58. We don't have reasonable transport. (BC)
_____ 59. When we don't like what someone has done, we tell them. (C)
_____ 60. We try to think of different ways to solve problems. (PS)

FAMILY ATTACHMENT AND CHANGEABILITY INDEX 8 (FACI8)

AUTHORS: Hamilton McCubbin, Anne Thompson, and Kelly Elver

PURPOSE: To measure family functioning.

DESCRIPTION: The FACI8 is a 16-item instrument designed to measure family functioning. It was specifically adapted from earlier scales for the study of African-American youth in residential treatment and their families. The FACI8 is based on the notion that families and youth create specific and predictable styles of functioning that can be measured and identified and that have predictive power in explaining which adolescents and young adults are most likely to respond to residential care and succeed in posttreatment living situations. The FACI8 was specifically developed to be ethnically sensitive but applicable to both Caucasian and African-American youth and their families. The FACI8 is available in both English and Spanish, and has two subscales: attachment (items 2, 5, 7, 9, 12, 13, 15, and 16) and changeability (items 1, 3, 4, 6, 8, 10, 11, and 14).

NORMS: The FACI8 has been studied with 1232 youth in residential treatment programs of whom 510 were African-American and 554 were Caucasian. The parents of these youths (N = 977) included 393 African-American and 475 Caucasian parents. The mean for all youths on the attachment subscale was 28.6 (SD = 6.2) and for parents was 29.6 (SD = 5.5). The overall mean for youth on changeability was 22.8 (SD = 6.8) and for parents was 23.5 (SD = 6.1). The means for Caucasian and African-American parents and youth are available in the primary reference.

SCORING: After reverse-scoring all items on the attachment subscale, the scores for the subscales and total scale are obtained by simply summing the item responses within each subscale and the total scale. This ensures that all items are scored in a positive direction.

RELIABILITY: The FACI8 has good internal consistency with an alpha for the youths' attachment scale of .73 and for the youth's changeability scale of .80. The alpha for the parents' attachment scale is .75 and for the changeability scale is .78. The FACI8 has fair stability with 6–12 month test-retest correlations that range from .26 to .48.

VALIDITY: The FACI8 has very good predictive validity showing significant effects for both youth and parent scores in predicting program completion and placement overall, for Caucasians, and for African-Americans with regard to parents' scores for program completion and youth scores for program placement.

PRIMARY REFERENCE: McCubbin, H. I., Thompson, A. I., and Elver, K. M. Family Attachment and Changeability Index 8 (FACI8). In H. I. McCubbin, A. I. Thompson, and M. A. McCubbin (1996). *Family Assessment: Re-*

siliency, Coping and Adaptation-Inventories for Research and Practice. Madison: University Wisconsin System, 725–751.

AVAILABILITY: After purchase of the primary reference, you may register by telephone at (608) 262-5070. The book provides instructions for permission to use the instrument.

FACI8

Decide how well each statement describes what is happening in your family. In the column headed **Now,** circle the number which best describes how often each thing is happening right now. In the column headed **Like,** circle the number which best describes how often you would like each thing to happen in your family.

For example, if you felt that most of the time it is all right for the members of your family to talk about their feelings, you would circle 4 in the NOW column. After you have finished all the items in the Now column, think about how often you would like these things to occur in your family in the future. For example, if you would like for the members of your family to be able to talk about their feelings all the time, you would circle 5 in the Like column.

IN MY FAMILY . . .	Now	Like
	Never / Sometimes / Half the time / More than half / Always	Never / Sometimes / Half the time / More than half / Always
1. In our family it is easy for everyone to express his/her opinion	1 2 3 4 5	1 2 3 4 5
2. It is easier to discuss problems with people outside the family than with other family members	1 2 3 4 5	1 2 3 4 5
3. Each family member has input in major family decisions	1 2 3 4 5	1 2 3 4 5
4. Family members discuss problems and feel good about the solutions	1 2 3 4 5	1 2 3 4 5
5. In our family everyone goes his/her own way	1 2 3 4 5	1 2 3 4 5
6. Family members consult other family members on their decisions	1 2 3 4 5	1 2 3 4 5
7. We have difficulty thinking of things to do as a family	1 2 3 4 5	1 2 3 4 5
8. Discipline is fair in our family	1 2 3 4 5	1 2 3 4 5
9. Family members feel closer to people outside the family than to other family members	1 2 3 4 5	1 2 3 4 5
10. Our family tries new ways of dealing with problems	1 2 3 4 5	1 2 3 4 5
11. In our family, everyone shares responsibilities	1 2 3 4 5	1 2 3 4 5
12. It is difficult to get a rule changed in our family	1 2 3 4 5	1 2 3 4 5
13. Family members avoid each other at home	1 2 3 4 5	1 2 3 4 5

14. When problems arise, we compromise	1	2	3	4	5	1	2	3	4	5
15. Family members are afraid to say what is on their minds	1	2	3	4	5	1	2	3	4	5
16. Family members pair up rather than do things as a total family	1	2	3	4	5	1	2	3	4	5

Copyright © H. I. McCubbin, D. Olson, Y. Lavee, and J. Patterson, 1984.

FACI8-SPANISH

Decida que tan bien cada declaración describe los que está sucediendo en su familia. En la columna que dice **Ahora,** encierre con un círculo el número que mejor describe la frecuencia con la que cada episodio sucede ahora. Bajo la columna **Gustaría,** encierre en un círculo el número que mejor describe la frecuencia con la que la gustaría que cada episodio sucediera.

Por ejemplo, si cree que es bueno que los miembros de la familia discutan sobre sus sentimientos la mayoría del tiempo, usted debe encerrar con un círculo el número 4 en la columna Ahora. Después de terminar con todas las declaraciones de la columna AHORA, piense en la frecuencia con la que le gustaría que estos episodios ocurrieran en su familia en el futuro. Por ejemplo, si le gustaría que los miembros de su familia hablaran sobre sus sentimientos todo el tiempo, usted debe encerrar en un círculo el 6 de la columna Gustaria.

	Ahora					Gustaría				
EN MI FAMILIA . . .	Nunca	A veces	La mitad del tiempo	Más de la mitad	Siempre	Nunca	A veces	La mitad del tiempo	Más de la mitad	Siempre
1. Es fácil para todos expresar su opinión	1	2	3	4	5	1	2	3	4	5
2. Es más fácil discutir los problemas con particulares que con miembros de la familia	1	2	3	4	5	1	2	3	4	5
3. Cada miembro da su parecer en decisiones familiares importantes	1	2	3	4	5	1	2	3	4	5
4. Los miembros discuten los problemas y se sienten bien sobre las soluciones	1	2	3	4	5	1	2	3	4	5
5. Cada uno toma por su lado	1	2	3	4	5	1	2	3	4	5
6. Todos consultan con otros miembros de la familia sobre las decisiones a tomar	1	2	3	4	5	1	2	3	4	5
7. Es difícil pensar en actividades que podemos realizar juntos	1	2	3	4	5	1	2	3	4	5
8. La disciplina es justa	1	2	3	4	5	1	2	3	4	5

9. Los miembros se sienten más cercanos a particulares que a los propios miembros de la familia	1	2	3	4	5	1	2	3	4	5
10. Probamos nuevos métodos de confrontar los problemas	1	2	3	4	5	1	2	3	4	5
11. Compartimos todas las responsabilidades	1	2	3	4	5	1	2	3	4	5
12. Es difícil cambiar una regla	1	2	3	4	5	1	2	3	4	5
13. Los miembros tratan de no tener nada ver los unos con otros	1	2	3	4	5	1	2	3	4	5
14. Cuando surgen problemas, cedemos para llegar a un acuerdo	1	2	3	4	5	1	2	3	4	5
15. Tememos decir lo que verdaderamente pensamos	1	2	3	4	5	1	2	3	4	5
16. Miembros de la familia se agrupan en vez de hacer las cosas todos juntos	1	2	3	4	5	1	2	3	4	5

Copyright © H. I. McCubbin, D. Olson, Y. Lavee, and J. Patterson, 1984.

FAMILY AWARENESS SCALE (FAS)

AUTHORS: Michael S. Kolevzon and Robert G. Green

PURPOSE: To measure family competence.

DESCRIPTION: The FAS is a 14-item instrument designed to measure family competence as described in the Beavers-Timberlawn Model of Family Competence. This model proposes that optimally functioning families can be distinguished from less competent families on the basis of several dimensions: family structure, mythology (how the family views itself), goal-directed negotiation, autonomy of its members, and the nature of family expression. The FAS can be administered to all members of a family able to understand the questions. As a relatively new instrument, the FAS does not have a great deal of psychometric data available, but it does appear to be one means of providing an overall view of family competence.

NORMS: The FAS was initially studied with 157 families who participated in a family therapy research project. All families had one child under supervision of the Corrections Department of the State of Virginia. The families were mainly white (79%), 36.9 single-parent, with a broad range of income levels. No actual norms are reported.

SCORING: Items 1 and 2 are scored on a 5-point scale while items 3 through 14 are scored on 9-point scales. Negatively worded items are reverse-scored and then all the items are summed to produce a range of 14 to 118, with higher scores meaning greater family competence.

RELIABILITY: The FAS has very good internal consistency, with alphas of .85 for children, .87 for mothers, and .88 for fathers. No test-retest data were reported.

VALIDITY: The FAS has some degree of concurrent validity, correlating at low but significant levels with trained raters of family competence who also used the Beavers-Timberlawn model. The FAS is also significantly correlated with the Parent-Adolescent Communication Inventory and the Dyadic Adjustment Scale. No other validity data were reported.

PRIMARY REFERENCE: Green, R. G., Kolevzon, M. S., and Vosler, N. R. (1985). The Beavers-Timberlawn Model of Family Competence and the Circumplex Model of Family Adaptability and Cohesion: Separate, but equal? *Family Process*, 24, 385–398. Instrument reproduced with permission of Michael S. Kolevzon and Robert G. Green.

AVAILABILITY: Dr. Michael S. Kolevzon, Florida International University School of Public Affairs and Services, Social Work Department, North Miami Beach, FL 33181.

FAS

PART I

Questions 1 and 2 each contain a group of statements that describe families. For each question please check the one blank for the statement that *most accurately describes* your family.

1. a. _____ No one person is really strong enough to be the leader in our family.
    b. _____ Our family has one stronq leader. The leader always makes the rules and enforces them.
    c. _____ Although we have a strong leader, *at times* we talk over decisions.
    d. _____ We *frequently* talk things over, but in the end one person is usually in charge.
    e. _____ Leadership is always shared between the adults in our family depending on the situation.

2. a. _____ In our family it seems that a parent and a child are always "teaming or ganging up" against other family members.
    b. _____ Frequently a parent and a child team up against other family members.
    c. _____ The adults are usually on the same side.
    d. _____ The adults are usually on the same side and generally they make a good learning team.
    e. _____ There is always a strong adult team in our family.

PART II

Questions 3 to 14 describe certain characteristics of all families on a 9-point scale. Please *circle* the number on the scale that best describes your family. *Please circle only one number for each item.*

3. How difficult is it for someone outside of your family to figure out which family members have power over other family members?

Very difficult   1   2   3   4   5   6   7   8   9   Very easy

4. How good a judge are individual family members of their own behaviors within your family?

Very good judge   1   2   3   4   5   6   7   8   9   Very poor judge

5. How good is your family at taking over and solving problems?

| Very good | | 1 | 2 | 3 | 4 | 5 | 6 | 7 | 8 | 9 | Very bad |

6. How *clearly* do the members of your family tell one another about their feelings and thoughts?

| Very clear | | 1 | 2 | 3 | 4 | 5 | 6 | 7 | 8 | 9 | Not clear |

7. How frequently do the members of your family say or admit that they are responsible for their own past and present behavior?

| Always | | 1 | 2 | 3 | 4 | 5 | 6 | 7 | 8 | 9 | Never |

8. How often do the members of your family speak for one another or act like they can read each other's minds?

| Frequently | 1 | 2 | 3 | 4 | 5 | 6 | 7 | 8 | 9 | Never |

9. How often are family members open and willing to listen to the statements of other family members?

| Usually | | 1 | 2 | 3 | 4 | 5 | 6 | 7 | 8 | 9 | Never |

10. How often do family members share their feelings with one another?

| Always | | 1 | 2 | 3 | 4 | 5 | 6 | 7 | 8 | 9 | Never |

11. How would you describe your family?

| Warm, Humerous, Optimistic | 1 | 2 | 3 | 4 | 5 | 6 | 7 | 8 | 9 | Pessimistic |

12. How much conflict is there generally in your family?

| Always | | 1 | 2 | 3 | 4 | 5 | 6 | 7 | 8 | 9 | Never |

13. How often are family members sensitive to, and understanding of, each others' feelings?

Always ———————————————————————— Never
        1   2   3   4   5   6   7   8   9

14. How many emotional problems does your family have compared *to most families*?

Far   ———————————————————————— Far
more   1   2   3   4   5   6   7   8   9 fewer

FAMILY BELIEFS INVENTORY (FBI)

AUTHORS: Patricia Vincent Roehling and Arthur L. Robin

PURPOSE: To measure unreasonable beliefs regarding parent-adolescent relationships.

DESCRIPTION: The FBI consists of two parallel forms for parents and adolescents and is designed to measure distorted beliefs regarding their relationships. The FBI for parents (FBI-P) assesses six distorted beliefs: ruination, perfectionism, approval, obedience, self-blame, and malicious intent. The FBI for adolescents (FBI-A) measures four beliefs: ruination, unfairness, autonomy, and approval. Each belief is assessed by 10 items linked to 10 vignettes depicting frequent sources of conflict between parents and teenagers. Two statements per vignette represent commonly held realistic beliefs; they were included to reduce any tendency toward response set. The FBI is based on a behavioral/family-systems account of family relations. Although it is much longer than other measures in this book, the FBI is one of the few measures, if not the only one, that examines the role of cognitive factors in parent-adolescent conflict. This instrument can be used as a measure of change, especially when changing cognitions is one of the targets of family-based intervention.

NORMS: The FBI was normed on 30 distressed (in treatment for parent-adolescent problems) and 30 nondistressed (satisfied with relationships and not in treatment) families. There were 10 female and 20 male adolescents (mean age = 14.4) in the distressed group and 9 males and 21 females (mean age = 14.9) in the nondistressed group. There were 8 single-parent families in the distressed group and 6 in the nondistressed group. The mean total score on the FBI for distressed fathers was 214 (SD = 25) and for nondistressed fathers was 186 (SD = 30). The mean total score for distressed mothers was 193 (SD = 35) and for nondistressed mothers 173 (SD = 42). The mean for distressed adolescents was 103 (SD = 31) and for nondistressed adolescents was 139 (SD = 22).

SCORING: Each item is rated on a 7-point Likert-type scale. Subscale scores are simply a sum of items in that subscale and range from 10 to 70. The total score is just a summing of all items and ranges from 60 to 420 for parents and 40 to 280 for adolescents. Higher scores represent greater adherence to a belief.

RELIABILITY: The FBI has fair to good internal consistency with alpha coefficients on all subscales except "approval" ranging from .67 to .84 for fathers, .65 to .78 for mothers, and .82 to .83 for adolescents. For approval, the alpha coefficients were .46 for fathers, .59 for mothers, and .72 for adolescents. No test-retest data are reported.

VALIDITY: The FBI has fair known-groups validity, distinguishing between distressed and nondistressed fathers on four of six subscales, and between distressed and nondistressed adolescents on three of four subscales. The FBI did not distinguish between distressed and nondistressed mothers.

PRIMARY REFERENCE: Roehling, P. V. and Robin, A. L. (1986). Development and validation of the Family Beliefs Inventory: A measure of unrealistic beliefs among parents and adolescents, *Journal of Consulting and Clinical Psychology*, 54, 693–697.

AVAILABILITY: Arthur L. Robin, Psychiatry/Psychology Department, Children's Hospital of Michigan, 3901 Beaubien Boulevard, Detroit, MI 48201.

FBI-P

We are interested in understanding how parents and their adolescents think about different situations. In order to help us do this we have created a questionnaire which describes a number of situations that might occur in daily life, each followed by several statements representing people's reactions to the situation.

Please read each situation and *imagine* that it is happening to you. Rate each statement on the degree to which you would agree with it. Because you may not have had the experiences described in some of the situations, it is important that you *imagine* that it is happening to you. Be sure that you don't rate the situation; just rate how much the statement is like the way you would think. Please rate every statement.

Who Should Be Youth's Friend

Your youth has recently begun spending a lot of time with an undesirable friend. This friend acts rudely toward you and your spouse, looks sleazy, skips school, smokes, and probably drinks. You suspect the friend may also be doing other things which you might disapprove of. You do not know the friend's family or what kind of people they are. You have begun to prohibit your youth from going places or doing things with this friend. Your youth objects strongly to your prohibitions. A number of very unpleasant disagreements have taken place between you and your youth over who should be his/her friends. You are concerned about what is going to happen next.

Please rate how strongly you agree or disagree with the following statements:

        1 = Do not agree at all
        2 = Agree very little
        3 = Agree a little
        4 = Moderately agree
        5 = Agree a lot
        6 = Mostly agree
        7 = Totally agree

_____ 1. A decent youth knows what kind of people to avoid and what kind to befriend.
_____ 2. Teenagers who get involved with undesirable friends end up getting into serious trouble and ruining their futures.
_____ 3. Youths do not always conform to the behavior of their peer groups.
_____ 4. Parents should not interfere with their youths' friends because the teenager will be very angry at the parents.
_____ 5. Teenagers who look for and find undesirable friends were not taught proper values by their parents.
_____ 6. Parents might occasionally offer advice about an adolescent's choice of friends.

_____ 7. Teenagers should respect their parents' judgments and follow their advice about friends.

_____ 8. Teenagers try to upset their parents by hanging out with the wrong type of people.

How Money Is Spent

Your adolescent spends money as if it were going out of style. He/she is constantly spending money on things like albums, video games, magazines, or junk food. You try to encourage your youth to put money to good use and buy things like clothing or books or even to save his/her money. But it is no use. As soon as your youth gets money, it is spent with nothing to show for it.

Please rate how strongly you agree or disagree with the following statements:

1 = Do not agree at all
2 = Agree very little
3 = Agree a little
4 = Moderately agree
5 = Agree a lot
6 = Mostly agree
7 = Totally agree

_____ 1. Parents should not upset their teenager by disapproving of the way he/she spends own money.

_____ 2. Adolescents should be allowed some freedom in deciding how their money is to be spent.

_____ 3. Teenagers who waste their money on junk learned these bad habits from their parents.

_____ 4. Teenagers should always follow their parents' advice about spending money.

_____ 5. Adolescents should help their parents by spending their own money on clothing, books, and other necessities.

_____ 6. If a person does not learn to spend money wisely as a youth, he/she will end up deeply in debt as an adult.

_____ 7. Parents should encourage their youths to save some money for the future.

_____ 8. Teenagers waste their parents' hard-earned money and don't care about their parents' financial position.

Being Nice to Teen's Friends

Your teenager has a group of friends who always seem to be calling or coming over. At times you feel as if you have no privacy. In addition, these friends are not as nice to you as you would like. They are loud and leave a mess. As a result, you are less than friendly towards them. You won't speak to them when they come over and you are not nice to them on the phone. This upsets your youth who is afraid that he/she will lose the friends.

Please rate how strongly you agree or disagree with the following statements:

1 = Do not agree at all
2 = Agree very little
3 = Agree a little
4 = Moderately agree
5 = Agree a lot
6 = Mostly agree
7 = Totally agree

____ 1. Adolescents should not invite back into their home friends who have annoyed their parents.

____ 2. Teenagers who bring all of their loud, messy friends over to visit want to harass their parents and drive them crazy.

____ 3. Generally, family members should treat each other's friends with courtesy.

____ 4. Adolescents should not choose friends who are unpleasant and discourteous.

____ 5. Parents should not anger teenagers by complaining about their friends' rude behavior.

____ 6. When visiting someone else's home, adolescents should be pleasant to their friend's parents.

____ 7. Parents who can not get along with their children's friends have serious personal inadequacies.

____ 8. Parents should speak out when their teenager's friends are rude or else the teenager will also become rude and discourteous.

Spending Time Away from Home

Your teenager has recently begun spending a lot of time with friends. They meet after school, go to the movies, go shopping, and spend weekends together. You are concerned that the family is not spending enough time together, and have suggested that your youth stay home with the family more often. However, your youth has not listened to your suggestions. Whenever you insist that the family spend more time together, an argument results. You may have to limit the amount of time your youth is permitted to spend with friends.

Please rate how strongly you agree or disagree with the following statements:

1 = Do not agree at all
2 = Agree very little
3 = Agree a little
4 = Moderately agree
5 = Agree a lot
6 = Mostly agree
7 = Totally agree

____ 1. There are some experiences which teenagers can better share with their friends than their families.

_____ 2. Parents should not limit the amount of time a youth spends away from home because this is likely to make the youth very angry.

_____ 3. Adolescents spend a lot of time away from home because their parents nag them a lot and make them miserable at home.

_____ 4. Parents know best how much time an adolescent should spend with friends and at home with parents.

_____ 5. It is important for teenagers to spend some time with their parents.

_____ 6. Teenagers should value a close relationship with their family and should not have to be asked to spend time at home.

_____ 7. Teenagers who spend too much time with their friends will be influenced in bad directions and will do things that could ruin their futures.

_____ 8. Teenagers who spend most of their time with their friends are trying to hurt their parents.

Using the Telephone

Your youth gets quite a few phone calls each evening and spends a half hour or more on the phone with each person who calls. When you want to use the phone, your teenager is often talking to a friend. You've asked your youth to make fewer or shorter calls, but all you have gotten is an angry refusal. Your youth states that he/she has a lot of important things to discuss. Often people tell you that they have been trying to call you, but your line is always busy. You're worried that you may be missing important calls. You are thinking about limiting your youth's phone privileges.

Please rate how strongly you agree or disagree with the following statements:

$$
\begin{aligned}
1 &= \text{Do not agree at all} \\
2 &= \text{Agree very little} \\
3 &= \text{Agree a little} \\
4 &= \text{Moderately agree} \\
5 &= \text{Agree a lot} \\
6 &= \text{Mostly agree} \\
7 &= \text{Totally agree}
\end{aligned}
$$

_____ 1. Parents should allow youths to have some telephone privileges.

_____ 2. Teenagers who spend hours on the telephone wish to anger their parents.

_____ 3. Parents should not restrict their adolescents' phone privileges because the teenagers might become very angry with their parents.

_____ 4. Youths should respect their parents' needs and ask permission before they use the telephone.

_____ 5. Teenagers learn to talk too much on the phone from parents who talk too much on the phone.

_____ 6. Teenagers who are constantly on the phone create serious problems for the family because important calls won't get through.

_____ 7. Teenagers should know that it is wrong to tie up the phone and should limit their calls without being asked.

_____ 8. Parents who are expecting a call should firmly instruct their adolescents to refrain from using the phone until the call is received.

Staying Out Past Curfew

When your teenager goes out on a date or with friends, you usually set a time by which he/she has to be home. Lately, your youth has been coming home one-half hour to an hour late, or he/she will call you at curfew time to request an extension. You have tried to talk to him/her about it, but arguments erupt. It is getting to the point where you cannot be sure when your teenager will be coming home. You are becoming increasingly angry.

Please rate how strongly you agree or disagree with the following statements:

$$1 = \text{Do not agree at all}$$
$$2 = \text{Agree very little}$$
$$3 = \text{Agree a little}$$
$$4 = \text{Moderately agree}$$
$$5 = \text{Agree a lot}$$
$$6 = \text{Mostly agree}$$
$$7 = \text{Totally agree}$$

_____ 1. Adolescents who stay out late with their friends are likely to get involved with sex, drugs, or alcohol and make mistakes which could ruin their lives.

_____ 2. When teenagers have a good reason to stay out later than planned, it is all right for parents to grant an extension.

_____ 3. Truly responsible youths should come home at a reasonable hour whether or not their parents set a curfew.

_____ 4. Youths should be discouraged from staying out past 2 A.M.

_____ 5. Teenagers should follow their parents' curfew because parents know what is best for them.

_____ 6. Adolescents stay out past their parents' curfew because their parents were so strict that they forced the adolescents to rebel.

_____ 7. Parents should not restrict their youths' curfew because the teenagers might get very angry at their parents.

_____ 8. Teenagers who come home late want to make their parents worry about them.

Cleaning One's Room

Your adolescent's room is a mess. Clothes are not folded or hung up properly. Games, books, records, and clothing are scattered around the room and the bed is not made. When you ask for the room to be cleaned, he/she says that it's his/her own room and since they have to live in it they should be able to keep it the way they like it. When your youth finally does agree to clean the room, you find that he/she has merely stuffed his/her clothes and other articles into drawers, closets or under their bed. You can't seem to win.

Please rate how strongly you agree or disagree with the following statements:

> 1 = Do not agree at all
> 2 = Agree very little
> 3 = Agree a little
> 4 = Moderately agree
> 5 = Agree a lot
> 6 = Mostly agree
> 7 = Totally agree

____ 1. Responsible youths should be neat and tidy and take care of their belongings without parental nagging.

____ 2. Parents have a right to request that youths try to keep their room looking decent.

____ 3. Teenagers who are not taught to take proper care of their belongings grow up to be irresponsible and sloppy in their lifestyle and work habits as adults.

____ 4. Teenagers should obey parents' requests to clean their rooms properly or be punished.

____ 5. Occasionally, parents might permit their youths to have a vacation from cleaning their room.

____ 6. Adolescents who refuse to clean their room or take care of their belongings were taught these bad habits by their parents.

____ 7. Parents should avoid nagging their teenagers about cleaning their room because nagging could lead to a bad parent-child relationship.

____ 8. Teenagers who fail to clean their rooms are purposely showing blatant disregard for their parents' feelings.

Talking Back to Parents

Your teenager has been developing the bad habit of talking back to you in a sarcastic, nasty tone of voice. This lack of respect is extremely annoying and has been occurring more frequently in recent weeks. When you talk to your youth about this rudeness, your youth states that he/she is only being honest about his/her feelings. The situation is rapidly deteriorating, and you are not sure how to handle it.

Please rate how strongly you agree or disagree with the following statements:

> 1 = Do not agree at all
> 2 = Agree very little
> 3 = Agree a little
> 4 = Moderately agree
> 5 = Agree a lot
> 6 = Mostly agree
> 7 = Totally agree

____ 1. Parents should avoid criticizing their teenagers for talking back because the teenagers will get very angry.

_____ 2. Adolescents should always talk to their parents in a courteous, respectful manner.

_____ 3. Youths should never be allowed to show disrespect toward their parents.

_____ 4. Teenagers talk back to their parents in order to hurt their feelings and get even with them for earlier punishments.

_____ 5. Youths who talk rudely to their parents grow up to be delinquent adults who can not respect authority.

_____ 6. It is natural for teenagers to get angry with their parents.

_____ 7. Teenagers treat their parents rudely because they have observed the parents treating each other disrespectfully.

_____ 8. There is reason for parental concern when youths begin to mouth off towards their parents.

Earning Money Away from Home

Your youth has become very interested in getting an after-school job at a local party store. This job would mean working long, late hours around the type of people you are not sure you want your youth to befriend. Besides, the job might interfere with homework and lead to lower school grades. When you try to discuss this calmly, it ends up in an argument. Your teenager accuses you of not trusting him/her.

Please rate how strongly you agree or disagree with the following statements:

$$
\begin{aligned}
1 &= \text{Do not agree at all} \\
2 &= \text{Agree very little} \\
3 &= \text{Agree a little} \\
4 &= \text{Moderately agree} \\
5 &= \text{Agree a lot} \\
6 &= \text{Mostly agree} \\
7 &= \text{Totally agree}
\end{aligned}
$$

_____ 1. Teenagers should understand that school comes before work and that they are too young for a late-night job.

_____ 2. It is wrong for parents to make their youth angry by refusing to permit them to have a part-time job.

_____ 3. It is important for teenagers to complete high school whether or not they have an after-school job.

_____ 4. A job can teach a teenager responsibility.

_____ 5. Adolescents who want an after-school job do not receive enough money from their parents.

_____ 6. If a youth works after school, his/her grades will seriously suffer, crippling his/her chances of going to college or getting a better job after high school graduation.

_____ 7. Teenagers should obey their parents' advice concerning jobs since the parents have had a lot of experience with work.

_____ 8. Teenagers work after school to get even with their parents for not giving them enough money.

Helping Out Around the House

You have assigned the following chores around the house to your youngster: cleaning up his/her bedroom, washing the dishes, taking out the trash, and helping with the dusting and vacuuming. Your teenager always complains that you have given too much work. There isn't enough time for fun things. The chores aren't always done, and when they are done, not properly. You end up getting into many arguments about chores with the teenager.

Please rate how strongly you agree or disagree with the following statements:

1 = Do not agree at all
2 = Agree very little
3 = Agree a little
4 = Moderately agree
5 = Agree a lot
6 = Mostly agree
7 = Totally agree

_____ 1. Teenagers should always do their share of work around the house without being asked.

_____ 2. The responsibility for doing chores around the house is something that the whole family should share.

_____ 3. Youths should unquestioningly do any tasks that their parents assign.

_____ 4. If a youth really hates doing chores it is better to do them yourself than to risk getting the youth angry at you.

_____ 5. It is reasonable to expect youths to help clean around the house.

_____ 6. If a youth fails to do what a parent asks it is because the parent has not earned the youth's respect.

_____ 7. A youth who fails to learn responsibility at home through doing chores will grow up to be lazy and irresponsible.

_____ 8. Teenagers fail to complete their chores because they wish to punish their parents and make them do the extra work.

FBI-A

We are interested in understanding how parents and their adolescents think about different situations. In order to help us do this we have created a questionnaire which describes a number of situations that might occur in daily life, each followed by several statements representing people's reactions to the situation.

Please read each situation and *imagine* that it is happening to you. Rate each statement on the degree to which you would agree with it. Because you may not have had the experiences described in some of the situations, it is important that you *imagine* that it is happening to you. Be sure that you don't rate the situation; just rate how much the statement is like the way you would think. Please rate every statement.

Who Should Be Youth's Friend

You have recently gotten to be close with a new friend. The two of you enjoy doing a lot of things together, including going to shopping malls, playing video games, and doing things after school together. Your parents do not like this friend at all. They complain that the friend talks rudely toward them, looks sloppy, skips school, and smokes and drinks. They also accuse your friend of doing other things which they disapprove. Recently, when you and your friend have wanted to do something together, your parents have dreamed up excuses to keep you home. They want to keep you from seeing this friend. A very unpleasant disagreement took place when you discussed this with them. You are not sure what will happen next.
Please rate how strongly you agree or disagree with the following statements:

1 = Do not agree at all
2 = Agree very little
3 = Agree a little
4 = Moderately agree
5 = Agree a lot
6 = Mostly agree
7 = Totally agree

_____ 1. Parents might occasionally offer advice about an adolescent's choice of friends.

_____ 2. If parents restrict a youth's friends, the youth will end up without any friends.

_____ 3. It is unfair for parents to restrict their teenagers from seeing certain friends.

_____ 4. There are times when parents offer their youths good advice about friends.

_____ 5. It is wrong for teenagers to upset their parents by spending time with friends whom the parents dislike.

_____ 6. Adolescents should be given the freedom to do whatever they chose with whomever they chose.

How Money Is Spent

You are able to make a small amount of money doing little jobs here and there and enjoy spending it. You spend your money on video games, record albums, concerts, and eating with your friends at places like McDonalds. Your parents, however, disapprove of how you spend your money. They accuse you of spending money as if it were going out of style. They are always telling you to save it or to start buying your own clothing or school supplies. You are really beginning to resent this.

Please rate how strongly you agree or disagree with the following statements:

    1 = Do not agree at all
    2 = Agree very little
    3 = Agree a little
    4 = Moderately agree
    5 = Agree a lot
    6 = Mostly agree
    7 = Totally agree

_____ 1. If parents do not approve of how a youth is spending money, the youth should change his/her spending habits.

_____ 2. Parents should encourage their youths to save some money for the future.

_____ 3. Adolescents should be allowed some freedom in deciding how their money is spent.

_____ 4. It is not fair for parents to tell teenagers how to spend the teenager's own money.

_____ 5. Adolescents should be permitted to spend their own money any way they please without parental interference.

_____ 6. If teenagers follow parents' suggestions for spending money, they will never get to have any fun or buy nice things.

Being Nice to Teen's Friends

You have a small group of friends whom you really like. They often telephone you or come over to visit you. You have noticed, however, that your parents are usually unfriendly to them. They accuse you and your friends of invading their privacy and of being loud and making a mess in the house. Your parents won't speak to your friends when they come over and are not nice to them on the phone. You are afraid that if something does not change soon, your friends are going to start feeling uncomfortable about calling or visiting you.

Please rate how strongly you agree or disagree with the following statements:

1 = Do not agree at all
2 = Agree very little
3 = Agree a little
4 = Moderately agree
5 = Agree a lot
6 = Mostly agree
7 = Totally agree

_____ 1. Generally, family members should treat each other's friends with courtesy.

_____ 2. If parents are rude to a teenager's friends, they will drive all of the friends away.

_____ 3. It is totally unfair for parents to be rude to their children's friends.

_____ 4. Parents should permit their adolescents' friends to do and say whatever they want when they visit in the home.

_____ 5. It is extremely upsetting if a youth's parents don't approve of his/her friends.

_____ 6. When visiting someone else's home, adolescents should be pleasant to their friends' parents.

Spending Time Away from Home

You have a couple of close friends with whom you spend a lot of time. You stay at each other's house on weekends, hang around together after school, go shopping and see movies together. Lately, your parents have been asking you to stay home with them more. When you insist on spending time with your friends, you end up getting into an argument. Your parents are now talking about limiting the time you spend away from home with friends.

Please rate how strongly you agree or disagree with the following statements:

1 = Do not agree at all
2 = Agree very little
3 = Agree a little
4 = Moderately agree
5 = Agree a lot
6 = Mostly agree
7 = Totally agree

_____ 1. There are some experiences which teenagers can better share with their friends than their families.

_____ 2. Parents should let their youths decide for themselves how and where to spend free time.

_____ 3. Teenagers who spend a lot of time away from home with their friends do not really care about their parents.

_____ 4. Youths whose parents make them stay home will stop being asked out and lose the friends that they have made.

_____ 5. It is terribly unfair for parents to ask their adolescents to stay home when they could be out having fun with their friends.

_____ 6. It is important for teenagers to spend some time with their parents.

Using the Telephone

You get quite a few phone calls from your friends every evening. Often you spend a half an hour or more on the phone with each person who calls. Your parents become upset when they catch you spending too much time on the phone. They say that someone may be trying to reach them. You, however, can not imagine who would be trying to call and have a lot of important things to say to your friends. Your parents are trying to limit your phone privileges, but you are resisting.

Please rate how strongly you agree or disagree with the following statements:

> 1 = Do not agree at all
> 2 = Agree very little
> 3 = Agree a little
> 4 = Moderately agree
> 5 = Agree a lot
> 6 = Mostly agree
> 7 = Totally agree

_____ 1. Teenagers should comply with their parents' request to talk less on the phone to avoid angering parents.

_____ 2. When someone is expecting a call, the line should be kept free until the call comes in.

_____ 3. If parents restrict the time their youth can talk on the phone, no one will ever call or be friendly with the youth.

_____ 4. It is unfair for parents to put limits on telephone time.

_____ 5. It is reasonable for parents to expect their youth to talk on the phone less than 45 minutes per day.

_____ 6. Youths should be permitted to have their own phones and spend as much time making calls as they please.

Staying Out Past Curfew

Your social life has really begun to improve. You have been spending many evenings hanging out with your friends or dating. Your parents always tell you to come home too early. Just as you start to have a really good time, it's time to go home. Most of your friends get to stay out later than you. Recently, you have been coming home one-half hour to one hour late, or calling your parents at curfew time to request an extension. Your parents are giving you a real hassle about this. When you try to explain your views to them, an argument starts up.

Please rate how strongly you agree or disagree with the following statements:

1 = Do not agree at all
2 = Agree very little
3 = Agree a little
4 = Moderately agree
5 = Agree a lot
6 = Mostly agree
7 = Totally agree

_____ 1. Teenagers whose parents make them come home early will lose all of their friends and be very depressed and lonely.

_____ 2. It is very unfair for parents to make teenagers come home earlier than their friends.

_____ 3. No matter what, adolescents should never stay out past their curfew because their parents will worry a lot and become upset.

_____ 4. Teenagers should be able to come home as late as they wish.

_____ 5. It is reasonable for parents to want to know what time their children are going to come home.

_____ 6. When teenagers have a good reason to stay out later than planned, it is allright to grant them an extension.

Cleaning One's Room

Your parents nag you daily to clean your room and take care of your belongings. They describe your room as a pig sty and complain about clothes being all over, the bed not made, and records and books being all over. You don't mind living in a messy room, but your parents can't stand even a little mess. This is hard to understand because you're the one who has to live in the room, not your parents. When you do clean your room, then they complain that you did not do a thorough job. You can't seem to win.

Please rate how strongly you agree or disagree with the following statements:

1 = Do not agree at all
2 = Agree very little
3 = Agree a little
4 = Moderately agree
5 = Agree a lot
6 = Mostly agree
7 = Totally agree

_____ 1. Youths should be permitted to decide for themselves how clean they want their rooms to be.

_____ 2. It is best for adolescents to obey their parents' demands to keep their room clean so that the parents won't get mad.

_____ 3. It is terribly unfair for parents to expect teenagers to keep their room as clean as the parents want.

_____ 4. Occasionally parents might permit their youths to have a vacation from cleaning their room.

_____   5.   If a teenager keeps the room as neat as parents demand, the parents will soon demand the teenager start cleaning the whole house, mow the grass, shovel snow, and do all kinds of extra chores.

_____   6.   Parents have the right to ask their teenagers to hang up their coats when they come home.

Talking Back to Parents

Your parents often accuse you of talking to them in a sarcastic, nasty tone of voice. They are always asking you a lot of nosy questions which you tell them you do not want to answer. You don't feel you are being nasty to them; you are merely being honest. There is no nice way to let your parents know that you don't want to answer their questions.

Please rate how strongly you agree or disagree with the following statements:

1 = Do not agree at all
2 = Agree very little
3 = Agree a little
4 = Moderately agree
5 = Agree a lot
6 = Mostly agree
7 = Totally agree

_____   1.   Teenagers should show their parents a certain amount of respect.

_____   2.   There are some areas of a teenager's life which are private and should not be shared with their parents.

_____   3.   Teenagers should be free to say whatever they wish to their parents without being accused of talking back.

_____   4.   It is terrible for adolescents to hurt their parents' feelings by talking back.

_____   5.   It is not fair for parents to ask teenagers very personal questions and then accuse them of talking back if the teenagers refuse to answer.

_____   6.   Teenagers who can not learn to stand up to their parents will be unable to stand up to others when they are adults.

Earning Money Away from Home

You have an opportunity to get a job at a local party store. The pay is very good. In fact, you'd be making more money than any of your friends. But, you would have to work long hours, and often wouldn't get home until very late. Your parents are afraid that your grades will suffer. Also, they don't like the people that hang out around the party store. You really want the job, but whenever you talk to your parents about it, you end up in an argument.

Please rate how strongly you agree or disagree with the following statements:

1 = Do not agree at all
2 = Agree very little
3 = Agree a little
4 = Moderately agree
5 = Agree a lot
6 = Mostly agree
7 = Totally agree

_____ 1.   A job teaches teenagers responsibility.

_____ 2.   It is important for teenagers to complete high school whether or not they have an after school job.

_____ 3.   Teenagers are perfectly capable of deciding whether they can handle a job and school without their parents' advice.

_____ 4.   Parents who stop their teenagers from having part-time jobs are acting unfairly.

_____ 5.   Teenagers should not upset their parents by wanting to take a job when it is against their parents' wishes.

_____ 6.   Without a job a teenager will never have the money to have a good time and will end up severely depressed and suicidal.

Helping Out Around the House

You have been given the following chores around the house by your parents: cleaning up your room, washing the dishes, taking out the garbage, and helping with the dusting and vacuuming. This is too much work. You complain, but your parents don't listen. You hate chores. They cut into time better spent with your friends. When you do the chores your parents bug you; they say you did a lousy job. You get into a big hassle and argument with your parents about chores.

Please rate how strongly you agree or disagree with the following statements:

1 = Do not agree at all
2 = Agree very little
3 = Agree a little
4 = Moderately agree
5 = Agree a lot
6 = Mostly agree
7 = Totally agree

_____ 1.   If teenagers have to do a lot of work around the house they will grow up to be dull, stupid, uninteresting bores that no one will like.

_____ 2.   It is terribly unfair for parents to make teenagers do a lot of work.

_____ 3.   It is reasonable for parents to expect their youths to do some work around the house.

_____ 4.   Teenagers should be able to decide for themselves how much work they want to do around the house.

_____ 5.   It is better to do what parents ask rather than risk them being mad at you.

_____ 6.   The responsibility for doing chores is something the whole family should share.

FAMILY CELEBRATIONS INDEX (FCEL)

AUTHORS: Hamilton I. McCubbin and Anne I. Thompson

PURPOSE: To measure a family's special events.

DESCRIPTION: The FCEL is a 9-item instrument designed to measure family celebrations, or the extent to which a family celebrates special events. The basis for this measure is that celebrations can be viewed as facilitators of family functioning and perhaps as indicators of family strengths.

NORMS: The FCEL was studied initially with 304 nonclinical families in Wisconsin. No other demographic data were reported. The mean score was 20.5 (SD = 3.1).

SCORING: Scores are assigned the following values and summed for a total score: "Never" = 0, "Seldom" = 1, "Often" = 2, "Always" = 3, "Not Applicable" = 0.

RELIABILITY: The FCEL has fair internal consistency with an alpha of .69. No data on stability were reported.

VALIDITY: The FCEL has good concurrent validity with significant correlations with several family scales: Flexibility, Coherence, Family Times and Routines Index, Family Satisfaction, and Family Traditions Scale.

PRIMARY REFERENCE: McCubbin, H. I. and Thompson, A. I. (eds.) (1991). *Family Assessment Inventories for Research and Practice*. Madison, WI: University of Wisconsin.

AVAILABILITY: Dr. Hamilton McCubbin, Dean, School of Family Resources and Consumer Services, Madison, WI 53706-1575.

FCEL

Please read each special event/occasion and decide how often your family *cele-brates* (i.e., takes time and effort to appreciate the event/special situation, etc.) on these occasions. Please circle the appropriate answer: Never (0), Seldom (1), Often (2), and Always (3). Please respond to all items.

We celebrate these special moments:	Never	Seldom	Often	Always	Not Applicable
1. Friend's special events	0	1	2	3	*No friends*
2. Children's birthday(s)	0	1	2	3	*No children*
3. Relatives' birthdays/anniversaries	0	1	2	3	*No relatives*
4. Spouses' birthdays	0	1	2	3	*No spouse*
5. Religious occasions (holy days, etc.)	0	1	2	3	
6. Yearly major holidays (4th of July, New Year)	0	1	2	3	
7. Occasions (i.e., Valentine's Day, Mother's Day)	0	1	2	3	
8. Special changes and events (i.e., graduation, promotion)	0	1	2	3	*None to celebrate*
9. Special surprises and successes (i.e., passed a test; good report card)	0	1	2	3	None to celebrate

Copyright © 1986 H. McCubbin.

FAMILY COPING COHERENCE INDEX (FCCI)

AUTHORS: Hamilton McCubbin, Andrea Larsen, and David Olson

PURPOSE: To measure family coherence.

DESCRIPTION: The FCCI is a 4-item instrument designed to measure Antonovsky's concept of a sense of coherence which families call upon to manage life changes and stresses. The FCCI emerged from the Family Crisis-Oriented Personal Evaluation Scales (F-COPES) to focus on the concept of coherence as a coping tool for families. The 4 items of the FCCI are conceptualized as defining the concepts of the sense of coherence. The FCCI is useful as a very short instrument to help identify one aspect of family coping.

NORMS: The FCCI has been studied with a number of samples including families of investment executives, Native Hawaiian families, and families of youth in residential treatment. The overall mean of the FCCI is reported as 16.0 (SD = 2.0).

SCORING: The FCCI is easily scored by simply summing the individual item scores.

RELIABILITY: The FCCI has fair internal consistency with a reported alpha of .71. The FCCI has very good stability with a reported test-retest correlation of .83.

VALIDITY: The FCCI has very good concurrent validity with reported strong correlations between the FCCI and several other instruments that measure the family's ability to call upon its appraisal skills and resources in order to manage stressful life events, strains, and changes.

PRIMARY REFERENCE: McCubbin, H. I., Larsen, A., and Olson, D. Family coping coherence index (FCCI). In H. I. McCubbin, A. I. Thompson, and M. A. McCubbin (1996). *Family Assessment: Resiliency, Coping and Adaptation. Inventories for Research and Practice.* Madison: University of Wisconsin, 703–712.

AVAILABILITY: Instruments may be used after purchase of the above reference and registration with Family Stress Coping, Coping and Health Project at (608) 262-5070. The book provides instructions for permission to use the instrument.

FCCI

Decide to what degree you either agree or disagree with each statement about your family. 0 = Strongly disagree, 4 = Strongly agree

When we face problems or difficulties in our family we cope by:	Strongly disagree	Disagree	Neutral	Agree	Strongly agree
1. Accepting stressful events as a fact of life	0	1	2	3	4
2. Accepting that difficulties occur unexpectedly	0	1	2	3	4
3. Defining the family problem in a more positive way so that we do not become too discouraged	0	1	2	3	4
4. Having faith in God	0	1	2	3	4

Copyright © H. I. McCubbin, A. Larsen, and D. Olson, 1982.

FAMILY COPING INDEX (FAMCI)

AUTHORS: Hamilton McCubbin, Anne Thompson, and Kelly Elver
PURPOSE: To measure family coping efforts.
DESCRIPTION: The FAMCI is a 24-item instrument designed to assess coping
   efforts of families of youth at risk, youth offenders, and youth in residential
   treatment programs. The FAMCI was developed as a measure that would be
   ethnically sensitive and applicable to families of both Caucasian and African-
   American youth. Development proceeded by systematically assessing self-
   reported coping responses of the families of youth offenders. Parents are
   asked to record on the FAMCI the degree to which they agree or disagree
   with the coping behavior listed on the questionnaire which describes how
   their family unit as a group typically responds to and copes with problems or
   difficulties. Since coping is an important target for intervention, the FAMCI
   is particularly useful as a measure to track changes in family coping as a result of therapeutic intervention. The FAMCI has three subscales: seeking
   professional and spiritual guidance (items 6, 9, 13, 16, 17, 19, and 22); seeking family and neighbor support (items 1, 2, 4, 5, 8, 10, 14, 21, and 23); and
   affirming the family's confidence (items 3, 7, 11, 12, 15, 18 20, and 24).
NORMS: The FAMCI has been studied with 477 families of youth in residential treatment programs including 191 African-American families and 286
   Caucasian families. For all families, on the total scale the mean was 84.6 (SD
   = 13.99). For African-American families, the mean was 89.6 (SD = 13.6) and
   for Caucasian families the mean was 81.192 (SD = 13.237). Data on the subscales are available in the primary reference.
SCORING: The FAMCI is easily scored by summing the responses on each of
   the items for the total score and for the subscale scores.
RELIABILITY: The FAMCI has very good internal consistency with an overall
   alpha of .85. The alphas for the subscales are .80, .78, and .70 for the seeking
   professional and spiritual guidance, seeking family and neighbor support,
   and affirming the family's confidence subscales, respectively. The FAMCI
   has very good stability, with test-retest correlations over a 6 to 12 month period of .56 for the total score and ranging from .41 to .57 for the subscales.
VALIDITY: The FAMCI has good predictive validity as determined by successfully predicting program completion and successful posttreatment adaptation. Only the subscale affirming the family's confidence, however, was
   related to successful posttreatment outcomes for African-American youth.
PRIMARY REFERENCE: McCubbin, H. I., Thompson, A. I., and Elver, K. M.
   Family coping index (FAMCI). In H. I. McCubbin, A. I. Thompson, and M.
   A. McCubbin (1996). *Family Assessment: Resiliency, Coping and Adaptation. Inventories for Research and Practice.* Madison: University of Wisconsin Press, 509–535.

AVAILABILITY: Instruments may be used after purchase of the above reference and registration with Family Stress Coping, Coping and Health Project at (608) 262-5070. The book provides instructions for permission to use the instrument.

FAMCI

First, read the list of "Response Choices" one at a time. Second, decide how well each statement describes your attitudes and behavior in response to problems or difficulties. If the statement describes your response very well, then circle the number 5 indicating that you **strongly agree;** if the statement does not describe your response at all, then circle the number 1 indicating that you **strongly disagree;** if the statement describes your response to some degree, then select a number 2, 3, or 4 to indicate how much you agree or disagree with the statement about your response.

When we face problems or difficulties in our family, we respond by:

	Strongly disagree	Moderately disagree	Neutral	Moderately agree	Strongly agree
1. Sharing our difficulties with relatives	1	2	3	4	5
2. Seeking encouragement and support from friends	1	2	0	4	5
3. Knowing we have the power to solve major problems	1	2	3	4	5
4. Seeking information and advice from persons in other families who have faced the same or similar problems	1	2	3	4	5
5. Seeking advice from relatives (grandparents, etc.)	1	2	3	4	5
6. Seeking assistance from community agencies and programs designed to help families in our situation	1	2	3	4	5
7. Knowing that we have the strength within our own family to solve our problems	1	2	3	4	5
8. Receiving gifts and favors from neighbors (e.g., food, taking in mail, etc.)	1	2	3	4	5
9. Seeking information and advice from the family doctor	1	2	3	4	5
10. Asking neighbors for favors and assistance	1	2	3	4	5
11. Facing the problems "head-on" and trying to get a solution right away	1	2	3	4	5
12. Showing that we are strong	1	2	3	4	5
13. Attending church services	1	2	3	4	5
14. Sharing concerns with close friends	1	2	3	4	5
15. Accepting that difficulties occur unexpectedly	1	2	3	4	5
16. Doing things with relatives (get-togethers, dinners, etc.)	1	2	3	4	5
17. Seeking professional counseling and help for family difficulties	1	2	3	4	5
18. Believing we can handle our own problems	1	2	3	4	5
19. Participating in church activities	1	2	3	4	5

20. Defining the family problem in a more positive way
    so that we do not become too discouraged   1   2   3   4   5
21. Asking relatives how they feel about problems we face   1   2   3   4   5
22. Seeking advice from a minister   1   2   3   4   5
23. Sharing problems with neighbors   1   2   3   4   5
24. Having faith in God   1   2   3   4   5

Copyright © H. I. McCubbin, D. Olson, and A. Larsen, 1981.

FAMILY COPING INVENTORY (FCI)

AUTHORS: Hamilton I. McCubbin, Pauline G. Boss, Lance R. Wilson, and Barbara B. Dahl

PURPOSE: To measure spouses' response to family stress.

DESCRIPTION: The FCI is a 70-item instrument designed to measure how spouses perceive their own responses to a family separation that is permanent (e.g., divorce), for an extended period (e.g., military assignments), or that recurs repeatedly (e.g., business travel). The theoretical bases for items on the FCI were social support theory, family stress theory, and psychological coping theory. The FCI has a number of factors depending upon whether the separation is long-term, recurrent short-term, or permanent (divorce). These are described in the scoring section. (The gender of items 10 and 42 can be changed for use with husbands.)

NORMS: The FCI has been used in several studies involving intact families where one spouse makes many short business trips, intact military families where spouses are separated for long periods of time, and divorced spouses. Actual norms are not available.

SCORING: The FCI is scored differently depending on the nature of the separation. For long-term separation, use items 3, 4, 6, 8, 12, 13, 14, 16, 18, 20, 28–30, 32, 33, 35, 41, 43, 45, 46, 54, 56, 57, 61, 63, 70. For recurrent short-term separation, use items 4, 32, 37, 39, 42, 45, 62, 65. For permanent separation, use items 1–9, 12–15, 17, 19–23, 26, 27, 29, 31–33, 36–38, 41, 43, 45–49, 51, 53–59, 63, 64, 66–68. In each case, items simply are summed for total scores.

RELIABILITY: Overall reliability coefficients are not available but individual factors on the FCI appear to have fair to good internal consistency with alphas that range from .71 to .86. Data on stability were not reported.

VALIDITY: The FCI has good factorial validity. The FCI also has fair known-groups validity, with two subscales and the overall score distinguishing between distressed and nondistressed wives coping with military separation.

PRIMARY REFERENCE: McCubbin, H. I. and Thompson, A. I. (eds.) (1991). *Family Assessment Inventories for Research and Practice*. Madison, WI: University of Wisconsin.

AVAILABILITY: Dr. Hamilton McCubbin, Dean, School of Family Resources and Consumer Services, Madison, WI 53706-1575.

FCI

Purpose:
FCI is designed to record the behaviors wives or husbands find helpful to them in managing family life when spouses are separated for short, long, or permanent periods of time. *Coping is defined as individual or group behavior used to manage the hardships and relieve the discomfort associated with life changes or difficult life events.*

Directions:
On the next pages is a list of "behaviors" or statements that spouses may or may not use to cope with a separation experience. Please carefully consider "how helpful" each of these behaviors has been to you in your adjustment to separation.

Circle one of the following responses for each statement:

3 = Very helpful
2 = Moderately helpful
1 = Minimally helpful
0 = Not helpful

Please be sure and record a response for every item.

COPING BEHAVIORS	Not helpful	Minimally helpful	Moderately helpful	Very helpful
1. Talking with other individuals in my same situation	0	1	2	3
2. Going to school	0	1	2	3
3. Learning new skills	0	1	2	3
4. Developing myself as a person	0	1	2	3
5. Making financial investments/savings	0	1	2	3
6. Doing things with the family	0	1	2	3
7. Involvement in religious activities	0	1	2	3
8. Trying to be a father and a mother to the children	0	1	2	3

	COPING BEHAVIORS	Not helpful	Minimally helpful	Moderately helpful	Very helpful
9.	Allowing myself to become angry	0	1	2	3
10.	Believing that my husband's career is most important	0	1	2	3
11.	Always depending upon friends to give me support	0	1	2	3
12.	Trying to maintain family stability	0	1	2	3
13.	Investing myself in my children	0	1	2	3
14.	Becoming more independent	0	1	2	3
15.	Reading	0	1	2	3
16.	Believing that the institutions that my spouse and I work for have my family's best interest in mind	0	1	2	3
17.	Taking advantage of local programs and services aimed at helping those in my situation	0	1	2	3
18.	Wishing my spouse (or former spouse) was not gone and that things were different	0	1	2	3
19.	Believing that my life would not be any better if my spouse were here (or my former spouse and I were still together)	0	1	2	3
20.	Building close relationships with people	0	1	2	3
21.	Taking advantage of professional counseling	0	1	2	3
22.	Involvement in activities specifically for someone in my situation	0	1	2	3
23.	Establishing a new life for myself	0	1	2	3
24.	Drinking alcohol	0	1	2	3
25.	Always counting on relatives to help me out	0	1	2	3

COPING BEHAVIORS	Not helpful	Minimally helpful	Moderately helpful	Very helpful
26. Being active in the local community	0	1	2	3
27. Doing things with relatives	0	1	2	3
28. Reliving the past; reflecting on the memorable moments	0	1	2	3
29. Crying	0	1	2	3
30. Believing that things will always work out	0	1	2	3
31. Dating	0	1	2	3
32. Talking to someone about how I feel	0	1	2	3
33. Showing that I'm strong	0	1	2	3
34. Using drugs	0	1	2	3
35. Making sure I take advantage of all the state and local economic benefits I have coming to me	0	1	2	3
36. Participating on a regular basis in planned activities conducted by others in my situation	0	1	2	3
37. Establishing a routine which is not dependent upon my spouse (or former spouse) being around	0	1	2	3
38. Believing that I am better at running the family and/or finances without my spouse or former spouse	0	1	2	3
39. Believing that this is our style of life and I should enjoy it	0	1	2	3
40. Always trusting my faith to pull me through	0	1	2	3
41. Doing more things with the children	0	1	2	3

COPING BEHAVIORS	Not helpful	Minimally helpful	Moderately helpful	Very helpful
42. Being a "good" wife and doing what my husband wants me to do	0	1	2	3
43. Believing in God	0	1	2	3
44. Doing volunteer work	0	1	2	3
45. Involvement in social activities (parties, etc.) with friends	0	1	2	3
46. Planning my future	0	1	2	3
47. Concentrating on hobbies (art, music, sewing, etc.)	0	1	2	3
48. Eating	0	1	2	3
49. Traveling	0	1	2	3
50. Always relying on myself to solve problems	0	1	2	3
51. Going shopping with the children or by myself	0	1	2	3
52. Reading about how other persons in my situation handle things	0	1	2	3
53. Seeking encouragement, guidance, and support from my parent(s)	0	1	2	3
54. Engaging in relationships and friendships which are satisfying to me	0	1	2	3
55. Sleeping	0	1	2	3
56. Keeping myself in shape and well-groomed	0	1	2	3
57. Watching television	0	1	2	3
58. Going to movies	0	1	2	3
59. Remodeling or redecorating the house	0	1	2	3

COPING BEHAVIORS	Not helpful	Minimally helpful	Moderately helpful	Very helpful
60. Engaging in club work (church, PTA, etc.)	0	1	2	3
61. Telling myself that I have many things I should be thankful for	0	1	2	3
62. Keeping problems to myself	0	1	2	3
63. Going shopping with friends	0	1	2	3
64. Advancing my professional career	0	1	2	3
65. Living up to what society wants me to do as a parent	0	1	2	3
66. Participating in gatherings and events with relatives	0	1	2	3
67. Socializing with friends of the opposite sex	0	1	2	3
68. Establish a new style of life—new friends, new activities, etc.	0	1	2	3
69. Always believing that nothing bad could ever happen to my children	0	1	2	3
70. Seeking out friends who understand how difficult it is for me at times	0	1	2	3

PLEASE Check all 70 items to be sure you have circled a number for each one.

Copyright © 1991 H. McCubbin and A. I. Thompson.

FAMILY CRISIS ORIENTED PERSONAL EVALUATION SCALES (F-COPES)

AUTHORS: Hamilton I. McCubbin, David H. Olson, and Andrea S. Larsen

PURPOSE: To measure family coping.

DESCRIPTION: The F-COPES is a 30-item instrument designed to identify problem-solving and behavioral strategies utilized by families in difficult or problematic situations. The F-COPES comprises five subscales: acquiring social support (items 1, 2, 5, 8, 10, 16, 20, 25, 29,); reframing (redefining stressful events to make them more manageable (items 3, 7, 11, 13, 15, 19, 22, 24); seeking spiritual support (items 1, 4, 23, 27, 30); mobilizing family to acquire and accept help (items 4, 6, 9, 21); and passive appraisal (ability to accept problematic issues (items 12, 17, 26, 28). The F-COPES is an important measure since it is one of the few available to deal with the crucial issue of a family's coping ability.

NORMS: The F-COPES has been studied with several thousand respondents, although specific demographic information was not reported. Norms were as follows: Total score—mean = 93.3 (SD = 13.62); acquiring social support—mean = 27.2 (SD = 6.4); reframing—mean = 30.2 (SD = 4.8), seeking spiritual support—mean = 16.1 (SD = 3.05); mobilizing of family— mean = 11.96 (SD = 3.4); and passive appraisal—mean = 8.55 (SD = 3.01).

SCORING: Items 12, 17, 26, and 28 (all on the passive appraisal subscale) are reverse-scored. Scores for subscales and total are derived simply by summing all item scores.

RELIABILITY: The F-COPES has very good internal consistency with an alpha of .86. Individual subscales have alphas that ranged from .63 to .83. The F-COPES also has good stability with a four-week test-retest correlation of .81. Individual subscales have test-retest correlations that ranged from .61 to .95.

VALIDITY: The F-COPES has very good factorial validity. The F-COPES also has good concurrent validity, correlating with several other family measures.

PRIMARY REFERENCE: McCubbin, H. I. and Thompson, A. I. (eds.) (1991). *Family Assessment Inventories for Research and Practice*. Madison, WI: University of Wisconsin.

AVAILABILITY: Dr. Hamilton McCubbin, Dean, School of Family Resources and Consumer Services, Madison, WI 53706-1575.

F-COPES

Purpose:

The Family Crisis Oriented Personal Evaluation Scales is designed to record effective problem-solving attitudes and behavior which families develop to respond to problems or difficulties.

Directions:

First, read the list of response choices one at a time.

Second, decide how well each statement describes your attitudes and behavior in response to problems or difficulties. If the statement describes your response *very well*, then circle the number 5 indicating that you STRONGLY AGREE; if the statement does not describe your response at all, then circle the number 1 indicating that you STRONGLY DISAGREE; if the statement describes your response to some degree, then select a number 2, 3, or 4 to indicate how much you agree or disagree with the statement about your response.

WHEN WE FACE PROBLEMS OR DIFFICULTIES IN OUR FAMILY, WE RESPOND BY:	Strongly disagree	Moderately disagree	Neither agree nor disagree	Moderately agree	Strongly agree
1. Sharing our difficulties with relatives	1	2	3	4	5
2. Seeking encouragement and support from friends	1	2	3	4	5
3. Knowing we have the power to solve major problems	1	2	3	4	5
4. Seeking information and advice from persons in other families who have faced the same or similar problems	1	2	3	4	5
S. Seeking advice from relatives (grandparents, etc.)	1	2	3	4	5
6. Seeking assistance from community agencies and programs designed to help families in our situation	1	2	3	4	5
7. Knowing that we have the strength within our own family to solve our problems	1	2	3	4	5

WHEN WE FACE PROBLEMS OR DIFFICULTIES IN OUR FAMILY, WE RESPOND BY:	Strongly disagree	Moderately disagree	Neither agree nor disagree	Moderately agree	Strongly agree
8. Receiving gifts and favors from neighbors (e.g., food, taking in mail, etc.)	1	2	3	4	5
9. Seeking information and advice from the family doctor	1	2	3	4	5
10. Asking neighbors for favors and assistance	1	2	3	4	5
11. Facing the problems "head-on" and trying to get solutions right away	1	2	3	4	5
12. Watching television	1	2	3	4	5
13. Showing that we are strong	1	2	3	4	5
14. Attending church services	1	2	3	4	5
15. Accepting stressful events as a fact of life	1	2	3	4	5
16. Sharing concerns with close friends	1	2	3	4	5
17. Knowing luck plays a big part in how well we are able to solve family problems	1	2	3	4	5
18. Exercising with friends to stay fit and reduce tension	1	2	3	4	5
19. Accepting that difficulties occur unexpectedly	1	2	3	4	5
20. Doing things with relatives (get-togethers, dinners, etc.)	1	2	3	4	5
21. Seeking professional counseling and help for family difficulties	1	2	3	4	5
22. Believing we can handle our own problems	1	2	3	4	5
23. Participating in church activities	1	2	3	4	5

WHEN WE FACE PROBLEMS OR DIFFICULTIES IN OUR FAMILY, WE RESPOND BY:	Strongly disagree	Moderately disagree	Neither agree nor disagree	Moderately agree	Strongly agree
24. Defining the family problem in a more positive way so that we do not become too discouraged	1	2	3	4	5
25. Asking relatives how they feel about problems we face	1	2	3	4	5
26. Feeling that no matter what we do to prepare, we will have difficulty handling problems	1	2	3	4	5
27. Seeking advice from a minister	1	2	3	4	5
28. Believing if we wait long enough, the problem will go away	1	2	3	4	5
29. Sharing problems with neighbors	1	2	3	4	5
30. Having faith in God	1	2	3	4	5

Copyright © 1991 H. McCubbin and A. I. Thompson.

FAMILY DISTRESS INDEX (FDI)

AUTHORS: Hamilton McCubbin, Anne Thompson, and Kelly Elver

PURPOSE: To measure family maladaptation.

DESCRIPTION: The FDI is an 8-item instrument to obtain family self-report observations regarding the occurrence of family hardships and challenges that reflect family disharmony and family intolerance. Severity of the distress is recorded by family members. Thus scores on the FDI reflect the degree to which families exhibit certain behaviors or patterns of functioning that reflect the family's continuous condition of disharmony and imbalance. In developing the FDI, items were selected that reflected conflict, reduced problem solving, tension, and disorientation in either a particular member of the family or the family unit as a whole. The FDI is very useful as a short form for quickly identifying family dysfunction.

NORMS: The FDI was studied with 191 families of Native Hawaiian ancestry and 524 midwestern farm families. The mean for the Native Hawaiian families was 4.2 (SD = 2.5) and for farm families was 3.7 (SD = 3.9).

SCORING: The FDI is easily scored by summing the individual item scores. Higher scores reflect greater family distress.

RELIABILITY: The FDI has very good internal consistency with an alpha of .87. Data on stability were not available.

VALIDITY: In the study of Native Hawaiian families, the FDI was strongly correlated with intense family pressures, having incendiary pattern of communication, and a lack of social support.

PRIMARY REFERENCE: McCubbin, H. I., Thompson, A. I., and Elver, K. M. Family Distress Index (FDI). In H. I. McCubbin, A. I. Thompson, and M. A. McCubbin (1996). *Family Assessment: Resiliency, Coping and Adaptation. Inventories for Research and Practice.* Madison: University of Wisconsin, 783–788.

AVAILABILITY: After purchasing the book cited above, you may register by telephone at (608) 262-5070. The book provides instructions for permission to use the instrument.

FDI

Please Circle 0, 1, 2 or 3 to record the degree to which each of the family pressures listed have been a problem in your family during the past 12 months.

Family Pressures:	Not a problem	Small problem	Medium problem	Large problem
1. A member appears to have emotional problems.	0	1	2	3
2. A member appears to depend on alcohol or drugs.	0	1	2	3
3. Increase in arguments between parent(s) and child(ren).	0	1	2	3
4. Increase in conflict among children in the family.	0	1	2	3
5. Increased disagreement about a member's friends or activities.	0	1	2	3
6. Increase in the number of problems or issues which don't get resolved.	0	1	2	3
7. Increase in the number of tasks or chores which don't get done.	0	1	2	3
8. Increased conflict with in-laws or relatives.	0	1	2	3

Copyright © H. I. McCubbin, A. J. Thompson, and K. M. Elver, 1983.

FAMILY EMOTIONAL INVOLVEMENT
AND CRITICISM SCALE (FEICS)

AUTHORS: Cleveland G. Shields, Peter Franks, J. J. Harp, S. H. McDaniel, and T. L. Campbell.

PURPOSE: To measure the expressed emotions in a family.

DESCRIPTION: This 14-item instrument measures two aspects of expressed emotions as theoretically related to psychopathology: emotional involvement (EI) in the family and perceived criticism (PC). Perceived criticism and emotional involvement (in particular, emotional overinvolvement), are useful when working with families with a member who is severely and persistently mentally ill. Higher criticism scores are associated with more health care visits for psychosocial and biomedical services. The FEICS is useful when monitoring families' health care utilization, including families with long-term care needs and mental health needs of children and grandchildren. The PC subscale is a good predictor of other mental health conditions, including depression and physical functioning. The FEIC is also useful when working with an enmeshed family or with child-parent conflicts.

NORMS: Normative data are available on a sample of 101 adult patients seen in a university medical clinic. The item average of the EI scale was 3.03 with a standard deviation of .91. The PC subscale had an average item score of 1.66 with a standard deviation of .67. Norms are also available for the FC subscale from a sample of 836 patients with an average age of 48.8 years at a family medical clinic. The mean score was 1.89 with a standard deviation of .79.

SCORING: Items 2 and 8 are reverse scored. The EI subscale is composed of the odd items, and total scores are the sum of item scores divided by 7. The PC subscale is composed of the even items, and total scores are the sum of the item responses divided by 7. Subscale scores range from 1 to 7 with higher scores reflecting more emotional involvement and perceived criticism from one's family.

RELIABILITY: The reliability of the PC and EI subscales was .82 and .74, respectively, for the sample of patients at a family medical clinic.

VALIDITY: The PC has very good concurrent validity and criterion-related validity. Scores correlated with two other measures of family functioning, mental health, Medicaid status, medical diagnosis, psychiatric status, and physical functioning. The separate subscale structure was supported with confirmatory factor analysis. Scores on the EI correlated with social support, cohesion, and adaptability in a family, which supports criterion validity.

PRIMARY REFERENCE: Shields, C. G., Franks. P., Harp, J. J., McDaniel, S. H., and Campbell, T. C. (1992). Development of the Family Emotional Involvement and Criticism Scale (FEICS): A self-report scale to measure expressed emotions, *Journal of Marital and Family Therapy,* 18, 395–407.

AVAILABILITY: Cleveland G. Shields, Ph.D., Family Medicine Center, 885 South Ave., Rochester NY 14620.

FEICS

Below are questions about your family. Please answer them as they relate to your experience with your family now.

		Almost never	Once in a while	Some	Often	Almost always
1.	I am upset if anyone else in my family is upset.	1	2	3	4	5
2.	My family approves of most everything I do.	1	2	3	4	5
3.	My family knows what I am feeling most of the time.	1	2	3	4	5
4.	My family finds fault with my friends.	1	2	3	4	5
5.	Family members give me money when I need it.	1	2	3	4	5
6.	My family complains about the way I handle money.	1	2	3	4	5
7.	My family knows what I am thinking before I tell them.	1	2	3	4	5
8.	My family approves of my friends.	1	2	3	4	5
9.	I often know what my family members are thinking before they tell me.	1	2	3	4	5
10.	My family complains about what I do for fun.	1	2	3	4	5
11.	If I am upset, people in my family get upset too.	1	2	3	4	5
12.	My family is always trying to get me to change.	1	2	3	4	5
13.	If I have no way of getting some-where my family will take me.	1	2	3	4	5
14.	I have to be careful what I do or my family will put me down.	1	2	3	4	5

FAMILY EMPOWERMENT SCALE (FES)

AUTHORS: Paul E. Koren, Neal DeChillo, and Barbara J. Friesen
PURPOSE: To measure empowerment in families with an emotionally disabled child.
DESCRIPTION: This 34-item instrument is designed to measure the empowerment of a parent or caregiver of an emotionally disabled child. The FES is based on a two-dimensional definition of empowerment: level of empowerment (including family, service system, and community/political levels of empowerment activities), and the expression of empowerment (including attitude, knowledge, and behaviors). Subscales scores are available for the three levels of empowerment: family (F; items 2, 4, 7, 9, 16, 21, 26, 27, 29, 31, 33, 34), service system (SS; items 1, 5, 6, 11, 12, 13, 18, 19, 23, 28, 30, 32), and community/political (C/P; items 3, 8, 10, 14, 15, 17, 20, 22, 24, 25). The FES is particularly useful in agencies whose delivery model features client empowerment as a goal.
NORMS: A sample of 86 parents involved in advisory empowerment activities (such as serving on task forces) had means of 49.89, 53.56, and 41.37 for the F, SS, and C/P subscales. A sample of 354 respondents not involved in advisory activities had means of 45.83, 48.60, and 31.44 for the F, SS, and C/P subscales. Additional means for five other empowerment activities are available in the primary reference.
SCORING: Subscale scores are the sum of the respective item scores. Scores on the F and SS range from 12 to 60. Scores on the C/P range from 10 to 50. Higher scores reflect more empowerment.
RELIABILITY: The FES has very good evidence of reliability. The internal consistency alphas for the F, SS, and C/P subscales were .88, .87, and .88, respectively. Test-retest reliability coefficients of stability over a several-week period were .83, .77, and .85 for the F, SS, and C/P subscales.
VALIDITY: Validity was addressed by first having a panel of experts classify items from the perspective of the two-dimensional framework of empowerment. Validity in the ratings is seen with kappa coefficients of agreement for multiple raters of .83, .70, and .77 for the F, SS, and C/P subscale items. Validity is also supported by factor analysis where the results generally support the three levels of empowerment that form the F, SS, and C/P subscales. The subscales are, however, highly correlated with each other. Finally, the FES has strong evidence of known-groups validity as seen with differences in scores for respondents involved in six empowerment activities compared to respondents not involved in empowerment activities.
PRIMARY REFERENCE: Koren, P. E., DeChillo, N., and Friesen, B. J. (1992). Measuring empowerment in families whose children have emotional disabilities: A brief questionnaire, *Rehabilitation Psychology*, 37, 305–321.

Instrument reproduced with permission of Paul E. Koren, Neal DeChillo, and Barbara Friesen.

AVAILABILITY: Paul E. Koren, Ph.D., Research and Training Center on Family Support and Children's Mental Health, Regional Research Institute for Human Services, Portland State University, P.O. Box 751, Portland, OR 97207-0751.

FES

Below are a number of statements that describe how a parent or caregiver of a child with an emotional problem may feel about his or her situation. For each statement, please circle the response that best describes how the statement applies to you.

1 = Not true at all
2 = Mostly not true
3 = Somewhat true
4 = Mostly true
5 = Very true

1. I feel that I have a right to approve all services my child receives.   1 2 3 4 5

2. When problems arise with my child, I handle them pretty well.   1 2 3 4 5

3. I feel I can have a part in improving services for children in my community.   1 2 3 4 5

4. I feel confident in my ability to help my child grow and develop.   1 2 3 4 5

5. I know the steps to take when I am concerned my child is receiving poor services.   1 2 3 4 5

6. I make sure that professionals understand my opinions about what services my child needs.   1 2 3 4 5

7. I know what to do when problems arise with my child.   1 2 3 4 5

8. I get in touch with my legislators when important bills or issues concerning children are pending.   1 2 3 4 5

9. I feel my family life is under control.   1 2 3 4 5

10. I understand how the service system for children is organized.   1 2 3 4 5

11. I am able to make good decisions about what services my child needs.   1 2 3 4 5

12. I am able to work with agencies and professionals to decide what services my child needs.   1 2 3 4 5

13. I make sure I stay in regular contact with professionals who are providing services to my child.   1   2   3   4   5

14. I have ideas about the ideal service system for children.   1   2   3   4   5

15. I help other families get the services they need.   1   2   3   4   5

16. I am able to get information to help me better understand my child.   1   2   3   4   5

17. I believe that other parents and I can have an influence on services for children.   1   2   3   4   5

18. My opinion is just as important as professionals' opinions in deciding what services my child needs.   1   2   3   4   5

19. I tell professionals what I think about services being provided to my child.   1   2   3   4   5

20. I tell people in agencies and government how services for children can be improved.   1   2   3   4   5

21. I believe I can solve problems with my child when they happen.   1   2   3   4   5

22. I know how to get agency administrators or legislators to listen to me.   1   2   3   4   5

23. I know what services my child needs.   1   2   3   4   5

24. I know what the rights of parents and children are under the special education laws.   1   2   3   4   5

25. I feel that my knowledge and experience as a parent can be used to improve services for children and families.   1   2   3   4   5

26. When I need help with problems in my family, I am able to ask for help from others.   1   2   3   4   5

27. I make efforts to learn new ways to help my child grow and develop.   1   2   3   4   5

28. When necessary, I take the initiative in looking for services for my child and family.   1   2   3   4   5

29. When dealing with my child, I focus on the good things as well as the problems.   1   2   3   4   5

30. I have a good understanding of the service system that my child is involved in.   1 2 3 4 5

31. When faced with a problem involving my child, I decide what to do and then do it.   1 2 3 4 5

32. Professionals should ask me what services I want for my child.   1 2 3 4 5

33. I have a good understanding of my child's disorder.   1 2 3 4 5

34. I feel I am a good parent.   1 2 3 4 5

Copyright © 1992 Regional Research Institute for Human Services. All rights reserved.

FAMILY FUNCTIONING SCALE (FFS)

AUTHORS: Mark L. Tavitian, Judith Lubiner, Laura Green, Lawrence C. Grebstein, Wayne F. Velicer

PURPOSE: To measure dimensions of family functioning.

DESCRIPTION: The FFS is a 40-item instrument designed to measure general dimensions of family functioning. The FFS attempts to overcome flaws in other family measurement devices. It is based on an eclectic, integrative view of family functioning. The measure was developed through a sequential method of scale development. The first step was to select relevant items from research, theory, and interviews with experts. This process led to creation of 210 items. After a pilot study with experts, 197 items were retained, balanced for positive and negative statements. The instrument then was studied on two large samples and reduced through factor analysis to the current 40-item scale with five factors: positive family affect, family communication, family conflicts, family worries, and family rituals/supports. However, the total score can be used. The FFS was seen to have many applications in research and treatment, including the possible development of family profiles of different problem populations.

NORMS: The FFS was studied with two samples with a total of 563 subjects, predominantly white (94.5%), single (54.5%, female (57.5%), and Catholic (52.5%). Subjects ranged in age from 12 to 64 with 47% being between the ages of 18 and 22. The average annual income for most subjects was over $30,000. All subjects were volunteers from a variety of sources including college students, church members, and people in therapy at a university clinic. Actual norms were not available.

SCORING: Items are scored on a 7-point Likert-type scale ("Never" = 1 and "Always" = 7). Items 4, 21, and 38 are first reverse-scored, then simply are summed for the subscale and total scale scores. Subscale scoring procedures are available from Lawrence Grebstein (address below).

RELIABILITY: The FFS has fair internal consistency with alphas that range from .90 for the positive family affect subscale to .74 for the conflicts subscale. The alpha for the total scale was not reported nor were test-retest data.

VALIDITY: Research described in the primary reference reveals that the FFS has good concurrent validity, as demonstrated by correlations with the FACES III measure of family functioning. It also successfully discriminated between two clinical groups and a group of "normals." The FFS also predicted individualization among late adolescents, suggesting good predictive validity. However, the most reliable of the subscales, positive family affect, was highly correlated with social desirability, suggesting the need for caution in interpreting that subscale.

PRIMARY REFERENCE: Tavitian, M. L., Lubiner, J. L., Green, L., Grebstein, L. C., and Velicer, W. F. (1987). Dimensions of family functioning, *Journal of Social Behavior and Personality*, 2, 191–204.

AVAILABILITY: Dr. Lawrence C. Grebstein, Department of Psychology, University of Rhode Island, Kingston, RI 02881.

FFS

This is a questionnaire about family life, which includes a variety of statements that describe families. Please rate how each statement describes your family at the present time. Use the following seven-point scale:

Never	Almost never	Rarely	Some-times	Frequently	Almost always	Always
1	2	3	4	5	6	7

For each statement, please circle the number that best expresses how you see your current family. Do not spend too much time on any one statement. If you read a statement that is too difficult for you to answer, please give your first reaction. Remember that there are no right or wrong answers, so please answer as honestly as you can. All of your responses will remain confidential.

Kindly rate each statement. Thank you for your cooperation.

1. Birthdays are important events in my family.   1 2 3 4 5 6 7

2. The children in my family fight with each other.   1 2 3 4 5 6 7

3. People in my family have to be reminded when they are asked to do something.   1 2 3 4 5 6 7

4. People in my family do not care enough about what I need.   1 2 3 4 5 6 7

5. Our family spends holidays together.   1 2 3 4 5 6 7

6. Members of my family argue about money.   1 2 3 4 5 6 7

7. My family accepts me as I am.   1 2 3 4 5 6 7

8. When someone in my family is angry, I feel worried.   1 2 3 4 5 6 7

9. People in my family listen when I speak.   1 2 3 4 5 6 7

10. I worry when I disagree with the opinions of other family members.   1 2 3 4 5 6 7

11. I feel respected by my family.   1 2 3 4 5 6 7

12. We pay attention to traditions in my family.   1 2 3 4 5 6 7

13. When things are not going well in my family I feel sick. 1 2 3 4 5 6 7

14. Our family celebrates special events, such as anniversaries and graduations. 1 2 3 4 5 6 7

15. People in my family hit each other. 1 2 3 4 5 6 7

16. When I have questions about personal relationships, I talk with family members. 1 2 3 4 5 6 7

17. I let my family know when I am sad. 1 2 3 4 5 6 7

18. The mood of one family member can spread to everyone in the house. 1 2 3 4 5 6 7

19. I let family members know when I am upset. 1 2 3 4 5 6 7

20. People in my family yell at each other. 1 2 3 4 5 6 7

21. My family sees me as a hopeless case. 1 2 3 4 5 6 7

22. It is hard for me to forget painful events that have happened in my family. 1 2 3 4 5 6 7

23. People in my family use my things without asking. 1 2 3 4 5 6 7

24. In my family we talk about what is right and wrong with regard to sex. 1 2 3 4 5 6 7

25. Family members are critical of each other's eating habits. 1 2 3 4 5 6 7

26. When things are going wrong in my family, someone gets blamed. 1 2 3 4 5 6 7

27. In my family we talk about the physical changes that go along with growing up. 1 2 3 4 5 6 7

28. I tell people in my family when I am angry with them. 1 2 3 4 5 6 7

29. Family members eat at least one meal a day together. 1 2 3 4 5 6 7

30. Family reunions are important to us. 1 2 3 4 5 6 7

31.	I have trouble sleeping when I think about family problems.	1	2	3	4	5	6	7
32.	We are interested in the history of our family.	1	2	3	4	5	6	7
33.	I feel loved by my family.	1	2	3	4	5	6	7
34.	When things are not going well in my family it affects my appetite.	1	2	3	4	5	6	7
35.	I let my family know when I feel afraid.	1	2	3	4	5	6	7
36.	People in my family are not interested in what I do.	1	2	3	4	5	6	7
37.	It is important to know the mood of certain family members.	1	2	3	4	5	6	7
38.	I feel like a stranger in my own house.	1	2	3	4	5	6	7
39.	We are friendly with other families.	1	2	3	4	5	6	7
40.	People in my family discuss their problems with me.	1	2	3	4	5	6	7

FAMILY HARDINESS INDEX (FHI)

AUTHORS: Marilyn A. McCubbin, Hamilton I. McCubbin, and Anne I. Thompson

PURPOSE: To measure family hardiness in resistance to stress.

DESCRIPTION: The FHI is a 20-item instrument designed to measure the characteristic of hardiness as a stress-resistance and adaptation resource in families. Hardiness is conceptualized as a buffer or mediating factor in mitigating the effects of stressors and demands. Hardiness specifically refers to the internal strength and durability of the family; hardiness is characterized by a sense of control over the outcomes of life events and hardships. The FHI has four subscales: co-oriented commitment, confidence, challenge, and control. However, the overall score seems the best indicator of hardiness.

NORMS: The FHI was studied initially with 304 nonclinical families in Wisconsin. No other demographic data are available. The overall mean was 47.4 (SD = 6.7).

SCORING: The FHI is easily scored by first reverse-scoring 9 items (1, 2, 3, 8, 10, 14, 16, 19, 20) and then summing all items for a total score.

RELIABILITY: The FHI has good internal consistency with an alpha of .82. Data on stability were not available.

VALIDITY: The FHI has fair concurrent validity with low but significant correlations with Family Flexibility (FACES II), Family Time and Routines Index, and Quality of Family Life Scale.

PRIMARY REFERENCE: McCubbin, H. I. and Thompson, A. I. (eds.) (1991). *Family Assessment Inventories for Research and Practice*. Madison, WI: University of Wisconsin.

AVAILABILITY: Dr. Hamilton McCubbin, Dean, School of Family Resources and Consumer Services, Madison, WI 53706-1575.

FHI

Please read each statement below and decide to what degree each describes your family. Is the statement False (0), Mostly false (1), Mostly true (2), or Totally true (3) about your family? Circle a number 0 to 3 to match your feelings about each statement. Please respond to each and every statement.

IN OUR FAMILY . . .	False	Mostly false	Mostly true	Totally true	Not applicable
1. Trouble results from mistakes we make.	0	1	2	3	NA
2. It is not wise to plan ahead and hope because things do not turn out anyway.	0	1	2	3	NA
3. Our work and efforts are not appreciated no matter how hard we try and work.	0	1	2	3	NA
4. In the long run, the bad things that happen to us are balanced by the good things that happen.	0	1	2	3	NA
5. We have a sense of being strong even when we face big problems.	0	1	2	3	NA
6. Many times I feel I can trust that even in difficult times things will work out.	0	1	2	3	NA
7. While we don't always agree, we can count on each other to stand by us in times of need.	0	1	2	3	NA
8. We do not feel we can survive if another problem hits us.	0	1	2	3	NA
9. We believe that things will work out for the better if we work together as a family.	0	1	2	3	NA

IN OUR FAMILY . . .	False	Mostly false	Mostly true	Totally true	Not applicable
10. Life seems dull and meaningless.	0	1	2	3	NA
11. We strive together and help each other no matter what.	0	1	2	3	NA
12. When our family plans activities we try new and exciting things.	0	1	2	3	NA
13. We listen to each other's problems, hurts, and fears.	0	1	2	3	NA
14. We tend to do the same things over and over . . . it's boring.	0	1	2	3	NA
15. We seem to encourage each other to try new things and experiences.	0	1	2	3	NA
16. It is better to stay at home than go out and do things with others.	0	1	2	3	NA
17. Being active and learning new things are encouraged.	0	1	2	3	NA
18. We work together to solve problems.	0	1	2	3	NA
19. Most of the unhappy things that happen are due to bad luck.	0	1	2	3	NA
20. We realize our lives are controlled by accidents and luck.	0	1	2	3	NA

Copyright © 1986 M. McCubbin and H. McCubbin. Copyright © 1991 H. McCubbin and A. I. Thompson.

FAMILY INVENTORY OF LIFE EVENTS AND CHANGES (FILE)

AUTHORS: Hamilton I. McCubbin, Joan M. Patterson, and Lance R. Wilson

PURPOSE: To measure family stress.

DESCRIPTION: The FILE is a 71-item instrument designed to measure the pile-up of life events experienced by a family as an index of family stress. Items for the FILE were guided by research and clinical experience on situational and developmental changes experienced by families at different stages in the life cycle and by life changes appearing on other inventories. The original 171 items were reduced through several studies to the current 71. The focus of the FILE is on change, with items intended to reflect a change of sufficient magnitude to require some adjustment in the pattern of family interaction. Although the FILE comprises several subscales, as can be seen from the instrument, only the total score is recommended for use.

NORMS: The FILE has been studied with a number of different samples including 1140 couples representative of seven stages of the life cycle. No other demographic data were available. Data are presented by the couple's stage in the life cycle, ranging from couples with no children to retired couples, followed by the mean score of the couples in that stage: couple (no children) = 478, preschool = 530, school age = 500, adolescent = 545, launching = 635, empty nest = 425, retirement = 395. Cut-off scores for each stage can be determined by using the mean score as moderate stress and then taking the mean and one standard deviation above the mean as high stress and the mean and one SD below the mean as low stress.

SCORING: The FILE can be completed separately by each partner or together; any item answered "yes" by either or both partners is assigned a score of "1." These scores are summed for the subscale and total scores. (There are four other methods of scoring, including the use of weights for each item, described in the primary reference.) Higher scores equal greater pile-up of family stress.

RELIABILITY: The FILE has good internal consistency with total scale alphas that range from .79 to .82. The subscales have lower alphas. The FILE also has very good stability with a four- to five-week test-retest correlation of .80.

VALIDITY: The FILE has fairly good concurrent validity, with several significant correlations with scales of the Family Environment Scales. The FILE also has good known-groups validity, distinguishing between families with chronically ill children who were high and low in family conflicts.

PRIMARY REFERENCE: McCubbin, H. I. and Thompson, A. I. (eds.) (1991). *Family Assessment Inventories for Research and Practice*. Madison, WI: University of Wisconsin.

AVAILABILITY: Dr. Hamilton McCubbin, Dean, School of Family Resources and Consumer Services, Madison, WI 53706-1575.

FILE

Purpose:
Over their life cycle, all families experience many changes as a result of normal growth and development of members and due to external circumstances. The following list of family life changes can happen in a family at any time. Because family members are connected to each other in some way, a life change for any one member affects all the other persons in the family to some degree.

"FAMILY" means a group of two or more persons living together who are related by blood, marriage or adoption. This includes persons who live with you *and* to whom you have a long-term commitment.

Directions:
Please read each family life change and decide whether it happened to any member of your family—*including* you. First, decide if it happened any time *during* the last 12 months and check YES or NO. Second, for *some family changes* decide if it happened any time *before* the last 12 months and check YES or NO. It is okay to check YES twice if it happened both times—before last year and during the past year.

		DID THE CHANGE HAPPEN IN YOUR FAMILY?			
		During Last 12 Months		*Before* Last 12 Months	
FAMILY LIFE CHANGES		Yes	No	Yes	No
I.	INTRA-FAMILY STRAINS				
1.	Increase of husband/father's time away from family	☐	☐	☐	☐
2.	Increase of wife/mother's time away from family	☐	☐	☐	☐
3.	A member appears to have emotional problems	☐	☐	☐	☐
4.	A member appears to depend on alcohol or drugs	☐	☐	☐	☐
5.	Increase in conflict between husband and wife	☐	☐	☐	☐

		DID THE CHANGE HAPPEN IN YOUR FAMILY?			
		During Last 12 Months		*Before* Last 12 Months	
	FAMILY LIFE CHANGES	Yes	No	Yes	No
6.	Increase in arguments between parent(s) and child(ren)	☐	☐	☐	☐
7.	Increase in conflict among children in the family	☐	☐	☐	☐
8.	Increased difficulty in managing teenage child(ren)	☐	☐	☐	☐
9.	Increased difficulty in managing school child(ren) (6–12 yrs.)	☐	☐	☐	☐
10.	Increased difficulty in managing preschool age child(ren) (2–6 yrs.)	☐	☐	☐	☐
11.	Increased difficulty in managing toddler(s) (1–2½ yrs.)	☐	☐	☐	☐
12.	Increased difficulty in managing infant(s) (0–1 yrs.)	☐	☐	☐	☐
13.	Increase in the amount of "outside activities" which the child(ren) are involved in	☐	☐	☐	☐
14.	Increased disagreement about a member's friends or activities	☐	☐	☐	☐
15.	Increase in the number of problems or issues which don't get resolved	☐	☐	☐	☐
16.	Increase in the number of tasks or chores which don't get done	☐	☐	☐	☐
17.	Increased conflict with in-laws or relatives	☐	☐	☐	☐

II. MARITAL STRAINS

| 18. | Spouse/parent was separated or divorced | ☐ | ☐ | ☐ | ☐ |

	FAMILY LIFE CHANGES	DID THE CHANGE HAPPEN IN YOUR FAMILY?			
		During Last 12 Months		*Before* Last 12 Months	
		Yes	No	Yes	No
19.	Spouse/parent has an "affair"	☐	☐	☐	☐
20.	Increased difficulty in resolving issues with a "former" or separated spouse	☐	☐	☐	☐
21.	Increased difficulty with sexual relationship between husband and wife	☐	☐	☐	☐

III. PREGNANCY AND CHILDBEARING STRAINS

22.	Spouse had unwanted or difficult pregnancy	☐	☐	☐	☐
23.	An unmarried member became pregnant	☐	☐	☐	☐
24.	A member had an abortion	☐	☐	☐	☐
25.	A member gave birth to or adopted a child	☐	☐	☐	☐

IV. FINANCE AND BUSINESS STRAINS

26.	Took out a loan or refinanced a loan to cover increased expenses	☐	☐	☐	☐
27.	Went on welfare	☐	☐	☐	☐
28.	Change in conditions (economic, political, weather) which hurts the family business	☐	☐	☐	☐
29.	Change in agriculture market, stock market, or land values which hurts family investments and/or income	☐	☐	☐	☐
30.	A member started a new business	☐	☐	☐	☐
31.	Purchased or built a home	☐	☐	☐	☐
32.	A member purchased a car or other major item	☐	☐	☐	☐

	FAMILY LIFE CHANGES	During Last 12 Months Yes	No	Before Last 12 Months Yes	No

DID THE CHANGE HAPPEN IN YOUR FAMILY?

	FAMILY LIFE CHANGES	During Last 12 Months		Before Last 12 Months	
		Yes	No	Yes	No
33.	Increasing financial debts due to overuse of credit cards	☐	☐	☐	☐
34.	Increased strain on family "money" for medical/dental expenses	☐	☐	☐	☐
35.	Increased strain on family "money" for food, clothing, energy, home care	☐	☐	☐	☐
36.	Increased strain on family "money" for child(ren)'s education	☐	☐	☐	☐
37.	Delay in receiving child support or alimony payments	☐	☐	☐	☐

V. WORK–FAMILY TRANSITIONS AND STRAINS

		During Last 12 Months		Before Last 12 Months	
38.	A member changed to a new job/career	☐	☐	☐	☐
39.	A member lost or quit a job	☐	☐	☐	☐
40.	A member retired from work	☐	☐	☐	☐
41.	A member started or returned to work	☐	☐	☐	☐
42.	A member stopped working for extended period (e.g., laid off, leave of absence, strike)	☐	☐	☐	☐
43.	Decrease in satisfaction with job/career	☐	☐	☐	☐
44.	A member had increased difficulty with people at work	☐	☐	☐	☐
45.	A member was promoted at work or given more responsibilities	☐	☐	☐	☐
46.	Family moved to a new home/apartment	☐	☐	☐	☐

			During Last 12 Months		Before Last 12 Months	
		DID THE CHANGE HAPPEN IN YOUR FAMILY?				
	FAMILY LIFE CHANGES	Yes	No	Yes	No	
47.	A child/adolescent member changed to a new school	☐	☐	☐	☐	

VI. ILLNESS AND FAMILY "CARE" STRAINS

48.	Parent/spouse became seriously ill or injured	☐	☐	☐	☐	
49.	Child became seriously ill or injured	☐	☐	☐	☐	
50.	Close relative or friend of the family became seriously ill	☐	☐	☐	☐	
51.	A member became physically disabled or chronically ill	☐	☐	☐	☐	
52.	Increased difficulty in managing a chronically ill or disabled member	☐	☐	☐	☐	
53.	Member or close relative was committed to an institution or nursing home	☐	☐	☐	☐	
54.	Increased responsibility to provide direct care or financial help to husband's and/or wife's parent(s)	☐	☐	☐	☐	
55.	Experienced difficulty in arranging for satisfactory child care	☐	☐	☐	☐	

VII. LOSSES

56.	A parent/spouse died	☐	☐	☐	☐	
57.	A child member died	☐	☐	☐	☐	
58.	Death of husband's or wife's parent or close relative	☐	☐	☐	☐	
59.	Close friend of the family died	☐	☐	☐	☐	

		DID THE CHANGE HAPPEN IN YOUR FAMILY?			
		During Last 12 Months		*Before* Last 12 Months	
	FAMILY LIFE CHANGES	Yes	No	Yes	No
60.	Married son or daughter was separated or divorced	☐	☐	☐	☐
61.	A member "broke up" a relationship with a close friend	☐	☐	☐	☐

VIII. TRANSITIONS "IN AND OUT"

62.	A member was married	☐	☐	☐	☐
63.	Young adult member left home	☐	☐	☐	☐
64.	A young adult member began college (or post high school training)	☐	☐	☐	☐
65.	A member moved back home or a new person moved into the household	☐	☐	☐	☐
66.	A parent/spouse started school (or training program) after being away from school for a long time	☐	☐	☐	☐

IX. FAMILY LEGAL VIOLATIONS

67.	A member went to jail or juvenile detention	☐	☐	☐	☐
68.	A member was picked up by police or arrested	☐	☐	☐	☐
69.	Physical or sexual abuse or violence in the home	☐	☐	☐	☐
70.	A member ran away from home	☐	☐	☐	☐
71.	A member dropped out of school or was suspended from school	☐	☐	☐	☐

Copyright © 1991 H. McCubbin and A. I. Thompson.

FAMILY INVENTORY OF RESOURCES FOR MANAGEMENT (FIRM)

AUTHORS: Hamilton I. McCubbin, Joan K. Comeau, and Jo A. Harkins

PURPOSE: To measure a family's repertoire of resources.

DESCRIPTION: The FIRM is a 69-item instrument designed to measure a family's resources in a number of areas: personal resources, family system, internal resources, and social support. The FIRM comprises four subscales, derived through factor analysis: family strengths I—esteem and communication (items 36, 38, 39, 44, 46, 50, 52, 53, 55, 58, 60, 62, 65, 67, 68); family strengths II—mastery and health (items 2, 3, 4, 6–9, 11, 13–15, 17, 18, 20, 22, 23, 26, 27, 29, 32); extended family social support (items 41, 48, 56, 66); and financial well-being (items 35, 37, 40, 42, 43, 47, 49, 51, 54, 57, 59, 61, 63, 64, 69). The remainder of the items on the FIRM provide information on sources of financial support and social desirability and are not considered part of the FIRM. The FIRM can be used to measure families' strengths and weaknesses regarding resources and for identifying resources that need to be increased or strengthened.

NORMS: The FIRM was studied with 322 families with a chronically ill child. No other demographic data are available. The means for the FIRM are: family strengths I = 35 (SD = 6); family strengths II = 35 (SD = 9); extended family social support = 9 (SD = 2); and financial well-being = 29 (SD = 9). The total mean for the four subscales = 110 (SD = 18).

SCORING: Reverse-score items that have an asterisk to the right of the item. Then sum all items for the subscale score and total score. The primary reference provides further instructions for scoring the other areas on the questionnaire as well as for developing a profile of family resources.

RELIABILITY: The FIRM has very good internal consistency, with an overall alpha of .89. All subscales have alphas of .85 except for extended family support (.62). Data on stability were not available.

VALIDITY: The FIRM has fair concurrent validity, correlating significantly with the Family Environment Scales. The two family strength subscales of the FIRM also distinguish between families with chronically ill children who were high or low in family conflict, indicating fair known-groups validity.

PRIMARY REFERENCE: McCubbin, H. I. and Thompson, A. I. (eds.) (1991). *Family Assessment Inventories for Research and Practice*. Madison, WI: University of Wisconsin.

AVAILABILITY: Dr. Hamilton McCubbin, Dean, School of Family Resources and Consumer Services, Madison, WI 53706-1575.

FIRM

Purpose:

FIRM—Family Inventory of Resources for Management was developed to record what social, psychological, community, and financial resources families believe they have available to them in the management of family life.

Directions:

To complete this inventory you are asked to read the list of "Family statements" one at a time. In each statement, "family" means your immediate family (mother and/or father and children). Then ask yourself: "How well does the statement describe our family situation?" Then make your decision by circling one of the following:

0 = Not at all—This statement does not describe our family situation. This does not happen in our family.

1 = Minimally—This statement describes our family situation only slightly. Our family may be like this once in a while.

2 = Moderately—This statement describes our family situation fairly well. Our family is like this some of the time.

3 = Very well—This statement describes our family very accurately. Our family is like this most of the time.

PLEASE BEGIN—Please read and record your decision for EACH and EVERY statement below.

	Not at all	Minimally	Moderately	Very well
FAMILY STATEMENTS				
1. We have money coming in from our investments (such as rental property, stocks, bonds, etc.)	0	1	2	3
2. Being physically tired much of the time is a problem in our family.*	0	1	2	3
3. We have to nag each other to get things done.*	0	1	2	3
4. We do not plan too far ahead because many things turn out to be a matter of good or bad luck anyway.*	0	1	2	3
5. Our family is as well adjusted as any family in this world can be.	0	1	2	3

FAMILY STATEMENTS	Not at all	Minimally	Moderately	Very well
6. Having only one person in the family earning money is or would be a problem in our family.*	0	1	2	3
7. It seems that members of our family take each other for granted.*	0	1	2	3
8. Sometimes we feel we don't have enough control over the direction our lives are taking.*	0	1	2	3
9. Certain members of our family do all the giving, while others do all the taking.*	0	1	2	3
10. We depend almost entirely upon financial support from welfare or other public assistance programs.*	0	1	2	3
11. We seem to put off making decisions.*	0	1	2	3
12. Family members understand each other completely.	0	1	2	3
13. Our family is under a lot of emotional stress.*	0	1	2	3
14. Many things seem to interfere with family members being able to share concerns.*	0	1	2	3
15. Most of the money decisions are made by only one person in our family.*	0	1	2	3
16. There are times when family members do things that make other members unhappy.*	0	1	2	3
17. It seems that we have more illness (colds, flu, etc.) in our family than other people do.*	0	1	2	3
18. In our family some members have many responsibilities while others don't have enough.*	0	1	2	3
19. No one could be happier than our family when we are together.	0	1	2	3
20. It is upsetting to our family when things don't work out as planned.*	0	1	2	3

		Not at all	Minimally	Moderately	Very well
FAMILY STATEMENTS					
21.	We depend almost entirely on income from alimony and/or child support.*	0	1	2	3
22.	Being sad or "down" is a problem in our family.*	0	1	2	3
23.	It is hard to get family members to cooperate with each other.*	0	1	2	3
24.	If our family has any faults, we are not aware of them.	0	1	2	3
25.	We depend almost entirely on social security retirement income.*	0	1	2	3
26.	Many times we feel we have little influence over the things that happen to us.*	0	1	2	3
27.	We have the same problems over and over—we don't seem to learn from past mistakes.*	0	1	2	3
28.	One or more working members of our family are presently unemployed.*	0	1	2	3
29.	There are things at home we need to do that we don't seem to get done.*	0	1	2	3
30.	We feel our family is a perfect success.	0	1	2	3
31.	We own land or property besides our place of residence.	0	1	2	3
32.	We seem to be so involved with work and or school activities that we don't spend enough time together as a family.*	0	1	2	3
33.	We own (are buying) a home (single family, condominium, townhouse, etc.).	0	1	2	3
34.	There are times when we do not feel a great deal of love and affection for each other.*	0	1	2	3

FAMILY STATEMENTS	Not at all	Minimally	Moderately	Very well
35. If a close relative were having financial problems we feel we could afford to help them out.	0	1	2	3
36. Friends seem to enjoy coming to our house for visits.	0	1	2	3
37. We feel we have a good retirement income program.	0	1	2	3
38. When we make plans we are almost certain we can make them work.	0	1	2	3
39. In our family we understand what help we can expect from each other.	0	1	2	3
40. We seem to have little or no problem paying our bills on time.	0	1	2	3
41. Our relatives seem to take from us, but give little in return.*	0	1	2	3
42. We would have no problem getting a loan at a bank if we wanted one.	0	1	2	3
43. We feel we have enough money on hand to cover small unexpected expenses (under $100).	0	1	2	3
44. When we face a problem, we look at the good and bad of each possible solution.	0	1	2	3
45. The member(s) who earn our family income seem to have good employee benefits (such as paid insurance, stocks, car, education, etc.).	0	1	2	3
46. No matter what happens to us, we try to look at the bright side of things.	0	1	2	3
47. We feel we are able to go out to eat occasionally without hurting our budget.	0	1	2	3
48. We try to keep in touch with our relatives as much as possible.	0	1	2	3

FAMILY STATEMENTS	Not at all	Minimally	Moderately	Very well
49. It seems that we need more life insurance than we have.*	0	1	2	3
50. In our family it is "okay" for members to show our positive feelings about each other.	0	1	2	3
51. We feel we are able to make financial contributions to a good cause (needy people, church, etc.).	0	1	2	3
52. We seem to be happier with our lives than many families we know.	0	1	2	3
53. It is "okay" for family members to express sadness by crying, even in front of others.	0	1	2	3
54. When we need something that can't be postponed, we have money in savings to cover it.	0	1	2	3
55. We discuss our decisions with other family members before carrying them out.	0	1	2	3
56. Our relative(s) are willing to listen to our problems.	0	1	2	3
57. We worry about how we would cover a large unexpected bill (for home, auto repairs, etc., for about $100).*	0	1	2	3
58. We get great satisfaction when we can help one another in our family.	0	1	2	3
59. In our family we feel it is important to save for the future.	0	1	2	3
60. The working members of our family seem to be respected by their co-workers.	0	1	2	3
61. We have written checks knowing there wasn't enough money in the account to cover it.*	0	1	2	3
62. The members of our family respect one another.	0	1	2	3

FAMILY STATEMENTS	Not at all	Minimally	Moderately	Very well
63. We save our extra spending money for special things.	0	1	2	3
64. We feel confident that if our main breadwinner lost his/her job, he/she could find another one.	0	1	2	3
65. Members of our family are encouraged to have their own interests and abilities.	0	1	2	3
66. Our relatives do and say things to make us feel appreciated.	0	1	2	3
67. The members of our family are known to be good citizens and neighbors.	0	1	2	3
68. We make an effort to help our relatives when we can.	0	1	2	3
69. We feel we are financially better off now than we were 5 years ago.	0	1	2	3

PLEASE Check all 69 items to be sure you have circled a number for each one. THIS IS IMPORTANT.

Copyright © 1991 H. McCubbin and A. I. Thompson.

FAMILY MEMBER WELL-BEING (FMWB)

AUTHORS: Hamilton McCubbin and Joan Patterson

PURPOSE: To measure adjustment of family members.

DESCRIPTION: The FMWB is an 8-item instrument that measures the degree to which a family member is adjusted in terms of concern about health, tension, energy, cheerfulness, fear, anger, sadness, and general concerns. The FMWB was developed by generating items related to family members' possible over-all emotional, social, interactional, and physical well-being. The FMWB is very useful as a short form for assessing the well-being of family members along several dimensions.

NORMS: The FMWB has been studied with a number of large samples including 297 investment executives and 234 spouses of investment executives, Midwest farm families involving 411 males and 389 females, 813 rural bank employees plus 448 of their spouses, and 524 male members of military families and 465 female members of military families. The means on the FMWB range from 37.5 (SD = 9.1) for Caucasian female members of military families to 45.5 (SD = 10.5) for spouses of investment executives.

SCORING: The FMWB is easily scored by simply summing item responses after reverse-scoring items 1, 2, 5, 6, 7, and 8. Higher scores are indicators of more positive family well-being.

RELIABILITY: The FMWB has very good internal consistency with an alpha of .85. Data on stability were not available.

VALIDITY: The FMWB has excellent concurrent validity as established through numerous studies. Well-being is significantly correlated with family members spending time together and spouse employment. Family well-being is also related to family coherence and meaning, social support, and family system resources. Family member well-being also predicted resiliency in farm families faced with economic pressures.

PRIMARY REFERENCE: McCubbin, H. I. and Patterson, J. Family Member Well-Being (FMWB). In H. I. McCubbin, A. I. Thompson, and M. A. McCubbin (1996). *Family Assessment: Resiliency, Coping and Adaptation. Inventories for Research and Practice.* Madison: University of Wisconsin, 753–782.

AVAILABILITY: After purchasing the book cited above, you may register by telephone at (608) 262-5070. The book provides instructions for permission to use the instrument.

FMWB

For each of the eight statements below, please note that the words at each end of the 0 to 10 scale describe opposite feelings. Please fill in the response along the bar which seems closest to how you have generally felt during the past month.

1. How *concerned or worried about your health* have you been? (During the past month)

   Not CONCERNED   Very
   at all   1 2 3 4 5 6 7 8 9 CONCERNED

2. How *relaxed or tense* have you been? (During the past month)

   Very   Very
   RELAXED   1 2 3 4 5 6 7 8 9 TENSE

3. How much *energy, pep, vitality* have you felt? (During the past month)

   No energy at all   Very energetic
   LISTLESS   1 2 3 4 5 6 7 8 9 DYNAMIC

4. How *depressed or cheerful* have you been? (During the past month)

   Very   Very
   DEPRESSED   1 2 3 4 5 6 7 8 9 CHEERFUL

5. How *afraid* have you been? (During the past month)

   Not   Very
   AFRAID   1 2 3 4 5 6 7 8 9 AFRAID

6. How *angry* have you been? (During the past month)

   Not ANGRY   Very
   at all   1 2 3 4 5 6 7 8 9 ANGRY

7. How *sad* have you been? (During the past month)

   Not SAD   Very
   at all   1 2 3 4 5 6 7 8 9 SAD

8. How *concerned or worries about the health of another family member* have you been? (During the past month)

   Not CONCERNED   Very
   at all   1 2 3 4 5 6 7 8 9 CONCERNED

Copyright © H. I. McCubbin and J. Patterson, 1983.

FAMILY-OF-ORIGIN SCALE (FOS)

AUTHORS: Alan J. Hovestadt, William T. Anderson, Fred P. Piercy, Samuel W. Cochran, and Marshall Fine

PURPOSE: To measure self-perceived levels of health in one's family of origin.

DESCRIPTION: The FOS is a 40-item instrument designed to measure one's perceptions of the "health" of one's family of origin. The FOS focuses on autonomy and intimacy as two key concepts in the life of a healthy family. In this model, the healthy family develops autonomy by emphasizing clarity of expression (CE; positive items 24 and 34, negative items 9 and 16), responsibility (R; positive items 11 and 38, negative items 5 and 18), respect for others (RO; positive items 15 and 19, negative items 4 and 28), openness to others (O; positive items 6 and 14, negative items 23 and 37), and acceptance of separation and loss (A; positive items 10 and 36, negative items 20 and 25). The healthy family is viewed as developing intimacy by encouraging expression of a range of feelings (RF; positive items 1 and 12, negative items 32 and 39), creating a warm atmosphere in the home, referred to as mood and tone (MT; positive items 29 and 40, negative items 2 and 22), dealing with conflict resolution without undue stress (C; positive items 27 and 31, negative items 7 and 13), promoting sensitivity or empathy (E; positive items 21 and 35, negative items 17 and 30), and developing trust in humans as basically good (T; positive items 3 and 8, negative items 26 and 33). The FOS is seen as especially useful in family therapy involving family-of-origin issues.

NORMS: The FOS was studied initially with 278 college students in Texas, including 39 black and 239 white students. No other demographic data were presented. Overall means did not distinguish significantly between blacks (147.0) and whites (144.1). Means (and standard deviations) for each construct, in the order presented above, were: CE—3.52 (1.12), R—3.43 (1.15), RO—3.50 (1.18), O—3.41 (1.15), A—3.44 (1.25), RF—3.57 (1.26), MT—4.06 (1.11), C—3.42 (1.21), E—3.51 (1.11), and T—3.78 (1.12).

SCORING: For each item, the most healthy response (noted above as positive items) receives a score of "5" while the least healthy (negative items) receives a score of "1." The total scores—the sum of each item—range from 40 to 200 with higher scores indicating perceptions of better family health.

RELIABILITY: The FOS has fair to good internal consistency, with an overall alpha of .75 and a standardized item alpha of .97. The FOS has good to excellent stability, with two-week test-retest correlations on the autonomy dimension that ranged from .39 to .88 with a median of .77 and on intimacy from .46 to .87 with a median of .73.

VALIDITY: The FOS has good known-groups validity, significantly discriminating between men in alcohol-distressed and nonalcohol-distressed marriages and between perceptions of current marriage and rationality of marriage partners. The FOS also was significantly correlated with perceived levels of health in respondents' current families.

PRIMARY REFERENCE: Hovestadt, A. J., Anderson, W. T., Piercy, F. A., Cochran, S. W., and Fine, M. (1985). A Family-of-Origin Scale, *Journal of Marital and Family Therapy*, 11, no. 3, 287–297. Instrument reprinted by permission of American Association for Marriage and Family Therapy.

AVAILABILITY: Journal article.

FOS

The family of origin is the family with which you spent most or all of your childhood years. This scale is designed to help you recall how your family of origin functioned.

Each family is unique and has its own ways of doing things. Thus, there are *no right or wrong choices* in this scale. What is important is that you respond as *honestly* as you can.

In reading the following statements, apply them to your family of origin, *as you remember it*. Using the following scale, circle the appropriate number. Please respond to each statement.

5 (SA) = Strongly agree that it describes my family of origin.
4 (A) = Agree that it describes my family of origin.
3 (N) = Neutral.
2 (D) = Disagree that it describes my family of origin.
1 (SD) = Strongly disagree that it describes my family of origin.

		SA	A	N	D	SD
1.	In my family, it was normal to show both positive and negative feelings.	5	4	3	2	1
2.	The atmosphere in my family usually was unpleasant.	5	4	3	2	1
3.	In my family, we encouraged one another to develop new friendships.	5	4	3	2	1
4.	Differences of opinion in my family were discouraged.	5	4	3	2	1
5.	People in my family often made excuses for their mistakes.	5	4	3	2	1
6.	My parents encouraged family members to listen to one another.	5	4	3	2	1
7.	Conflicts in my family never got resolved.	5	4	3	2	1
8.	My family taught me that people were basically good.	5	4	3	2	1
9.	I found it difficult to understand what other family members said and how they felt.	5	4	3	2	1

		SA	A	N	D	SD
10.	We talked about our sadness when a relative or family friend died.	5	4	3	2	1
11.	My parents openly admitted it when they were wrong.	5	4	3	2	1
12.	In my family, I expressed just about any feeling I had.	5	4	3	2	1
13.	Resolving conflicts in my family was a very stressful experience.	5	4	3	2	1
14.	My family was receptive to the different ways various family members viewed life.	5	4	3	2	1
15.	My parents encouraged me to express my views openly.	5	4	3	2	1
16.	I often had to guess at what other family members thought or how they felt.	5	4	3	2	1
17.	My attitudes and my feelings frequently were ignored or criticized in my family.	5	4	3	2	1
18.	My family members rarely expressed responsibility for their actions.	5	4	3	2	1
19.	In my family, I felt free to express my own opinions.	5	4	3	2	1
20.	We never talked about our grief when a relative or family friend died.	5	4	3	2	1
21.	Sometimes in my family, I did not have to say anything, but I felt understood.	5	4	3	2	1
22.	The atmosphere in my family was cold and negative.	5	4	3	2	1
23.	The members of my family were not very receptive to one another's views.	5	4	3	2	1
24.	I found it easy to understand what other family members said and how they felt.	5	4	3	2	1
25.	If a family friend moved away, we never discussed our feelings of sadness.	5	4	3	2	1

		SA	A	N	D	SD
26.	In my family, I learned to be suspicious of others.	5	4	3	2	1
27.	In my family, I felt that I could talk things out and settle conflicts.	5	4	3	2	1
28.	I found it difficult to express my own opinions in my family.	5	4	3	2	1
29.	Mealtimes in my home usually were friendly and pleasant.	5	4	3	2	1
30.	In my family, no one cared about the feelings of other family members.	5	4	3	2	1
31.	We usually were able to work out conflicts in my family.	5	4	3	2	1
32.	In my family, certain feelings were not allowed to be expressed.	5	4	3	2	1
33.	My family believed that people usually took advantage of you.	5	4	3	2	1
34.	I found it easy in my family to express what I thought and how I felt.	5	4	3	2	1
35.	My family members usually were sensitive to one another's feelings.	5	4	3	2	1
36.	When someone important to us moved away, our family discussed our feelings of loss.	5	4	3	2	1
37.	My parents discouraged us from expressing views different from theirs.	5	4	3	2	1
38.	In my family, people took responsibility for what they did.	5	4	3	2	1
39.	My family had an unwritten rule: Don't express your feelings.	5	4	3	2	1
40.	I remember my family as being warm and supportive.	5	4	3	2	1

Copyright © 1985 American Association for Marriage and Family Therapy.

FAMILY ORGANIZED COHESIVENESS SCALE (FOC)

AUTHOR: Lawrence Fischer

PURPOSE: To measure organized cohesiveness in a family.

DESCRIPTION: This 13-item instrument measures the respondent's perception of how cohesiveness is organized in his or her family. The FOC measures four aspects of organized cohesiveness: cohesion, sharedness, clarity of leadership, and clarity of rules. The instrument was designed as part of the California Family Health Project, which evaluated family life and the health of husbands and wives in a sample of 225 families. For husbands in the study, organized cohesiveness was positively correlated with general well-being, and inversely correlated with depression and problem drinking. Scores also correlated with well-being and depression for the wives of the sample. Wives' scores on cohesiveness also correlated negatively with anxiety.

NORMS: Normative data are not available.

SCORING: Items 2, 4, and 9 are reverse scored. Total score on the FOC is the sum of the item scores. Scores range from 13 to 78.

RELIABILITY: The original FOC had 29 items and had a reliability coefficient of .88. The 13-item version has an alpha coefficient of .80.

VALIDITY: Scores on the FOC were correlated with a number of health-related variables for husbands and wives as described above. Scores also were correlated with self-esteem for husbands and wives. Scores on the FOC were different for families categorized as "balanced," "traditional," "disconnected," or "emotionally strained." These findings tend to support the criterion-related and concurrent validity of the FOC.

PRIMARY REFERENCE: Fischer, L., Ransom, D. C., Terry, H. E., and Burge, S. (1992). The California Family Health Project: IV. Family structure/organization and adult health. *Family Process,* 31, 399–419.

AVAILABILITY: Lawrence Fischer, Ph.D., University of California San Francisco, School of Medicine, 500 Parnassus Avenue, MU-3 East, Box 0900, San Francisco, CA, 94143-0900.

FOC

The following items will tell us about your family's attitudes and beliefs. Record in the space the number that best corresponds to your family's current attitude about each item. Please answer the items about your current family (you, your spouse/partner, your children). Also, answer the items according to YOUR FAMILY'S OPINION which may not be the same as your own. Use the following scale:

1 = Strongly disagree
2 = Disagree
3 = Mildly disagree
4 = Mildly agree
5 = Agree
6 = Strongly agree

_____ 1. Family members spend much of their free time together.
_____ 2. It is hard to know what the rules are in our family because they are always changing.
_____ 3. It is easy to know who the leader is in our family.
_____ 4. It is unclear what will happen when rules are broken in our family.
_____ 5. It is clear about what is best for family members.
_____ 6. Family togetherness is important.
_____ 7. In our family everybody knows what is expected of them.
_____ 8. It is clear who makes the decisions.
_____ 9. Members of our family are not very involved with each other.
_____ 10. In our family, we are alike in how we think and feel.
_____ 11. Family members share the same friends.
_____ 12. Family members feel very close to each other.
_____ 13. When our family gets together for activities, everybody is present.

FAMILY PRESSURES SCALE—ETHNIC (FPRES-E)

AUTHORS: Hamilton McCubbin, Anne Thompson, and Kelly Elver

PURPOSE: To measure severity of pressure in a family system.

DESCRIPTION: The FPRES-E is a 64-item inventory designed to be inclusive of pressures related to the life experience of families of color and to obtain an index of the severity of the pressure in the family system. The FPRES-E is adapted from the Family Inventory of Life Events and Changes in an effort to create a measure that is more culturally sensitive to the special pressures and stressors experienced by Native American families, including families of Hawaiian ancestry. Because the FPRES-E is one of the few measures available that makes a specific effort to be sensitive to the needs of Native American families, it is an important measure for assessing stresses within those families.

NORMS: The FPRES-E was studied with 174 families of Native Hawaiian ancestry. The mean score was 19.3 (SD = 10.6).

SCORING: The total score for FPRES-E is obtained by simply summing up all item responses.

RELIABILITY: The FPRES-E has excellent internal consistency with an alpha of .92. No data on stability were available.

VALIDITY: The FPRES-E was found to be the strongest predictor of family distress in a study of Native Hawaiian families, thereby showing good predictive validity.

PRIMARY REFERENCE: McCubbin, H. I., Thompson, A. I., and Elver, K. M. Family Pressures Scale—Ethnic (FPRES-E). In H. I. McCubbin, A. I. Thompson, and M. A. McCubbin (1996). *Family Assessment: Resiliency, Coping and Adaptation. Inventories for Research and Practice.* Madison: University of Wisconsin, 227–236.

AVAILABILITY: After purchasing the book cited above, you may register at the following number (608) 262-5070. The book provides instructions for permission to use the instrument.

FPRES-E

Please Circle 0, 1, 2, or 3 to record the degree to which each of the family pressures listed has been a problem in your family during the past 12 months.

Family Pressures:	Not a problem	Small problem	Medium problem	Large problem
1. Increase of husband/father's time away from family	0	1	2	3
2. A child member was treated badly because of racial prejudice	0	1	2	3
3. A member did not get a job because of racial prejudice	0	1	2	3
4. Close relative or friend of the family became seriously ill	0	1	2	3
5. A member became physically disabled or chronically ill	0	1	2	3
6. Increased difficulty in managing a chronically ill or disabled member	0	1	2	3
7. Member or close relative was committed to an institution or nursing home	0	1	2	3
8. Increased difficulty in resolving issues with a "former" or separated spouse	0	1	2	3
9. Increased responsibility to provide direct care or financial help to husband's and/or wife's parent(s)	0	1	2	3
10. A parent/spouse died	0	1	2	3
11. A child member died	0	1	2	3
12. Death of husband's or wife's parent or close relative	0	1	2	3
13. Increased difficulty with sexual relationship between husband and wife	0	1	2	3
14. Married son or daughter was separated or divorced	0	1	2	3
15. A member went to jail or juvenile detention	0	1	2	3
16. A member was picked up by police or arrested	0	1	2	3
17. Physical or sexual abuse or violence in the home	0	1	2	3
18. Delay in receiving child support or alimony payments	0	1	2	3
19. A member ran away from home	0	1	2	3
20. A member dropped out of school or was suspended from school	0	1	2	3
21. We worry that our ethnicity/roots are dying	0	1	2	3
22. A member appears to have emotional problems				
23. We worry that we are losing our ethnic values	0	1	2	3
24. A member appears to depend on alcohol or drugs	0	1	2	3
25. We worry that the land we were promised will never come to us	0	1	2	3
26. Increase in conflict between husband and wife	0	1	2	3
27. Worry that our children aren't interested in the family ethnicity/roots	0	1	2	3

28.	Increase in arguments between parent(s) and child(ren)	0	1	2	3
29.	We worry that use of our native language will fade away	0	1	2	3
30.	Increase in conflict among children in the family	0	1	2	3
31.	We worry that tension/conflict in the home hurts children's learning	0	1	2	3
32.	Increased disagreement about a member's friends or activities	0	1	2	3
33.	We worry that parents are not able to spend time with children to encourage learning	0	1	2	3
34.	Increase in the number of problems or issues which don't get resolved	0	1	2	3
35.	We worry that children want to quit school early	0	1	2	3
36.	Increase in the number of tasks or chores which don't get done	0	1	2	3
37.	We worry about children joining neighborhood/city gangs	0	1	2	3
38.	Spouse had unwanted or difficult pregnancy	0	1	2	3
39.	Worry that children will join groups abusing alcohol/drugs	0	1	2	3
40.	An unmarried member became pregnant	0	1	2	3
41.	We worry that jobs will not be available for children in the future	0	1	2	3
42.	A member had an abortion	0	1	2	3
43.	We worry that they will not have enough money for the children's education	0	1	2	3
44.	A member gave birth to or adopted a child	0	1	2	3
45.	We worry that the family will not be able to take care of the elders in the future	0	1	2	3
46.	We worry that the elders will become a burden upon the children in the future	0	1	2	3
47.	Went on welfare	0	1	2	3
48.	Increased conflict with in-laws or relatives	0	1	2	3
49.	Took out a loan or refinanced a loan to cover increased expenses	0	1	2	3
50.	Increased strain on family "money" for medical/dental expenses	0	1	2	3
51.	Purchased or built a home	0	1	2	3
52.	A member purchased a car or other major item	0	1	2	3
53.	A member changed to a new job/career	0	1	2	3
54.	Increasing financial debts due to overuse of credit cards	0	1	2	3
55.	Increased strain on family "money" for food, clothing, energy, home care	0	1	2	3
56.	A member lost or quit a job	0	1	2	3
57.	Increased strain on family "money" for child(ren)'s education	0	1	2	3
58.	Decrease in satisfaction with job/career	0	1	2	3
59.	A member started or returned to work	0	1	2	3
60.	A member had increased difficulty with people at work	0	1	2	3
61.	Family moved to a new home/apartment	0	1	2	3
62.	A member stopped working for extended period (e.g., laid off, leave of absence, strike)	0	1	2	3

63. Experienced difficulty in arranging for satisfactory   0   1   2   3
    child care
64. We worry that they cannot pay for health insurance   0   1   2   3
    in the future

Copyright © H. I. McCubbin, A. I. Thompson, and K. M. Elver, 1993.

FAMILY PROBLEM SOLVING COMMUNICATION (FPSC)

AUTHORS: Marilyn McCubbin, Hamilton McCubbin, and Anne Thompson

PURPOSE: To measure family communication.

DESCRIPTION: The FPSC is a 10-item instrument designed to measure the two dominant patterns in family communication that appear to play a major part in the way families cope with hardship and catastrophes. The instrument was developed specifically for family stress and resiliency research, and measures both positive and negative patterns of communication. The FPSC is based on the conceptual notion that the quality of family communication determines how families manage tension and strain and develop a satisfactory level of family functioning. Available in both English and Spanish, the FPSC comprises two subscales: incendiary communication (items 1, 3, 5, 7, and 9) and affirming communication (items 2, 4, 6, 8, and 10).

NORMS: The FPSC has been studied with several populations including 1404 employees of a national insurance company, 107 mothers of children with a cardiac illness, 92 fathers of children with a cardiac illness, 72 mothers of children with diabetes, 62 fathers of children with diabetes, 189 families of Native Hawaiian ancestry, 743 rural bank employees, 413 spouses of rural bank employees, 297 investment executives, and 233 spouses of investment executives. Means on the total FPSC range from 18.746 (SD = 4.83) for single-parent families of Native Hawaiian ancestry to 22.697 (SD = 4.66) for employees of a national insurance company. Total score and subscale score means and standard deviations for all the groups studied are available in the primary reference.

SCORING: The FPSC is scored two ways. For developing a total score, reverse-score items 1, 5, and 7 and sum all item responses. To score the subscales separately, items 3 and 9 of the incendiary communication subscale should be reverse scored and items on each subscale should be summed; this will ensure that incendiary communication is a negative form of communication and affirming communication will be positive.

RELIABILITY: The FPSC has excellent internal consistency with an alpha of .89 for the total scale and alphas of .78 and .86 for incendiary and affirming communication, respectively. The FPSC has excellent stability with a reported test-retest correlation of .86.

VALIDITY: The FPSC has very good concurrent validity with correlations in expected directions between the FPSC and several other valid measures of family functioning and of family well-being.

PRIMARY REFERENCE: McCubbin, M. A., McCubbin, H. I., and Thompson, A. Family Problem Solving Communication (FPSC). In H. I. McCubbin, A. I. Thompson, and M. A. McCubbin (1996). *Family Assessment: Resiliency,*

Coping and Adaptation. Inventories for Research and Practice. Madison: University of Wisconsin, 639–686.

AVAILABILITY: After purchasing the book cited above, you may register by telephone at (608) 262-5070. The book provides instructions for permission to use the instrument.

FPSC

When our family struggles with problems or conflicts which upset us, I would describe my family in the following way:	False	Mostly false	Mostly true	True
1. We yell and scream at each other.	0	1	2	3
2. We are respectful of each others' feelings.	0	1	2	3
3. We talk things through till we reach a solution.	0	1	2	3
4. We work hard to be sure family members were not hurt, emotionally or physically.	0	1	2	3
5. We walk away from conflicts without much satisfaction.	0	1	2	3
6. We share with each other how much we care for one another.	0	1	2	3
7. We make matters more difficult by fighting and bring up old matters.	0	1	2	3
8. We take the time to hear what each other has to say or feel.	0	1	2	3
9. We work to be calm and talk things through.	0	1	2	3
10. We get upset, but we try to end our conflicts on a positive note.	0	1	2	3

Copyright © M. A. McCubbin, H. I. McCubbin, and A. I. Thompson, 1988.

FAMILY RESPONSIBILITY INDEX (FRI)

AUTHOR: Patricia M. Bjorkquist

PURPOSE: To measure the division of family-role responsibilities.

DESCRIPTION: The FRI is a 53-item instrument designed to measure behaviorally the way spouses divide family-role responsibilities. The FRI was designed to sample a balance of traditionally masculine and feminine tasks, including an evaluation of degree of responsibility. The instrument is designed to elicit a direct assessment of specific behaviors; attitudes and beliefs are not evaluated. The 53 items are divided into 10 separate areas of typical family responsibilities.

NORMS: The FRI was initially studied with 122 respondents comprising 61 dual career couples. One spouse in each couple was a faculty member in a university, while the other was either a full-time student or employed full-time in a professional occupation. Actual norms are not provided.

SCORING: The 53 items are rated on a 5-point scale regarding the extent of the respondent's responsibility for each task during a typical week. Items that do not apply are rated as 0, leaving a total possible range from 0 to 265.

RELIABILITY: Reliability was measured by correlations between spouses on the 53 FRI behaviors. In two administrations of the FRI, these correlations averaged .82 and .79, suggesting good agreement.

VALIDITY: The author reports good face and content validity due to inclusion of a representative composite of tasks. Validity coefficients were computed by correlating data from interviews with 10 of the couples regarding contribution to domestic responsibilities and their scores on the FRI. The mean correlations were .88 for husbands and .86 for wives.

PRIMARY REFERENCE: Alley, P. M. (1984). The Family Responsibility Index: A behavioral measure of marital work allocation, *Journal of Personality Assessment*, 48, 3–5. Instrument reprinted with permission.

AVAILABILITY: Dr. Patricia Bjorkquist, 3054A Glen Creek Road, NW, Salem, OR 97304.

FRI

This survey represents a refinement of several previous studies attempting to understand how husbands and wives in dual career families arrange their domestic situations. Please answer all of the questions. If you wish to comment on any questions or qualify your answers, please feel free to use the space in the margins. Your comments will be read and taken into account.

Thank you for your help.

During a typical working week, who is responsible for each of the following tasks? (Circle the appropriate number.)

		Wife always	Wife more	H/W Equally or both	Husband more	Husband always	Does not apply
Yardwork							
1.	Mow lawn	5	4	3	2	1	0
2.	Trim and/or edge lawn	5	4	3	2	1	0
3.	Plant and tend flower garden	5	4	3	2	1	0
4.	Plant and tend vegetable garden	5	4	3	2	1	0
5.	Water lawn and garden	5	4	3	2	1	0
6.	Service lawn and garden tools	5	4	3	2	1	0
7.	Trim bushes, fertilize lawn, and garden	5	4	3	2	1	0
Laundry							
1.	Wash clothes	5	4	3	2	1	0
2.	Put clean clothes away	5	4	3	2	1	0
3.	Iron clothes	5	4	3	2	1	0

		Wife always	Wife more	H/W Equally or both	Husband more	Husband always	Does not apply
House Care and Upkeep							
1.	Indoor painting	5	4	3	2	1	0
2.	Outdoor painting	5	4	3	2	1	0
3.	Physical upkeep of house exterior	5	4	3	2	1	0
4.	Household repairs	5	4	3	2	1	0
5.	Household remodeling	5	4	3	2	1	0
6.	Put on storm windows and/or screens	5	4	3	2	1	0
Kitchen Clean-up							
1.	Put dishes in dishwasher/wash dishes	5	4	3	2	1	0
2.	Empty dishwasher/dry dishes and put dishes away	5	4	3	2	1	0
3.	Clean stove, counters, and table	5	4	3	2	1	0
Family Business							
1.	Balance checkbook	5	4	3	2	1	0
2.	Pay bills	5	4	3	2	1	0
3.	Prepare income tax forms	5	4	3	2	1	0

		Wife always	Wife more	H/W Equally or both	Husband more	Husband always	Does not apply
4.	Make major financial decisions (e.g., buy insurance, select financial investments)	5	4	3	2	1	0

Housecleaning

1.	Clean bathroom	5	4	3	2	1	0
2.	Vacuum rugs	5	4	3	2	1	0
3.	Wash floors	5	4	3	2	1	0
4.	Dust furniture	5	4	3	2	1	0
5.	Change beds	5	4	3	2	1	0
6.	Care for indoor plants	5	4	3	2	1	0
7.	Make beds	5	4	3	2	1	0
8.	Empty garbage	5	4	3	2	1	0

Car Care

1.	Check and add gas, oil, water, battery fluid	5	4	3	2	1	0
2.	Decide when car needs servicing and take to garage	5	4	3	2	1	0
3.	Buy and change tires or take to garage to have tires changed	5	4	3	2	1	0
4.	Perform routine car servicing (e.g., change oil, antifreeze)	5	4	3	2	1	0

		Wife always	Wife more	H/W Equally or both	Hus- band more	Hus- band always	Does not apply
Heavy Housecleaning							
1.	Wash windows and drapes/curtains	5	4	3	2	1	0
2.	Wash walls	5	4	3	2	1	0
3.	Clean refrigerator and stove	5	4	3	2	1	0
4.	Shampoo rugs and furniture	5	4	3	2	1	0
5.	Polish floors	5	4	3	2	1	0
Family Care							
1.	Buy clothes for self	5	4	3	2	1	0
2.	Buy clothes for other family members	5	4	3	2	1	0
3.	Make dental and doctor appointments	5	4	3	2	1	0
4.	Take children to dentist/doctor	5	4	3	2	1	0
5.	Stay with children when sick	5	4	3	2	1	0
6.	Care for family pets	5	4	3	2	1	0
7.	Take care of preschool children	5	4	3	2	1	0
8.	Teach, help, and discipline:						
	—girls, age 6–18	5	4	3	2	1	0
	—boys, age 6–18	5	4	3	2	1	0

		Wife always	Wife more	H/W Equally or both	Hus-band more	Hus-band always	Does not apply
9.	Arrange for child care	5	4	3	2	1	0
10.	Organize family recreation and entertainment	5	4	3	2	1	0
11.	Keep in touch with relatives and good friends	5	4	3	2	1	0

Preparing Meals

1.	Plan meals/buy food	5	4	3	2	1	0
2.	Prepare meals	5	4	3	2	1	0

Copyright © 1981 Patricia M. Alley, Ph.D.

FAMILY SCHEMA—ETHNIC (FSCH-E)

AUTHORS: Hamilton McCubbin, Anne Thompson, Kelly Elver, and Kera Carpenter

PURPOSE: To measure family world view.

DESCRIPTION: The FSCH-E is a 39-item instrument designed to measure the degree to which a family has cultivated a family schema, a world view inclusive of cultural and ethnic values which is an important part of the family's identity. Family schema is conceptualized as a generalized structure of shared values, beliefs, goals, expectations, and priorities. The schema is seen as shaped and adopted by the family unit, thus providing a generalized informational structure through which information is processed. Family schemas are seen as evolving over time and serving as a world view and framework for families to evaluate crisis situations and to affirm their established patterns of functioning. The family schema has as one of its central functions the development of family meanings. The FSCH-E is one of the few measures available to evaluate this perspective of family functioning and as such should be particularly helpful for both researchers and practitioners.

NORMS: The FSCH-E was studied with 141 families of Native Hawaiian ancestry. The mean score was 90.3 (SD = 12.3).

SCORING: The FSCH-E is easily scored by summing the individual item responses.

RELIABILITY: The FSCH-E has very good internal consistency with an alpha of .87. The FSCH-E is also very stable with a several-week test-retest correlation of .82.

VALIDITY: In a study of Native Hawaiian families, the FSCH-E was positively correlated with family problem-solving communication and family sense of coherence. The FSCH-E is seen as a valid measure for evaluating family meanings, values, and world views with items that reflect cultural or ethnically oriented factors of family life as part of the family's schema.

PRIMARY REFERENCE: McCubbin, H. I., Thompson, A. I., Elver, K. M., and Carpenter, K. Family Schema—Ethnic (FSCH-E). In H. I. McCubbin, A. I. Thompson, and M. A. McCubbin (1996). *Family Assessment: Resiliency, Coping and Adaptation-Inventories for Research and Practice.* Madison: University Wisconsin System, 713–721.

AVAILABILITY: After purchasing the book cited above, you may register at the following telephone number (608) 262-5070. The book provides instructions for permission to use the instrument.

FSCH-E

Decide how well each statement describes your family. If the statement describes your family well, circle #3, True. If the statement does not fit your family, circle 0, False. If the statement fits your family to some degree, circle #2, Mostly True. Circle #1 if the statement describes your family a little.

In our family:	False	Mostly false	Mostly true	True
1. We believe that the land we live on is an important part of who we are.	0	1	2	3
2. If we have more than we need, we share with others.	0	1	2	3
3. We give up things we want for the good of others.	0	1	2	3
4. Children are precious because they carry our spirit on to the future.	0	1	2	3
5. We believe that if we destroy the land, water, and air, we are hurting ourselves.	0	1	2	3
6. We will sacrifice personal goals for the family.	0	1	2	3
7. We help each other without being asked.	0	1	2	3
8. We believe children need strict discipline.	0	1	2	3
9. We don't hold grudges, we forgive and move on.	0	1	2	3
10. We expect members to place the family first.	0	1	2	3
11. When there are problems, family members will come home to help out.	0	1	2	3
12. We encourage family members to take advantage of opportunities even if it means moving away.	0	1	2	3
13. Our ethnic/cultural roots (e.g., being Caucasian, African-American, Native American, Hawaiian, Hispanic, Alaskan, Asian) give strength to us.	0	1	2	3
14. Music teaches us about our ethnic/cultural roots.	0	1	2	3
15. Dancing teaches us about our ethnic/cultural roots.	0	1	2	3
16. Using our native language helps us appreciate and value our ethnic/cultural roots.	0	1	2	3
17. When we try to fit in, we lose our identity.	0	1	2	3
18. We don't make a big deal of things.	0	1	2	3
19. In our family, we do not keep secrets for very long.	0	1	2	3
20. We believe that all families must take care of the land, water, and air.	0	1	2	3
21. When we try to fit in, we lose our self-respect.	0	1	2	3
22. We do things for pleasure, not for personal gain.	0	1	2	3
23. We value and respect our elders (grandparents, parents, etc.).	0	1	2	3
24. Children are respected.	0	1	2	3
25. We do a lot to hold on to our ethnic/cultural identity and beliefs.	0	1	2	3

26.	We are easygoing and open to others.	0	1	2	3
27.	We believe that the future will depend on our taking care of the land, water, and air.	0	1	2	3
28.	We believe that giving to others or sharing is important.	0	1	2	3
29.	Grandparents, aunts, and uncles have some say in the decisions we make.	0	1	2	3
30.	We teach children to support each other.	0	1	2	3
31.	Storytelling is how we pass on information about our ethnic/cultural roots.	0	1	2	3
32.	We are taught not to say anything that might upset others.	0	1	2	3
33.	We only take from the land and water what we feel is necessary.	0	1	2	3
34.	Happiness is more important than success.	0	1	2	3
35.	We teach our children to listen to our elders and their opinions.	0	1	2	3
36.	We practice and believe in traditions and celebrations.	0	1	2	3
37.	We believe it is good to say what we feel or think in front of others.	0	1	2	3
38.	We try to make our ethnic/cultural roots a part of our daily lives.	0	1	2	3
39.	Children should be seen and not heard.	0	1	2	3

Copyright © H. I. McCubbin, A. J. Thompson, and K. M. Elver, 1992.

FAMILY SENSE OF COHERENCE (FSOC) AND FAMILY
ADAPTATION SCALES (FAS)

AUTHORS: Aaron Antonovsky and Talma Sourani

PURPOSE: To measure the sense of coherence and sense of adaptation of families.

DESCRIPTION: The FSOC and FAS are jointly developed 26-item and 10-item scales (respectively) designed to measure a family's sense of coherence and sense of adaptation to internal and external environments. Family coherence is defined as an orientation that expresses confidence that internal and external stimuli are structured and predictable, resources are available to meet demands from those stimuli, and the demands are worthy challenges. The theory underlying both measures is that the higher the sense of family coherence, the greater the adaptation or satisfaction with its adaptation to the family's internal and external environments. Both scales are related to theory on the importance of family coherence. The measures can be used together or separately, and may be used to target changes in the course of family therapy.

NORMS: The two scales were initially studied on 60 married couples in a central Israeli city. All the men were at least 40% disabled from 2 to 10 years, aged 25 to 50, married, with at least one child at home. The focus on one disabled spouse was a result of the study's focus on coping with a crisis. All families were characterized as being from a working-class population, although 48.3% were unemployed, and 38.4% had 5 to 8 years of schooling. The mean score on the FSOC for husbands was 128.63 (SD = 33.35) and for wives was 130.85 (SD = 33.99). Scores on the FAS were not reported.

SCORING: The FSOC is scored on sliding scales from 1 to 7 with higher scores indicating a stronger sense of coherence. Reverse-score items 1, 3, 5, 6, 9, 10, 13, 15, 18, 21, 22, 24, 25 so that "7" is always a high sense of coherence. The total scale score is obtained by summing all items after reverse-scoring. The FAS is scored the same way as the FSOC with items 1, 2, 4, 6, 9, and 10 reverse-scored.

RELIABILITY: Both measures have good to excellent internal consistency. The FSOC has an alpha of .92 while the alpha for the FAS was .87.

VALIDITY: Both scales may be seen as having good concurrent validity since they appear conceptually and empirically to measure two different concepts but are highly correlated with each other. Also, husbands' scores on both measures are significantly correlated with wives' scores. In addition, both scales are significantly correlated with social workers' ratings of overall adaptation of the families in the study.

PRIMARY REFERENCE: Antonovsky, A. and Sourani, T. (1988). Family sense of coherence and family adaptation, *Journal of Marriage and the Family*,

50, 79–92. Instrument reprinted with permission of the National Council on Family Relations.

AVAILABILITY: Journal article.

FSOC

This questionnaire contains questions about the way your family handles various daily problems. The questions relate to your immediate family: spouse and children. In answering, try to think of the behavior of the entire family, and not only of specific individuals. But don't include little children to whom the questions don't apply. There are no right or wrong answers. Each family has its own way of behaving in different situations.

Please circle the number that comes closest to your feelings about each situation. Each item is on a different 7-point scale.

1.   Is there a feeling in your family that *everyone* understands everyone else well?

```
             1      2      3      4      5      6      7
      There's full under-                    There's no under-
      standing among all                     standing among
      family members.                        family members.
```

2.   When you have to get things done which depend on cooperation among all members of the family, your feeling is:

```
             1      2      3      4      5      6      7
      There's almost no                      The things will
      chance that the                        always get done.
      things will get done.
```

3.   Do you have the feeling that it's always possible, in your family, to get help one from another when a problem arises?

```
             1      2      3      4      5      6      7
      You can always                         You can't get
      get help from all                      help from
      family members                         family members
```

4.   Let's assume that unexpected guests are about to arrive and the house isn't set up to receive them. Does it seem to you that

```
             1      2      3      4      5      6      7
      The job will fall                      All the members of the
      on one person.                         family will pitch in to
                                             get the house ready.
```

5. In case an important decision has to be taken which concerns the whole family, do you have the feeling that

             1   2   3   4   5   6   7

A decision will always be taken that's for the good of all family members.
          The decision that will be taken won't be for the good of all family members.

6. Family life seems to you

             1   2   3   4   5   6   7

Full of interest.
          Totally routine.

7. Does it happen that someone in the family feels as if it isn't clear to him/her what his/her jobs are in the house?

             1   2   3   4   5   6   7

This feeling exists all the time.
          This feeling exists very rarely.

8. When a problem comes up in the family (like: unusual behavior of a family member, an unexpected overdraft in the bank account, being fired from work, unusual tension), do you think that you can together clarify how it happened?

             1   2   3   4   5   6   7

Very little chance.
          To a great extent.

9. Many people, even those with a strong character, sometimes feel like sad sacks (losers). In the past, has there been a feeling like this in your family?

             1   2   3   4   5   6   7

There's never been a feeling like this in the family.
          This feeling always exists.

10. Think of a situation in which your family moved to a new house. Does it seem to you that

             1   2   3   4   5   6   7

All family members would be able to adjust easily to the new situation.
          It would be very hard for family members to adjust to the new situation.

11. Let's assume that your family has been annoyed by something in your neighborhood. Does it seem to you that

            1   2   3   4   5   6   7

Nothing can be done to prevent the annoyance.   It's possible to do a great deal to prevent the annoyance.

12. Until now your family life has had

            1   2   3   4   5   6   7

No clear goals or purpose at all.   Very clear goals and purpose.

13. When you think about your family life, you very often

            1   2   3   4   5   6   7

Feel how good it is to be alive.   Ask yourself why the family exists.

14. Let's say you're tired, disappointed, angry, or the like. Does it seem to you that *all* the members of the family will sense your feelings?

            1   2   3   4   5   6   7

No one will sense my feelings.   All the family members will sense my feelings.

15. Do you sometimes feel that there's no clear and sure knowledge of what's going to happen in the family?

            1   2   3   4   5   6   7

There's no such feeling at all.   There's always a feeling like this.

16. When the family faces a tough problem, the feeling is

            1   2   3   4   5   6   7

There's no hope of overcoming the difficulties.   We'll overcome it all.

17. To succeed in things that are important to the family or to one of you

            1   2   3   4   5   6   7

Isn't important in the family.   Is a very important thing for all family members.

18.   To what extent does it seem to you that family rules are clear?

	1	2	3	4	5	6	7

The rules in
the family are
completely clear.

The rules aren't
clear at all.

19.   When something very difficult happened in your family (like a critical illness of a family member), the feeling was

	1	2	3	4	5	6	7

There's no point
in going on living
in the family.

This is a challenge to go
on living in the family
despite everything.

20.   When you think of possible difficulties in important areas of family life, is the feeling

	1	2	3	4	5	6	7

There are many
problems which
have no solution.

It's possible in
every case to
find a solution.

21.   Think of your feeling about the extent of planning money matters in your family

	1	2	3	4	5	6	7

There's full
planning of
money matters.

There's no planning
about money matters
at all in the family.

22.   When you're in the midst of a rough period, does the family

	1	2	3	4	5	6	7

Always feel cheered
up by the thought
about better things
that can happen.

Feel disappointed
and despairing
about life.

23.   Does it happen that you feel that there's really not much meaning in maintaining the family framework?

	1	2	3	4	5	6	7

We always
have this
feeling.

We've never had
a feeling like this
in our family.

24.   Think of your feeling about the extent of order in your home. Is the case that

            1   2   3   4   5   6   7
       The house is   The house isn't
       well-ordered.   at all ordered.

25.   Let's assume that your family is the target of criticism in the neighborhood.
       Does it seem to you that your reactions will be

            1   2   3   4   5   6   7
       The whole family will   Family members will
       join together against   move apart from
       the criticism.   each other.

26.   To what extent do family members share sad experiences with each other?

            1   2   3   4   5   6   7
       There's complete   We don't share our
       sharing with all   sad experiences
       family members.   with family members.

Please circle the number that comes closest to your feelings about each situation.

1. Are you satisfied in belonging to your family?

1	2	3	4	5	6	7
I'm completely satisfied						I'm not satisfied

2. Are you satisfied about the way the children are being raised? (like with their education, their behavior, their activities?)

1	2	3	4	5	6	7
I'm completely satisfied						I'm not satisfied

3. Are you satisfied with the family's way of life?

1	2	3	4	5	6	7
I'm not satisfied						I'm completely satisfied

4. Are you satisfied with the possibility of expressing what you feel in your family?

1	2	3	4	5	6	7
I'm completely satisfied						I'm not satisfied

5. Are you satisfied with the extent to which family members are close to each other?

1	2	3	4	5	6	7
I'm not satisfied						I'm completely satisfied

6. Are you satisfied with how the family spends its leisure time?

1	2	3	4	5	6	7
I'm completely satisfied						I'm not satisfied

7. Are you satisfied with the way family members communicate with each other?

1	2	3	4	5	6	7
I'm not satisfied						I'm completely satisfied

8.   Are you satisfied with how your family fits into the neighborhood?

         1   2   3   4   5   6   7
      I'm not   I'm completely
      satisfied   satisfied

9.   Are you satisfied with the social relations your family has?

         1   2   3   4   5   6   7
      I'm completely   I'm not
      satisfied   satisfied

10. Are you satisfied with the way the family relates to the wishes of all the
     family members?

         1   2   3   4   5   6   7
      I'm completely   I'm not
      satisfied   satisfied

Copyright © 1988 National Council on Family Relations.

FAMILY TIMES AND ROUTINES INDEX (FTRI)

AUTHORS: Hamilton I. McCubbin, Marilyn A. McCubbin, and Anne I. Thompson

PURPOSE: To measure family integration and stability.

DESCRIPTION: The FTRI is a 32-item instrument that examines family time together and routines families adopt as indicators of family integration and stability. This integration includes effective ways of meeting common problems and the ability to handle major crises. As can be seen from the measure, FTRI measures a number of areas of family life, and includes 8 factors reflecting those areas. However, the FTRI can be used as an overall index by simply using the total score. As such, it is a very useful measure to evaluate the ways families handle everyday chores and routines.

NORMS: The FTRI was studied with 304 nonclinical families. No other demographic data were reported. The overall mean for the presence or absence of family routines was 63.5 (SD = 10.8).

SCORING: The FTRI provides two scores, one for the extent to which each of the two routines is true for the family and one for the extent to which the routine is viewed as important. Overall scores are derived by simply summing all items. For the "importance" scale, NI = 0, SI = 1, VI = 2, NA = 0.

RELIABILITY: The FTRI has excellent internal validity with an alpha of .88. Data on stability were not available.

VALIDITY: The FTRI has good concurrent validity, with significant correlations with the Family Bonding scale of FACES II, Family Coherence scale of F-COPES, Family Celebrations Index, and Quality of Family Life.

PRIMARY REFERENCE: McCubbin, H. I. and Thompson, A. I. (eds.) (1991). *Family Assessment Inventories for Research and Practice*. Madison, WI: University of Wisconsin.

AVAILABILITY: Dr. Hamilton McCubbin, Dean, School of Family Resources and Consumer Services, Madison, WI 53706-1575.

FTRI

Directions:

First, read the following statements and decide to what extent each of these routines listed below is false or true about your family. Please circle the number (0, 1, 2, 3) which best expresses your family experiences: False (0), Mostly false (1), Mostly true (2), True (3).

Second, determine the importance of each routine to keeping your family together and strong: (NI = Not important, SI = Somewhat important, VI = Very important). Please circle the letters (NI, SI, or VI) which best express how important the routines are to your family. If you do not have children, relatives, teenagers, etc., please circle NA = Not Applicable.

| | | | | | How Important to Keeping the Family Together and Strong | | |
| | | | | | Important to family | | |
ROUTINES	False	Mostly false	Mostly true	True	Not	Some-what	Very	Not applic-able

Workday and Leisure-Time Routines

1. Parent(s) have some time each day for just talking with the children.	0	1	2	3	NI	SI	VI	NA
2. Working parent has a regular play time with the children after coming home from work.	0	1	2	3	NI	SI	VI	NA
3. Working parent takes care of the children sometime almost every day.	0	1	2	3	NI	SI	VI	NA

| | | | How Important to Keeping the Family Together and Strong | | | |
| | | | Important to family | | | |
ROUTINES	False	Mostly false	Mostly true	True	Not	Some-what	Very	Not applic-able
4. Nonworking parent and children do something together outside the home almost every day (e.g., shopping, walking, etc.).	0	1	2	3	NI	SI	VI	NA
5. Family has a quiet time each evening when everyone talks or plays quietly.	0	1	2	3	NI	SI	VI	NA
6. Family goes some place special together each week.	0	1	2	3	NI	SI	VI	NA
7. Family has a certain family time each week when they do things together at home.	0	1	2	3	NI	SI	VI	NA
8. Parents read or tell stories to the children almost every day.	0	1	2	3	NI	SI	VI	NA
9. Each child has some time each day for playing alone.	0	1	2	3	NI	SI	VI	NA
10. Children/Teens play with friends daily.	0	1	2	3	NI	SI	VI	NA

ROUTINES

ROUTINES	False	Mostly false	Mostly true	True	How Important to Keeping the Family Together and Strong — Important to family			
					Not	Some-what	Very	Not applic-able
Parents' Routines								
11. Parents have a certain hobby or sport they do together regularly.	0	1	2	3	NI	SI	VI	NA
12. Parents have time with each other quite often.	0	1	2	3	NI	SI	VI	NA
13. Parents go out together one or more times a week.	0	1	2	3	NI	SI	VI	NA
14. Parents often spend time with teenagers for private talks.	0	1	2	3	NI	SI	VI	NA
Family Bedtime Routines								
15. Children have special things they do or ask for each night at bedtime (e.g., story, good-night kiss, hug).	0	1	2	3	NI	SI	VI	NA
16. Children go to bed at the same time almost every night.	0	1	2	3	NI	SI	VI	NA

| | | | | How Important to Keeping the Family Together and Strong | | | |
| | | | | Important to family | | | |
ROUTINES	False	Mostly false	Mostly true	True	Not	Some-what	Very	Not applic-able
Family Meals								
17. Family eats at about the same time each night.	0	1	2	3	NI	SI	VI	NA
18. Whole family eats one meal together daily.	0	1	2	3	NI	SI	VI	NA
Extended Family Routines								
19. At least one parent talks to his/her parents regularly.	0	1	2	3	NI	SI	VI	NA
20. Family has regular visits with the relatives.	0	1	2	3	NI	SI	VI	NA
21. Children/teens spend time with grandparents quite often.	0	1	2	3	NI	SI	VI	NA
22. We talk with/write to relatives usually once a week.	0	1	2	3	NI	SI	VI	NA

ROUTINES	False	Mostly false	Mostly true	True	How Important to Keeping the Family Together and Strong			
					Important to family			Not applic-able
					Not	Some-what	Very	
Leaving and Coming Home								
23. Family checks in or out with each other when someone leaves or comes home.	0	1	2	3	NI	SI	VI	NA
24. Working parent comes home from work at the same time each day.	0	1	2	3	NI	SI	VI	NA
25. Family has certain things they almost always do to greet each other at the end of the day.	0	1	2	3	NI	SI	VI	NA
26. We express caring and affection for each other daily.	0	1	2	3	NI	SI	VI	NA
Family Disciplinary Routines								
27. Parents have certain things they almost always do each time the children get out of line.	0	1	2	3	NI	SI	VI	NA
28. Parents discuss new rules for children/teenagers with them quite often.	0	1	2	3	NI	SI	VI	NA

ROUTINES	False	Mostly false	Mostly true	True	How Important to Keeping the Family Together and Strong		
					Important to family		Not applic-able
					Not	Some-what	Very
Family Chores							
29. Children do regular household chores.	0	1	2	3	NI	SI	VI	NA
30. Mothers do regular household chores.	0	1	2	3	NI	SI	VI	NA
31. Fathers do regular household chores.	0	1	2	3	NI	SI	VI	NA
32. Teenagers do regular household chores.	0	1	2	3	NI	SI	VI	NA

Copyright © 1986 H. McCubbin and M. McCubbin. Copyright © 1991 H. McCubbin and A. I. Thompson.

FAMILY TRADITIONS SCALE (FTS)

AUTHORS: Hamilton I. McCubbin and Anne I. Thompson

PURPOSE: To measure family traditions.

DESCRIPTION: The FTS is a 20-item instrument designed to measure the extent to which a family is involved in maintaining traditions around transitions and/or changes in the family. The basis for the scale is that higher scores presumably reflect a more integrated, stable family. The FTS measures four types of traditions: holidays, changes (e.g., marriage), religious occasions, and special events. However, the FTS is best used by utilizing the overall score.

NORMS: The FTS was studied with 304 nonclinical families. No other demographic data were reported. The mean was 26.3 (SD = 4.4).

SCORING: The FTS is easily scored by giving each "yes" 1 point and then summing those items for a total score.

RELIABILITY: The FTS has very good internal consistency with an alpha of .85. No data on stability were available.

VALIDITY: There is little validity data for the FTS, although a correlation with the Family Celebrations Index suggests some degree of concurrent validity

PRIMARY REFERENCE: McCubbin, H. I. and Thompson, A. I. (eds.) (1991). *Family Assessment Inventories for Research and Practice*. Madison, WI: University of Wisconsin.

AVAILABILITY: Dr. Hamilton McCubbin, Dean, School of Family Resources and Consumer Services, Madison, WI 53706-1575.

FTS

In our family we may have traditions. *Traditions* are those things *we do as a family* . . . things such as decorating a tree at Christmas, which we always do, which we have *done in the past* which we are *likely to continue to do*, and which we *value and/or respect*. Which of the following traditions apply to your family? *Please circle yes (Y) or no (N) for each item. Please respond to each and every statement.*

		This is a tradition in our family	
Traditions Around Holidays		YES	NO
1.	Decoration (house, room, table, tree, etc.)	Y	N
2.	Gift giving and sharing	Y	N
3.	Place of gathering (i.e., grandparents' home, etc.)	Y	N
4.	Special rules and duties for everyone to follow	Y	N
5.	Special activities (i.e., going caroling)	Y	N
6.	People to include (i.e., special friends/relatives)	Y	N

Traditions Around Changes (i.e., marriage, death, etc.)

7.	Where ceremony is held (i.e., same church, etc.)	Y	N
8.	Who is involved in ceremony (i.e., same minister)	Y	N
9.	Type of ceremony (i.e., religious, private, etc.)	Y	N
10.	Type of rules to follow (i.e., passing down of heirlooms, reception after wedding/funeral, etc.)	Y	N
11.	Special experiences (i.e., songs, dances, food, etc.)	Y	N
12.	Special rituals (i.e., choose names, planting of a tree, having special flowers, etc.)	Y	N

Religious Occasions

13.	Who leads the service	Y	N
14.	How children participate in service	Y	N
15.	Special rules to follow (i.e., fasting, etc.)	Y	N
16.	Special location (i.e., church, park, in the home, etc.)	Y	N

Family Special Events (i.e., reunions, etc.)

17.	Which members participate	Y	N
18.	Location of the family event	Y	N
19.	Experiences at the event (i.e., food, music, etc.)	Y	N
20.	Activities at the family event (i.e., baseball, etc.)	Y	N

Copyright © 1986 H. McCubbin.

FETAL HEALTH LOCUS OF CONTROL SCALE (FHLC)

AUTHORS: Sharon M. Labs and Sandy K. Wurtele

PURPOSE: To measure expectancies for locus of control with respect to maternal health behaviors.

DESCRIPTION: The FHLC is an 18-item instrument used to measure expectancies regarding locus of control for maternal health behavior. The goal of use of FHLC is to facilitate predictions of identifiable antecedent factors that could contribute to compliance with health-related recommendations during pregnancy. The final version of the FHLC is the product of pretesting of a face valid 85-item questionnaire and factor analysis that led to the current 18-item version. The FHLC is divided into three 6-item subscales: internal (I; items 1, 6, 8, 12, 15, and 17), chance (C; items 2, 4, 9, 11, 14, and 16), and powerful others (P; items 3, 5, 7, 10, 13, and 18). The FHLC is readable at the ninth to tenth grade level and low in social desirability response set. The FHLC is particularly useful in predicting maternal health-related behaviors; it therefore can allow targeting of intervention efforts for those women who may be most at risk.

NORMS: The FHLC was normed on 65 pregnant women attending an obstetrics clinic in a southeastern city. The mean age was 26.5, 94% were married, 86% were white (13% black, 1% Hispanic) with most respondents reporting annual incomes from $15,000 to $35,000. The mean scores on the FHLC subscales were: I = 46.84 (SD = 5.76), C = 24.56 (SD = 10.44), and P = 26.70 (SD = 10.24).

SCORING: Items are scored on a 9-point scale from "strongly disagree" (0) to "strongly agree" (9). Subscale (and total scale) scores are simply a sum of the individual items (subscale range = 0 to 54).

RELIABILITY: The FHLC has very good internal consistency, with alpha coefficients of .88 (I), .83 (C), and .76 (P). Stability of the FHLC also is very good with test-retest reliabilities over a two-week period of .80 (I), .86 (C), and .67 (P).

VALIDITY: The internal subscale has good known-groups validity, significantly distinguishing between women who intended and did not intend to take childbirth classes. The I and C subscales also predicted smoking status of pregnant women, and the I subscale also distinguished caffeine intake among pregnant women.

PRIMARY REFERENCE: Labs, S. M., and Wurtele, S. K. (1986). Fetal Health Locus of Control Scale: Development and validation, *Journal of Consulting and Clinical Psychology*, 54 (6), 814–819.

AVAILABILITY: Dr. Sharon M. Labs, Oregon Health Sciences University, Department of Medical Psychology, Portland, OR 97201.

FHLC

This is a questionnaire designed to determine the way in which women of childbearing age view various health issues concerning pregnancy.

Each item is a belief statement with which you can either agree or disagree. Beside each statement is a scale which ranges from strongly disagree (0) to strongly agree (9). For each item, we would like you to circle the number that best represents the extent to which you agree or disagree with the statement. *The more strongly you agree with a statement, the higher will be the number you circle. The more strongly you disagree with a statement, the lower will be the number you circle.* Please be sure that you answer every item and that you circle *only one* number per item.

Remember, this is a measure of your personal beliefs. There are no right or wrong answers. Answer these items carefully, but do not spend too much time on any one item. As much as possible, try to respond to each item independently. As much as you can, try not to be influenced by your previous choices. It is very important that you respond according to your actual beliefs and not according to how you feel that you should believe or how you think that we want you to believe.

		Strongly disagree			Slightly disagree			Slightly agree			Strongly agree
1.	By attending prenatal classes taught by competent health professionals, I can greatly increase the odds of having a healthy, normal baby.	0 1 2 3 4 5 6 7 8 9

| 2. | Even if I take excellent care of myself when I am pregnant, fate will determine whether my child will be normal or abnormal. | 0 1 2 3 4 5 6 7 8 9 |

| 3. | My baby will be born healthy only if I do everything my doctor tells me to do during pregnancy. | 0 1 2 3 4 5 6 7 8 9 |

| 4. | If my baby is born unhealthy or abnormal, nature intended it to be that way. | 0 1 2 3 4 5 6 7 8 9 |

		Strongly disagree				Slightly disagree			Slightly agree			Strongly agree

5. The care I receive from health professionals is what is responsible for the health of my unborn baby.

0 1 2 3 4 5 6 7 8 9

6. My unborn child's health can be seriously affected by my dietary intake during pregnancy.

0 1 2 3 4 5 6 7 8 9

7. Health professionals are responsible for the health of my unborn child.

0 1 2 3 4 5 6 7 8 9

8. If I get sick during pregnancy, consulting my doctor is the best thing I can do to protect the health of my unborn child.

0 1 2 3 4 5 6 7 8 9

9. No matter what I do when I am pregnant, the laws of nature determine whether or not my child will be normal.

0 1 2 3 4 5 6 7 8 9

10. Doctors and nurses are the only ones who are competent to give me advice concerning my behavior during pregnancy.

0 1 2 3 4 5 6 7 8 9

11. God will determine the health of my child.

0 1 2 3 4 5 6 7 8 9

12. Learning how to care for myself before I become pregnant helps my child to be born healthy.

0 1 2 3 4 5 6 7 8 9

13. My baby's health is in the hands of health professionals.

0 1 2 3 4 5 6 7 8 9

14. Fate determines the health of my unborn child.

0 1 2 3 4 5 6 7 8 9

		Strongly disagree				Slightly disagree			Slightly agree		Strongly agree

15. What I do right up to the time that my baby is born can affect my baby's health.　　0　1　2　3　4　5　6　7　8　9

16. Having a miscarriage means to me that my baby was not destined to live.　　0　1　2　3　4　5　6　7　8　9

17. Before becoming pregnant, I would learn what specific things I should do and not do during pregnancy in order to have a healthy, normal baby.　　0　1　2　3　4　5　6　7　8　9

18. Only qualified health professionals can tell me what I should and should not do when I am pregnant.　　0　1　2　3　4　5　6　7　8　9

INDEX OF BROTHER AND SISTER RELATIONS (IBR and ISR)

AUTHOR: Walter W. Hudson, Gordon MacNeil, and J. Dierks

PURPOSE: To measure problems with siblings.

DESCRIPTION: The IBR and ISR are 25-item instruments designed to measure the degree or magnitude of problems clients have in their relationships with brothers or sisters. The instruments are identical except for the words "brother" or "sister" depending upon to whom the client is referring. The IBR and ISR are designed to be easily read by children although they are not recommended for children under the age of 12. The IBR and ISR are two of several instruments of the WALMYR Assessment Scales package that are reproduced here, all of which are administered and scored the same way.

NORMS: Data are not available. However, the IBR and ISR have two cutting scores.

SCORING: Like most WALMYR Assessment Scales instruments, the IBR and ISR are scored by first reverse-scoring items listed at the bottom of the page (on both scales, items 1, 4, 5, 7–9, 11, 12, 15–18, 21, and 25), summing the scores, subtracting the number of completed items, multiplying this figure by 100, and dividing by the number of items completed times 6. This will produce a range from 0 to 100 with higher scores indicating greater magnitude or severity of problems. The IBR and ISR have two cutting scores. The first is a score of 30 (±5); scores below this point indicate absence of a clinically significant problem in this area. Scores above 30 suggest the presence of a clinically significant problem. The second cutting score is 70. Scores above this point nearly always indicate that clients are experiencing severe stress with a clear possibility that some type of violence could be considered or used to deal with problems. The practitioner should be aware of this possibility.

RELIABILITY: The IBR and ISR have excellent internal consistency with alphas in excess of .90. No data on stability are available.

VALIDITY: The IBR and ISR are reported to have very good content, factorial, and construct validity, with validity coefficients of .60 or larger.

PRIMARY REFERENCE: Hudson, W. W. (1997). *The WALMYR Assessment Scales Scoring Manual.* Tallahassee, FL: WALMYR Publishing Company.

AVAILABILITY: This scale cannot be reproduced or copied in any manner and must be obtained by writing to the WALMYR Publishing Company, PO Box 12217, Tallahassee, FL 32317-2217 or by calling (850) 383-0045.

INDEX OF BROTHER RELATIONS (IBR)

Name: _____ Today's Date: _____

This questionnaire is designed to measure the way you feel about your brother. It is not a test so there are no right or wrong answers. Answer each item as carefully and as accurately as you can by placing a number beside each one as follows.

    1 = None of the time
    2 = Very rarely
    3 = A little of the time
    4 = Some of the time
    5 = A good part of the time
    6 = Most of the time
    7 = All of the time

---

1. _____ I get along very well with my brother.
2. _____ My brother acts like he doesn't care about me.
3. _____ My brother treats me badly.
4. _____ My brother really seems to respect me.
5. _____ I can really trust my brother.
6. _____ My brother seems to dislike me.
7. _____ My brother really understands me.
8. _____ My brother seems to like me very much.
9. _____ My brother and I get along well together.
10. _____ I hate my brother.
11. _____ My brother seems to like having me around.
12. _____ I really like my brother.
13. _____ I really feel that I am disliked by my brother.
14. _____ I wish I had a different brother.
15. _____ My brother is very nice to me.
16. _____ My brother seems to respect me.
17. _____ My brother thinks I am important to him.
18. _____ My brother is a real source of pleasure to me.
19. _____ My brother doesn't seem to even notice me.
20. _____ I wish my brother was dead.
21. _____ My brother regards my ideas and opinions very highly.
22. _____ My brother is a real "jerk".
23. _____ I can't stand to be around my brother.
24. _____ My brother seems to look down on me.
25. _____ I enjoy being with my brother.

Copyright (c) 1992, Walter W. Hudson   **Illegal to Photocopy or Otherwise Reprodu**

1, 4, 5, 7, 8, 9, 11, 12, 15, 16, 17, 18, 21, 25.

INDEX OF SISTER RELATIONS (ISR)

Name: _____ Today's Date: _____

This questionnaire is designed to measure the way you feel about your sister. It is not a test so there are no right or wrong answers. Answer each item as carefully and as accurately as you can by placing a number beside each one as follows.

    1 = None of the time
    2 = Very rarely
    3 = A little of the time
    4 = Some of the time
    5 = A good part of the time
    6 = Most of the time
    7 = All of the time

1. _____ I get along very well with my sister.
2. _____ My sister acts like she doesn't care about me.
3. _____ My sister really treats me badly.
4. _____ My sister really seems to respect me.
5. _____ I can really trust my sister.
6. _____ My sister seems to dislike me.
7. _____ My sister really understands me.
8. _____ My sister seems to like me very much.
9. _____ My sister and I get along well together.
10. _____ I hate my sister.
11. _____ My sister seems to like having me around.
12. _____ I really like my sister.
13. _____ I really feel that I am disliked by my sister.
14. _____ I wish I had a different sister.
15. _____ My sister is very nice to me.
16. _____ My sister seems to respect me.
17. _____ My sister thinks I am important to her.
18. _____ My sister is a real source of pleasure to me.
19. _____ My sister doesn't seem to even notice me.
20. _____ I wish my sister was dead.
21. _____ My sister regards my ideas and opinions very highly.
22. _____ My sister is a real "jerk".
23. _____ I can't stand to be around my sister.
24. _____ My sister seems to look down on me.
25. _____ I enjoy being with my sister.

Copyright (c) 1992, Walter W. Hudson   **Illegal to Photocopy or Otherwise Reproduce**

1, 4, 5, 7, 8, 9, 11, 12, 15, 16, 17, 18, 21, 25.

INDEX OF FAMILY RELATIONS (IFR)

AUTHOR: Walter W. Hudson

PURPOSE: To measure family relationship problems.

DESCRIPTION: The IFR is a 25-item scale designed to measure the extent, severity, or magnitude of problems that family members have in their relationships with one another. The IFR allows the respondent to characterize the severity of family problems in a global fashion and can be regarded as an overall measure of intrafamilial stress. It can be used with one client or with two or more family members who each evaluate the overall family environment. The IFR has two cutting scores. The first is a score of 30 (±5); scores below this point indicate absence of a clinically significant problem in this area. Scores above 30 suggest the presence of a clinically significant problem. The second cutting score is 70. Scores above this point nearly always indicate that clients are experiencing severe stress with a clear possibility that some type of violence could be considered or used to deal with problems. The practitioner should be aware of this possibility. Another advantage of the IFR is that it is one of several scales of the WALMYR Assessment Scales package reproduced here, all of which are administered and scored the same way.

NORMS: The IFR was developed with 518 respondents, including single and married individuals, clinical and nonclinical populations, and college students and nonstudents. Respondents were primarily Caucasian, but also included Japanese and Chinese Americans, and a smaller number of other ethnic groups. The IFR is not recommended for use with children under the age of 12. Actual norms are not available.

SCORING: Like most WALMYR Assessment Scales instruments, the IFR is scored by first reverse-scoring items listed at the bottom of the page (1, 2, 4, 5, 8, 14, 15, 17, 18, 20, 21, and 23), summing the scores, subtracting the number of completed items, multiplying this figure by 100, and dividing by the number of items completed times 6. This will produce a range from 0 to 100 with higher scores indicating greater magnitude or severity of problems.

RELIABILITY: The IFR has a mean alpha of .95, indicating excellent internal consistency, and an excellent (low) Standard Error of Measurement of 3.65. Test-retest data are not available.

VALIDITY: The IFR has excellent known-groups validity, significantly distinguishing respondents designated by themselves and their counselors as having family relationships problems. The IFR also has good construct validity, correlating poorly with measures with which it should not correlate, and correlating well with other measures with which it should correlate such as other parent-child and family relationship ratings.

PRIMARY REFERENCE: Hudson, W. W. (1997). *The WALMYR Assessment Scales Scoring Manual.* Tallahassee, FL: WALMYR Publishing Company.

AVAILABILITY: This scale cannot be reproduced or copied in any manner and must be obtained by writing to the WALMYR Publishing Company, PO Box 12217, Tallahassee, FL 32317-2217 or by calling (850) 383-0045.

INDEX OF FAMILY RELATIONS (IFR)

Name: _____ Today's Date: _____

This questionnaire is designed to measure the way you feel about your family as a whole. It is not a test, so there are
right or wrong answers. Answer each item as carefully and as accurately as you can by placing a number beside each o
as follows.

    1 = None of the time
    2 = Very rarely
    3 = A little of the time
    4 = Some of the time
    5 = A good part of the time
    6 = Most of the time
    7 = All of the time

1. ____ The members of my family really care about each other.
2. ____ I think my family is terrific.
3. ____ My family gets on my nerves.
4. ____ I really enjoy my family.
5. ____ I can really depend on my family.
6. ____ I really do not care to be around my family.
7. ____ I wish I was not part of this family.
8. ____ I get along well with my family.
9. ____ Members of my family argue too much.
10. ____ There is no sense of closeness in my family.
11. ____ I feel like a stranger in my family.
12. ____ My family does not understand me.
13. ____ There is too much hatred in my family.
14. ____ Members of my family are really good to one another.
15. ____ My family is well respected by those who know us.
16. ____ There seems to be a lot of friction in my family.
17. ____ There is a lot of love in my family.
18. ____ Members of my family get along well together.
19. ____ Life in my family is generally unpleasant.
20. ____ My family is a great joy to me.
21. ____ I feel proud of my family.
22. ____ Other families seem to get along better than ours.
23. ____ My family is a real source of comfort to me.
24. ____ I feel left out of my family.
25. ____ My family is an unhappy one.

Copyright (c) 1992, Walter W. Hudson   **Illegal to Photocopy or Otherwise Reprod**

1, 2, 4, 5, 8, 14, 15, 17, 18, 20, 21, 23.

INDEX OF PARENTAL ATTITUDES (IPA)

AUTHOR: Walter W. Hudson

PURPOSE: To measure a parent's relationship problems with a child.

DESCRIPTION: The IPA is a 25-item instrument designed to measure the extent, severity, or magnitude of parent-child relationship problems as seen and reported by a parent. The child may be of any age, from infant to adult. The IPA has two cutting scores. The first is a score of 30 (±5); scores below this point indicate absence of a clinically significant problem in this area. Scores above 30 suggest the presence of a clinically significant problem. The second cutting score is 70. Scores above this point nearly always indicate that clients are experiencing severe stress with a clear possibility that some type of violence could be considered or used to deal with problems. The practitioner should be aware of this possibility. Another advantage of the IPA is that it is one of several scales of the WALMYR Assessment Scales package reproduced here, all of which are administered and scored the same way.

NORMS: The 93 respondents who participated in the development of this scale all were seeking counseling services for personal or interpersonal problems. No other demographic data are available, nor are actual norms.

SCORING: Like most WALMYR Assessment Scales instruments, the IPA is scored by first reverse-scoring items listed at the bottom of the page (2, 3, 5, 8, 12, 14–16, 21, and 24) summing the scores, subtracting the number of completed items, multiplying this figure by 100, and dividing by the number of items completed times 6. This will produce a range from 0 to 100 with higher scores indicating greater magnitude or severity of problems.

RELIABILITY: The IPA has a mean alpha of .97, indicating excellent internal consistency, and an excellent (low) Standard Error of Measurement of 3.64. Test-retest data are not available.

VALIDITY: The IPA has excellent known-groups validity, significantly distinguishing between groups of clients designated by themselves and their counselors as having or not having relationship problems with their children. The IPA also has fair construct validity, correlating moderately with variables with which it is predicted it would correlate moderately, and correlating highly with other measures with which it should correlate including other measures of parent-child and family relationships.

PRIMARY REFERENCE: Hudson, W. W. (1997). *The WALMYR Assessment Scales Scoring Manual.* Tallahassee, FL: WALMYR Publishing Company.

AVAILABILITY: This scale cannot be reproduced or copied in any manner and must be obtained by writing to the WALMYR Publishing Company, PO Box 12217, Tallahassee, FL 32317-2217 or by calling (850) 383-0045

INDEX OF PARENTAL ATTITUDES (IPA)

Name: _____ Today's Date: _____

This questionnaire is designed to measure the degree of contentment you have in your relationship with your child. It is [not] a test, so there are no right or wrong answers. Answer each item as carefully and as accurately as you can by placing a number beside each one as follows.

1 = None of the time
2 = Very rarely
3 = A little of the time
4 = Some of the time
5 = A good part of the time
6 = Most of the time
7 = All of the time

1. _____ My child gets on my nerves.
2. _____ I get along well with my child.
3. _____ I feel that I can really trust my child.
4. _____ I dislike my child.
5. _____ My child is well behaved.
6. _____ My child is too demanding.
7. _____ I wish I did not have this child.
8. _____ I really enjoy my child.
9. _____ I have a hard time controlling my child.
10. _____ My child interferes with my activities.
11. _____ I resent my child.
12. _____ I think my child is terrific.
13. _____ I hate my child.
14. _____ I am very patient with my child.
15. _____ I really like my child.
16. _____ I like being with my child.
17. _____ I feel like I do not love my child.
18. _____ My child is irritating.
19. _____ I feel very angry toward my child.
20. _____ I feel violent toward my child.
21. _____ I feel very proud of my child.
22. _____ I wish my child was more like others I know.
23. _____ I just do not understand my child.
24. _____ My child is a real joy to me.
25. _____ I feel ashamed of my child.

Copyright (c) 1992, Walter W. Hudson   Illegal to Photocopy or Otherwise Reproduce

2, 3, 5, 8, 12, 14, 15, 16, 21, 24.

KANSAS FAMILY LIFE SATISFACTION SCALE (KFLS)

AUTHORS: Walter R. Schumm, Anthony P. Jurich, and Stephen R. Bollman
PURPOSE: To measure satisfaction with family life.
DESCRIPTION: The KFLS is a 4-item instrument designed to assess satisfaction with three key types of family relationships and with satisfaction with family life as a whole. The three types of family relationship are marriage, parent-child, and sibling. The KFLS is designed to be used in interview or questionnaire formats and with families containing a mother, father, and preferably at least two children. It is one of the few available family satisfaction measures, and is easily completed in less than three minutes. The KFLS also has been used with Mexican-American families and Korean wives of American men. Two forms of the KFLS (father/mother and adolescent) are reproduced here.
NORMS: The KFLS was studied initially in a midwestern sample of 620 families with a mean duration of marriage of 21.4 years, mean age for husbands of 44.5, mean age for wives of 41.6, mean age for children of 15.3 years; 34.5% of husbands and 31.5% of wives had less than a high school education, and 19.7% of husbands and 9.7% of wives had college degrees; 8.4% of husbands were unemployed and 48% of wives were not employed outside the home; 55.6% of respondents were from urban areas. The mean score for fathers was 24.19 (SD = 3.46), for mothers 24.44 (SD = 3.16), and for children 23.52 (SD = 3.94).
SCORING: The KFLS is easily scored by adding up the scores for each item for a potential range of 4 to 28.
RELIABILITY: The KFLS has good internal consistency, with alphas that range from .79 to .83. No data on stability were reported.
VALIDITY: The KFLS has good construct validity, with significant correlations in predicted directions with satisfaction with quality of life (positive), locus of control (positive), and religiosity (negative). Income was not correlated with scores on the KFLS.
PRIMARY REFERENCE: Schumm, W. R., Jurich, A. P., and Bollman, S. R. (1986). Characteristics of the Kansas Family Life Satisfaction Scale in a regional sample, *Psychological Reports*, 58, 975–980.
AVAILABILITY: The Free Press.

KFLS Father/Mother Version

For each of the following four questions please indicate your satisfaction by recording your answer in the space to the left of the item. Use the following scale to indicate your response:

1 = Extremely dissatisfied
2 = Dissatisfied
3 = Somewhat dissatisfied
4 = Mixed
5 = Somewhat satisfied
6 = Satisfied
7 = Extremely satisfied

_____ 1. How satisfied are you with your family life?
_____ 2. How satisfied are you with your relationship with your spouse?
_____ 3. How satisfied are you with your relationship with your child(ren)?
_____ 4. How satisfied are you with your children's relationship with each other? (Answer only if you have more than one child.)

KFLS Adolescent Version

For each of the following four questions please indicate your satisfaction by recording your answer in the space to the left of the item. Use the following scale to indicate your response:

1 = Extremely dissatisfied
2 = Dissatisfied
3 = Somewhat dissatisfied
4 = Mixed
5 = Somewhat satisfied
6 = Satisfied
7 = Extremely satisfied

_____ 1. How satisfied are you with your family life?
_____ 2. How satisfied are you with your parents' relationship with each other?
_____ 3. How satisfied are you with your relationship with your parents?
_____ 4. How satisfied are you with your relationship with your brothers and/or sisters? (Answer only if you have a sibling.)

KANSAS PARENTAL SATISFACTION SCALE (KPS)

AUTHORS: Walter R. Schumm and Justin Hall

PURPOSE: To measure satisfaction with parenting.

DESCRIPTION: The KPS is a 3-item instrument designed to measure satisfaction with oneself as a parent, the behavior of one's children, and one's relationship with one's children. The KPS is easily completed in less than two minutes, and is one of the few scales available to directly measure satisfaction with parenting. It has been used with Caucasian as well as Korean-American couples.

NORMS: The KPS was studied initially on two samples. The first involved 84 randomly selected married mothers in three Korean communities. The second involved parents from 22 Southern Baptist churches involved in a nationwide parents' enrichment program. Some 24% of parents were in their twenties, about half were in their thirties, and most of the remainder were in their forties; 11.6% of fathers and 24% of mothers had a high school degree or less, and 23.1% of fathers and 20.4% of mothers had finished college; 88.5% of fathers and 44.5% of mothers were employed outside the home. For the first sample (mothers only), with items on a 7-point satisfaction response scale (reprinted here), the mean for the total scale was 17.4 (SD = 2.20), and for the second sample, with items modified to a 5-point Likert scale, the mean for fathers was 8.12 (SD = 2.26) and for mothers was 7.79 (SD = 2.05).

RELIABILITY: The KPS has very good internal consistency, with alphas that range from .78 to .85. No data on stability were reported.

VALIDITY: The KPS has good concurrent validity, correlating significantly with marital satisfaction and the Rosenberg Self-Esteem Scale.

PRIMARY REFERENCE: James, D. E. et al. (1985). Characteristics of the Kansas Parental Satisfaction Scale among two samples of married parents, *Psychological Reports*, 57, 163–169.

AVAILABILITY: The Free Press.

KPS

For each of the following questions please indicate your satisfaction by recording your answer in the space to the left of the item. Use the following scale to indicate your response:

1 = Extremely dissatisfied
2 = Very dissatisfied
3 = Somewhat dissatisfied
4 = Mixed
5 = Somewhat satisfied
6 = Very satisfied
7 = Extremely satisfied

_____ 1. How satisfied are you with the behavior of your children?

_____ 2. How satisfied are you with yourself as a parent?

_____ 3. How satisfied are you with your relationship with your children?

LEVEL OF EXPRESSED EMOTION (LEE)

AUTHORS: John D. Cole and Shahe S. Kazarian

PURPOSE: To measure expressed emotion.

DESCRIPTION: The LEE is a 60-item instrument designed to measure perceived emotional climate in a person's influential relationships. Expressed emotion (EE) is becoming a very important variable in the research on the influence of family environment on schizophrenia and therapies designed to deal with that influence. The research generally indicates that people diagnosed with schizophrenia who are discharged to home environments that have a high level of expressed emotion tend to relapse at a much greater rate than those who are discharged to homes with low expressed emotion. Items for the LEE were selected to reflect a theoretical framework about EE, and factor analysis of the scale did in fact reveal four factors (specific items available from the author) that suggest the scale does adequately measure a comprehensive theoretical framework about EE. The four subscales are intrusiveness, emotional response, attitude toward illness, and tolerance/ expectation. This scale is an important addition to the basic research on functioning of families with a member who has been diagnosed as schizophrenic, as well as a valuable tool to assess the impact of therapeutic programs on families' levels of expressed emotion.

NORMS: The LEE was originally studied with 46 subjects, all of whom had been diagnosed with schizophrenia, of whom 36 were in outpatient programs and 10 were in inpatient programs for the treatment of schizophrenia. The mean age of the subjects was 35.7 years (SD = 10.4), with females accounting for 60.9% of the sample. Although means and standard deviations were not available in the original article, subsequent research used the median score for a high-low splitting of LEE scores. The median for the new sample of people with schizophrenia was 9, so that high LEE scores can be assumed to be above 9 and low LEE scores below 9. Higher scores are associated with higher rates of readmission.

SCORING: Information about scoring the LEE can be obtained from the author.

RELIABILITY: The LEE has excellent internal consistency, with a KR-20 coefficient for the overall scale of .95 with the subscales ranging from .84 to .89. Stability of the LEE was very good, with a six-week test-retest correlation on a subsample of .82 for the overall scale.

VALIDITY: The LEE has a very good concurrent and predictive validity. The LEE correlated highly and significantly with the Influential Relationships Questionnaire, which measures the presence of overprotection, criticism, and lack of care. The LEE does not differ significantly between the mean scores of males and females, nor does age affect overall LEE score. The subsequent research shows the LEE has very good predictive validity, with higher LEE scores consistently predicting readmission to the hospital of individuals diagnosed as schizophrenic.

PRIMARY REFERENCE: Cole, J. D. and Kazarian, S. S. (1988). The Level of Expressed Emotion Scale: A new measure of expressed emotion, *Journal of Clinical Psychology,* 44, 392–397.

AVAILABILITY: S. S. Kazarian, Ph.D., London Psychiatric Hospital, 850 Highbury Avenue, London, Ontario, Canada, N6A 4H1. Reprinted by permission of the authors. Contact the authors for scoring instructions at (519) 455-5110—telephone; (519) 455-3011—fax.

LEE

YOUR NAME: _____ AGE: _____ SEX: (circle one) Male   Female
                                                                DATE: _____
MARITAL STATUS: (circle one)
    Single   Married/Common-law   Separated   Divorced   Widowed

Indicate who has been the most influential person in your life over the past three
months: (circle one)
Mother   Father   Brother   Sister   Spouse
Other relative (e.g., Aunt, Grandfather)   Friend
Other (Please specify) _____

Have you been living with your influential person during the past three months?
(circle one)   Yes   No

How many waking hours on a typical weekday have you been spending with your
influential person during the past three months? _____ hours per week day

How many waking hours on a typical weekend have you been spending with your
influential person during the past three months? _____ hours per weekend

Read each statement and decide whether it is true or false as applied to your influential person. If it is true, circle the letter T. If it is false, circle the letter F.

T   F   1. Understands if sometimes I don't want to talk.
T   F   2. Calms me down when I'm upset.
T   F   3. Says I lack self-control.
T   F   4. Is tolerant with me even when I'm not meeting his/her expectations.
T   F   5. Doesn't butt into my conversations.
T   F   6. Doesn't make me nervous.
T   F   7. Says I just want attention when I say I'm not well.
T   F   8. Makes me feel guilty for not meeting his/her expectations.
T   F   9. Isn't overprotective with me.
T   F   10. Loses his/her temper when I'm not feeling well.
T   F   11. Is sympathetic towards me when I'm ill or upset.
T   F   12. Can see my point of view.
T   F   13. Is always interfering.
T   F   14. Doesn't panic when things start going wrong.
T   F   15. Encourages me to seek outside help when I'm not feeling well.
T   F   16. Doesn't feel that I'm causing him/her a lot of trouble.
T   F   17. Doesn't insist on doing things with me.
T   F   18. Can't think straight when things go wrong.
T   F   19. Doesn't help me when I'm upset or feeling unwell.
T   F   20. Puts me down if I don't live up to his/her expectations.
T   F   21. Doesn't insist on being with me all the time.
T   F   22. Blames me for things not going well.
T   F   23. Makes me feel valuable as a person.

T F 24. Can't stand it when I'm upset.
T F 25. Leaves me feeling overwhelmed.
T F 26. Doesn't know how to handle my feelings when I'm not feeling well.
T F 27. Says I cause my troubles to occur in order to get back at him/her.
T F 28. Understands my limitations.
T F 29. Often checks up on me to see what I'm doing.
T F 30. Is able to be in control in stressful situations.
T F 31. Tries to make me feel better when I'm upset or ill.
T F 32. Is realistic about what I can and cannot do.
T F 33. Is always nosing into my business.
T F 34. Hears me out.
T F 35. Says it's not OK to seek professional help.
T F 36. Gets angry with me when things don't go right.
T F 37. Always has to know everything about me.
T F 38. Makes me feel relaxed when he/she is around.
T F 39. Accuses me of exaggerating when I say I'm unwell.
T F 40. Will take it easy with me, even if things aren't going right.
T F 41. Insists on knowing where I'm going.
T F 42. Gets angry with me for no reason.
T F 43. Is considerate when I'm ill or upset.
T F 44. Supports me when I need it.
T F 45. Butts into my private matters.
T F 46. Can cope well with stress.
T F 47. Is willing to gain more information to understand my condition, when I'm not feeling well.
T F 48. Is understanding if I make mistakes.
T F 49. Doesn't pry into my life.
T F 50. Is impatient with me when I'm not well.
T F 51. Doesn't blame me when I'm feeling unwell.
T F 52. Expects too much from me.
T F 53. Doesn't ask a lot of personal questions.
T F 54. Makes matters worse when things aren't going well.
T F 55. Often accuses me of making things up when I'm not feeling well.
T F 56. "Flies off the handle" when I don't do something well.
T F 57. Gets upset when I don't check in with him/her.
T F 58. Gets irritated when things don't go right.
T F 59. Tries to reassure me when I'm not feeling well.
T F 60. Expects the same level of effort from me, even if I don't feel well.

Copyright © 1992 John D. Cole, Ph.D., and Shahe S. Kazarian, Ph.D.

MEMORY AND BEHAVIOR PROBLEMS CHECKLIST (MBPC)

AUTHORS: Steven H. Zarit and Judy M. Zarit

PURPOSE: To measure problem behaviors in dementia patients and the effects on caregivers.

DESCRIPTION: The MBPC consists of a 32-item checklist of behaviors and a 9-item checklist of activities of daily living that are designed to determine how frequently a dementia patient engages in problem behaviors and which problems are especially upsetting for family members. The instrument is designed to be used by an interviewer who asks the questions to a family member or caretaker. The checklist is not designed to be handed to respondents to complete by themselves. Each problem is scored twice, once regarding the frequency of the problem and once regarding the caregiver's reaction to it. The reactions score indicates how much difficulty caregivers are having coping with dementia-related problems.

NORMS: Not available.

SCORING: The behavior checklist is scored by summing all item scores to indicate the overall severity of current problems, with higher scores indicating greater severity. Items rated as "7" are scored as "5" for estimating severity. The reaction checklist is scored by summing all items, with higher scores indicating greater difficulty in coping. The activities of daily living checklist is scored in the same way.

RELIABILITY: The MBPC has fair reliability, with Guttman split-half reliabilities of .65 for the problem checklist and .66 for the distress ratings. The MBPC has fair stability with test-retest correlations of .80 for the problem checklist and .56 for distress ratings. Data are not reported for the activities of daily living checklist.

VALIDITY: The MBPC has good concurrent validity, with significant correlations between the Frequency of Problem Behavior Checklist and the Mental Status Questionnaire, the Face-Hand Test, and the Folstein Mini-Mental State Examination. A significant correlation was found between distress ratings and the Brief Symptom Inventory.

PRIMARY REFERENCE: Zarit, S. H., et al. (1985). *The Hidden Victim of Alzheimer's Disease: Families Under Stress*. New York: New York University Press.

AVAILABILITY: The Free Press.

MBPC

Instructions to Caregiver:

"I am going to read you a list of common problems. Tell me if any of these problems have occurred during the past week. If so, how often have they occurred? If not, has this problem ever occurred?" Hand the subject the card on which the frequency ratings are printed.

Frequency Ratings

```
0  =  Never occurred
1  =  Occurred frequently in the past but not in the past three months
2  =  Has occurred recently, but not in the past week
3  =  Has occurred 1 or 2 times in the past week
4  =  Has occurred 3 to 6 times in the past week
5  =  Occurs daily or more often
7  =  This problem would occur, if the patient wasn't supervised
```

Reaction Ratings: For current problems (frequency ratings 2 through 7), ask: "How much does this problem bother or upset you when it happens?"

Reaction Ratings

```
0  =  Not at all
1  =  A little
2  =  Moderately
3  =  Very much
4  =  Extremely
```

Behaviors	Frequency	Reaction
1. Asking the same question over and over again	0 1 2 3 4 5 7	0 1 2 3 4
2. Trouble remembering recent events (e.g., items in the newspaper, on TV)	0 1 2 3 4 5 7	0 1 2 3 4
3. Trouble remembering significant events from the past	0 1 2 3 4 5 7	0 1 2 3 4
4. Mixing up past and present (e.g., thinking a deceased parent is alive)	0 1 2 3 4 5 7	0 1 2 3 4

Behaviors	Frequency	Reaction
5. Losing or misplacing things	0 1 2 3 4 5 7	0 1 2 3 4
6. Hiding things	0 1 2 3 4 5 7	0 1 2 3 4
7. Unable to find way about indoors	0 1 2 3 4 5 7	0 1 2 3 4
8. Unable to find way about outdoors, for example, on familiar streets	0 1 2 3 4 5 7	0 1 2 3 4
9. Wandering or getting lost	0 1 2 3 4 5 7	0 1 2 3 4
10. Not recognizing a familiar place	0 1 2 3 4 5 7	0 1 2 3 4
11. Not recognizing familiar people	0 1 2 3 4 5 7	0 1 2 3 4
12. Not recognizing a familiar object	0 1 2 3 4 5 7	0 1 2 3 4
13. Forgetting what day it is	0 1 2 3 4 5 7	0 1 2 3 4
14. Unable to start activities by self (besides ADLs)	0 1 2 3 4 5 7	0 1 2 3 4
15. Unable to keep occupied or busy by self	0 1 2 3 4 5 7	0 1 2 3 4
16. Follows you around	0 1 2 3 4 5 7	0 1 2 3 4
17. Being constantly restless or agitated	0 1 2 3 4 5 7	0 1 2 3 4
18. Spending long periods of time inactive	0 1 2 3 4 5 7	0 1 2 3 4
19. Being constantly talkative	0 1 2 3 4 5 7	0 1 2 3 4
20. Talking little or not at all	0 1 2 3 4 5 7	0 1 2 3 4
21. Being suspicious or accusative	0 1 2 3 4 5 7	0 1 2 3 4

Behaviors	Frequency	Reaction
22. Doing things in public that embarrass you	0 1 2 3 4 5 7	0 1 2 3 4
23. Waking you up at night	0 1 2 3 4 5 7	0 1 2 3 4
24. Appears sad or depressed	0 1 2 3 4 5 7	0 1 2 3 4
25. Appears anxious or worried	0 1 2 3 4 5 7	0 1 2 3 4
26. Becomes angry	0 1 2 3 4 5 7	0 1 2 3 4
27. Strikes out or tries to hit	0 1 2 3 4 5 7	0 1 2 3 4
28. Destroying property	0 1 2 3 4 5 7	0 1 2 3 4
29. Engaging in behavior that is potentially dangerous to others or self	0 1 2 3 4 5 7	0 1 2 3 4
30. Seeing or hearing things that are not there (hallucinations or illusions)	0 1 2 3 4 5 7	0 1 2 3 4
31. Any other problems (specify):	0 1 2 3 4 5 7	0 1 2 3 4
32. Any other problems (specify):	0 1 2 3 4 5 7	0 1 2 3 4

Activities of Daily Living

The following activities of daily living are scaled differently than other behavior problems, and should be viewed separately in estimating overall severity of a patient's deficits. Administration and scoring are the same as for the Behaviors checklist.

Frequency Ratings

0 = Independent
1 = Needs supervision
2 = Needs some assistance to complete task
3 = Totally independent

Activity	Frequency	Reaction
1. Eating	0 1 2 3	0 1 2 3 4

Activity	Frequency	Reaction
2. Dressing	0 1 2 3	0 1 2 3 4
3. Shaving or putting on make-up	0 1 2 3	0 1 2 3 4
4. Taking medications	0 1 2 3	0 1 2 3 4
5. Bathing	0 1 2 3	0 1 2 3 4
6. Going to the bathroom (indicate if incontinent of bowel or bladder; score 2 if occasionally incontinent, 3 if incontinent most or all of the time)	0 1 2 3	0 1 2 3 4

Other Activities

Activity	Frequency	Reaction
7. Walking	0 1 2 3	0 1 2 3 4

    0   As usual
    1   Slower than usual
    2   Unsteady or shuffling gait
    3   Unable to walk

Activity	Frequency	Reaction
8. Watching television	0 1 2 3	0 1 2 3 4

    0   As usual
    1   Watches more than usual
    2   Watches less than usual (may watch for brief periods)
    3   No longer able to watch

Activity	Frequency	Reaction
9. Telephone	0 1 2 3	0 1 2 3 4

    0   As usual
    1   Unable to dial many numbers
    2   Can only engage in brief conversations
    3   Unable to use

PARENT AFFECT TEST (PAT)

AUTHOR: Marsha M. Linehan

PURPOSE: To measure parental affect In response to child behaviors.

DESCRIPTION: The PAT is a 40-item instrument designed to measure two aspects of parental response to child behavior: anger and pleasure. These two aspects form the two subscales of the PAT. Anger is assessed in terms of one's responses to negative child behaviors. Pleasure measures affective responses to positive child behaviors. These two emotions are considered salient in the maintenance of punitive or abusive behavior towards children. The PAT is useful in monitoring interventions with abusive parents or siblings. The positive and negative child behaviors that are contained in the PAT were designed to span various developmental age groups, but basically are appropriate for parents with a child aged 2 to 11 years old. The instrument's development followed excellent procedures that exemplify sound psychometrics.

NORMS: A sample of 49 mothers and fathers from the general population reported means of 98.02 (SD = 8.79) for mothers and 95.58 (SD = 7.22) for fathers on the anger subscale. The mothers had a mean of 130.34 (SD = 9.62) and fathers had a mean of 121.01 (SD = 12.47) on the pleasure subscale.

SCORING: Each item is scored on a range from 1 to 7; points within each item must be rearranged so that "7" is consistently the high score on either anger or pleasure. The score for anger is the sum of items 1, 2, 3, 4, 7, 8, 10, 13, 14, 17, 20, 22, 25, 26, 29, 32, 36, 37, 39, 40. The score on the pleasure subscale is the sum of responses on items 5, 6, 9, 11, 12, 15, 16, 18, 19, 21, 23, 24, 27, 28, 30, 31, 33, 34, 35, 38. The subscales are designed to be treated separately and are not to be combined to form a total score. Higher scores reflect more affect. Thorough instructions and scoring sheets accompany the PAT and are available from the author.

RELIABILITY: The PAT has excellent internal consistency coefficients of .92 and .96 for the anger and pleasure subscales. Data on stability were not available.

VALIDITY: The subscales have good evidence of concurrent validity. For mothers, the anger subscale correlated with a measure of self-reported anger, a spouse's report of anger, and negatively correlated with self-reported frequency and intensity of feeling pleasure by the respondent. The anger subscale was not correlated with a measure of social desirability, although the pleasure subscale was slightly correlated with social desirability. Fathers' anger subscale scores correlated with social desirability, with self-reported intensity of anger and correlated negatively with self-reported frequency and intensity of feeling pleasure. The fathers' pleasure scores were negatively correlated with two other measures of anger.

PRIMARY REFERENCE: Linehan, M. M., Paul, E., and Egan, K. J. (1983). The Parent Affect Test: Development, validity and reliability, *Journal of Clinical Child Psychology*, 12, 161–166. Instrument reproduced with permission of Marsha Linehan and the American Psychological Association.
AVAILABILITY: Marsha M. Linehan, Ph.D., Department of Psychology, University of Washington, Seattle, WA 98195.

PAT

The purpose of this inventory is to study parent responses to typical behaviors of children. On the following pages are situations you probably have experienced, followed by scales of certain personal feelings and reactions. You are to pick *one* child in your family whose age falls in the range of 2 through 11 years, and fill out the whole inventory on that child.

There are 40 child behaviors described in this questionnaire. Think about each one and imagine that this particular child is ACTUALLY DOING IT. Then, rate what your response would be on *each* scale under *each* behavior. Do this by putting a check in the middle of *one* space on each scale to indicate the degree to which you would have that reaction or feeling. Please do not omit any situation.

1. My child gets into some things that don't belong to him/her . . . I would

Feel good	___:__:__:__:__:__	Feel bad
Feel angry	___:__:__:__:__:__	Feel pleased
Feel relaxed	___:__:__:__:__:__	Feel tense
Want to hug/kiss	___:__:__:__:__:__	Want to hit/spank
Want to yell at	___:__:__:__:__:__	Want to praise
Want to send child to room	___:__:__:__:__:__	Want to be with child

2. My child does not listen to me . . . I would

Feel pleased	___:__:__:__:__:__	Feel angry
Feel bad	___:__:__:__:__:__	Feel good
Want to hit/spank	___:__:__:__:__:__	Want to hug/kiss
Want to yell at	___:__:__:__:__:__	Want to praise
Feel tense	___:__:__:__:__:__	Feel relaxed
Want to send child to room	___:__:__:__:__:__	Want to be with child

3. My child talks back to me . . . I would

Feel relaxed	___:__:__:__:__:__	Feel tense
Feel angry	___:__:__:__:__:__	Feel pleased
Want to be with child	___:__:__:__:__:__	Want to send child to room
Want to yell at	___:__:__:__:__:__	Want to praise
Want to hug/kiss	___:__:__:__:__:__	Want to hit/spank
Feel bad	___:__:__:__:__:__	Feel good

4. My child comes home dirty and messy . . . I would

Feel good	:	:	:	:	:	Feel bad
Want to yell at	:	:	:	:	:	Want to praise
Feel pleased	:	:	:	:	:	Feel angry
Feel tense	:	:	:	:	:	Feel relaxed
Want to hug/kiss	:	:	:	:	:	Want to hit/spank
Want to send child to room	:	:	:	:	:	Want to be with child

5. My child shares a favorite possession with a friend . . . I would

Feel good	:	:	:	:	:	Feel bad
Feel angry	:	:	:	:	:	Feel pleased
Feel relaxed	:	:	:	:	:	Feel tense
Want to hug/kiss	:	:	:	:	:	Want to hit/spank
Want to yell at	:	:	:	:	:	Want to praise
Want to send child to room	:	:	:	:	:	Want to be with child

6. My child acts respectful toward me . . . I would

Feel pleased	:	:	:	:	:	Feel angry
Feel bad	:	:	:	:	:	Feel good
Want to hit/spank	:	:	:	:	:	Want to hug/kiss
Want to yell at	:	:	:	:	:	Want to praise
Feel tense	:	:	:	:	:	Feel relaxed
Want to send child to room	:	:	:	:	:	Want to be with child

7. My child leaves his/her belongings all over the house . . . I would

Feel relaxed	:	:	:	:	:	Feel tense
Feel angry	:	:	:	:	:	Feel pleased
Want to be with child	:	:	:	:	:	Want to send child to room
Want to yell at	:	:	:	:	:	Want to praise
Want to hug/kiss	:	:	:	:	:	Want to hit/spank
Feel bad	:	:	:	:	:	Feel good

8. My child interrupts me while I am on the phone (eating dinner, etc.) . . . I would

Feel good	:	:	:	:	:	Feel bad
Want to yell at	:	:	:	:	:	Want to praise
Feel pleased	:	:	:	:	:	Feel angry
Feel tense	:	:	:	:	:	Feel relaxed
Want to hug/kiss	:	:	:	:	:	Want to hit/spank
Want to send child to room	:	:	:	:	:	Want to be with child

9. My child makes a good decision . . . I would

Feel good	__:_:_:_:_:_:_	Feel bad
Feel angry	__:_:_:_:_:_:_	Feel pleased
Feel relaxed	__:_:_:_:_:_:_	Feel tense
Want to hug/kiss	__:_:_:_:_:_:_	Want to hit/spank
Want to yell at	__:_:_:_:_:_:_	Want to praise
Want to send child to room	__:_:_:_:_:_:_	Want to be with child

10. My child carelessly spills something (a drink, plate of food, etc.) . . . I would

Feel pleased	__:_:_:_:_:_:_	Feel angry
Feel bad	__:_:_:_:_:_:_	Feel good
Want to hit/spank	__:_:_:_:_:_:_	Want to hug/kiss
Want to yell at	__:_:_:_:_:_:_	Want to praise
Feel tense	__:_:_:_:_:_:_	Feel relaxed
Want to send child to room	__:_:_:_:_:_:_	Want to be with child

11. My child expresses the desire to be with me . . . I would

Feel relaxed	__:_:_:_:_:_:_	Feel tense
Feel angry	__:_:_:_:_:_:_	Feel pleased
Want to be with child	__:_:_:_:_:_:_	Want to send child to room
Want to yell at	__:_:_:_:_:_:_	Want to praise
Want to hug/kiss	__:_:_:_:_:_:_	Want to hit/spank
Feel bad	__:_:_:_:_:_:_	Feel good

12. My child learns something new quickly . . . I would

Feel good	__:_:_:_:_:_:_	Feel bad
Want to yell at	__:_:_:_:_:_:_	Want to praise
Feel pleased	__:_:_:_:_:_:_	Feel angry
Feel tense	__:_:_:_:_:_:_	Feel relaxed
Want to hug/kiss	__:_:_:_:_:_:_	Want to hit/spank
Want to send child to room	__:_:_:_:_:_:_	Want to be with child

13. My child criticizes me as a parent . . . I would

Feel good	__:_:_:_:_:_:_	Feel bad
Feel angry	__:_:_:_:_:_:_	Feel pleased
Feel relaxed	__:_:_:_:_:_:_	Feel tense
Want to hug/kiss	__:_:_:_:_:_:_	Want to hit/spank
Want to yell at	__:_:_:_:_:_:_	Want to praise
Want to send child to room	__:_:_:_:_:_:_	Want to be with child

14.   My child does not do his/her household chores . . . I would

Feel pleased	_____:___:___:___:___:___	Feel angry
Feel bad	_____:___:___:___:___:___	Feel good
Want to hit/spank	_____:___:___:___:___:___	Want to hug/kiss
Want to yell at	_____:___:___:___:___:___	Want to praise
Feel tense	_____:___:___:___:___:___	Feel relaxed
Want to send child to room	_____:___:___:___:___:___	Want to be with child

15.   When I play a game with my child he/she smiles a lot . . . I would

Feel relaxed	_____:___:___:___:___:___	Feel tense
Feel angry	_____:___:___:___:___:___	Feel pleased
Want to be with child	_____:___:___:___:___:___	Want to send child to room
Want to yell at	_____:___:___:___:___:___	Want to praise
Want to hug/kiss	_____:___:___:___:___:___	Want to hit/spank
Feel bad	_____:___:___:___:___:___	Feel good

16.   My child takes good care of his/her belongings . . . I would

Feel good	_____:___:___:___:___:___	Feel bad
Want to yell at	_____:___:___:___:___:___	Want to praise
Feel pleased	_____:___:___:___:___:___	Feel angry
Feel tense	_____:___:___:___:___:___	Feel relaxed
Want to hug/kiss	_____:___:___:___:___:___	Want to hit/spank
Want to send child to room	_____:___:___:___:___:___	Want to be with child

17.   When getting dressed to leave the house, my child dawdles and fools around . . . I would

Feel good	_____:___:___:___:___:___	Feel bad
Feel angry	_____:___:___:___:___:___	Feel pleased
Feel relaxed	_____:___:___:___:___:___	Feel tense
Want to hug/kiss	_____:___:___:___:___:___	Want to hit/spank
Want to yell at	_____:___:___:___:___:___	Want to praise
Want to send child to room	_____:___:___:___:___:___	Want to be with child

18.   My child comes to me and gives me a kiss . . . I would

Feel pleased	_____:___:___:___:___:___	Feel angry
Feel bad	_____:___:___:___:___:___	Feel good
Want to hit/spank	_____:___:___:___:___:___	Want to hug/kiss
Want to yell at	_____:___:___:___:___:___	Want to praise
Feel tense	_____:___:___:___:___:___	Feel relaxed
Want to send child to room	_____:___:___:___:___:___	Want to be with child

19. My child greets me pleasantly when I come home . . . I would

Feel relaxed ___ : _ : _ : _ : _ : _ : ___ Feel tense
Feel angry ___ : _ : _ : _ : _ : _ : ___ Feel pleased
Want to be with child ___ : _ : _ : _ : _ : _ : ___ Want to send child to room
Want to yell at ___ : _ : _ : _ : _ : _ : ___ Want to praise
Want to hug/kiss ___ : _ : _ : _ : _ : _ : ___ Want to hit/spank
Feel bad ___ : _ : _ : _ : _ : _ : ___ Feel good

20. My child asks me repeatedly if he/she can have something . . . I would

Feel good ___ : _ : _ : _ : _ : _ : ___ Feel bad
Want to yell at ___ : _ : _ : _ : _ : _ : ___ Want to praise
Feel pleased ___ : _ : _ : _ : _ : _ : ___ Feel angry
Feel tense ___ : _ : _ : _ : _ : _ : ___ Feel relaxed
Want to hug/kiss ___ : _ : _ : _ : _ : _ : ___ Want to hit/spank
Want to send child ___ : _ : _ : _ : _ : _ : ___ Want to be with child
to room

21. My child chooses to eat a well-balanced meal . . . I would

Feel good ___ : _ : _ : _ : _ : _ : ___ Feel bad
Feel angry ___ : _ : _ : _ : _ : _ : ___ Feel pleased
Feel relaxed ___ : _ : _ : _ : _ : _ : ___ Feel tense
Want to hug/kiss ___ : _ : _ : _ : _ : _ : ___ Want to hit/spank
Want to yell at ___ : _ : _ : _ : _ : _ : ___ Want to praise
Want to send child ___ : _ : _ : _ : _ : _ : ___ Want to be with child
to room

22. My child complains . . . I would

Feel pleased ___ : _ : _ : _ : _ : _ : ___ Feel angry
Feel bad ___ : _ : _ : _ : _ : _ : ___ Feel good
Want to hit/spank ___ : _ : _ : _ : _ : _ : ___ Want to hug/kiss
Want to yell at ___ : _ : _ : _ : _ : _ : ___ Want to praise
Feel tense ___ : _ : _ : _ : _ : _ : ___ Feel relaxed
Want to send child ___ : _ : _ : _ : _ : _ : ___ Want to be with child
to room

23. My child seems happy . . . I would

Feel relaxed ___ : _ : _ : _ : _ : _ : ___ Feel tense
Feel angry ___ : _ : _ : _ : _ : _ : ___ Feel pleased
Want to be with child ___ : _ : _ : _ : _ : _ : ___ Want to send child to room
Want to yell at ___ : _ : _ : _ : _ : _ : ___ Want to praise
Want to hug/kiss ___ : _ : _ : _ : _ : _ : ___ Want to hit/spank
Feel bad ___ : _ : _ : _ : _ : _ : ___ Feel good

24. My child enjoys the outdoors and nature . . . I would

Feel good	:	:	:	:	:	:	Feel bad
Want to yell at	:	:	:	:	:	:	Want to praise
Feel pleased	:	:	:	:	:	:	Feel angry
Feel tense	:	:	:	:	:	:	Feel relaxed
Want to hug/kiss	:	:	:	:	:	:	Want to hit/spank
Want to send child to room	:	:	:	:	:	:	Want to be with child

25. I ask my child to do something and he/she gets really angry . . . I would

Feel good	:	:	:	:	:	:	Feel bad
Feel angry	:	:	:	:	:	:	Feel pleased
Feel relaxed	:	:	:	:	:	:	Feel tense
Want to hug/kiss	:	:	:	:	:	:	Want to hit/spank
Want to yell at	:	:	:	:	:	:	Want to praise
Want to send child to room	:	:	:	:	:	:	Want to be with child

26. My child begins yelling . . . I would

Feel pleased	:	:	:	:	:	:	Feel angry
Feel bad	:	:	:	:	:	:	Feel good
Want to hit/spank	:	:	:	:	:	:	Want to hug/kiss
Want to yell at	:	:	:	:	:	:	Want to praise
Feel tense	:	:	:	:	:	:	Feel relaxed
Want to send child to room	:	:	:	:	:	:	Want to be with child

27. I ask my child to do something for me and he/she does it . . . I would

Feel relaxed	:	:	:	:	:	:	Feel tense
Feel angry	:	:	:	:	:	:	Feel pleased
Want to be with child	:	:	:	:	:	:	Want to send child to room
Want to yell at	:	:	:	:	:	:	Want to praise
Want to hug/kiss	:	:	:	:	:	:	Want to hit/spank
Feel bad	:	:	:	:	:	:	Feel good

28. My child acts respectfully toward someone in authority . . . I would

Feel good	:	:	:	:	:	:	Feel bad
Want to yell at	:	:	:	:	:	:	Want to praise
Feel pleased	:	:	:	:	:	:	Feel angry
Feel tense	:	:	:	:	:	:	Feel relaxed
Want to hug/kiss	:	:	:	:	:	:	Want to hit/spank
Want to send child to room	:	:	:	:	:	:	Want to be with child

29. I repeat more than once what I want my child to do, and he/she still doesn't do it . . . I would

Feel good	:	:	:	:	:	Feel bad
Feel angry	:	:	:	:	:	Feel pleased
Feel relaxed	:	:	:	:	:	Feel tense
Want to hug/kiss	:	:	:	:	:	Want to hit/spank
Want to yell at	:	:	:	:	:	Want to praise
Want to send child to room	:	:	:	:	:	Want to be with child

30. My child hugs me . . . I would

Feel pleased	:	:	:	:	:	Feel angry
Feel bad	:	:	:	:	:	Feel good
Want to hit/spank	:	:	:	:	:	Want to hug/kiss
Want to yell at	:	:	:	:	:	Want to praise
Feel tense	:	:	:	:	:	Feel relaxed
Want to send child to room	:	:	:	:	:	Want to be with child

31. I explain to my child why he/she needs to stop some bad behavior and he/she obeys me . . . I would

Feel relaxed	:	:	:	:	:	Feel tense
Feel angry	:	:	:	:	:	Feel pleased
Want to be with child	:	:	:	:	:	Want to send child to room
Want to yell at	:	:	:	:	:	Want to praise
Want to hug/kiss	:	:	:	:	:	Want to hit/spank
Feel bad	:	:	:	:	:	Feel good

32. My child puts his/her feet on the furniture . . . I would

Feel good	:	:	:	:	:	Feel bad
Want to yell at	:	:	:	:	:	Want to praise
Feel pleased	:	:	:	:	:	Feel angry
Feel tense	:	:	:	:	:	Feel relaxed
Want to hug/kiss	:	:	:	:	:	Want to hit/spank
Want to send child to room	:	:	:	:	:	Want to be with child

33. My child helps out with the household chores without being asked . . . I would

Feel good	:	:	:	:	:	:	Feel bad
Feel angry	:	:	:	:	:	:	Feel pleased
Feel relaxed	:	:	:	:	:	:	Feel tense
Want to hug/kiss	:	:	:	:	:	:	Want to hit/spank
Want to yell at	:	:	:	:	:	:	Want to praise
Want to send child to room	:	:	:	:	:	:	Want to be with child

34. My child joins me in an activity (walking, bowling, swimming, etc.) of mine . . . I would

Feel pleased	:	:	:	:	:	:	Feel angry
Feel bad	:	:	:	:	:	:	Feel good
Want to hit/spank	:	:	:	:	:	:	Want to hug/kiss
Want to yell at	:	:	:	:	:	:	Want to praise
Feel tense	:	:	:	:	:	:	Feel relaxed
Want to send child to room	:	:	:	:	:	:	Want to be with child

35. My child is honest and confides a mistake he/she has made . . . I would

Feel relaxed	:	:	:	:	:	:	Feel tense
Feel angry	:	:	:	:	:	:	Feel pleased
Want to be with child	:	:	:	:	:	:	Want to send child to room
Want to yell at	:	:	:	:	:	:	Want to praise
Want to hug/kiss	:	:	:	:	:	:	Want to hit/spank
Feel bad	:	:	:	:	:	:	Feel good

36. My child starts crying when I punish him/her . . . I would

Feel good	:	:	:	:	:	:	Feel bad
Want to yell at	:	:	:	:	:	:	Want to praise
Feel pleased	:	:	:	:	:	:	Feel angry
Feel tense	:	:	:	:	:	:	Feel relaxed
Want to hug/kiss	:	:	:	:	:	:	Want to hit/spank
Want to send child to room	:	:	:	:	:	:	Want to be with child

37. My child pesters other children . . . I would

Feel good	:	:	:	:	:	:	Feel bad
Feel angry	:	:	:	:	:	:	Feel pleased
Feel relaxed	:	:	:	:	:	:	Feel tense
Want to hug/kiss	:	:	:	:	:	:	Want to hit/spank
Want to yell at	:	:	:	:	:	:	Want to praise
Want to send child to room	:	:	:	:	:	:	Want to be with child

38.　While playing at sports, my child does very well . . . I would

Feel pleased ____:___:___:___:___:___ Feel angry
Feel bad ____:___:___:___:___:___ Feel good
Want to hit/spank ____:___:___:___:___:___ Want to hug/kiss
Want to yell at ____:___:___:___:___:___ Want to praise
Feel tense ____:___:___:___:___:___ Feel relaxed
Want to send child ____:___:___:___:___:___ Want to be with child
to room

39.　My child asks me repeatedly if he/she can do something . . . I would

Feel relaxed ____:___:___:___:___:___ Feel tense
Feel angry ____:___:___:___:___:___ Feel pleased
Want to be with child ____:___:___:___:___:___ Want to send child to room
Want to yell at ____:___:___:___:___:___ Want to praise
Want to hug/kiss ____:___:___:___:___:___ Want to hit/spank
Feel bad ____:___:___:___:___:___ Feel good

40.　My child does not clean up his/her room . . . I would

Feel good ____:___:___:___:___:___ Feel bad
Want to yell at ____:___:___:___:___:___ Want to praise
Feel pleased ____:___:___:___:___:___ Feel angry
Feel tense ____:___:___:___:___:___ Feel relaxed
Want to hug/kiss ____:___:___:___:___:___ Want to hit/spank
Want to send child ____:___:___:___:___:___ Want to be with child
to room

PARENT'S REPORT (PR)

AUTHORS: Eleanor Dibble and Donald J. Cohen

PURPOSE: To measure parental style.

DESCRIPTION: The PR is a 56-item instrument designed to measure a parent's perception of his or her own parental style in relation to a particular child. The PR was devised by selecting from the literature 16 categories of parental behavior that covered the domain of parenting styles, including eight socially desirable (positive) categories and eight socially undesirable (negative) categories. Three behaviorally descriptive items were written for each category. Initial empirical work led to the development of the 56-item questionnaire reproduced here. On 23 of the items, parents evaluate themselves on two complementary scales, how they really are and how the ideal parent would be. Differences in scores between the two scales then can be used either for further investigation or clinical intervention. The forms for mother and father are identical except for identifying which parent fills out the form (the mother's PR is reproduced here).

NORMS: The PR was studied initially with five groups of parents and one group of teachers; although an exact N is not provided, over 450 sets of parents and five teachers participated. The children evaluated were described as including "normal" and "behaviorally disturbed" children, some of whom were subjects in an epidemiological study of twins and siblings, and others who were inpatients in a pediatric service and children's clinic. No other demographic data were reported, nor were actual norms reported.

SCORING: The 56 items of the PR are presented as 7-item (0–6) Likert-type scales. Scores are derived by simply adding up the individual item scores for a total score that could range from 0 to 336.

RELIABILITY: Specific reliability coefficients were not reported. The authors report good test-retest reliability. The lack of difference between mothers' and fathers' responses between test and retest was seen as additional evidence of reliability.

VALIDITY: No specific data are reported. The authors claim factorial validity and state that a research social worker's ratings correlated significantly with most ratings of both mothers and fathers.

PRIMARY REFERENCE: Dibble, E. and Cohen, D. J. (1974). Comparison instruments for measuring children's competence and parental style, *Archives of General Psychiatry*, 30, 805–815.

AVAILABILITY: Journal article.

PR—Mother

This is about ways parents and children do things together. There are two answers for each of the first 23 questions. One is how you really act. The other answer is how you think a perfect or absolutely ideal parent would act toward this child.

All parents are different and all children are different. For the first answer, it is important to think how YOU really act. For the second answer, think about WHAT WOULD BE BEST FOR THIS ONE CHILD. There are two columns for each sentence. Within each column is a scale from 0 to 6. First, check the box in the first column that describes you today. Second, check the box from the second column that describes the ideal parent.

	COLUMN 1 How I Really Am							COLUMN 2 How the Ideal Parent Would Be						
	Never	Almost never	Seldom	Half the time	Frequently	Almost always	Always	Never	Almost never	Seldom	Half the time	Frequently	Almost always	Always
	0	1	2	3	4	5	6	0	1	2	3	4	5	6
I see both the child's good points and his/her faults.														
I let him/her know that I feel hurt if he/she does not do what he/she is told.														
I ask others what he/she does while he/she is away from me.														

	COLUMN 1 — How I Really Am							COLUMN 2 — How the Ideal Parent Would Be						
	Never 0	Almost never 1	Seldom 2	Half the time 3	Frequently 4	Almost always 5	Always 6	Never 0	Almost never 1	Seldom 2	Half the time 3	Frequently 4	Almost always 5	Always 6
I speak in a strong way in order to teach him/her how to behave.														
I think of things that will please him/her.														
I forget things he/she has told me.														
I avoid talking to him/her after he/she displeases me.														
I care about him/her, even when he/she does less well than I know he/she could.														
I let him/her know that if he/she really cared he/she wouldn't do things to cause me worry.														
I get angry about little things he/she does.														

	COLUMN 1 How I Really Am							COLUMN 2 How the Ideal Parent Would Be						
	Never 0	Almost never 1	Seldom 2	Half the time 3	Frequently 4	Almost always 5	Always 6	Never 0	Almost never 1	Seldom 2	Half the time 3	Frequently 4	Almost always 5	Always 6
I lose my temper when he/she does not do as I ask.														
I consider his/her needs and interests when making my own plans.														
I am unaware of what he/she thinks or feels.														
I withdraw from being with my child when he/she displeases me.														
I like to hug and kiss him/her.														
I let him/her dress as he/she wants.														
I can predict how he/she will respond or feel about something new.														

411

	COLUMN 1 How I Really Am							COLUMN 2 How the Ideal Parent Would Be						
	Never	Almost never	Seldom	Half the time	Frequently	Almost always	Always	Never	Almost never	Seldom	Half the time	Frequently	Almost always	Always
	0	1	2	3	4	5	6	0	1	2	3	4	5	6
I accept a decision even if it's not the way I think.														
I make clear rules for him/her to follow.														
I let him/her express his/her feelings about being punished or restricted.														
I change rules.														
I let myself be talked out of things.														
I tell him/her that I worry about how he/she will turnout because of his/her bad behavior.														

The remainder of the questions ask about your child's behaviors.

	Never	Almost never	Seldom	Half the time	Fre-quently	Almost always	Always
	0	1	2	3	4	5	6
Fusses and cries when he/she must give up something he/she wants							
Talks and acts happily and with excitement about things that interest him/her							
Tries to strike up friendships with other children by approaching them to play							
Even a slight distraction will make him/her forget what he/she is doing							
Happy to accept a toy or other object and is satisfied to keep it, look at it, and play with it							
Does things vigorously. Likes to use his/her strength							
Uninvolved when there are happy events, like trips, visits, new toys, treats, and parties							
Makes a great effort to do something that is difficult for him/her by reaching, pulling, or dragging							
Active, impossible to keep up with him/her							

	Never	Almost never	Seldom	Half the time	Fre- quently	Almost always	Always
	0	1	2	3	4	5	6
Pushes other children and adults in an unfriendly way							
Can pay attention for a long time to something							
Lies down, rests his/her head, or falls asleep instead of playing							
Shies away from getting attention. Moves away from people							
Is afraid to go near novel and strange things or moving toys, noisy toys, or balloons							
Is cheerful, smiles and laughs a lot							
Carries on and won't cooperate with routine activities such as washing, eating, or going to bed							
Watches and follows what you are doing when shown how a toy works, how it moves, or makes sounds							
Tries to please others							
Bites, hits, kicks, and tries to hurt you							
Gives long attention to objects, toys, or books that interest him/her							
Seems to have little zest for normal activities. Acts tired							

	Never	Almost never	Seldom	Half the time	Fre-quently	Almost always	Always
	0	1	2	3	4	5	6
Would rather be left alone if you try to play with him/her or talk to him/her							
Is afraid to go close to or touch insects, dogs, cat, or other animals							
Seems to enjoy most of the things that he/she does							
Will keep pushing you for something else when you give him/her a toy or something							
Pays close attention when you show him/her something							
Shows sympathy for others who are having trouble or are sad							
Is a talkative child who expresses himself/herself in language or near-language							
Tends to be resistent and unfriendly							
Sucks his/her thumb, twiddles his/her hair, or does something by habit							
Enjoys being played with							
Is unhappy being with people and being the center of attention							
Likes to feel, smell, taste, pound, squeeze, or examine new things and toys							

415

PARENT-CHILD RELATIONSHIP SURVEY (PCRS)

AUTHORS: Mark A. Fine, J. R. Moreland, and Andrew Schwebel

PURPOSE: To measure the quality of parent-child relationships.

DESCRIPTION: The PCRS is a 24-item instrument designed to measure adults' perceptions of their parent-child relationship. The instrument originally was developed to assess the effects of divorce on adult children of divorced parents, although the instrument appears useful for assessing the relationship of any children to their parents, perhaps even minors. The PCRS comes in two forms, one for assessing the child's relationship with the mother and one for assessing the child's relationship with the father. Both forms are identical except that the words "father" and "mother" are interchangeable, so only one is reprinted here. However, different factors emerged on the forms for father and mother. The factors for the father version are: positive affect (items 3, 14, and 18–24), father involvement (items 1, 2, 6, 9, 10, and 16), communication (items 7, 8, and 15–17), and anger (item 13). For the mother version, the factors are: positive affect (items 1–3, 6, 7, and 15–23), resentment/role confusion (items 9 and 14), identification (items 13, 23, and 24), and communication (items 4, 5, 7, 8, and 15–17).

NORMS: The PCRS was studied originally with 241 college students, of whom 100 were male and 141 female, with a mean age of 19.6 years (SD = 4.5). Fifty-six males and 85 females were from continuously intact families and were used as a control group to be compared with the remaining 100 students who were from divorced families. Total score means for mother-child relationships were as follows: males from divorced families, 16.7; males from intact families, 16.4; females from divorced families, 17.3; females from intact families, 18.9. For father-child relationships, total score means were: males from divorced families, 15.5; males from intact families, 19.3; females from divorced families, 14.8; females from intact families, 19.3. Respondents from divorced families generally perceived their relationships with both parents significantly more negatively than those from intact families.

SCORING: The PCRS is easily scored by reverse-scoring negatively worded items (9, 13, 14) and then summing individual item scores and dividing by the number of items on that factor for the subscale (mean) score; the total score is the sum of the means of the subscales.

RELIABILITY: The PCRS has excellent internal consistency, with alphas for the father subscales that range from .89 to .94 with an overall alpha of .96, and alphas for the mother subscales that range from .61 (identification) to .94 with an overall alpha of .94. No data on stability were provided.

VALIDITY: The PCRS has good known-groups and predictive validity, significantly discriminating between children from divorced and intact families.

PRIMARY REFERENCE: Fine, M. A. and Schwebel, A. I. (1983). Long-term effects of divorce on parent-child relationships, *Developmental Psychology*, 19, 703–713. Instrument reprinted with permission from M. A. Fine.

AVAILABILITY: Dr. Mark A. Fine, Department of Psychology, University of Dayton, Dayton, OH 45469-1430.

PCRS

Father Scale

Please complete the following items about your father.

1. How much time do you feel you spend with your father?
   (1 = almost none, 7 = a great deal)

   1 2 3 4 5 6 7

2. How well do you feel you have been able to maintain a steady relationship with your father?
   (1 = not at all, 7 = extremely)

   1 2 3 4 5 6 7

3. How much do you trust your father?
   (1 = not at all, 7 = a great deal)

   1 2 3 4 5 6 7

4. How confident are you that your father would not ridicule or make fun of you if you were to talk about a problem?
   (1 = not at all, 7 = extremely)

   1 2 3 4 5 6 7

5. How confident are you that your father would help you when you have a problem?
   (1 = not at all, 7 = extremely)

   1 2 3 4 5 6 7

6. How close do you feel to your father?
   (1 = very distant, 7 = very close)

   1 2 3 4 5 6 7

7. How comfortable would you be approaching your father about a romantic problem?
   (1 = not at all, 7 = extremely)

   1 2 3 4 5 6 7

8. How comfortable would you be talking to your father about a problem at school?
   (1 = not at all, 7 = extremely)

   1 2 3 4 5 6 7

9. How confused are you about the exact role your father is to have in your life?
   (1 = not at all, 7 = a great deal)

   1 2 3 4 5 6 7

10. How accurately do you feel you understand your father's feelings, thoughts, and behavior?
    (1 = not at all, 7 = a great deal)

    1 2 3 4 5 6 7

11. How easily do you accept the weaknesses in your father?
    (1 = not at all, 7 = extremely)

    1 2 3 4 5 6 7

12. To what extent do you think of your father as an adult with a life of his own, as opposed to thinking of him only as your father?
(1 = think of as only a father, 7 = see as adult with life of his own)   1 2 3 4 5 6 7

13. How often do you get angry at your father?
(1 = almost never, 7 = quite often)   1 2 3 4 5 6 7

14. In general, how much do you resent your father?
(1 = not at all, 7 = a great deal)   1 2 3 4 5 6 7

15. How well do you communicate with your father?
(1 = not at all, 7 = extremely)   1 2 3 4 5 6 7

16. How well does your father understand your needs, feelings, and behavior?
(1 = not at all, 7 = extremely)   1 2 3 4 5 6 7

17. How well does your father listen to you?
(1 = not at all, 7 = extremely)   1 2 3 4 5 6 7

18. How much do you care for your father?
(1 = not at all, 7 = a great deal)   1 2 3 4 5 6 7

19. When you are away from home, how much do you typically miss your father?
(1 = not at all, 7 = a great deal)   1 2 3 4 5 6 7

20. How much do you respect your father?
(1 = not at all, 7 = a great deal)   1 2 3 4 5 6 7

21. How much do you value your father's opinion?
(1 = not at all, 7 = a great deal)   1 2 3 4 5 6 7

22. How much do you admire your father?
(1 = not at all, 7 = a great deal)   1 2 3 4 5 6 7

23. How much would you like to be like your father?
(1 = not at all, 7 = a great deal)   1 2 3 4 5 6 7

24. How much would you be satisfied with your father's life-style as your own?
(1 = not at all, 7 = extremely)   1 2 3 4 5 6 7

PARENTAL AUTHORITY QUESTIONNAIRE (PAQ)

AUTHOR: John R. Buri

PURPOSE: To measure parental authority.

DESCRIPTION: The PAQ is a 30-item instrument designed to measure parental authority, or disciplinary practices, from the point of view of the child (of any age). The PAQ has three subscales based on prototypes of parental authority: permissive—relatively warm, nondemanding, noncontrolling parents (P: items 1, 6, 10, 13, 14, 17, 19, 21, 24, 28); authoritarian—parents who value unquestioning obedience and attempt to control their children's behavior, often through punitive disciplinary procedures (A: items 2, 3, 7, 9, 12, 16, 18, 25, 26, 29); and authoritative—falling somewhere between the other two dimensions, using firm, clear but flexible and rational modes of parenting (F: items 4, 5, 8, 11, 15, 20, 22, 23, 27, 30). The mother and father forms are identical except for appropriate references to gender.

NORMS: The PAQ initially was studied with 119 female undergraduates (mean age = 18.7) and 111 male undergraduates (mean age = 19.9). Actual norms were not available.

SCORING.   The PAQ is scored easily by summing the individual items to comprise the subscale scores. Scores on each subscale range from 10 to 30.

RELIABILITY: The PAQ has good internal consistency with alphas that range from .74 to .87 for the subscales. The stability of the PAQ also is very good, with two-week test-retest reliabilities that range from .77 to .92.

VALIDITY: The PAQ has fairly good construct validity, with authoritarianism inversely correlated with respondents' self-esteem and authoritativeness positively related to self-esteem. Permissiveness was not related to self-esteem.

PRIMARY REFERENCE: Buri, J. R. (1991). Parental Authority Questionnaire, *Journal of Personality and Social Assessment*, 57, 110–119.

AVAILABILITY: Dr. John R. Buri, Department of Psychology, University of St. Thomas, 2115 Summit Avenue, St. Paul, MN 55105.

PAQ Pertaining to Mothers

Instructions: For each of the following statements, circle the number of the 5-point scale (1 = *strongly disagree,* 5 = *strongly agree*) that best describes how that statement applies to you and your mother. Try to read and think about each statement as it applies to you and your mother during your years of growing up at home. There are no right or wrong answers, so don't spend a lot of time on any one item. We are looking for your overall impression regarding each statement. Be sure not to omit any items.

1 = Strongly disagree
2 = Disagree
3 = Neither agree nor disagree
4 = Agree
5 = Strongly agree

1. While I was growing up my mother felt that in a well-run home the children should have their way in the family as often as the parents do.   1 2 3 4 5

2. Even if her children didn't agree with her, my mother felt that it was for our own good if we were forced to conform to what she thought was right.   1 2 3 4 5

3. Whenever my mother told me to do something as I was growing up, she expected me to do it immediately without asking any questions.   1 2 3 4 5

4. As I was growing up, once family policy had been established, my mother discussed the reasoning behind the policy with the children in the family.   1 2 3 4 5

5. My mother has always encouraged verbal give-and-take whenever I have felt that family rules and restrictions were unreasonable.   1 2 3 4 5

6. My mother has always felt that what children need is to be free to make up their own minds and to do what they want to do, even if this does not agree with what their parents might want.   1 2 3 4 5

7. As I was growing up my mother did not allow me to question any decision she had made.   1 2 3 4 5

8. As I was growing up my mother directed the activities and decisions of the children in the family through reasoning and discipline.   1 2 3 4 5

9. My mother has always felt that more force should be used by parents in order to get their children to behave the way they are supposed to.   1 2 3 4 5

10. As I was growing up my mother did *not* feel that I needed to obey rules and regulations of behavior simply because someone in authority had established them.   1 2 3 4 5

11. As I was growing up I knew what my mother expected of me in my family, but I also felt free to discuss those expectations with my mother when I felt that they were unreasonable.   1 2 3 4 5

12. My mother felt that wise parents should teach their children early just who is boss in the family.   1 2 3 4 5

13. As I was growing up, my mother seldom gave me expectations and guidelines for my behavior.   1 2 3 4 5

14. Most of the time as I was growing up my mother did what the children in the family wanted when making family decisions.   1 2 3 4 5

15. As the children in my family were growing up, my mother consistently gave us direction and guidance in rational and objective ways.   1 2 3 4 5

16. As I was growing up my mother would get very upset if I tried to disagree with her.   1 2 3 4 5

17. My mother feels that most problems in society would be solved if parents would *not* restrict their children's activities, decisions, and desires as they are growing up.   1 2 3 4 5

18. As I was growing up my mother let me know what behavior she expected of me, and if I didn't meet those expectations, she punished me.   1 2 3 4 5

19. As I was growing up my mother allowed me to decide most things for myself without a lot of direction from her.   1 2 3 4 5

20. As I was growing up my mother took the children's opinions into consideration when making family decisions, but she would not decide for something simply because the children wanted it.   1 2 3 4 5

21. My mother did not view herself as responsible for directing and guiding my behavior as I was growing up.   1 2 3 4 5

22. My mother had clear standards of behavior for the children in our home as I was growing up, but she was willing to adjust those standards to the needs of each of the individual children in the family.   1 2 3 4 5

23. My mother gave me direction for my behavior and activities as I was growing up and she expected me to follow her direction, but she was always willing to listen to my concerns and to discuss that direction with me.   1 2 3 4 5

24. As I was growing up my mother allowed me to form my own point of view on family matters and she generally allowed me to decide for myself what I was going to do.   1 2 3 4 5

25. My mother has always felt that most problems in society would be solved if we could get parents to strictly and forcibly deal with their children when they don't do what they are supposed to as they are growing up.   1 2 3 4 5

26. As I was growing up my mother often told me exactly what she wanted me to do and how she expected me to do it.   1 2 3 4 5

27. As I was growing up my mother gave me clear direction for my behaviors and activities, but she was also understanding when I disagreed with her.   1 2 3 4 5

28. As I was growing up my mother did not direct the behaviors, activities, and desires of the children in the family.   1 2 3 4 5

29. As I was growing up I knew what my mother expected of me in the family and she insisted that I conform to those expectations simply out of respect for her authority.   1 2 3 4 5

30. As I was growing up, if my mother made a decision in the family that hurt me, she was willing to discuss that decision with me and to admit it if she had made a mistake.   1 2 3 4 5

PARENTAL BONDING INSTRUMENT (PBI)

AUTHORS: Gordon Parker, Hilary Tupling, and L. B. Brown

PURPOSE: To measure parental bonding.

DESCRIPTION: The PBI is a 25-item instrument designed to measure parent-child bonds from the perspective of the child. The PBI actually measures parental behaviors and attitudes as perceived by the child (who may be an adult). The PBI was constructed on the basis of two variables deemed important in developing a bond between parent and child: caring (with the opposite extreme being indifference or rejection), and overprotection (with the opposite extreme being encouragement of autonomy and independence). From an initial scale of 114 items, pilot research and factor analysis produced the current 25-item scale with two subscales, care (12 items; 1, 2, 4, 5, 6, 11, 12, 14, 16, 17, 18, 24) and overprotection (remaining 13 items). The subscales can be used separately or integrated into a single bonding scale.

NORMS: The PBI was studied initially with 65 medical students, 43 psychiatric nurses, 13 technical college students, and 29 parents of school children. Respondents were roughly equivalent in terms of sex. Mean scores were 24.9 for the care subscale and 13.3 for overprotection. A sample of 410 patients attending three general practitioners revealed care means of 26.9 for women and 23.08 for men, and overprotection means of 13.3 for women and 12.5 for men.

SCORING: The PBI is scored on a Likert-type scale ranging from 0 ("very like") to 3 ("very unlike"). Items 1, 5, 6, 8–13, 17, 19, 20 are reverse-scored. The 12 items of the care subscale allow a maximum score of 36 and the 13 items of the overprotection subscale allow a maximum score of 39.

RELIABILITY: The PBI has good to excellent internal consistency, with split-half reliability coefficients of .88 for care and .74 for overprotection. The PBI also has good stability, with three-week test-retest correlations of .76 for care and .63 for overprotection.

VALIDITY: The PBI has good concurrent validity, correlating significantly with independent rater judgments of parental caring and overprotection. Overall, mothers were viewed as significantly more caring than fathers.

PRIMARY REFERENCE: Parker, G., Tupling, H., and Brown, L. B. (1979). A Parental Bonding Instrument, *British Journal of Medical Psychology*, 52, 1–10.

AVAILABILITY: Journal article.

PBI

This questionnaire lists various attitudes and behaviors of parents. As you remember your mother/father in your first 16 years, would you place a tick in the most appropriate brackets next to each question.

		Very like	Moderately like	Moderately unlike	Very unlike
1.	Spoke to me with a warm and friendly voice	( )	( )	( )	( )
2.	Did not help me as much as I needed	( )	( )	( )	( )
3.	Let me do those things I liked doing	( )	( )	( )	( )
4.	Seemed emotionally cold to me	( )	( )	( )	( )
5.	Appeared to understand my problems and worries	( )	( )	( )	( )
6.	Was affectionate to me	( )	( )	( )	( )
7.	Liked me to make my own decisions	( )	( )	( )	( )
8.	Did not want me to grow up	( )	( )	( )	( )
9.	Tried to control everything I did	( )	( )	( )	( )
10.	Invaded my privacy	( )	( )	( )	( )
11.	Enjoyed talking things over with me	( )	( )	( )	( )
12.	Frequently smiled at me	( )	( )	( )	( )
13.	Tended to baby me	( )	( )	( )	( )
14.	Did not seem to understand what I needed or wanted	( )	( )	( )	( )
15.	Let me decide things for myself	( )	( )	( )	( )
16.	Made me feel I wasn't wanted	( )	( )	( )	( )
17.	Could make me feel better when I was upset	( )	( )	( )	( )

		Very like	Moder- ately like	Moder- ately unlike	Very unlike
18.	Did not talk with me very much	( )	( )	( )	( )
19.	Tried to make me dependent on her/him	( )	( )	( )	( )
20.	Felt I could not look after myself unless she/he was around	( )	( )	( )	( )
21.	Gave me as much freedom as I wanted	( )	( )	( )	( )
22.	Let me go out as often as I wanted	( )	( )	( )	( )
23.	Was overprotective of me	( )	( )	( )	( )
24.	Did not praise me	( )	( )	( )	( )
25.	Let me dress in any way I pleased	( )	( )	( )	( )

PARENTAL NURTURANCE SCALE (PNS)

AUTHORS: John R. Buri, T. M. Misukanis, and R. A. Mueller

PURPOSE: To measure parental nurturance.

DESCRIPTION: The PNS is a 24-item instrument designed to measure parental nurturance from the point of view of the child (of any age). Parental nurturance includes parental approval, acceptance, and affirmation of their children. With nurturance assumed to be an important factor in the development of children's self-esteem, the PNS can be a valuable tool for helping assess the child's perception of change in nurturance as a result of family counseling. Identical forms of the PNS are used for both mothers and fathers changing only gender references as appropriate.

NORMS: The PNS was studied with 128 undergraduate students in a large midwestern liberal arts college. The students were all white, predominantly Catholic and middle class. There were 61 females and 67 males with a mean age of 19.1 years. Actual norms were not provided.

SCORING: The PNS is easily scored by summing up individual items for a total score. Items 1, 3, 7, 8, 11, 13, 14, 16, 18, 19, 21, and 24 are reverse-scored.

RELIABILITY: The PNS has excellent internal consistency, with alphas of .95 for mothers and .93 for fathers. The PNS also has excellent stability with test-retest reliabilities of .92 for mothers and .94 for fathers (the time interval for the testing was not reported).

VALIDITY: The PNS has good concurrent validity, with significant positive correlations with self-esteem for both mother's and father's PNS.

PRIMARY REFERENCE: Buri, J. R. (1989). Self-esteem and appraisals of parental behavior, *Journal of Adolescent Behavior*, 4, 33–49. Instrument reprinted by permission of Sage Publications, Inc.

AVAILABILITY: Journal article.

PNS

For each of the following statements, indicate the number on the 5-point scale below that best describes how that statement applies to you and your mother. Try to read and think about each statement as it applies to you and your mother during your years of growing up at home. There are no right or wrong answers, so don't spend a lot of time on any one item. We are looking for your overall impression regarding each statement. Be sure not to omit any items. Record your answer in the space to the left.

1 = Strongly disagree
2 = Disagree
3 = Neither agree nor disagree
4 = Agree
5 = Strongly agree

_____ 1. My mother seldom says nice things about me.
_____ 2. I am an important person in my mother's eyes.
_____ 3. My mother often acts as if she doesn't care about me.
_____ 4. My mother enjoys spending time with me.
_____ 5. My mother expresses her warmth and affection for me.
_____ 6. My mother is easy for me to talk to.
_____ 7. I am tense and uneasy when my mother and I are together.
_____ 8. I feel that my mother finds fault with me more often than I deserve.
_____ 9. My mother takes an active interest in my affairs.
_____ 10. I feel very close to my mother.
_____ 11. My mother does not understand me.
_____ 12. My mother believes in me.
_____ 13. I don't feel that my mother enjoys being with me.
_____ 14. My mother doesn't really know what kind of person I am.
_____ 15. My mother is a warm and caring individual.
_____ 16. My mother does not feel that I am important and interesting.
_____ 17. My mother is very interested in those things that concern me.
_____ 18. My mother is often critical of me and nothing I do ever seems to please her.
_____ 19. My mother seldom shows me any affection.
_____ 20. My mother consoles me and helps me when I am unhappy or in trouble.
_____ 21. My mother is generally cold and removed when I am with her.
_____ 22. I receive a lot of affirmation from my mother.
_____ 23. My mother is very understanding and sympathetic.
_____ 24. My mother does not really care much what happens to me.

Copyright © 1989 Sage Publications, Inc.

PARENTAL TOLERANCE SCALE (PTS)

AUTHOR: Richard J. Butler

PURPOSE: To measure parental tolerance to children's enuresis.

DESCRIPTION: The PTS is a 16-item instrument designed to measure parental tolerance to their child's nocturnal enuresis. Parental tolerance has emerged as the most important predictor of parents who prematurely withdraw their children from treatment for nocturnal enuresis. The original versions of this scale contained 20 items, and much of the data about these scales are based on the 20-item scale. However, subsequent research has yielded the current 16-item scale. The scale originally was applied only to mothers, but subsequent unpublished research suggests that fathers of children with nocturnal enuresis respond in very similar ways to mothers. Items 1–7 on the scale provide a measure of support and items 8–16 provide a measure of intolerance. Items lower down the scale represent increasingly more intolerant attitudes. The PTS can be used to identify parental intolerance, so that intervention can begin prior to parents withdrawing from treatment.

NORMS: The scale was initially studied with two samples of parents of children with enuresis in England, the first sample comprising 68 mothers, and the second sample involving 134 mothers. The norms for the scale were published using the 20-point version; norms with the 16-point version are available from the author.

SCORING: The PTS is easily scored by scoring "one" for each "yes" response. The scores for items 1–7 are summed to provide the measure of support, and the scores for items 8–16 are summed to provide a measure of intolerance.

RELIABILITY: Data on reliability were not available in the original articles.

VALIDITY: The PTS has good predictive validity, consistently predicting premature dropout of parents from treatment for their children's nocturnal enuresis. The PTS also has good concurrent validity, correlating with a number of other variables related to parental anger, attributions, and concerns regarding their children's enuresis.

PRIMARY REFERENCE: Butler, R. J., Brewin, C. R., and Forsythe, W. I. (1986). Maternal attributions and tolerance for nocturnal enuresis, *Behaviour Research and Therapy,* 24, 307–312; Butler, R. J., Redfern, E. J., and Forsythe, I. (1993). The maternal tolerance scale and nocturnal enuresis, *Behaviour Research and Therapy,* 31, 433–436.

AVAILABILITY: Dr. R. J. Butler, Consultant Clinical Psychologist, Leeds Community and Mental Health Services, High Royds Hospital, Menston, Ilkley, West Yorkshire LS29 6AQ; Fax 01943 870471.

PTS

Circle either YES or NO depending on how true the statement is for you.

1.	I feel sorry for any child who wets the bed.	Yes	No
2.	I try to help him/her not to be upset.	Yes	No
3.	It's a pity the bedwetting stops him/her doing so many things.	Yes	No
4.	It's embarassing to be a bedwetter.	Yes	No
5.	I don't mind the washing because he/she can't help it.	Yes	No
6.	I tell him/her it does not matter.	Yes	No
7.	Bedwetting usually clears up on its own.	Yes	No
8.	I find it difficult to get used to wet beds.	Yes	No
9.	After a wet bed I show him/her I am disappointed.	Yes	No
10.	I try to make him/her realize the unpleasantness the bedwetting causes for others.	Yes	No
11.	The bedwetting is a nuisance to the rest of us.	Yes	No
12.	I don't see why my child can't be dry when other children can.	Yes	No
13.	Children could stop bedwetting if they tried hard enough.	Yes	No
14.	If he/she would grow up a bit we wouldn't have all the trouble with wet beds.	Yes	No
15.	I punish my child for bedwetting.	Yes	No
16.	A smack following bedwetting never did any harm.	Yes	No

PARENTING SCALE (PS)

AUTHORS: David S. Arnold, Susan G. O'Leary, Lisa S. Wolff, and Maureen M. Acker

PURPOSE: To measure dysfunctional discipline practices.

DESCRIPTION: The PS is a 30-item instrument designed to measure dysfunctional discipline practices in parents of young children. The PS is perhaps the first paper and pencil questionnaire to be developed specifically for identifying dysfunctional discipline activities of parents. Unlike more global measures of parental attitudes and beliefs, the items on the PS are specific enough to target these areas for intervention regarding parent training. The PS does not appear necessarily tied to the frequency of child misbehavior so that it may even allow for early identification of at-risk parents and for intervention directed at dysfunctional discipline practices before severe child behavior problems develop. The PS comprises three subscales (items 1, 5, 13, and 27 are not on the subscales): laxness (items 7, 8, 12, 15, 16, 19, 20, 21, 24, 26, and 30); overreactivity (items 3, 6, 9, 10, 14, 17, 18, 22, 25, and 28); and verbosity (items 2, 4, 7, 9, 11, 23, and 29).

NORMS: The PS was initially developed with 168 mothers of children 18 to 48 months old (the mean age of the children was 24 months). The mean age of the mothers was 31.2 years with a mean family income of $35,000 per year and a mean level of mothers' education of 14.9 years. Sixty-five of the mothers had reported to a clinic because of extreme difficulties in handling their children; the rest were mothers whose children attended a university preschool or who had volunteered to participate in the study. In a subsample of clinic and nonclinic mothers, scores on the PS were as follows: for the clinic group total score M = 3.1 (SD = .7); for laxness, M = 2.8 (SD = 1.0); overreactivity, M = 3.0 (SD = 1.0); and verbosity, M = 3.1 (SD = 1.0). For the nonclinic group, total score M = 2.6 (SD = .6); laxness, M = 2.4 (SD = .8); overreactivity, M = 2.4 (SD = .7); and verbosity, M = 2.6 (SD = .6).

SCORING: Each item receives a score from 1 to 7, where 7 is the "ineffective" end of the item. The following items have 7 on the left side (the others on the right): 2, 3, 6, 9, 10, 13, 14, 17, 19, 20, 23, 26, 27, and 30. To compute the total score average the responses on all items; to compute a subscale score, average the responses on the items on that subscale.

RELIABILITY: The PS has good internal consistency with alphas for the total score of .84, and for laxness, .83, for overreactivity, .82, and for verbosity, .63. The PS also has very good test stability with two-week test-retest correlations of .84 for the total score and .83, .82, and .79 for the laxness, overreactivity, and verbosity subscales, respectively.

VALIDITY: The PS has very good concurrent and discriminant validity. The PS significantly distinguishes between clinic and nonclinic mothers on the laxness, overreactivity, and total scales. The PS also was significantly correlated with the Child Behavior Checklist on the total scale and all subscales and was negatively correlated with the Locke-Wallace Marital Adjustment Inventory (with lower scores on the Marital Adjustment test indicating greater marital discord). The PS also was significantly correlated with observations of parenting behavior.

PRIMARY REFERENCE: Arnold, D. S., O'Leary, S. G., Wolff, L. S., and Acker, M. M. (1993). The parenting scale: A measure of dysfunctional parenting in discipline situations, *Psychological Assessment,* 5, 137–144.

AVAILABILITY: Susan G. O'Leary, David S. Arnold, Lisa S. Wolff, and Maureen M. Acker, Psychology Department, State University of New York at Stonybrook, Stonybrook, NY, 11794. Reprinted with permission of Dr. O'Leary.

PS

At one time or another, all children misbehave or do things that could be harmful, that are "wrong," or that parents don't like. Examples include:

hitting someone	whining	throwing food
forgetting homework	not picking up toys	lying
having a tantrum	refusing to go to bed	wanting a cookie before dinner
running into the street	arguing back	coming home late

Parents have many different ways or styles of dealing with these types of problems. Below are items that describe some styles of parenting.

For each item, fill in the circle that best describes your style of parenting during the past two months with the child indicated above.

1. When my child misbehaves . . .
    I do something right away   I do something about it later

    1 2 3 4 5 6 7

2. Before I do something about a problem . . .
    I give my child several reminders or warnings.   I use only one reminder or warning.

    7 6 5 4 3 2 1

3. When I'm upset or under stress . . .
    I am picky and on my child's back.   I am no more picky than usual.

    7 6 5 4 3 2 1

4. When I tell my child not to do something . . .
    I say very little.   I say a lot.

    1 2 3 4 5 6 7

5. When my child pesters me . . .
    I can ignore the the pestering.   I can't ignore the pestering.

    1 2 3 4 5 6 7

6. When my child misbehaves . . .
    I usually get into a long argument with my child.   I don't get into an argument.

    7 6 5 4 3 2 1

7. I threaten to do things that . . .
    I am sure I can carry out.   I know I won't actually do.

    1 2 3 4 5 6 7

8. I am the kind of parent that . . .
    sets limits on what my child is allowed to do.   lets my child do whatever he or she wants.

    1 2 3 4 5 6 7

9. When my child misbehaves . . .
I give my child a
long lecture.   I keep my talks short
                                                 and to the point.
                    7 6 5 4 3 2 1

10. When my child misbehaves . . .
I raise my voice or yell.   I speak to my child calmly.
                    7 6 5 4 3 2 1

11. If saying no doesn't work right away . . .
I take some other kind
of action.   I keep talking and try to
                                                 get through to my child.
                    1 2 3 4 5 6 7

12. When I want my child to stop doing something . . .
I firmly tell my child   I coax or beg my child
to stop.   to stop.
                    1 2 3 4 5 6 7

13. When my child is out of my sight . . .
I often don't know what   I always have a good idea
my child is doing.   of what my child is doing.
                    7 6 5 4 3 2 1

14. After there's been a problem with my child . . .
I often hold a grudge.   things get back to
                                                 normal quickly.
                    7 6 5 4 3 2 1

15. When we're not at home . . .
I handle my child the   I let my child get away
way I do at home.   with a lot more.
                    1 2 3 4 5 6 7

16. When my child does something I don't like . . .
I do something about it   I often let it go.
every time it happens.
                    1 2 3 4 5 6 7

17. When there's a problem with my child . . .
things build up and I do   things don't get out
things I don't mean to do.   of hand.
                    7 6 5 4 3 2 1

18. When my child misbehaves, I spank, slap, grab, or hit my child . . .
never or rarely.   most of the time.
                    1 2 3 4 5 6 7

19. When my child doesn't do what I ask . . .
I often let it go or end   I take some other action.
up doing it myself.
                    7 6 5 4 3 2 1

20. When I give a fair threat or warning . . .
I often don't carry it out.   I always do what I said.
                    7 6 5 4 3 2 1

21. If saying no doesn't work . . .
I take some other kind
of action.   I offer my child something
nice so he/she will behave.

            1 2 3 4 5 6 7

22. When my child misbehaves . . .
I handle it without
getting upset.   I get so frustrated or angry
that my child can see I'm
upset.

            1 2 3 4 5 6 7

23. When my child misbehaves . . .
I make my child tell me
why he/she did it.   I say "No" or take some
other action.

            7 6 5 4 3 2 1

24. If my child misbehaves and then acts sorry . . .
I handle the problem   I let it go that time.
like I usually would.

            1 2 3 4 5 6 7

25. When my child misbehaves . . .
I rarely use bad
language or curse.   I almost always use bad
language.

            1 2 3 4 5 6 7

26. When I say my child can't do something . . .
I let my child do it   I stick to what I said.
anyway.

            7 6 5 4 3 2 1

27. When I have to handle a problem . . .
I tell my child I'm sorry   I don't say I'm sorry.
about it.

            7 6 5 4 3 2 1

28. When my child does something I don't like, I insult my child, say mean
things, or call my child names . . .
never or rarely.   most of the time.

            1 2 3 4 5 6 7

29. If my child talks back or complains when I handle a problem . . .
I ignore the complaining   I give my child a talk
and stick to what I said.   about not complaining.

            1 2 3 4 5 6 7

30. If my child gets upset when I say "No," . . .
I back down and give   I stick to what I said.
in to my child.

            7 6 5 4 3 2 1

PERINATAL GRIEF SCALE (PGS)

AUTHORS: Louise Potvin, Judith Lasker, and Tori Toediter

PURPOSE: To measure bereavement in pregnancy-related loss.

DESCRIPTION: The PGS is a 33-item instrument designed to measure bereavement in perinatal loss (abortion, ectopic pregnancy, fetal death, and neonatal death), including the entire pregnancy and postpartum period. The scale was developed to provide a short version of a more extensive perinatal grief scale that was considered too long to be easily utilized. The PGS has three subscales revealed in factor analysis: active grief (items 1, 4, 7, 10, 13, 16, 19, 22, 25, 28, 31); difficulty coping (items 2, 5, 8, 11, 14, 17, 20, 23, 26, 29, 32); and despair (items 3, 6, 9, 12, 15, 18, 21, 24, 27, 30, 33).

NORMS: The PGS was investigated with 138 women who had experienced a perinatal loss. The mean age was 28.5 years, with a mean of 13.5 years of education; 86% were white, 1% were black, and the rest were Hispanic and "other." The mean for active grief was 35.75 (SD = 10.14), for difficulty coping was 24.09 (SD = 9.03), for despair was 22.26 (SD = 7.41), and for the total scale was 82.10 (SD = 23.61).

SCORING: The PGS is easily scored by summing items on the 5-point Likert-type scales for each subscale and for the total score. Items 11 and 32 should be reverse-scored.

RELIABILITY: The PGS has excellent internal consistency, with an overall alpha of .92 (subscales ranged from .86 to .92). The PGS has good stability, with 12- to 15-week test-retest correlations ranging from .59 to .66, even though it was expected that scales at the second time of testing should be substantially lower.

VALIDITY: The PGS has good factorial validity, although other types of validity information are not available. This form correlates .98 with the longer form of the PGS.

PRIMARY REFERENCE: Potvin, L., Lasker, J., and Toediter, T. (1989). Measuring grief: A short version of the perinatal grief scale, *Journal of Psychopathology and Behavioral Assessment*, 11, 29–45.

AVAILABILITY: Journal article.

PGS

Using the following scale, please indicate the extent you agree or disagree with each of the following items. Please record your answer in the space to the left of each item.

$$
\begin{aligned}
1 &= \text{Strongly disagree} \\
2 &= \text{Disagree} \\
3 &= \text{Neither agree nor disagree} \\
4 &= \text{Agree} \\
5 &= \text{Strongly agree}
\end{aligned}
$$

____ 1. I feel depressed.
____ 2. I find it hard to get along with certain people.
____ 3. I take medicine for my nerves.
____ 4. I feel empty inside.
____ 5. I can't keep up with my usual activities.
____ 6. I feel guilty when I think about the baby.
____ 7. I feel a need to talk about the baby.
____ 8. I have considered suicide since the loss.
____ 9. I feel physically ill when I think about the baby.
____ 10. I am grieving for the baby.
____ 11. I feel I have adjusted well to the loss.
____ 12. I feel unprotected in a dangerous world since he/she died.
____ 13. I am frightened.
____ 14. I have let people down since the baby died.
____ 15. I try to laugh but nothing seems funny anymore.
____ 16. I very much miss the baby.
____ 17. I get cross at my friends and relatives more that I should.
____ 18. The best part of me died with the baby.
____ 19. It is painful to recall memories of the loss.
____ 20. Sometimes I feel like I need a professional counselor to help me get my life together again.
____ 21. I blame myself for the baby's death.
____ 22. I get upset when I think about the baby.
____ 23. I feel as though I am just existing and am not really living since he/she died.
____ 24. I feel worthless since he/she died.
____ 25. I cry when I think about him/her.
____ 26. I feel somewhat apart and remote even among friends.
____ 27. It is safer not to love.
____ 28. Time passes so slowly since the baby died.
____ 29. I find it difficult to make decisions since the baby died.
____ 30. I worry about what my future will be.
____ 31. I feel so lonely since he/she died.
____ 32. It feels great to be alive.
____ 33. Being a bereaved parent means being a second-class citizen.

REALIZATIONS OF FILIAL RESPONSIBILITY (RFR)

AUTHOR: Wayne C. Seelbach

PURPOSE: To measure level of filial aid received by an aged parent.

DESCRIPTION: The RFR is a 19-item instrument designed to measure an aged parent's perception of the level of aid and support received from his or her children. Filial responsibility was defined operationally as scores on items derived from surveys concerning sources of aid and assistance received by parents from their children. The RFR can be very useful in assessing the level of support received by the elderly and by evaluating changes in that support following intervention with their families.

NORMS: The RFR was studied initially with 595 elderly persons living in Philadelphia; 74.3% were black, 25.7% were white; median age was 70 years and the entire group was living in poverty. No actual norms were reported.

SCORING: The first 6 items on the RFR are scored on a 6-point Likert-type scale. Remaining items are scored on a scale from −1 (someone other than an offspring provided the aid) to 0 (no need for aid, or a need is not met) to +1 (a child provided the aid). Proximity is scored as +1 = close, 0 = not too far, and −1 = distant. Frequency of visits is scored as +1 = visits at least weekly, 0 = at least monthly but not weekly, and −1 = less than monthly. The last two items are averaged if there is more than one child. All scores are totaled with results ranging from negative (receipt of no aid from children) to positive (high levels of aid and support) numbers.

RELIABILITY: No data were reported.

VALIDITY: Although validity data on the RFR are generally absent, some indirect concurrent validity information is available. Scores are significantly associated with sex (females were more likely than males to report high filial support), marital status (widowed or nonmarried reported higher levels of support than married), income (those with higher income reported less support), and health status (persons in better health reported less support). No differences due to race were found.

PRIMARY REFERENCE: Seelbach, W. C. (1978). Correlates of aged parents' filial responsibility expectations and realizations, *The Family Coordinator*, 27, 341–350. Instrument reprinted by permission of the National Council of Family Relations.

AVAILABILITY: Dr. Wayne Seelbach, Executive Assistant to the President, Lamar University, P.O. Box 10001, Beaumont, TX 77710.

RFR

For each of the first six items, please record the number that comes closest to what you believe about what your children should be like. Record your answer in the space to the left of each item and determine your answer from the following scale:

1 = Strongly disagree
2 = Disagree
3 = Somewhat disagree
4 = Somewhat agree
5 = Agree
6 = Strongly agree

"1" Means you strongly disagree that your children should be that way, and "6" means you strongly agree that your children should be that way.

_____ 1. Married children should live close to parents.
_____ 2. Children should take care of their parents, in whatever way necessary, when they are sick.
_____ 3. Children should give their parents financial help.
_____ 4. If children live nearby after they grow up, they should visit their parents at least once a week.
_____ 5. Children who live at a distance should write to their parents at least once a week.
_____ 6. The children should feel responsible for their parents.

For the next 11 items, please record "−1" if someone other than your child provided aid, "0" if there is no need for aid in that area, and "+1" if one of your children provided aid.

_____ 1. Shopping for groceries
_____ 2. Preparing hot meals
_____ 3. Cleaning house
_____ 4. Doing laundry
_____ 5. Accompanying old parent when paying bills
_____ 6. Accompanying old parent when cashing check
_____ 7. Paying rent
_____ 8. Paying mortgage
_____ 9. Heavy work around the house
_____ 10. Going to movie, church, meetings, visiting friends
_____ 11. Walking up and down stairs

For each child, circle "−1" if the child lives distant from you, "0" if the child lives not too far, and "+1" if the child lives close.

	−1	0	+1
Child 1	Distant	Not too far	Close
Child 2	Distant	Not too far	Close
Child 3	Distant	Not too far	Close
Child 4	Distant	Not too far	Close
Child 5	Distant	Not too far	Close

For the last item, for each child, circle "−1" if the child visits less than once a month, "0" if the visits were at least monthly and "+1" if visits are at least weekly.

	−1	0	+1
Child 1	Visits less than once a month	Visits at least monthly but not weekly	Visits at least weekly
Child 2	Visits less than once a month	Visits at least monthly but not weekly	Visits at least weekly
Child 3	Visits less than once a month	Visits at least monthly but not weekly	Visits at least weekly
Child 4	Visits less than once a month	Visits at least monthly but not weekly	Visits at least weekly
Child 5	Visits less than once a month	Visits at least monthly but not weekly	Visits at least weekly

Copyright © 1978 National Council on Family Relations.

SELF-REPORT FAMILY INSTRUMENT (SFI)

AUTHORS: W. Robert Beavers, Robert B. Hampson, and Yosef F. Hulgus

PURPOSE: To measure family competence.

DESCRIPTION: The SFI is a 36-item instrument based on the Beavers-Timber-lawn Model of Family Competence in which several dimensions of family functioning are proposed to distinguish competent from less competent families. These dimensions include family structure, mythology, goal-directed negotiation, autonomy of family members, the nature of family expression, and family style. All members of the family who can understand the items can be administered the SFI. Factor analysis reveals five sub-dimensions of the SFI: family conflict (items 5, 6, 7, 8, 10, 14, 18, 24, 25, 30, 31, and 34), family communication (items 11, 23, 26, and 29), family cohesion (items 2, 15, 19, 27, and 36), directive leadership (items 8, 16, and 32), and family health (all remaining items except 1, 9, 13, 20 and 22). A sixth dimension is composed of items 1, 9, 13, 20, and 22, although this subscale was not empirically determined. The SFI can be used as a total scale or the subscales can be used separately.

NORMS: Data are based on two nonclinical samples of college students (n = 279 and n = 205). Additionally, 71 families who had previously been in treatment completed the measure. No other demographic or normative data are available.

SCORING: The following items are reverse-scored: 5, 6, 7, 8, 10, 14, 18, 19, 23, 24, 25, 27, 29, 30, 31, 34. The scores on the six factors are summed and then divided by the number of items included in the particular factor; subscale scores can be summed for an overall score.

RELIABILITY: The internal consistency of the SFI is reported for the two samples of college students. For the larger sample the internal consistency was good, .85 using Cronbach's alpha. For the other sample, the alpha coefficient was .78.

VALIDITY: The SFI has a fair amount of concurrent validity, with subscales of the SFI correlating with the subscales of FACES-II, several factors of the Bloom Family Functioning Scale, and ratings of a clinical sample of 71 families. There is also some preliminary information on known-groups validity, with the subscales of health and expressiveness able to distinguish between outside-rated groups of high and low functioning families.

PRIMARY REFERENCE: Beavers, W. R., Hampson, R. B., and Hulgus, Y. F. (1985). Commentary: The Beavers systems approach to family assessment, *Family Process*, 24, 398–405. Instrument reproduced with permission of Yosef F. Hulgus and *Family Process*.

AVAILABILITY: W. Robert Beavers, M.D., Southwest Family Institute, 12532 Nuestra, Dallas, TX 75230.

SFI

For each question, mark the answer that best fits how you see your family now. If you feel that your answer is between two of the labeled numbers (the odd numbers), then choose the even number that is between them.

		YES: Fits our family very well		SOME: Fits our family some		NO: Does not fit our family
1.	Family members pay attention to each other's feelings.	1	2	3	4	5
2.	Our family would rather do things together than with other people.	1	2	3	4	5
3.	We all have a say in family plans.	1	2	3	4	5
4.	The grownups in this family understand and agree on family decisions.	1	2	3	4	5
5.	The grownups in the family compete and fight with each other.	1	2	3	4	5
6.	There is closeness in my family but each person is allowed to be special and different.	1	2	3	4	5
7.	We accept each other's friends.	1	2	3	4	5
8.	There is confusion in our family because there is no leader.	1	2	3	4	5
9.	Our family members touch and hug each other.	1	2	3	4	5
10.	Family members put each other down.	1	2	3	4	5

		YES: Fits our family very well		SOME: Fits our family some		NO: Does not fit our family
11.	We speak our minds, no matter what.	1	2	3	4	5
12.	In our home, we feel loved.	1	2	3	4	5
13.	Even when we feel close, our family is embarrassed to admit it.	1	2	3	4	5
14.	We argue a lot and never solve problems.	1	2	3	4	5
15.	Our happiest times are at home.	1	2	3	4	5
16.	The grownups in this family are strong leaders.	1	2	3	4	5
17.	The future looks good to our family.	1	2	3	4	5
18.	We usually blame one person in our family when things aren't going right.	1	2	3	4	5
19.	Family members go their own way most of the time.	1	2	3	4	5
20.	Our family is proud of being close.	1	2	3	4	5
21.	Our family is good at solving problems together.	1	2	3	4	5
22.	Family members easily express warmth and caring towards each other.	1	2	3	4	5
23.	It's okay to fight and yell in our family.	1	2	3	4	5
24.	One of the adults in this family has a favorite child.	1	2	3	4	5

		YES: Fits our family very well		SOME: Fits our family some		NO: Does not fit our family
25.	When things go wrong we blame each other.	1	2	3	4	5
26.	We say what we think and feel.	1	2	3	4	5
27.	Our family members would rather do things with other people than together.	1	2	3	4	5
28.	Family members pay attention to each other and listen to what is said.	1	2	3	4	5
29.	We worry about hurting each other's feelings.	1	2	3	4	5
30.	The mood in my family is usually sad and blue.	1	2	3	4	5
31.	We argue a lot.	1	2	3	4	5
32.	One person controls and leads our family.	1	2	3	4	5
33.	My family is happy most of the time.	1	2	3	4	5
34.	Each person takes responsibility for his/her behavior.	1	2	3	4	5

35.   On a scale of 1 to 5, I would rate my family as:

1	2	3	4	5

My family
functions very
well together

My family does
not function well
together at all.
We really need
help.

36.   On a scale of 1 to 5, I would rate the independence in my family as:

1	2	3	4	5

No one is indepen-
dent. There are no
open arguments. Fam-
ily members rely on
each other for satis-
faction rather than on
outsiders.

Sometimes indepen-
dent. There are some
disagreements. Family
members find satis-
faction both within and
outside the family.

Family members usu-
ally go their own way.
Disagreements are
open. Family mem-
bers look outside the
family for satisfaction.

SOCIAL SUPPORT INDEX (SSI)

AUTHORS: Hamilton McCubbin, Joan Patterson, and Thomas Glynn

PURPOSE: To measure family social support.

DESCRIPTION: The SSI is a 17-item instrument designed to measure the degree to which families find support in their communities. Social support has been found in a number of studies to be an important buffer against family crisis factors, and to be a factor in family resilience in promoting family recovery, and as a mediator of family distress. Thus this measure is a particularly important instrument for examining the extent of community-based social support as an ingredient in family resiliency. The SSI has been used with thousands of families in Western Europe and in the United States including families of rural bank employees and families with different ethnic backgrounds including Asian, Native Hawaiian, Caucasian, African-American and those of mixed races.

NORMS: The SSI has been studied with thousands of families including farm families, Native Hawaiian families, military families, families of investment executives, and families of rural bank employees. The means on the SSI range from 35.8 (SD = 7.9) for 720 rural bank employees to 46.4 (SD = 8.2) for 423 midwestern farm families. Specific means and standard deviations for a number of these groups are available in the primary reference.

SCORING: The score for the SSI is obtained by summing the individual items after items 7, 9, 10, 13, 14, and 17 are reverse scored to ensure that all items are scored in the same, positive, direction.

RELIABILITY: The SSI has very good internal consistency with an alpha across several samples of .82. The SSI is also reported as having good stability with a test-retest correlation of .83.

VALIDITY: The SSI has good concurrent validity as it is correlated with a criterion of family well-being, and shows that community/social support varies across stages of the family life cycle from the lowest point of the school-age stage to its highest at the empty-nest stage. The SSI also has been found to be an important predictor of family resilience and is positively correlated with families' confidence in coping with situations. Among families of minority ethnic background, the SSI was negatively correlated with family distress, and positively correlated with family well-being.

PRIMARY REFERENCE: McCubbin, H. I., Patterson, J., and Glynn, T. Social Support Index (SSI). In H. I. McCubbin, A. I. Thompson, and M. A. McCubbin (1996). *Family Assessment: Resiliency, Coping and Adaptation. Inventories for Research and Practice.* Madison: University of Wisconsin, 357–389.

AVAILABILITY: After purchasing the book cited above, you may register by telephone at (608) 262-5070. The book provides instructions for permission to use the instrument.

SSI

Read the statements below and decide for your family whether you: (1) Strongly disagree; (2) Disagree; are (3) Neutral; (4) Agree; or (5) Strongly agree and circle that number.

Please indicate how much you agree or disagree with each of the following statements about your community and family:

	Strongly disagree	Disagree	Neutral	Agree	Strongly agree
1. If I had an emergency, even people I do not know in this community would be willing to help.	0	1	2	3	4
2. I feel good about myself when I sacrifice and give time and energy to members of my family.	0	1	2	3	4
3. The things I do for members of my family and they do for me make me feel part of this very important group.	0	1	2	3	4
4. People here know they can get help from the community if they are in trouble.	0	1	2	3	4
5. I have friends who let me know they value who I am and what I can do.	0	1	2	3	4
6. People can depend on each other in this community.	0	1	2	3	4
7. Members of my family seldom listen to my problems or concerns; I usually feel criticized.	0	1	2	3	4
8. My friends in this community are a part of my everyday activities.	0	1	2	3	4
9. There are times when family members do things that make other members unhappy.	0	1	2	3	4
10. I need to be very careful how much I do for my friends because they take advantage of me.	0	1	2	3	4
11. Living in this community gives me a secure feeling.	0	1	2	3	4
12. The members of my family make an effort to show their love and affection for me.	0	1	2	3	4
13. There is a feeling in this community that people should not get too friendly with each other.	0	1	2	3	4
14. This is not a very good community to bring children up in.	0	1	2	3	4
15. I feel secure that I am as important to my friends as they are to me.	0	1	2	3	4
16. I have some very close friends outside the family who I know really care for me and love me.	0	1	2	3	4
17. Member(s) of my family do not seem to understand me; I feel taken for granted.	0	1	2	3	4

Copyright © H. I. McCubbin, J. Patterson, and T. Glynn, 1982.

INSTRUMENTS FOR CHILDREN

ADOLESCENT CONCERNS EVALUATION (ACE)

AUTHOR: David W. Springer

PURPOSE: To measure potential runaway behavior in adolescents.

DESCRIPTION: The ACE is a 40-item instrument designed to identify youths who are at risk of running away. The ACE consists of four separate yet interdependent domains: Family (items 1–12); School (items 13–21); Peer (items 22–28); and Individual (depression; items 29–40). There are no other instruments that can serve as indicators of adolescents who may be at risk of running away from home, or that have the capacity to track progress of treatment with runaway youths. The four domains of the ACE are based on review of the literature showing that these areas are important predictors of runaway potential. The ACE does not necessarily resolve why a particular youth may be at risk of running away from home; it mainly serves as an indicator that a youth may be at risk of running away. The ACE can be used not only to assess runaway behavior but to measure whether interventions used with runaway youths are effective.

NORMS: The ACE was initially developed with a clinical sample of 110 youths and a nonclinical sample of 117 youths. The clinical sample consisted of youths housed at a runaway shelter in Tallahassee, Florida as well as youths detained at three juvenile assessment centers in Florida. The clinical sample was made up of students in grades 6–12 at a high school in Tallahassee. The mean age of participants was 14.9 years. The subjects included 114 males and 113 females; 40 subjects were African-American, 18 were Hispanic, 9

American Indian, 147 white, 6 Asian and 4 identified themselves as "other." In the nonclinical sample only one participant reported ever having run away, and in the clinical sample 76 reported running away (69.1%) and 54% reported themselves as throwaways. Actual means and standard deviations were not reported.

SCORING: The ACE is scored by first reverse-scoring the positively worded items (2, 3, 5, 8, 11–13, 17, 18, 22, 24, 27, 28, 34, and 36), then summing all items. Thus, higher scores suggest greater runaway potential.

RELIABILITY: The ACE has excellent internal consistency with alphas for all four domains of .89 and above. The SEM was also computed for each domain and showed an excellent low SEM which range from .206 to .265. Data on stability were not reported.

VALIDITY: The ACE has excellent known-groups validity and construct validity. The ACE on all four domains significantly distinguished between the clinical and nonclinical samples. The ACE also correctly classified clinical and nonclinical subjects correctly using discriminant function analysis. The ACE demonstrated good discriminant construct validity by not correlating with items that were predicted not to correlate with the ACE. The ACE also showed excellent convergent construct validity correlating with several measures with which it was predicted to correlate such as the Index of Family Relations, the Generalized Contentment Scale, and the Hare Self-Esteem Scale.

PRIMARY REFERENCE: Springer, D. W. (1998). Validation of the adolescent concerns evaluation (ACE): Detecting indicators of runaway behavior in adolescence, *Social Work Research*, 22, 241–250.

AVAILABILITY: Dr. David W. Springer, University of Texas at Austin, School of Social Work, Austin, Texas 78712-1203.

ACE

The following statements are meant to describe how you see the world around you. Since these are your personal views, there are no right or wrong answers. Please answer as honestly as possible. Some items ask about relationships with parents. If you are not living with a parent, then for those items think about your primary adult caretaker(s). Circle the one response for each item which best describes how you see things at this time.

Please rate how strongly you agree or disagree with each statement, where:

1 = Strongly disagree
2 = Disagree
3 = Neither agree nor disagree
4 = Agree
5 = Strongly agree

FIRST, THINK ABOUT YOUR FAMILY LIFE.

1.	I am not comfortable talking to my parents about my problems.	1	2	3	4	5
2.	My mother and I get along well.	1	2	3	4	5
3.	My father and I get along well.	1	2	3	4	5
4.	My parents do not understand me.	1	2	3	4	5
5.	I enjoy spending time with my family.	1	2	3	4	5
6.	I do not feel safe in my home.	1	2	3	4	5
7.	I am not listened to in my family.	1	2	3	4	5
8.	My feelings are respected in my family.	1	2	3	4	5
9.	My parents demand too much from me.	1	2	3	4	5
10.	The rules in my family are not fair.	1	2	3	4	5
11.	I feel my parents trust me.	1	2	3	4	5
12.	All in all, I like my family.	1	2	3	4	5

NOW, THINK ABOUT YOUR EXPERIENCES WITH SCHOOL.

13.	I have good relationships with my teachers.	1	2	3	4	5
14.	My teachers are too hard on me.	1	2	3	4	5

15.	I get into trouble at school.	1	2	3	4	5
16.	School is easier for other people than it is for me.	1	2	3	4	5
17.	Finishing high school is important to me.	1	2	3	4	5
18.	School is helping me prepare for my future.	1	2	3	4	5
19.	I am not usually happy with my grades.	1	2	3	4	5
20.	My friends generally do not go to school.	1	2	3	4	5
21.	I do not enjoy school.	1	2	3	4	5

NOW, THINK ABOUT YOUR EXPERIENCES WITH YOUR PEERS.

22.	I am well liked by my peers.	1	2	3	4	5
23.	I do not fit in with my peers.	1	2	3	4	5
24.	My peers seem to respect me.	1	2	3	4	5
25.	I do not feel like part of the group.	1	2	3	4	5
26.	My parents do not approve of my peers.	1	2	3	4	5
27.	My peers seem to care about me.	1	2	3	4	5
28.	I have a lot of fun with my peers.	1	2	3	4	5

FINALLY, THINK ABOUT YOUR FEELINGS ABOUT YOUR LIFE.

29.	I feel depressed a lot of the time.	1	2	3	4	5
30.	I feel hopeless about my situation.	1	2	3	4	5
31.	I think about suicide.	1	2	3	4	5
32.	I feel worthless.	1	2	3	4	5
33.	I can't do anything right.	1	2	3	4	5
34.	I handle my problems well.	1	2	3	4	5
35.	I feel trapped.	1	2	3	4	5
36.	I feel good about myself.	1	2	3	4	5
37.	I deal well with stress.	1	2	3	4	5

38. I feel angry a lot of the time.   1   2   3   4   5

39. I do not feel like I have control   1   2   3   4   5
     over my life.

40. I feel that others would be glad if   1   2   3   4   5
     I wasn't around.

Copyright © 1997 David William Springer.

ADOLESCENT COPING ORIENTATION FOR PROBLEM EXPERIENCES (A-COPE)

AUTHORS: Joan M. Patterson and Hamilton I. McCubbin

PURPOSE: To measure adolescent coping behaviors.

DESCRIPTION: The A-COPE is a 54-item instrument designed to measure the behaviors adolescents find helpful in managing problems or difficult situations. Given the pressures on adolescents in American society, and the often difficult transition from childhood to adolescence, the availability of a measure like A-COPE seems very important for intervention programs working with adolescents. The items on the scale were developed both from literature review and interviews with adolescents regarding life changes. The A-COPE comprises 12 factors described in the primary reference, although the total score can be used as an overall measure of coping.

NORMS: The A-COPE has been used with several samples of adolescents including 185 female and 241 male junior and senior high school students and 709 adolescents from families enrolled in a large health maintenance organization in a midwestern city. Actual norms are not available, although total mean scores for adolescents who were in residential treatment for social adjustment problems were 168.7 (SD = 26.3). There were no differences in A-COPE scores based on race.

SCORING: The A-COPE is easily scored by summing item scores for a total score; items 7, 8, 19, 24, 26, 28, 42, 46, 49 are reverse-scored.

RELIABILITY: The subscales of A-COPE have fair to good internal consistency, with alphas that range from .50 to .75. Data on stability were not available. However, reliability data from the Young Adult—COPE, which is only slightly modified from A-COPE (and is described in the primary reference), show an overall alpha of .82 and good stability with a test-retest correlation of .83.

VALIDITY: The A-COPE has fair predictive validity, with several correlations in predicted directions with use of illicit substances including alcohol and marijuana.

PRIMARY REFERENCE: McCubbin, H. I. and Thompson, A. I. (eds.) (1991). *Family Assessment Inventories for Research and Practice*. Madison, WI: University of Wisconsin.

AVAILABILITY: Dr. Hamilton McCubbin, Dean, School of Family Resources and Consumer Services, Madison, WI 53706-1575.

A-COPE

Purpose:
A-COPE is designed to record the behaviors adolescents find helpful in managing problems or difficult situations which happen to them or members of their families.

COPING is defined as individual or group behavior used to manage the hardships and relieve the discomfort associated with life changes or difficult life events.

Directions:
Read each of the statements below which describes a behavior for coping with problems.

Decide *how often* you do each of the described behaviors when you face difficulties or feel tense. Even though you may do some of these things just for fun, please indicate ONLY how often you do each behavior as a way to cope with problems.

Circle one of the following responses for each statement:
1 = Never   2 = Hardly ever   3 = Sometimes   4 = Often   5 = Most of the time

Please be sure and circle a response for each statement.

NOTE: Anytime the words parent, mother, father, brother, or sister are used, they also mean stepparent, stepmother, etc.

When you face difficulties or feel tense, how often do you	Never	Hardly ever	Some-times	Often	Most of the time
1. Go along with parents' requests and rules	1	2	3	4	5
2. Read	1	2	3	4	5
3. Try to be funny and make light of it all	1	2	3	4	5
4. Apologize to people	1	2	3	4	5
5. Listen to music—stereo, radio, etc.	1	2	3	4	5
6. Talk to a teacher or counselor at school about what bothers you	1	2	3	4	5
7. Eat food	1	2	3	4	5

When you face difficulties or feel tense, how often do you	Never	Hardly ever	Some- times	Often	Most of the time
8. Try to stay away from home as much as possible	1	2	3	4	5
9. Use drugs prescribed by a doctor	1	2	3	4	5
10. Get more involved in activities at school	1	2	3	4	5
11. Go shopping; buy things you like	1	2	3	4	5
12. Try to reason with parents and talk things out; compromise	1	2	3	4	5
13. Try to improve yourself (get body in shape, get better grades, etc.)	1	2	3	4	5
14. Cry	1	2	3	4	5
15. Try to think of the good things in your life	1	2	3	4	5
16. Be with a boyfriend or girl- friend	1	2	3	4	5
17. Ride around in the car	1	2	3	4	5
18. Say nice things to others	1	2	3	4	5
19. Get angry and yell at people	1	2	3	4	5
20. Joke and keep a sense of humor	1	2	3	4	5
21. Talk to a minister/priest/rabbi	1	2	3	4	5
22. Let off steam by complaining to family members	1	2	3	4	5
23. Go to church	1	2	3	4	5

When you face difficulties or feel tense, how often do you	Never	Hardly ever	Some-times	Often	Most of the time
24. Use drugs (not prescribed by doctor)	1	2	3	4	5
25. Organize your life and what you have to do	1	2	3	4	5
26. Swear	1	2	3	4	5
27. Work hard on schoolwork or other school projects	1	2	3	4	5
28. Blame others for what's going wrong	1	2	3	4	5
29. Be close with someone you care about	1	2	3	4	5
30. Try to help other people solve their problems	1	2	3	4	5
31. Talk to your mother about what bothers you	1	2	3	4	5
32. Try, on your own, to figure out how to deal with your problems or tension	1	2	3	4	5
33. Work on a hobby you have (sewing, model building, etc.)	1	2	3	4	5
34. Get professional counseling (not from a school teacher or school counselor)	1	2	3	4	5
35. Try to keep up friendships or make new friends	1	2	3	4	5
36. Tell yourself the problem is not important	1	2	3	4	5
37. Go to a movie	1	2	3	4	5
38. Daydream about how you would like things to be	1	2	3	4	5

When you face difficulties or feel tense, how often do you	Never	Hardly ever	Some-times	Often	Most of the time
39. Talk to a brother or sister about how you feel	1	2	3	4	5
40. Get a job or work harder at one	1	2	3	4	5
41. Do things with your family	1	2	3	4	5
42. Smoke	1	2	3	4	5
43. Watch TV	1	2	3	4	5
44. Pray	1	2	3	4	5
45. Try to see the good things in a difficult situation	1	2	3	4	5
46. Drink beer, wine, liquor	1	2	3	4	5
47. Try to make your own decisions	1	2	3	4	5
48. Sleep	1	2	3	4	5
49. Say mean things to people; be sarcastic	1	2	3	4	5
50. Talk to your father about what bothers you	1	2	3	4	5
51. Let off steam by complaining to your friends	1	2	3	4	5
52. Talk to a friend about how you feel	1	2	3	4	5
53. Play video games (Space Invaders, Pac-Man), pool, pinball, etc.	1	2	3	4	5
54. Do a strenuous physical activity (jogging, biking, etc.)	1	2	3	4	5

Copyright © 1991 H. McCubbin and A. I. Thompson.

ASSERTIVENESS SCALE FOR ADOLESCENTS (ASA)

AUTHORS: Dong Yul Lee, Ernest T. Hallberg, Alan G. Slemon, and Richard F. Haase

PURPOSE: To Measure assertiveness of adolescents in specific situations.

DESCRIPTION: The ASA is a 33-item instrument designed for children in grades 6 through 12. It describes 33 interpersonal situations and provides the respondent with three options as to what he or she would usually do in each situation. The three options are classified as assertive, unassertive, and aggressive or passive-aggressive. The instrument has three purposes: (1) to obtain children's reports about their typical behavior that could be used by practitioners to identify interpersonal problem areas, (2) to be used as a screening device for intervention or prevention programs, and (3) to be used as a research tool in investigating assertiveness.

NORMS: Initial studies used 682 students in grades 6 through 12 in Canada. The children included 323 boys and 359 girls and were from two elementary and three secondary schools. Means are available for boys and girls at each grade level and range from 19.81 to 23.48.

SCORING: One of each of the three options for each situation has been designated as the ("appropriate") assertive response. Each of these responses is assigned one point and the scores are summed, producing an overall assertiveness score that can range from 0 to 33 (higher scores reflect greater assertiveness). "A" is the assertive response for items 6, 10, 14, 20, 21,23, 26, 28, 29, 31, 32; "B" is assertive for items 9, 7, 9, 12, 15, 18, 19, 22, 25, 27, 30, 33; and "C" is assertive for items 2, 3, 4, 5, 8, 11, 13, 16, 17, and 24.

RELIABILITY: Based on a subsample of 55 children, the Kuder-Richardson formula 20 indicated fairly good internal consistency while the test-retest reliability (stability) was very good with a correlation over a four-week interval of .84

VALIDITY: The ASA has fair validity in several areas. Concurrent validity based on correlations with two other measures was rather low (.33 for selected items from the Gambrill-Richey Assertiveness inventory and .55 with the Children's Action Tendency Scale) although both were statistically significant. However the ASA did distinguish between known groups on several dimensions (e.g., leaders versus non-leaders), appears to be sensitive to the effects of group assertion training sessions, and does not appear to be confounded with aggression or social desirability response set (based on lack of a significant relationship with the Crowne-Marlowe Social Desirability Scale). The ASA also was negatively correlated with irrational beliefs (the more assertive, the less respondents held irrational beliefs based on the Irrational Belief Questionnaire.)

PRIMARY REFERENCE: Lee, D. Y., Hallberg, E. T., Slemon, A. G., and Haase, R. F. (1985) An Assertiveness Scale for Adolescents, *Journal of Clinical Psychology*, 41, 51–57. Instrument reproduced by permission of D. Y. Lee.

AVAILABILITY: Dr. Dong Yul Lee, Department of Educational Psychology, Faculty of Education, University of Western Ontario, London, Ontario, Canada N6G 1G7

ASA

On the next few pages, you will see several situations that you may or may not have met in the past. We would like to know *what you would usually do in each situation*. Please circle the letter of the response that best describes what you would do in this situation.

1. You and your best friend have four tickets for the football game. Your other two friends do not show up, leaving you both with an extra ticket. Your best friend says, "If you give me your extra ticket, I will try to sell both." Your best friend does sell both, but doesn't give you your share of the money.
   A. You accept your friend's actions because you think that your friend earned the extra money by selling your ticket.
   B. You say calmly, "Give me my money."
   C. You say, "You crook. I am telling you now that if you don't give me the money it will be the end of our friendship."

2. Your mother has sent you shopping for food. The supermarket is busy and you are waiting patiently at the check-out. Your mother has told you to hurry. Suddenly a woman behind you pushes you with her shopping cart and says, "Hey, you don't mind if I go first, do you? I'm in a hurry."
   A. You are not happy with the way she treats you, but you calm yourself down and say, "Okay," and let the woman go first.
   B. You push the woman's cart and say, "You've got your nerve butting in like that," and refuse to give her your place in the line.
   C. You say, "Yes, I can see that, but I am in a hurry too. Please wait your turn or go to another check-out."

3. A school friend of yours has been spreading lies about you. As a result, most of your other friends now avoid you and talk about you behind your back. Today you happen to run into your school friend in the cafeteria. You are greeted as if nothing has happened.
   A. You talk with your friend, and pretend that you do not know about the lies your friend has told.
   B. You say, "Well, well, I'm glad I have finally caught up with you. We have a little matter to settle, liar."
   C. You say, "I am hurt by the rumors that you have been spreading about me. I thought you were my friend, and I am surprised that you did this to me. If you have a reason, I would like you to tell me so that we can get this matter sorted out."

4.   You often do favors for your friends. One of your friends, however, requests
      many more favors than the others. In fact, you think that some of this
      friend's requests are unreasonable, and that you are being used. Today
      this friend again asks for a favor.
      A.   You do the favor because friendship is very important to you.
      B.   You make up an excuse and tell your friend that you are too busy to
            help today.
      C.   You say to your friend, "lately you have been asking for a lot of fa-
            vors and some of them are unreasonable. This time I will say no.
            Friendship is a two-way street."

5.   You are a member of the school basketball team. The coach has promised
      that everyone will get a chance to play in this game. There are only five
      minutes left to play in the game and the coach hasn't put you in yet.
      A.   You get up, walk over to the coach, swear, and stomp out.
      B.   You stay on the bench. You think that you can learn a lot of things by
            watching others play.
      C.   You approach the coach and remind him that you haven't been in the
            game yet.

6.   Today you got back your graded test paper. After talking with your class-
      mates, you feel that one of your answers was not graded fairly. Later in
      the day your teacher greets you in the corridor.
      A.   You say, "Hello. By the way, I believe that one of my answers was
            not graded fairly. Could we go over this together?"
      B.   You say, "Hello. I think you have been very unfair to me."
      C.   You don't think that this is the time to argue over a grade so you sim-
            ply say "Hi," and continue walking.

7.   A classmate of yours missed a test and asks you for your test paper when
      you are walking home together. You know that the teacher is going to give
      the same test to those that missed the first one. You don't think that it is
      fair to allow your friend to get a good grade by studying only the answers
      to the questions on the test.
      A.   You refuse to give your test paper to your friend and say that you are
            no longer friends.
      B.   You refuse to give your test paper to your friend and explain why you
            think it would be wrong for your friend to use it.
      C.   Keeping a good classmate means a lot to you, so you give your
            classmate your test paper.

8.   Your favorite teacher asks you to volunteer one or two hours a day to help
      with an extracurricular project. You are doing well in his class, but are
      behind in some of your other subjects and are afraid that you might fail.
      A.   You say, "I will think about it," and then do your best to avoid that
            teacher.
      B.   You are not happy about doing it, but you are afraid that the
            teacher's feelings will be hurt if you refuse. You agree to work on the
            project.
      C.   You say "No," and explain that you would like to help, but you need
            the time to catch up on your other subjects.

9.   You are having dinner at a friend's house. After sitting down at the table
      you discover that everything is served on your plate, including a vegetable
      you hate. This vegetable has made you sick in the past. Your friend's
      mother says, "The rule in this house is that you eat everything on your
      plate."
      A.   You don't wish to cause any embarrassment at your friend's house,
            so you force yourself to eat the vegetable.
      B.   You tell her that in the past this vegetable has made you sick and
            that you don't think it would be wise for you to eat it now.
      C.   You say nothing, but to show your displeasure you get up quietly,
            leave the table, and go home.

10.   You are standing in a line at the popcorn booth in the movie theater. The
      show is going to start in a few minutes and you don't want to miss the
      beginning. Finally you get to the counter. As the girl is about to serve you,
      a man behind you shouts his order and the girl starts to serve him first.
      A.   You simply say, "Sorry, I was next," and proceed to order your pop-
            corn.
      B.   You say to the man, "You've got your nerve pushing in like that," and
            then say to the girl, "What's the idea of serving him first?"
      C.   You are upset, but you wait until the girl asks for your order. You de-
            cide that you'll never go back to that movie theater again.

11.   You buy a game at a store. When you get home you discover that some
      of the pieces are missing. You go back to the store to ask for a refund or
      a replacement. When you talk to the cashier about it, she says "That's too
      bad," but does nothing about it.
      A.   You say nothing, leave the store, and decide never to go back there
            again.
      B.   You get angry at the cashier, throw the game on the floor, and walk
            out.
      C.   You say, "I know it's too bad, but I insist that the game be replaced or
            that a refund be given."

12.   Your teacher singles you out in class by saying loudly, "Your answers to
      these problems are very similar to those of one of your classmates. I'll let
      it pass this time, but don't let it happen again." You didn't copy anybody's
      work and your teacher is wrong in suggesting that you cheated.
      A.   You don't say anything, pick up a book, and start reading it as if you
            had never been spoken to.
      B.   You say, "I didn't cheat, and I resent the suggestion that I did."
      C.   You are angry, but don't say anything, hoping you will be able to get
            back at the teacher later.

13.   You are traveling by bus to another city. The bus is crowded and you are
       sitting in the no smoking section. The man sitting beside you is smoking
       one cigarette after another. You are beginning to feel sick.
       A.   You do nothing, fight off the smoke and hope that the driver will
             come and give him a warning.
       B.   You angrily stare at him and hope that he will get the message soon.
       C.   You say to the man, "I would appreciate it if you would stop smoking
             because it is making me sick. You know this is a no smoking section."

14.   It is Saturday and you have just finished doing your chores. Now you
       would like to go out and play with your friends. Your mother, however,
       tells you that you are to babysit your younger sister for the afternoon.
       A.   You say, "I would like to go out and play with my friends."
       B.   You don't want to babysit, but you say, "Yes, mother."
       C.   You ignore your mother's request and walk out of the house.

15.   During an exam the student behind you asks for a Kleenex. Since you
       have some, you pass one back. The teacher sees this and accuses you
       of cheating.
       A.   You are upset, but say, "I'm sorry," and continue working on the
             exam.
       B.   You tell the teacher that the student behind you asked for a Kleenex
             and that you passed one back.
       C.   Realizing that only your friend can help you, you look back at your
             friend hoping that he will speak on your behalf.

16.   Your best friend has continually borrowed money from you for several days
       and hasn't paid you back. Today you don't have the money and need a
       dollar to buy lunch. You ask your best friend for some money and are
       refused.
       A.   Although you are hurt, you say nothing and decide that this is the
             end of your friendship.
       B.   You say, "Isn't it great when you continually ask me for money and I
             give it to you? Well, from now on you can forget about asking me for
             any more money."
       C.   You say,"I've been lending money to you for several days and it
             bugs me that you can't return the favor just once."

17.   You are waiting in line at a store. The customer in front of you has been
       chatting to the cashier for at least five minutes. It is almost supper time
       and you are in a hurry to get home.
       A.   You say nothing, and walk out of the store, without getting what you
             came for.
       B.   You interrupt the cashier and the other customer and say, "Hey,
             don't you people think it's about time that you shut up? Can't you see
             that I've been waiting here for more than five minutes?"
       C.   You say, "Excuse me, I have waited quite some time and would like
             to be served now."

18. Today is Wednesday and your science notebook is due on Friday. One of your friends who is behind in this subject asks to borrow your notebook to catch up. You need to do some more work on the notebook yourself.

    A. You lend your notebook for the sake of your friendship even though you have more work to do on it yourself.

    B. You say, "No, you may not have it. I still have work to do on it before Friday."

    C. You say, "Let me think about it," and then try to avoid him, hoping he will not ask you again.

19. You are waiting at the bus stop with a lot of packages. When the bus arrives it is almost full and you are lucky to get the last seat. After you sit down you notice that you have dropped one of your packages. When you leave your seat to pick it up, someone else takes your seat.

    A. You don't want to make a big fuss over a seat, so you say nothing and stand up in the aisle.

    B. You say, "Excuse me, that's my seat."

    C. You stare angrily at the person, hoping the person will get the message and give up the seat.

20. You and your classmate have just completed a school project together. You, however, have done most of the work. The teacher is very pleased, especially with the drawings you did. The teacher asks which one of you did the drawings. Before you can say anything, your classmate claims credit for doing them.

    A. You say, "That's not true. I did the drawings."

    B. You ignore what has been said because you don't want to embarrass your classmate in front of your teacher.

    C. You say to your teacher, "He is a liar," and say to your classmate, "I will never work on another project with you again '

21. Your teacher has told you that you have been doing very well in class lately, and that your grade will go up from the B you received on your first report card. She has said that you might get an A. Today you receive your final mark and discover with disbelief that it is still a B.

    A. You ask the teacher why you were given a B when you were told that your grade would be higher.

    B. You accept the fact that you received only a B, because you feel that you must have done something recently to change the teacher's mind.

    C. You say nothing to your teacher, but spread the word among your friends that your teacher lied to you.

22. You have agreed to babysit for your neighbor for 75¢ an hour. You don't really like the neighbor's kids because they always give you a hard time at bedtime. Tonight is worse than usual. When your neighbor comes home, he says that he will pay you only 50¢ an hour.
    A. You say nothing, take the 50¢ an hour, and decide that you will never babysit his kids again.
    B. You say, "You promised me 75¢ an hour. It is only fair that you give it to me."
    C. You accept the 50¢ an hour because it is better than nothing, and go home very unhappy.

23. You are playing baseball with your friends in the backyard. One of them accidentally breaks a neighbor's window. Later, when the neighbor comes home, you are called over and blamed for breaking the window. Your neighbor says, "I know you did it. Be more careful next time."
    A. You tell her that it was an accident, but that you didn't do It.
    B. You say nothing, but the next day break another window on purpose.
    C. You say, "Okay," and accept the blame so that your friend will not get in trouble.

24. Your mother's friend comes over to your house and asks you to run an errand for her. It's time to go to your swimming lesson and if you do this errand you will be late. To make matters worse, your mother supports her friend's request.
    A. You refuse to do the errand, and tell your mother's friend that she should do it herself.
    B. You say nothing and do the errand, even though you'll be late for your swimming lesson.
    C. You tell your mother and her friend that you have a swimming lesson, and that you will be late if you run this errand.

25. You and your two friends are hungry, so you go to the nearest snack bar. The waitress takes your orders—two hamburgers with the works, and one without onion. You hate onions. When she brings back the hamburgers, all three have onions on them.
    A. You say nothing, and scrape the onion off the hamburger.
    B. You call the waitress over and tell her that you ordered a hamburger without onion. You ask her to get another one with no onions.
    C. You get angry at the waitress and say, "You are dumb, lady. I told you I didn't want any onions."

26. Your best friend has asked to borrow the ring that your parents gave you for doing well in school last year. You value this ring very much and don't want to lend it, even to your best friend.
    A. You say, "No, this ring is very special to me and I wouldn't lend it to anyone."
    B. You don't want to hurt your friend, so you let your best friend borrow the ring.
    C. You say, "Well, let me think about it," and then try your best to avoid your friend so that you won't have to lend the ring.

27. You are at the beach. It is very crowded but you find a very good spot and place your towel there while you go swimming. When you get back to your spot you find that someone has moved your towel and two people are lying there.
   A. You say nothing, pick up your towel, and look for another spot.
   B. You tell the people that you were there first, and ask them to move to another spot.
   C. You say nothing but angrily stare at them, hoping that they get the message and move to a different place.

28. After school you stop at the corner store to buy some candy. As soon as you get outside, you realize that you have not been given the correct change. You go back into the store and tell the cashier, but are not believed.
   A. You say to the cashier, "You should believe me. I know that you don't have to give me the five cents but I would appreciate it."
   B. You tell the cashier that you will never come back to this store again, and that you will tell your friends not to come here, either.
   C. You forget about trying to correct the error, and tell yourself that you won't let this happen again.

29. Your parents have just given you a new book. You proudly show it to your sister who immediately wants to borrow it for a day. You don't want to lend it at this time because you have not had a chance to read it yourself. Your sister, however, insists on borrowing it
   A. You tell your sister that you don't want to lend it to her until you have had a chance to read it yourself
   B. You say nothing and give the book to your sister, because you do not wish to argue with her.
   C. You get angry at your sister for asking to borrow something that is yours.

30. You went with your friend to the hospital after school because your friend sprained an ankle in Phys. Ed class. You are late for dinner and your father asks you for an explanation. You tell him the truth. He calls you a liar, and tells you to go to your room without supper.
   A. You go to your room, thinking that this is the only way to keep peace in your family.
   B. You again tell your father what happened and suggest that he call the hospital and your teacher.
   C. You say to your father, "I've had enough. I don't deserve this type of treatment. I won't go to my room."

31. You and your friend go over to a classmate's home. You don't know the classmate that well and her/his parents are not home. While watching TV the classmate offers you and your friend cigarettes. Your friend accepts and they light up. You don't want to smoke, but your friend and classmate tease you and laugh.
     A.   You stand firm by simply saying, "No, I don't want to smoke, but I guess you're in the mood for some jokes."
     B.   You don't really want to, but you do because you don't want them to laugh at you.
     C.   You don't say anything, but get up and leave the house, not wanting to return.

32. A close friend of yours is nominated to be captain of the basketball team. Another player, whom you believe would make a better captain, is also nominated. You are to vote by raising your hand. If you do not vote for your friend, you may hurt your friend's feelings.
     A.   You vote for the player who you believe will be the best captain.
     B.   You don't want your close friend to feel hurt, so you say "This is dumb, I'm not going to vote."
     C.   All of a sudden you remember that you have something else to do, excuse yourself, and say, "Go ahead and vote without me."

33. You have been looking forward to going to your friend's place after school to listen to a new record, and your mother has given you her permission. You rush home from school, drop off your books, and are about to leave when you mother says, "I'd like you to vacuum the living room. We're going to have company tonight and I'm very busy."
     A.   You pretend that you did not hear what your mother said and walk out.
     B.   You say to your mother, "You told me I could go out. It's not fair to ask me to stay home at the last minute."
     C.   You say to your mother, "You're always interrupting my plans," and rush out the door.

BEHAVIORAL SELF-CONCEPT SCALE (BSCS)

AUTHORS: Robert L. Williams and Edward A. Workman

PURPOSE: To measure children's self-concept.

DESCRIPTION: The BSCS is a 36-item instrument designed to measure children's school-related self-concept. The rationale for this instrument is that experiences in the classroom have a significant impact on the child's self-concept. The BSCS is actually a measure of behavioral self-concept in that children are asked to specify which member of 36 pairs of academic behaviors they are better at. The BSCS can be administered orally or in writing.

NORMS: The BSCS was initially developed on 86 male and female fourth and fifth grade students. No other demographic information or norms are provided.

SCORING: The respondent's self-concept for a specific activity is determined by summing the number of times a student ranks that activity over other activities. There appear to be four major activities—reading, mathematics, spelling and writing, and play, which includes drawing and singing. Higher scores indicate higher self-concept for that particular activity.

RELIABILITY: The BSCS has fair stability, with three-week test-retest correlations that range from .59 to .90. No data on internal consistency are available.

VALIDITY: No validity data were reported although the BSCS appears to have fair face and content validity for the specific academic areas selected.

PRIMARY REFERENCE: Williams, R. L. and Workman, E. A. (1978). The development of a behavioral self-concept scale, *Behavior Therapy*, 9, 680–681. Instrument reproduced with permission of Robert L. Williams.

AVAILABILITY: Dr. Robert L. Williams, University of Tennessee, Educational and Counseling Psychology, Knoxville, TN 37996-3400.

BSCS

Instructions to be read to the students: "All of us are better at some things than we are at others. The sheets I have given you describe activities we do at school. Each item lists two of those activities. As I read each item, *underline* the activity you're better at. For example, for item 1 if you are better at solving math problems in class than you are reading the language book at school, you would underline solving math problems in class. However, if you are better at reading the language book at school, what would you underline for that item? . . . That's correct. Now, do you have any questions as to what you are to do? . . . All right, let's actually do item 1."

1. Solving math problems in class   Reading the language book at school

2. Spelling   Writing school assignments

3. Drawing in art class   Reading the science book at school

4. Playing games during gym or recess   Singing in music class

5. Reading the social studies book at school   Spelling

6. Writing, school assignments   Drawing in art class

7. Reading the language book at school   Playing games during gym or recess

8. Singing in music class   Solving math problems in class

9. Reading the science book at school   Reading the social studies book at school

10. Spelling   Drawing in art class

11. Playing games during gym or recess   Writing school assignments

12. Reading the language book at school   Singing in music class

13. Solving math problems in class   Reading the science book at school

14. Reading the social studies book at school   Playing games during gym or recess

15.	Drawing in art class	Reading the language book at school
16.	Singing in music class	Spelling
17.	Writing school assignments	Solving math problems in class
18.	Reading the science book at school	Playing games during gym or recess
19.	Reading the language book at school	Reading the social studies book at school
20.	Drawing in art class	Singing in music class
21.	Spelling	Reading the science book at school
22.	Solving math problems in class	Reading the social studies book at school
23.	Singing in music class	Writing school assignments
24.	Playing games during gym or recess	Drawing in art class
25.	Reading the science book at school	Reading the language book at school
26.	Reading the social studies book	Singing in music class
27.	Playing games during gym or recess	Spelling
28.	Drawing in art class	Solving math problems in class
29.	Reading the science book at school	Writing school assignments
30.	Reading the language book at school	Spelling
31.	Reading the social studies book at school	Drawing in art class
32.	Solving math problems in school	Playing games during gym or recess
33.	Writing school assignments	Reading the language book at school

34.	Singing in music class	Reading the science book at school
35.	Spelling	Solving math problems in class
36.	Writing school assignments	Reading the social studies book at school

BEHAVIOR RATING INDEX FOR CHILDREN (BRIC)

AUTHORS: Arlene R. Stiffman, John G. Orme, Deborah A. Evans, Ronald A. Feldman, and Phoebe A. Keeney

PURPOSE: To measure children's behavior problems.

DESCRIPTION: The BRIC is a 13-item instrument designed to be used as a rating scale by people in children's environments—such as parents, teachers, other caretakers, and children themselves—to measure the degree of children's behavior problems. The measure is brief, easy to use, and can be used by multiple respondents to evaluate children of all ages. It also can be used in group and classroom settings. The behavioral problems included on the BRIC are those that appeared repeatedly in previous research. This is a promising instrument that overcomes the limitations of many other related measures for evaluating children's behavior since the BRIC takes only a few minutes to complete, can be used for longitudinal studies, and can be scored quickly and easily by hand.

NORMS: The BRIC was initially studied with over 600 children enrolled in a group field experiment, some of whom were recruited because one or both parents were in treatment for a diagnosed mental illness. In addition, 486 parents or guardians of the children, 198 teachers, and 13 participant observers filled out the BRIC. All members of all groups did not participate in all aspects of the initial research. No actual norms were reported.

SCORING: The BRIC is scored on a 5-point Likert-type scale (1–5), omitting items 1, 6, and 10, which are not problem-oriented items. The scores are transformed into a potential range of 0 to 100 by adding up all the item scores, subtracting from that figure the total number of items (out of 10) completed, multiplying that figure by 100, and dividing that result by the total number of items completed times 4. High scores indicate more severe behavioral problems. The authors report that response bias was not a problem, with only one respondent completing positively and negatively worded items in the same extreme fashion.

RELIABILITY: The BRIC has fair to good internal consistency, with alphas ranging from .80 to .86 for adults and .60 to .70 for children. The BRIC is a fairly stable instrument when completed by adults, with one- to four-week test-retest correlations ranging from .71 to .89, but only .50 for children. Interrater reliability for adults was fair with a correlation coefficient of .51.

VALIDITY: The BRIC has good concurrent validity. The correlation between children's scores on the BRIC as reported by parents and children's treatment status (receiving or not receiving treatment for behavioral problems) was .65 (p < .001). There also was a .76 (p < .001) correlation between scores on the BRIC and scores on the widely used 118-item Child Behavior Checklist. The BRIC uses a score of 30 as a rough clinical cutting point, with higher scores suggesting problems requiring more intensive examination and possible intervention.

PRIMARY REFERENCE: Stiffman, A. R., Orme, J. G., Evans, D. A., Feldman, R. A., and Keeney, P. A. (1984). A brief measure of children's behavior problems: The Behavior Rating Index for Children, *Measurement and Evaluation in Counseling and Development*, 16, 83–90.

AVAILABILITY: Journal article.

BRIC

For each item, please record the number that comes closest to your observations of the child. Record your answer in the space to the left of each item, using the following scale:

$$1 = \text{Rarely or never}$$
$$2 = \text{A little of the time}$$
$$3 = \text{Some of the time}$$
$$4 = \text{A good part of the time}$$
$$5 = \text{Most or all of the time}$$

IN GENERAL, HOW OFTEN DOES THIS CHILD:

_____ 1. Feel happy or relaxed?

_____ 2. Hide his/her thoughts from other people?

_____ 3. Say or do really strange things?

_____ 4. Not pay attention when he/she should?

_____ 5. Quit a job or task without finishing it?

_____ 6. Get along well with other people?

_____ 7. Hit, push, or hurt someone?

_____ 8. Get along poorly with other people?

_____ 9. Get very upset?

_____ 10. Compliment or help someone?

_____ 11. Feel sick?

_____ 12. Cheat?

_____ 13. Lose his/her temper?

Copyright © 1983 Arlene R. Stiffman.

BODY INVESTMENT SCALE (BIS)

AUTHORS: Israel Orbach and Mario Mikulincer

PURPOSE: To measure emotional investment in the body.

DESCRIPTION: The BIS is a 24-item instrument designed to measure children's emotional investment in their body, especially as it pertains to self-destructive behavior. In particular, the BIS was developed because of increasing emphasis on the study of suicidal behavior as it pertains to the bodily experiences of the suicidal person. Since suicidal behavior involves a physical attack on the body, and it is believed that such attacks may be related to attitudes and feelings about the body, it is important to have a way of measuring an individual's emotional investment in his or her body. The BIS is a useful measure not only for identifying bodily experiences that may be related to self-destructive tendencies and potential suicide, but may also be useful in exploring related disordered behavior such as eating disorders, drug abuse, and experiences of physical and sexual abuse. The BIS comprises four subscales: image, feelings and attitudes toward the body (items 5, 10, 13, 16, 17, and 21); comfort in touch (items 2, 6, 9, 11, 20, and 23); body care (items 1, 4, 8, 12, and 19), and body protection (items 3, 7, 15, 18, 22, and 24).

NORMS: The BIS was developed in a series of four studies using both hospitalized and community youngsters in Israel. Study I involved several hundred community and hospitalized children in which the BIS items were developed. The second study involved 104 suicidal patients involving 75 boys and 29 girls with a mean age of 16.6 years (SD = 1.88), and a nonsuicidal inpatient group consisting of 102 children of which 78 were boys and 24 were girls with a mean age of 17.19 (SD = 2.07), and a control group of participants outside of the hospital involving 69 boys and 46 girls with a mean age of 16.3 years. The third study involved 11 boys and 14 girls with a mean age of 16.72 years, all of whom were suicidal inpatients and 17 boys and 10 girls with a mean age of 17.40 years who were nonsuicidal inpatients and a community control group of 13 boys and 22 girls with a mean age of 15.26 years. The fourth study involved 20 boys and 37 girls who were suicidal inpatients with a mean age of 16.61 years, and 22 boys and 23 girls who were nonsuicidal inpatients with a mean age of 17.66 years and a community control group of 26 boys and 20 girls with a mean age of 16.41 years. Means and standard deviations for each of the subscales for control, nonsuicidal, and suicidal groups, broken down by gender, are available in the original article.

SCORING: The BIS is easily scored by first reverse-scoring items 2, 3, 5, 7, 9, 11, 13, 17, and 22, and then summing all item responses and dividing by the number of responses for the average for each subscale.

RELIABILITY: The BIS has good to excellent internal consistency with an alpha of .75 for body image, .85 for body touch, .86 for body care, and .92 for body protection. No data on stability were reported.

VALIDITY: The BIS has established very good known-groups validity and construct validity. The BIS significantly distinguishes suicidal inpatients from control respondents and from nonsuicidal inpatients. The factors of the BIS also were significantly correlated with different aspects of suicidal tendencies and were significantly related to bodily experiences such as physical anhedonia (a major distortion in body perception characteristic of suicidal individuals).

PRIMARY REFERENCE: Orbach, I. and Mikulincer, M. (1998). The body investment scale: Construction and validation of a body experience scale, *Psychological Assessment,* 10, 415–425.

AVAILABILITY: Dr. Israel Orbach, Department of Psychology, Bar-ilan University, Ramat-gan 52900, Israel; E-mail: orbachi@mail.biu.ac.il.

BIS

The following is a list of statements about one's experience, feelings, and attitudes of his/her body. There are no right or wrong answers. We would like to know what *your* experience, feelings, and attitudes of your body are. Please read each statement carefully and evaluate how it relates to you by checking the degree to which you agree or disagree with it. If you do not agree at all: circle (1). If you do not agree: circle (2). If you are undecided: circle (3). If you agree: circle (4). If you strongly agree: circle (5). Try to be as honest as you can. Thank you for your time and cooperation.

1. I believe that caring for my body will improve my well-being.   1   2   3   4   5

2. I don't like it when people touch me.   1   2   3   4   5

3. It makes me feel good to do something dangerous.   1   2   3   4   5

4. I pay attention to my appearance.   1   2   3   4   5

5. I am frustrated with my physical appearance.   1   2   3   4   5

6. I enjoy physical contact with other people.   1   2   3   4   5

7. I am not afraid to engage in dangerous activities.   1   2   3   4   5

8. I like to pamper my body.   1   2   3   4   5

9. I tend to keep a distance from the person with whom I am talking.   1   2   3   4   5

10. I am satisfied with my appearance.   1   2   3   4   5

11. I feel uncomfortable when people get too close to me physically.   1   2   3   4   5

12. I enjoy taking a bath.   1   2   3   4   5

13. I hate my body.   1   2   3   4   5

14. In my opinion it is very important to take care of the body.   1   2   3   4   5

15. When I am injured, I immediately take care of the wound.   1   2   3   4   5

16. I feel comfortable with my body.   1   2   3   4   5

17. I feel anger toward my body.   1   2   3   4   5

18. I look in both directions before crossing the street.   1   2   3   4   5

19. I use body care products regularly.   1   2   3   4   5

20. I like to touch people who are close to me.   1   2   3   4   5

21. I like my appearance in spite of its imperfections.   1   2   3   4   5

22. Sometimes I purposely injure myself.   1   2   3   4   5

23. Being hugged by a person close to me can comfort me.   1   2   3   4   5

24. I take care of myself whenever I feel a sign of illness.   1   2   3   4   5

CHILD DENTAL CONTROL ASSESSMENT (CDCA)

AUTHORS: Philip Weinstein, Peter Milgrom, Olafur Hoskuldsson, Daniel Golletz, Ellen Jeffcott, and Mark Koday

PURPOSE: To measure children's control strategies at the dentist.

DESCRIPTION: The CDCA is a 20-item instrument designed as a situationally
specific measure of control strategies for children visiting the dentist. The
CDCA is based on the importance of individuals feeling "in control," especially the desire to exercise control over the environment in stressful dental
and medical settings. The CDCA is based on the evidence that style of coping varies across situations for children as well as adults, so that the effect of
desire for control also may vary depending upon the setting. This suggests
the need for situationally specific measures of control; there have been few if
any measures such as this developed for children. This measure is based on
the finding that children who reported pain and perceived lack of control
were 16 times less likely to return to the same dentist than those who did not
experience pain or lack of control The CDCA also allows tracking of intervention studies that would enhance children's control in dental care settings.
The current version of the CDCA has 20 items, most of which have two to
three parts.

NORMS: The CDCA was developed with a series of pilot and subsequent studies with a group of school children in Seattle, Washington. The main study
involved 180 children who were 8 to 14 years old, 58.9% female, in third and
fifth grade classrooms in two Catholic schools, with a mean age of 10.8
years. The children were drawn from a multiracial population with a broad
range of socioeconomic backgrounds. Factor analysis revealed five subscales. The first subscale is dentist-mediated control (items 2, 3, 4, 5, and 6)
with a mean of 6.9 (SD = 2.7) where 15 represents the need for maximum
control. The second subscale was active coping (items 16, 17, and 18) with a
mean of 3.2 (SD = 2.2) where 9 represents a need for maximum control. Factor 3 is cognitive withdrawal (items 8, 13, and 15) with a mean of 2.6 (SD =
1.9) where 9 indicates a need for maximum control. Factor 4 is reassurance
(items 1 and 13) with a mean of 3.0 (SD = 1.3) where 6 is a need for maximal control. The last factor is physical escape (items 7, 9, and 10) with a
mean of 2.4 (SD = 1.8) where 9 indicates a desire for maximal control. The
subscales have been rescaled so that 100 indicates the need for maximal control so that the following mean scores can provide norms: dentist-mediated
control = 46; active coping = 36; cognitive withdrawal = 29; reassurance =
50; and physical escape = 27.

SCORING: The subscales and the total score are simple sums of individual item
scores with "True" receiving a score of 3, "Sometimes" a score of 2, and

"False" a score of 1. Each of the subscales is expressed as the average of the items completed.

RELIABILITY: The subscales had only fair internal consistencies with alpha coefficients of the respective subscales, in order, being .68, .70, .60, .55, and .52. No data on stability were presented.

VALIDITY: The CDCA has good concurrent validity with all subscales significantly related to the Childrens' Fear Survey Schedule, and all but the first subscale being significantly related to children's expressed fear of returning to the dentist.

PRIMARY REFERENCE: Weinstein, P. et al. (1996). Situation-specific child control: A visit to the dentist, *Behaviour Research and Therapy,* 34, 11–21.

AVAILABILITY: Dr. Peter Milgrom, Dental Public Health Sciences, University of Washington, Box 357475, Seattle, WA 98195-7475. Reprinted with permission of the authors.

CDCA

Please circle either True (T), Sometimes (S), or False (F) to each question. Try your best to answer even if you are not sure.

Each question in this next section has two parts: What happened at the *last* appointment and what you want at the *next* visit.

		True	Sometimes	False
1a.	*At the last visit* the dentist told me everything would be okay.	T	S	F
1b.	*Next time* I want the dentist to tell me everything will be okay.	T	S	F
2a.	*At the last visit* the dentist asked me how I felt.	T	S	F
2b.	*Next time* I want the dentist to ask me how I feel.	T	S	F
3a.	*At the last visit* I asked the dentist questions.	T	S	F
3b.	*At the last visit* the dentist did not answer my questions.	T	S	F
3c.	*Next time* I want the dentist to answer my questions.	T	S	F
4a.	*At the last visit* the dentist let me have a rest.	T	S	F
4b.	*Next time* I want to have a rest.	T	S	F
5a.	*At the last visit* I asked the dentist to stop.	T	S	F
5b.	*At the last visit* the dentist didn't stop when I asked.	T	S	F
5c.	*Next time* I want the dentist to stop when I ask.	T	S	F
6a.	*At the last visit* someone in my family was in the room with me.	T	S	F
6b.	*Next time* I want someone in my family in the room with me.	T	S	F
7a.	*At the last visit,* they asked me to breathe some special stuff.	T	S	F
7b.	*Next time* I want them to ask me to breathe the special stuff.	T	S	F
8a.	*At the last visit* I was very sleepy.	T	S	F
8b.	*Next time* I want to be sleepy again.	T	S	F
9a.	*At the last visit* they let me watch what was going on.	T	S	F
9b.	*Next time* I want them to let me watch what is going on.	T	S	F
10a.	*At the last visit* they told me how long things would last.	T	S	F
10b.	*Next time* I want them to tell me how long things will last.	T	S	F
11a.	*At the last visit* the dentist told me what was going to happen.	T	S	F
11b.	*Next time* I want the dentist to tell me what will happen.	T	S	F

12a.	*At the last visit* I tried not to think about what the dentist was doing.	T	S	F
12b.	*Next time* I do not want to think about what the dentist is doing.	T	S	F
13a.	*At the last visit* someone told me a story.	T	S	F
13b.	*Next time* I want someone to tell me a story.	T	S	F
14a.	*At the last visit* the dentist told me I was doing a good job.	T	S	F
14b.	*Next time* I want the dentist to tell me I am doing a good job.	T	S	F
15a.	*At the last visit* I tried to think about something else while the dentist worked.	T	S	F
15b.	*Next time* I want to think about something else while the dentist works.	T	S	F
16a.	*At the last visit* the dentist asked me to hold the suction.	T	S	F
16b.	*Next time* I want to hold the suction.	T	S	F
17a.	*At the last visit* I tried to keep myself from getting scared.	T	S	F
17b.	*Next time* I will try to keep myself from getting scared.	T	S	F
18a.	*At the last visit* I tried hard to keep myself calm.	T	S	F
18b.	*Next time* I will try hard to keep myself calm.	T	S	F
19a.	*At the last visit* I listened to music.	T	S	F
19b.	*Next time* I want to listen to music.	T	S	F
20a.	*At the last visit* I felt so sick I wanted to leave.	T	S	F
20b.	*Next time* I'll want to leave if I feel sick.	T	S	F

CHILD REPORT OF POSTTRAUMATIC SYMPTOMS AND PARENT REPORT OF POSTTRAUMATIC SYMPTOMS (CROPS/PROPS)

AUTHORS: Ricky Greenwald and Allen Rubin

PURPOSE: To measure child and parent reports of children's posttraumatic symptoms.

DESCRIPTION: The CROPS is a 25-item instrument for measuring a child's self-report of posttraumatic symptoms. The PROPS is a 30-item instrument designed to measure the parent's report of the child's posttraumatic symptoms. These two measures were developed based on the increasing recognition of the widespread nature of child trauma and its detrimental effect on psychosocial development and quality of life. Any number of situations could induce traumatic reactions in children ranging from abuse to natural disaster or violence. Thus it is very important to have a very simple direct measure of children's own assessment of their posttraumatic reactions. However, the nature of this problem is such that while children can report on some aspects of their feelings, they may be poor observers of their own behavior. Thus the PROPS was developed to enhance the observations of the children's behavior regarding posttraumatic stress. These two scales make important contributions for assessing the existence of posttraumatic symptoms in children, but also can be very important to evaluate changes in posttraumatic stress status due to clinical interventions. Both scales were developed to include those symptoms that the empirical literature has identified as related to traumatic stress in children as well as to reflect the *DSM-IV.*

NORMS: The CROPS and PROPS were developed using community samples of children in grades 4 through 8 in two urban schools and grades 3 through 6 in two rural schools and their parents. One hundred and fifty-two questionnaires from the urban schools and 54 from the rural schools were eventually returned. Of those who indicated ethnicity, 53% were African-American, 23% were Hispanic, 17% were white, and 7% were other. The median age of students was 11.5 years with 51% being girls and 49% being boys. The mean on the CROPS was 19.7 (SD = 10.4), and on the PROPS the mean was 18.3 (SD = 11.7). The SEM on the CROPS was .73 and on the PROPS was .81.

SCORING: Each scale is easily scored by summing item responses. The total possible range of scores on the CROPS was 0 to 52 and on the PROPS was 0 to 60, with higher scores on both scales indicating higher degrees of posttraumatic stress.

RELIABILITY: The CROPS and PROPS have excellent internal consistency with the alpha for CROPS of .91 and the alpha for PROPS at .93. Both measures also were stable with four-to-six-week test-retest correlation of .80 on CROPS and .79 for PROPS.

VALIDITY: The CROPS and PROPS appear to have very good concurrent validity as evidenced by correlations between both the CROPS and PROPS and clinician ratings based on the Lifetime Incidence of Traumatic Events Checklist, indicating what types of trauma or losses a child had experienced at what age and how many times. The correlations between the LITE ratings and both the CROPS and PROPS were significant at the .001 level supporting the concurrent validity of both measures. Suggested cutting points based on the ratings on the LITE are 16 for the PROPS and 19 for the CROPS with scores above the cutting point indicating greater problems in the area of post-traumatic stress.

PRIMARY REFERENCE: Greenwald, R. and Rubin, A. (1999). Assessment of posttraumatic symptoms in children: Development and preliminary validation of parent and child scales, *Research on Social Work Practice,* 9, 61–75.

AVAILABILITY: Dr. Ricky Greenwald at rickygr@childtrauma.com.

CROPS

Mark how true each statement feels for you *in the past week.* Don't skip any, even if you're not sure. There is no right or wrong answer. Answer by circling 0 for none, 1 for some, and 2 for lots.

0 = None
1 = Some
2 = Lots

1.	I daydream.	0	1	2
2.	I "space out" when people are talking to me.	0	1	2
3.	I find it hard to concentrate.	0	1	2
4.	I think about bad things that have happened.	0	1	2
5.	I try to forget about bad things that have happened.	0	1	2
6.	I avoid reminders of bad things that have happened.	0	1	2
7.	I worry that bad things will happen.	0	1	2
8.	I do special things to make sure nothing bad happens.	0	1	2
9.	I do some things that I'm probably too old for.	0	1	2
10.	It is hard for me to go to sleep at night.	0	1	2
11.	I have bad dreams or nightmares.	0	1	2
12.	I get headaches.	0	1	2
13.	I get stomachaches.	0	1	2
14.	I feel sick or have pains.	0	1	2
15.	I feel tired or have low energy.	0	1	2
16.	I feel all alone.	0	1	2
17.	I feel strange or different than other kids.	0	1	2
18.	I feel like there's something wrong with me.	0	1	2
19.	I feel like it's my fault when bad things happen.	0	1	2
20.	I'm a jinx, or bad-luck charm.	0	1	2
21.	I feel sad or depressed.	0	1	2
22.	I don't feel like doing much.	0	1	2
23.	Things make me upset or mad.	0	1	2
24.	I'm on the lookout for bad things that might happen.	0	1	2
25.	I am nervous or jumpy.	0	1	2

Crops 1.0 copyright © Ricky Greenwald, 1996.

PROPS

Mark how well each item describes your child *in the past week.* Circle the 0 if the item is *not true* or *rarely true* of the child. Circle the 1 if the item is *somewhat* or *sometimes true* of the child. Circle the 2 if the item is *very true* or *often true* of the child. Don't skip any, even if you're not sure.

0 = None
1 = Some
2 = Lots

1.	Difficulty concentrating	0	1	2
2.	Mood swings	0	1	2
3.	Thinks of bad memories	0	1	2
4.	Spaces out	0	1	2
5.	Feels too guilty	0	1	2
6.	Anxious	0	1	2
7.	Irrational fears	0	1	2
8.	Repeats the same game or activity	0	1	2
9.	Clings to adults	0	1	2
10.	Avoids former interests	0	1	2
11.	Fights	0	1	2
12.	Bossy with peers	0	1	2
13.	Sad or depressed	0	1	2
14.	Hyper-alert	0	1	2
15.	Feels picked on	0	1	2
16.	Gets in trouble	0	1	2
17.	Worries	0	1	2
18.	Fearful	0	1	2
19.	Withdrawn	0	1	2
20.	Nervous	0	1	2
21.	Startles easily	0	1	2
22.	Irritable	0	1	2
23.	Quick temper	0	1	2
24.	Argues	0	1	2
25.	Secretive	0	1	2
26.	Doesn't care anymore	0	1	2
27.	Difficulty sleeping	0	1	2
28.	Nightmares or bad dreams	0	1	2
29.	Stomachaches	0	1	2
30.	Headaches	0	1	2

PROPS 1.1 copyright © Ricky Greenwald, 1996.

CHILDHOOD PERSONALITY SCALE (CPS)

AUTHORS: Eleanor Dibble and Donald J. Cohen

PURPOSE: To measure a child's general personality and competence.

DESCRIPTION: The CPS is a 40-item instrument designed to be completed by a parent as a way of measuring a child's personality and competence. The CPS was designed by selecting 24 behavior categories that covered the broad domain of descriptors for children's behavior and writing two behaviorally descriptive items for each category, half of which are viewed as socially desirable (positive), and half of which are viewed as socially undesirable (negative). Each parent is asked to rate on a 7-point scale (0–6) the degree to which he or she perceived each of the items to be an accurate description of the child's behavior during the preceding two months. Following preliminary testing, the scale was reduced to 40 items as reproduced here.

NORMS: The CPS was studied initially with five groups of parents and one group of teachers; although an exact number is not provided, over 450 sets of parents and five teachers participated. Some of the children evaluated were described as including "normal," and others as "behaviorally disturbed"; some were subjects in an epidemiological study of twins and siblings, and others were inpatients in a pediatric service and children's clinic. No other demographic data were reported, nor were actual norms reported.

SCORING: The 40 items of the CPS are presented as 7-item (0–6) Likert-type scales. Scores are derived by simply adding up the individual item scores. The final 25 items request respondents to answer in two ways for comparison purposes: How they are and how the ideal parent would be.

RELIABILITY: Specific reliability coefficients were not reported for the CPS. However, the authors report good split-half reliability, and good test-retest reliability, with few if any significant differences between mothers and fathers between test and retest.

VALIDITY: The authors report good face validity. The CPS also shows good concurrent validity, demonstrating significant correlations with a variety of ratings and measures in a nursery school setting such as active coping, originality and tractability, dependency, play involvement, maturity, and fearfulness.

PRIMARY REFERENCE: Dibble, E. and Cohen, D. J. (1974). Companion instruments for measuring children's competence and parental style, *Archives of General Psychiatry*, 30, 805–815.

AVAILABILITY: Journal article.

CPS

The purpose of this questionnaire is to get a picture of each child's personality as he or she typically has been for the last two months. Some of the sentences may describe this child very well. Other sentences will not be at all like this child. There are seven columns after each sentence. For each sentence, check the column that is most true of this child's personality and the way he acts.

	Never	Almost never	Seldom	Half the time	Fre-quently	Almost always	Always
	1	2	3	4	5	6	7
Will talk or babble to you about his/her toys, clothes, and what he/she is doing							
Tends to be fussy and complains. Generally is not satisfied							
Plays for a long time in the same way with one toy or thing. Repeats over and over.							
Smiles to a friendly person							
Turns his/her head away or looks down in an uncomfortable way when people pay attention to him/her							
Tries out a toy in many different ways. Is curious about what he/she can get something to do							
Quickly shows his/her anger and frustration if he/she can't get something done that he/she is working on							

	Never	Almost never	Seldom	Half the time	Fre- quently	Almost always	Always
	1	2	3	4	5	6	7
Persists in trying to do something, even if he/she has some small problems along the way							
Likes to be with people rather than by himself/herself							
Loses interest in what he/she has started doing. Goes from one thing to another							
Is agreeable to play with something, take a walk, wash up, or eat when someone suggests it							
Can get away from you "quick as a flash" when he/she wants to							
Sits without doing anything unless another person tries hard to get him/her interested							
Babbles or talks with delight. Gets pleasure out of almost everything							
Jumps, runs, and is on the move. Can't seem to be still for long							

There are two columns for each sentence. Within each column is a scale from 0 to 6. First, check the box in the first column that describes you today. Second, check the box from the second column that describes the ideal parent.

	COLUMN 1 How I Really Am							COLUMN 2 How the Ideal Parent Would Be						
	Never	Almost never	Seldom	Half the time	Frequently	Almost always	Always	Never	Almost never	Seldom	Half the time	Frequently	Almost always	Always
	0	1	2	3	4	5	6	0	1	2	3	4	5	6
I tell him/her how happy he/she makes me.														
I like him/her to do things his/her way.														
I encourage him/her to tell me what he/she is thinking and feeling.														
I make decisions with him/her.														
I see to it that he/she obeys what he/she is told.														
I ignore misbehavior.														

491

	COLUMN 1 How I Really Am							COLUMN 2 How the Ideal Parent Would Be						
	Never 0	Almost never 1	Seldom 2	Half the time 3	Frequently 4	Almost always 5	Always 6	Never 0	Almost never 1	Seldom 2	Half the time 3	Frequently 4	Almost always 5	Always 6
I forget rules that have been made.														
I explain to him/her why he/she is being punished.														
I warn him/her about future punishments to prevent him/her from acting badly.														
I feel close to him/her both when he/she is happy and when he/she is worried.														
I let him/her know all I have done for him/her when I want him/her to obey.														
I check on what he's/she's doing and whom he/she is seeing all during the day.														
I use physical punishment.														

	COLUMN 1 How I Really Am							COLUMN 2 How the Ideal Parent Would Be						
	Never 0	Almost never 1	Seldom 2	Half the time 3	Frequently 4	Almost always 5	Always 6	Never 0	Almost never 1	Seldom 2	Half the time 3	Frequently 4	Almost always 5	Always 6
I give him/her a lot of care and attention.														
I prefer going places and doing things without him/her.														
I avoid looking at him/her when I am disappointed in him/her.														
I enjoy listening to him/her and doing things with him/her.														
I am aware of his/her need for privacy.														
I know how he/she feels without his/her saying.														
I let him/her help me decide about things that affect him/her.														

	COLUMN 1 How I Really Am							COLUMN 2 How the Ideal Parent Would Be						
	Never	Almost never	Seldom	Half the time	Frequently	Almost always	Always	Never	Almost never	Seldom	Half the time	Frequently	Almost always	Always
	0	1	2	3	4	5	6	0	1	2	3	4	5	6
I punish him/her for disobeying.														
I allow things to be left undone.														
I enforce rules depending upon my mood.														
I set limits for activities to help him/her stay out of trouble.														
I keep reminding him/her of past bad behavior.														

CHILD'S ATTITUDE TOWARD FATHER (CAF) AND MOTHER (CAM) SCALES

AUTHOR: Walter W. Hudson

PURPOSE: To measure problems children have with their parents.

DESCRIPTION: The CAF and CAM are 25-item instruments designed to measure the extent, degree, or severity of problems a child has with his or her father or mother. The instruments are identical except for the interchangeable use of the word "father" or "mother." The CAF and CAM have two cutting scores. The first is a score of 30 (±5); scores below this point indicate absence of a clinically significant problem in this area. Scores above 30 suggest the presence of a clinically significant problem. The second cutting score is 70. Scores above this point nearly always indicate that clients are experiencing severe stress with a clear possibility that some type of violence could be considered or used to deal with problems. The practitioner should be aware of this possibility. An advantage of these instruments is that they are administered and scored in the same way as the other scales of the WALMYR Assessment Scales package reproduced here.

NORMS: The CAF and CAM were developed using 1072 students of heterogeneous backgrounds from the seventh through twelfth grades. Respondents were Caucasian, Japanese and Chinese Americans, and a smaller number of members of other ethnic groups. The scales are not recommended for use with children under the age of 12. Actual norms are not available.

SCORING: Like most WALMYR Assessment Scales instruments, the CAF and CAM are scored by first reverse-scoring items listed at the bottom of the page (2, 3, 8, 12, 14–16, 21, and 24), summing the scores, subtracting the number of completed items, multiplying this figure by 100, and dividing by the number of items completed times 6. This will produce a range from 0 to 100 with higher scores indicating greater magnitude or severity of problems.

RELIABILITY: The CAF has a mean alpha of .95 and an excellent (low) Standard Error of Measurement of 4.56; the CAM has a mean alpha of .94 and a Standard Error of Measurement of 4.57; both possess excellent internal consistency. Both measures also have excellent stability with one-week test-retest correlations of .96 (CAF) and .95 (CAM).

VALIDITY: The CAF and CAM have excellent known-groups validity, both significantly distinguishing between children who rate themselves as having relationship problems with their parents and those who don't. The CAF and CAM also have good predictive validity, significantly predicting children's responses to questions regarding problems with their parents.

PRIMARY REFERENCE: Hudson, W. W. (1997). *The WALMYR Assessment Scales Scoring Manual.* Tallahassee, FL: WALMYR Publishing Company.

AVAILABILITY: This scale cannot be reproduced or copied in any manner and must be obtained by writing to the WALMYR Publishing Company, PO Box 12217, Tallahassee, FL 32317-2217 or by calling (850) 383-0045.

CHILD'S ATTITUDE TOWARD FATHER (CAF)

Name: _____ Today's Date: _____

This questionnaire is designed to measure the degree of contentment you have in your relationship with your father. It not a test, so there are no right or wrong answers. Answer each item as carefully and as accurately as you can by placing number beside each one as follows.

1 = None of the time
2 = Very rarely
3 = A little of the time
4 = Some of the time
5 = A good part of the time
6 = Most of the time
7 = All of the time

1. _____ My father gets on my nerves.
2. _____ I get along well with my father.
3. _____ I feel that I can really trust my father.
4. _____ I dislike my father.
5. _____ My father's behavior embarrasses me.
6. _____ My father is too demanding.
7. _____ I wish I had a different father.
8. _____ I really enjoy my father.
9. _____ My father puts too many limits on me.
10. _____ My father interferes with my activities.
11. _____ I resent my father.
12. _____ I think my father is terrific.
13. _____ I hate my father.
14. _____ My father is very patient with me.
15. _____ I really like my father.
16. _____ I like being with my father.
17. _____ I feel like I do not love my father.
18. _____ My father is very irritating.
19. _____ I feel very angry toward my father.
20. _____ I feel violent toward my father.
21. _____ I feel proud of my father.
22. _____ I wish my father was more like others I know.
23. _____ My father does not understand me.
24. _____ I can really depend on my father.
25. _____ I feel ashamed of my father.

Copyright (c) 1992, Walter W. Hudson   **Illegal to Photocopy or Otherwise Reprod**

2, 3, 8, 12, 14, 15, 16, 21, 24.

CHILD'S ATTITUDE TOWARD MOTHER (CAM)

Name: _____ Today's Date: _____

This questionnaire is designed to measure the degree of contentment you have in your relationship with your mother. It is not a test, so there are no right or wrong answers. Answer each item as carefully and as accurately as you can by placing a number beside each one as follows.

    1 = None of the time
    2 = Very rarely
    3 = A little of the time
    4 = Some of the time
    5 = A good part of the time
    6 = Most of the time
    7 = All of the time

---

1. ____ My mother gets on my nerves.
2. ____ I get along well with my mother.
3. ____ I feel that I can really trust my mother.
4. ____ I dislike my mother.
5. ____ My mother's behavior embarrasses me.
6. ____ My mother is too demanding.
7. ____ I wish I had a different mother.
8. ____ I really enjoy my mother.
9. ____ My mother puts too many limits on me.
10. ____ My mother interferes with my activities.
11. ____ I resent my mother.
12. ____ I think my mother is terrific.
13. ____ I hate my mother.
14. ____ My mother is very patient with me.
15. ____ I really like my mother.
16. ____ I like being with my mother.
17. ____ I feel like I do not love my mother.
18. ____ My mother is very irritating.
19. ____ I feel very angry toward my mother.
20. ____ I feel violent toward my mother.
21. ____ I feel proud of my mother.
22. ____ I wish my mother was more like others I know.
23. ____ My mother does not understand me.
24. ____ I can really depend on my mother.
25. ____ I feel ashamed of my mother.

Copyright (c) 1992, Walter W. Hudson   **Illegal to Photocopy or Otherwise Reproduce**

2, 3, 8, 12, 14, 15, 16, 21, 24.

CHILDREN'S ACTION TENDENCY SCALE (CATS)

AUTHOR: Robert H. Deluty

PURPOSE: To measure assertiveness in children

DESCRIPTION: This 39-item instrument measures assertive, aggressive, and submissive behavior in children. The scale was originally developed with three pairs of possible responses to each of the 13 conflict situations; the three pairs of responses represent all combinations of assertive, aggressive, or submissive ways of behaving in the conflict. For each of the pairs of alternatives the child is asked to select one which best describes how he or she would behave. For young children, below a fourth or fifth grade level, the items can be read aloud, although this may require frequent repetition of the items. A valid short version can be created by eliminating items 3, 12, and 13. The opening paragraph on the questionnaire ordinarily is not included.

NORMS: The CATS was originally tested on a sample of 46 parochial school children from grades three, four, and six. There was a total of 27 boys and 19 girls. The mean aggressiveness score was 7.93 for boys and 5.05 for girls. The average assertiveness scores were 14.48 for boys and 16.21 for girls. The average submissiveness score was 7.59 for boys and 8.74 for girls. The means are based on a 30-item instrument. Norms also are available for public school children.

SCORING: The respondent is instructed to read both alternatives in each item and circle the one alternative from each pair that is most like how he or she would behave. Scores on each of the three dimensions are the total number of aggressive, assertive, and submissive alternatives circled as coded in parentheses next to each situation. These codes are not included on the questionnaire for respondents. Since each situation has all possible combinations of aggressive, assertive, and submissive responses, a child could select any one type of alternative twice. For this reason scores on the scales range from 0 to 26, but all three scales must total 39 for the long form. Higher scores reflect more aggression, assertion, and submission.

RELIABILITY: Reliability has been estimated with internal consistency and test-retest reliability methods with the parochial school sample. The coefficients of internal consistency using split-half reliability were .77, .63, and .72 for the aggressiveness, assertiveness, and submission scales. Test-retest reliability over a four-month interval was .48, .60, and .57. While the test-retest reliability may seem low, for a children's measure over a four-month period, this is acceptable.

VALIDITY: The CATS generally has very good validity data. Construct and concurrent validity are demonstrated in correlations with scores on a self-esteem measure, and peer and teacher rating of interpersonal behavior.

Scores also discriminate between samples of clinically aggressive and normal subjects indicating good known-groups validity. Behavioral observations also provide validity support.

PRIMARY REFERENCE: Deluty, R. H. (1979). Children's Action Tendency Scale: A self-reported measure of aggressiveness, assertiveness, and submissiveness in children, *Journal of Consulting and Clinical Psychology*, 47, 1061–1071. Instrument reproduced with permission of Robert Deluty and the American Psychological Association.

AVAILABILITY: Robert H. Deluty, Ph.D., Department of Psychology, University of Maryland, Baltimore County, Baltimore, MD 21228.

CATS

Below are thirteen situations. After each you are asked to decide what you would do in that situation by selecting *one* of the choices from each of the three pairs of alternatives. Indicate your answer by circling either alternative "a" or alternative "b." Remember to select one answer for each of the 36 pairs of choices. We are concerned with what you *would* do and not with what you *should* do. There are no "right" or "wrong" answers. You are not going to be graded on this, so please be honest.

1. You're playing a game with your friends. You try your very best but you keep making mistakes. Your friends start teasing you and calling you names. What would you do?

   a. Punch the kid who's teasing me the most, *or* (Agg)
   b. Quit the game and come home (Sub)

   a. Tell them to stop because they wouldn't like it if I did it to them (As), *or*
   b. Punch the kid who's teasing me the most

   a. Quit the game and come home, *or*
   b. Tell them to stop because they wouldn't like it if I did it to them

2. You and a friend are playing in your house. Your friend makes a big mess, but your parents blame you and punish you. What would you do?

   a. Ask my friend to help me clean up the mess, *or* (As)
   b. Refuse to talk to or listen to my parents the next day (Agg)

   a. Clean up the mess, *or* (Sub)
   b. Ask my friend to help me clean up the mess

   a. Refuse to talk to or listen to my parents the next day, *or*
   b. Clean up the mess

3. One morning before class, a friend comes over to you and asks if they can copy your homework. They tell you that if you don't give them your answers, they'll tell everyone that you're really mean. What would you do?

   a. Tell them to do their own work, *or* (As)
   b. Give them the answers (Sub)

   a. Tell them that I'll tell everyone they're a cheater, *or* (Agg)
   b. Tell them to do their own work

   a. Give them the answers, *or*
   b. Tell them that I'll tell everyone they're a cheater.,

4. You're standing in line for a drink of water. A kid your age and size walks over and just shoves you out of line. What would you do?

    a.   Push the kid back out of line, or (Agg)
    b.   Tell the kid, "You've no right to do that." (As)

    a.   I'd go to the end of the line, or (Sub)
    b.   Push the kid back out of line

    a.   Tell the kid, "You've no right to do that," or
    b.   I'd go to the end of the line

5. You lend a friend your favorite book. A few days later it is returned, but some of the pages are torn and the cover is dirty and bent out of shape. What would you do?

    a.   Ask my friend, "How did it happen?" or (As)
    b.   Call the kid names (Agg)

    a.   Ignore it, or (Sub)
    b.   Ask my friend, "How did it happen?"

    a.   Call the kid names, or
    b.   Ignore it

6. You're coming out of school. A kid who is smaller and younger than you are throws a snowball right at your head. What would you do?

    a.   Beat the kid up, or (Agg)
    b.   Ignore it (Sub)

    a.   Tell the kid that throwing at someone's head is very dangerous, (As)
         or
    b.   Beat the kid up

    a.   Ignore it, or
    b.   Tell the kid that throwing at someone's head is very dangerous

7. You see some kids playing a game. You walk over and ask if you can join. They tell you that you can't play with them because you're not good enough. What would you do?

    a.   Ask them to give me a chance, or (As)
    b.   Walk away, feeling hurt (Sub)

    a.   Interfere with their game so that they won't be able to play, or (Agg)
    b.   Ask them to give me a chance

    a.   Walk away, feeling hurt, or
    b.   Interfere with their game so that they won't be able to play

8. You're watching a really terrific show on television. In the middle of the show, your parents tell you that it's time for bed and turn off the TV. What would you do?

   a. Scream at them "I don't want to!" *or* (Agg)
   b. Start crying (Sub)

   a. Promise to go to bed early tomorrow night if they let me stay (As) up late tonight, *or*
   b. Scream at them, "I don't want to!"

   a. Start crying, *or*
   b. Promise to go to bed early tomorrow night if they let me stay up late tonight

9. You're having lunch in the cafeteria. Your friend has a big bag of delicious chocolates for dessert. You ask if you can have just one, but your friend says, "No." What would you do?

   a. Offer to trade something of mine for the chocolate, *or* (As)
   b. Call the kid mean and selfish (Agg)

   a. Forget about it and continue eating my lunch, *or* (Sub)
   b. Offer to trade something of mine for the chocolate

   a. Call the kid mean and selfish, *or*
   b. Forget about it and continue eating my lunch

10. A kid in your class brags that they're much smarter than you. However, you know for sure that the kid is wrong and that really you're smarter. What would you do?

    a. Tell the kid to shut up, *or* (Agg)
    b. Suggest that we ask each other questions to find out who is smarter (As)

    a. Ignore the kid and just walk away, *or* (Sub)
    b. Tell the kid to shut up

    a. Suggest that we ask each other questions to find out who is smarter, *or*
    b. Ignore the kid and just walk away

11. You and another kid are playing a game. The winner of the game will win a really nice prize. You try very hard, but lose by just one point. What would you do?

    a. Tell the kid that they cheated, *or* (Agg)
    b. Practice, so I'll win the next time (As)

a. Go home and cry, *or* (Sub)
b. Tell the kid that they cheated

a. Practice, so I'll win the next time, *or*
b. Go home and cry

12. Your parents do something that really bugs you. They know that it bugs you, but they just ignore how you feel and keep doing it anyway. What would you do?

a. Get back at them by doing something that bugs them, *or* (Agg)
b. Tell them that they are bugging me (As)

a. Try to ignore it, *or* (Sub)
b. Get back at them by doing something that bugs them

a. Tell them that they are bugging me, *or*
b. Try to ignore it

13. You're playing with a friend in your house and you're making a lot of noise. Your parents get really angry and start yelling at you for making so much noise. What would you do?

a. Find something else to do, *or* (Sub)
b. Ignore their yelling and continue to make noise (Agg)

a. Tell them, "I'm sorry, but I can't play the game without making noise," *or* (As)
b. Find something else to do

a. Ignore their yelling and continue to make noise, *or*
b. Tell them, "I'm sorry, but I can't play the game without making noise."

CHILDREN'S ATTRIBUTIONAL STYLE
QUESTIONNAIRE—REVISED (CASQ-R)

AUTHORS: M. Thompson, N. J. Kaslow, B. Weiss, and S. Nolen-Hoeksema
PURPOSE: To measure children's attributional style.
DESCRIPTION: The CASQ-R is a 24-item instrument designed to measure attributional style for children. The measure is a revision of an earlier longer questionnaire, and tests the attributional reformulation of the learned helplessness model of depression in children. Research has shown that children who report more depressive symptoms tend to blame themselves for negative events (internal) and view the causes of these events as consistent over time (stable) and generalizable across situations (global). Conversely, these children tend to attribute positive events to factors outside of themselves (external) and to view the causes of those events as inconsistent over time (unstable) and situation specific (specific). The CASQ-R, therefore, can be a useful measure to help practitioners in both assessing and trying to modify children's depressive feelings and behaviors.
NORMS: The CASQ-R was studied with 1086 children, 9 to 12 years old (mean age = 10.34, SD = 1.03) who were elementary and middle school students in nine public schools in a southeastern city. The sample was 48% male and 52% female with 56% being African-American and 44% Caucasian. Students were from a variety of middle-income and lower-income neighborhoods. The means and standard deviations for the CASQ-R were reported by gender, race, and age. For boys the mean overall score was 4.83 (SD = 3.36); for girls the mean overall score was 4.91 (SD = 3.42). For African-American children the mean overall score was 4.93 (SD = 3.22); for Caucasian children, the mean overall score was 4.78 (SD = 3.60). For children 9 and 10 years old, the mean overall score was 4.73 (SD = 3.35); for children 11 and 12 years old, the mean overall score was 5.13 (SD = 3.66). The original article also reports subscale scores in that half of the 24 forced-choice items address positive outcomes and half address negative outcomes. The subscale scores are also reported by gender, race, and age. The means for the overall score range from 4.87 (SD = 3.39) to 4.96 (SD = 3.49) over two times of testing.
SCORING: The CASQ-R includes 24 forced-choice items, half addressing positive outcomes and half addressing negative outcomes. Following each item, in parentheses, is the choice (A or B) leading to a score of 1 for that item. Positive events include internality: items 5(A), 8(A), 23(A), and 24(B); stability: items 9(A), 17(A), 18(B), and 19(A); globality: items 1(A), 13(B), 16(B), and 20(B). The composite score for positive events (CP) is the sum of these subscales, with higher scores indicating a less depressive attributional style. Negative events are internality: items 2(B), 3(B), 10(A), and 21(A); stability: items 6(A), 12(B), 14(A), and 15(B); globality: items 4(B), 7(B),

11(B), and 22(A). The composite score for negative events (CN) equals the sum of these subscales, with higher scores indicating a more depressed attributional style. For the overall composite score (CP – CN), lower scores indicate more depressive attributional styles.

RELIABILITY: The CASQ-R has only fair internal consistency with alphas for the overall composite score equaling .61. Alphas for the positive composite and the negative composite were lower and ranged from .45 to .60. Stability of the CASQ-R was also established by calculating test-retest reliabilities over 6 months with an overall composite correlation of .53 suggesting fair stability over such a long period of time. The data also are available in the original article for the subscales and separately by gender, age, and race categories.

VALIDITY: The CASQ-R has established good concurrent validity with the overall, positive, and negative composite scores all correlating significantly and in the predicted direction with scores on the Vanderbilt Depression Inventory. Overall children with more maladaptive attributional styles on the CASQ-R reported more symptoms of depression on the Vanderbilt Depression Inventory.

PRIMARY REFERENCE: Thompson, M., Kaslow, N. J., Weiss, B., and Nolen-Hoeksema, S. (1998). Children's attributional style questionnaire—revised: Psychometric examination, *Psychological Assessment, 10*, 166–170.

AVAILABILITY: Nadine Kaslow, Ph.D., Emory University, Department of Psychiatry, Grady Health System, 80 Butler St. S. E., Atlanta, GA 30335.

CASQ-R

1. You get an "A" on a test.
    A. I am smart
    B. I am good in the subject that the test was in.

2. Some kids that you know say that they do not like you.
    A. Once in a while people are mean to me.
    B. Once in a while I am mean to other people.

3. A good friend tells you that he hates you.
    A. My friend was in a bad mood that day.
    B. I wasn't nice to my friend that day.

4. A person steals money from you.
    A. That person is not honest.
    B. Many people are not honest.

5. Your parents tell you something that you make is very good.
    A. I am good at making some things.
    B. My parents like some things I make.

6. You break a glass.
    A. I am not careful enough.
    B. Sometimes I am not careful enough.

7. You do a project with a group of kids and it turns out badly.
    A. I don't work well with people in that particular group.
    B. I never work well with groups.

8. You make a new friend.
    A. I am a nice person.
    B. The people that I meet are nice.

9. You have been getting along well with your family.
    A. I am usually easy to get along with when I am with my family.
    B. Once in a while I am easy to get along with when I am with my family.

10. You get a bad grade in school.
    A. I am not a good student
    B. Teachers give hard tests.

11. You walk into a door and you get a bloody nose.
    A. I wasn't looking where I was going.
    B. I have been careless lately.

12. You have a messy room.
    A. I did not clean my room that day.
    B. I usually do not clean my room.

13. Your mother makes you your favorite dinner.
    A. There are a few things that my mother will do to please me.
    B. My mother usually likes to please me.

14. A team that you are on loses a game.
    A. The team members don't help each other when they play together.
    B. That day the team members didn't help each other.

15. You do not get your chores done at home.
    A. I was lazy that day.
    B. Many days I am lazy.

16. You go to an amusement park and you have a good time.
    A. I usually enjoy myself at amusement parks.
    B. I usually enjoy myself in many activities.

17. You go to a friend's party and you have fun.
    A. Your friend usually gives good parties.
    B. Your friend gave a good party that day.

18. You have a substitute teacher and she likes you.
    A. I was well behaved during class that day
    B. I am almost always well behaved during class.

19. You make your friends happy.
    A. I am usually a fun person to be with.
    B. Sometimes I am a fun person to be with.

20. You put a hard puzzle together.
    A. I am good at putting puzzles together.
    B. I am good at doing many things.

21. You try out for a sports team and do not make it.
    A. I am not good at sports.
    B. The other kids who tried out were very good at sports.

22. You fail a test.
    A. All tests are hard.
    B. Only some tests are hard.

23. You hit a home run in a ball game.
    A. I swung the bat just right.
    B. The pitcher threw an easy pitch.

24. You do the best in your class on a paper.
    A. The other kids in my class did not work hard on their papers.
    B. I worked hard on the paper.

CHILDREN'S BELIEFS ABOUT PARENTAL DIVORCE SCALE (CBAPS)

AUTHORS: Lawrence A. Kurdek and Berthold Berg

PURPOSE: To measure children's beliefs about parental divorce.

DESCRIPTION: The CBAPS is a 36-item instrument designed to measure children's problematic beliefs about their parents' divorce. Despite the importance to the helping professions of the topic of divorce and its impact on children, few if any measures are available to study this phenomenon. The CBAPS contains six subscales, each with six items (described below), that were selected on the basis of the problematic beliefs cited in the clinical literature. The scale began as a projective test that was revised into a 70-item yes/no objective scale. Item analyses of these 70 items and rewriting to control for a yes/no response set led to the current 36-item version.

NORMS: A total of 170 children from three samples formed the basis for the norming of this measure. The samples included 63 children recruited from court records of divorces in Ohio, 63 from grades 3–6 of a public elementary school, and 44 from grades 7–9 of a junior high school. The total sample included 84 boys and 86 girls. The mean age was 11.06 years and all but two were white. All children had divorced parents. Following are the mean scores and standard deviations for each subscale: peer ridicule and avoidance (items 1, 7, 13, 19, 25, 31)—mean = 1.45, SD = 1.44; paternal blame (items 2, 8, 14, 20, 26, 32)—mean = 1.72, SD = 1.79; fear of abandonment (items 3, 9, 15, 21, 27, 33)—mean = 1.33, SD = 1.56; maternal blame (items 4, 10, 16, 22, 28, 34)—mean = 0.85, SD = 1.41; hope of reunification (items 5, 11, 17, 23, 29, 35)—mean = 1.26, SD = 1.65; self-blame (items 6, 12, 18, 24, 30, 36)—mean = 1.55; SD = 1.38. The mean for the total score was 8.20 with a standard deviation of 4.98.

SCORING: The CBAPS is keyed for problematic responding. A yes response on items 1, 2, 3, 4, 6, 9, 11, 12, 14–20, 22, 23, 27, 29, 30, 35, 36 and a no response on items 5, 7, 8, 13, 21, 24–26, 28, 31–34 indicate a problematic response. Scores for the six subscales are derived by simply summing the number of problematic beliefs within each subscale with a total possible score of six. A total score is derived by summing up the number of problematic beliefs across all items with a total possible score of 36.

RELIABILITY: The CBAPS has good internal consistency, with a Cronbach's alpha for the total score of .80. The alphas for the subscales, in the order presented above were .62, .78, .73, .77, .78 and .54. Stability of the CBAPS was fair, with a nine-week test-retest reliability coefficient of .65 and subscale coefficients, in the same order as above, of .41, .72, .53, .51, .51, and .43 (all statistically significant).

VALIDITY: The CBAPS has fair concurrent validity, with problematic beliefs generally related to self-reported maladjustment. The total scores were significantly related to high anxiety, low self-concept regarding relations with parents, and low social support. The instrument was subjected to a factor analysis that showed all but the fear of abandonment and self-blame subscales emerging as separate and relatively independent factors.

PRIMARY REFERENCE: Kurdek, L. A. and Berg, B. (1987). Children's Beliefs About Parental Divorce Scale: Psychometric characteristics and concurrent validity, *Journal of Consulting and Clinical Psychology*, 55, 712–718.

AVAILABILITY: Professor Larry Kurdek, Wright State University, Department of Psychology, Dayton, OH 45435-0001.

CBAPS

On the following pages are some statements about children and their separated parents. Some of them are true about how you think and feel, so you will want to check YES. Some are NOT TRUE about how you think or feel so you will want to check NO. There are no right or wrong answers. Your answers will just tell us some of the things you are thinking now about your parents' separation.

1.	It would upset me if other kids asked a lot of questions about my parents.	☐ Yes	☐ No
2.	It was usually my father's fault when my parents had a fight.	☐ Yes	☐ No
3.	I sometimes worry that both my parents will want to live without me.	☐ Yes	☐ No
4.	When my family was unhappy it was usually because of my mother.	☐ Yes	☐ No
5.	My parents will always live apart.	☐ Yes	☐ No
6.	My parents often argue with each other after I misbehave.	☐ Yes	☐ No
7.	I like talking to my friends as much now as I used to.	☐ Yes	☐ No
8.	My father is usually a nice person.	☐ Yes	☐ No
9.	It's possible that both my parents will never want to see me again.	☐ Yes	☐ No
10.	My mother is usually a nice person.	☐ Yes	☐ No
11.	If I behave better I might be able to bring my family back together.	☐ Yes	☐ No
12.	My parents would probably be happier if I were never born.	☐ Yes	☐ No
13.	I like playing with my friends as much now as I used to.	☐ Yes	☐ No
14.	When my family was unhappy it was usually because of something my father said or did.	☐ Yes	☐ No
15.	I sometimes worry that I'll be left all alone.	☐ Yes	☐ No
16.	Often I have a bad time when I'm with my mother.	☐ Yes	☐ No
17.	My family will probably do things together just like before.	☐ Yes	☐ No
18.	My parents probably argue more when I'm with them than when I'm gone.	☐ Yes	☐ No
19.	I'd rather be alone than play with other kids.	☐ Yes	☐ No
20.	My father caused most of the trouble in my family.	☐ Yes	☐ No
21.	I feel that my parents still love me.	☐ Yes	☐ No
22.	My mother caused most of the trouble in my family.	☐ Yes	☐ No
23.	My parents will probably see that they have made a mistake and get back together again.	☐ Yes	☐ No
24.	My parents are happier when I'm with them than when I'm not.	☐ Yes	☐ No
25.	My friends and I do many things together.	☐ Yes	☐ No
26.	There are a lot of things about my father I like.	☐ Yes	☐ No

27. I sometimes think that one day I may have to go live with a friend or relative.   ☐ Yes   ☐ No

28. My mother is more good than bad.   ☐ Yes   ☐ No

29. I sometimes think that my parents will one day live together again.   ☐ Yes   ☐ No

30. I can make my parents unhappy with each other by what I say or do.   ☐ Yes   ☐ No

31. My friends understand how I feel about my parents.   ☐ Yes   ☐ No

32. My father is more good than bad.   ☐ Yes   ☐ No

33. I feel my parents still like me.   ☐ Yes   ☐ No

34. There are a lot of things about my mother I like.   ☐ Yes   ☐ No

35. I sometimes think that once my parents realize how much I want them to they'll live together again.   ☐ Yes   ☐ No

36. My parents would probably still be living together if it weren't for me.   ☐ Yes   ☐ No

Copyright © 1987 American Psychological Association. Reprinted by permission.

CHILDREN'S COGNITIVE ASSESSMENT QUESTIONNAIRE (CCAQ)

AUTHORS: Sheri Zatz and Laurie Chassin

PURPOSE: To measure the cognitions associated with test anxiety.

DESCRIPTION: This 40-item instrument measures self-defeating and self-enhancing cognitions associated with test anxiety. The instrument was originally developed for hypothesis testing on the relationship of cognition to test anxiety and task performance. The theoretical perspective asserts that self-defeating thoughts inhibit one's performance while self-enhancing thoughts facilitate performance. The CCAQ focuses on negative self-evaluations (NSE) and positive self-evaluations (PSE) as reflecting self-defeating and self-enhancing cognitions, respectively. It also assesses self-distracting thoughts (called off-task thoughts; OFFT) and cognitions which focus one's attention to the task (called on-task thoughts; ONT). The four aspects of the CCAQ are used as subscales. The CCAQ is particularly useful for practitioners in school settings or residential programs where academic performance is frequently found to be an antecedent to clinical problems and in cognitive therapy.

NORMS: The CCAQ was developed on a sample of 294 fifth and sixth grade children. Fifty-seven percent were female, 89 percent were white, and 55 were from working class families. Subjects were screened for test anxiety and were categorized into three groups: low anxiety ($n = 69$), moderate anxiety ($n = 106$) and high anxiety ($n = 119$). The mean scores on the negative evaluation subscale were .6, 1.4, and 2.7 for the low, moderate, and high anxious subsamples, respectively. Off-task thought means were 2.2, 3.5, and 4.4 for the three respective groups. Mean scores on the positive evaluation subscale were 6.1, 5.7, and 5.2 for the three groups. The mean scores on the on-task thoughts subscale were 6.8, 6.9, and 6.4 for the low, moderate, and high anxious subsamples.

SCORING: Each of the 40 items is answered True or False. Total scores for the four subscales are the number of items answered "true," and they range from 0 to 10. Higher scores reflect more thoughts associated with test anxiety.

RELIABILITY: The subscales had moderate to good internal consistency using coefficient alpha: PSE = .74, NSE = .82, ONT = .67, OFFT = .72. Test-retest reliability correlations for a six-week period were PSE = .71, NSE = .69, ONT = .69, OFFT = .63, which are fairly strong for a children's instrument measured over such a long period.

VALIDITY: The validity of the CCAQ was tested with known-groups procedures. The group of highly anxious children scored differently from less anxious children on all four subscales of the CCAQ. In general, the more anxious children revealed more negative evaluation and off-task thought, and less anxious children scored higher on positive evaluation. The CCAQ subscales have good concurrent validity, with subscales correlating with test anxiety. For the sample of females, only the NSE and OFFT scores correlated with test anxiety.

PRIMARY REFERENCE: Zatz, S. and Chassin, L. (1983). Cognitions of test-anxious children, *Journal of Consulting and Clinical Psychology*, 51, 526–534. Instrument reproduced with permission of the American Psychological Association.

AVAILABILITY: Journal article.

CCAQ

Listed below are four sets of statements. Indicate whether each is true or false of your thoughts while taking the test by circling T (true) or F (false).

Negative evaluations

T	F	The others probably think I'm dumb.
T	F	I have a bad memory.
T	F	I'm doing poorly.
T	F	I can't do this—I give up.
T	F	Everyone usually does better than me.
T	F	I must be making many mistakes.
T	F	I don't do well on tests like this.
T	F	I am too dumb to do this.
T	F	I'm doing worse than the others.
T	F	I really feel stupid.

Off-task thoughts

T	F	I wish I were playing with my friends.
T	F	I am nervous and worried.
T	F	I wish I were home.
T	F	I wish this was over.
T	F	My mind keeps wandering.
T	F	I keep on daydreaming.
T	F	I wonder what the examiner is going to find out about me.
T	F	I can't seem to sit still.
T	F	Pretty soon I'll get to do something else.
T	F	I am hungry.

Positive evaluations

T	F	I am fast enough to finish this.
T	F	I do well on tests like this.
T	F	I usually do better than the others.
T	F	I am bright enough to do this.
T	F	This test is easy for me to do.
T	F	I am doing the best that I can.
T	F	I usually catch on quickly to new things.
T	F	I am doing better than the others.
T	F	I am sure to do fine on this.
T	F	I am able to do well on different things.

On-task thoughts

T	F	Stay calm and relaxed.
T	F	The harder it gets, the more I need to try.
T	F	Try a different plan.
T	F	One step at a time.
T	F	I have a plan to solve this.
T	F	Keep looking for a solution.
T	F	Work faster.
T	F	Pay attention.
T	F	I've almost got it now—keep working.
T	F	Don't think about anything but solving the problem.

CHILDREN'S LONELINESS QUESTIONNAIRE (CLQ)

AUTHOR: Steven R. Asher

PURPOSE: To measure children's feelings of loneliness.

DESCRIPTION: The CLQ includes 16 primary items focused on children's feelings of loneliness, feelings of social adequacy versus inadequacy, and subjective estimations of peer status. Eight "filler" items that ask about children's hobbies and other activities are included to help children feel more relaxed and open about expressing their feelings. Specific instructions, including the way children are taught to use the 5-point scale, are available in Asher et al. (1984). In addition to identifying children who feel lonely, this instrument may be used to examine variables related to that loneliness.

NORMS: A study of an earlier version of the questionnaire was conducted on third to sixth grade children. After modifying the questionnaire, more recent data were collected from 200 children in the third to sixth grades in one elementary school. These children included 89 girls and 111 boys; 80% were white, 16% black, and 4% Asian or Hispanic. All socioeconomic groups seemed represented. No actual norms were reported.

SCORING: Items 2, 5, 7, 11, 13, 15, 19, and 23 are the "filler" items and are not scored. Scores for the 16 5-point items are totaled, producing a potential range of 16 to 80. Items 6, 9, 12, 14, 17, 18, 20, 21, and 24 are reverse-scored. Higher scores reflect more loneliness.

RELIABILITY: The CLQ has excellent internal consistency, with an alpha of .90 for the 16 primary items. A one year test-retest correlation of .55 suggests good long-term stability.

VALIDITY: The major form of validity reported on the CLQ is a type of known-groups validity: the CLQ was significantly and negatively correlated with positive social status (lower loneliness associated with higher status) and positively correlated with negative status. In addition, the CLQ distinguished between rejected children and children from other status groups (neglected, controversial, and popular).

PRIMARY REFERENCE: Asher, S. R. and Wheeler, V. A. (1985). Children's loneliness: A comparison of rejected and neglected peer status, *Journal of Consulting and Clinical Psychology*, 53, 500–505. Instrument reproduced with permission of Steven R. Asher and the American Psychological Association.

AVAILABILITY: Dr. Steven R. Asher, University of Illinois, Bureau of Educational Research, 1310 South Sixth Street, Champaign, IL 61820.

CLQ

Below are 24 statements. Please read each statement and indicate how true it is for you using the following rating scale:

1 = That's always true about me
2 = That's true about me most of the time
3 = That's sometimes true about me
4 = That's hardly ever true about me
5 = That's not true at all about me

Please record your answer in the space to the left of each item.

_____ 1. It's easy for me to make new friends at school.
_____ 2. I like to read.
_____ 3. I have nobody to talk to in my class.
_____ 4. I'm good at working with other children in my class.
_____ 5. I watch TV a lot.
_____ 6. It's hard for me to make friends at school.
_____ 7. I like school.
_____ 8. I have lots of friends in my class.
_____ 9. I feel alone at school.
_____ 10. I can find a friend in my class when I need one.
_____ 11. I play sports a lot.
_____ 12. It's hard to get kids in school to like me.
_____ 13. I like science.
_____ 14. I don't have anyone to play with at school.
_____ 15. I like music.
_____ 16. I get along with my classmates.
_____ 17. I feel left out of things at school.
_____ 18. There are no other kids I can go to when I need help in school.
_____ 19. I like to paint and draw.
_____ 20. I don't get along with other children in school.
_____ 21. I'm lonely at school.
_____ 22. I am well liked by the kids in my class.
_____ 23. I like playing board games a lot.
_____ 24. I don't have any friends in class.

CHILDREN'S PERCEIVED SELF-CONTROL (CPSC) SCALE

AUTHOR: Laura Lynn Humphrey

PURPOSE: To measure children's perceptions of their self-control.

DESCRIPTION: This 11-item instrument measures self-control from a cognitive-behavioral perspective. The theory asserts that self-control is a personal competency which can solidify treatment gains and promote health and adjustment in children. Self-control includes problem recognition, commitment, protracted self-regulation, and habit reorganization. The instrument has subscales which measure three aspects of self-control: interpersonal self control (ISC), personal selfcontrol (PSC), and self evaluation (SE). Total scores on the CPSC also can be used. The measure has a similar form developed for teachers' assessment of a child's self-control.

NORMS: The CPSC was developed on a sample of suburban, middle class, fourth and fifth graders (372 boys and 391 girls). For boys, the mean scores were 4.96, 2.12, and 1.37 on the ISC, PSC and SE subscales; the mean on the total CPSC was 5.34 with a standard deviation of 3.08. For girls the mean scores were 5.92, 2.32, and 1.39 on the ISC, PSC and SE; the mean of the total scale was 5.82 with a standard deviation of 2.17.

SCORING: Each item is answered as either 1, "usually yes" or 0, "usually no," according to whether the content describes the child. Items reflecting poor self-control are reverse-scored. Total scores range from 0 to 11, with higher scores reflecting more self-control. Subscale items are: ISC: 1, 2, 3, 4; PSC: 5, 6, 7; SE: 8 and 9 and ranges are 0 to 4, 0 to 3, and 0 to 2, respectively.

RELIABILITY: Reliability is reported in terms of test-retest correlations over a two to three-week period. Total scores correlated .71, while the subscales were correlated as follows: ISC = .63, PSC = .63, SE. = 56. No data on internal consistency were reported.

VALIDITY: The concurrent validity evidence has been minimal. Scores on the total CPSC were not correlated with several expected criteria. Correlations were high, however, between the ISC and naturalistic observations, although scores were uncorrelated with the Child Behavior Rating Scale on academic achievement.

PRIMARY REFERENCE: Humphrey, L. L. (1982). Children's and teachers' perspectives on children's self-control: The development of two rating scales, *Journal of Consulting and Clinical Psychology*, 50, 624–633. Instrument reproduced with permission of Laura Humphrey and the American Psychological Association.

AVAILABILITY: Laura Humphrey, Ph.D., Department of Psychiatry, Northwestern University Medical School, 320 E. Huron, Chicago, IL 60611.

CPSC

Below are eleven statements. Please consider each in terms of whether it is usually true for you or not. Answer each according to the following scale.

1 = Usually yes
0 = Usually no

Record your answer in the space to the left of the statement.

_____   1.   If someone bothers me when I'm busy I ignore him/her.
_____   2.   When the teacher is busy I talk to my friends.
_____   3.   When someone pushes me I fight them.
_____   4.   I think about other things while I work.
_____   5.   It's hard to keep working when my friends are having fun.
_____   6.   It's hard to wait for something I want.
_____   7.   I make mistakes because I work too fast.
_____   8.   I know when I'm doing something wrong without someone telling me.
_____   9.   If my work is too hard I switch to something else.
_____ 10.   After I do something it's hard to tell what will happen next.
_____ 11.   It's hard for me to finish my work if I don't like it.

CHINESE WAYS OF COPING QUESTIONNAIRE (CWCQ)

AUTHOR: David W. Chan

PURPOSE: To measure coping.

DESCRIPTION: The CWCQ is a 16-item scale designed to measure coping activities among Chinese secondary school students and teachers. From an original 66 items, the scale was reduced in a series of studies to the present 16 items. It includes four subscales: rational problem solving (items 1, 5, 9, and 13); resigned distancing (items 2, 6, 10 and 14); seeking support and ventilation (items 3, 7, 11, and 15); and passive wishful thinking (items 4, 8, 12, and 16). The scale is in Chinese although English translations also are presented on the scale. The importance of the CWCQ is that it extends work on previous English language scales into the Chinese context and language, and shows that the coping activities identified in the scale were used in Chinese student and adult efforts to cope with events in daily living.

NORMS: Although the CWCQ was originally developed on samples involving secondary school students and teachers, the most recent research involved 412 secondary school teachers with a mean age of 31.06 (SD = 7.74); 180 subjects were male and 222 were female with 6 not reporting gender. The mean number of years of teaching was 7.78. Mean scores were presented only for subscales. The mean on the rational problem solving subscale was 11.14 (SD = 2.04); the mean for seeking support/ventilation was 10.63 (SD = 2.26); the mean for resigned distancing was 8.16 (SD = 2.05); and the mean for passive wishful thinking was 8.41 (SD = 2.27).

SCORING: The CWCQ is scored by a simple sum of individual item scores. This results in a range from 0 to 48.

RELIABILITY: The CWCQ has fair internal consistency with an alpha of .62 for resigned distancing and alphas ranging from .70 to .74 for the other three subscales. The overall alpha for the entire scale was not presented. There were no data available on stability.

VALIDITY: The concurrent validity of the CWCQ was examined through structural equation modeling, and it was found that the direct effect of stressors on distress is greatly reduced when coping strategies as measured by the CWCQ are utilized. The data were obtained by analyzing the CWCQ in a complex model involving a measure of teacher stress and a measure of psychological distress all of which were presented to respondents in Chinese versions and then analyzed through structural equation modeling.

PRIMARY REFERENCE: Chan, D. W. (1998). Stress, coping strategies, and psychological distress among secondary school teachers in Hong Kong, *American Educational Research Journal, 35,* 145–163.

AVAILABILITY: David W. Chan, Department of Educational Psychology, Faculty of Education, The Chinese University of Hong Kong, Shatin, New Territories, Hong Kong. Copyright © 1998 David W. Chan.

CWCQ

The following statements describe the ways people cope with their life events and how they feel. Please indicate, by circling the appropriate number (0, 1, 2, or 3), to what extent you use the following ways of coping.

0 = bú shìyòng huò méi yǒuyòng
Does not apply or not used
1 = yǒu shíhou yòng
Used somewhat
2 = hěnduō shí yòng
Used quite a lot
3 = jīngcháng yòng
Used a great deal

1. Wǒ fānfù sīliang wǒ huì zěnyàng shuō huò zěnyàng zuò.   0 1 2 3
I thought about what I would say or do.
2. Wǒ ruòwúqíshì, jiù xiàng shìqing méi yǒu fāshēng guo.   0 1 2 3
I acted as if nothing had happened.
3. Wǒ xiàng biérén sùshuō zì jǐ de gǎnshòu.   0 1 2 3
I talked to someone about my feelings.
4. Wǒ huànxiǎng shìqing jiāng huì shì rúhé jiéguǒ de.   0 1 2 3
I fantasized that things would turn out in some specific ways.
5. Wǒ zuò hǎo zhǔnbèi qù miànduì zuì ēliè de qíng kuàng.   0 1 2 3
I made preparations to face the worst.
6. Wǒ xiāngxìn mìngyùn, yǒu shí wǒ zhǐshì yùshang huài   0 1 2 3
yùnqi ba! *I believed in fate, knowing that sometimes I just
had bad luck.*
7. Wǒ zhǎo rén qīngtán, qú duō xiē liǎojiě qíng kuàng.   0 1 2 3
I talked to people to understand more about the situation.
8. Wǒ fā bái rì mèng huò huànxiǎng zìjǐ chǔ shēn yú yí ge   0 1 2 3
jiào hǎo de shíjiān huò qíngjìng.
I daydreamed or fantasized myself in a better time or place.
9. Wǒ zhīdao yīnggāi zuò xiē shénme, yīncǐ wǒ jiābèi nǔlì qù   0 1 2 3
zuò, shù tǐ chénggōng. *I knew what needed to be done,
so I worked extra hard to make things work.*
10. Wǒ chángshì wàngjì zhěngjiàn shì.   0 1 2 3
I tried to forget the whole incident.
11. Wǒ shèfǎ biǎodá zìjǐ de gǎnshòu.   0 1 2 3
I expressed my feelings in one way or another.
12. Wǒ xīwàng shìqing huì guòqu huò yǐ mǒuzhǒng fāngshì wánjié. 0 1 2 3
I wished that things would pass or end in some specific ways.
13. Wǒ shǐ zìjǐ gǎibiàn huò zuò gèrén de chéngzhǎng.   0 1 2 3
I made myself change or grow as an individual.
14. Wǒ chángshì zànshí fàngxia nàxiē wèntí, qù xiūxi huò dùjià.   0 1 2 3
*I put aside the problems for the time being by taking a rest
or going on a vacation.*
15. Wǒ xiàng wǒ zūnjìng de qīnqi huò péngyou qǐngjiào.   0 1 2 3
I sought advice from relatives or friends I respected.
16. Wǒ dànyuàn kěyǐ gǎibiàn yǐ fāshēng de shìqing huò zìjǐ   0 1 2 3
de gǎnshòu. *I wished I could change what actually
happened or my own feelings.*

COMMON BELIEF INVENTORY FOR STUDENTS (CBIS)

AUTHORS: Stephen R. Hooper and C. Clinton Layne

PURPOSE: To measure rationality in children.

DESCRIPTION: The CBIS is a 44-item instrument that was developed to measure the eleven irrational beliefs that Albert Ellis suggests are commonly held by people in general. Although total scores on this instrument can be used, each of the eleven beliefs is related to four items on the scale and each of the eleven can be scored separately. The numbers in parentheses on the instrument correspond to the eleven beliefs. (To summarize, the beliefs are as follows: 1. the idea one must be loved by everyone; 2. the idea one must be thoroughly competent; 3. the belief that certain people are wicked and warrant punishment; 4. the belief that it is awful and catastrophic when things do not go your way; 5. the idea that human happiness is determined by external events and not within human control; 6. the idea that if something is dangerous or fearsome, one should be concerned about it; 7. the belief that it is easier to avoid than to face certain of life's difficulties; 8. the belief that one should be dependent on others; 9. the idea that one's past history determines one's present behavior; 10. the belief that one should be quite upset over others' problems or disturbances; 11. the idea that there are perfect solutions to human problems and that it is catastrophic if the solutions are not found.) The CBIS appears to hold promise for standardized clinical assessment of rational thinking in children. All of the items are constructed so that the more one adheres to any of the statements (the higher the score), the more irrational the thinking. The authors are in the process of examining the factor structure of the CBIS, with plans to transform the scores on the CBIS into standard score units, thus allowing practitioners to compare CBIS scores with other standardized measures.

NORMS: The CBIS was initially developed using two groups of fourth through seventh graders totaling several thousand boys and girls. Newer data have been collected on a sample of 1500 fourth through seventh graders to further examine and perhaps standardize the CBIS. Actual norms are not available, but for one sample of 1226 students, the mean overall score was 74.4, with means on the individual beliefs ranging from 4.4 to 8.1.

SCORING: Each item is scored on a scale from 0 to 4; the four items pertaining to each of the eleven beliefs are summed to obtain the score for that belief, and all 44 items are summed to obtain the total score. Total scores can range from 0 to 176.

RELIABILITY: The CBIS has excellent internal consistency, with an alpha of .85 for the total scale and split-half reliability of .88. The CBIS also has excellent stability with test-retest correlations of .84 over a six-week period.

VALIDITY: The CBIS has demonstrated fair concurrent validity in correlating significantly with the FCMAS which measures trait anxiety in children. The CBIS also was found in two studies to be sensitive to clinical changes following treatment using rational therapy techniques.

PRIMARY REFERENCE: Hooper, S. R. and Layne, C. C. (1983). The Common Belief Inventory for Students: A measure of rationality in children, *Journal of Personality Assessment*, 47, 85–90. Instrument reproduced with permission of Stephen R. Hooper. The authors would appreciate correspondence from other investigators using the CBIS and would be happy to serve as consultants.

AVAILABILITY: Dr. Stephen R. Hooper, Bradley Hospital, Department of Psychology, 1011 Veterans Memorial Parkway, East Providence, RI 02915.

CBIS

The following are common beliefs which most people your age think. Please indicate the number that shows how often you think that belief. Remember this is about how you usually think. Please take your time and answer every question.

0 = Never (0%)
1 = Sometimes (25%)
2 = Half the time (50%)
3 = Almost always (75%)
4 = Always (100%)

_____ 1. If a person doesn't have any friends, that means that nobody likes him. (1)
_____ 2. I believe I should be different from what I am. (9)
_____ 3. I should be a better person. (7)
_____ 4. I believe I need to change some things about myself. (9)
_____ 5. I believe I should be smarter than I am. (7)
_____ 6. I believe that I should be better looking. (7)
_____ 7. A person who doesn't have any friends has got to be unhappy. (1)
_____ 8. I worry about many things. (6)
_____ 9. It's only human to be upset when things don't go my way. (5)
_____ 10. I believe that it helps to worry about some things. (6)
_____ 11. I am unlucky. (11)
_____ 12. I believe I need to always think of other peoples' feelings first instead of my own. (10)
_____ 13. I believe I need more confidence in myself. (2)
_____ 14. I feel bad about many things that I have done. (4)
_____ 15. I feel bad when I fail at something. (2)
_____ 16. I believe I would like myself better if I had more friends. (2)
_____ 17. I worry about what other people are thinking about me. (1)
_____ 18. I always get upset if something important doesn't go the way I want. (4)
_____ 19. I believe some people don't treat me the way they ought to. (5)
_____ 20. Most of the time when I get upset it's because someone else made me mad or hurt my feelings. (5)
_____ 21. I believe that how other people treat me makes a difference in how much I like myself. (5)
_____ 22. I believe that I am selfish because I usually please myself first and other people second. (10)
_____ 23. If a close friend has his feelings hurt, and if I feel badly too, then that tells me how much I really like that person. (10)
_____ 24. I believe that everyone should always know what they want to do in life. (11)
_____ 25. I believe that what a person does tells me everything about that person. (9)
_____ 26. Sometimes things happen to me that just shouldn't happen. (11)
_____ 27. When I make a mistake I feel awful. (2)
_____ 28. People have no right to make me feel bad. (3)

_____ 29. It's terrible when people make fun of me. (1)
_____ 30. People who do bad things should always be punished. (3)
_____ 31. Children who don't do their school work should always be punished. (3)
_____ 32. Kids who do bad things are bad people. (3)
_____ 33. I feel awful if I don't get what I want. (4)
_____ 34. School is terrible if I don't do well. (4)
_____ 35. I always worry about how well I am doing in school.
_____ 36. I am always afraid that dogs will bite me. (6)
_____ 37. I can't work alone. (8)
_____ 38. It's easier to quit a game I am losing than to finish it. (7)
_____ 39. I believe that it is better for my parents to do the things that are hard for me to do. (8)
_____ 40. I always have trouble doing things by myself. (8)
_____ 41. I always need other people to tell me how to do things. (8)
_____ 42. I feel terrible when my friends get yelled at in school. (10)
_____ 43. Things should always turn out the way I plan them. (11)
_____ 44. Life isn't as good as it should be because of things that happened when I was little. (9)

COMPANION ANIMAL BONDING SCALE (CABS)

AUTHORS: Robert H. Poresky, Charles Hendrix, Jacob E. Mosier, and Marvin L. Samuelson

PURPOSE: To measure the extent of child-animal activities.

DESCRIPTION: The CABS is an 8-item instrument designed to measure the extent of human-animal bonding based on extent of human-animal activities. The basis for this scale is the research evidence that bonding between humans and animals can have salutary effects on humans such as reducing feelings of loneliness and alienation. The CABS focuses on the quality of the relationship between human and pet rather than on the fact of pet ownership alone. The scale has two forms: the contemporary form reproduced here, and the "past" form, in which the present tense ("are," "do") is changed to the past tense ("were," "did"). The scale is viewed as a useful tool for examining the extent of human–animal bonding and its effect on emotional and social development.

NORMS: The CABS initially was studied on 121 students ranging in age from 15 to 47 years (mean age, 26.4, SD = 4.5). The respondents were students from high schools and universities in Kansas and included 53 women and 68 men. On the past scale, the mean score was 26.7 (SD = 5.7). The mean score on the form was 28.6 (SD = 6.3).

SCORING: The CABS is scored by summing the individual items (always = 5, never = 1). The possible range is from 8 to 40.

RELIABILITY: The CABS has good internal consistency, with Cronbach's alphas of .77 for the past and .82 for the contemporary scales. No test-retest data were reported.

VALIDITY: The CABS has fair concurrent validity, with significant correlations with the Pet Attitude Scale of .42 and .38 for the past and contemporary scales respectively.

PRIMARY REFERENCE: Poresky, R. H., Hendrix, C., Mosier, J. E., and Samuelson, M. L. (1987). The Companion Animal Bonding Scale: Internal reliability and construct validity, *Psychological Reports*, 60, 743–746.

AVAILABILITY: Journal article.

CABS

The following questions concern your relationship with your companion animal/pet. Please indicate how often you engage In each activity with your pet.

1 = Always
2 = Generally
3 = Often
4 = Rarely
5 = Never

____ 1. How often are you responsible for your companion animal's care?
____ 2. How often do you clean up after your companion animal?
____ 3. How often do you hold, stroke, or pet your companion animal?
____ 4. How often does your companion animal sleep in your room?
____ 5. How often do you feel that your companion animal is responsive to you?
____ 6. How often do you feel that you have a close relationship with your companion animal?
____ 7. How often do you travel with your companion animal?
____ 8. How often do you sleep near your companion animal?

COMPULSIVE EATING SCALE (CES)

AUTHORS: Dona M. Kagan and Rose L. Squires

PURPOSE: To measure uncontrollable eating.

DESCRIPTION: This 8-item instrument measures compulsive eating which is associated with obesity. More specifically, the CES assesses the inability to control one's eating behaviors in terms of overeating and eating during times when one is not necessarily hungry. The CES is one of the few instruments on eating which was developed for high school students and for males and females, alike. It is also appropriate for adults.

NORMS: The CES was developed on a sample of over 2000 high school students. Normative data were not reported.

SCORING: All items are rated on 5-point scales, but have different categories for various items. The letters used in the rating are converted to numbers as follows: a = 1, b = 2, c = 3, d = 4 and e = 5. Scores are the sum of the item ratings, and range from 8 to 40. Higher scores indicate more compulsivity in one's eating.

RELIABILITY: The CES has fair internal consistency, with an alpha of .75. Data on test-retest reliability were not presented.

VALIDITY: The CES was first utilized in research on the prevalence of eating disorders among high school students. The measure predicted differences among subjects categorized as normal eaters, borderline eaters and disordered eaters. Support for the instrument's concurrent validity is found in correlations with self-discipline and rebelliousness.

PRIMARY REFERENCE: Kagan, D. M. and Squires, R. L. (1984). Eating disorders among adolescents: Patterns and prevalence. *Adolescence*, 19, 15–29. Instrument reproduced with permission of Dona M. Kagan and Libra Publishers.

AVAILABILITY: Journal article.

CES

How often do you do each of the following activities? Circle the one answer for each question that comes closest to describing you.

1. Eat because you are feeling lonely.
   a. Never   b. Once or twice a year   c. Once a month   d. Once a week
   e. More than once a week

2. Feel completely out of control when it comes to food.
   a. Never   b. Once or twice a year   c. Once a month   d. Once a week
   e. More than once a week

3. Eat so much that your stomach hurts.
   a. Never   b. Once or twice a year   c. Once a month   d. Once a week
   e. More than once a week

4. Eat too much because you are upset or nervous.
   a. Never   b. Once or twice a year   c. Once a month   d. Once a week
   e. More than once a week

5. Eat too much because you are bored.
   a. Never   b. Once or twice a year   c. Once a month   d. Once a week
   e. More than once a week

6. Go out with friends just for the purpose of over-stuffing yourselves with food.
   a. Never   b. Once or twice a year   c. Once a month   d. Once a week
   e. More than once a week

7. Eat so much food so fast that you don't know how much you ate or how it tasted.
   a. Never   b. Once or twice a year   c. Once a month   d. Once a week
   e. More than once a week

8. Get out of bed at night, go into the kitchen, and finish the remains of some delicious food, because you knew it was there.
   a. Never   b. Once or twice a year   c. Once a month   d. Once a week
   e. More than once a week

CONCERN OVER WEIGHT AND DIETING SCALE (COWD)

AUTHORS: Dona M. Kagan and Rose L. Squires

PURPOSE: To measure dieting behavior.

DESCRIPTION: This 14-item instrument measures concerns over weight and dieting as symptoms of eating disorders. The instrument was originally developed in a study of the prevalence rate of eating disorders in high school students, and its clinical utility has yet to be established. The COWD was found to be independent of compulsive eating, suggesting that a concern over one's weight and dieting are not a consequence of compulsive eating. The COWD is most useful with bulimic and anorectic clients, or clients who self-impose restrictive diets.

NORMS: The COWD was developed on a sample of over 2000 high school students. Normative data are not available.

SCORING: All items are rated on 5-point scales, although there are different response categories for various items. The letters used in rating one's responses are converted to the following numeric values: a = 1, b = 2, c = 3, d = 4 and, e = 5. Scores are the sum of all item responses and range from 14 to 70. Higher scores indicate greater concern over one's weight and diet.

RELIABILITY: The COWD was tested for internal consistency using Cronbach's alpha. The instrument has very good reliability, with a correlation coefficient of .88. Evidence of test-retest reliability was not available.

VALIDITY: Evidence of known-groups validity is found with differences in COWD scores for subjects categorized as normal eaters, borderline eaters, and disordered eaters. The COWD also has good evidence of concurrent validity correlating with self-discipline and rebelliousness.

PRIMARY REFERENCE: Kagan, D. M. and Squires, R. L. (1984). Eating disorders among adolescents: Patterns and prevalence, *Adolescence*, 19, 15–29. Instrument reproduced with permission of Dona Kagan and Libra Publications.

AVAILABILITY: Journal article.

COWD

For the following questions please answer each by circling the alternative that is most true for you.

1. The worst thing about being fat is:
   a. No opinion   b. Getting teased   c. Feeling unsexy   d. Being unpopular
   e. Feeling bad about yourself

2. What is the greatest amount of weight you ever lost on a diet?
   a. Never on a diet   b. 10 lbs   c. 11–19 lbs   d. 20–29 lbs.
   e. 30 lbs or more

3. Do you think you are overweight now?
   a. Don't know   b. No   c. Yes: by less than 10 lbs   d. Yes: 10–19 lbs
   e. Yes: by 20 lbs or more

4. How often do you skip one meal so you will lose weight?
   a. Never   b. Once or twice a year   c. Once a month   d. Once a week
   e. More than once a week

5. How often do you avoid eating fattening foods like candy so you will lose weight?
   a. Never   b. Once or twice a year   c. Once a month   d. Once a week
   e. More than once a week

6. How often do you hate yourself or feel guilty because you cannot stop overeating?
   a. Never   b. Once or twice a year   c. Once a month   d. Once a week
   e. More than once a week

7. How often do you go without eating solid food for 24 hours or more so you will lose weight?
   a. Never   b. Once or twice a year   c. Once a month   d. Once a week
   e. More than once a week

8. If a special weight-control course were offered at this school, would you take it?
   a. No opinion   b. No   c. Probably no   d. Probably yes
   e. Definitely yes

9. How often do you feel guilty after eating?
   a. Never   b. Once in a while   c. Frequently   d. Very frequently
   e. All the time

10. How often are you aware of the calorie content of the food you eat?
    a. Never   b. Once in a while   c. Frequently   d. Very frequently
    e. All the time

11. How old were you when you first started worrying about your weight?
     a. Never   b. 12 years or less   c. 13–14 years   d. 15–16 years
     e. 17–18 years

How many times have you tried each of the weight-loss methods listed below?

12. Diet medicine (pills, liquids, or powders).
     a. Never   b. Once   c. Twice   d. Three times   e. More than three times

13. Health spa or exercise class (including aerobic dancing).
     a. Never   b. Once   c. Twice   d. Three times   e. More than three times

14. Diet published in a book or magazine or recommended by a friend or
     relative.
     a. Never   b. Once   c. Twice   d. Three times   e. More than three times

DEPRESSION SELF-RATING SCALE (DSRS)

AUTHOR: Peter Birleson

PURPOSE: To measure the extent and severity of depression in children.

DESCRIPTION: The DSRS is an 18-item instrument designed specifically to measure depression in children between the ages of 7 and 13. Because of the age group, the items on the scale are written in particularly simple language and responses categories are not complicated. Initial items were developed by identifying from the literature items associated with depressive symptomatology in childhood. Bias due to response set is avoided by wording some items positively and some negatively. The scale includes items dealing with mood, physiological and somatic complaints, and cognitive aspects of depression. The DSRS has a rough cutting score of 13 which was found to discriminate between depressed and nondepressed children.

NORMS: The initial study (referenced below) was conducted on four groups of children ($N = 53$), including depressed and nondepressed children from a child psychiatric clinic, and children from a residential school for "maladjusted children" and a "normal" school in Britain. A second study (Asarnow and Carlson, 1985) was conducted on 85 consecutively admitted child psychiatric inpatients in the United States (this study used a modified scale with additional items but analyzed data based on the original 18-item scale). The initial study was divided fairly evenly between boys and girls across the range of all income groups. The second study contained 22 girls and 60 boys from a wide range of socioeconomic levels (63 white, 9 black, and 10 Hispanic respondents).

SCORING: The DSRS items are scored on a 3-point scale, with positively worded items ranging from 0 to 2 and negatively worded items ranging from 2 to 0. These responses are totaled, so the range of possible scores is 0 to 36.

RELIABILITY: Alphas in the two studies were .86 and .73, indicating fair internal consistency. The test-retest reliability coefficient was .80, showing good stability.

VALIDITY: The DSRS has good concurrent validity, correlating .81 with the Children's Depression Inventory. In both studies, the DSRS showed good known-groups validity, significantly discriminating between depressed and nondepressed children with very few false positive errors (classifying nondepressed children as depressed).

PRIMARY REFERENCE: Birleson, Peter (1981). The validity of depression disorders in childhood and the development of a self-rating scale: A research report, *Journal of Child Psychology and Psychiatry*, 22, 73–88. Instrument reproduced with permission of Peter Birleson and Pergamon Press.

AVAILABILITY: Dr. Peter Birleson, Royal Children's Hospital, Fleminton Road, Parkville, Victoria 3052, Australia.

DSRS

Please answer as honestly as you can by indicating at the left the number that best refers to how you have felt over the past week. There are no right answers; it is important to say how *you* have felt.

1 = Most of the time
2 = Sometimes
3 = Never

___ 1. I look forward to things as much as I used to.
___ 2. I sleep very well.
___ 3. I feel like crying.
___ 4. I like to go out to play.
___ 5. I feel like running away.
___ 6. I get tummy aches.
___ 7. I have lots of energy.
___ 8. I enjoy my food.
___ 9. I can stick up for myself.
___ 10. I think life isn't worth living.
___ 11. I am good at things I do.
___ 12. I enjoy the things I do as much as I used to.
___ 13. I like talking about my family.
___ 14. I have horrible dreams.
___ 15. I feel very lonely.
___ 16. I am easily cheered up.
___ 17. I feel so sad I can hardly stand it.
___ 18. I feel very bored.

DRINKING MOTIVES QUESTIONNAIRE (DMQ)

AUTHOR: M. Lynne Cooper

PURPOSE: To measure drinking motives.

DESCRIPTION: The DMQ is a 20-item instrument designed to measure adolescents' motivations for using alcohol. The DMQ is based on earlier hypotheses that drinking motives can be characterized along two underlying dimensions of the outcomes an individual hopes to achieve by drinking. Individuals may drink to obtain a positive outcome or to avoid a negative outcome. In addition, drinking may be responsive to internal rewards or to external rewards such as social approval. Thus, there are four possible classes of motives: (1) internally generated, positive reinforcement motives (drinking to enhance positive mood or well-being); (2) externally generated positive reinforcement motives (drinking to obtain positive social rewards); (3) internally generated negative reinforcement motives (drinking to reduce or regulate negative emotions); and (4) externally generated, negative reinforcement motives (drinking to avoid social censure or rejection). In addition, numerous treatment approaches to alcohol abuse focus on the motivational underpinnings of drinking behavior without being able to directly assess drinking motives. The use of this scale, therefore, not only can help identify differences in drinking motives, but also can provide important leads for the focusing of individualized treatment. Factor analysis revealed four factors or subscales within the DMQ: social (items 1, 3, 5, 11, and 14); coping (items 4, 6, 7, 15, and 17); enhancement (items 2, 9, 10, 13, and 18); and conformity (items 8, 12, 16, 19, and 20).

NORMS: The DMQ was initially studied with 1243 adolescents who were a subsample of a larger sample; all the respondents in this study claim to have previously drunk alcohol. There are roughly equivalent numbers of male and female respondents with whites consisting of 58% of the sample and the remainder mainly African-American. The mean age of the adolescents was 17.3 years, and 7% of the respondents 16 and over were high school dropouts. Ninety-five percent of the respondents had drunk alcohol within the past six months; 48% of these also reported experiencing at least one problem related to alcohol use. Means of the four subscales are broken down by gender, race, and age in the original article. The overall means for each of the individual subscales are as follows: social = 2.46 (SD = .98); coping = 1.60 (SD = .75); enhancement = 2.15 (SD = 1.01); and conformity = 1.38 (SD = .61).

SCORING: The items on the DMQ typically are read to respondents as indicated on the questionnaire. Relative frequency of drinking for each of the 20 reasons is then rated by respondents on a 1–6 scale. The scores for each of the subscales are obtained by summing the items on that subscale, with higher scores suggesting greater endorsement of the motives on each subscale.

RELIABILITY: The DMQ has very good internal consistency, with alphas for the four subscales ranging from .84 to .88. No data on stability were reported.

VALIDITY: The results on the DMQ were generally similar across most demographic subgroups. In addition, the set of four drinking motives individually and in combination accounted for significant amounts of the variation in predicting the quantity and frequency of alcohol use and abuse. This suggests good predictive validity for the DMQ.

PRIMARY REFERENCE: Cooper, M. L. (1994). Motivations for alcohol use among adolescents: Development and validation of a four-factor model, *Psychological Assessment, 6*, 117–128.

AVAILABILITY: Copyright American Psychological Association; reprinted by permission of the author. Copies can be obtained from the author: M. Lynne Cooper, Department of Psychology, University of Missouri—Columbia, Columbia, MO 65211.

DMQ

Instructions (for interviewer-administered format)

Below is a list of reasons people give for drinking alcohol. There are no right or wrong answers to these questions. We just want to know about the reasons why you usually drink when you do.

Thinking now of all the times you drink, and using the following scale record your answer in the space next to the question.

$$1 = Never$$
$$2 = Almost\ never$$
$$3 = Some\ of\ the\ time$$
$$4 = About\ half\ of\ the\ time$$
$$5 = Most\ of\ the\ time$$
$$6 = Almost\ always$$

____ 1. How often do you drink because it helps you enjoy a party?
____ 2. How often do you drink because you like the feeling?
____ 3. How often would you say you drink to be sociable?
____ 4. How often do you drink to forget your worries?
____ 5. How often do you drink because it makes social gatherings more fun?
____ 6. How often do you drink because it helps you when you feel depressed or nervous?
____ 7. How often do you drink to cheer up when you're in a bad mood?
____ 8. How often do you drink because your friends pressure you to drink?
____ 9. How often do you drink because it's fun?
____ 10. How often do you drink because it's exciting?
____ 11. How often do you drink because it improves parties and celebrations?
____ 12. How often do you drink so that others won't kid you about not drinking?
____ 13. How often do you drink to get high?
____ 14. How often do you drink to celebrate a special occasion with friends?
____ 15. How often do you drink because you feel more self-confident or sure of yourself?
____ 16. How often do you drink so you won't feel left out?
____ 17. How often do you drink to forget about your problems?
____ 18. How often do you drink because it gives you a pleasant feeling?
____ 19. How often would you say you drink to fit in with a group you like?
____ 20. How often do you drink to be liked?

EYBERG CHILD BEHAVIOR INVENTORY (ECBI)

AUTHOR: Sheila Eyberg

PURPOSE. To measure conduct-problem behaviors in children.

DESCRIPTION: The ECBI is a 36-item instrument designed to measure conduct-problem behaviors in children and adolescents. This is one of the most widely used parent-rating scales. It measures a range of problem behaviors including aggression, noncompliance, temper tantrums, disruptive and annoying behaviors, stealing, lying, and so on. The ECBI is used by parents to rate children between the age of 2 and 17. It can be used as a measure to screen "normal" from conduct-problem children and for measuring change due to treatment.

NORMS: The ECBI has been studied with a number of samples. One study involved 1003 children selected on a stratified random sample basis from children in grades 1 to 12 from Seattle Public Schools. The sample was 52% male, 78% white, 8% black, 7% Asian and 7% mixed; 80% of the scales were completed by mothers, and 81% of the children had no repeated history of treatment for learning disability or behavioral problems. The mean intensity score for the 36 behaviors for the nonproblem sample was 92.1 (SD = 27.0); the mean problem score was 5.9 (SD = 6.3). The mean intensity score for children receiving treatment for learning disability was 110.88 (SD = 26.99) and the mean problem score was 9.97 (SD = 6.12). For children receiving treatment for behavior problems, the mean intensity score was 135.0 (SD = 32.9) and the problem score was 15.0 (SD = 6.61).

SCORING: The ECBI has two scores. The intensity score is the total frequency of occurrence for the 36 behaviors and the problem score is the total number of behaviors for which the response is "Yes." There are two clinical cutting scores: 127 on intensity and 11 on problem, with higher scores suggesting the need for treatment.

RELIABILITY: The ECBI has excellent internal consistency, with an alpha of .93 for intensity and .91 for problem. Date on stability were not available, though the ECBI is reported to have good stability.

VALIDITY: The ECBI has good concurrent and known-group validity, significantly correlating with independent observations of children's behavior, temperamental characteristics of the child, and distinguishing conduct-disordered children from nonclinic children.

PRIMARY REFERENCE: Burns, G. L. and Patterson, D. R. (1990). Conduct problem behaviors in a stratified random sample of children and adolescents: New standardization data on the Eyberg Child Behavior Inventory, *Psychological Assessment*, 2, 391–397.

AVAILABILITY: Dr. Sheila Eyberg, Department of Clinical and Health Psychology, University of Florida, Box J-165 HSC, Gainesville, FL 32610.

ECBI

Below are a series of phrases that describe children's behavior. Please (1) circle the number describing how often the behavior currently occurs with your child, and (2) circle either "yes" or "no" to indicate whether the behavior is currently a problem.

	Never	Seldom	Some-times	Often	Always	Is this a problem for you?	
						How often does this occur with your child?	
1. Dawdles in getting dressed	1	2	3	4	5	6	7	Yes No
2. Dawdles or lingers at mealtime	1	2	3	4	5	6	7	Yes No
3. Has poor table manners	1	2	3	4	5	6	7	Yes No
4. Refuses to eat food presented	1	2	3	4	5	6	7	Yes No
5. Refuses to do chores when asked	1	2	3	4	5	6	7	Yes No
6. Slow in getting ready for bed	1	2	3	4	5	6	7	Yes No
7. Refuses to go to bed on time	1	2	3	4	5	6	7	Yes No
8. Does not obey house rules on own	1	2	3	4	5	6	7	Yes No

			How often does this occur with your child?						Is this a problem for you?	
		Never	Seldom		Some-times	Often		Always		
9.	Refuses to obey until threatened with punishment	1	2	3	4	5	6	7	Yes	No
10.	Acts defiant when told to do something	1	2	3	4	5	6	7	Yes	No
11.	Argues with parents about rules	1	2	3	4	5	6	7	Yes	No
12.	Gets angry when doesn't get own way	1	2	3	4	5	6	7	Yes	No
13.	Has temper tantrums	1	2	3	4	5	6	7	Yes	No
14.	Sasses adults	1	2	3	4	5	6	7	Yes	No
15.	Whines	1	2	3	4	5	6	7	Yes	No
16.	Cries easily	1	2	3	4	5	6	7	Yes	No
17.	Yells or screams	1	2	3	4	5	6	7	Yes	No
18.	Hits parents	1	2	3	4	5	6	7	Yes	No
19.	Destroys toys and other objects	1	2	3	4	5	6	7	Yes	No

How often does this occur with your child?

Is this a problem for you?

		Never	Seldom	Some-times		Often	Always		
20.	Is careless with toys and other objects	1	2 3	4	5	6	7	Yes	No
21.	Steals	1	2 3	4	5	6	7	Yes	No
22.	Lies	1	2 3	4	5	6	7	Yes	No
23.	Teases or provokes other children	1	2 3	4	5	6	7	Yes	No
24.	Verbally fights with friends own age	1	2 3	4	5	6	7	Yes	No
25.	Verbally fights with sisters and brothers	1	2 3	4	5	6	7	Yes	No
26.	Physically fights with friends own age	1	2 3	4	5	6	7	Yes	No
27.	Physically fights with sisters and brothers	1	2 3	4	5	6	7	Yes	No
28.	Constantly seeks attention	1	2 3	4	5	6	7	Yes	No
29.	Interrupts	1	2 3	4	5	6	7	Yes	No
30.	Is easily distracted	1	2 3	4	5	6	7	Yes	No
31.	Has short attention span	1	2 3	4	5	6	7	Yes	No

543

	How often does this occur with your child?						Is this a problem for you?
	Never	Seldom	Some-times	Often		Always	
32. Fails to finish tasks or projects	1	2 3	4	5	6	7	Yes No
33. Has difficulty entertaining self alone	1	2 3	4	5	6	7	Yes No
34. Has difficulty concentrating on one thing	1	2 3	4	5	6	7	Yes No
35. Is overactive or restless	1	2 3	4	5	6	7	Yes No
36. Wets the bed	1	2 3	4	5	6	7	Yes No

544

FAMILY, FRIENDS, AND SELF FORM (FFS)

AUTHORS: Dwayne Simpson and Anthony A. McBride

PURPOSE: To measure social relationships and psychological adjustment of youth.

DESCRIPTION: The FFS is a 3-part instrument with a total of 60 items designed to provide a comprehensive assessment of youth involving family setting and relations, peer activities and involvement, and personal perceptions of self and environment as well as psychological adjustment. Although originally developed as measures to use in tracking problem behaviors of adolescents involving drug and alcohol use, school problems, and legal involvement, these scales appear to have broader value for assessment of adolescents at risk. The three parts of the FFS comprise numerous subscales. The parts are described as A, B, C, with the numbers indicating the items on each part. For Family scales the "warmth" subscale includes items A-1, A-2, A-8, A-10, A-15, A-19, A-22, A-25, A-27, A-31, and A-32. The second subscale under Family scales, "control," includes items A-3, A-7, A-12, A-20, A-24, A-26, and A-30. The third family scale, called "conflict," includes items A-6, A-11, A-14, and A-18. There are four Friends subscales. The first is "peer activity," including items A-4, A-9, A-16, A-21, and A-29. The second Friends scale is called "trouble," including items B-7, B-8, B-11, B-12, B-14, B-17, and B-18. The third Friends subscale, "familiarity with parents," includes items B-2, B-4, B-10, and B-15. The fourth is called "conventional involvement" and includes items B-1, B-3, B-5, B-6, B-9, B-13, B-16. The last set of scales is called "Self-Rating." The first Self-Rating subscale is "self-esteem" which includes items A-5, A-13, A-17, A-23, and A-28. The second Self-Rating scale, "environment," includes items C-2, C-3, C-4, C-6, C-8, and C-10. The final Self-Rating subscale is called "school satisfaction" and includes items C-1, C-5, C-7, and C-9. The FFS scales capture useful and predictive measures of family and peer relationships as well as psychological adjustment of adolescent clients.

NORMS: The FFS scales have been studied with over 1500 youths including Hispanic, African-American, and white respondents. The most recent study involved 700 Mexican-American youths, age 13 to 18, of whom 73% were male and 26% female with an average age of 14.8 years. All respondents had been admitted to drug abuse prevention programs located throughout Texas. Means and standard deviations were not reported in the article, but are available from the authors at their website, noted below.

SCORING: Generally the items are read aloud to respondents who then respond with an answer card which includes the categories described to the right of each scale. It also seems possible for respondents to complete the scale as a paper and pencil questionnaire. Each of the three parts is easily scored by summing item responses for each subscale; the following items should be re-verse-scored before the scale scores are computed: A-12, A-20, A-26, B-6.

RELIABILITY: The subscales have good to excellent internal consistency, with alphas ranging from .725 for conventional involvement to .912 for warmth. No data on stability were reported.

VALIDITY: The FFS appears to have good predictive validity. With the exception of "control," all of the FFS scales had significant correlations with the respective diagnostic indices that were based on counselor ratings completed on the sample youth at intake of their drug prevention program. In particular, three of the Friends scales—trouble, peer activity, and conventional involvement—were significantly correlated with the counselor diagnosis of drug problems. Thus, these scales appear to be valuable for further study of intervention with problems of adolescent drug abuse.

PRIMARY REFERENCE: Simpson, D. D. and McBride, A. A. (1992). Family, friends, and self (FFS) assessment scales for Mexican-American youth, *Hispanic Journal of Behavioral Sciences,* 14, 327–340.

AVAILABILITY: At www.ibr.tcu.edu; click on "forms," "adolescents." Scales reprinted by permission of the authors.

FFS

PART A

INSTRUCTIONS TO BE READ ALOUD TO RESPONDENT: I would now like to ask you some questions about *you and your parents, family, and friends.* Using the answer card that I will give you, tell me your answer after I read each question.

READ EACH ITEM AND CIRCLE ANSWER.

		Never	Rarely	Some-times	Often	Almost always
1.	Is there a feeling of togetherness in your family?	0	1	2	3	4
2.	Are there times each day when your family is all together?	0	1	2	3	4
3.	Are there exact rules you have to follow in your family?	0	1	2	3	4
4.	Do you spend time hanging out with your friends?	0	1	2	3	4
5.	Can you think of things that you like about yourself?	0	1	2	3	4
6.	Do members of your family say bad things about each other?	0	1	2	3	4
7.	How often do your parents punish you in some way when you do something wrong?	0	1	2	3	4
8.	How often do your parents try to understand what you need to be happy?	0	1	2	3	4
9.	Do you spend a lot of your free time with friends?	0	1	2	3	4
10.	How often does your family sit down to eat together at the same time?	0	1	2	3	4
11.	How often do members of your family get really mad at one another?	0	1	2	3	4
12.	Do you make more decisions than your parents about things you do and places you go?	0	1	2	3	4
13.	Are you proud of how you act and the things you do?	0	1	2	3	4
14.	How often do your family members hit or yell at each other?	0	1	2	3	4
15.	How often do your parents pay attention to what you say?	0	1	2	3	4
16.	How often do you and your friends spend time together after school?	0	1	2	3	4
17.	Do you think you have a lot to be proud of?	0	1	2	3	4
18.	Are there many arguments or fights in your family?	0	1	2	3	4

19.	How often do your parents try to cheer you up when you're sad?	0	1	2	3	4
20.	Do your parents let you go anywhere you please without asking?	0	1	2	3	4
21.	Do your best friends spend a lot of time hanging out?	0	1	2	3	4
22.	How often do your parents tell you they love and care about you?	0	1	2	3	4
23.	Are you happy and satisfied with yourself?	0	1	2	3	4
24.	How often do your parents make decisions for you?	0	1	2	3	4
25.	When you have a problem, does someone in your family help you out?	0	1	2	3	4
26.	Do your parents let you off easy when you do something wrong?	0	1	2	3	4
27.	How often do your parents really listen to your problems?	0	1	2	3	4
28.	When you do something, do you think you do it well?	0	1	2	3	4
29.	Do you spend time at your friends' houses?	0	1	2	3	4
30.	Are there definite rules set in your family?	0	1	2	3	4
31.	How often do your parents make you feel they love you?	0	1	2	3	4
32.	How often does your family try to do things that are fun for everyone?	0	1	2	3	4

PART B

In this part, I would like to ask you some questions about your *friends*. Using the Answer Card that I will give you, tell me your answer after I read each question.

How many of your friends—

		None	A Few	Some	Most	All
1.	like to play sports?	0	1	2	3	4
2.	know your parents?	0	1	2	3	4
3.	get all good grades at school?	0	1	2	3	4
4.	do your parents like?	0	1	2	3	4
5.	like school?	0	1	2	3	4
6.	do homework after school or at night?	0	1	2	3	4
7.	do things that might get them into trouble with the law?	0	1	2	3	4
8.	have ever used a weapon (like a gun, knife, or club) in a serious fight?	0	1	2	3	4
9.	want to go to college?	0	1	2	3	4
10.	like your parents?	0	1	2	3	4

11.	have been in trouble with the police because of alcohol or drugs?	0	1	2	3	4
12.	have quit or want to quit school?	0	1	2	3	4
13.	are in clubs or other organizations such as scouts?	0	1	2	3	4
14.	have damaged other peoples' property on purpose?	0	1	2	3	4
15.	do your parents know?	0	1	2	3	4
16.	like to read books after school?	0	1	2	3	4
17.	have ever been stopped or picked up by the police?	0	1	2	3	4
18.	do things that might get them into trouble at school?	0	1	2	3	4

PART C

In this part, I would like to ask you some questions about various *people and things in your life.* Using the answer card that I will give you, tell me your answer after I read each question.

How do you feel about—

		Very unhappy	Mostly unhappy	Neither happy nor unhappy	Mostly happy	Very happy
1.	your school?	0	1	2	3	4
2.	your family?	0	1	2	3	4
3.	the house or place where you live?	0	1	2	3	4
4.	the things you and your family have, like bicycles, cars, boats, TVs, radios, and other things?	0	1	2	3	4
5.	your teachers at school?	0	1	2	3	4
6.	the amount of money that you and your family have?	0	1	2	3	4
7.	the courses you are taking at school?	0	1	2	3	4
8.	the way you get along with your parents?	0	1	2	3	4
9.	your school principal?	0	1	2	3	4
10.	your life in general?	0	1	2	3	4

HARE SELF-ESTEEM SCALE (HSS)

AUTHOR: Bruce R. Hare

PURPOSE: To measure self-esteem in school-age children.

DESCRIPTION: The HSS is a 30-item instrument that measures self-esteem of school age children 10 years old and above. The HSS consists of three 10-item subscales that are area-specific (peer, school, and home) and presented as distinct units. The sum of all 30 items is viewed as a general self-esteem measure. Items were chosen to include both self-evaluative and other-evaluative items. The items are also intended to induce respondents to report a general sense of the self-feeling within each area. The rationale for concluding that the sum of the three subscales produces an overall measure of self-esteem is that peer, home, and school are the major areas of interaction for the child in which he or she develops a sense of self-worth. Thus, they represent something close to the child's universe for self-evaluation. The HSS can be administered individually or in groups, orally or in writing.

NORMS: The HSS was tested on fifth and eighth graders. Subsamples included 41 blacks and 207 whites, 115 boys and 137 girls. Means for all the subsamples are available, the mean ranges from 90.4 to 95 with a group mean of 91.1 for all subsamples.

SCORING: After reverse-scoring negatively worded items, the items for the subscales are summed using the following scale: a = 1, b = 2, c = 3, d = 4. The three subscale scores are totaled to produce the score for the general self-esteem scale. Higher scores indicate higher self-esteem.

RELIABILITY: No internal consistency data are reported. Test-retest correlations indicate good stability, with three-month correlations ranging from .56 to .65 for the three subscales and .74 for the general scale.

VALIDITY: The HSS general scale correlated .83 with both the Coopersmith Self-Esteem Inventory and the Rosenberg Self-Esteem Scale, indicating excellent concurrent validity. The HSS subscales also correlate significantly with changes in life status and with predicted area-specific activities (e.g., reading achievement scores with school subscale). This suggests that changes in area-specific sources of self-esteem do not result in changes in the level of general self-esteem.

PRIMARY REFERENCE: Hare, B. R. (1985). The HARE general and area-specific (school, peer, and home) self-esteem scale. Unpublished manuscript, Department of Sociology, SUNY Stony Brook, Stony Brook, New York (mimeo.). Instrument reproduced with permission of Bruce R. Hare.

AVAILABILITY: The Free Press.

HSS

Peer Self-Esteem Scale

In the blank provided, please write the letter of the answer that best describes how you feel about the sentence. These sentences are designed to find out how you generally feel when you are with other people your age. There are no right or wrong answers.

a = Strongly disagree
b = Disagree
c = Agree
d = Strongly agree

_____ 1. I have at least as many friends as other people my age.
_____ 2. I am *not* as popular as other people my age.
_____ 3. In the kinds of things that people my age like to do, I am at least as good as most other people.
_____ 4. People my age often pick on me.
_____ 5. Other people think I am a lot of fun to be with.
_____ 6. I usually keep to myself because I am *not* like other people my age.
_____ 7. Other people wish that they were like me.
_____ 8. I wish I were a different kind of person because I'd have more friends.
_____ 9. If my group of friends decided to vote for leaders of their group I'd be elected to a high position.
_____ 10. When things get tough, I am *not* a person that other people my age would turn to for help.

Home Self-Esteem Scale

In the blank provided, please write the letter of the answer that best describes how you feel about the sentence. These sentences are designed to find out how you generally feel when you are with your family. There are no right or wrong answers.

a = Strongly disagree
b = Disagree
c = Agree
d = Strongly agree

_____ 1. My parents are proud of the kind of person I am.
_____ 2. No one pays much attention to me at home.
_____ 3. My parents feel that I can be depended on.
_____ 4. I often feel that if they could, my parents would trade me in for another child.
_____ 5. My parents try to understand me.
_____ 6. My parents expect too much of me.
_____ 7. I am an important person to my family.
_____ 8. I often feel unwanted at home.

_____ 9. My parents believe that I will be a success in the future.
_____ 10. I often wish that I had been born into another family.

School Self-Esteem Scale

In the blank provided, please write the letter of the answer that best describes how you feel about the sentence. These sentences are designed to find out how you generally feel when you are in school. There are no right or wrong answers.

$$a = \text{Strongly disagree}$$
$$b = \text{Disagree}$$
$$c = \text{Agree}$$
$$d = \text{Strongly agree}$$

_____ 1. My teachers expect too much of me.
_____ 2. In the kinds of things we do in school, I am at least as good as other people in my classes.
_____ 3. I often feel worthless in school.
_____ 4. I am usually proud of my report card.
_____ 5. School is harder for me than most other people.
_____ 6. My teachers are usually happy with the kind of work I do.
_____ 7. Most of my teachers do *not* understand me.
_____ 8. I am an important person in my classes.
_____ 9. It seems that no matter how hard I try, I never get the grades I deserve.
_____ 10. All and all, I feel I've been very fortunate to have had the kinds of teachers I've had since I started school.

HOMEWORK PROBLEM CHECKLIST (HPC)

AUTHORS: Kathleen M. Anesko, Geryl Scholock, Rafael Ramirez, and Frederick M. Levine

PURPOSE: To measure children's homework problems.

DESCRIPTION: The HPC is a 20-item instrument designed to measure the frequency and intensity of children's homework problems. The items were generated from literature reviews and interviews with parents and professionals who work with elementary school children. The checklist is simply filled out by parents and appears to be a good instrument for assessing difficulties children are having with homework.

NORMS: The HPC was investigated with the parents of 319 children in grades 2 through 4. The children included 172 girls and 147 boys ages 6–10 (mean = 8.4 years). The sample was largely white and middle class. For males, the means were 11.71 (SD = 8.18) for second grade, 12.73 (SD = 9.63) for third grade, and 11.84 (SD = 8.72) for fourth grade. For girls, for the respective grades, the means were 8.28 (SD = 6.18), 8.84 (SD = 7.26), and 10.34 (SD = 7.62). Boys had significantly more homework problems than girls regardless of grade in school.

SCORING: The HPC is easily scored by summing the four-point items (0 = never to 3 = very often) for a total score that can range from 0 to 60. Higher scores equal greater homework problems.

RELIABILITY: The HPC has excellent internal consistency, with an alpha of .91. No data on stability were reported.

VALIDITY: The HPC has good known-groups validity, significantly discriminating between children rated by their parents as "below" versus "on or above" grade level. The HPC also is sensitive to change produced by an intervention program.

PRIMARY REFERENCE: Anesko, K. M., Scholock, G., Ramirez, R., and Levine, F. M. (1987). The Homework Problem Checklist: Assessing children's homework difficulties, *Behavioral Assessment*, 9, 179–185.

AVAILABILITY: Journal article.

HPC

Please circle one:

Child performs: (−1) below grade level in most subjects
                 (0)   on grade level in most subjects
                 (+1) above grade level in most subjects

For each statement, circle one:	Never (0)	At times (1)	Often (2)	Very often (3)
Fails to bring home assignment and necessary materials (textbook, dittos, etc.)	0	1	2	3
Doesn't know exactly what homework has been assigned.	0	1	2	3
Denies having homework assignment.	0	1	2	3
Refuses to do homework assignment.	0	1	2	3
Whines or complains about homework.	0	1	2	3
Must be reminded to sit down and start homework.	0	1	2	3
Procrastinates, puts off doing homework.	0	1	2	3
Doesn't do homework satisfactorily unless someone is in the room.	0	1	2	3
Doesn't do homework satisfactorily unless someone does it with him/her.	0	1	2	3
Daydreams or plays with objects during homework session.	0	1	2	3
Easily distracted by noises or activities of others.	0	1	2	3
Easily frustrated by homework assignment.	0	1	2	3
Fails to complete homework.	0	1	2	3
Takes unusually long time to do homework.	0	1	2	3

For each statement, circle one:	Never (0)	At times (1)	Often (2)	Very often (3)
Responds poorly when told by parent to correct homework.	0	1	2	3
Produces messy or sloppy homework.	0	1	2	3
Hurries through homework and makes careless mistakes.	0	1	2	3
Shows dissatisfaction with work, even when he/she does a good job.	0	1	2	3
Forgets to bring assignment back to class.	0	1	2	3
Deliberately fails to bring assignment back to class.	0	1	2	3

HOPELESSNESS SCALE FOR CHILDREN (HSC)

AUTHOR: Alan F. Kazdin

PURPOSE: To measure hopelessness in children.

DESCRIPTION: This 17 item instrument measures cognitions of hopelessness, a construct pertinent to depression and suicidal ideation. Hopelessness is defined as negative expectations about oneself and the future. The HSC was modeled after the Hopelessness Scale for Adults by Beck, Weissman, Lester, and Trexler (1974). It has a second grade reading comprehension level, making it useful for children 7 years and older. Scores on the HSC have been shown to be associated with severity of depression and self-esteem. Moreover, the well established correlation between depression and suicidal intent is minimized when hopelessness is statistically controlled, suggesting the HSC is an important measure to use when working with suicidal clients.

NORMS: The HSC was developed on a sample of 66 children from an inpatient psychiatric unit. The research protocol required that these subjects show no evidence of a confused state, uncontrolled seizures, or dementia. The average IQ score was 92.9. Fifty-three children were white, thirteen were female. The age range for the sample was 5 to 13 with a mean age of 10.5. The mean score on the HSC was 5.2 with a standard deviation of 3.2.

SCORING: Items are answered "true" or "false." Items keyed for true answers are 2, 8, 9, 10, 12, 13, 14, 15, and 17. The remaining items are keyed false. Scores are the number of items answered in agreement with the key, and range from 0 to 17, with higher scores reflecting greater hopelessness.

RELIABILITY: Internal consistency is fair, with a coefficient alpha of .71, and split-half reliability of .70. These coefficients are relatively low but acceptable for a children's measure.

VALIDITY: Concurrent validity is demonstrated by correlations between the HSC and three measures of depression. Scores were inversely correlated with self-esteem. Research on known-groups validity indicated scores discriminated between suicidal and nonsuicidal children.

PRIMARY REFERENCE: Kazdin, A. E., French, N. H., Unis, A. S., Esveldt-Dawson, K., and Sherick, R. B. (1983) Hopelessness, depression, and suicidal intent among psychiatrically disturbed children, *Journal of Consulting and Clinical Psychology*, 51, 504–510. Instrument reproduced with permission of Alan Kazdin and the American Psychological Association.

AVAILABILITY: Alan E. Kazdin, Ph.D., Professor of Psychiatry and Psychology, Western Psychiatric Institute and Clinic, 3811 O'Hare Street, Pittsburgh, PA 15213.

HSC

Instructions to be read to the child: "These sentences are about how some kids feel about their lives. Your answers let us know about how kids feel about things.

"I am going to read each sentence to you. I'd like you to tell me if the sentence is *true* for you or *false* for you. If the sentence is how you feel, you would say it is *like you* or *true*. If the sentence is *not* how you think you feel, you would say it is *not* like you or *false*.

"There are no right or wrong answers. Just tell me if the sentence is like you or not like you—true or false."

T	F	1.	I want to grow up because I think things will be better.
T	F	2.	I might as well give up because I can't make things better for myself.
T	F	3.	When things are going badly, I know they won't be as bad all of the time.
T	F	4.	I can imagine what my life will be like when I'm grown up.
T	F	5.	I have enough time to finish the things I really want to do.
T	F	6.	Some day, I will be good at doing the things that I really care about.
T	F	7.	I will get more of the good things in life than most other kids.
T	F	8.	I don't have good luck and there's no reason to think I will when I grow up.
T	F	9.	All I can see ahead of me are bad things, not good things.
T	F	10.	I don't think I will get what I really want.
T	F	11.	When I grow up, I think I will be happier than I am now.
T	F	12.	Things just won't work out the way I want them to.
T	F	13.	I never get what I want, so it's dumb to want anything.
T	F	14.	I don't think I will have any real fun when I grow up.
T	F	15.	Tomorrow seems unclear and confusing to me.
T	F	16.	I will have more good times than bad times.
T	F	17.	There's no use in really trying to get something I want because I probably won't get it.

HOSPITAL FEARS RATING SCALE (HFRS)

AUTHORS: Barbara G. Melamed and Mark A. Lumley

PURPOSE: To measure anxiety in response to medical and hospital concerns.

DESCRIPTION: The HFRS is a 25-item instrument which assesses the magnitude of fear one has in response to a variety of medical and hospital stimuli. The HFRS has three subscales: medical fear (MF; items 1–8), hospital fear (HF; items 9–16), and nonmedically related items (items 17–25). The nonmedical subscale can serve as a baseline for comparison with the specific hospital-related fears. The HFRS is useful when working with children troubled by or concerned about pending medical or hospital procedures. Scores can be used to monitor progress of a fear reduction program.

NORMS: Normative data are not available.

SCORING: All fear stimuli are rated on a 1 to 5 scale. Scores are the sum of item scores. Scores on the MF and HF range from 8 to 40. Scores on the nonmedical subscale range from 9 to 45. A higher score reflects a greater magnitude of fear.

RELIABILITY: Reliability studies of the HFRS have been very limited. One study reports test-retest reliability of .74.

VALIDITY: The HFRS has good support for its validity. Scores on the HFRS correlated with age, the number of disruptive behaviors displayed in the operating room, and days needed for recovery. The HFRS has been shown to be sensitive to measuring change over the course of medical care. Known-group validity is suggested by differences in scores for subjects exposed to an anxiety reducing pre-operation program and those not exposed.

PRIMARY REFERENCE: Melamed, B. G. and Lumley, M. A. (1990). Hospital Fears Rating Scale. In M. Hersen and A. S. Bellack (eds.), *Dictionary of Behavioral Assessment Techniques*. New York: Pergamon Press, pp. 252–253. Instrument reproduced with permission of Barbara G. Melamed.

AVAILABILITY: Barbara G. Melamed, Ph.D., Professor and Dean, Ferkauf Graduate School of Psychology, Yeshiva University, 1300 Morris Park Avenue, Bronx, NY 10461.

HFRS

In response to each stimulus, use the following scale and rate your degree of fear. Record your rating in the space next to the item.

1 = Not afraid
2 = A little fear
3 = Some fear
4 = Moderate fear
5 = Very afraid

_____ 1. Sharp objects
_____ 2. Having to go to the hospital
_____ 3. Going to the dentist
_____ 4. Going to the doctor
_____ 5. Getting a shot
_____ 6. Getting a haircut
_____ 7. Getting car sick
_____ 8. Deep water or the ocean
_____ 9. Germs or getting seriously ill
_____ 10. The sight of blood
_____ 11. Being alone without your parents
_____ 12. Having an operation
_____ 13. Getting a cut or injury
_____ 14. Getting sick at school
_____ 15. Not being able to breathe
_____ 16. Persons wearing masks
_____ 17. Spiders
_____ 18. Making mistakes
_____ 19. Going to bed in the dark
_____ 20. Strange or mean looking dogs
_____ 21. Flying in an airplane
_____ 22. Getting punished
_____ 23. Thunderstorms
_____ 24. Ghosts or spooky things
_____ 25. Falling from high places

IMPULSIVITY SCALE (IS)

AUTHORS: Paul P. Hirschfield, Brian Sutton-Smith, and B. G. Rosenberg

PURPOSE: To measure impulsivity in children.

DESCRIPTION: This 19-item instrument assesses impulsivity, and is arranged in a true-false format for easy administration. The instrument defines impulsivity as the tendency toward restlessness, rule-breaking, and indulgence in horseplay. Each item is phrased one way with another parallel item worded in the reverse. Only one set of the 19 items should be used; the other may serve as a parallel form. The instrument has potential use with children with problems in control or with oppositional and acting out disorders.

NORMS: The instrument was developed on 127 fifth and sixth grade students. The mean score was 8.24.

SCORING: When a respondent's item answer corresponds to the item key, it is given a score of 1. The nonparenthetical items are scored True while those within parentheses are keyed False. Total scores range from 0 to 19.

RELIABILITY: Internal consistency data were not reported. Stability was good with test-retest correlations of .85.

VALIDITY: This instrument has good criterion-referenced concurrent validity, correlating significantly with teacher ratings of school children. Scores are also correlated with behavioral observations by teachers and the researcher in the classroom.

PRIMARY REFERENCE: Hirschfield, P. P. (1965). Response set in impulsive children, *Journal of Genetic Psychology*, 107, 117–126. Instrument reproduced with permission of Paul P. Hirschfield.

AVAILABILITY: Dr. Paul P. Hirschfield, Hirschfield and Associates, 529 Pharr Road, Atlanta, GA 30305.

IS

Decide whether each statement is true as applied to you or false as applied to you. If a statement is True or Mostly True as applied to you, circle T. If a statement is False or Mostly False as applied to you, circle F.

T F 1. I like to keep moving around.
      (I don't like to keep moving around.)
T F 2. I make friends quickly.
      (I don't make friends quickly.)
T F 3. I like to wrestle and to horse around.
      (I don't like to wrestle and to horse around.)
T F 4. I like to shoot with bows and arrows.
      (I don't like to shoot with bows and arrows.)
T F 5. I must admit I'm a pretty good talker.
      (I must admit that I'm not a good talker.)
T F 6. Whenever there's a fire engine going someplace, I like to follow it.
      (If there's a fire engine going someplace, I don't usually like to follow it.)
T F 7. My home life is not always happy.
      (My home life is always happy.)
T F 8. When things get quiet, I like to stir up a little fuss.
      (I usually don't like to stir up a little fuss when things get quiet.)
T F 9. I am restless.
      (I am not restless.)
T F 10. I don't think I'm as happy as other people.
      (I think I'm as happy as other people.)
T F 11. I get into tricks at Halloween.
      (I don't get into tricks at Halloween.)
T F 12. I like being "it" when we play games of that sort.
      (I don't like being "it" when we play games of that sort.)
T F 13. It's fun to push people off the edge into the pool.
      (It's not fun to push people off the edge into the pool.)
T F 14. I play hooky sometimes.
      (I never play hooky.)
T F 15. I like to go with lots of other kids, not just one.
      (I usually like to go with one kid, rather than lots of them.)
T F 16. I like throwing stones at targets.
      (I don't like throwing stones at targets.)
T F 17. It's hard to stick to the rules if you're losing the game.
      (It's not hard to stick to the rules even if you are losing the game.)
T F 18. I like to dare kids to do things.
      (I don't like to dare kids to do things.)
T F 19. I'm not known as a hard and steady worker.
      (I'm known as a hard and steady worker.)

INDEX OF PEER RELATIONS (IPR)

AUTHOR: Walter W. Hudson

PURPOSE: To measure problems with peers.

DESCRIPTION: The IPR is a 25-item instrument designed to measure the extent, severity, or magnitude of a problem the respondent has with peers. The IPR can be used as a global measure of relationship problems with peers or one or more specific peer reference groups can be considered. A note stating which reference group is being used should be placed at the top of the questionnaire. The IPR has two cutting scores. The first is a score of 30 (±5); scores below this point indicate absence of a clinically significant problem in this area. Scores above 30 suggest the presence of a clinically significant problem. The second cutting score is 70. Scores above this point nearly always indicate that clients are experiencing severe stress with a clear possibility that some type of violence could be considered or used to deal with problems. The practitioner should be aware of this possibility. Another advantage of the IPR is that it is one of several scales of the WALMYR Assessment Scales package reproduced here, all of which are administered and scored the same way.

NORMS: The norms for the IPR were developed with a sample of 107 clients currently engaged in counseling of whom 50 were evaluated by their therapists as not having problems with peers. Means for these groups on the IPR are 55.9 and 20.8, respectively, although these means are based on scales with 5 rather than 7 response categories. No other demographic information was provided, although the sample was described as diverse with respect to gender, ethnicity, and social class.

SCORING: Like most WALMYR Assessment Scales instruments, the IPR is scored by first reverse-scoring items listed at the bottom of the page (1, 4, 7, 8, 11, 12, 15–18, 21, 22), summing the scores, subtracting the number of completed items, multiplying this figure by 100, and dividing by the number of items completed times 6. This will produce a range from 0 to 100 with higher scores indicating greater magnitude or severity of problems.

RELIABILITY: The IPR has a mean alpha of .94 indicating excellent internal consistency, and an excellent (low) Standard Error of Measurement of 4.44. Test-retest data are not available.

VALIDITY: The IPR has excellent known-groups validity, significantly distinguishing between clients judged by themselves and their therapists as either having or not having peer relationship problems.

PRIMARY REFERENCE: Hudson, W. W. (1997). *The WALMYR Assessment Scales Scoring Manual*. Tallahassee, FL: WALMYR Publishing Company.

AVAILABILITY: This scale cannot be reproduced or copied in any manner and must be obtained by writing to the WALMYR Publishing Company, PO Box 12217, Tallahassee, FL 32317-2217 or by calling (850) 383-0045.

INDEX OF PEER RELATIONS (IPR)

Name: _____ Today's Date: _____

PEER GROUP _____

This questionnaire is designed to measure the way you feel about the people you work, play, or associate with most of the time; your peer group. It is not a test, so there are no right or wrong answers. Place the name of your peer group at the top of the page in the space provided. Then answer each item as carefully and as accurately as you can by placing a number beside each one as follows.

    1 = None of the time
    2 = Very rarely
    3 = A little of the time
    4 = Some of the time
    5 = A good part of the time
    6 = Most of the time
    7 = All of the time

1. ____ I get along very well with my peers.
2. ____ My peers act like they don't care about me.
3. ____ My peers treat me badly.
4. ____ My peers really seem to respect me.
5. ____ I don't feel like am "part of the group".
6. ____ My peers are a bunch of snobs.
7. ____ My peers understand me.
8. ____ My peers seem to like me very much.
9. ____ I really feel "left out" of my peer group.
10. ____ I hate my present peer group.
11. ____ My peers seem to like having me around.
12. ____ I really like my present peer group.
13. ____ I really feel like I am disliked by my peers.
14. ____ I wish I had a different peer group.
15. ____ My peers are very nice to me.
16. ____ My peers seem to look up to me.
17. ____ My peers think I am important to them.
18. ____ My peers are a real source of pleasure to me.
19. ____ My peers don't seem to even notice me.
20. ____ I wish I were not part of this peer group.
21. ____ My peers regard my ideas and opinions very highly.
22. ____ I feel like I am an important member of my peer group.
23. ____ I can't stand to be around my peer group.
24. ____ My peers seem to look down on me.
25. ____ My peers really do not interest me.

Copyright (c) 1992, Walter W. Hudson   Illegal to Photocopy or Otherwise Reprod

1, 4, 7, 8, 11, 12, 15, 16, 17, 18, 21, 22.

INVENTORY OF PARENT AND PEER ATTACHMENT (IPPA)

AUTHORS: Gay C. Armsden and Mark T. Greenberg

PURPOSE: To measure attachment to parents and peers.

DESCRIPTION: The IPPA consists of three 25-item instruments that measure one's attachment to parents and peers. The inventory has separate scales to measure attachment to mother, father, and close friends. The instrument considers these significant others as a source of psychological security. Each instrument yields three subscales, although the use of total scores is recommended over subscale scores. The three subscales are trust (T), communication (C), and alienation (A); all items for the A subscale are reverse-scored, so that the subscale is actually the absence of alienation in one's attachment to parents and peers. While the IPPA was originally developed for late adolescence, it is actually useful for ages 10 to 20.

NORMS: The scoring procedure has changed since the IPPA was originally published. There are no norms for the current version of the IPPA.

SCORING: All three instruments are scored independently. Total attachment scores for mother and father are the sum of all items after reverse-scoring items 3, 6, 8, 9, 10, 11, 14, 17, 18, 23. Subscale scores are developed using the following procedures: $T = 1 + 2 + 4 + 13 + 14 + 21 + 23 + 24$; $C = 6 + 8 + 16 + 17 + 20 + 26 + 28$; $A = 1 + 9 + 12 + 18 + 19 + 22 + 25 + 27$. Total peer attachment scores are the sum of all items after reverse-scoring items 4, 5, 9, 10, 11, 18, 22, and 23. Subscale scores are derived from the following procedures: $T = 6 + 8 + 12 + 13 + 14 + 15 + 19 + 20 + 21$; $C = 1 + 2 + 3 + 7 + 16 + 17 + 24 + 25$; $A = 4 + 9 + 10 + 11 + 18 + 22 + 23$. Higher scores indicate more attachment.

RELIABILITY: The original form of the IPPA did not separate mother from father attachment. The T, C, and A subscales of this prototype had internal consistency alphas of .91, .91, and .86, respectively. The peer scale had internal consistency coefficients of .91, .87, and .72 for the T, C, and A subscales. Test-retest reliability coefficients over a three-week interval were excellent: .93 for the prototype parent attachment scale and .86 for the peer attachment.

VALIDITY: The IPPA has excellent concurrent validity. Scores correlate with several measures of psychological well-being, including self-concept, self-esteem, positiveness, life satisfaction, problem solving, and locus of control. Scores are negatively correlated with depression and loneliness. Scores also correlate with several measures of family functioning. The IPPA also has good known-groups validity with scores discriminating delinquent from nondelinquent youngsters.

PRIMARY REFERENCE: Armsden, G. C. and Greenberg, M. T. (1987). The Inventory of Parent and Peer Attachment: Individual differences and the relationship to psychological well-being in adolescence, *Journal of Youth and Adolescence*, 16, 427–454. Instruments reproduced with permission of Mark T. Greenberg.

AVAILABILITY: Instruments and a short manual are available for $5.00 from Mark T. Greenberg, Ph.D., Department of Psychology, NI-25, University of Washington, Seattle, Washington 98195.

IPPA

This questionnaire asks about your relationships with important people in your life—your mother, your father, and your close friends. Please read the directions to each part carefully.

PART I

Each of the following statements asks about your feeling about your *mother*, or the woman who has acted as your mother. If you have more than one person acting as your mother (e.g., a natural mother and a stepmother) answer the questions for the one you feel has most influenced you.

Please read each statement and circle the *ONE* number that tells how true the statement is for you now.

		Almost never or never true	Not very often true	Some-times true	Often true	Almost always or always true
1.	My mother respects my feelings.	1	2	3	4	5
2.	I feel my mother does a good job as my mother.	1	2	3	4	5
3.	I wish I had a different mother.	1	2	3	4	5
4.	My mother accepts me as I am.	1	2	3	4	5
5.	I like to get my mother's point of view on things I'm concerned about.	1	2	3	4	5
6.	I feel it's no use letting my feelings show around my mother.	1	2	3	4	5
7.	My mother can tell when I'm upset about something.	1	2	3	4	5

		Almost never or never true	Not very often true	Some- times true	Often true	Almost always or always true
8.	Talking over my problems with my mother makes me feel ashamed or foolish.	1	2	3	4	5
9.	My mother expects too much from me.	1	2	3	4	5
10.	I get upset easily around my mother.	1	2	3	4	5
11.	I get upset a lot more than my mother knows about.	1	2	3	4	5
12.	When we discuss things, my mother cares about my point of view.	1	2	3	4	5
13.	My mother trusts my judgment.	1	2	3	4	5
14.	My mother has her own problems, so I don't bother her with mine.	1	2	3	4	5
15.	My mother helps me to understand myself better.	1	2	3	4	5
16.	I tell my mother about my problems and troubles.	1	2	3	4	5
17.	I feel angry with my mother.	1	2	3	4	5
18.	I don't get much attention from my mother.	1	2	3	4	5

		Almost never or never true	Not very often true	Some-times true	Often true	Almost always or always true
19.	My mother helps me to talk about my difficulties.	1	2	3	4	5
20.	My mother under-stands me.	1	2	3	4	5
21.	When I am angry about something, my mother tries to be understanding.	1	2	3	4	5
22.	I trust my mother.	1	2	3	4	5
23.	My mother doesn't understand what I'm going through these days.	1	2	3	4	5
24.	I can count on my mother when I need to get something off my chest.	1	2	3	4	5
25.	If my mother knows something is bother-ing me, she asks me about it.	1	2	3	4	5

PART II

This part asks about your feeling about your *father*, or the man who has acted as your father. If you have more than one person acting as your father (e.g., natural and stepfathers) answer the questions for the one you feel has most influenced you.

		Almost never or never true	Not very often true	Some-times true	Often true	Almost always or always true
1.	My father respects my feelings.	1	2	3	4	5

		Almost never or never true	Not very often true	Some-times true	Often true	Almost always or always true
2.	I feel my father does a good job as my father.	1	2	3	4	5
3.	I wish I had a different father.	1	2	3	4	5
4.	My father accepts me as I am.	1	2	3	4	5
5.	I like to get my father's point of view on things I'm concerned about.	1	2	3	4	5
6.	I feel it's no use letting my feelings show around my father.	1	2	3	4	5
7.	My father can tell when I'm upset about something.	1	2	3	4	5
8.	Talking over my problems with my father makes me feel ashamed or foolish.	1	2	3	4	5
9.	My father expects too much from me.	1	2	3	4	5
10.	I get upset easily around my father.	1	2	3	4	5
11.	I get upset a lot more than my father knows about.	1	2	3	4	5
12.	When we discuss things, my father cares about my point of view.	1	2	3	4	5
13.	My father trusts my judgment.	1	2	3	4	5

		Almost never or never true	Not very often true	Some-times true	Often true	Almost always or always true
14.	My father has his own problems, so I don't bother him with mine.	1	2	3	4	5
15.	My father helps me to understand myself better.	1	2	3	4	5
16.	I tell my father about my problems and troubles.	1	2	3	4	5
17.	I feel angry with my father.	1	2	3	4	5
18.	I don't get much atten-tion from my father.	1	2	3	4	5
19.	My father helps me to talk about my difficulties.	1	2	3	4	5
20.	My father under-stands me.	1	2	3	4	5
21.	When I am angry about something, my father tries to be understanding.	1	2	3	4	5
22.	I trust my father.	1	2	3	4	5
23.	My father doesn't understand what I'm going through these days.	1	2	3	4	5
24.	I can count on my father when I need to get something off my chest.	1	2	3	4	5

	Almost never or never true	Not very often true	Some-times true	Often true	Almost always or always true
25. If my father knows something is bothering me, he asks me about it.	1	2	3	4	5

PART III

This part asks about your feelings about your relationships with your close friends. Please read each statement and circle the *ONE* number that tells how true the statement is for you now.

	Almost never or never true	Not very often true	Some-times true	Often true	Almost always or always true
1. I like to get my friends' point of view on things I'm concerned about.	1	2	3	4	5
2. My friends can tell when I'm upset about something.	1	2	3	4	5
3. When we discuss things, my friends care about my point of view.	1	2	3	4	5
4. Talking over my problems with my friends makes me feel ashamed or foolish.	1	2	3	4	5
5. I wish I had different friends.	1	2	3	4	5
6. My friends under-stand me.	1	2	3	4	5

		Almost never or never true	Not very often true	Some-times true	Often true	Almost always or always true
7.	My friends help me to talk about my diffi-culties.	1	2	3	4	5
8.	My friends accept me as I am.	1	2	3	4	5
9.	I feel the need to be in touch with my friends more often.	1	2	3	4	5
10.	My friends don't under-stand what I'm gong through these days.	1	2	3	4	5
11.	I feel alone or apart when I'm with my friends.	1	2	3	4	5
12.	My friends listen to what I have to say.	1	2	3	4	5
13.	I feel my friends are good friends.	1	2	3	4	5
14.	My friends are fairly easy to talk to.	1	2	3	4	5
15.	When I am angry about something, my friends try to be understanding.	1	2	3	4	5
16.	My friends help me to understand myself better.	1	2	3	4	5
17.	My friends care about how I am.	1	2	3	4	5
18.	I feel angry with my friends.	1	2	3	4	5

	Almost never or never true	Not very often true	Some- times true	Often true	Almost always or always true
19. I can count on my friends when I need to get something off my chest.	1	2	3	4	5
20. I trust my friends.	1	2	3	4	5
21. My friends respect my feelings.	1	2	3	4	5
22. I get upset a lot more than my friends know about.	1	2	3	4	5
23. It seems as if my friends are irritated with me for no reason.	1	2	3	4	5
24. I can tell my friends about my problems and troubles.	1	2	3	4	5
25. If my friends know something is bothering me, they ask me about it.	1	2	3	4	5

MOOD THERMOMETERS (MT)

AUTHOR: Bruce W. Tuckman

PURPOSE: To measure moods.

DESCRIPTION: This 5-item instrument quickly and accurately measures subjective feeling states at any particular moment. The MT was designed for use with adolescents, though it is clearly useful for all age groups. The instrument was developed from the position that mood represents one's awareness of well-being and ill-being. The five mood states measured are tension, confusion, anger, fatigue, and depression. The thermometers may be used as individual indices or combined to measure two factors of mood: anger and poorness of mood.

SCORING: Each thermometer may be used as an index of the mood state with scores ranging from 0 to 100. Some are upside-down in order to reduce any response set. Poorness of mood scores is determined by adding the scores for tension, confusion, fatigue, and depression, and dividing by four. Anger is scored on a 0 to 100 index.

NORMS: Normative data are not available. As a measure of the immediate awareness of one's mood states, normative data are also less useful. That is, as state measures, scores fluctuate continuously and may be influenced by different environments.

RELIABILITY: Factor analysis was used to show the internal association of the four items of poorness of mood, a method of providing evidence about internal consistency. Test-retest reliability evidence suggests a variable which is a state and not a trait, with correlations ranging from .50 to .64, and averaging .57.

VALIDITY: The MT has good concurrent validity, correlating with the Profile of Mood Scale. The MT also has evidence of known-groups validity, as seen in distinguishing scores of students participating in a regular physical education class from scores of students involuntarily assigned to special programs which were disfavored by the students.

PRIMARY REFERENCE: Tuckman, B. W. (1988). The scaling of mood, *Educational and Psychological Measurement*, 48, 419–427. Instrument reproduced with permission of Bruce Tuckman and *Educational and Psychological Measurement*.

AVAILABILITY: Journal article.

MT

HOW I FEEL RIGHT NOW

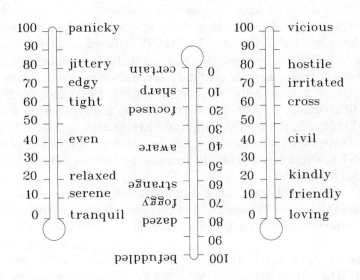

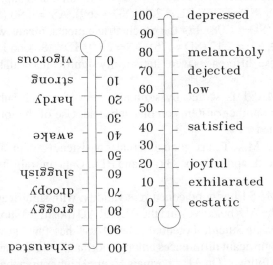

There are five thermometers to measure your feelings. Mark a line on each one to show how "high" or "low" you feel. Each one measures a different feeling. Don't just mark them all the same. For two of them, you have to turn the paper over. Give your real, honest feeling. Don't just make something up.

Copyright © 1986 Bruce W. Tuckman.

MULTI-ATTITUDE SUICIDE TENDENCY SCALE (MAST)

AUTHORS: Israel Orbach, Ilana Milstein, Dov Har-Even, Alan Apter, Sam Tiano, and Avner Elizur

PURPOSE: To measure suicide tendency in adolescents.

DESCRIPTION: The MAST is a 30-item instrument designed to measure suicide tendency among adolescents. The MAST is based on the premise that suicidal behavior evolves around a basic conflict among attitudes toward life and death. Factor analysis confirmed four subscales that deal with these conflicts: attraction to life (AL; items 1, 5, 6, 13, 18, 25, 28), repulsion by life (RL; items 2, 9, 14–16, 21, 30), attraction to death (AD; items 8, 17, 19, 22, 23, 26, 27), and repulsion by death (RD; items 3, 4, 7, 10–12, 20, 24, 29). Given the high frequency of suicide behavior among adolescents, the MAST is a very important scale for assessing and monitoring changes in suicide tendencies.

NORMS: The MAST was studied with two samples of adolescents in Israel including a total of 79 male and 67 female "normal" respondents, 33 male and 46 female suicidal adolescents, and 20 male and 14 female nonsuicidal psychiatric patients. The age range was 13 to 18 years. For the "normal" group the means were: AL = 4.13 (SD = .46), RL = 1.70 (SD = .60), AD = 2.30 (SD = .76), and RD = 3.02 (SD = .80). For the suicidal group, the means were AL = 3.68 (SD = .76), RL = 2.53 (SD = .69), AS = 2.90 (SD = .70), and RD = 2.92 (SD = 1.08). For the psychiatric patients, means were: AL = 3.70 (SD = .76), RL = 2.12 (SD = .76), AS = 2.40 (SD = .86), and RD = 3.07 (SD = .95). These differences were statistically significant on all but the RD subscale.

SCORING: The MAST is scored by summing items for each subscale and dividing by the number of items on that subscale. Use of the total score is not recommended.

RELIABILITY: The MAST has good internal consistency, with alphas that range from .76 (RL and AD) to .83 (AL and RD). Data on stability were not reported.

VALIDITY: The MAST has good concurrent validity, with significant correlations between the AL (negative) and the RL and AD (positive) subscales and the Israeli Index of Suicide Potential. The MAST has fair known-groups validity, with significant differences among "normal," suicidal, and psychiatric patients as follows: On AL, "normals" scored higher than the other two groups; on RL all three groups differed, with the suicidal group scoring highest and the "normal" group scoring lowest; and on AD, the suicidal group scored highest.

PRIMARY REFERENCE: Orbach, I., Milstein, I., Har-Even, D., Apter, A., Tiano, S., Elizur, A. (1981). A Multi-Attitude Suicide Tendency Scale for adolescents, *Psychological Assessment*, 3, 398–404.

AVAILABILITY: Dr. Israel Orbach, Department of Psychology, Bar-Ilan University, Ramat-Gan 52900, Israel.

MAST

This is a questionnaire of attitudes about life and death. It is not an examination and there are no right or wrong answers. Please fill out the questionnaire according to what *you* think and feel. This is what is important to us.

Please read every sentence carefully and rate it on the degree to which you agree with it.

If the sentence reflects what you never feel and think, please circle *Strongly disagree* (1).

If the sentence reflects what you feel and think rarely, please circle *Don't agree* (2).

If the sentence reflects what you feel and think *sometimes*, please circle *Sometimes agree; sometimes disagree* (3).

If the sentence reflects what you feel and think *most* of the time, please circle *Agree* (4).

If the sentence reflects strongly what you feel and think *all* of the time, please circle *Strongly agree* (5).

Thank you for your cooperation.

		Strongly disagree	Don't agree	Sometimes agree; sometimes disagree	Agree	Strongly agree
1.	Most of the time I feel happy.	1	2	3	4	5
2.	Life seems to be one long and difficult struggle.	1	2	3	4	5
3.	I fear the idea that there is no return from death.	1	2	3	4	5
4.	I fear death because all my mental and spiritual activity will stop.	1	2	3	4	5
5.	Even though things may be tough at times, I think it's worth living.	1	2	3	4	5

		Strongly disagree	Don't agree	Sometimes agree; sometimes disagree	Agree	Strongly agree
6.	I feel that close people make me feel good.	1	2	3	4	5
7.	I fear death because my identity will disappear.	1	2	3	4	5
8.	I know people who have died and I believe that I will meet them when I die.	1	2	3	4	5
9.	I don't ask for help even when things are very tough for me.	1	2	3	4	5
10.	Thinking about death gives me the shivers.	1	2	3	4	5
11.	I am afraid of death because my body will rot.	1	2	3	4	5
12.	I fear death because it means that I will not be able to experience and think anymore.	1	2	3	4	5
13.	I can see myself as being very successful in the future.	1	2	3	4	5
14.	I feel that I am not important to my family.	1	2	3	4	5
15.	Sometimes I feel that my family will be better off without me.	1	2	3	4	5
16.	Sometimes I feel that my problems can't be solved.	1	2	3	4	5
17.	Death can change things for the better.	1	2	3	4	5

		Strongly disagree	Don't agree	Sometimes agree; sometimes disagree	Agree	Strongly agree
18.	I like to do many things.	1	2	3	4	5
19.	Death is actually eternal life.	1	2	3	4	5
20.	The thought that one day I will die frightens me.	1	2	3	4	5
21.	I don't like to spend time with my family.	1	2	3	4	5
22.	Many problems can be solved by death only.	1	2	3	4	5
23.	I believe that death can bring a great relief for suffering.	1	2	3	4	5
24.	I fear death because all my plans will come to an end.	1	2	3	4	5
25.	I am very hopeful.	1	2	3	4	5
26.	In some situations it is better to die than go on living.	1	2	3	4	5
27.	Death can be a state of rest and calm.	1	2	3	4	5
28.	I enjoy many things in life.	1	2	3	4	5
29.	Death frightens me more than anything else.	1	2	3	4	5
30.	No one really loves me.	1	2	3	4	5

MULTIGROUP ETHNIC IDENTITY MEASURE (MEIM)

AUTHOR: Jean S. Phinney

PURPOSE: To measure ethnic identity.

DESCRIPTION: The MEIM is a 12-item instrument designed to measure ethnic identity, particularly among adolescents. The MEIM provides a means of examining young people's degree of identification with their ethnic group, regardless of the unique characteristics of their ethnic group. The MEIM is useful with samples that are ethnically diverse or of unknown ethnicity. The measure also permits comparison of correlates of ethnic identity across different samples, such as the relationship of ethnic identity to any number of psychological variables. The MEIM allows the exploration of commonalities across groups as well as the differences among groups in the development of ethnic identity. The current version of the MEIM comprises two factors: ethnic identity search (items 1, 2, 4, 8, and 10), and affirmation, belonging, and commitment (items 3, 5, 6, 7, 9, 11, and 12). The first factor is thought to be a developmental and cognitive component and the second factor is an affective component. The data presented here are from research on an earlier 14-item scale; data on the 12-item scale are available from the author.

NORMS: The MEIM was studied with 417 high school participants (182 males and 235 females) attending an urban school with an ethnically diverse student body. The mean age was 16.5 years, and respondents were from diverse socioeconomic backgrounds. The sample included 134 Asian-Americans, 131 African-Americans, 89 Hispanics, 49 students with mixed backgrounds, 12 whites, and 10 other. An additional 136 respondents who were attending a large urban university (47 males and 89 females) participated in the study. That sample included 58 Hispanics, 35 Asian-Americans, 23 whites, 11 African-Americans, 8 mixed backgrounds, and 1 American Indian. The mean age was 20.2. Overall means on the 14-item scale for ethnic identity were 2.94 (SD = .50) for the high school students and 3.0 (SD = .59) for the college students. Norms for the revised 12-item version with two factors are available from the author.

SCORING: The MEIM is scored by simply summing all items for each subscale and the total scale and deriving the mean by dividing by the number of items on each subscale and the total number of items. Higher scores indicate stronger ethnic identity.

RELIABILITY: The MEIM has good internal consistency with alphas for subscales above .80 across a wide range of ethnic groups and ages. No data on stability were available.

VALIDITY: Unpublished research obtainable from the author has more evidence of validity of the MEIM. Published research shows some degree of concurrent validity of the MEIM with statistically significant positive correlations between the MEIM and the Rosenberg Self-Esteem Inventory for Minority Students as predicted by the literature.

PRIMARY REFERENCE: Phinney, J. S. (1992). The multigroup ethnic identity measure: A new scale for use with diverse groups, *Journal of Adolescent Research*, 7, 156–176.

AVAILABILITY: Written permission is not required for use of the measure. The author requests a summary of results and copies of any papers or publications that result from using the measure: Jean S. Phinney, Ph.D., Department of Psychology, California State University, Los Angeles, CA 90032-8227. Reprinted by permission of the author.

MEIM

In this country, people come from many different countries and cultures, and there are many different words to describe the different backgrounds or *ethnic groups* that people come from. Some examples of the names of ethnic groups are Hispanic or Latino, Black or Latino, Black or African-American, Asian-American, Native American or American Indian, Mexican American, and Caucasian or White. These questions are about your ethnicity or your ethnic group and how you feel about it or react to it.

Please fill in: In terms of ethnic group, I consider myself to be _____

Use the numbers below to indicate how much you agree or disagree with each statement.

1 = Strongly disagree
2 = Disagree
3 = Agree
4 = Strongly agree

____ 1. I have spent time trying to find out more about my ethnic group, such as its history, traditions, and customs.

____ 2. I am active in organizations or social groups that include mostly members of my own ethnic group.

____ 3. I have a clear sense of my ethnic background and what it means for me.

____ 4. I think a lot about how my life will be affected by my ethnic group membership.

____ 5. I am happy that I am a member of the group I belong to.

____ 6. I have strong sense of belonging to my own ethnic group.

____ 7. I understand pretty well what my ethnic group membership means to me.

____ 8. In order to learn more about my ethnic background, I have often talked to other people about my ethnic group.

____ 9. I have a lot of pride in my ethnic group.

____ 10. I participate in cultural practices of my own group, such as special food, music, or customs.

____ 11. I feel a strong attachment towards my own ethnic group.

____ 12. I feel good about my cultural or ethnic background.

____ 13. My ethnicity is

____ (1) Asian or Asian-American, including Chinese, Japanese, and others

____ (2) Black or African-American

____ (3) Hispanic or Latino, including Mexican-American, Central American, and others

____ (4) White, Caucasian, Anglo, European American; not Hispanic

____ (5) American Indian/Native American

____ (6) Mixed; Parents are from two different groups

____ (7) Other (write in): _____

____ 14. My father's ethnicity is (use numbers above)

____ 15. My mother's ethnicity is (use numbers above)

NOWICKI-STRICKLAND LOCUS OF CONTROL SCALE (N-SLCS)

AUTHORS: Stephen Nowicki, Jr, and Bonni R. Strickland

PURPOSE: To measure locus of control in children.

DESCRIPTION: The N-SLCS is a 40-item instrument designed to measure whether or not a child believes that reinforcement comes to him or her by chance or fate (external locus of control) or because of his or her own behavior (internal locus of control). Locus of control in children is important because a number of studies have shown that it is related to several other behaviors and attitudes including some involving academic achievement. Thus, a child who is relatively high in internal locus of control will view himself or herself as more in control of his or her life. The N-SLCS has been used with children from the third grade up. It also has been modified for use by college-age and adult respondents by changing the word "kids" to "people" and deleting items about parents.

NORMS: The N-SLCS was developed in a series of studies involving over 1000 male and female children from the third to the twelfth grade. the students were primarily white with representation from all socioeconomic levels. Means for males and females are available and range from 11.01 to 18.80, with students' responses becoming more internal with age.

SCORING: The N-SLCS is scored by adding up the number of items that are scored "correctly," The correct responses are "yes" for items 1, 3, 5, 7, 8, 10–12, 14, 16–19, 21, 23, 24, 27, 29, 31, 33, 35–39, and "no" for the remainder. Higher scores reflect more external locus of control.

RELIABILITY: The N-SLCS has only fair internal consistency overall, with split-half reliabilities increasing with age: .32 for grades 3 through 5, .68 for grades 6 through 8, .74 for grades 6 through 11, and .81 for grade 12. Stability of the instrument is fair, with six-week test-retest correlations of .63 for the third grade, .66 for the seventh grade, and .71 for the tenth grade.

VALIDITY: The N-SLCS has fair concurrent validity, correlating significantly with three other measures of locus of control. The N-SLCS also has been shown to correlate with a number of other academic and nonacademic behaviors, although race, socioeconomic level, and sex tend to mediate some of those findings. Further, the N-SLCS also has been found to be sensitive to change due to a therapeutically designed camping experience. The N-SLCS was found not to be affected by social desirability response set.

PRIMARY REFERENCE: Nowicki, S. and Strickland, B. R., (1973) A locus of control scale for children, *Journal of Consulting and Clinical Psychology* 40, 148–154. Instrument reproduced with permission of Stephen Nowicki and the American Psychological Association.

AVAILABILITY: Dr. Stephen Nowicki, Jr., Department of Psychology, Emory University Atlanta, GA 30322.

N-SLCS

Please circle Yes or No for each question as it applies to you.

Yes No 1. Do you believe that most problems will solve themselves if you just don't fool with them?

Yes No 2. Do you believe that you can stop yourself from catching a cold?

Yes No 3. Are some kids just born lucky?

Yes No 4. Most of the time do you feel that getting good grades means a great deal to you?

Yes No 5. Are you often blamed for things that just aren't your fault?

Yes No 6. Do you believe that if somebody studies hard enough he or she can pass any subject?

Yes No 7. Do you feel that most of the time it doesn't pay to try hard because things never turn out right anyway?

Yes No 8. Do you feel that if things start out well in the morning it's going to be a good day no matter what you do?

Yes No 9. Do you feel that most of the time parents listen to what their children have to say?

Yes No 10. Do you believe that wishing can make good things happen?

Yes No 11. When you get punished does it usually seem it's for no good reason at all?

Yes No 12. Most of the time do you find it hard to change a friend's opinion?

Yes No 13. Do you think that cheering more than luck helps a team to win?

Yes No 14. Do you feel that it's nearly impossible to change your parent's mind about anything?

Yes No 15. Do you believe that your parents should allow you to make most of your own decisions?

Yes No 16. Do you feel that when you do something wrong there's very little you can do to make it right?

Yes No 17. Do you believe that most kids are just born good at sports?

Yes No 18. Are most of the other kids your age stronger than you are?

Yes No 19. Do you feel that one of the best ways to handle most problems is just not to think about them?

Yes No 20. Do you feel that you have a lot of choice in deciding who your friends are?

Yes No 21. If you find a four-leaf clover do you believe that it might bring you good luck?

Yes No 22. Do you often feel that whether you do your homework has much to do with what kind of grades you get?

Yes No 23. Do you feel that when a kid your age decides to hit you, there's little you can do to stop him or her?

Yes No 24. Have you ever had a good luck charm?

Yes No 25. Do you believe that whether or not people like you depends on how you act?

Yes No 26. Will your parents usually help you if you ask them to?

Yes No 27. Have you felt that when people were mean to you it was usually for no reason at all?

Yes	No	28.	Most of the time, do you feel that you can change what might happen tomorrow by what you do today?
Yes	No	29.	Do you believe that when bad things are going to happen they just are going to happen no matter what you try to do to stop them?
Yes	No	30.	Do you think that kids can get their own way if they just keep trying?
Yes	No	31.	Most of the time do you find it useless to try to get your own way at home?
Yes	No	32.	Do you feel that when good things happen they happen because of hard work?
Yes	No	33.	Do you feel that when somebody your age wants to be your enemy there's little you can do to change matters?
Yes	No	34.	Do you usually feel that it's easy to get friends to do what you want them to?
Yes	No	35.	Do you usually feel that you have little to say about what you get to eat at home?
Yes	No	36.	Do you feel that when someone doesn't like you there's little you can do about it?
Yes	No	37.	Do you usually feel that it's almost useless to try in school because most other children are just plain smarter than you are?
Yes	No	38.	Are you the kind of person who believes that planning ahead makes things turn out better?
Yes	No	39.	Most of the time, do you feel that you have little to say about what your family decides to do?
Yes	No	40.	Do you think it's better to be smart than to be lucky?

OREGON MENTAL HEALTH REFERRAL
CHECKLIST (OMHRC)

AUTHOR: Kevin Corcoran

PURPOSE: To identify youth in the juvenile justice system in need of a mental health referral.

DESCRIPTION: The OMHRC is a 32-item checklist of which 31 items are specific mental health symptoms or problems which might warrant a mental health referral. The final item is the respondent's judgment of a need for a mental health referral. Total scores may be used to measure the magnitude of mental health problems, or individual items used to determine if a mental health referral is warranted (e.g., tortures animals). The OMHRC was developed with a panel of 15 administrators and providers from juvenile justice and mental health systems using the multidimensional scaling and cluster analytic procedures of concept mapping. The instrument has been tested on three samples: first-time offenders, adjudicated youth, and incarcerated offenders. The OMHRC is available in three parallel versions in order to assess the need for a mental health referral from the perspective of the youth, his or her parent, and a provider in the juvenile justice or mental health systems. The youth self-report version is reprinted here. Each version has three parallel forms in order to assess the mental health symptomatology over an 18-month period, and is printed on non-reproduction paper to share the completed form between juvenile justice and mental health agencies and to establish a cumulative record over time. The parent and youth versions of the OMHRC are available in Spanish, although there are no psychometric data on those versions.

NORMS: Each item on the OMHRC is designed to facilitate clinical decision making. From a sample of 146 adjudicated youths, those reporting they had seen a mental health professional for a personal problem had a mean and standard deviation of 5.4 and 3.1 on a 30-item prototype. Those who reported never having seen a mental health professional had a mean of 4.1 and a standard deviation of 3.4.

SCORING: Endorsement of any particular item may warrant a mental health referral depending on the severity of the symptom. Items are organized in descending order from those with the highest triage rating to the lowest, according to a panel of providers and administrators in mental health and juvenile justice. Total scores are the sum of the first 31 items which are endorsed. Scores range from zero to 31; higher scores reflect more symptoms.

RELIABILITY: The internal consistency of a prototype of the OMHRC was .72. The interrater agreement between juvenile justice counselors and parents was .48.

VALIDITY: The validity of the OMHRC was estimated with concurrent validity procedures. Scores on a prototype correlated with previous mental health history and external symptomatology using the Child Behavior Checklist. Total scores also differentiated youth with different mental health histories, which supports known-groups validity. The items of the OMHRC cluster around symptoms characteristic of youth in the juvenile justice and mental health systems, as determined by a panel of 15 administrators and providers. Triage ratings of the items by the panel were correlated with those of a child psychiatrist (r = .95).

PRIMARY REFERENCE: Corcoran, K. and Feyerherm, W. H. (1998). Building bridges between the juvenile justice and mental health systems: Validation of the Oregon Mental Health Referral Checklist. Unpublished manuscript.

AVAILABILITY: In public domain and may be copied *ad libitum.* NCR paper versions available from Kevin Corcoran, Ph.D., J.D., Graduate School of Social Work, Portland State University, POB 751, Portland OR 97201.

OMHRC

Below are 32 statements that might describe you. Please check the *dark* circle for each item which describes you. Unless told otherwise, consider whether each item describes you *within the past 6 months.* If the phrase only describes you *a little,* please check the *light* circle.

This statement describes me.

This statement describes me *a little.*

1. I have made a plan to commit suicide.   O   O
2. I have attempted suicide at least once in my life.   O   O
3. I feel like killing somebody.   O   O
4. I have had hallucinations (seen or heard things that weren't there when *not* on drugs or alcohol).   O   O
5. I have a strong belief that something is true when most people say it isn't (e.g., someone is out to get me).   O   O
6. While *not* on drugs or alcohol, have you lost touch with reality (felt "crazy")?   O   O
7. Have you intentionally harmed or injured an animal?   O   O
8. Have you started a fire that was dangerous or could have done harm or damage?   O   O
9. Have you sexually assaulted another or taken sexual advantage of another in the past 6 months?   O   O
10. I have used drugs or alcohol in the past 6 months.   O   O
11. Have you had frequent sex with people, or used sex to start a relationship?   O   O
12. Have you [I have] physically harmed yourself (such as cutting yourself, or putting a cigarette out on your skin)?   O   O
13. Have you *ever* been abused sexually or forced into a sexual activity?   O   O
14. Have you seen horrible/traumatic things or severe violence, including domestic violence?   O   O
15. I have threatened or intentionally harmed others.   O   O
16. I have explosive outbursts or sometimes throw fits.   O   O
17. I have intentionally destroyed someone else's belongings/property (e.g., vandalism).   O   O
18. Have you run away from your home or residence in the past 6 months?   O   O
19. I feel depressed *most* of the time.   O   O
20. I feel a sense of grief or deep loss for no reason at all.   O   O
21. I feel out of control of my emotions.   O   O
22. I frequently feel confused or get distracted easily and get off task.   O   O
23. I feel overactive or hyperactive.   O   O
24. I have thoughts I can't get out of my mind or behavior I can't stop.   O   O
25. On a typical day my moods are extreme and change dramatically (e.g., going quickly from happy to sad).   O   O
26. My moods seem extreme or different from others in the same situation.   O   O
27. I feel withdrawn or isolated from others.   O   O

28. I have difficulty sleeping, including nightmares.   o o
29. I have lost/gained a noticeable amount of weight in the past 6   o o
    months.
30. I feel anxious or worried most of the time.   o o
31. I feel angry much of the time or argue a lot.   o o
32. Do you need to see a mental health counselor?   o o

PAIN RESPONSE INVENTORY (PRI)

AUTHORS: Lynn S. Walker, Craig A. Smith, Judy Garber, and Deborah A. Van Slyke

PURPOSE: To measure children's coping responses to pain.

DESCRIPTION: The PRI is a 60-item instrument designed to measure children's coping responses to recurrent pain. The PRI assesses three broad coping factors—active, passive, and accommodative—with each of these factors consisting of subscales representing specific strategies for coping with pain. The PRI was developed to provide for practitioners a measure suitable for school-age children with chronic or recurrent pain, specifically, recurrent abdominal pain which is the most common recurrent pain complaint of childhood. The theoretical and empirical literature was used to develop this measure which identifies different types of strategies for coping with pain; this is of particular interest because different strategies may be amenable to change through clinical interventions. There are 13 subscales on the PRI: problem solving (items 1, 8, 19, 32, 47); acceptance (items 4, 14, 19, 24, 37, 38, 53); seeking social support (items 28, 45, 46, 49, 51, 58); rest (items 6, 16, 26, 39, 55); massage/guard (items 21, 29, 41); condition-specific strategies (items 7, 17, 27, 35, 56); self-isolation (items 5, 15, 25, 38, 54); behavioral disengagement (items 3, 13, 23, 36, 52); catastrophizing (items 11, 18, 30, 42, 57); minimizing pain (items 9, 20, 33); self-encouragement (items 31, 43, 59); distract/ignore (items 10, 34, 44, 48, 60); and stoicism (items 2, 12, 22, 40, 50). The overall strategies are: Passive Coping (subscales behavioral disengagement, self-isolation, catastrophizing); Active Coping (subscales problem solving, seeking social support, rest, massage/guard, condition-specific strategies); and Accommodative Coping (subscales acceptance, minimizing pain, self-encouragement and distract/ ignore). The subscale Stoicism is not included on any of the overall strategies.

NORMS: The PRI was initially developed on three samples. Sample 1 was 688 school children in Nashville, Tennessee with a mean age of 11.79 of whom 59% were female. Sixty-four percent of the sample was Caucasian, 23% were African-American, and 13% were other ethnicities. Sample 2 included 158 new patients with abdominal pain at a pediatric clinic with a mean age of 11.92; 56% were female and 96% were Caucasian. The third sample involved 175 former pediatric abdominal pain patients with a mean age of 15.46 of whom 62% were female. A control sample of 49 well former patients who had participated in an earlier study also were involved; they had a mean age of 15.38 and 47% were female. The means on the three broad coping factors are as follows for the total school sample: on Active Coping M = 1.93 (SD = .70), Passive Coping, M = 1.13 (SD = .68), and Accommodative Coping, M = 1.49 (SD = .80). For clinic patients, on Active Coping, M = 2.28

(SD = .60); Passive Coping, M = 1.10 (SD = .77); and on Accommodative Coping, M = 1.98 (SD = .71). For former patients, on Active Coping, M = 2.07 (SD = .56); Passive Coping, M = 1.08 (SD = .64); and Accommodative Coping, M = 2.04 (SD = .70). The mean scores are available in the original article for all 13 subscales.

SCORING: Each subscale is scored by computing the mean of the item responses for that subscale. The three overall coping strategies are scored by computing the mean of the subscales for each coping strategy.

RELIABILITY: The PRI has fair to good internal consistency with alphas on the subscales that range from .66 to .91. Alphas for the broad coping factors ranged from .64 to .82. The PRI has fair stability with a 1-week test-retest correlation for the school sample that ranged from .46 to .71 for the subscales with a median of .59. For the clinic subsample, 6-month test-retest correlations ranged from .34 to .46.

VALIDITY: The PRI has established good construct validity with correlations with scores on the Abdominal Pain Index and measures of somatization symptoms, functional disability, and depressive symptoms. For example, the overall strategy of passive coping was associated with negative outcomes including higher levels of pain. Individual subscales also were associated in a variety of ways with a number of other measures involving pain and pain-related states. Several of the subscales and the passive coping and accommodative coping overall strategies also were statistically significant predictors of changes in pain and somatization symptoms. There also were several statistically significant differences among nonrecovered, recovered, and well patients on several of the subscales and on the three coping strategies, thus suggesting good known-groups validity.

PRIMARY REFERENCE: Walker, L. S., Smith C. A., Garber, J., and Van Slyke, D. A. (1997). Development and validation of the Pain Response Inventory for children, *Psychological Assessment,* 9, 392–405.

AVAILABILITY: Dr. Lynn S. Walker, Division of Adolescent Medicine, 436 Medical Center South, Vanderbilt University Medical Center, Nashville, TN 37232. Reprinted by permission of the author.

PRI

Please circle the number that comes closest to describing you. When you have a bad stomachache, how often do you:

		Never	Once in a while	Some-times	Often	Always
1.	Try hard to do something about it?	0	1	2	3	4
2.	Keep your feelings to yourself?	0	1	2	3	4
3.	Tell yourself that you can't deal with it, and quit trying?	0	1	2	3	4
4.	Try to get used to it?	0	1	2	3	4
5.	Get as far away from other people as you can?	0	1	2	3	4
6.	Lie down to try to feel better?	0	1	2	3	4
7.	Eat something?	0	1	2	3	4
8.	Try to do something to make it go away?	0	1	2	3	4
9.	Tell yourself that it doesn't matter that much to you?	0	1	2	3	4
10.	Do something you enjoy so you won't think about it?	0	1	2	3	4
11.	Think to yourself that it's never going to stop?	0	1	2	3	4
12.	Not let other people see what you're going through?	0	1	2	3	4
13.	Give up trying to feel better?	0	1	2	3	4
14.	Try to accept it?	0	1	2	3	4
15.	Go off by yourself?	0	1	2	3	4
16.	Try not to move around too much?	0	1	2	3	4
17.	Drink something?	0	1	2	3	4
18.	Feel like you can't stand it anymore?	0	1	2	3	4
19.	Try to think of a way that you could make it better?	0	1	2	3	4
20.	Tell yourself that it isn't that big a deal?	0	1	2	3	4
21.	Rub your stomach to try to make it better?	0	1	2	3	4
22.	Not tell anyone how you're feeling?	0	1	2	3	4
23.	Think to yourself that there's nothing you can do, so you don't even try?	0	1	2	3	4
24.	Try to learn to live with it?	0	1	2	3	4
25.	Stay away from people?	0	1	2	3	4
26.	Try to rest?	0	1	2	3	4
27.	Try to go to the bathroom?	0	1	2	3	4
28.	Talk to someone to find out what to do?	0	1	2	3	4

29.	Bend over or curl up to try to feel better?	0	1	2	3	4
30.	Think to yourself that it's going to get worse?	0	1	2	3	4
31.	Tell yourself you can get over the pain?	0	1	2	3	4
32.	Try to figure out what to do about it?	0	1	2	3	4
33.	Tell yourself that it's not that bad?	0	1	2	3	4
34.	Try to think of something pleasant to take your mind off the pain?	0	1	2	3	4
35.	Be careful about what you eat?	0	1	2	3	4
36.	Give up since nothing helps?	0	1	2	3	4
37.	Tell yourself that's just the way it goes?	0	1	2	3	4
38.	Try to be alone?	0	1	2	3	4
39.	Try to keep still?	0	1	2	3	4
40.	Keep others from knowing how much it hurts?	0	1	2	3	4
41.	Hold your stomach to try to make it better?	0	1	2	3	4
42.	Think to yourself that you might be really sick?	0	1	2	0	4
43.	Tell yourself to keep going even though it hurts?	0	1	2	3	4
44.	Try not to think about it?	0	1	2	3	4
45.	Ask someone for help?	0	1	2	3	4
46.	Talk to someone who will understand how you feel?	0	1	2	3	4
47.	Think hard about what to do?	0	1	2	3	4
48.	Think of things to keep your mind off the pain?	0	1	2	3	4
49.	Stay close to someone who cares about you?	0	1	2	3	4
50.	Keep quiet about it?					
51.	Ask someone for ideas about what you can do?	0	1	2	3	4
52.	Not even try to do anything about it because it won't help?	0	1	2	3	4
53.	Tell yourself, "That's life."?	0	1	2	3	4
54.	Try to get away from everyone?	0	1	2	3	4
55.	Stop what you're doing to see if it will help?	0	1	2	3	4
56.	Take some medicine?	0	1	2	3	4
57.	Think to yourself that something might be really wrong with you?	0	1	2	3	4
58.	Talk to someone so that you'll feel better?	0	1	2	3	4
59.	Tell yourself you can deal with the pain?	0	1	2	3	4
60.	Try to forget about it?	0	1	2	3	4

PEER AND SELF-RATING SCALE (PSRS)

AUTHORS: R. A. Glow and P. H. Glow

PURPOSE: To measure symptoms of attention deficit disorder.

DESCRIPTION: This 50-item instrument is designed to measure symptoms of attention deficit/hyperactivity in peers and self. The names of the peers to be rated are listed across the top of the PSRS. After rating the peers the respondent rates him/herself. The PSRS reproduced here is designed for rating six peers, but may be modified in order to rate a different number. The PSRS has six subscales: shyness-sensitivity (SS; items 5, 7, 10, 12, 15, 32, 34); inconsideration (I; items 9, 11, 24, 27, 31, 35, 37, 39, 44, 45, 48); effectiveness (E; items 3, 14, 19, 23, 26, 36, 40, 50); popularity (P; items 13, 33, 38, 47), bullying (B; items 22, 29, 46, 49). Peer ratings of attention deficit behaviors have the advantage of allowing the use of several raters sharing the same observations base, as in rating by members in group treatment, or residents in a group home, or siblings in a family.

NORMS: Normative data are not reported in the primary reference.

SCORING: All items not composing one of the subscales are decoys and are excluded from scoring. Subscale scores are the sum of the number of ratings for each child rated, including the respondent himself or herself. Except for scores on the E and P subscales, higher scores reflect greater ratings of attention deficit behaviors.

RELIABILITY: The internal consistency of the six subscales is very good. The alpha coefficients were .89, .98, .98, .97, .87, and .91 for the SS, I, H, E, P, and B subscales, respectively.

VALIDITY: The PSRS has generally good validity, with extensive research, including factor analysis, multimethod-multitrait analyses of discriminant and convergent validity and predictive validity among the ratings of peers, parents, and teachers (e.g., correlation between peers' and teachers' ratings was .93). The major limitation to the instrument is that peers seem to have difficulty discriminating hyperactivity from inconsideration and effectiveness; effectiveness, in fact, correlated with hyperactivity.

PRIMARY REFERENCE: Glow, R. A. and Glow, P. H. (1980). Peer and Self-rating: Children's perception of behavior relevant to hyperkinetic impulse disorder, *Journal of Abnormal Child Psychology*, 8, 471–490. Instrument reproduced with permission of Peter H. Glow.

AVAILABILITY: Dr. Peter H. Glow, Professor of Psychology, Department of Psychology, The University of Adelaide, G.P.O. Box 498, Adelaide South Australia, Australia 5001.

These questions will help us to find out how well children can notice other children's behavior. At the top of the page are the names of some of the children in this class. If your own name is among those at the top, cross it out and do not put any marks in the column underneath it. At the side of the page are some questions. Read each question carefully and think about whether it applies to any of the people whose names are at the top. Put a cross, X, under the name of each person whose name answers the question. For example if one of the children whose name is at the top is taller than most, you would put a cross under his or her name. Remember to look at all the names. Do each question in turn.

NAMES

1. Who is taller than most?

2. Who fidgets with things?

3. Who is clumsy?

4. Who gets angry when they don't get their own way?

5. Who usually gets chosen last to join in activities?

6. Who is rude to the teacher?

7. Who never seems to be having a good time?

8. Who can't sit still?

9. Who does or says things without thinking?

10. Who is too shy to make friends?

11. Who is mean and cruel to other children?

12. Who is unhappy or sad?

13. Who is your close friend?

14. Who does strange things?

15. Who gets upset when asked to answer questions in class?

16. Who bothers people when they are trying to work?

17. Who is smaller than most?

18. Who thinks of interesting things to do?

19. Who daydreams?

20. Who never seems to get upset by things?

21. Who wants to be the teacher's pet?

22. Who gives dirty looks?

23. Who always seems to understand things?

24. Who acts like a baby?

25. Who always messes around and gets into trouble?

26. Who often has to be reminded of things?

27. Who tries to get others into trouble?

28. Who doesn't pay attention to the teacher?

29. Who says they can beat everybody up?

30. Who gets very upset by tests?

31. Who exaggerates and makes up stories?

32. Who is not noticed much?

33. Who is fun to do things with?

34. Who has very few friends?

35. Who wants to show off in front of the class?

36. Who can be relied upon?

37. Who complains a lot?

38. Who is especially nice?

39. Who blames the others?

40. Who helps the others?

41. Whose feelings are easily hurt?

42. Who is good at sports?

43. Who often doesn't want to play?

44. Who borrows things without asking?

45. Who thinks they are better than everyone else?

46. Who makes fun of people?

47. Who is liked by everyone?

48. Who can't wait their turn?

49. Who tells other children what to do?

50. Who always does what they are told?

When you have finished, go back and put a circle around every question that applies to you. For example, if *you* are taller than most, you put a circle around question 1. Remember to read through all the questions.

Copyright © 1992 R. A. and P. H. Glow.

599

PERSISTENCE SCALE FOR CHILDREN (PS)

AUTHORS: Dubi Lufi and Arie Cohen

PURPOSE: To measure persistence in children.

DESCRIPTION: The PS is a 40-item instrument designed to measure persistence in children or the ability to continue to work at a difficult or even insoluble task, especially over the long run. Persistence is seen as an important characteristic in education and in personality development in general. Persistence may be a personality trait that is especially important in the developmental stages of young people where success hinges on continuing to study or train for many years. This scale is seen as useful for research and possibly even for monitoring clinical efforts to improve children's persistence.

NORMS: The PS initially was studied with 322 Israeli boys and girls aged 7 to 13. The means varied slightly by age and ranged from 20.33 (SD = 3.73) to 24.43 (SD = 4.87) with the youngest children having the lowest means.

SCORING: The PA is simply scored by adding up all items except 5, 10, 15, 20, and 25. These items are "yes" responses except for items 1, 6, 8, 9, 12, 17, 19, 23, 26, 29, 30, 32, 33, 36, 38–40.

RELIABILITY: The PS has fair internal consistency, with an alpha of .66, and very good stability, with a six-month test-retest correlation of .77.

VALIDITY: The PS has good known-groups validity, significantly distinguishing between gymnasts who stayed active in a gymnastics program and those who dropped out. The PS also has good concurrent validity, correlating significantly with the Locus of Control Scale, the Revised Children's Manifest Anxiety Scale, and the extrapunitive and impunitive subscales of the Rosenzweig Picture Frustration Study.

PRIMARY REFERENCE: Lufi, D. and Cohen, A. (1987). A scale for measuring persistence in children, *Journal of Personality Assessment*, 51, 178–185.

AVAILABILITY: Journal article.

PS

Please answer *yes* or *no* to all of the items. In case you have not encountered the situation described in the item, imagine what you would do if faced with such a situation.

		Yes	No
1.	I often do not complete many activities I begin.	——	——
2.	I usually persist in what I am doing.	——	——
3.	When I read a book, I do not like to take breaks until I finish it.	——	——
4.	Even if I fail to solve a problem, I try again and again and hope that I will find the solution.	——	——
5.	When I read a newspaper, I read all the articles on the front page.	——	——
6.	While I am doing my homework, I like to take breaks.	——	——
7.	When I read a book, I do not skip any pages.	——	——
8.	I need lots of encouragement in order to complete many things.	——	——
9.	I do not keep on working after the time given for the work is over.	——	——
10.	I often stay up all night to study.	——	——
11.	If I have decided not to eat chocolate, I will not eat it even if someone offers me some.	——	——
12.	If I have started a game of chess and it seems like it is going to take a long time, I prefer to stop playing.	——	——
13.	When I am at a party, I will stay even if it is boring.	——	——
14.	When I do not understand something, I will ask my teacher again and again until I understand.	——	——
15.	When I fail in something, I am willing to try again and again forever.	——	——
16.	If I go fishing, I will continue fishing even if I do not succeed in the first hour.	——	——
17.	When I go to a movie and find it boring, I do not stay to the end.	——	——
18.	I help other children when I can.	——	——
19.	I won't try to solve a problem again and again if I don't find the solution the first time I try it.	——	——
20.	I always tell the truth.	——	——
21.	When I take part in an argument, I do not stop until everything is clear.	——	——
22.	When I do not understand something, I usually ask for an explanation.	——	——
23.	Only the knowledge that I will succeed on a test makes me study.	——	——
24.	I do not stop my work even if it is very difficult.	——	——
25.	I like all the people I know.	——	——
26.	I will stop my work on time even if I do not finish it.	——	——

		Yes	No
27.	I will continue my hobby even though I haven't had much success at it.	___	___
28.	When I am in the classroom, I try to answer all the questions asked in the class.	___	___
29.	I will not go to school when I feel bad.	___	___
30.	When I have difficulties doing something, I prefer to get help from an adult rather than doing it by myself.	___	___
31.	When I watch television, I like to see the programs from the beginning to the end.	___	___
32.	I study at home only when I have to be prepared for class the next day.	___	___
33.	When I clean my room, I prefer not to do it all at once.	___	___
34.	When I check my bicycle, I do it very carefully.	___	___
35.	If I were kicked out of work for no reason, I would not leave until I got a proper explanation.	___	___
36.	When I go jogging (running), I like to take breaks.	___	___
37.	If I try to solve a mathematical problem, I will not stop until I find a solution or a different approach.	___	___
38.	Usually I do not watch television programs to the end.	___	___
39.	I do not persist in most of the things I do.	___	___
40.	I usually give up easily when I do not succeed.	___	___

PERSONAL ATTRIBUTE INVENTORY FOR CHILDREN (PAIC) AND NONSEXIST PERSONAL ATTRIBUTE INVENTORY (NPAIC)

AUTHOR: Thomas S. Parish

PURPOSE: To measure children's self concept.

DESCRIPTION: This 48-item adjective checklist is designed to measure children's self concept. The checklist format allows it to be completed quickly. The focus of the PAIC is on evaluative and affective descriptions of either one's self or another, such as a parent. The instrument does not evaluate cognitions or behaviors. The instructions for the PAIC have a blank at the end. Consequently, the measure can also be used to assess a child's impression of someone else, such as a parent or sibling. This is accomplished by replacing the word "you" in the blank with the other person's name. Thus, the scale has potential for use in family therapy or in parent-child conflicts. A shorter 32-adjective form (NPAIC) is also available. This form is considered nonsexist as many of the adjectives reflecting either gender are removed.

NORMS: The PAIC has been tested on over 1000 children (450 males and 586 females). The mean score was 12.01 (SD = 3.02) for males and 12.41 (SD = 2.75) for females. Additional normative data are available.

SCORING: The child is asked to put an X in the box next to the 15 adjectives that best describe him or her or the other person he or she is rating. Twenty-four of the adjectives are positive (marked with asterisks here) and 24 are negative. The PAIC scores are the total number of positive adjectives checked and range from 0 to 15.

RELIABILITY: Especially for a children's measure, this instrument has excellent test-retest reliability, .73 for a sample of school children, over a four-week period. The instrument was less stable for third graders (.66) than for sixth graders (.87) over the same period. The evidence of stability is good, as children change so quickly that lower coefficients are anticipated. Evidence of internal consistency is not reported.

VALIDITY: The PAIC has good concurrent validity, demonstrated by significant correlations with the Piers-Harris Children's Self-Concept Scale. While the magnitude of the concurrent validity correlations was less for third than for sixth graders, the evidence is generally supportive.

PRIMARY REFERENCE: Parish, T. S. and Taylor, J. C. (1978). The Personal Attribute Inventory for Children: A report on its validity and reliability as a self-concept scale, *Educational and Psychological Measurement*, 38, 565–569. For the adult form, see Parish, T. S., Bryant, W., and Shirazi, A. (1976). The personal attribute inventory, *Perceptual and Motor Skills*, 42, 715–720. Instruments reprinted with permission.

AVAILABILITY: Thomas S. Parish, Professor, College of Education, Kansas State University, Manhattan, KS 66506.

PAIC

Read through this list of words, then put an X on the line beside the 15 words that best describe you.

____ Afraid	____ Happy*
____ Angry	____ Healthy*
____ Awkward	____ Helpful*
____ Bad	____ Honest*
____ Beautiful*	____ Jolly*
____ Bitter	____ Kind*
____ Brave*	____ Lazy
____ Calm*	____ Lovely*
____ Careless	____ Mean
____ Cheerful*	____ Nagging
____ Complaining	____ Nice*
____ Cowardly	____ Polite*
____ Cruel	____ Pretty*
____ Dirty	____ Rude
____ Dumb	____ Selfish
____ Fairminded*	____ Show-off
____ Foolish	____ Strong*
____ Friendly*	____ Sweet*
____ Gentle*	____ Ugly
____ Gloomy	____ Unfriendly
____ Good*	____ Weak
____ Great*	____ Wise*
____ Greedy	____ Wonderful*
____ Handsome*	____ Wrongful

NPAIC

Read through this list of words, then put an X on the line beside the 10 words that best describe you.

____ Angry	____ Helpful*
____ Awkward	____ Honest*
____ Calm*	____ Jolly*
____ Careless	____ Kind*
____ Complaining	____ Lazy
____ Cowardly	____ Lovely*
____ Dirty	____ Mean
____ Dumb	____ Nagging
____ Fairminded*	____ Nice*
____ Foolish	____ Polite*
____ Friendly *	____ Rude
____ Gentle*	____ Ugly
____ Good*	____ Unfriendly
____ Greedy	____ Wise*
____ Happy*	____ Wonderful*
____ Healthy*	____ Wrongful

REASON FOR LIVING INVENTORY
FOR ADOLESCENTS (RFL-A)

AUTHORS: Augustine Osman, William R. Downs, Tracia M. Besett, Beverly
A. Kopper, Francisco X. Barrios, and Marsha M. Linehan

PURPOSE: To measure adaptive characteristics of suicidal adolescents.

DESCRIPTION: This 32-item instrument measures a range of beliefs and attitudes which differentiate suicidal from nonsuicidal adolescents. It was developed from a number of studies using rigorous research methods in an
effort to identify the reasons a teenager does not commit suicide; that is, a
youth's reasons for living. The RFL-A is designed to ascertain why a person
does not commit suicide from five different dimensions: future optimism (FO
= items 4, 11, 13, 15, 19, 25, and 28), suicide-related concerns (SRC = items
2, 8, 20, 21, 26, and 32), family alliance (FA = items 1, 7, 12, 17, 23, and 24),
peer acceptance and support (PAS = items 5, 6, 10, 16, 22, and 27), and self-
acceptance (SA = items 3, 9, 14, 18, 29, and 31). The RFL-A may be used
with total scale scores or individual subscale scores for more precision.

NORMS: Normative data are available for a number of samples. For a sample
of 300 teenage high school boys (averaging 16 years of age) the means (and
standard deviations) for the FO, SRC, FA, PAS, and SA were 5.07 (1.04), 4.23
(1.63), 4.80 (1.19), 4.84 (1.05), and 4.83 (1.13), respectively. For a sample of
354 high school girls, the means (and standard deviations) were 4.93 (.98),
4.76 (1.13), 4.82 (.96), and 4.60 (1.09) for the FO, SRC, FA,
PAS, and SA subscales, respectively. The average total score was 4.77 (SD =
.98) for boys and 4.71 (SD = .87) for girls. In contrast, a sample of suicidal
psychiatric patients had means (and standard deviations) of 4.18 (1.16), 2.97
(1.39), 3.54 (1.39), 4.05 (1.24), and 3.70 (1.19) on the FO, SRC, FA, PAS,
and SA subscales. The average total RFL-A score was 3.70 (.90) for suicidal
psychiatric patients.

SCORING: A total score on the RFL-A is the sum of the item scores divided by
32. Subscale scores are the sum of the particular item scores divided by either
6 or 7. Total scores and subscale scores range from 1 to 6 with higher scores
evidencing more reasons for living.

RELIABILITY: The internal consistency of the RFL-A and the subscales has
been estimated in a number of studies. The reliability has been excellent for
total scores, often .95 or higher, and the internal consistency of subscales
ranged from .89 to .94 in one study and from .92 to .95 in another.

VALIDITY: The multidimensionality of the five-subscale structure has been
supported in a number of studies. Moreover, the RFL-A has excellent concurrent validity, as seen by the correlation of RFL-A scores with measures of
suicidality, hopelessness, and depression. Scores on the instrument also distinguished suicidal psychiatric patients from nonsuicidal psychiatric patients

and from nonsuicidal high school students. The differences in scores between suicidal patients and the nonsuicidal patients and students strongly support the known-groups validity of the RFL-A and the subscales.

PRIMARY REFERENCE: Osman, O., Downs, W. R., Kopper, B. A., Barrios, F. X., Besett, T. M., Linehan, M. M., Baker, M. T., and Osman, J. R. (1998). The Reasons for Living Inventory for Adolescents (RFL-A): Development and psychometric properties, *Journal of Clinical Psychology,* 54, 1063–1078.

AVAILABILITY: Augustine Osman, Ph.D., University of Northern Iowa, Department of Psychology, Cedar Falls, IA 50614-0505.

RFL-A

This questionnaire lists specific *reasons* that people sometimes have *for not committing suicide,* if the thought were to occur to them or if someone were to suggest it to them. Please read each statement carefully, and then choose a number that best describes how *important* each reason is to you for *not* committing suicide.

Use the scale below and circle the appropriate number in the space to the right of each statement. Please use the whole range of choices so as not to rate only at the middle (2, 3, 4, 5) or only at the extremes (1, 6).

How *important* to you is this *reason for not committing suicide?*	Not at all important	Quite unimportant	Somewhat unimportant	Somewhat important	Quite important	Extremely important
1. Whenever I have a problem, I can turn to my family for support or advice.	1	2	3	4	5	6
2. It would be painful and frightening to take my own life.	1	2	3	4	5	6
3. I accept myself for what I am.	1	2	3	4	5	6
4. I have a lot to look forward to as I grow older.	1	2	3	4	5	6
5. My friends stand by me whenever I have a problem.	1	2	3	4	5	6
6. I feel loved and accepted by my close friends.	1	2	3	4	5	6
7. I feel emotionally close to my family.	1	2	3	4	5	6
8. I am afraid to die, so I would not consider killing myself.	1	2	3	4	5	6
9. I like myself just the way I am.	1	2	3	4	5	6
10. My friends care a lot about me.	1	2	3	4	5	6
11. I would like to accomplish my plans or goals in the future.	1	2	3	4	5	6
12. My family takes the time to listen to my experiences at school, work, or home.	1	2	3	4	5	6
13. I expect many good things to happen to me in the future.	1	2	3	4	5	6
14. I am satisfied with myself.	1	2	3	4	5	6
15. I am hopeful about my plans or goals for the future.	1	2	3	4	5	6
16. I believe my friends appreciate me when I am with them.	1	2	3	4	5	6
17. I enjoy being with my family.	1	2	3	4	5	6
18. I feel that I am an OK person.	1	2	3	4	5	6
19. I expect to be successful in the future.	1	2	3	4	5	6
20. The thought of killing myself scares me.	1	2	3	4	5	6
21. I am afraid of using any method to kill myself.	1	2	3	4	5	6

22.	I can count on my friends to help if I have a problem.	1	2	3	4	5	6
23.	Most of the time, my family encourages and supports my plans or goals.	1	2	3	4	5	6
24.	My family cares about the way I feel.	1	2	3	4	5	6
25.	My future looks quite hopeful and promising.	1	2	3	4	5	6
26.	I am afraid of killing myself.	1	2	3	4	5	6
27.	My friends accept me for what I really am.	1	2	3	4	5	6
28.	I have many plans I am looking forward to carrying out in the future.	1	2	3	4	5	6
29.	I feel good about myself.	1	2	3	4	5	6
30.	My family cares a lot about what happens to me.	1	2	3	4	5	6
31.	I am happy with myself.	1	2	3	4	5	6
32.	I would be frightened or afraid to make plans for killing myself.	1	2	3	4	5	6

Copyright © 1996 Osman, Downs, Besett, Kopper, Barrios and Linehan.

ROSENBERG SELF-ESTEEM SCALE (RSE)

AUTHOR: Morris Rosenberg

PURPOSE: To measure self-esteem.

DESCRIPTION: The RSE is a 10-item Guttman scale with one dimension that was originally designed (1962) to measure the self-esteem of high school students. Since its development, the scale has been used with a number of other groups including adults with a variety of occupations. One of its greatest strengths is the amount of research that has been conducted with a wide range of groups on this scale over the years.

NORMS: The original research on the RSE was conducted on some 5000 high school students of varying ethnic backgrounds. Subsequent research involved thousands of college students and other adults from a range of professions and occupations. Norms are available for many of those groups.

SCORING: As a Guttman scale, scoring is based on a somewhat complicated method of combined ratings. Low self-esteem responses are "disagree" or "strongly disagree" on items 1, 3, 4, 7,10, and "strongly agree" or "agree" on items 2, 5, 6, 8, 9. Two or three out of three correct responses to items 3, 7, and 9 are scored as one item. One or two out of two correct responses for items 4 and 5 are considered as a single item; items 1, 8, and 10 are scored as individual items; and combined correct responses (one or two out of two) to items 2 and 6 are considered to be a single item. The scale might also be scored by a simple totaling of the individual 4-point items after reverse-scoring the negatively worded items.

RELIABILITY: The RSE has a Guttman scale coefficient of reproducibility of .92, indicating excellent internal consistency. Two studies of two-week test-retest reliability show correlations of .85 and .88, indicating excellent stability.

VALIDITY: A great deal of research demonstrates the concurrent, known-groups, predictive, and construct validity of the RSE. The RSE correlates significantly with other self-esteem measures such as the Coopersmith Self-Esteem Inventory. Similarly, the RSE correlates in predicted directions with measures of depression, anxiety, and peer-group reputation, demonstrating good construct validity by correlating with measures with which it should theoretically correlate and not correlating with those with which it should not.

PRIMARY REFERENCE: Rosenberg, M. (1979). *Conceiving the Self.* New York: Basic Books. Instrument reproduced with permission of Morris Rosenberg.

AVAILABILITY: Dr. Morris Rosenberg, Department of Sociology, University of Maryland, College Park, MD 20742.

RSE

Please record the appropriate answer for each item, depending on whether you strongly agree, agree, disagree, or strongly disagree with it.

$$1 = \text{Strongly agree}$$
$$2 = \text{Agree}$$
$$3 = \text{Disagree}$$
$$4 = \text{Strongly disagree}$$

____ 1. On the whole, I am satisfied with myself.
____ 2. At times I think I am no good at all.
____ 3. I feel that I have a number of good qualities.
____ 4. I am able to do things as well as most other people.
____ 5. I feel I do not have much to be proud of.
____ 6. I certainly feel useless at times.
____ 7. I feel that I'm a person of worth
____ 8. I wish I could have more respect for myself.
____ 9. All in all, I am inclined to think that I am a failure.
____ 10. I take a positive attitude toward myself.

SCALE OF RACIAL SOCIALIZATION
FOR ADOLESCENTS (SORS-A)

AUTHOR: Howard C. Stevenson, Jr.

PURPOSE: To measure racial socialization.

DESCRIPTION: The SORS-A is a 45-item scale designed to assess the degree of acceptance of racial socialization attitudes or race-related messages of child rearing within African-American culture. The SORS-A focuses on a multidimensional understanding of African-American life experience, identifying several key areas germane to African-American family functioning. The SORS-A has four subscales: spiritual and religious coping (items, in order of their factor loading, 22, 13, 21, 40, 7, 4, and 28); extended family caring (items 11, 8, 27, 10, 15, 9, 12, 30, 6, 24, and 2); cultural pride reinforcement (items 18, 20, 23, 43, 33, 29, 39, 16, and 17); and racism awareness teaching (items 41, 19, 42, 37, 38, 1, 3, 26, 30, and 45). A fifth factor called life achievement and struggling (items 5, 14, 25, 31, 32, 34, 35, 36, and 44) is also developed but was considered to be less empirically sound than the first four factors.

NORMS: The SORS-A was initially studied with 236 inner-city African-American adolescents, of whom 156 were female and 80 were male, with a mean age of 14.6 years. The students were participating in a larger study to assess relationships among kinship support and racial identity attitudes and racial socialization. The mean for the total scale was 170.1 (SD = 16.2). The means for the subscales were as follows: spiritual and religious coping, 26.8 (SD = 4.9); family rearing, 44.4 (SD = 5.9); cultural pride reinforcement, 27.7 (SD = 4.3); racism awareness teaching, 38.8 (SD = 6.7); and life achievement and struggling, 18.4 (SD = 3.7).

SCORING: The SORS-A is scored by summing all items for the total score, and summing individual items within each subscale for the subscale score. The items are scored along a 5-point Likert type scale ranging from "Strongly disagree" to "Strongly agree."

RELIABILITY: The SORS-A has fair reliability with an alpha for the total scale of .75. The alphas for the subscales range from .48 for life achievement and struggling to .74 for spiritual and religious coping. No data on stability were presented.

VALIDITY: The main data on validity come from factor analyses with moderate correlations between factors, suggesting a common theme among the four unique aspects of racial socialization. The racism awareness teaching factor does not significantly correlate with the remaining factors, suggesting that it is unique. The factor analyses suggest that racial socialization has two dimensions. These two dimensions were called proactive and protective regarding adolescents' perceptions of racial socialization.

PRIMARY REFERENCE: Stevenson, H. C., Jr. (1994). Validation of the scale of racial socialization for African-American adolescents: Steps toward multidimensionality, *Journal of Black Psychology,* 20, 445–468.

AVAILABILITY: Dr. Howard C. Stevenson, Jr., University of Pennsylvania, Graduate School of Education, School, Community and Child Clinical Psychology, 3700 Walnut St., Philadelphia, PA 19104-6216. Reprinted with permission of the author.

SORS-A

Circle the number on the line, depending on whether you 1—Disagree a lot, 2—Disagree a little, 3—Not sure, 4—Agree a little, 5—Agree a lot with the statement. Circle only one number per question. Thank you.

1. Our society is fair toward black people.   1   2   3   4   5

2. Grandparents help parents to make decisions.   1   2   3   4   5

3. Black children will feel good about being black in a school with mostly white children.   1   2   3   4   5

4. It is important for families to go to church or mosque where spiritual growth can happen.   1   2   3   4   5

5. Families should talk about black slavery with their children.   1   2   3   4   5

6. Relatives can help black parents raise their children.   1   2   3   4   5

7. Religion is an important part of a person's life.   1   2   3   4   5

8. Racism and discrimination are the hardest things a black child has to face.   1   2   3   4   5

9. Having large families can help many black families survive life struggles.   1   2   3   4   5

10. Families of black children should teach them to be proud to be black.   1   2   3   4   5

11. Children should be taught that all races are equal.   1   2   3   4   5

12. Children who have good times with their relatives become better people.   1   2   3   4   5

13. A belief in God can help a person deal with tough life struggles.   1   2   3   4   5

14. A mostly black school will help black children learn more than a mostly white school.   1   2   3   4   5

15. Spending good time with relatives is just as important for parents as it is for their children.   1   2   3   4   5

16. Black parents should teach their children about racism.   1   2   3   4   5

17. Black parents should talk about their roots to African culture to their children.   1   2   3   4   5

18. Relatives can teach children things that parents may not know.   1   2   3   4   5

19. Families who talk about racism to their children will lead them to doubt themselves.   1   2   3   4   5

20. Schools should be required to teach all children about black history.   1   2   3   4   5

21. Depending on religion and God can help a person make good life decisions.   1   2   3   4   5

22. Families who talk openly about religion or God are helping their children grow.   1   2   3   4   5

23. Teachers should make it so black children can see signs of black culture in the classroom.   1   2   3   4   5

24. Only people who are blood-related to you should be called your "family."   1   2   3   4   5

25. Getting a good education is still the best way for a black child to survive racism.   1   2   3   4   5

26. "Don't forget who your people are because you may need them someday."   1   2   3   4   5

27. When children are younger than 5, racism doesn't bother them.   1   2   3   4   5

28. Spiritual battles that people fight are more important than the physical battles.   1   2   3   4   5

29. Teaching children about black history will help them to survive a hostile world.   1   2   3   4   5

30. "Train up a child in the way he should go, and he will not turn away from it."   1   2   3   4   5

31. A black child has to work twice as hard in order to get ahead in this world.   1   2   3   4   5

32. Watching parents struggle to find work can make many black children wonder if it is worth it to try and succeed in the world.   1   2   3   4   5

33. Parents can teach children to be proud to be black   1   2   3   4   5
without saying a word.

34. Black children at a mostly black school will feel   1   2   3   4   5
better about themselves than those who go to a
mostly white school.

35. Black parents need to teach their children how to   1   2   3   4   5
live in two worlds: one black and one white.

36. Light-skin black persons often think they are better   1   2   3   4   5
than darker skinned blacks.

37. Whites do not have more opportunities than blacks.   1   2   3   4   5

38. A black child or teenager will not be harassed   1   2   3   4   5
simply because s/he is black.

39. More job opportunities would be open to African-   1   2   3   4   5
Americans if people were not racist.

40. Black children should be taught early that God can   1   2   3   4   5
protect them from racial hatred.

41. Whites do not think of black people as lazy or   1   2   3   4   5
aggressive today like they used to believe 30
or more years ago.

42. Black parents should not teach their children   1   2   3   4   5
to speak their mind because they could be
attacked by others in society.

43. If black parents teach their children that blacks   1   2   3   4   5
don't always have the same opportunities as
whites, they may help them to survive racism
and be successful.

44. Black children don't have to know about Africa   1   2   3   4   5
in order to survive life in America.

45. My family taught me very little about racism   1   2   3   4   5
in America.

Copyright © Howard C. Stevenson.

SELF-CONCEPT SCALE FOR CHILDREN (SC)

AUTHOR: Lewis P. Lipsitt

PURPOSE: To measure the self-concept of children.

DESCRIPTION: The SC consists of 22 descriptive adjectives tapping children's feelings about themselves, which are responded to on 5-point scales. Three of these adjectives, items 10, 17, and 20, are considered negative while the rest are positive. The SC is one of the few self-report measures available that can be used with children from approximately the fourth grade up. Higher scores on the SC reflect higher self-concept (i.e., less self-disparagement).

NORMS: The original study involved 138 boys and 160 girls in the fourth through sixth grades. No real norms are available although the mean score for all children was 86.75. There were no differences based on grade or sex.

SCORING: After the three negatively worded items are reverse-scored, the scores on the individual 22 items are totaled, producing a potential range of 22 to 110.

RELIABILITY: No data on internal consistency are reported. However, two-week test-retest correlations range from .73 to .91, indicating good stability.

VALIDITY: The only validity data reported show that the SC correlates significantly and in predicted directions with scores on the Children's Manifest Anxiety Scale. Thus, the greater the anxiety level, the lower the score on the SC.

PRIMARY REFERENCE: Lipsitt, L. P. (1958). A Self-Concept Scale for Children and its relationship to the children's form of the Manifest Anxiety Scale, *Child Development*, 29, 463–472. Instrument reproduced with permission of L. P. Lipsitt.

AVAILABILITY: Journal article or Dr. L. P. Lipsitt, Department of Psychology, Brown University, Providence, RI 02912.

SC

Select the phrase that comes closest to the way you are by recording the appropriate number to the left of each statement. Select only one of them. Do the best you can.

$$
\begin{array}{rcl}
1 & = & \text{Not at all} \\
2 & = & \text{Not very often} \\
3 & = & \text{Some of the time} \\
4 & = & \text{Most of the time} \\
5 & = & \text{All of the time}
\end{array}
$$

_____ 1. I am friendly.
_____ 2. I am happy.
_____ 3. I am kind.
_____ 4. I am brave.
_____ 5. I am honest.
_____ 6. I am likable.
_____ 7. I am trusted.
_____ 8. I am good.
_____ 9. I am proud.
_____ 10. I am lazy.
_____ 11. I am loyal.
_____ 12. I am cooperative.
_____ 13. I am cheerful.
_____ 14. I am thoughtful.
_____ 15. I am popular.
_____ 16. I am courteous.
_____ 17. I am jealous.
_____ 18. I am obedient.
_____ 19. I am polite.
_____ 20. I am bashful.
_____ 21. I am clean.
_____ 22. I am helpful.

SELF-CONTROL RATING SCALE (SCRS)

AUTHORS: Philip C. Kendall and L. E. Wilcox

PURPOSE: To measure children's self-control.

DESCRIPTION: The SCRS is a 33-item instrument designed to measure the degree to which a child's behavior can be described as self-controlled (versus impulsive). The SCRS is administered by an observer who rates the child. The SCRS is based on a cognitive-behavioral model of self-control. It was developed because of a general absence of measures for assessing children's self-control and the need for an instrument that could be used to assess changes due to treatment.

NORMS: The SCRS has been studied with several samples of elementary school age children. Further demographic data and actual norms are not available. However, boys score significantly higher than girls, and persons scoring at or above 160 to 165 are said to be candidates for treatment for difficulties with self-control.

SCORING: The SCRS is easily scored by summing item scores, with higher scores indicating a greater lack of self-control.

RELIABILITY: The SCRS has excellent internal consistency, with an alpha of .98. The SCRS also has very good stability with a test-retest correlation of .84.

VALIDITY: The SCRS has very good construct validity, with significant correlations or lack of correlations in predicted directions with the Peabody Picture Vocabulary Test, Matching Familiar Figures, Porteus Maze, and observer ratings of behaviors. The SCRS also has good known-groups validity, significantly distinguishing between groups with high and low rates of off-task behaviors.

PRIMARY REFERENCE: Kendall, P. C. and Wilcox, L. E. (1979). Self-Control in children: Development of a rating scale, *Journal of Consulting and Clinical Psychology*, 47, 1020–1029.

AVAILABILITY: Dr. Philip Kendall, Department of Psychology, Temple University, 478 Weiss Hall, Philadelphia, PA 19122.

SCRS

Please rate this child according to the descriptions below by circling the appropriate number. The underlined 4 in the center of each row represents where the average child would fall on this item. Please do not hesitate to use the entire range of possible ratings.

1. When the child promises to do something, can you count on him/her to do it?

   1 2 3 <u>4</u> 5 6 7
   Always   Never

2. Does the child butt into games or activities even when he/she hasn't been invited?

   1 2 3 <u>4</u> 5 6 7
   Never   Often

3. Can the child deliberately calm down when he/she is excited or all wound up?

   1 2 3 <u>4</u> 5 6 7
   Yes   No

4. Is the quality of the child's work all about the same or does it vary a lot?

   1 2 3 <u>4</u> 5 6 7
   Same   Varies

5. Does the child work for long-range goals?

   1 2 3 <u>4</u> 5 6 7
   Yes   No

6. When the child asks a question, does he/she wait for an answer, or jump to something else (e.g., a new question) before waiting for an answer?

   1 2 3 <u>4</u> 5 6 7
   Waits   Jumps

7. Does the child interrupt inappropriately in conversations with peers, or wait his/her turn to speak?

   1 2 3 <u>4</u> 5 6 7
   Waits   Interrupts

8. Does the child stick to what he/she is doing until he/she is finished with it?

   1 2 3 <u>4</u> 5 6 7
   Yes   No

9. Does the child follow the instructions of responsible adults?

   1 2 3 <u>4</u> 5 6 7
   Always   Never

10. Does the child have to have everything right away?

    1 2 3 <u>4</u> 5 6 7
    No   Yes

11. When the child has to wait in line, does he/she do so patiently?

    1 2 3 <u>4</u> 5 6 7
    Yes   No

12. Does the child sit still?

    1 2 3 <u>4</u> 5 6 7
    Yes   No

13. Can the child follow suggestions of others in group projects, or does he/she insist on imposing his/her own ideas?

    1 2 3 <u>4</u> 5 6 7
    Able to   Imposes
    follow

14. Does the child have to be reminded several times to do something before he/she does it?

1 2 3 <u>4</u> 5 6 7
Never   Always

15. When reprimanded, does the child answer back inappropriately?

1 2 3 <u>4</u> 5 6 7
Never   Always

16. Is the child accident prone?

1 2 3 <u>4</u> 5 6 7
No   Yes

17. Does the child neglect or forget regular chores or tasks?

1 2 3 <u>4</u> 5 6 7
Never   Always

18. Are there days when the child seems incapable of settling down to work?

1 2 3 <u>4</u> 5 6 7
Never   Often

19. Would the child more likely grab a smaller toy today or wait for a larger toy tomorrow, if given the choice?

1 2 3 <u>4</u> 5 6 7
Wait   Grab

20. Does the child grab for the belongings of others?

1 2 3 <u>4</u> 5 6 7
Never   Often

21. Does the child bother others when they're trying to do things?

1 2 3 <u>4</u> 5 6 7
No   Yes

22. Does the child break basic rules?

1 2 3 <u>4</u> 5 6 7
Never   Always

23. Does the child watch where he/she is going?

1 2 3 <u>4</u> 5 6 7
Always   Never

24. In answering questions, does the child give one thoughtful answer, or blurt out several answers all at once?

1 2 3 <u>4</u> 5 6 7
One   Several
answer

25. Is the child easily distracted from his/her work or chores?

1 2 3 <u>4</u> 5 6 7
No   Yes

26. Would you describe this child more as careful or careless?

1 2 3 <u>4</u> 5 6 7
Careful   Careless

27. Does the child play well with peers (follows rules, waits turn, cooperates)?

1 2 3 <u>4</u> 5 6 7
Yes   No

28. Does the child jump or switch from activity to activity rather than sticking to one thing at a time?

1 2 3 <u>4</u> 5 6 7
Sticks to   Switches
one

29. If a task is at first too difficult for the child, will he/she get frustrated and quit, or first seek help with the problem?

     1   2   3   <u>4</u>   5   6   7
     Seek help   Quit

30. Does the child disrupt games?

     1   2   3   <u>4</u>   5   6   7
     Never   Often

31. Does the child think before he/she acts?

     1   2   3   <u>4</u>   5   6   7
     Always   Never

32. If the child paid more attention to his/her work, do you think he/she would do much better than at present?

     1   2   3   <u>4</u>   5   6   7
     No   Yes

33. Does the child do too many things at once, or does he/she concentrate on one thing at a time?

     1   2   3   <u>4</u>   5   6   7
     One thing   Too
                  many

Copyright © 1979 Phillip C. Kendall, Ph.D.

SPIDER PHOBIA QUESTIONNAIRE
FOR CHILDREN (SPQ-C)

AUTHORS: Merel Kindt, Jos F. Brosschot, and Peter Muris

PURPOSE: To measure spider phobia.

DESCRIPTION: The SPQ-C is a 29-item questionnaire designed to assess fear of spiders in children. There are relatively few self-report instruments that can reliably assess the degree of fear of children who suffer from a specific fear or phobia. The SPQ-C is perhaps one of the few questionnaires designed to assess specific fear, in this case fear of spiders. Given the fact that specific fears like spider phobia can be a serious concern in children because their severity or duration may undermine normal development, the SPQ-C is a welcome development focusing on children's, rather than adults', phobic responses to specific animals.

NORMS: The SPQ-C was initially studied with 1258 children, including 598 boys and 660 girls who were elementary school students aged 8 to 12. The mean for boys was 4.2 (SD = 4.0) and the mean for girls was 8.7 (SD = 5.9). Means for age groups from 8 to 12 are available in the original article. Among a group of girls selected for validity testing, the mean SPQ-C score for a spider phobic group was 19.4 (SD = 2.6) and for the nonphobic group the mean score was .9 (SD = .4).

SCORING: The SPQ-C is easily scored by summing the scores of all items to indicate the degree of spider fear; the following items are reverse-scored prior to summing: 6, 12, 14, 16, 17, 19, 24, and 26.

RELIABILITY: The SPQ-C has very good internal consistency with a Kuder-Richardson Formula 20 correlation of .89. The SPQ-C also has very good stability with 7-week test-retest correlations that range from .50 to .70.

VALIDITY: The SPQ-C has very good known-groups validity, significantly distinguishing between a spider phobic and nonphobic group of elementary school girls. The SPQ-C also significantly differentiated spider phobic and nonphobic girls on the scores of the Behavioral Approach Test.

PRIMARY REFERENCE: Kindt, M., Brosschot, J. F., and Muris, P. (1996). Spider phobia questionnaire for children (SPQ-C): a psychometric study and normative data, *Behaviour Research and Therapy*, 34, 277–282.

AVAILABILITY: Dr. Merel Kindt, Department of Medical, Clinical, and Experimental Psychology, Faculties of Medicine and Health Sciences, Maastricht University, PO Box 616, 6200MP, Maastricht, The Netherlands. Reprinted by permission of the authors.

SPQ-C

Indicate whether you agree or disagree with each statement by circling True or Not True.

1.	I avoid being in gardens or parks because spiders might be there.	True	Not true
2.	Even a toy spider in my hand scares me a bit.	True	Not true
3.	Whenever I see a spider on television I close my eyes.	True	Not true
4.	I dislike looking at pictures of spiders.	True	Not true
5.	When there is a spider above my bed, I'm only able to sleep if somebody takes the spider away.	True	Not true
6.	I enjoy looking at spiders weaving webs.	True	Not true
7.	Even the thought of touching a spider scares me.	True	Not true
8.	Whenever somebody tells me that there are spiders near me, I start looking around and get nervous.	True	Not true
9.	If I think there are spiders in the closet, I keep the door of the closet closed.	True	Not true
10.	If I'm about to put my shoes on, I would feel very uneasy if a spider would creep out of one of them.	True	Not true
11.	If I see a spider, I feel tense.	True	Not true
12.	I enjoy reading a story about spiders.	True	Not true
13.	It makes me feel sick when I see a spider.	True	Not true
14.	Spiders can be useful because they eat flies.	True	Not true
15.	Thinking of spiders makes me shiver.	True	Not true
16.	Some spiders are quite funny to watch.	True	Not true
17.	I think other children are always a bit scared of grabbing a spider.	True	Not true
18.	The way spiders walk is an ugly sight.	True	Not true
19.	I dare to touch a spider with a long stick.	True	Not true
20.	If I happened to find a spider while playing, I would probably run away.	True	Not true
21.	Spiders scare me more than any other animal.	True	Not true
22.	I would rather stay away from countries where there are a lot of poisonous spiders.	True	Not true
23.	I'm careful picking fruit because there might be spiders in between the fruit.	True	Not true
24.	I stay calm if there are spiders around.	True	Not true
25.	When the teacher speaks of spiders I would rather leave the classroom.	True	Not true
26.	Spider webs are very beautiful.	True	Not true
27.	I stop reading a story if it is about spiders.	True	Not true
28.	If I think that I will run into a spider on my way to school, I'll take another route, even if this makes me come too late to school.	True	Not true
29.	I'm scared of spiders, and of centipedes and of caterpillars.	True	Not true

YOUNG CHILDREN'S SOCIAL DESIRABILITY SCALE (YCSD)

AUTHORS: LeRoy H. Ford and Barry M. Rubin

PURPOSE: To measure need for social approval in young children.

DESCRIPTION: The 26-item forced-choice YCSD considers social desirability as a form of defensive denial. The research indicates the instrument is a measure of general motivation to comply with social demands. The instrument may be administered in writing or read aloud to young children or respondents with limited reading ability. The forced-choice format helps control for an acquiescence response set.

NORMS: Normative data are available on three samples of preschool children with a total sample size of 437. A mean score of 16.36 and a standard deviation of approximately 4.85 are reported for the combined sample. Additional normative data are available from the primary reference.

SCORING: In selecting the alternative when verbally presented. the child must repeat at least one word or phrase from the statement. The key words are identified by italics on the instrument. The first two items are warm-up items and are not to be scored. The socially desirable response is the second alternative in items 3, 6, 7, 10, 11, 14, 15, 17, 18, 22–24, 27. and the first alternative in the remainder. Scores are the total number of socially desirable responses. Scores range from 0 to 28.

RELIABILITY: The reliability data tend to be very dependent on the age of the children. For example, the internal consistency was .48 and .51 for young boys and girls, respectively. For older children it was .79 for boys and .84 for girls. In a third sample, internal consistency using Kuder-Richardson was .83 for older boys and .85 for older girls. Over a five-week period, the test-retest correlation was. 58.

VALIDITY: The validity of the YCSD was tested using concurrent procedures. Scores on the YCSD correlated with vocabulary IQ suggesting that children with higher verbal intelligence are more likely to idealize social norms and indicate adherence to them. Validity was also demonstrated in three experiments. In general, the results indicate that children who score high on the YCSD respond more positively to interpersonal demands than children who score low on the measure.

PRIMARY REFERENCE: Ford, L. H. and Rubin, B. M. (1970). A social desirability questionnaire for young children, *Journal of Consulting and Clinical Psychology*, 35, 195–204. Instrument reproduced with permission of the American Psychological Association.

AVAILABILITY: Journal article.

YCSD

Below are twenty-eight sets of statements. Indicate which is most true for you by circling the number to the left of the choice.

1.   *1.*   Do you *sometimes* play with toys? or
         2.   Do you *never play* with toys?

2.   *1.*   Do you *always* play all by yourself? or
         2.   Do you *sometimes* play with other children?

3.   *1.*   Do you *sometimes argue* with your mother? or
         2.   Do you *never argue* with your mother?

4.   *1.*   Are you *always polite* to older people? or
         2.   Are you *sometimes not polite* to older people?

5.   *1.*   Do you *never shout* when you feel angry? or
         2.   Do you *sometimes shout* when you feel angry?

6.   *1.*   Do you *sometimes* tell a little *lie*? or
         2.   Do you *never* tell a little *lie*?

7.   *1.*   Do you *sometimes hit* another boy or girl?
         2.   Do you *never hit* another boy or girl?

8.   *1.*   Do you *always help* people? or
         2.   Do you *sometimes not help* people?

9.   *1.*   Do you *never show off* to your friends? or
         2.   Do you *sometimes show off* to your friends?

10.   *1.*   Do you *sometimes say mean things* to people? or
         2.   Do you *never say mean things* to people?

11.   *1.*   Do you *sometimes feel like throwing* or *breaking* things? or
         2.   Do you *never feel like throwing* or *breaking* things?

12.   *1.*   Do you feel that your parents are *always right*? or
         2.   Do you sometimes feel that your parents are *not always right*?

13.   *1.*   Do you *never* act *naughty*? or
         2.   Do you *sometimes* act *naughty*?

14.   *1.*   Do you *sometimes do other things* instead of what your teacher tells you to do? or
         2.   Do you *always do what* your *teacher tells you* to do?

15.   *1.* Do you *sometimes do things* you're *not supposed to do*? or
       2. Do you *never do things* you're *not supposed to* do?

16.   *1.* Do you think your *teachers know more* than you do? or
       2. Do you think you *know more* than your teacher does? *(I know more)*

17.   *1.* Do you *sometimes want things* your *parents don't want you* to have? or
       2. Do you *never want things* your *parents don't want you* to have?

18.   *1.* Does it *sometimes bother* you *when you don't get your way*? or
       2. Does it *never bother* you *when you don't get your way*?

19.   *1.* Do you *always listen* to your parents? or
       2. Do you *sometimes not listen* to your parents?

20.   *1.* Do you *always wash* your *hands* before every meal? or
       2. Do you *sometimes not wash* your *hands* before every meal?

21.   *1.* Do you *never feel like making fun* of other people? or
       2. Do you *sometimes feel like making fun* of other people?

22.   *1.* Do you *sometimes forget* to say "please" and "thank you"? or
       2. Do you *never forget* to say "please" and "thank you"?

23.   *1.* Does it *sometimes bother you to share things* with your friends? or
       2. Does it *never bother you to share things* with your friends?

24.   *1.* Do you *sometimes want to do things* your *parents tell you not to do*?
       2. Do you *never want to do things* your *parents tell you not* to do?

25.   *1.* Do you *never get angry*? or
       2. Do you *sometimes get angry*?

26.   *1.* Are you *always nice* to people? or
       2. Are you *sometimes not nice* to people?

27.   *1.* Do you *sometimes not do the right things*? or
       2. Do you *always do the right things*?

28.   *1.* Do you *always tell the truth*? or
       2. Do you *sometimes not tell the truth*?

YOUTH COPING INDEX (YCI)

AUTHORS: Hamilton McCubbin, Anne Thompson, and Kelly Elver

PURPOSE: To measure youth coping.

DESCRIPTION: The YCI is a 31-item instrument designed to measure youth coping with an ethnically sensitive instrument. The YCI was developed specifically for the study of African- American youth in residential treatment. The YCI is an adaptation of the Adolescent Coping Orientation for Problem Experiences instrument which identifies the coping repertoires of respondents. The YCI has five subscales that assess the degree to which youth use certain coping behaviors and strategies to manage life's stressors and strains. The subscales are: youth spiritual and personal development (items 2, 3, 4, 5, 8, 10, 11, 14, 21, 24, 27, 30, and 31); youth positive appraisal and problem solving (items 1, 6, 7, 12, 13, 16, 20, 22, 28, and 29); and youth incendiary communication and tension management (items 9, 15, 17, 18, 19, 23, 25, and 26). The YCI is particularly suited as a measure for evaluating the effect of intervention from intake to completion of treatment programs.

NORMS: The YCI was studied with 430 youth in residential treatment programs. The overall mean for the total scale was 93.5 (SD = 16.2). The overall mean on the total scale for African-American youth (N = 193) was 95.4 (SD = 16.8) and for Caucasian youth (N = 237) 91.8 (SD = 15.5). The norms for the subscales for the total sample and for African-American and Caucasian youth are available in the primary reference.

SCORING: After reverse-scoring item 17, the scores for the YCI and the subscales are obtained by simply summing item responses.

RELIABILITY: The YCI has very good internal consistency with an alpha for the total scale of .86. Alphas for the subscales range from .70 to .84. The YCI has good stability with a long term (6–15 months) test-retest correlation of .43.

VALIDITY: The YCI has very good predictive validity, successfully predicting program completion and successful adaptation for youths in residential treatment. The percentage of accuracy of prediction for successful program completion was 75% and for unsuccessful program completions 91%. The percentage of accuracy of prediction for successful 12-month adaptation was 76.2% and for unsuccessful 12-month adaptation, 71.4%.

PRIMARY REFERENCE: McCubbin, H. I., Thompson, A. I., and Elver, K. M. Youth Coping Index (YCI). In H. I. McCubbin, A. I. Thompson, and M. A. McCubbin (1996). *Family Assessment: Resiliency, Coping and Adaptation. Inventories for Research and Practice.* Madison: University of Wisconsin, 585–611.

AVAILABILITY: After purchasing the book cited above, you may register by telephone at (608) 262-5070. The book provides instructions for permission to use the instrument.

YCI

Read each of the statements below which describes a behavior for coping with problems. Decide *how often* you do each of the described behaviors when you face difficulties or feel tense. Even though you may do some of these things just for fun, please indicate ONLY how often you do each behavior as a way to cope with problems.

Circle one of the following responses for each statement:

1 = Never   2 = Hardly ever   3 = Sometimes   4 = Often   5 = Most of the time

Note: Anytime the words parent, mother, father, brother or sister are used, they also mean step-parent, step-mother, etc.

When you face difficulties or feel tense, how often do you:	Never	Hardly ever	Sometimes	Often	Most of the time
1. Apologize to people	1	2	3	4	5
2. Talk to a teacher or counselor at school about what bothers you	1	2	3	4	5
3. Read	1	2	3	4	5
4. Get more involved in activities at school	1	2	3	4	5
5. Try to improve yourself (get body in shape, get better grades, etc.)	1	2	3	4	5
6. Try to reason with parents and talk things out; compromise	1	2	3	4	5
7. Try to think of the good things in your life	1	2	3	4	5
8. Say nice things to others	1	2	3	4	5
9. Get angry and yell at people	1	2	3	4	5
10. Work hard on schoolwork or other school projects	1	2	3	4	5
11. Pray	1	2	3	4	5
12. Try, on your own, to figure out how to deal with your problems or tensions	1	2	3	4	5
13. Try to make your own decisions	1	2	3	4	5
14. Go to church	1	2	3	4	5
15. Swear	1	2	3	4	5
16. Organize your life and what you have to do	1	2	3	4	5
17. Go along with parents' requests and rules	1	2	3	4	5
18. Blame others for what's going wrong	1	2	3	4	5
19. Tell yourself the problem is not important	1	2	3	4	5
20. Try to help other people solve their problems	1	2	3	4	5
21. Get professional counseling (not from a school teacher or school counselor)	1	2	3	4	5
22. Try to keep up friendships or make new friends	1	2	3	4	5

23.	Daydream about how you would like things to be	1	2	3	4	5
24.	Play video games (Space Invaders, Pac-Man), pool, pinball, etc.	1	2	3	4	5
25.	Let off steam by complaining to your friends	1	2	3	4	5
26.	Say mean things to people; be sarcastic	1	2	3	4	5
27.	Do things with your family	1	2	3	4	5
28.	Talk to a friend about how you feel	1	2	3	4	5
29.	Try to see the good things in a difficult situation	1	2	3	4	5
30.	Work on a hobby you have (sewing, model building, etc.)	1	2	3	4	5
31.	Do a strenuous physical activity (jogging, biking, etc.)	1	2	3	4	5

Copyright © H. I. McCubbin, A. I. Thompson, and K. M. Elver, 1995.

REFERENCES

Acierno, R., Hersen, M., and Ammerman, R. T. (1994). Overview of the issues in prescriptive treatments. In M. Hersen and R. T. Ammerman (eds.), *Handbook of Prescriptive Treatment*, pp. 3–30. New York: Plenum.

Adorno, T. W., Frenkel-Brunswick, E., Levinson, D. J., and Sanford, R. N. (1950). *The Authoritarian Personality.* New York: Harper.

American Psychiatric Association (1994). *Diagnostic and Statistical Manual.* 4th edition. Washington, D.C.: American Psychiatric Association.

American Psychological Association, American Educational Research Association, and National Council on Measurement in Education (1985). *Standards For Educational and Psychological Testing.* Washington, D.C.: American Psychological Association.

Anastasi, A. (1988). *Psychological Testing,* 6th edition. New York: Macmillan.

Andrulis, R. S. (1977). *Adult Assessment: A Sourcebook of Tests and Measures of Human Behavior.* Springfield, Ill.: Charles C. Thomas.

Asarnow, J. R. and Carlson, G. A. (1982). Depression self-rating: Utility with child psychiatric inpatients, *Journal of Consulting and Clinical Psychology, 53,* 491–499.

Asher, D. R., Hymel, S., and Renshaw, P. D. (1984). Loneliness in children, *Child Development,* 55, 1457–1464.

Austin, C. D. (1981). Client assessment in context, *Social Work Research and Abstracts,* 17, 4–12.

Babbie, E. (1983). *The Practice of Social Research,* 3rd edition. Belmont, Calif.: Wadsworth.

Barlow, D. H. (ed.) (1981). *Behavioral Assessment of Adult Disorders.* New York: Guilford.

Barlow, D. (ed.). (1994). *Clinical Handbook of Psychological Disorders: A Step-by-Step Treatment Manual.* 2nd edition. New York: Guilford Press.

――― (1985). *Clinical Handbook of Psychological Disorders.* New York: Guilford.

―――, Hayes, S. C., and Nelson, R. O. (1984). *The Scientist Practitioner: Research and Accountability in Clinical and Educational Settings.* New York: Pergamon.

―――, and Hersen, M. (1984). *Single Case Experimental Designs: Strategies for Studying Behavior Change.* 2nd edition. New York: Pergamon.

Beach, S. R. H. and Arias, I. (1983). Assessment of perceptual discrepancy: Utility of the primary communication inventory, *Family Process,* 22, 309–316.

Beck, A. T., Ward, C. H., Mendelson, M., Mock, J., and Erbaugh, J. (1961). An inventory for measuring depression, *Archives of General Psychiatry,* 4, 561–571.

―――, Weissman, A., Lester, D. and Trexler, L. (1974). The measurement of pessimism: The Hopelessness Scale, *Journal of Consulting and Clinical Psychology,* 42, 861–865.

Beere, C. A. (1979). *Women and Women's Issues: A Handbook of Tests and Measures.* San Francisco: Jossey-Bass.

Bellack, A. S. and Hersen, M. (1977). The use of self-report inventories in behavioral assessment. In J. D. Cone and R. P. Hawkins (eds.), *Behavioral Assessment: New Directions in Clinical Psychology,* pp. 52–76. New York: Brunner/Mazel.

――― (eds.) (1988). *Behavioral Assessment: A Practical Handbook.* 3rd edition. New York: Pergamon.

Bernstein, D. A., and Allen, G. J. (1969). Fear Survey Schedule (II): Normative data and factor analyses based upon a large college sample. *Behaviour Research and Therapy,* 1969, 7, 403–407.

Bloom, M. (1975). *The Paradox of Helping. Introduction to the Philosophy of Scientific Practice.* New York: John Wiley.

――― and Fischer, J. (1982). *Evaluating Practice: Guidelines for the Accountable Professional.* Englewood Cliffs, N.J.: Prentice Hall.

―――, Fischer, J., and Orme, J. (1994). *Evaluating Practice: Guidelines for the Accountable Professional,* 2nd Edition. Englewood Cliffs, N.J.: Prentice Hall.

―――. (1999). *Evaluating Practice: Guidelines for the Accountable Professional,* 3rd edition. Boston: Allyn & Bacon.

Blumenthal, M. and Dielman, T. (1975). Depression symptomatology and role function in a general population, *Archives of General Psychiatry,* 32, 985–991.

Brodsky, S. L. and Smitherman, H. O. (1983). *Handbook of Scales for Research in Crime and Delinquency.* New York: Plenum.

Buros, O. K. (ed.) (1978). *The Eighth Mental Measurements Yearbook,* Vols. I and II. Highland Park, N.J.: Gryphon Press.

Cattell, R. B. (1966). The scree test for the number of factors, *Multivariate Behavioral Research,* 1, 245–276.

Cautela, J. R. (1977). *Behavior Analysis Forms for Clinical Intervention.* Champaign, Ill.: Research Press.

———— (1981). *Behavior Analysis Forms for Clinical Intervention,* Vol. 2. Champaign, Ill.: Research Press.

Chambless, D. L., et al. (1996). An update on empirically validated theories, *The Clinical Psychologist,* 49, 5–18.

Chun, K.-T., Cobb, S., and French, J. R., Jr. (1975). *Measures for Psychological Assessment: A Guide to 3,000 Original Sources and Their Application.* Ann Arbor, Mich.: Institute for Social Research.

Ciarlo, J. A., et al. (1986). *Assessing Mental Health Treatment Outcome Measurement Techniques.* Rockville, Md.: National Institutes of Mental Health (DHHS Publication No. (ADM) 86-1301).

Ciminero, A. R., Calhoun, K. S., and Adams, H. E. (eds.). (1977). *Handbook of Behavioral Assessment.* New York: John Wiley.

Colby, K. M. (1980). Computer Psychotherapists. In J. B. Sidowski, J. H. Johnson, and T. A. Williams (eds.), *Technology in Mental Health Care Delivery Systems,* pp. 109–117. Norwood, N.J.: Ablex.

Comrey, A. L., et al. (1973). *A Sourcebook for Mental Health Measures.* Los Angeles: Human Interaction Research Institute.

————, Barker, T., and Glaser, E. (1975). *A Sourcebook for Mental Health Measure.* Los Angeles: Human Interaction Research Institute.

———— (1978). Common methodological problems in factor analytic studies, *Journal of Consulting and Clinical Psychology,* 46, 648–659.

Cone, J. D. and Hawkins, R. P. (eds.) (1977). *Behavioral Assessment: New Directions in Clinical Psychology.* New York: Brunner/Mazel.

Conoley, J. C. and Kramer, J. J. (1995). *The Twelfth Mental Measurements Yearbook.* Lincoln, Neb.: Buros Institute of Mental Measurement.

Conway, J. B. (1977). Behavioral self-control of smoking through aversion conditioning and self-management, *Journal of Consulting and Clinical Psychology,* 45, 348–357.

Corcoran, K. J. (1988). Selecting a measuring instrument. In R. M. Grinnell, Jr., *Social Work Research and Evaluation,* 3rd edition. Itasca, Ill.: F. E. Peacock.

———— (ed.) (1992). *Structuring Change: Effective Practice for Common Client Problems.* Chicago: Lyceum Books.

———— (1993). Practice evaluation: Problems and promises of single-system design in clinical practice. *Journal of Social Service Research,* 18, 147–159.

———— (1997). The use of rapid assessment instruments as outcomes measures. In Edward Mullen and Jennifer L. Magnabosco (eds.), *Outcomes Measurements in the Human Services,* pp. 137–143. Washington, D.C.: NASW Press.

———— and Vandiver, V. L. (1996). *Maneuvering the Maze of Managed Care: Skills for Mental Health Practitioners.* New York: The Free Press.

Cormier, S. and Cormier, B. (1998). *Interviewing Strategies for Helpers: Fundamental Skills and Cognitive Behavioral Interventions.* Pacific Grove, Calif.: Brooks/Cole.

Cronbach, L. J. (1970). *Essentials of Psychological Testing,* 3rd edition. New York: Macmillan.

Dana, R. H. (1993). *Multicultural Assessment Perspective for Professional Psychology.* Boston: Allyn & Bacon.

Epstein, L. H. (1976). Psychophysiological measurement in assessment. In M. Hersen and A. S. Bellack (eds.), *Behavioral Assessment: A Practical Handbook,* pp. 207–232. New York: Pergamon.

Erdman, H. P., Klein, M. H., and Greist, J. H. (1985). Direct patient computer interviewing, *Journal of Consulting and Clinical Psychology,* 53(6), 760–773.

Fenigstein, A., Scheier, M. F., and Buss, A. H. (1975). Public and private self-consciousness: Assessment and theory, *Journal of Consulting and Clinical Psychology,* 43, 522–527.

Fischer, J. (1981). The Social Work Revolution, *Social Work,* 26, 199–207.

———— (1994). Empirically based practice: The end of ideology? *Journal of Social Service Research,* 17.

———— and Gochros, H. (1975). *Planned Behavior Change: Behavior Modification in Social Work.* New York: The Free Press.

Fowler, D. (1985). Landmarks in Computer-Assisted Psychological Assessment, *Journal of Consulting and Clinical Psychology,* 53(6), 748–759.

Fredman, N. and Sherman, R. (1987). *Handbook of Measurement for Marriage and Family Therapy.* New York: Brunner/Mazel.

Gambrill, E. (1983). *Casework: A Competency-Based Approach.* Englewood Cliffs, N.J.: Prentice Hall.

Gerson, M. J. (1984). Splitting: The development of a measure, *Journal of Clinical Psychology,* 40, 157–162.

Golden, C. J., Sawicki, R. F., and Franzen, M. D. (1984). Test construction. In G. Goldstein and M. Hersen (eds.), *Handbook of Psychological Assessment,* pp. 19–37. New York: Pergamon.

Goldman, B. A. and Busch, J. C. (1978). *Directory of Unpublished Experimental Mental Measures,* Vol. II. New York: Human Sciences Press.

——— (1982). *Directory of Unpublished Experimental Mental Measures,* Vol. III. New York: Human Sciences Press.

——— and Sanders, J. L. (1974). *Directory of Unpublished Experimental Mental Measures,* Vol. I. New York: Behavioral Publications.

Goldman, J., Stein, C. L., and Guerry, S. (1983). *Psychological Methods of Clinical Assessment.* New York: Pergamon.

Goldstein, G. and Hersen M. (eds.) (1990). *Handbook of Psychological Assessment.* 2nd edition. New York: Pergamon.

Gottman, J. M. and Leiblum, S. R. (1974). *How to Do Psychotherapy and How to Evaluate It.* New York: Holt.

Grotevant, H. D. and Carlson, C. I. (eds.) (1989). *Family Assessment: A Guide to Methods and Measures.* New York: Guilford.

Hammill, D. H. D., Brown, L., and Bryant, B. R. (1989). *A Consumer's Guide to Tests in Print.* Austin, Tex.: Pro-Ed.

Haynes, S. N. (1978). *Principles of Behavioral Assessment.* New York: Gardner.

——— (1983). Behavioral assessment. In M. Hersen, A. E. Kazdin, and A. S. Bellack (eds.), *The Clinical Psychology Handbook,* pp. 397–425. New York: Pergamon.

——— and Wilson, C. C. (1979). *Behavioral Assessment.* San Francisco: Jossey-Bass.

Hersen, M. and Bellack, A. S. (eds.) (1981). *Behavioral Assessment: A Practical Handbook.* 2nd edition. New York: Pergamon.

——— (1988). *Dictionary of Behavioral Assessment Techniques.* New York: Pergamon.

Holman, A. M. (1983). *Family Assessment: Tools for Understanding and Intervention.* Beverly Hills: Sage.

Hoon, E. F. and Chambless, D. (1987). Sexual Arousability Inventory (SAI) and Sexual Arousability Inventory—Expanded (SAI-E). In C. M. Davis and W. L. Yarber (eds.), *Sexuality-Related Measures: A Compendium*. Syracuse, N.Y.: Graphic Publishing.

Hudson, W. W. (1978). First axioms of treatment, *Social Work*, 23, 65–66.

——— (1981). Development and use of indexes and scales. In R. M. Grinnell (ed.), *Social Work Research and Evaluation*, pp. 130–155. Itasca, Ill.: F. E. Peacock.

——— (1982). *The Clinical Measurement Package: A Field Manual*. Chicago: Dorsey Press.

——— (1985). *The Clinical Assessment System*. University of Arizona, School of Social Work, Tempe, Arizona 85287 (computer program).

——— (1997). *WALMYR Assessment Scales Scoring Manual*. Tallahassee, Fla.: WALMYR Publishing Co.

Humphrey, L. L. (1982). Children's and teachers' perceptions on children's self-control: The development of two rating scales. *Journal of Consulting and Clinical Psychology*, 50, 624–633.

Jacob, T. and Tennenbaum, D. L. (1988). *Family Assessment: Rationale, Methods, and Future Directions*. New York: Plenum.

Jayaratne, S. and Levy, R. L. (1979). *Empirical Clinical Practice*. New York: Columbia University Press.

Johnson, O. G. (1976). *Tests and Measurements in Child Development* (Vols. 1 and 2). San Francisco: Jossey-Bass.

Johnson, S. M. and Bolstad, O. D. (1973). Methodological issues in natural observation: Some problems and solutions for field research. In L. A. Hammerlynck, L. C. Handy, and E. J. Mash (eds.), *Behavior Change: Methodology, Concepts, and Practice*. Champaign, Ill.: Research Press.

Johnson, O. G. and Bommarito, J. W. (1971). *Tests and Measurements in Child Development: A Handbook*. San Francisco: Jossey-Bass.

Kallman, W. M. and Feuerstein, M. (1986). Psychophysiological Procedures. In A. R. Ciminero, C. S. Calhoun, and H. E. Adams (eds.), *Handbook of Behavioral Assessment*, 2nd edition, Chapter 10. New York: John Wiley.

Kamphaus, R. W. and Frick, P. J. (1996). *Clinical Assessment of Child and Adolescent Personality and Behavior*. Boston: Allyn & Bacon.

Karger, H. J. and Levine, J. (1999). *The Internet and Technology for the Human Services*. New York: Longman.

Kazdin, A. F. (1979). Situational specificity: The two-edged sword of behavioral assessment, *Behavioral Assessment*, 1, 57–76.

——— (1980). *Research Design in Clinical Psychology*. New York: Harper and Row.

——— (1982). Observer effects: Reactivity of direct observation. In D. P. Hartman (ed.), *Using Observers to Study Behavior: New Directions for Methodology of Social and Behavioral Science*, pp. 5–19. San Francisco: Jossey-Bass.

——— (1982). *Single-Case Research Designs: Methods for Clinical and Applied Settings*. New York: Oxford University Press.

Kendall, P. C. and Hollon, S. D. (eds.) (1981). *Assessment Strategies for Cognitive-Behavioral Interventions*. New York: Academic Press.

Kestenbaum, C. J. and Williams, D. T. (eds.) (1988). *Handbook of Clinical Assessment of Children and Adolescents*. Austin, Tex.: Pro-Ed.

Kratochwill, T. R. (ed.) (1978). *Single-Subject Research: Strategies for Evaluating Change*. New York: Academic Press.

Lake, D. G., Miles, M. B., and Earle, R. B., Jr. (1973). *Measuring Human Behavior: Tools for the Assessment of Social Functioning*. New York: Teachers College Press.

Lambert, M. J., Christensen, E. R., and DeJulio, S. S. (eds.) (1983). *The Assessment of Psychotherapy Outcome*. New York: Wiley and Sons.

Lang, P. J. (1977). Physiological assessment of anxiety and fear. In D. D. Cone and R. P. Hawkins (eds.), *Behavioral Assessment: New Directions in Clinical Psychology*, pp. 178–195. New York: Brunner/Mazel.

Lauffer, A. (1982). *Assessment Tools for Practitioners, Managers, and Trainers*. Beverly Hills, Calif.: Sage Publications.

Levitt, J. L. and Reid, W. J. (1981). Rapid-assessment instruments for practice, *Social Work Research and Abstracts*, 17, 13–19.

Levy, L. H. (1983). Trait approaches. In M. Hersen, A. E. Kazdin, and A. S. Bellack (eds.), *The Clinical Psychology Handbook*, pp. 123–142. New York: Pergamon.

Linehan, Marsha M. (1985). The reason for living scale. In P. A. Keller and L. G. Ritt (eds.), *Innovations in Clinical Practice: A Source Book* (vol. 4). Sarasota, Fla.: Professional Resource Exchange.

Mash, L. and Terdal, L. (eds.) (1988). *Behavioral Assessment of Childhood Disorders*, 2nd edition. New York: Guilford.

Mathews, A. M., Gelder, M. G., and Johnston, D. W. (1981). *Agoraphobia: Nature and Treatment*. New York: Guilford.

McCormick, I. A. (1984). A simple version of the Rathus Assertiveness Schedule, *Behavior Assessment*, 7, 95–99.

McCubbin, H. I. and Thompson, A. I. (eds.) (1991). *Family Assessment: Inventories for Research and Practice.* Madison: University of Wisconsin.

McCubbin, H. I., Thompson, A. I., and McCubbin, M. A. (1996). *Family Assessment: Resilience, Coping and Adaptation. Inventories for Research and Practice.* Madison: University of Wisconsin Press.

McDonald, A. P. and Games, R. G. (1972). Ellis's irrational values, *Rational Living,* 7, 25–28.

McDowell, I. and Newell, C. (1996). *Measuring Health: A Guide to Rating Scales and Questionnaires.* 2nd edition. New York: Oxford University Press.

McReynolds, P. (1981) (ed.). *Advances in Psychological Assessment,* Vol. V, San Francisco: Jossey-Bass.

Merluzzi, T. V., Glass, C. R., and Genest, M. (eds.) (1981). *Cognitive Assessment.* New York: Guilford.

Miller, D. C. (1977). *Handbook of Research Design and Social Measurement.* 3rd edition. New York: Longman.

Minuchin, S. (1974). *Families and Family Therapy.* Cambridge, Mass.: Harvard University Press.

Mischel, W. (1968). *Personality and Assessment.* New York: John Wiley.

——— (1981). *Introduction to Personality.* New York: Holt.

Mitchell, J. V. (ed.) (1985). *The Ninth Mental Measurement Yearbook.* Lincoln, Neb.: University of Nebraska Press.

Moos, R. H. (1974). *Evaluating Treatment Environments: A Social Ecological Approach.* New York: John Wiley.

——— (1975a). Assessment and impact of social climate. In P. McReynolds (ed.), *Advances in Psychological Assessment,* Vol. 3. San Francisco: Jossey-Bass.

——— (1975b). *Evaluating Correctional and Community Settings.* New York: John Wiley.

——— (1979). *Evaluating Educational Environments.* San Francisco: Jossey-Bass.

Mosher, D. L. and Sirkin, M. (1984). Measuring a macho personality constellation, *Journal of Research in Personality,* 18, 150–163.

Nathan, P. E. and Gorman, J. M. (eds.) (1998). *A Guide to Treatments That Work.* New York: Oxford University Press.

Nay, W. R. (1979). *Multimethod Clinical Assessment.* New York: Gardner.

Nelsen, J. C. (1985). Verifying the independent variable in single-subject research, *Social Work Research and Abstracts,* 21, 3–8.

Nelson, R. O. (1981). Realistic dependent measures for clinical use, *Journal of Consulting and Clinical Psychology,* 49, 168–182.

———— and Barlow, D. H. (1981). Behavioral assessment: Basic strategies and initial procedures. In D. H. Barlow (ed.), *Behavioral Assessment of Adult Disorders,* pp. 13–43. New York: Guilford.

Nunnally, J. C. (1978). *Psychometric Theory,* 2nd edition. New York: McGraw-Hill.

Nurius, P. S. and Hudson, W. W. (1993). *Human Services: Practice, Evaluation, and Computers.* Pacific Grove, Calif.: Brooks/Cole.

Ogles, B. M. and Masters, K. S. (1996). *Assessing Outcome in Clinical Practice.* Boston: Allyn & Bacon.

Olin, J. T. and Keatinge, C. (1998). *Rapid Psychological Assessment.* New York: Wiley.

Ollendick, T. H. and Hersen, M. (1992). *Handbook of Child and Adolescent Assessment.* Des Moines, Iowa: Allyn & Bacon.

Pecora, P. et al. (1995). *Evaluating Family-Based Services.* Hawthorne, N.Y.: Aldine de Gruyter.

Phares, E. J. and Erskine, N. (1984). The measurement of selfism, *Educational and Psychological Measurement,* 44, 597–608.

Pikoff, H. B. (1996). *Treatment Effectiveness Handbook: A Reference Guide to the Key Research Reviews in Mental Health and Substance Abuse.* Buffalo, N.Y.: Data for Decisions.

Rathus, S. A. (1973). A 30-item schedule for assessing assertive behavior, *Behavior Therapy* 4, 398–406.

Ray, W. J. and Raczynski, J. M. (1981). Psychophysiological assessment. In M. Hersen and A. S. Bellack (eds.), *Behavioral Assessment: A Practical Handbook,* 2nd edition. New York: Pergamon.

Reckase, M. D. (1984). Scaling techniques. In G. Goldstein and M. Hersen (eds.), *Handbook of Psychological Assessment,* pp. 38–53. New York: Pergamon.

Rehm, L. P. (1981). Assessment of depression. In M. Hersen and A. S. Bellack (eds.), *Behavioral Assessment: A Practical Handbook,* pp. 246–295. New York: Pergamon.

Reid, W. J. (1997). Evaluating the dodo's verdict: Do all interventions have equal outcomes? *Research on Social Work Practice,* 21, 5–16.

Reynolds, C. R. and Kamphaus, R. W. (eds.) (1990). *Handbook of Psychological and Educational Assessment of Children.* New York: Guilford.

Richardson, F. C. and Suinn, R. M. (1972). The Mathematics Anxiety Rating Scale: Psychometric data, *Journal of Counseling Psychology,* 19, 551–554.

Roberts, R. E. and Attkisson, C. C. (1984). Assessing client satisfaction among Hispanics, *Evaluation and Program Planning,* 6, 401–413.

Robinson, J. P. and Shaver, P. R. (1973). *Measures of Social Psychological Attitudes,* revised edition. Ann Arbor, Mich.: Institute for Social Research.

Roth, A. and Foragy, P. (1996). *What Works for Whom? A Critical Review of Psychotherapy Research.* New York: Guilford.

Rugh, J. D., Gable R. S., and Lemke, R. R. (1986). Instrumentation for behavioral assessment. In A. R. Ciminero, K. S. Calhoun, and H. E. Adams (eds.), *Handbook of Behavioral Assessment,* 2nd edition, Chapter 4. New York: John Wiley.

Rutter, M., Tuma, A. H., and Lann, I. S. (eds.) (1988). *Assessment and Diagnosis in Child Psychopathology.* New York, Guilford.

Sanderson, W. C. and Woody, S. (1995). Manuals for empirically validated treatments. *The Clinical Psychologist,* 48, 7–11.

Sawin, K. J. and Harrington, M. (1994). *Measures of Family Functioning for Research and Practice.* New York: Springer.

Scholl, G. and Schnur, R. (1976). *Measures of Psychological, Vocational and Educational Functioning in the Blind and Visually Handicapped.* New York: American Foundation for the Blind.

Schutte, N. S. and Malouff, J. M. (1995). *Sourcebook of Adult Assessment Strategies.* New York: Plenum.

Sederer, L. I. and Dickey, B. (eds.). (1996). *Outcomes Assessment in Clinical Practice.* Baltimore: Williams & Wilkins.

Schwartz, A. and Goldiamond, I. (1975). *Social Casework: A Behavioral Approach.* New York: Columbia University Press.

Shelton, J. L. and Levy, R. L. (1981). *Behavioral Assignments and Treatment Compliance: A Handbook of Clinical Strategies.* Champaign, Research Press.

Shorkey, C. T. and Whiteman, V. (1977). Development of the Rational Behavior Inventory: Initial validity and reliability, *Educational and Psychological Measurement,* 37, 527–534.

Slack, W. V., Hicks, G. P., Reed, C. Z., and Van Cura, L. J. (1966). A computer-based medical history system, *New England Journal of Medicine,* 274, 194–198.

Smith, M. C. and Thelen, M. N. (1984) Development and validation of a test for bulimia, *Journal of Consulting and Clinical Psychology,* 52, 863–872.

Southworth, L. E., Burr, R. L., and Cox, A. E. (1981). *Screening and Evaluating the Young Infant: A Handbook of Instruments to Use from Infancy to Six Years.* Springfield, Ill.: C. C. Thomas.

Spielberger, C. D., Jacobs, G., Russel, S., and Crane, R. S. (1983). Assessment of anger: The state-trait anger scale. In J. N. Butcher and C. D. Spielberger (eds.), *Advances in Personality Assessment,* Vol. 2, pp. 159–187. Hillsdale, N.J.: Lawrence Erlbaum Associates.

Stiles, W. B. (1980). Measurement of the impact of psychotherapy sessions, *Journal of Consulting and Clinical Psychology* 48, 176–185.

Sundberg, N. D. (1977). *Assessment of Persons.* Englewood Cliffs, N.J.: Prentice Hall.

Suzuki, L. A., Meller, P. J., and Ponterotto, J. G. (eds.). (1996). *Handbook of Multicultural Assessment: Clinical, Psychological and Educational Applications.* San Francisco: Jossey-Bass.

Sweetland, R. C. and Keyser, D. J. (1991). *Tests: A Comprehensive Reference,* 3rd edition. Austin, Tex.: Pro-Ed.

Tan, A. L., Kendis, R. J., Fine, J. T., and Porac, J. (1977). A short measure of Eriksonian ego identity, *Journal of Personality Assessment,* 41, 279–284.

Thomas, E. J. (1978). Research and service in single-case experimentation: Conflicts and choices, *Social Work Research and Abstracts,* 14, 20–31.

Thompson, C. (ed.) (1989). *The Instruments of Psychiatric Research.* New York: John Wiley.

Thyer, B., Papsdorf, J., Himle, D., and Bray, H. (1981). Normative data on the Rational Behavior Inventory: A further study, *Educational and Psychological Measurement,* 41, 757–760.

Thyer, B. A. and Wodarski, J. S. (eds.) (1998). *Handbook of Empirical Social Work Practice. Vol. 1. Mental Disorders.* New York: Wiley.

Toseland, R. W. and Reid, W. J. (1985). Using rapid assessment instruments in a family service agency, *Social Casework,* 66, 547–555.

Touliatos, J., Perlmutter, B. F., and Straus, M. A. (eds.) (1990). *Handbook of Family Measurement Techniques.* Newbury Park, Calif.: Sage.

van Riezen, H. and Segal, M. (1988). *Comparative Evaluation of Rating Scales for Clinical Psychopharmacology.* New York: Elsevier.

Videcka-Sherman, L. and Reid, W. J. (eds.) (1990). *Advances in Clinical Social Work Research.* Silver Spring, Md.: National Association of Social Workers.

Waskow, I. E. and Parloff, M. B. (eds.) (1975). *Psychotherapy Change Measures.* Rockville, Md.: National Institute of Mental Health.

Webb, E. J., Campbell, D. T., Schwartz, R. D., and Sechrest, L. (1966). *Unobtrusive Measures: Nonreactive Research in the Social Sciences.* Chicago: Rand McNally.

———— Campbell, D. T., Schwartz, R. D., Sechrest, L., and Grove, J. B. (1981). *Nonreactive Measures in the Social Sciences.* 2nd edition. Boston: Houghton Mifflin.

Wetzler, S. (ed.) (1989). *Measuring Mental Illness: Psychometric Assessment for Clinicians.* Washington, D.C.: American Psychiatric Association.

Wicker, A. W. (1981). Nature and assessment of behavior settings: Recent contributions from the ecological perspective. In P. McReynolds (ed.), *Advances in Psychological Assessment,* Vol. V, pp. 22–61. San Francisco: Jossey-Bass.

Wincze, J. P. and Lange, J. D. (1982). Assessment of sexual behavior. In D. H. Barlow (ed.), *Behavioral Assessment of Adult Disorder,* pp. 301–328. New York: Guilford.

Wittenborn, J. R. (1984). Psychological assessment in treatment. In G. Goldstein and M. Hersen (eds.), *Handbook of Psychological Assessment,* pp. 405–410. Elmsford, N.Y.: Pergamon Press.

Wodarski, J. S. and Thyer, B. A. (eds.) (1998). *Handbook of Empirical Social Work Practice. Vol. 2. Social Problems and Practice Issues.* New York: Wiley.

Woody, R. H. (ed.) (1980). *Encyclopedia of Clinical Assessment,* Vols. I and II. San Francisco: Jossey-Bass.

Zung, W. K. (1965). A self-rating depression scale. *Archives of General Psychiatry,* 12, 63–70.

———— (1974). *The Measurement of Depression.* Milwaukee: Lakeside Laboratories.